A Colony of Citizens

A Colony

Citizens

REVOLUTION & SLAVE EMANCIPATION

IN THE FRENCH CARIBBEAN, 1787–1804

LAURENT DUBOIS

Published for the Omohundro Institute of Early American History and Culture, Williamsburg, Virginia, by the University of North Carolina Press, Chapel Hill and London

The Omohundro Institute of Early American History and Culture is sponsored jointly by the College of William and Mary and the Colonial Williamsburg Foundation. On November 15, 1996, the Institute adopted the present name in honor of a bequest from Malvern H. Omohundro, Jr.

Set in Monticello and Bickham types
by Tseng Information Systems, Inc.
Manufactured in the United States of America

Library of Congress
Cataloging-in-Publication Data
Dubois, Laurent, 1971–
A colony of citizens : revolution and slave
emancipation in the French Caribbean,
1787–1804 / Laurent Dubois.
    p. cm.
Includes bibliographical references and index.
ISBN 0-8078-2874-2 (cloth : alk. paper) —
ISBN 0-8078-5536-7 (pbk. : alk. paper)
1. West Indies, French—History.   2. Slaves—
Emancipation—West Indies, French—History.
3. Slave insurrections—West Indies, French—
History.   I. Title.
F2151.D83   2004
326'.8'0972976–dc22   2003019519

The paper in this book meets the guidelines for permanence
and durability of the Committee on Production Guidelines
for Book Longevity of the Council on Library Resources.

This volume received indirect support from an
unrestricted book publications grant awarded to the
Institute by the L. J. Skaggs and Mary C. Skaggs
Foundation of Oakland, California.

cloth 08 07 06 05 04   5 4 3 2 1
paper 08 07 06 05 04   5 4 3 2 1

For Guadeloupe

ACKNOWLEDGMENTS

This book was born of travels back and forth across the Atlantic, from Michigan to Aix-en-Provence, from Guadeloupe to Paris, travels through which I have accumulated unpayable debts and invaluable friendships. It began as a dissertation at the University of Michigan, where I was surrounded by nurturing teachers. Throughout, Fernando Coronil inspired and pushed me with his intellect and passion for the possibilities of using knowledge for the present and the future. I thank him for his example and friendship. Rebecca Scott's contagious energy and intellectual example shaped this project, and she constantly communicated to me both the opportunities and responsibilities that come with historical work. Julius Scott, who travels in the same historical waters I do, has inspired me through his ability to bring to life the world of the Caribbean in ways I can only hope to emulate. Ruth Behar, David Bien, Frederick Cooper, Simon Gikandi, and Ann Stoler all contributed in important ways to the evolution of the project. I owe a great deal to my fellow travelers at Michigan, who heard more than they wanted to about Guadeloupe as we grew into an intellectual family. Martha Baker, Paul Eiss, Mandana Limbert, Setrag Manoukian, and Steven Pierce read drafts of various chapters. David Pedersen always got me thinking about my categories. And with Aims McGuinness I shared the joys of writing about seemingly marginal places.

During my first year of research in Aix-en-Provence, conversations with Marie-Josée Bussenius, Priska Dégras, Edris Makward, and Adlai Murdoch gave early direction to my research. Conversations with Assia Djebar, whose work of memory is a model for me, stirred my imagination. As I first stumbled into the archives, I had the remarkable luck of finding Stewart King there. Stewart was working in the notarial registers of Saint-Domingue for his dissertation, now a book, and with startling generosity showed me his methods, including his well-constructed database, on which I modeled much of my research. It was also in Aix that I met Gary Wilder, and our conversations over French cafeteria food initiated an enduring intellectual camaraderie. Gary's humor keeps me laughing even when he isn't around, his work has influenced this book profoundly, and the promise of continuing discussions with him has made the work of research and writing worthwhile.

A fortuitous encounter at the Archives nationales in Paris led to a fruitful dialogue with Patrick Weil, whose input has been fundamental in the development of my ideas on citizenship and the meaning of Republican culture. His center (CEPIC) provided a home base in Paris, and he helped me bring the eighteenth century into dialogue with the twentieth, both through the seminar he organized and by inviting me to be part of a government commission on immigration reform in the summer of 1997. Conversations with Erik Bleich and Daniel Cohen, fellow researchers at the CEPIC during 1996–1997, as well as with Carlo Celius and Myriam Cottias, were also vital in the development of ideas. Patrick furthermore opened doors that enabled me to publish a part of my dissertation in 1998 under the title *Les Esclaves de la République: L'Histoire oubliée de la première émancipation, 1789-1794*, with Editions Calmann-Lévy (Paris, 1998). My editor there, Olivier Nora, was generous to take a risk on the book. The reviews of *Les Esclaves de la République* and the conversations I had with readers helped me to rethink and expand my ideas herein. Michel Giraud's enthusiasm for the book honored and encouraged me. And there was little more I could wish for once I learned my book was being sold at the supermarket in Basse-Terre.

For my 1996–1997 year in Paris, I thank the Franco-American Commission for Educational Exchange, which oversaw the Fulbright grant that allowed me to do my research. Further research in France and Guadeloupe was funded by a grant from the Georges Lurcy Charitable and Educational Trust. The beginnings of the project were nurtured by a Pre-Dissertation Fellowship from the Council for European Studies at Columbia University and a Hewlett-Rackham dissertation grant from the University of Michigan. The staffs of the Archives nationales and the Bibliothèque nationale in Paris, the Archives historiques de l'armée de terre in Vincennes, the Centre des archives d'outre-mer in Aix-en-Provence, the Archives départementales de la Guyane, the William L. Clements Library at the University of Michigan in Ann Arbor, and the Library of Congress provided invaluable assistance through my years of research. And Laird Pruixsma did me an enormous service by creating a computer program that converts Republican dates to Gregorian ones.

For his teachings I thank Erol Josué, who introduced me to the world of Vodou in Paris and in so doing changed my vision of the past and the present. I also thank Lionel Saintval for his friendship. In Guadeloupe, Brigitte and Hugues Delannay were infinitely hospitable; their vision of their island's history shaped this project, and their family introduced me to Voukoum. During trips to Guadeloupe and Paris, I was also lucky enough to come to know Daniel Maximin, whose writing, cultural work, and enthusiasm for bringing history alive inspired me throughout this undertaking. I thank Ghislaine Bouchet, the Director of the Archives départementales de la Guadeloupe, for her hospitality, as well as Carlomann Bassette, Christian Froleau, Dimitri Garnier, and Sainte-Croix Lacour. Fréderic Régent, who knows more than anyone about the archives and the history of revolutionary Guadeloupe, generously shared portions of his dissertation-in-progress with me. He is the only person with whom I could hotly debate precisely which wigmaker from Basse-Terre had signed a certain petition. I am also grateful to Fabien Marius-Hatchi for sharing his work with me.

My participation in the Atlantic History Seminar at the Charles Warren Center for Studies in American History at Harvard University in the summer of 1997 and comments by David Armitage, Bernard Bailyn, Eliga Gould, and my future colleague Susan Sleeper-Smith were essential in the evolution of the project. A year at the W. E. B. DuBois Institute for Afro-American Research at Harvard University in 1998–1999, funded in part by a grant from the Ford Foundation, allowed me crucial time to reshape my dissertation into a manuscript. During that year, I was grateful for the companionship of Mickaëlla Périna, whose work on Martinique influenced my thinking on citizenship, as well as Fabien Eboussi-Boulaga, Patricia Sullivan, and Richard Turits.

In 1999, some of my work on Hugues was published in the *William and Mary Quarterly* under the title "The Price of Liberty: Victor Hugues and the Administration of Freedom in Guadeloupe, 1794–1798" (3d Ser., LVI [1999], 363–392). Three dauntingly expert reviewers gave me excellent suggestions on the work, as did Philip Morgan, and the experience was fundamental in refining my ideas on Hugues's regime. I was also lucky to get to know Suzanne Desan, who wrote me detailed thoughts about my dissertation that pushed me to think more carefully about gender and emancipation. The responses and insights of Sue Peabody, whose work was an inspiration early on, have shaped the present version of this work. The input of David Brion Davis, Seymour Drescher, Malick Ghachem, David Geggus, John Garrigus, and Marixa Lasso also shaped the revisions of my manuscript. And at Michigan State I have had the pleasure to work with wonderful and supportive colleagues. Funding from the Center for Latin American and Caribbean Studies helped me as I was revising the manuscript. Anna and Chris

Celenza gave me helpful suggestions. Darlene Clark Hine provided a grant from the Comparative Black History Ph.D. Program for illustrations, and Anne Meyering helped me track many of them down.

Thanks to Elaine Maisner, the manuscript made its way to the University of North Carolina Press and the Omohundro Institute of Early American History and Culture. I am profoundly grateful for the care with which the book has been edited there. Two insightful anonymous reviewers helped me reshape and expand the work. Kathryn Burdette was a model editor, coming to be quite an expert on Guadeloupe herself, and Fredrika J. Teute was a careful and supportive critic. Working with the two of them has taught me that a writer has no better friend than a good editor.

As I have forged ahead in this research without ever knowing exactly where I was going, my family has been a source of support and, when necessary, teasing. My brother Joel Dubois has been a constant companion in this intellectual journey. Monique Dubois-Dalcq listened to my stories from the archives and read my writing with a careful eye, and Heinz Arnheiter's geneticist vision never ceased to challenge me. To André Dubois I am indebted for the lesson that the greatest gift is to work at what you love—and for the patience with which he helped me find that gift. Marie-Claude Dubois has, more than anyone, taught me the spirit of French history and has read the many versions of this work with care, devotion, and insight. If I have pursued and written down these stories, it is only thanks to what all of them have taught me. What has made all these travels a journey in the true sense of the word has been making them with Katharine Brophy Dubois, who is as much the author of this work, and the paths it has come out of, as am I.

CONTENTS

MAPS & ILLUSTRATIONS

ABBREVIATIONS

ADG
  Archives départementales de la Guadeloupe, Bisdary
    Section 2 E (Notariat)
ADGn
  Archives départementales de la Guyane, Cayenne
    Série X
AHAT
  Archives historique de l'armée de terre, Vincennes
    X i, 13, 18, 80 (Troupes coloniales)
    B 9, 2 (Correspondance Indes occidentales)
AN
  Archives nationales, Paris
    107, AP, 127–130 (Gallifet Papers)
    AD VII, 21, 22 (Archives imprimées)
    AF III, 209 (Directory Regime)
    C 181, 464, 466, 513, 518, 577 (Elections)
    D XXV (Comité colonial)
    Marine, AA (Actes du pouvoir souverain)
BN
  Bibliothèque nationale, Paris
    Manuscrits occidentaux, France
      Nouvelles acquisitions, 6894, and 12101 T. 1–3
        (Correspondance de Toussaint L'Ouverture)
CAOM
  Centre des Archives d'outre-mer, Aix-en-Provence
    B 250 (Correspondance au départ)
    C 7A (Correspondance à l'arrivée, Guadeloupe, régistres 46–55)
    DFC (Dépôt des fortifications des colonies, cartons 28, 29)
    Etat civil Guadeloupe
    F 3, 23, 58 (Fonds Moreau de St.-Méry)
    G 1, 500–504 (Recensements Guadeloupe)
    Notariat Guadeloupe

INTRODUCTION

On June 30, 1997, a public ritual took place in the town hall of Pantin, just outside Paris. It was organized by members of the *sans-papiers* movement, which had emerged as the most important defender of the rights of undocumented immigrants in France. The assistant to the Socialist mayor presided, wearing his tricolor sash to signal that he was acting as a Republican official. One by one, ten sans-papiers presented themselves, each accompanied by two French citizens who declared their wish to become his or her godparents. All three then signed a document that was given to the sans-papiers to be carried as an unofficial identity card, the mark of a symbolic and legal bond meant both to help them in their dealings with state officials and to make a political statement of solidarity. Each of the godmothers and godfathers was given a pin composed of a black and a white string tied together in a knot, whose peculiarity was (as the maker of the pins put it) that the more you pulled on it, the tighter it became.

When all ten groups had signed the documents, the mayor thanked them and invited them to champagne and orange juice. Before he broke up the assembly, however, a young Haitian sans-papier named Erol Josué interrupted him and asked whether he might speak. Josué was a musician and a dancer as well as an *oungan*—Vodou priest—who had lived in France for four years and who conducted ceremonies in Paris and its suburbs. "I—we—want to thank all those who have come forward to help us," he said, then launched into a praise song to Agwé, a *lwa*, or deity, of Vodou who lives under the ocean and protects those who are on journeys. Josué then sang to Lasirèn, Agwé's consort, who is the patron of musicians. It was a call for help that told the lwa that the assembled group was blocked at the crossroads and needed guidance to move forward. When he stopped singing, Josué told the crowd: "Just as you help us, we will help you, in our own way."

This event was part of the larger sans-papiers movement, through which victims of restrictive French immigration laws publicly announced their status as sans-papiers residents and challenged the laws excluding them from documentation and the rights that flowed from it. Through a wave of church occupations and demonstrations in 1996 and 1997, the sans-papiers phrased their demands in a universalist language of Republican rights. Yet their political strategy also included a stream of demonstrations in which their origins—whether Chinese, Malian, or Haitian—were put forward through music, dress, and banners written in various foreign languages. The sans-papiers movement braided together the seemingly incommensurable ideals of universalism and cultural difference; by propounding universalism in foreign languages, they presented themselves as foreign cultures at home in France. In doing so, they phrased the issue, not as one about the assimilation of outsiders, but rather as one about a republic that was violating the rights of men and women who were part of its past, present, and future. When Erol Josué sang his praise song during the *parrainage républicain*, he suggested that the Republic itself was not only giving but also receiving the blessings of those who had traveled to France. As Josué knew, somewhere Agwé and Lasirèn were citizens. They were part of the Republic's past and, through Josué's praise song, its present. In bringing the lwa into the Republican ceremony, Josué spoke the memory of a silenced history of the Republic and suggested that a different past might be necessary to make a different future.

This book, too, tells a different history of the Republic: how, at the end of the eighteenth century, the actions of slaves-turned-citizens in the Caribbean transformed Europe and the Americas. During the early 1790s, slave insurgents gave new content to the abstract universality of the language of rights, expanding the scope of political culture as they demanded Republican citizenship and racial equality. Developments in the Antilles outran the political imagination of the metropole in the transformation—and universalization—of the idea of rights. Out of alliances between slave insurgents and Republican officials there, a new colonial order emerged, one in which the principles of universalism were put into effect through regimes that applied the same constitution in the metropole and colony and granted all people within the French Empire the same rights. The universalism of the Republic gained potent, and unexpected, meaning through slave insurgents' demands for inclusion, a transformation that marked a powerful blow to the system of slavery. These were crucial steps in the broader march toward emancipation throughout the Americas and Europe.[1]

1. On the concept of transculturation, see Fernando Ortiz, *Cuban Counterpoint: Tobacco and Sugar*, trans. Harriet de Onís (Durham, N.C., 1995). My work responds to Paul Gilroy's call for a more profound examination of the role of the "Black Atlantic," and notably the Haitian Revolution, in constructing the forms of

The enslaved revolutionaries challenged the racialized colonial system of the day, deploying the language of Republican rights and the promise of individual liberty against a social order based on the denial of their humanity. In winning back the natural rights the Enlightenment claimed as the birthright to all people, however, the formerly enslaved laid bare a profound tension within the ideology of rights they had made their own. The right to individual freedom they had gained was, inevitably, a strike against the property rights claimed by their former masters. The 1789 Declaration of the Rights of Man and Citizen defended both the natural right to freedom and the right to private property: in the Caribbean, where much of the propertyowners' wealth was invested in human beings, the contest between the two sets of rights raised profound questions about the nature and meaning of rights. Emancipation, furthermore, struck at the foundations of an economic system deemed central to the functioning of a French Empire at war with powerful rival empires. As in later post-emancipation contexts in the Americas, freed people sought to fulfill the promises of freedom by seeking economic autonomy while former masters did their best to preserve their power over their former slaves' labor. Colonial authorities—charged with overseeing abolition while continuing plantation production—negotiated this conflict by combining emancipation with new forms of labor coercion and racial exclusion. The result was a "Republican racism" that excluded the former slaves from full equality and justified the continued exploitation of their labor, arguing their incapacity to live as free and independent citizens.[2]

Colonial administrators in the revolutionary French Caribbean confronted, essentially for the first time, the dilemmas of a Republican im-

---

modern democracy; see *The Black Atlantic: Modernity and Double-Consciousness* (Cambridge, Mass., 1993). In pursuing this goal, I build on the foundations set by Julius Sherrard Scott III, "The Common Wind: Currents of Afro-American Communication in the Era of the Haitian Revolution" (Ph.D. diss., Duke University, 1987), and Robin Blackburn, *The Overthrow of Colonial Slavery, 1776-1848* (London, 1988).

2. Among the many works on emancipation, the two that have most influenced me in my interpretations here are Thomas C. Holt, *The Problem of Freedom: Race, Labor, and Politics in Jamaica and Britain, 1832-1938* (Baltimore, 1992), and Rebecca J. Scott, *Slave Emancipation in Cuba: The Transition to Free Labor, 1860-1899* (Princeton, N.J., 1985); see also Frederick Cooper, Thomas C. Holt, and Rebecca J. Scott, eds., *Beyond Slavery: Explorations of Race, Labor, and Citizenship in Postemancipation Societies* (Chapel Hill, N.C., 2000).

perialism in which colonial exploitation had to be institutionalized and justified within an ideological system based on the principle of universal rights. The solutions these administrators crafted were a foundation for the forms of governance employed by the French "imperial nation-state" of the nineteenth and twentieth centuries. In this empire, as in the revolutionary French Caribbean, the colonized sometimes used claims to universal rights in demands for representation. But even as the colonial state presented itself as the bearer of the liberatory possibilities of democracy, administrators argued that the majority of the colonized did not have the cultural and intellectual capacities necessary to responsibly exercise political rights. The promise of access to rights was extended by the colonial administration but was constantly deferred to some unspecified moment in the future. This enduring and effective set of political habits of colonial universalism was a continuation, and expansion, of the strategies used in containing the liberty of the freed people of the revolutionary French Caribbean.[3]

This book has been shaped by the rich work produced in colonial studies during the late twentieth century, which has argued for the centrality of colonialism not only in the economy of Europe but also in the formation of Western political and cultural forms. Much of the theorizing in colonial studies, however, has been driven by the histories of nineteenth- and twentieth-century northern European empires in Africa and Asia and has overlooked the earlier period of colonization by Spain, Portugal, France, and England in the Americas. But integrating the history of the Americas, and the Caribbean in particular, into both studies of European history and the history of empire can provide us with new perspectives. And it can help us appreciate one of the major implications, and ironies, of the story I tell here: Central aspects of the universalism presented by imperial powers of the nineteenth and twentieth centuries (as well as in the world order of the twenty-first) as products of Europe's intellectual heritage in fact originated in the colonial Caribbean. The democratic possibilities imperial powers would claim they were bringing to the colonies had in fact been forged, not within the boundaries of Europe, but through the struggles over rights that spread through-

3. My thoughts on the comparisons between the late eighteenth century and later developments in French imperial policy have been shaped by conversations with Gary Wilder, whose work I draw on for the term "imperial nation-state"; see his "Subject-Citizens and Interwar France: Negritude, Colonial Humanism, and the Imperial Nation-State" (Ph.D. diss., University of Chicago, 1999).

out the Atlantic empires. The challenges posed by colonial insurgents in the Americas—the most revolutionary of them the enslaved rebels of the French Caribbean—created a democratic culture that was later presented as a gift from Europe and a justification for expanding imperialism.[4]

Michel-Rolph Trouillot has stressed that one of the more radical transformations of the Age of Revolution has been pushed to the margins of both historiography and historical consciousness in Europe and North America. To counteract this tendency and to place the battles over slavery and the actions of the enslaved themselves at the center of our understanding of modern political culture's emergence, new approaches to the study of the history of ideas must be developed. The revolutionaries of the Caribbean, both free and enslaved, left many traces of their intellectual and political visions in the archives. They are, however, often fragmentary and hidden. In order to find and interpret these traces, I have drawn on a variety of historical methodologies—materialist and discursive—as well as on symbolic anthropology, seeking to understand how Republican political ideas became embedded in the eighteenth-century Caribbean and were transformed through the actions of slaves-turned-citizens. My goal has been to illustrate the possibilities of bringing together history, anthropology, and literary criticism in order to propose a new vision of the foundations of democracy.[5]

4. Fernando Coronil has emphasized that in rethinking the history of the West it is crucial to draw on "a long Caribbean and Latin American tradition of critical reflection concerning colonialism and modern imperialism." Because of the "much longer entanglement of European colonialism and imperialism," he suggests, the history of these regions can provide a useful perspective on the "mutual constitution" of Europe and its colonies. See *The Magical State: Nature, Money, and Modernity in Venezuela* (Chicago, 1997), 13–14. A compelling exploration of the impact of the Haitian Revolution on philosophical developments in Europe is Susan Buck-Morss, "Hegel and Haiti," *Critical Inquiry*, XXVI (2000), 821–865. The history of the Americas, notably Haiti, is included in the collection by Gyan Prakash, ed., *After Colonialism: Imperial Histories and Postcolonial Displacements* (Princeton, N.J., 1995); on the ways the Caribbean struggles of the 1790s "presaged" later "tensions" in imperial governance, see "Introduction," Frederick Cooper and Ann Laura Stoler, eds., *Tensions of Empire: Colonial Cultures in a Bourgeois World* (Berkeley, Calif., 1997), 1–56, esp. 2.

5. See Michel-Rolph Trouillot, *Silencing the Past: Power and the Production of History* (Boston, 1995), esp. chaps. 2, 3. The pace of research on the history of the revolutionary French Caribbean has thankfully accelerated during the past decades. The historiography on Guadeloupe during the revolutionary period, for instance, has been expanded enormously by Fréderic Régent, who has produced the

This work focuses to a large extent on, and therefore risks privileging, struggles surrounding political forms—citizenship, rights, the Republic—that are still powerfully associated in the minds of many with European political and intellectual history. Like other scholars who have worked on the Caribbean in this period, I hope to help make it impossible in the future to screen out the profound contribution made by events in the Caribbean to the development of these political forms. What is it that distinguishes the Caribbean social and political context from that of Europe? The overwhelming importance of enslaved labor in these societies is, of course, a central factor. The plantation system shaped the social world of the Caribbean, and it shaped the ideologies of those invested in justifying slavery. It also involved the infusion of African culture and ideologies into the region. As John Thornton has written of the eighteenth-century Americas, "African culture was not surviving: It was arriving." Throughout the plantation societies of the Caribbean, African languages were spoken, African stories and African histories were remembered, and African religions were practiced and adapted through their encounters with one another and the order of the colonial Caribbean.[6]

The size, and origins, of African populations varied from island to island. In colonial Saint-Domingue, more than half the enslaved had been born in and spent a significant part of their lives in Africa, a fact of profound importance to the course of the insurrection and the fight for independence. In contrast, Guadeloupe, which was economically marginal in the French Caribbean and supplied by only a small number of French slave ships, had a less Africanized population, of which only a fifth or perhaps a quarter was African-born. In both Saint-Domingue and especially Guadeloupe, slave insurgents at various moments voiced their claims in terms of Republican rights. In Guadeloupe, the use of this language became the primary vehicle for slave demands. The more complex, varied, and widespread forms of insurrectionary and political strategies manifested in Saint-Domingue provide us with a number of specific examples, brought to light by Thornton as well as Carolyn Fick, in which African political ideology, religious practices, and military techniques played im-

most thorough work to date on the subject, "Entre esclavage et liberté: Esclaves, libres, et citoyens de couleur en Guadeloupe de 1789 à 1802, une population en Révolution" (Ph.D. diss., Université Paris I, 2002).

6. John K. Thornton, *Africa and Africans in the Making of the Atlantic World, 1400–1800* (Cambridge, 1998), 320.

Introduction

portant roles. References to African cultural forms, in contrast, are rare in the case of Guadeloupe.

In spite of these differences, Saint-Domingue and Guadeloupe had in common with each other, and with all eighteenth-century Caribbean societies, something fundamental: they had been shaped by several centuries of interaction and confrontation between a variety of heterogeneous European, African, and native American cultures. Fernando Ortiz's term "transculturation" best names this complex process through which new communities were forged in the fires of empire. Out of the world created by transculturation emerged the political transformations of the 1790s and the democratic ideals that drove them; these transformations, in turn, played a crucial role in defining the course and impact of a revolutionary decade that must be understood as containing both a French and a Caribbean revolution. These two revolutions emerged symbiotically as news, ideologies, and people crisscrossed the Atlantic, as actors in the Caribbean deployed the ideals and symbols of republicanism and pushed the meaning of citizenship and national belonging in new directions. The culmination of their action was the 1794 abolition of slavery, which was the era's most radical political shift and had ramifications that reached deep into France and the rest of Europe. The larger transatlantic social changes and political culture that emerged from this period, then, were profoundly shaped by the European-African transculturation in the Caribbean.

This period of Atlantic revolution involved both the demolition of oppressive political hierarchies and the creation of new forms of political exclusion. In metropolitan France, eloquent voices arguing in favor of granting citizenship to women were drowned out by those who asserted that women did not have the capacity for political participation. In this book, I draw on the insightful scholarship on these debates, which has examined the use of universalist language in support of exclusionary policies. There are important parallels between the justifications used for the exclusion of women in the metropole and those used against people of African descent in the colonies. And, in demanding rights, both groups similarly sought to deploy and expand the universalist language of rights wielded by those who excluded them. At the same time, economic exigencies on the plantation societies of the Caribbean, which during the Revolution continued to be seen primarily as sources of sugar and coffee, shaped the forms of Republican political exclusion that took root there. In the wake of emancipation, continuing racial exclusion was justified by invoking the economic needs of the threatened nation and ultimately defining the rights of freed people by the roles they had occupied when they were enslaved. Racial and gendered exclusions, meanwhile, were intertwined in ways that made men's and women's experiences of freedom very different.[7]

The processes of revolution I examine here led to the creation of two nations with very different futures: France and Haiti. My account, however, focuses neither on Paris nor Saint-Domingue but rather Guadeloupe, where slavery was first abolished in 1794 and then reestablished in 1802. The little-known history of this island does not provide a story of a nation's birth or of a successful process of emancipation. But precisely for that reason it highlights the dramatic possibilities opened up in the 1790s—when France and the Caribbean were united in a Republican colonial project based on granting rights to people of all colors—and the contradictions at the heart of this project, which led to its brutal demolition in 1802. A focus on the island, and particularly on two communities, Basse-Terre and Trois-Rivières, allows us to see how those who were enslaved and won their freedom both shaped and experienced the transformations of the age. This work presents a historical anthropology that begins by describing both the forces that shaped the French Caribbean and those that inhabited and reshaped it from within, then braids together the history of debates about slavery and citizenship that took place in the centers of political power with a social and political history of African-descended communities in Guadeloupe. By placing a microhistory of these communities within the context of a broader Atlantic tale, I show how they made profound and lasting intellectual contributions to the revolutionary political culture of the age.

7. On gender and the French Revolution, the literature is vast, but three works that have influenced my analysis are Joan Wallach Scott's analysis of Olympe de Gouges in *Only Paradoxes to Offer: French Feminists and the Rights of Man* (Cambridge, Mass., 1996); Lynn Hunt, *The Family Romance of the French Revolution* (Berkeley, Calif., 1992); Suzanne Desan, "'Constitutional Amazons': Jacobin Women's Clubs in the French Revolution," in Bryant T. Ragan, Jr., and Elizabeth A. Williams, eds., *Recreating Authority in Revolutionary France* (New Brunswick, N.J., 1992), 11–35; see also Sue Peabody, who is exploring this issue in greater detail in her work; see her "Gendered Access to Freedom: Manumission and Emancipation during the Ancien Régime and the Revolution," in Pamela Scully and Diana Paton, *Gender and Emancipation in the Atlantic World*, forthcoming.

In the first part of the book, "Prophecy, Revolt, and Emancipation, 1787–1794," I use a revolt in Trois-Rivières in 1793 as a lens to examine how conflicts over the meaning of the Republic in the Antilles, and particularly the intervention of slave insurgents into those conflicts, brought about emancipation and with it an expansion of the possibilities of Republican political culture. After introducing the Trois-Rivières revolt in Chapter 1, I begin Chapter 2 by presenting a "social cartography" of the slave society of Guadeloupe during the years leading up to manumission. I suggest that this ethnographic description of Guadeloupe's plantation society should be placed within an understanding of the "natural" spaces in which sugar was grown in the center and other crops were grown on the margins. These spaces were constructed and dominated by the plantation economy, but they were also home to other relationships, hidden histories worth seeking out, histories of layered labor hidden behind the histories of revolt. Chapter 3, "Prophetic Rumor," examines how the new political culture of the French Revolution became part of the struggles in Guadeloupe and the Greater Caribbean. In Saint-Domingue, where a major slave insurrection broke out in 1791, as well as in Guadeloupe and Martinique, *gens de couleur* and slaves began using the language of rights in pursuit of equality and freedom. They incorporated themselves strategically, and successfully, into debates about how the colonies should be governed and about what their own juridical status should be. Spreading and mobilizing around rumors of imminent emancipation, they invoked as-yet-unmade decisions on the part of the metropole and in so doing contributed to the increasing intervention of metropolitan authorities into colonial governance. Their actions brought about the victory of a form of colonial assimilationism that insisted the rights of man and the laws that flowed from them were equally applicable in the metropole and the colonies.

Chapter 4, "The Insurgent Republic," details the Trois-Rivières insurrection and its impact. There, insurgents transformed the meaning of political belonging as they forcibly integrated themselves into the Republic. Using the language of citizenship to explain their actions—instead of taking flight—they demonstrated a strong, and ultimately well-placed, sense that by invoking political solidarity with Republican whites they would be thanked rather than punished. Enslaved blacks radicalized the political conflict in Guadeloupe, and their example spurred certain "new citizens" to argue that slaves should be transformed into citizens in order to defend the Republic in Guadeloupe. In Part I, then, the events at Trois-Rivières reflect the larger movement for freedom and equality that shook the French Caribbean between 1789 and 1794. The struggle ended in victory: the prophecies of imminent liberation that circulated among the slaves were ultimately realized because of the slave insurrections they had helped inspire. As I discuss in Chapter 5, in 1794 the National Convention ratified a local decision made in Saint-Domingue in 1793, abolishing slavery throughout the French Empire. The enslaved had radically expanded the terms of Republican citizenship and fundamentally transformed the political culture of the Age of Revolution.

Part II, "The Meaning of Citizenship, 1794–1798," examines Victor Hugues's regime in Guadeloupe and emancipation's impact on its social world. This regime constructed the new society in the Antilles with little or no direction from the metropole, and altercations arose over the meaning of freedom between ex-slaves, ex-masters, and Republican administrators. As a result, a contradictory order combining racial equality with new forms of racial exclusion emerged on the island. Chapter 6 begins with an exploration of the ideas of eighteenth-century abolitionist thinkers; of particular note is the influential marquis de Condorcet, who argued that ex-slaves would be incapable of acting as free citizens and that their rights should be limited, at least temporarily, after emancipation. As I show in Chapter 7, "Worthy of the Nation," Hugues drew on the ideas of gradual abolitionists in constructing his regime in Guadeloupe. Invoking national responsibility, he forced ex-slaves to stay on the plantations where they had previously lived, arguing that they owed the Republic for freeing them and that they should pay it back by continuing to work as plantation laborers. Now called *cultivateurs*, many new citizens in Guadeloupe profited little from the change in their status. At the same time, emancipation did bring about changes in the life on Guadeloupe's plantations.

Hugues also recruited huge numbers of ex-slaves in a massive campaign against the English. The decree of slave emancipation became a powerful weapon of war that altered the military situation in the eastern Caribbean. In Chapter 8, "War and Emancipation," Republican troops, a majority of whom were ex-slaves, waged campaigns as they fanned out from Guadeloupe into Saint Vincent, Saint Lucia, and Grenada in 1795 and 1796. Emancipation transformed war in the region as the French joined slave rebels, disaffected gens de couleur, and groups such as the Black Caribs in attacking the British. Service in the Republican army, or on the Republican corsairs that roved the waters, opened up opportunities for male ex-slaves. Furthermore, the possibilities afforded by the economy of war affected families and friends in the towns, as did the so-cial status and new connections that came with military service.

Despite the limitations imposed by Hugues's regime, ex-slaves mo-bilized their rights in the struggle for better lives, and in so doing they changed the social world of Guadeloupe. Before emancipation, the en-slaved had been excluded from the legal sphere and did not have the capacity to create legal documents in their own names. When freedom came, the former slaves took advantage of their new legal rights by fill-ing the *état civil* and notary registers of Guadeloupe, leaving testimony to the uses they made of their legal freedom and its expansion. Chap-ter 9, "The Mark of Freedom," examines their struggles against the re-strictions on their freedom and their mobilization of rights in pursuit of social and economic power. Documentation such as that presented in the état civil was, however, produced at the intersection of individual action and a state project of documentation that sought to control the movement of the freed people on the island. The censuses produced by Hugues in 1796 and 1797 exemplify the effort to develop new forms of surveillance in spite of the principle of juridical equality. In both the registers and the censuses, the contest over the use of racial categories provides a fascinat-ing glimpse at the shift in racial thinking within emancipation.

Chapter 10, "The Revolution's Spiral," explores the later years of Hugues's regime and the Republic's retreat from equality. Hugues re-sponded and contributed to this retreat by increasingly describing colo-nial society as a place of corruption and degradation where democracy was dangerous and impossible to apply. Certain new citizens in Guade-loupe thus revolted in 1798 against Hugues and for a different political system in which blacks rather than whites would rule. This revolt, dis-cussed in Chapter 11, was the first of ever more powerful uprisings de-fending republicanism against a French nation retreating from it. The contradictions that became apparent during the era of emancipation ex-ploded with a violence that illuminated the radical potential, and danger, of the aspirations of freed people for full equality and citizenship.

Part III, "The Boundaries of the Republic, 1798–1804," turns to the period when the project of emancipation was slowly dismantled, and ultimately reversed, in a bloody conflict over the meaning of "repub-lic." Chapter 13, "Defending the Republic," examines the regimes that succeeded Hugues's between 1798 and 1800, when former planters in exile as well as merchants and even former abolitionists began criticiz-ing the effects of manumission in the Caribbean. In Guadeloupe, these threats to freedom encouraged some to resist the 1798 replacement of Victor Hugues by the commissioner Étienne Desfourneaux—eventually deposed by a popular uprising, only to be replaced by new agents who continued his policies. In late 1799, a new regime came into power in France: the Consulate, whose most powerful member was Napoléon Bonaparte. Broad changes in colonial governance followed, which Chapter 14, "The New Imperial Order," explores. Informed by colonial administrators' increasingly harsh remarks on the effects of emancipation, a new commissioner, Lacrosse, quickly stirred up resistance through his arrests of several popular officers and his attacks on the rights of the cultivateurs. Soon a revolt among the soldiers of Guadeloupe forced Lacrosse into exile in Dominica, from which he and other administrators planned to isolate the rebels of Guadeloupe and their government. Behind him lay the force of Bonaparte himself, who sent two missions—the Leclerc expedition to Saint-Domingue and the Richepance expedition to Guadeloupe—to prepare for a reestablishment of slavery.

From within the new social order of Guadeloupe, men and women followed the changes occurring in the metropole and made difficult choices between loyalty to an increasingly threatening French government and loyalty to the Republican ideals of equality the government had once proclaimed. As metropolitan authorities struck at the policies of racial equality of the previous years, men and women in the Antilles began to seek alternatives, both through projects to gain national independence and through individual efforts to maintain freedom. Ultimately, many chose to fight and die for a republic that France had abandoned. Chapter 15, "Vivre libre ou mourir!" tells the story of their little-known struggle and ultimate defeat in a mass suicide at a plantation near the town of Matouba. As Chapter 16, "The Exiled Republic," explores, insurgents continued to fight from the mountains of Guadeloupe and from elsewhere in the Caribbean, even as French actions against them inspired accelerating resistance in Saint-Domingue. Without mentioning slavery, the French military government, followed by the civilian government of Lacrosse and his successor Daniel Lescallier, brutally repressed opposition and reestablished slavery. The short experiment in emancipation had ended in Guadeloupe, leaving deep traces on the landscape of that island and of the Atlantic world. Meanwhile, across the water, the stories of what had happened in Guadeloupe continued to spur on the fighting in Saint-Domingue, ultimately leading to the creation of the Republic of Haiti in 1804.

The events of this period left a profound mark on the French Caribbean and metropolitan France, but for a long time they were silenced in official national histories. In the late twentieth century, however, activists, historians, and writers in the Caribbean have increasingly sought to reconstruct and revive this past and make it part of contemporary cultural consciousness. Novelists have played a particularly important role in this movement, and throughout this book I engage with two works of literature that are perhaps the best-known accounts (and indeed until now almost the only ones available in English) of the history of Guadeloupe during this period: the Cuban writer Alejo Carpentier's *Explosion in a Cathedral (El siglo de las luces)*, which is based on the life of Victor Hugues, and the Guadeloupean writer Daniel Maximin's *Lone Sun (L'Isolé soleil)*. These novels are part of a corpus of Caribbean literature that has sought to recover and evoke the histories of these islands and has played a crucial role in drawing attention to the region's past. Maximin's novel evokes the layered historical landscape of the region at the heart of this study. In *Lone Sun*, as in his other novels, Maximin describes a world caught between the constant, veiled threats of the Soufrière volcano, almost perpetually shrouded in mist, and the dangerous ocean and its hurricanes. Nature and history conspire in buffeting the area, whose topography is sedimented with a multiplicity of pasts rooted in the ecology of the island but defined by the meeting of continents. *Lone Sun* tells the history of the revolutionary period in Guadeloupe by chronicling the character Marie-Gabriel's attempt to write the history of her island. Seeking to make "truth serve the imagination and not the opposite," she uses the "journal of Jonathan," a diary left behind by one of her ancestors, as her antidote to the silences of official history. The journal, constituted in the novel by a slave gathering fragments from books and newspapers—and drawn by Maximin from actual eighteenth-century works—coexists with other forms of memory, such as song, through which the actions of maroons, of African gods, of women are written back into history as unacknowledged sources of historical change. By combining existing historical sources with invented ones and placing them as historical documents within his novel, Maximin confronts the silences of the archives by creating an archive containing histories that, if they are impossible to recover, are necessary to remember.[8]

8. Daniel Maximin, *Lone Sun* (Charlottesville, Va., 1989), 10; see also his *Soufrières* (Paris, 1987), and *L'Ile et une nuit* (Paris, 1995); Alejo Carpentier, *Explosion in a Cathedral* (New York, 1963). History has long been a preoccupation of Caribbean novelists. In the original preface to *The Kingdom of This World* (New

Maximin's work, like that of the Martinican writers Edouard Glissant and Patrick Chamoiseau, raises the question of whether the stories of slaves can in fact ever be recovered through archival documents recorded by the masters and institutions who held them in bondage. The same question has long preoccupied social historians working on slavery. Novelists and historians have, of course, developed very different responses to the problem, and by understanding the difference between their approaches rather than conflating them, we can perhaps open the way to a productive dialogue between the two genres for narrating the past. Inspired and instructed by the discipline of social history, this work tells the stories of the enslaved and freed people of Guadeloupe, of their struggles within and against slavery, and of their attempts to shape the meaning of liberty, citizenship, and racial equality. Yet, Maximin's evocation of the historical landscape of Guadeloupe has also shaped my efforts. His novels helped me recognize details I might otherwise have missed in the documents and helped me transform these details into the narrative I have presented here. As I researched and wrote this work, I watched Maximin and other Antilleans make the past into part of the contemporary landscape, through monuments built in Guadeloupe and Paris and through the commemoration of the 1848 abolition of slavery. And I learned how the past has been reworked for the present in other ways, in rituals that bring together Haitians, Guadeloupeans, and Martinicans in the basement Vodou temples of Paris and its suburbs. There, oungans and *manbos* (priestesses) call down unruly and unpredictable lwa who carry the marks of slavery and revolution and who address concerns of those gathered for them. I offer up this book in the hopes that it will find its place at the crossroads of France and the Caribbean, where the past of the Republic is brought into dialogue with its present.[9]

York, 1967), a novel about the Haitian Revolution, Alejo Carpentier coined the term "magical realism," suggesting that this literary style was necessary to capture the true history of the Caribbean. Two works that deal with French Caribbean literature's handling of history are Simon Gikandi, *Writing in Limbo: Modernism and Caribbean Literature* (Ithaca, N.Y., 1992); Mireille Rosello, *Littérature et identité créole aux Antilles* (Paris, 1992).

9. Edouard Glissant calls for "a prophetic vision of the past" in *Caribbean Discourse: Selected Essays*, trans. J. Michael Dash (Charlottesville, Va., 1989); see also Patrick Chamoiseau, *Texaco* (Paris, 1992).

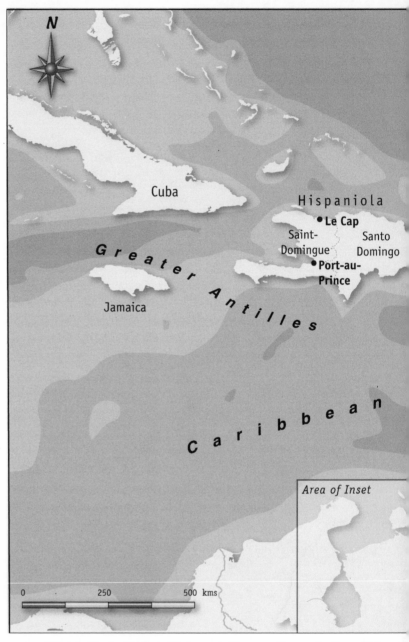

MAP I. West Indies in the Late Eighteenth Century. *Drawn by Gerry Krieg*

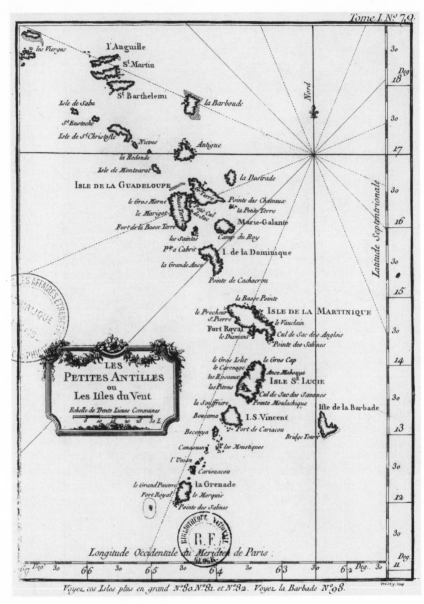

les Vierges

l'Anguille

St Martin

St Barthelemi

la Barboude

Isle de Saba

St Eustache

Isle de St Christofle

Nieves

Antigue

la Redonde

Isle de Montsarat

la Desirade

ISLE DE LA GUADELOUPE

Basse Terre

le Gros Morne

Pointe des Châteaux

le Marigot

Petit Cul de Sac

la Petite Terre

Fort de la Basse Terre

Marie-Galante

les Saintes

Camp du Roy

Pte a Cabrit

I. de la Dominique

la Grande Ance

Pointe de Cachacrou

la Basse Pointe

le Precheur

ISLE DE LA MARTINIQUE

S. Pierre

le Vauclain

Fort Royal

Cul de Sac des Anglois

le Diamant

Pointe des Salines

le Gros Ilet

le Gros Cap

le Carenage

Ance Mabouya

los Byocaux

ISLE Ste LUCIE

les Pitons

Cul de Sac des Savanes

la Souffriere

Pointe Moulachique

Boucama

Isle de la Barbade

I. S. Vincent

Becouya

Port de Cariacou

Bridge Town

Canaouan

los Moustiques

l'Union

Cariouacou

le Grand Pauvre

la Grenade

Fort Royal

le Marquis

Pointe des Salines

Nord

Latitude Septentrionale

LES
PETITES ANTILLES
OU
Les Isles du Vent

Echelle de Trente Lieues Communes

5   10   15   20   25   30 L.

Longitude Occidentale du Meridien de Paris

Deg. 30   66   30   65   30   64   30   63   30   62   Deg. 30

18   Deg.
30
17
30
16
30
15
30
14
30
13
30
12
30   Deg. 11

Voyez ces Isles plus en grand N.º 80. N.º 81. et N.º 82. Voyez la Barbade N.º 98.

MAP 2. "Les Petites Antilles; ou, Les Isles du Vent." Eighteenth century.
Cliché Bibliothèque nationale de France, Paris

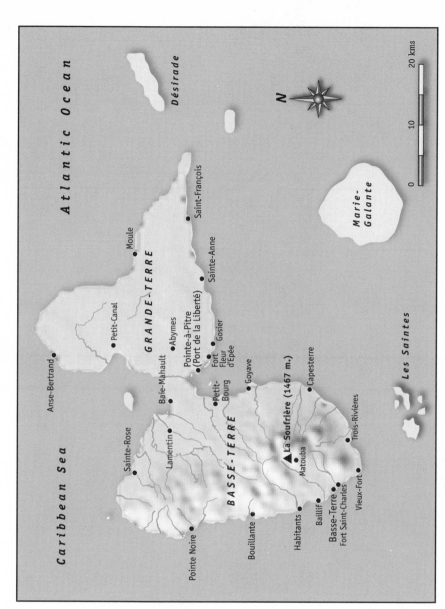

MAP 3. Guadeloupe in the Late Eighteenth Century. *Drawn by Gerry Krieg*

Part One

PROPHECY,

REVOLT, &

EMANCIPATION,

1787–1794

Chapter 1

INSURRECTION & THE LANGUAGE OF RIGHTS

During the night of Saturday, April 20, 1793, hundreds of enslaved blacks revolted in the area surrounding the village of Trois-Rivières, Guadeloupe. They killed twenty-two whites and ransacked a chosen set of plantations. They then locked up those plantations, posted sentries to prevent further looting, and marched out of Trois-Rivières toward the nearby capital of the island, Basse-Terre. There, soldiers and citizens heard news of the massacre, formed an armed troop, and marched out of town to put down the revolt. At dawn, the two groups met.

The soldiers prepared to fight, but the rebels were quiet, orderly, and unaggressive as they approached. When they were finally within firing range, a soldier shouted, "Who goes there?"

The blacks responded, "Citizens and friends!"

Six soldiers moved toward the insurgents, holding their bayonets in front of them. As one witness reported:

> One of the slaves began to speak and asked if we were citizens, patri-
> ots; the response came that yes, we were; in that case, he said, we
> are friends, we have come to save you, and hate only those aristocrats
> who want to kill you. We have no bad intentions; we want to fight
> for the Republic, the law, the nation, order. (These are their actual
> words.) We asked them if they had as leaders some *hommes de couleur*
> or whites; they responded no, that they acted on their own.

Four insurgent leaders discussed the situation with the white officers, describing what had happened in Trois-Rivières. The officers in turn explained that, in order to avoid panic, the soldiers should escort the enslaved into Basse-Terre, where they would be placed into custody. The insurgents agreed; they allowed the soldiers to surround them, and as they were marched into town they repeatedly shouted, "Vive la République!" The authorities placed them under guard at Fort Saint-Charles but did not disarm them. Under interrogation, the rebels explained that their royalist masters had armed them as part of an anti-Republican plot. Rather than act against the republic toward which they felt loyalty, they rose up against their masters and killed them.[1]

Victor Collot, then the governor of the island, arrived later in the day. He was shocked to discover that many of the local officials felt sympathetic toward the rebels and even claimed that they had saved Guadeloupe from a conspiracy linking the British and royalist planters. In a memoir published a few years later in the United States, Collot described how, after the "243 blacks slaughtered 22 whites . . . in the most barbaric fashion," the insurgents, "far from fleeing—which is the natural movement of the guilty, and especially of the African when he is not guided by whites—asked to come to Basse-Terre under the protection of the *Comité de sûreté générale*." When he arrived in Basse-Terre, Collot found the insurgents in the courtyard of the fort, "still soiled with the blood of their victims, clothed in their loot, armed with sabers, guns, and bayonets." He had to order them twice before they put down their arms. And he found the members of the comité insubordinate as well. They rejected his proposal to "lock the blacks up in a fort or on a ship in the harbor until the date of their trial . . . alleging that this would prejudice the trial, and that national commissioners had to know of an event of such importance, which had saved the colony." They further infuriated Collot by ruling that visitors had open access to the imprisoned rebels and that the rebel leader, Jean-Baptiste, was "free to come and go at all times, in order to better inform the comité of what occurred." Even more surprising, they agreed to Jean-Baptiste's request that twenty of the prisoners be allowed to go out each day.[2]

Collot wrote that "posterity" would never believe that the inhabitants of Basse-Terre, who had "always distinguished themselves by their wisdom and their patriotism," were made to "suffer such indignities." The comité, animated by criminal "Robespierrean principles," ignored "that, in a Republic, the good of the people resides in the virtues of the magistrates." Collot had watched one comité member recover "stolen pieces of

1. The quotes and the account are from the *Journal républicain de la Guadeloupe*, Apr. 24, 1793, in CAOM, C 7A, 47, 124.

2. Georges Henri Victor Collot, *Précis d'événements qui se sont passés à la Guadeloupe pendant l'administration de Georges Henri Victor Collot, depuis le 20 mars, 1793, jusqu'au 22 avril, 1794* (Philadelphia, 1795), 5–6. On Collot's career, see Anne Pérotin-Dumon, *Etre patriote sous les tropiques* (Basse-Terre, Guadeloupe, 1985), 179–182.

Prophecy, Revolt, & Emancipation, 1787–1794

furniture" that were "buried in the shacks of the Africans." "If you did not share in their crimes," he accused, "you would have had them condemned as thieves." He went on,

> But instead of that, what did the comité do? They proposed to form them into a legion! A regiment of assassins whose function would be to execute the laws made by the *Commission générale extraordinaire* or to be more precise of the comité; we were to employ them to chase, gun down, drown all those who held property regardless of their political opinions; these loyal satellites would have put themselves in the place of the soldiers, crying VIVE LA LIBERTÉ![3]

When Collot published this account in 1795, its prime villains—rebel slaves—no longer existed as such. The enslaved had been freed and declared citizens in all the French colonies as of February 1794, when the Jacobin-controlled National Convention in France ratified the abolition of slavery proclaimed several months earlier by Republican commissioners in Saint-Domingue. And the Jacobins he railed against were no longer in power; in the Thermidorean reaction during mid-1794, their leader Maximilien Robespierre was executed and the Reign of Terror was ended, with moderate Republicans taking control. Collot wrote from Philadelphia, where many émigrés from France and the Caribbean had fled to wait and watch events unfold. Throughout his memoir, written to defend himself against accusations that he had, through design or incompetence, lost Guadeloupe to the British in 1794, he presented himself as a victim of the Jacobins, whom he called "bloodthirsty savages." The anti-Jacobinism of Collot's account was similar to that found in many other texts of the time, but it also made particular claims about what many whites considered the most dangerous aspects of post-emancipation Guadeloupe and Saint-Domingue. Collot's most virulent accusation in the section quoted above is that the Jacobins actually wanted to turn the enslaved who had revolted into a Republican legion—that brutal murderers of whites would be welcomed into the fold of the French nation and even hailed as its defenders. In his description of the misdeeds propagated by Republican officials during

3. Collot, *Précis d'événements*, 7. Because of the continual importance of the marking of race in the larger struggles over the meaning of citizenship, I have in most cases chosen to preserve the original terms in text, both in the case of *noirs* (blacks) or *nègres* (negroes) and with terms such as *gens de couleur* (free people of color) and *mulâtre* (mulatto).

the Trois-Rivières revolt lay in microcosm a critique of the entire political project that had taken hold in the French Caribbean since 1793. In Saint-Domingue, armies composed of ex-slaves, under the black leader François Dominique Toussaint L'Ouverture, were fighting for the Republic against Spain and England; in Guadeloupe, the French administrator Victor Hugues was overseeing Republican military and political expansion also based on armies composed in large part of ex-slaves. What Collot saw as an insane Jacobin project had taken root: enslaved blacks had become citizens and formed legions that were turned against the internal and external enemies of the Republic.

Collot's retrospective version of the 1793 events in Trois-Rivières contrasted sharply with the report of the Comité de sûreté générale. They produced their assessment the month after the insurrection, in a series of meetings and interrogations driven by fears of a deluge of royalist conspiracies. Accepting and expanding on the accusations made by the enslaved themselves, the report declared the rebels innocent, identifying royalist conspirators as the original source of the trouble and casting the killings as a heroic Republican action. The often confused report, however, structured the events of the revolt by describing the white actors behind each of the black rebels involved. Despite its sharp political opposition to Collot's narrative, the comité report was therefore similar in at least one respect: neither depicted the enslaved themselves as an independent political force. The source of the uprising—and therefore its explanation—resided elsewhere, in political conflicts begun in the metropole and transported to the Caribbean. The genesis for the violence was the ideology of either the Jacobins or the royalists; the power of the enslaved as soldiers existed to be appropriated by one or another political party. The difference between the two accounts lay in which of the white political groups was blamed for igniting the black rebels' violence.[4]

Yet, if the Trois-Rivières revolt—and the larger process of slave insurrection that shook the edifice of slavery in the Americas during the 1790s—is to be understood, it must be through an exploration of how enslaved insurgents heard, spoke, and ultimately transformed an evolving Republican language of rights. By the time of the revolt in 1793, France had seen four years of terrifyingly swift and sweeping transformations whose acceleration toward a Jacobin climax was near culmination. Since 1789, ships had continually brought more and more surprising

4. "Rapport du Comité de sûreté générale à la Commission générale et extraordinaire de la Guadeloupe," May 8, 1793, in AN, D XXV, 129, 1008.

Prophecy, Revolt, & Emancipation, 1787–1794

news to the Caribbean, new laws and pronouncements often rescinded by the next set of orders: news of the storming of the Bastille, the abolition of aristocratic privileges, the confiscation of church property, the onset of war with the English, and ultimately the execution of the king himself. These ships also brought symbols of the Revolution—tricolor pins, new uniforms for soldiers and militias, banners carrying revolutionary slogans—that were signs of a larger, contested project of building a democratic nation. Struggles over the definition of citizenship took on particular inflections in the colonial setting, where social relations were defined by racial hierarchies tied to regimes of plantation labor. As they moved back and forth across the Atlantic during those years, the evolving ideologies and practices surrounding citizenship took on new meanings and had unexpected ramifications. In the French Antilles, groups driven by different histories and harboring different hopes participated in this broader conflict over the meaning of the Republic, engaging in increasingly murderous power struggles.

Writing the history of this period raises a set of difficult questions: What was the relationship between the Revolution in France and that in the Caribbean? In what ways did the ideas surrounding political rights and national citizenship during this period drive the changes that took place in the Antilles? Answering such questions requires reframing them. To begin with, we need to see the Enlightenment itself in an Atlantic context molded by colonial expansion and the institution of slavery. The mass enslavement of Africans on New World plantations and their resistance shaped eighteenth-century visions of human nature and human rights. The interlinked revolutions of the late eighteenth century—American, French, and Haitian—emerged from imperialism and were forged by a spectrum of political actors embedded in the social order of empire. The Caribbean, like the broader Atlantic world, played an essential role in the emergence of a new political culture during the late eighteenth century.[5]

The French Revolution set in motion political, military, and juridical changes that created an opening for demands by free people of color and slaves in the nation's Caribbean colonies. But the demands they made

5. On the links between slave resistance and Enlightenment thinking, see Michèle Duchet, *Anthropologie et histore au siècle des lumières* (Paris, 1971). For the term "political culture," see Keith Michael Baker, *Inventing the French Revolution: Essays on French Political Culture in the Eighteenth Century* (Cambridge, Mass., 1990); Lynn Hunt, *Politics, Culture, and Class in the French Revolution* (Berkeley, Calif., 1984).

and the strategies they used in making them sprang from a long tradition of resistance firmly rooted in these plantation societies. From the cross-roads of these two histories came insurrection and ultimately a radical reversal of the social order. Neither histories that focus narrowly on the "contagion" of French revolutionary ideas into the region nor that deny the importance of such ideas to the actions of the enslaved can tell the full story of this Caribbean revolution. The challenge is to write an ac-count that places the Caribbean people of African descent, both free and enslaved, at the heart—rather than on the margins—of the political and intellectual transformations of the age.

Historians of the French Revolution have explored in detail how the political culture of republicanism was shaped through violent struggles over the boundaries of citizenship in metropolitan France between 1789 and 1794, and some have given much attention to debates about colo-nial policy that then raged in Paris. But they have traditionally paid less attention to the crucial chapter in the history of Republican political cul-ture written during those same years in the plantation societies of the French Caribbean, where the movement that transformed slaves into free citizens gave new content to the universalism that was the centerpiece of Republican political culture.[6]

How and why these radical transformations occurred in the French Caribbean has long perplexed observers. In 1795, François Polverel—the son of the commissioner who, along with his colleague Léger Félicité Sonthonax, had abolished slavery in Saint-Domingue in 1793—intro-duced a pamphlet on the events of the previous years by noting: "In the colonies, the French Revolution encountered obstacles that were larger and more difficult to overcome than those it saw in the metropole." The interests of the *colons*, suggested Polverel, as well as "the servitude and degradation in which the largest class of men in the colony lived; the long experience they had of their chains; their respect for their masters,

6. I am indebted to Rebecca J. Scott for suggesting this formulation to me. It draws also on Ada Ferrer, *Insurgent Cuba: Race, Nation, and Revolution, 1868-1898* (Chapel Hill, N.C., 1999). C. L. R. James, in *The Black Jacobins: Toussaint L'Ouverture and the San Domingo Revolution* (New York, 1963), highlighted the ways the revolution in Saint-Domingue both responded to and surpassed the radi-cal transformations of the French Revolution. Robin Blackburn, *The Overthrow of Colonial Slavery, 1776-1848* (London, 1988), and Carolyn E. Fick, *The Making of Haiti: The Saint Domingue Revolution from Below* (Knoxville, Tenn., 1990), have also argued for the centrality of slave insurrections in the political transformations of the period.

whom they considered a race superior to themselves," made it seem that the "eternal principles consecrated in the Declaration of Rights" would never take root in the colonies.

A violent upheaval achieved what the [National] Assembly had avoided: the chains of the cultivateurs, which could have been removed by degrees, were shattered with a roar. Five hundred thousand men took back their rights, of which they had been deprived for the profit of a few hundred individuals. The National Convention legalized this emancipation, and extended its effects to all of its colonies. Free France has only free men among its children; soon this happy revolution will spread its blessings to the possessions of the other powers, and the day when Europe will see the head of its last tyrant fall will be the end of the slavery of Africans and Indians in the New World.[7]

"What were the causes, what were the events that precipitated, in Saint-Domingue, this massive change?" asked Polverel. "How did the *noirs*, so recently burdened under the whip, like animals, pass suddenly to the natural state of man? How did they become nearly the only population, and the only defenders, of the French territory? That is what I propose to explain." Unfortunately, Polverel's account, like the competing interpretations of the Trois-Rivières insurrection, concentrated almost entirely on the political conflicts between whites, and so he ultimately fails to answer his own question. In the following chapters, through a *récit des événements* that places the Trois-Rivières insurrection in the context of the revolutionary period of 1789 and 1794, I seek to show how groups of insurgents in the Caribbean "took back their rights" by acting as, and therefore becoming, Republican citizens.[8]

7. François Polverel, *A la commission des colonies, coup-d'oeil impartial sur Saint-Domingue; ou, Notions sur les événements qui ont eu lieu dans cette isle depuis le commencement de la révolution . . . adressées au Comité de salut public, le 19 messidor, l'an deuxième de la république* (Paris, 1794), 9–10.

8. Polverel, *Coup d'oeil impartial sur Saint-Domingue*, 10.

Chapter 2

A SOCIAL CARTOGRAPHY

In Alejo Carpentier's novel of the Haitian Revolution, *The Kingdom of This World*, an enslaved man named Ti Noel visits the maroon leader Makandal in his hideout and sees "an account book stolen from the plantation's bookkeeper, its pages showing heavy signs drawn in charcoal." Out of this stolen register, whose purpose had been to order the daily labor of the enslaved, Makandal has created something very different. Across a landscape divided into plantations, each with its population of human property, he has identified those who are willing to help him terrorize slave masters. The register maps out a network that spans the plantations and traces out a community tied together by a mission of resistance—a diagram of revolt rather than production.[1]

The enslaved, freed people of color, and masters in the Caribbean created societies layered with competing and interdependent social and economic networks. Although the economic exigencies of transatlantic commercial networks between particular colonies and their metropoles drove and defined the land use on Caribbean islands, a thriving contraband trade crossed imperial boundaries, connecting the diverse colonies in the Caribbean. And, while plantations produced staple crops of sugar, coffee, and cotton for metropolitan consumption, the enslaved developed parallel economies on the margins of these plantations.

In the 1830s, the abolitionist Victor Schoelcher visited a plantation in Martinique where a huge mango tree stood in the middle of a cane field, stunting the cane that grew in its shade. The planter would have cut down the tree, but it was owned by an enslaved man, who had already promised to pass it on to his descendants. According to Schoelcher, there were similar cases involving fruit trees owned by slaves on other plantations. "Alongside the property that the law guarantees and protects for those who are free, another form of property has developed

1. Alejo Carpentier, *The Kingdom of This World* (New York, 1967), 30.

among those who are not free, guaranteed not by written laws but by habit, with the consent of all classes of colonial society," claimed another text of the period. "The slave uses this property as he wishes; he passes it on to his children. . . . No master . . . would consider taking away the property of one of his slaves; whoever did so would be dishonored in the eyes of the entirety of colonial society." By cultivating their gardens and participating in informal market economies—as well as by joining or supporting communities of maroons—enslaved blacks in the late eighteenth and early nineteenth centuries created and cultivated networks that crisscrossed, and therefore undermined, the highly structured world of the plantations. Out of the networks they developed, typified by Makandal's account book, arose the insurrections that brought profound challenges and changes to the meaning of rights during the 1790s. And, once the enslaved gained emancipation, their understanding of what freedom meant grew out of the range of possibilities they had developed within slavery.[2]

Eighteenth-century maps of the Caribbean highlighted the plantations, roads, and port towns that focused on the production and export of commodities to the metropole. However, like the correspondence of administrators concerned with maintaining the social and economic order of the colony, these maps also sometimes identified other patterns and practices that emerged within and against this order. Such sources present a social cartography of eighteenth-century Guadeloupe, a world formed by the interaction of colonial policy and daily practice and by the negotiation between plantation masters and the enslaved who survived and resisted them.

The Emergence of the French Caribbean

French acquisition of Caribbean colonies began in 1625, under the rule of Louis XIII, when Cardinal Richelieu sent a mission to create a settlement on the small island of Saint Christopher. There, French and English settlers, along with the Caribs of the island, developed a fragile peace. The French settlement suffered from disease and periodic wars,

2. Victor Schoelcher, *Des colonies françaises: Abolition immédiate de l'esclavage* (1842; Paris, 1998), 10; Dale W. Tomich, *Slavery in the Circuit of Sugar: Martinique and the World Economy, 1830-1848* (Baltimore, 1990), chap. 8, esp. 274; Gabriel Lafond de Lurcy, *Un Mot sur l'émancipation de l'esclavage et sur le commerce maritime de la France . . .* (Paris, 1844), 17; for a broader look at the market system, see also Sidney W. Mintz, *Caribbean Transformations* (New York, 1989).

however, and several of its members envisioned setting up colonies on the three neighboring islands of Guadeloupe, Martinique, and Dominica, which remained entirely in Carib hands despite several European attempts at colonization. In 1635, Richelieu's newly formed *Compagnie des îles d'Amérique* funded colonization missions in Martinique and in Guadeloupe. On both islands, relationships with the Caribs quickly deteriorated, and by 1641 the French had expelled most Caribs from Guadeloupe.[3]

The Compagnie des îles d'Amérique ran the colonies until 1664, when the *Compagnie des Indes occidentales* gained a monopoly of French Caribbean commerce. These organizations granted concessions to settlers, who created a growing number of plantations during the seventeenth century while bringing in a steady stream of white *engagés* (indentured laborers) and enslaved Africans to work on them. In 1655, there were thirteen thousand whites and ten thousand Africans in the French Caribbean colonies, including Saint Christopher, with Martinique and Guadeloupe each containing about five thousand whites. The white population in Guadeloupe declined during the next decade, and, in 1671, slaves already made up 57 percent of the total population of approximately 7,500. By that time, the plantations on the island were quite varied: some focused on the relatively small-scale production of provisions or tobacco; others diversified and included indigo, ginger, and some sugarcane among their crops; still others focused exclusively on sugar production, anticipating the sort of plantation that ultimately would dominate the island.[4]

Martinique and Guadeloupe developed at roughly similar rates until 1671. At that point, the central administration of the French islands was transferred from Saint Christopher to Martinique, with long-lasting consequences for Guadeloupe. As the official seat, Martinique also gained commercial primacy with the metropole, leaving Guadeloupe dependent on Martinique's officials and merchants. This administrative hierarchy strengthened after 1674, when the royal government dissolved the Compagnie des Indes occidentales and brought Guadeloupe and Martinique under its direct control.[5]

3. Lucien-Réné Abénon, *La Guadeloupe de 1671 à 1759: Etude politique, économique et sociale*, 2 vols. (Paris, 1987), I, 15–19; Robin Blackburn, *The Making of New World Slavery: From the Baroque to the Modern, 1492–1800* (London, 1997), 279–281.

4. Blackburn, *New World Slavery*, 282; Abénon, *La Guadeloupe*, I, 31, 120–121.

5. Blackburn, *New World Slavery*, 282; Abénon, *La Guadeloupe*, I, 62–74.

Prophecy, Revolt, & Emancipation, 1787–1794

A few decades later, a new French colony emerged on the western part of the island of Hispaniola. It would ultimately far outshine Guadeloupe and Martinique and indeed all the other slave colonies of the Americas. In the early seventeenth century, French settlers had started encroaching on this Spanish colony, and in 1697 the Spanish crown officially ceded the western third of the island to the French. During the first decades of the eighteenth century, this new colony, Saint-Domingue, experienced a startling economic expansion. The French soon covered many of its rich plains, especially in the well-watered northern province, with sugar plantations. Saint-Domingue became the preferred destination for French slaving and shipping vessels, to the detriment of Martinique and particularly Guadeloupe.[6]

Still, France's new, wealthy colony fell under the same restrictions as its precursors in the eastern Caribbean. Through the Compagnie des Indes occidentales and the royal administration that followed, the *exclusif* (monopoly) governed the French colonial economy during the eighteenth century. In the early years of the colonies, most trade had been with foreign vessels, but French statesman Jean-Baptiste Colbert changed that and created a system whereby only ships from French ports could trade with the colonies. On all levels—from the purchasing of plantations and laborers to the maintenance of mills, to the sale and shipment of sugar and coffee—the metropole controlled the economic choices of planters. The planters, in turn, were legally required to buy and sell commodities through official trade routes and official institutions, which set prices and determined the amounts that would be purchased. Furthermore, colonial representation was very limited: until the Revolution, the French islands never had powerful assemblies of the kind common in the British islands.[7]

Planters chafed against these restrictions and against their limited capacity to change them. Many found themselves chronically indebted to metropolitan merchants, and bankruptcies were common. The planters believed, with good reason, that they could get better prices and make greater profits in a more open economic system. At the same time, the centralized structure of the French colonies aided the development of

6. On the development of Saint-Domingue, see Charles Frostin, *Les Révoltes blanches à St.-Domingue aux XVIIe et XVIIIe siècles* (Paris, 1975); Carolyn E. Fick, *The Making of Haiti: The Saint-Domingue Revolution from Below* (Knoxville, Tenn., 1990), chap. 1.

7. Blackburn, *New World Slavery*, 281–283.

FIGURE I. Plantation outside Basse-Terre. Early nineteenth century.
Engraving by Joseph Coussin. ©*Arch. dép. de la Guadeloupe, G 116*

---

a plantation economy from which many planters and merchants profited enormously. France's Caribbean colonies in the seventeenth century had lagged behind Great Britain's, notably Barbados, in growth; but during the eighteenth century France outpaced chief competitor England in productivity. The French islands had distinct ecological advantages: for one thing, they comprised twice as much land as the British islands. Saint-Domingue was more than double the size of Jamaica, at 10,714 square miles versus 4,411, and Guadeloupe and Martinique were, at 563 and 425 square miles respectively, much larger than Barbados (166) and Antigua (108). The French were also generally better supplied with the water that was vital to sugar production. These natural advantages were supplemented, however, by projects carried out by the royal government. The plains of the western province of Saint-Domingue, for instance, developed flourishing sugar plantations in the late eighteenth century as the direct result of government-sponsored irrigation works. Construction of roads and ports also helped develop the plantation economy.[8]

Although less important and profitable than Saint-Domingue, Guadeloupe was essential to the French sugar boom of the eighteenth century. On the flanks of the Soufrière volcano, plantations grew in richly watered areas such as Trois-Rivières, which was noted for its "beautiful sugar" in the Abbé Raynal's voluminous description of the European colonies. By the beginning of the eighteenth century, sugar had become the dominant crop, and Guadeloupe's population increased by leaps and bounds. In 1700, it was eleven thousand (58 percent enslaved), and by 1720 it had more than doubled to twenty-four thousand (70 percent enslaved). By 1751, the population had doubled again to fifty thousand (82 percent enslaved).[9]

At the time of the Seven Years' War (1756–1763), then, Caribbean colonies had become profoundly important to France, just as they had to Britain. As part of the campaigns of this transatlantic conflict, the British occupied Guadeloupe from 1759 to 1763, and a pamphlet war erupted in London over the question of which possession was more useful to the British Empire: Canada or Guadeloupe? One 1760 pamphlet estimated that the exports of Guadeloupe alone were roughly equivalent to those of all eight of the British Caribbean islands at the time. In 1761, an English merchant who lived on the occupied island argued that, if faced with a choice between Canada and Guadeloupe, Britain should take the latter. The land was rich and could produce a great deal of sugar; "thirty thousand acres in the West Indies would increase the value of Britain and America both, more than three hundred thousand either in Europe or America could possibly do." Basse-Terre, he noted, was teeming with

8. Ibid., 431–444, esp. 438; on the irrigation projects, see James E. McClellan II, *Colonialism and Science: Saint Domingue in the Old Regime* (Baltimore, 1992), 72.

9. See Guillaume-Thomas-François Raynal, *Histoire philosophique et politique des établissements et du commerce des Européens dans les deux Indes*, 10 vols. (Geneva, 1782), VII, 92–93; on the expansion of Guadeloupe's sugar economy, see Abénon, *La Guadeloupe*, I, 127–138. For the population statistics, see Christian Schnakenbourg, "Statistiques pour l'histoire de l'économie de plantation en Guadeloupe et en Martinique, 1635–1835," *Bulletin de la Société d'histoire de la Guadeloupe*, XXXI (1977), 1–121, esp. 37–38. These statistics are for the island of Guadeloupe itself and do not include the small populations of the island's dependencies of Marie-Galante and Les Saintes.

water and land not only for sugar but for other products such as cinnamon. The writer also argued that the British could easily lose control of the North American colonies, with their vast, unsettled territory, but keep control of a small island such as Guadeloupe. In the end, the French made the choice the author of the work had counseled for the British: through the Treaty of Paris in 1763, they surrendered the entirety of Canada in return for regaining control of Guadeloupe and Martinique.[10]

The British occupation of Guadeloupe had transformed the island, stimulating an era of unparalleled economic development. The extent of the British influence on the island can be divined in part from the fact that, during the four-year occupation, British slavers imported 15,215 slaves into the island, greater than the 14,003 imported directly by French slavers into Guadeloupe over the entire eighteenth century. When it was under French control, many slaves came into the colony via transshipment from Martinique or contraband rather than directly from slave-trading vessels. Such practices continued under the British: census data indicate an increase of approximately 30,000 slaves during the occupation. The slave imports were part of a broad project of development that expanded the island's sugar industry enormously; between 1761 and 1762 alone, the number of sugar plantations on the colony increased from 339 to 420. Although the exact range of the expansion in sugar production is controversial, some have estimated an increase of up to five times during the occupation, and more reliable statistics show coffee production likely increased to the same extent. More than a hundred ships a year came to trade in Guadeloupe not only from Britain but also from North America. Although some English merchants and planters came to Guadeloupe during this period, the vast majority of those who profited from the expansion were French planters already established there before the occupation. The rest of the Caribbean also felt the impact of the war and the occupation; the loss of Canada meant that French settlement and trade in the Americas became almost entirely focused on the islands, and the next decades saw unprecedented economic expansion all around, with slave imports reaching their highest levels.[11]

10. *Reasons for Keeping Guadaloupe at a Peace, Preferable to Canada, Explained in Five Letters, from a Gentleman in Guadaloupe, to His Friend in London* (London, 1761), 22. On the "pamphlet war," which at one point involved Benjamin Franklin, see Theodore Draper, *A Struggle for Power: The American Revolution* (New York, 1996), 3–25.

11. See Abénon, *La Guadeloupe*, II, 218–222. The information on slave imports

One major geographical impact of the British occupation of Guadeloupe was the development of a new city that was to become the economic
center of the island. In order to sustain their development of Guadeloupe,
the British created a port on the Rivière Salée, the small ocean channel
that separates the two halves of Guadeloupe, transforming Pointe-à-Pitre
from a swampy backwater into a bustling port town. This usurped the
role traditionally held by Basse-Terre, which had always been the major
port and governmental capital of the island, instigating a strong rivalry
between the two cities that exploded during the revolutionary period
—and indeed continued into the twenty-first century. When, in 1798,
metropolitan authorities briefly declared Pointe-à-Pitre (then called Port
de la Liberté) the administrative capital of the island, one of Basse-
Terre's merchants reminded them that, whereas the new capital was a
"noxious city, built in a swamp," Basse-Terre was a "healthy city, bathed
in water and rivers, where the inhabitants breathe a truly European air
. . . provided with good drinking water, hospitals, and institutions for
civilians and the military." A decade earlier, however, a visitor who was
perhaps less biased had noted that the government buildings there were
little more than "wooden shacks that are in danger of falling apart," a
condition the revolutionary period could only have worsened. Nevertheless, although Pointe-à-Pitre continued to be the largest and most active
city on the island and its largest commercial point, within a year Basse-
Terre regained its status as the administrative capital of the island, which
it retains to this day.[12]

In 1794, an English priest described the view of Basse-Terre from
the sea: "We were becalmed off the town, and had a beautiful view of
the country round it, which rising gradually inland, presents a varied
amphitheater of plantations, woods, hills, and valleys, interspersed with
elegant and well-built houses, ornamented by many fine plantations of
palms, cocoa-nut, and other tall and majestic trees." A 1791 account also
described the area around Basse-Terre as a "vast amphitheater." It is in

---

comes from *The Transatlantic Slave Trade: A Database on CD-ROM* (Cambridge,
1999).

12. For M. Albert's letter of year VI (1798), see AN, C 518, no. 183, I, 194; on the
development of the cities during the eighteenth century, see Anne Pérotin-Dumon,
"Commerce et travail dans les villes coloniales des lumières," *Revue française d'histoire d'outre-mer*, LXXV (1988), 31–78; Pérotin-Dumon, *La Ville aux Iles, la ville
dans l'île: Basse-Terre et Pointe-à-Pitre, Guadeloupe, 1650–1820* (Paris, 2000),
chaps. 3, 4.

FIGURE 2. "La Ville de la Basse Terre dans l'isle de la Guadeloupe."
Late eighteenth century. Engraving by Nicolas-Marie Ozanne.
Cliché Bibliothèque nationale de France, Paris

---

this theater, a small piece of the broader French colonial world, that we now set our scene.[13]

Soufrières

In the late 1760s, military cartographers created a detailed map of Guadeloupe, which consists of sixteen parts and would cover a space about fifty feet square if it were all pieced together. One sees a widely developed island, with most of the land divided into plantations connected by a network of roads and identified with particular owners. Only two areas were not divided in this way: the "Bas-Fonds" north of Pointe-à-Pitre and the middle of the island of Basse-Terre, north of the Soufrière volcano, which was identified as an "inaccessible core." Between the heights of the Soufrière volcano and the sea lay a multiform progression, from a site of maroon refuges to the regions of coffee production, then sugar production, and finally to the site of metropolitan authority housed in the official buildings of the capital city of Basse-Terre.

13. Cooper Willyams, *An Account of the Campaign in the West Indies, in the Year 1794* . . . (1796; rpt., Basse-Terre, 1990), 95; Louis Bovis, *Historique des événements qui se sont passés à la Basse-Terre, ville capitale de l'île Guadeloupe, depuis la révolution* (Basse-Terre, Guadeloupe, 1791), 2.

Prophecy, Revolt, & Emancipation, 1787–1794

FIGURE 3. "La Basse-Terre, vue prise de la Batterie de l'Impératrice (Guadeloupe)." Early nineteenth century. Lithograph by Emile Vernier. *Cliché Bibliothèque nationale de France, Paris*

Opposing the regions of the plantations were the paths "inaccessible" to the mapmakers and to officials but inhabited nonetheless. When the Guadeloupean-born poet Nicolas Léonard journeyed up the Soufrière volcano in the late 1780s, the surrounding dense, tropical nature amazed him. Having lost his way, he came across a small house and a plot of land cultivated by a family consisting of an eighty-year-old man and his many children, along with one slave. They lived in isolation, in one room, surviving off what they grew and wove from the surrounding jungle.[14]

14. See the "Carte générale de l'isle de Guadeloupe, 1768," BN, cartes et plans, Société hydrologique, portfolio 155, div. 2, 14. The gorgeously painted original version of this map, whose assembly depends on the geographical knowledge of the researcher, was used to make a smaller and more manageable version as well; see Nicolas Germain Léonard, "Lettre sur un voyage aux Antilles," in *Ouevres de M. Léonard* . . . (Paris, 1797–1798), I, 214.

These heights also sheltered maroon communities. The presence of the maroons, who comprised about 2 percent of the population of the island during the eighteenth century, was a persistent counterpoint to the regular functioning of the plantation. Their raids were a constant threat; the administration employed the *maréchaussée* (police) to hunt them down, and newspapers published descriptions of captured maroons whose owners were unknown. Although they had escaped from the plantations, maroons also depended on them—often through contacts with the slaves there—for food and information. Little was known of how the maroons lived or where their villages were, but at least one map marked the tracks they made as they escaped: a detailed topographical survey made around 1807. This map shows all the ravines heading up from Basse-Terre, past Matouba, and stops at the Soufrière volcano. Near the top of the map, one path diverges. Heading toward the summit of the mountain, a path called Chemin du Grand Marron eventually disappears. Its other fork, which turns back down the slope toward the ocean, is named Chemin du Petit Marron. *Grand marronnage* represented a definitive break from the plantation, a disappearance, and *petit marronnage* represented a short-term escape with the intention of returning. That these two choices were common enough to be marked as names for the paths that led either to permanent freedom or back to the plantation suggests that they were established routes—familiar enough on the island to be known to a French mapmaker.[15]

Maroons were not the only ones who left traces on the land in their attempts to carve out spaces for themselves in the colony. In the 1770s, military administrators in Basse-Terre claimed that the indiscriminate chopping of trees on the slopes above the town was destroying strategic, protected sites vital to the defense of the island. Some of those who had chopped down trees or shrubs were known plantation owners, and they were in a few cases ordered to replant in certain areas. Much of the

15. CAOM, Dépôt des fortifications des colonies (hereafter cited as DFC), Guadeloupe, 460-A. The map dates from 1807–1808. On the percentage of maroons in Guadeloupe, see Léo Elisabeth, "Résistances des esclaves aux XVIIe et XVIIIe siècles dans les colonies françaises d'Amérique, principalement aux îles du Vent," in Marcel Dorigny, ed., *Les Abolitions de l'esclavage de L. F. Sonthonax à V. Schoelcher, 1793, 1794, 1848* (Paris, 1995), 78–86. For general studies on marronnage, see Yvan Debbasch, "Le Marronage: Essai sur la désertion de l'esclave antillais," *L'Année sociologique* (1961), 1–112; Gabriel Debien, "Le Marronage aux Antilles françaises au XVIIIe siècle," *Caribbean Studies*, VI (1966), 3–44.

Prophecy, Revolt, & Emancipation, 1787–1794

damage, however, had been done by "a number of *petits habitants* [poor whites] whose names are unknown." "These habitants are clearing not only the plain between the mountains but also the slopes, and if we don't stop them, there will soon be a new opening onto the plain and therefore onto Basse-Terre, which is vital for us to avoid." Furthermore, a chaotic network of trails had developed, linking Basse-Terre, Trois-Rivières, and the slopes above and between the two towns. The military officials saw in this the creation of routes that could be used by enemy forces in case of an invasion of the island. But the illegal cutting of the trees and the creation of new paths were testament to the attempts of poor whites, and likely gens de couleur and slaves as well, to build houses, keep their fires burning, and facilitate their daily movement from place to place.[16]

The administrative concern about the downing of trees was part of a larger set of conflicts over the use of the natural resources of the colony, such as water. In 1788, a land surveyor named Mallet inspected and reported on the water supply of the city of Basse-Terre and the neighboring *bourg* of Saint-François. He tracked the "cours d'eau" from the center of the town near the ocean, up to where the water supplied the hospital and the garrison, and beyond to the slopes above. What he found shocked him: "It is surprising that no one has brought the administrators of this colony to look upon the bad quality of this water. . . . It is certain that a number of people have died because of it." The disturbance of the water in the ravine by fishermen and the overgrowth of plants made the water fetid and dirty; one of the main streams passed through a "vinaigrerie," which poisoned the water, and through a number of latrines before reaching the hospital, the garrison, and the town proper.[17]

The canals Mallet inspected drew water from the streams in order to supply both agricultural needs and the population of the town. Water was crucial for plantations, particularly sugarmills, and as such its distribution was often established through legal documents. In Trois-Rivières, Augustin Delignières, while introducing sugar on a plantation, had a statement drawn up by a notary attesting that his diversion of water from the Carbet River would not interfere with any other plantations. In another agreement—which highlights the detailed distribution of water—

16. "Mémoire sur les défrichis et les inconvenients qui en résultent pour la défense du pays," "Ordonnance concernant la conservation des bois de l'isle de Guadeloupe et dépendances," both in CAOM, DFC, Guadeloupe, carton 28, nos. 289, 318.

17. Mallet, "Visite des eaux de la ville de Basse-Terre et bourg St. Francois de l'isle de Guadeloupe," in CAOM, DFC, Guadeloupe, carton 29, no. 414.

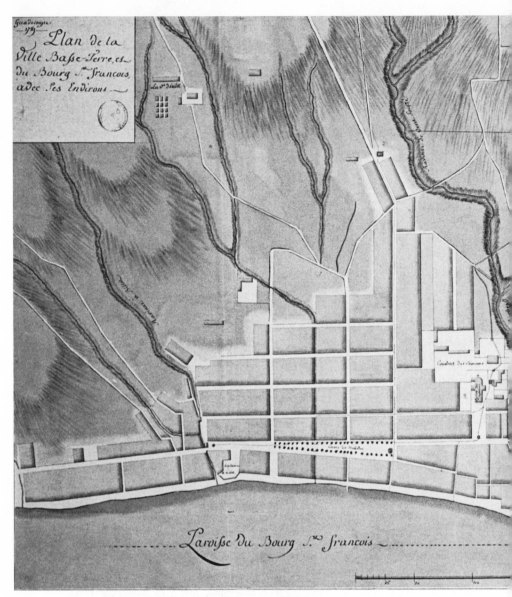

MAP 4. "Plan de la ville Basse-Terre, et du bourg St. François, avec les environs." 1787. The town of Basse-Terre and its neighboring bourg of Saint-François are depicted here. *C.A.O.M. Aix-en-Provence (France), F 3, 288, no. 62. Tous droits réservés*

Paroisse de la Ville Basse Terre

a small landowner in Trois-Rivières allowed another owner to build a canal across his land. In return he gained the right to use for himself a "filet" of water three inches wide.[18]

The life of Basse-Terre formed around water. The Rivière Galion and the Rivières des Pères bordered the town, and the Rivières aux Herbes divided its center. Throughout Basse-Terre, according to a Danish visitor of the late eighteenth century, stood "bubbling fountains that distribute water as fresh and clear as crystal." A large one graced the town's main axis, the tree-lined Champ de Mars, whose very name evoked the political presence of the metropole. So did the government buildings clustered along this road. To the east, the avenues led to Fort Saint-Charles, which dominated the town, and to the west the avenues, dotted with fountains, led into Saint-François, the commercial heart of the city. It was there that some of the local gens de couleur lived, such as one "André mulâtre libre," whose property was fed by some of the canals Mallet inspected. Indeed, the Danish visitor observed "a multitude of gardens," most of which were traversed by "running water" that allowed their owners to grow "the most delicate vegetables": artichokes, asparagus, and peas.[19]

All of these uses of water were threatened by a series of illicit practices Mallet identified in his report. The large pierced stone that regulated the flow of water to the fountains of the Champ de Mars was often "overturned by the negroes, in order to divert the water." On Saturdays and Sundays the slaves redirected the water for bathing and washing clothes, which sent soap and lime into the water supply. They also diverted water to the gardens they kept on the plantations. The ditches they (along with some white fishermen) dug destroyed the canals, lowering the level of the water and creating stagnant pools. In certain places, Mallet could barely identify the outlines of the original canals, which were covered with plants and destroyed by the holes that fed a network of irrigation ditches.[20]

The official ownership of resources such as water, land, and of course the slaves themselves was contested within and without the plantation in ways denied by official contracts and regulations. Ownership over the bodies of the enslaved, for instance, was asserted even after they had es-

18. CAOM, Notariat Guadeloupe, Barbier, 53, Dec. 13, 1791, Jan. 13, 1792.

19. Mallet, "Visite des eaux," in CAOM, DFC, Guadeloupe, carton 29, no. 414; Paul Erdman Isert, *Voyages en Guinée et dans les îles caraïbes en Amérique* ([1793]; Paris, 1989); Pérotin-Dumon, *La Ville*, chap. 7, esp. 377–379.

20. Mallet, "Visite des eaux," in CAOM, DFC, Guadeloupe, carton 29, no. 414.

Prophecy, Revolt, & Emancipation, 1787–1794

FIGURE 4. One of the rivers flowing through the town of Basse-Terre. Early nineteenth century. Engraving by Joseph Coussin. ©*Arch. dép. de la Guadeloupe, G 39*

caped from the plantation. The planter Delignières, in addition to notarizing his right over the water of the Carbet River, made another agreement in renting the plantation where he was introducing sugarcane: as was the common practice, both he and the sister who owned the plantation were to consider the slaves who had marooned as part of the property. They were, in the words of the notary act, to be considered "present, though absent." But, even if legal documents could assert the ownership of Delignières over absent slaves, and even if Mallet could assert the right of plantations and official fountains to water use over that of slaves or poor whites tending gardens, the actual practice of marronnage and appropriation of resources betrayed the confidence of these documents.[21]

21. "Présents, quoique absents," in CAOM, Notariat Guadeloupe, Barbier, 52, Jan. 25, 1791. On this common practice, see Debbasch, "Le Marronage," *L'Année sociologique* (1961), 1–112.

Contraband and Community

From towns like Basse-Terre and Trois-Rivières, commodities traveled across the Atlantic to the port towns of France to have a wide-ranging impact on the economy of eighteenth-century Europe. Sugar, in particular, transformed patterns of trade and consumption as it turned from a luxury into a necessity. In France, the capital generated by the slave economy helped fuel the growth leading up to the French Revolution. C. L. R. James famously linked the Caribbean and French Revolutions in *The Black Jacobins*:

> "Sad irony of human history," comments [Jean] Jaurès. "The fortunes created at Bordeaux, at Nantes, by the slave-trade, gave to the bourgeoisie that pride which needed liberty and contributed to human emancipation." ... Nearly all the industries which developed in France during the eighteenth century had their origin in goods or commodities destined either for the coast of Guinea or for America. The capital for the slave-trade fertilized them; though the bourgeoisie traded in other things than slaves, upon the success or failure of the traffic everything else depended.[22]

The plantation economy, and the traffic in humans that sustained it, produced fortunes in France. Profits from the French slave trade itself were extremely variable, but some slave-trading families made enough to invest in industries linked to colonial commerce, such as textile production. Others invested directly in the Caribbean colonies, where they acquired plantations (sometimes through the bankruptcy of planters to whom they had given loans) they placed in the hands of local managers.

---

22. See Sidney W. Mintz, *Sweetness and Power: The Place of Sugar in Modern History* (New York, 1985); C. L. R. James, *The Black Jacobins: Toussaint L'Ouverture and the San Domingo Revolution* (New York, 1963), 47–48. James's claim never incited the kind of debate that has surrounded Eric Williams's parallel arguments about the importance of slavery in the development of British industry; see Williams, *Capitalism and Slavery* (1944; Chapel Hill, N.C., 1994); for criticisms, see Seymour Drescher, *Econocide: British Slavery in the Era of Abolition* (Pittsburgh, 1977); Drescher, "The Decline Thesis of British Slavery since *Econocide,*" *Slavery and Abolition: A Journal of Comparative Studies*, VII (1986), 3–24; David Eltis, *Economic Growth and the Ending of the Atlantic Slave Trade* (New York, 1987). See also more generally Philip D. Curtin, *The Rise and Fall of the Plantation Complex: Essays in Atlantic History* (Cambridge, 1990); David Eltis and James Walvin, eds., *The Abolition of the Atlantic Slave Trade: Origins and Effect in Europe, Africa, and the Americas* (Madison, Wisc., 1981).

More important, however, were the profits gained by merchants involved in reexporting colonial sugar to the rest of Europe.[23]

In sharp contrast to Britain, which consumed most of the sugar produced in its colonies domestically, the majority of the products that arrived in French ports from the Caribbean were consumed outside of France. Between 1785 and 1789, for instance, an average of roughly 90 percent of the coffee, 70 percent of the sugar, and 75 percent of colonial commodities as a whole were reexported. Products from the Caribbean colonies made up half of France's total exports. The port town of Bordeaux, a major arrival point for ships coming from across the Atlantic, boomed in the late eighteenth century as a result of its major role in this trade. As the foundation for the Caribbean plantation economy, the slave trade therefore played a crucial role in the economic and social development of eighteenth-century France. The colonial economy stimulated a social and economic transformation that was essential to the rise of a wealthy and powerful bourgeoisie determined to challenge their exclusion from the society of the ancien régime.[24]

The structure of the French colonial economy also created numerous tensions, notably between metropolitan merchants and the planters of the Caribbean. Although increasingly weakened by the end of the eighteenth century, the exclusif still dominated the economic life of the French Caribbean. The very restrictiveness of the exclusif and the in-

23. On the French slave trade, see Curtin, *The Atlantic Slave Trade: A Census* (Madison, Wisc., 1969), chap. 6; Robert Louis Stein, *The French Slave Trade in the Eighteenth Century: An Old Regime Business* (Madison, Wisc., 1979), esp. chap. 10; on Nantes, see Olivier Pétré-Grenouilleau, *L'Argent de la traite: Milieu négrier, capitalisme, et développement: Un modèle* (Paris, 1996). A detailed study of one merchant house in Bordeaux is Françoise Thésée, *Négociants bordalais et colons de Saint-Domingue; liaisons d'Habitations: La Maison Henry Romberg, Bapst et Cie, 1783-1793* (Paris, 1972).

24. For a history of the French Revolution that highlights the importance of the colonial trade, see Georges Lefebvre, *The Coming of the French Revolution, 1789*, trans. R. R. Palmer (Princeton, N.J., 1947). On Bordeaux as a slave-trading port, see Eric Saugera, *Bordeaux, port négrier: Chronologie, économie, idéologie, XVIIe–XIXe siècles* (Paris, 1995). For the statistics on colonial reexportation, see Jean Tarrade, *Le Commerce colonial de la France à la fin de l'ancien régime: L'Evolution du régime de 'l'exclusif' de 1763-1789* (Paris, 1972), II, 754-755; see also Patrick Villiers, "The Slave and Colonial Trade in France Just before the Revolution," in Barbara L. Solow, ed., *Slavery and the Rise of the Atlantic System* (Cambridge, 1991), 210-236. On the comparison between French and British trade, see Blackburn, *New World Slavery*, 444-449.

ability of the metropole to supply the growing colonies with what they needed helped produce a thriving contraband business, which created links between the colonies of different empires and redefined their economies. The proximity of English and Dutch islands provided ample opportunities for illegal trade. Sugar was shipped out, untaxed, along illegal routes, as were coffee and cotton; food, wine, and other perishables were traded; and slaves were brought into the colony from the British or Dutch islands. The contraband trade provided a livelihood for individuals who existed on the margins of colonial society, flouting official control. The practices of *coureurs-des-îles* (Frenchmen who traded with Carib communities during the sixteenth and seventeenth centuries) continued into the eighteenth century; white sailors and traders—sometimes joined as well by freed slaves—plied the coasts of other islands and traded with English, Dutch, and Caribs.[25]

The island of Guadeloupe, particularly the city of Basse-Terre, had an especially well developed illegal trade because of its marginal position within the French Caribbean colonies. In the second half of the eighteenth century, few French boats making the transatlantic voyage even stopped in Guadeloupe, preferring the richer ports of Saint-Domingue and the more developed Martinique. Saint-Pierre was the administrative and trade center for the French in the eastern Caribbean, through which Guadeloupean planters had to export their crops and import goods whose prices were increased by Martinican middlemen. These conditions made smuggling an economic necessity for many. In 1770, an estimated 40 to 50 percent of the island's trade took place through illicit means. Sometimes boats from Guadeloupe on legitimate missions carried contraband, notably when they traveled to the neighboring British colony of Dominica. Ships from Martinique as well as from the British, Spanish, and Dutch islands also brought contraband to Guadeloupe; so did schooners from the North American colonies and, later, the United States.[26]

25. See Philip P. Boucher, *Cannibal Encounters: Europeans and Island Caribs, 1492–1763* (Baltimore, 1992); Peter Hulme, *Colonial Encounters: Europe and the Native Caribbean, 1492–1797* (London, 1986).

26. See Pérotin-Dumon, "Commerce et travail," *Revue française d'histoire d'outre-mer*, LXXV (1988), 31–78, esp. 35–40. Between thirteen and one hundred ships visited Guadeloupe annually, with an average of 67 visits per year between 1781 and 1792, compared to an average of 105 per year in Martinique during the same period. Furthermore, those stopping in Guadeloupe were much more often

Basse-Terre's situation in Guadeloupe made it an ideal center for contraband. Most ships arriving in the colony stopped in Pointe-à-Pitre; from there, smaller boats shipped goods to Basse-Terre and, in turn, from Basse-Terre to other seaside towns nearby. Basse-Terre, therefore, was a center for the comings and goings of small boats owned and managed by whites or gens de couleur and often manned by enslaved sailors. These boats could as easily ship contraband as they did legal imports. They were ideally suited for the former, which was often carried out at night, when arriving ships anchored along the coast or in sheltered bays, signaling contacts ashore to row out to meet them. Thus the administrative capital of the island was also a hub of illegal trade that sustained the town's economy.[27]

In the decades before the French Revolution, administrators in Guadeloupe repeatedly identified contraband as a serious subversion of metropolitan authority. In 1773, when the *Chambre d'agriculture de la Guadeloupe* requested the creation of a separate government on the island, one of their main arguments was the need for a local administrative body to control the continual illegal trade with nearby islands such as Dominica. A memoir from 1787 suggests that—despite changes in the administration of Guadeloupe and increased policing—contraband had risen. The visits made by officials to inspect ships entering and leaving the ports were inefficient and superficial, because they were done when the ships were completely loaded. Besides, "as everyone knows, it is along the coasts, and in the bays, that the contraband is conducted." The only solution, the writer suggested, was to police the open waters between the island and nearby Dominica; otherwise the "foreigners" would continue to navigate "in full security and tranquillity." "Isn't this the moment to redouble our surveillance in order to conserve, for the metropole, the products of these islands . . . which our neighbors constantly try to usurp through all conceivable means?"[28]

In 1789 and 1790, with the advent of the French Revolution, the

---

on intra-Caribbean or American journeys rather than transatlantic ones. See the "Recensement général de la colonie pour la population et la culture pendant l'année 1790," in CAOM, DFC, Guadeloupe, carton 29, no. 443.

27. Pérotin-Dumon, *La Ville*, 216–220.

28. "Mémoire de la chambre d'agriculture de la Guadeloupe, sur la demande d'un gouvernement indépendant de la Martinique," "Mémoire sur la contrebande aux îles du Vent," both in CAOM, DFC, Guadeloupe, carton 28, nos. 247, 285; see also Raynal, *Histoire philosophique et politique*, VII, 92–93.

monopoly was one of the most vociferously attacked aspects of governmental policy. If it was clear to those white planters who attacked the exclusif how many possibilities would open up if this monopoly trade were eliminated, it is in no small part because the profits of contraband were already well known. The illicit trade created, through contacts between the small islands of the eastern Caribbean and the various zones of the Greater Caribbean, a parallel economic network that linked English, Dutch, French, Spanish, and Caribs. This set of relationships was later exploited by the Republican administration of Victor Hugues, who turned smuggling and piracy into official wartime policy and crafted a military alliance with the Black Caribs of Saint Vincent.

The contraband trade set up multiple links between the islands of various colonial powers. In the face of an official policy that sought to make the transatlantic connection between metropole and colony the main course for the transmission of economic and political power, another set of routes connected the Caribbean, creating other identities that depended less on the metropole and more on the Creole culture within the Lesser Antilles. These routes created another map, organized, not according to the demands of the metropolitan centers of empire, but according to the needs of the various social groups of the Caribbean. Among these groups, of course, the majority of population were slaves themselves who, even as they were locked within the oppressive conditions of slavery, were able to carve out spaces of autonomy and develop connections that transcended the economic and political order of the plantation society.

Slavery and the Social Contract

The French Caribbean of the late eighteenth century has been described as a collection of "five island colonial units"—Martinique, Guadeloupe, and the three provinces of Saint-Domingue—along with French Guiana. Of these, the three provinces of Saint-Domingue were demographically and economically the most important, boasting a population in 1789 of approximately 465,000 slaves, 30,000 whites, and 28,000 gens de couleur. The most marginal area was French Guiana, sparsely populated by 1,307 whites, 494 gens de couleur, 10,748 slaves, and 812 Indians. Martinique's population of approximately 101,600—83,000 slaves, 10,600 whites, and 5,000 gens de couleur—was a bit smaller than that of Guadeloupe, which according to a 1790 census was 107,228. There were 90,134 slaves, about 85 percent of the population, 13,969 whites, and 3,125 gens de couleur.[29]

Guadeloupe's economic marginality within this broader system and its dependence on contraband had important demographic effects on its slave population. Because French slavers made Guadeloupe the last destination after Saint-Domingue and Martinique, Guadeloupe was consistently undersupplied in slaves as well as in other materials. Over the course of the eighteenth century, only 1.6 percent of slaves brought to the French Caribbean on French slavers were brought to Guadeloupe, with 10.9 percent going to Martinique and 74.3 percent going to Saint-Domingue. Guadeloupe received less than 1 percent of slaves between 1700 and 1750 (less than the Guianas and Louisiana), and this increased to only around 2 percent between 1750 and 1800. Even if one factors in the large number of slaves brought in by the British during the Seven Years' War, the number of slaves recorded arriving in Guadeloupe in the entire eighteenth century totaled only about forty-six thousand. Although the natural growth rate of the enslaved population was higher than in Saint-Domingue, running a bit over 3 percent between 1770 and 1789, a 110 percent increase took place between 1753 and 1788. Guadeloupe's enslaved population grew as it did because of the constant arrival of slaves via transshipment from Martinique as well as through an illegal but well-known trade that brought slaves from nearby English and Dutch colonies to Guadeloupe. Slaves who arrived in the French colony from these other islands diversified the slave population, bringing not only new languages and religious practices but also news and stories from their former homes. In fact, some of them might well have maintained connections with their former communities.[30]

29. Curtin, *Rise and Fall*, 159; for the population of Saint-Domingue and Martinique, see Blackburn, *The Overthrow of Colonial Slavery, 1776–1848* (London, 1988); for Guiana, see Yves Bénot, *La Guyane sous la Révolution française; ou, L'Impasse de la révolution pacifique* (Kourou, 1997), 15; for the Guadeloupe census, see "Recensement général de la colonie pour la population et la culture pendant l'année 1790," in CAOM, DFC, Guadeloupe, carton 29, no. 443. These statistics probably underestimated the actual population of slaves, since masters throughout the Caribbean often underreported slave numbers to decrease their tax liability.

30. For the statistics on slave imports, see *The Transatlantic Slave Trade: A Database on CD-ROM*. Among French slave traders from the port of Nantes, of 737 ships that made the journey from Africa to the Antilles between 1707 and 1763, only 12 (1.6 percent) stopped in Guadeloupe; 264 (35.8 percent) stopped in Mar-

Many of the enslaved in Guadeloupe, of course, had been torn from communities across the Atlantic, in Africa. They, too, brought diverse cultures, languages, and histories to the island. Among those brought directly to Guadeloupe by slave traders arriving from Africa, almost a quarter came from ports in West-Central Africa, which exported massive numbers of Congo slaves during the eighteenth century. Just under 20 percent came from the Bight of Biafra, home to various groups including the Igbos, whereas 12 percent arrived from the Bight of Benin, the oldest of the slave-trading regions and home to groups such as the Aradas, the Fons, and the Nagos. Smaller percentages came from other regions of Africa, and the origins of many others on these vessels were not identified. Since so many slaves came to Guadeloupe via routes that left their arrivals unrecorded, however, the extent to which these percentages can be applied more broadly to the African slave population of the island is uncertain. So, too, is the percentage of eighteenth-century Guadeloupe's slaves born in Africa. In a survey of about 10 percent of the enslaved population between 1770 and 1789, 20 percent were identified as African-born, whereas nearly 60 percent were born in the colony itself. The remaining 20 percent had no origin indicated, possibly because they had been purchased through a contraband trade. Even if we assume half of those with unidentified origin had been born in Africa, this means that less than a third of the island's population were African. The contrast with Saint-Domingue is striking. In 1789, two-thirds of the slaves in France's "pearl" were African-born.[31]

-----

tinique; and the rest (62.6 percent) went to Saint-Domingue. After 1763 and the British occupation of Guadeloupe, the number of ships stopping in Guadeloupe increased only slightly: of 1,427 ships from Nantes that traveled from Africa to the Antilles between 1763 and 1793, 32 (2.2 percent) stopped in Guadeloupe, with only 53 (3.7 percent) stopping in Martinique; 94.1 percent of slave ships went only to Saint-Domingue (Jean Mettas, *Répertoire des expéditions négrières françaises au XVIIIe siècle*, ed. Serge Daget, 2 vols. [Paris, 1984]). On the growth rate and the contraband supply of slaves, see Nicole Vanony-Frisch, "Les Esclaves de la Guadeloupe à la fin de l'ancien régime d'après les sources notariales (1770–1789)," *Bulletin de la Société d'histoire de la Guadeloupe*, LXIII–LXIV (1985), 3–165, esp. 156; Lucien-Réné Abénon, "Le Problème des esclaves de contrabande à la Guadeloupe pendant la première moitié du XVIIIe siècle," *Bulletin de la Société d'histoire de la Guadeloupe*, XXXVIII (1978), 49–58.

31. Vanony-Frisch, "Les Esclaves," *Bulletin de la Société d'histoire de la Guadeloupe*, LXIII–LXIV (1985), 3–165, esp. 154–157; Fick, *Making of Haiti*, 25. There is no complete, exhaustive study of slave origins in Guadeloupe. For an examination of one African ethnicity in the French Antilles, see Josette Fallope, "Contri-

Eighty percent of the enslaved in Guadeloupe lived on rural plantations. Among the 90,139 slaves listed in the 1790 census, roughly 55,000 were field laborers, half of these working on sugar plantations and the other half working on cotton and coffee plantations. Of the roughly 51,279 cultivated acres on the island (which covered less than half of its overall surface), 22,686 were used to grow sugarcane, with the rest divided between cotton, coffee, and food for local consumption. During the previous decade, the number of plantations had decreased even as the amount of land cultivated had expanded, which suggests that certain planters had expanded their holdings, driving others out of business. But business was good: between 1781 and 1792, sugar exports increased by 220 percent, and coffee exports more than doubled. The economy, however, fluctuated a great deal from year to year. These cycles of boom and bust had a profound impact on the lives of the planters as well as on the material conditions of the enslaved, who were likely to find themselves working more and eating less in times of economic strain.[32]

Such was the statistical landscape of the island—a plantation society centered on production for the metropole, harboring a majority population of slaves. The lives of this majority were governed by contracts not of their own choosing, transformed through ordered and registered sales, and administered by official policy. On the plantation, most slaves worked long days in the fields, organized into work groups led by a slave the French called a *commandeur* and the English called a "driver." Work varied depending on the period of the year; during the sugarcane harvest, from the end of December until July, slaves worked all day and all night, cutting the cane and then processing it in the sugarmills. On coffee plantations, picking was concentrated from September to December but also took place during other months, notably March. Outside the harvest season, slaves took up a variety of other agricultural tasks with occasional periods of less-intense labor, such as the month of December on sugar plantations. The rhythm of labor was different for slaves who worked as domestics in the master's house, with the women often working as nurses, cooks, or laundresses. An elite group of slaves, whose jobs

bution de Grand Lahou au peuplement afro-caribéen," in Serge Daget, ed., *De la traite à l'esclavage: Actes du colloque international sur la traite des noirs, Nantes, 1985* (Paris, 1988), 9–24.

32. Schnakenbourg, "Statistiques pour l'histoire de l'économie," *Bulletin de la Société d'histoire de la Guadeloupe*, XXXI (1977), 1–121, esp. 55, 57, 63, 87, 105, 113–120. These statistics are drawn from official sources and so do not account for contraband trade.

allowed them a certain freedom of movement and the occasional possibility for money-making, worked as hunters or fishermen or as artisans—masons, barrelmakers, carpenters, and blacksmiths. The pace and intensity of the work depended on the product: sugar plantations were the largest, often employing hundreds of slaves; cotton plantations were usually smaller, as were coffee plantations, which were usually located on mountainous terrain and were often the province of new landowners, such as gens de couleur. In Guadeloupe, and especially in the region of Basse-Terre, most plantations were run by their owners and not by managers working for absentee planters. The functioning of these individual plantations depended on a social structure that enforced the exclusion of slaves from personhood—and from the all-important ability to make contracts.[33]

The policing of this social structure depended on a group that occupied a paradoxical place within it: the gens de couleur. This "intermediate" category between free whites and the enslaved was made up of those of African descent who were no longer enslaved. Many, but not all, in this group also had some European ancestry. Although their liberty guaranteed them many of the legal rights denied to the slaves, they were also subject to a battery of discriminatory legislation. The limits on their freedom helped drive many men in this group to volunteer for the militia service, an arena in which they could demonstrate their value and loyalty to colonial society. During the second half of the eighteenth century, hommes de couleur came to occupy a central place in the local militias, particulary Saint-Domingue's. Free-colored units from that colony were an important part of the French expeditionary forces that supported the

33. Vanony-Frisch, "Les Esclaves," *Bulletin de la Société d'histoire de la Guadeloupe*, LXIII–LXIV (1985), 3–165, chap. 7; see also generally Gabriel Debien, *Les Esclaves aux Antilles françaises (XVIIe–XVIIIe siècles)* (Basse-Terre, Guadeloupe, 1974); on plantation harvesting schedules, see 139, 143. On the sexual division of labor on the plantations, see Arlette Gautier, *Les Soeurs de Solitude: La Condition féminine dans l'esclave aux Antilles du XVII au XIX siècle* (Paris, 1985), particularly chap. 7. Detailed documents about the functioning of one plantation in the area of Basse-Terre between 1689 and 1754 can be found in the papers of Michel Bouquet in AN, T 268, 1; see also Poyen Sainte-Marie, *De l'exploitation de sucreries; ou, Conseils d'un vieux planteur aux jeunes agriculteurs des colonies* (Basse-Terre, Guadeloupe, 1792). For Saint-Domingue, see the documents of the Gallifet plantation in Saint-Domingue, located in AN, 107, AP, 127–130; Debien, "Les Esclaves des plantations Mauger à Saint-Domingue, 1763–1802," *Bulletin de la Société d'histoire de la Guadeloupe*, XLIII–XLIV (1980), 31–164.

American Revolution, participating in the 1779 siege of Savannah. In Guadeloupe in 1780, 1,200 of the 3,400 militia troops were "colored." Saint-Domingue also had free-colored officers, but Guadeloupe's militia officers were always white.[34]

During times of war, service in the militia and in other military units was also a route to freedom for enslaved men. In the second half of the eighteenth century, French Caribbean administrations established "liberty taxes"—which ranged from five hundred to two thousand livres, increasing toward the end of the century—and levied them against masters who wished to free one of their slaves. The policy was an attempt to limit manumissions as well as to raise money for the colonial state. This tax, however, was waived if the enslaved man in question served a certain term in the militia. The master avoided paying for his good deed, and the enslaved man gained his freedom, though only after many years of difficult military service. In the meantime, the colonial government had the use of an additional soldier.[35]

In Saint-Domingue, opportunities for freedom were available more consistently throughout the later eighteenth century through service in the maréchaussée, the colonial police force. In 1787, as officials in the eastern Caribbean buckled down on contraband, they also drew on the example of Saint-Domingue in calling for the formation of brigades for the "internal policing" of Martinique, Guadeloupe, Saint Lucia, and Tobago. "Considering how important it is that the agriculture of these islands, which is in the hands of the slaves, be actively protected by a disciplined corps of police," administrators laid out a detailed plan for the composition and the work of the maréchaussée. The officers of the corps were to be all white and made up of army officers or soldiers who were literate and "good subjects." The main body of the corps, however, would be drawn from the existing free-colored militia companies. A distinction was made between the two groups in these militias: there was to be a preference for free volunteers as opposed to those who were serving to gain their freedom. The free would serve in the maréchaussée for eight years; the enslaved serving for liberty would remain for twelve.[36]

34. Stewart R. King, *Blue Coat or Powdered Wig: Free People of Color in Pre-revolutionary Saint-Domingue* (Athens, Ga., 2001), chap. 4; John D. Garrigus, "Catalyst or Catastrophe? Saint-Domingue's Free Men of Color and the Battle of Savannah, 1779–1782," *Revista interamericana*, XXII, nos. 1–2 (1992), 109–124; Pérotin-Dumon, *La Ville*, 674–676.

35. King, *Blue Coat*, 56, 108; Pérotin-Dumon, *La Ville*, 672–675.

36. "Projet: Ordonnance du roi, portant création de compagnies de maréchaus-

The English sailor Henry Schroeder might have witnessed the mobilization of gens de couleur and slaves for the maréchaussée when he landed in Guadeloupe in 1787 and saw that "a considerable number of negro troops were training, consisting of mulattos and negroes." Schroeder also encountered a figure who symbolized the important possibilities this kind of military service could hold for social advancement in the colony: "A commissioned officer, a man of colour, of the black corps, who kept a rum store on the beach." The officer granted Schroeder and the other sailors credit at his store and appeared not to keep very close accounts of what they consumed. The day before the sailors left, however, the officer appeared on the boat and gave the captain a detailed bill of all his sailors had spent. The captain refused to pay and abused and insulted the de couleur officer, who responded with dignity and politely shook hands with the sailors before leaving the ship. The next day, when the captain set sail without having settled his debt, the battery on the shore fired a shot and a boatful of French soldiers rowed out to the ship. They commanded the captain to return to Basse-Terre, where authorities forced him to pay not only for what the sailors had consumed but for the damage they had inflicted during a bar fight. At least in this case, an homme de couleur of rank in the military was able to count on the support of other soldiers in the defense of his economic interests.[37]

Ironically, the gens de couleur and the slaves who gained status—and in so doing undermined the racial order of the plantation society—were also central in preserving slavery. The job of the maréchaussée, proposed in 1787, in addition to maintaining order in the colonies, was to "stop deserters, vagabonds, untrustworthy outlaws, and maroons, and to make sure the slaves follow the laws." Their routine was to involve the surveillance of the slaves both in the countryside and in their gathering places in

sée affectées à la police intérieure des isles . . ." (1787), in CAOM, DFC, Guadeloupe, carton 29, no. 411. Maréchaussée regulations restated and extended traditional provisions for policing first institutionalized on a large scale with the Code noir in 1685; see Louis Sala-Moulins, *Le Code noir; ou, Le Calvaire de Canaan* (Paris, 1988); Antoine Gisler, *L'Esclavage aux Antilles françaises XVIIe–XIXe siècles* (Fribourg, Switzerland, 1965), esp. chap. 2. On the maréchaussée in Saint-Domingue, see King, *Blue Coat*, 56–60. For parallel contemporary developments in metropolitan France, see Robert M. Schwartz, *Policing the Poor in Eighteenth-Century France* (Chapel Hill, N.C., 1988), esp. chap. 7.

37. William Butterworth [Henry Schroeder], *Three Years Adventures, of a Minor, in England, Africa, the West Indies, South-Carolina and Georgia* (Leeds, 1831), 289–290, 312–313.

Prophecy, Revolt, & Emancipation, 1787–1794

the towns, including the potentially lucrative shops and "cabarets established for the slaves," which by law could be owned only by gens de couleur. The owners of these establishments were allowed only to "sell either wine, rum, or other liquors at the door of their cabarets" and could open their shops only between sunrise and sunset; they were responsible for preventing slaves from eating, drinking, or gambling in their establishments. The *auberge* was a crucial center of social life for whites, and the owners were important figures; in Trois-Rivières, the *aubergiste* Louis Robert was by far the most common witness for notary acts of all kinds, including those of *mulâtres libres* who were buying or emancipating slaves. The regulation of the cabarets was likely an attempt to curtail the formation of a parallel gathering place for slaves while also placing gens de couleur as the mediators between the world of the free and that of the slaves. Owners of cabarets were also prohibited from "accepting payment in sugar, cotton, coffee, or other goods," limiting the economic access of slaves who might barter with goods they had grown, stolen, or acquired through trade in the markets.[38]

The regulation of other kinds of "slave gatherings at crossroads or in the countryside" was the subject of several other of the maréchaussée's intended duties. According to the 1787 regulations, they were "to visit the different crossroads of the towns and the countryside to dissipate slave gatherings; to seize those who are gambling and the money that is in the game and to immediately bring the guilty to prison." Any free people caught gambling with slaves could be punished with a month in prison, with harsher penalties for recidivists. White plantation owners who allowed "the 'calandats' and nocturnal dances that take place to the sound of the drum" in the houses of their slaves could be fined. When the maréchaussée was "informed of these dances or of any tumultuous gatherings of negroes during the night," its job was to "disperse these assemblies" and to report them so the guilty master could be punished.[39]

38. "Projet," in CAOM, DFC, Guadeloupe, carton 29, no. 411. Louis Robert was the witness in approximately one-third of the acts (CAOM, Notariat Guadeloupe, Barbier, 51–53).

39. "Projet," in CAOM, DFC, Guadeloupe, carton 29, no. 411. Such stipulations were already present in Articles 16 and 17 of the Code noir of 1685, which made "attroupements" of slaves illegal, whether for weddings or any other celebrations. Such gatherings were especially outlawed in "isolated places," and punishment for slaves who were caught at such gatherings could go as far as the death penalty for recidivists. The term *calandat* did not appear, however, in the Code

The *calandats*—"tumultuous" gatherings of slaves—were seen as a threat throughout the Antilles. They not only provided a space in which slaves from different plantations could act in a community but were also known to be the site of religious rituals whose practice frightened and mystified whites. Since the seventeenth century, the policy of suppressing slave gatherings had gone hand-in-hand with the encouragement of slave participation in official religious holidays. As part of a larger policy meant to encourage religious instruction among the slaves, Article 6 of the *Code noir* had outlawed masters from working their slaves on Sundays and on holy days. This rule had clearly been the subject of complaints in the colonies; as early as 1763, the *préfet apostolique* of the Dominicans in Martinique had requested a special dispensation for the colonies that would reduce the number of holy days. Such a policy was in fact instituted in 1787 by Louis XVI, who received permission from the pope to give a special order decreasing the number of religious holidays in the colonies to ten. The declaration noted that the large number of holidays "occasioned serious inconveniences, either from the scandal caused among those who observed them or from the disorders that are always the result of idleness." Clearly, the slaves' appropriation of sacred days as a way of breaking the routine of work and plantation life had disturbed colonial officials. The limitation of the number of holidays would, the king hoped, encourage "our subjects in the colonies to fulfill more zealously the duties that religion requires of them on these solemn days."[40]

During his 1787 visit to the island, Schroeder spent a Sunday on a "summit of a hill" outside of Basse-Terre. The "congregated negroes and others" formed circles, Schroeder wrote, with the young people sitting at the center; each group—the "sambo," "mustees," "mulattoes," "blacks" —had its own circle. Women, particularly the well-dressed domestic servants, gathered separately, performing a "mazy dance" and "singing." They danced "unencumbered by their dress, which consisted of a white

---

noir; it came into use during the eighteenth century. See Gisler, *L'Esclavage*, 21–22; Sala-Moulins, *Le Code noir*.

40. Déclaration de Louis XVI, Versailles, Jan. 28, 1787, in CAOM, Généralités, box 86, 785; see also Gisler, *L'Esclavage*, 24, and Leslie G. Desmangles, *The Faces of the Gods: Vodou and Roman Catholicism in Haiti* (Chapel Hill, N.C., 1992), on colonial policy and fear of Vodou in Saint-Domingue; on slave dances and religious rituals in Saint-Domingue, see Médéric-Louis Élie Moreau de Saint-Méry, *Description topographique, physique, civile, politique, et historique de la partie française de l'isle Saint-Domingue* . . . (Philadelphia, 1797), I, 63–70.

FIGURE 5. "Cudgelling Match between English and French Negroes in the Island of Dominica. . . ." 1779. Engraving by Agostino Brunias. *Cliché Bibliothèque nationale de France, Paris*

dimity petticoat, very short; a shawl tastefully tied round the head; and another hanging pendant, like a sash, the ends being tied together on the shoulders." They also wore a lot of jewelry: "Many-coloured beads glittered on the arms and wrists of most of them; large ear-rings, considered ornamental, distinguished some; and all sported necklaces round their necks, some of which the finest sculptors might be proud to copy, as models of symmetry." The men divided themselves into teams identified by flags of different colors and competed against one another in martial arts, including stick-fighting and head-butting, or "tupping." For this sport, which had distinct African roots, some of them had cut their hair to form a kind of cushion. They fought to music played on "humstrums, an instrument somewhat like a guitar; drums; and rattles, made by enclosing a small number of pebbles in the firm textured shell of a cocoa nut, of themselves more discordant than the drone of a bagpipe." Another group of men and women "amused themselves dancing to African music, produced from drums of different sizes, or any sonorous body." One of them was "a raisin jar, which was placed between the legs of a person sitting on the ground, who produced a sound, by beating the open end thereof."[41]

During the same period, another visitor, Nicolas Léonard, witnessed a wedding ceremony among slaves on the Desmarêts plantation, just above Basse-Terre. "Different nations of blacks appeared," he wrote, "distinguished by their flags." The bride, dressed in white, danced in the center of a circle with her eyes to the ground while different women presented themselves and challenged her by dancing in front of her, then placed a coin in the apron she was wearing. "The nations each had their particular dances; hers was limited to small and measured movements of her feet." Others sang wedding songs punctuated by choruses, clapped, or twirled while knocking calabashes together. Men played drums and laughed at the joking gestures of the female dancers, and the celebration continued until it began to rain.[42]

Such vibrant gatherings, which brought together the free and the enslaved, from plantation and town, provided the foundation for the circulation of news and for networks that would become so important in organizing the revolts of the early 1790s. The administrators who pushed for an injunction against the celebration of feast days and who ordered the maréchaussée to police and disperse these assemblies perceived this potential. Nonetheless, such gatherings persisted. In 1790, a writer in Pointe-à-Pitre argued for increased policing to fight the "desertion, lack of discipline and banditry among the negroes, which have advanced to such a point that it is a danger to public security; groups of blacks and deserters are camped in the woods throughout our islands, promising the same revolutions that Jamaica and Dominica have suffered." He also suggested that the authorities should take upon themselves to systematically destroy "poisonous plants, especially in those areas frequented by negroes" in order to "take from their hands the tools of their ven-

41. Butterworth, *Three Years Adventures*, 300–305. On the African roots of head-butting, see W. Jeffrey Bolster, *Black Jacks: African American Seamen in the Age of Sail* (Cambridge, Mass., 1997), 119–120, which discusses Schroeder's (Butterworth's) account of Guadeloupe.

42. Léonard, "Lettre," in *Ouevres de M. Léonard*, I, 207. This text, originally published in 1787, was an account of a journey to Guadeloupe that took place sometime after 1783. See also Gautier, *Les Soeurs de Solitude*, 99–106, on practices and debates surrounding slave marriages in the Antilles.

FIGURE 6. "Le Mariage des nègres." 1794. Engraving by Freret.
Private collection

---

geance and hatred." By then, slavery was increasingly under assault both
in the Caribbean and in the metropole. Over the preceding decades, partially in response to the strain placed on plantation slavery by slave resistance, various French writers had denounced the immorality of slavery.
Their works, which responded to the struggles of slaves in the Caribbean, in turn inspired new attacks against slavery on both sides of the
Atlantic.[43]

43. Dubuc de Marentille, *De l'esclavage des nègres dans les colonies de l'Amérique* (Pointe-à-Pitre, Guadeloupe, 1790), 26, in AN, AD VII, 21 A, no. 4. The
author was referring to maroon wars and slave revolts that had taken place in the
previous decades in these British colonies.

The Roots of French Antislavery

In February 1788, Jacques-Pierre Brissot de Warville founded the *Société des amis des noirs*, whose members eventually included French revolutionary figures such as the marquis de Condorcet, the Abbé Grégoire, the comte de Mirabeau, and the marquis de Lafayette. What united them beyond an interest in the problem of slavery was a political project that emphasized the need for the unity of the national territory—including the colonies—in relation to a supreme national authority. The creation of this society, whose immediate inspiration was the British movement for the abolition of the slave trade, was part of a long tradition of political thought concerning slavery. Drawing on earlier criticisms of slavery, which included those written by French missionaries in the Caribbean in the seventeenth and early eighteenth centuries, the baron de Montesquieu attacked the morality and philosophical legitimacy of the institution in his 1721 *Persian Letters* and again in his 1748 *Spirit of Laws*; so did Jean-Jacques Rousseau, most notably in the 1762 *Social Contract*, and François Arouet de Voltaire in a 1768 dialogue called *L'A,B,C*. Both Rousseau and Voltaire also dealt with slavery in novels, the latter most famously in a scene in *Candide* where the characters meet a mutilated slave. That passage might have been inspired by a reading of the English novel *Oroonoko*, by Aphra Behn, which told the story of an enslaved African prince. First translated into French in 1745, it was among the nine most read English novels in France between 1760 and 1780. It inspired a similar French novel called *Ziméo* (1769), which in turn inspired antislavery articles during these years. These works were part of a broader move in novels, plays, memoirs, and travel accounts to portray the enslaved as noble and generous individuals who were unfairly oppressed. This tradition flourished at the end of the 1780s with the publications of Bernardin de Saint-Pierre's *Paul et Virginie* (1788) and Joseph Lavallée's 1789 novel *Le Nègre comme il y a peu de blancs*, written with the goal of "making it so the noirs are loved." Antislavery sentiments found their place within certain articles of the *Encyclopédie* (edited by Dénis Diderot and published between 1751 and 1765) as well as in the *Encyclopédie méthodique* (1782). Physiocrats broadcast opposition to slavery through their writings, notably through the *Ephémérides du citoyen*. They, along with other French antislavery thinkers, took inspiration from the actions of the Quakers in North America and the writings of Anthony Benezet.[44]

44. Edward Derbyshire Seeber, *Anti-slavery Opinion in France during the Sec-*

Criticisms of slavery were part of the Enlightenment philosophes' concern with the creation of societies and states in which individuals would see their rights guaranteed and their potential for reason and progress freed from oppression. In extending the compass of human legitimacy, philosophes used the figure of the slave to show the absurdity and waste generated by tyranny. Their evocations of the suffering and resistance of the enslaved, however, were linked to the pressure placed on the slave system by daily resistance and marronnage during the eighteenth century. The consolidation of maroon groups throughout the Caribbean, along with the consistent slave revolts (such as the poisonings attributed to Makandal during the 1750s in Saint-Domingue) forced administrators to reflect on the brutality of slavery and the danger resistance posed to whites.

For planters, the response to slave resistance was commonly to intensify repression and steadfastly defend the strict hierarchy of colonial society as the only way of preventing slaves—and gens de couleur—from ever imagining their equality to whites. Yet, for a number of colonial administrators, slave resistance represented the beginning of a crisis within slave society, and they sought to develop policies that might ease the violence of masters and slave rebels alike. There is no simple correlation between slave resistance and the development of antislavery discourse; although the Dutch and Portuguese colonies were the sites of the largest and most powerful maroon communities, large antislavery currents did not flow through their metropoles. In the French colonial world, however, there were numerous links between reform-minded administrators and Enlightenment thinkers who wrote about slavery and colonialism. To cite one example, the comte de Mirabeau, a key member of the Société des amis des noirs, was influenced by the letters written to him by his brother, who served from 1753 to 1755 as the governor of Guadeloupe.

---

ond Half of the Eighteenth Century (Baltimore, 1937), esp. 28–34, 59, 63–67, 76–77, 84–89, 104, 148–150, 175, 178–179, and bibliography; for Montesquieu's attack on slavery, see Montesquieu, The Spirit of Laws: A Compendium of the First English Edition, ed. David Wallace Carrithers (Berkeley, Calif., 1977), particularly book 15. On the Physiocrats' opposition to slavery, and the work of Condorcet, see Chapter 6, below. On the Société des amis des noirs, see Blackburn, Overthrow of Colonial Slavery, 169–170; Daniel P. Resnick, "The Société des amis des noirs and the Abolition of Slavery," French Historical Studies, VII (1972), 558–569; Marcel Dorigny and Bernard Gainot, La Société des amis des noirs, 1788–1799: Contribution à l'histoire de l'abolition de l'esclavage (Paris, 1998), which includes the complete register of the society's meetings.

Such connections facilitated intellectual and political discussions about the viability of slavery.[45]

Metropolitan France also became the site of direct challenges to the legality of slavery on the part of slaves themselves. During the second half of the eighteenth century, in a series of highly publicized trials, black slaves who had been brought by their masters to Paris demanded —and often won—their freedom. The lawyers who argued their cases, many of them in the Admiralty Court of Paris, did so on the basis of a common-law tradition (which they in fact developed as they invoked it) that outlawed slavery in metropolitan France. Some royal officials reacted sharply to these trials and to the presence of ex-slaves in cities such as Paris by putting in place a series of measures aimed at excluding those defined as "blacks," who were explicitly identified as a danger to the national body, from the territory of France. In the 1780s, the *Police des noirs* required blacks who lived in France to carry identity papers *(cartouches)* proving their status and right to be in the country; they could be stopped and questioned on the streets, then deported to the colonies if they lacked papers. One advocate of the removal of all Africans from France argued that their presence led to a situation in which "the public houses are infected; the colors mingle together; the blood degenerates." "Black" prostitutes spread venereal disease, he argued, and he further denounced "bizarre marriages of black men with white women and white men with negresses, monstrous unions of slave with free, by which are graced creatures of neither one or the other species, forming an oddity which will soon disfigure the children of the state." Yet the presence of slaves in France and their legal struggles for liberty combined with other circumstances to increase sympathy for the political and moral concerns raised by slavery.[46]

Among the most powerful attacks against slavery came the massive project overseen by the Abbé Raynal, one of whose main contributors

45. Michèle Duchet, *Anthropologie et histoire au siècle des lumières* (Paris, 1971), 137–180, esp. 160–161. See also Elisabeth, "Résistances," in Dorigny, ed., *Les Abolitions de l'esclavage*, 78–86; Malick Walid Ghachem, "Sovereignty and Slavery in the Age of Revolution: Haitian Variations on a Metropolitan Theme" (Ph.D. diss., Stanford University, 2001). On Dutch antislavery, see the essays in Gert Oostindie, ed., *Fifty Years Later: Antislavery, Capitalism, and Modernity in the Dutch Orbit* (Pittsburgh, 1996).

46. Sue Peabody, *"There Are No Slaves in France": The Political Culture of Race and Slavery in the Ancien Régime* (New York, 1996), esp. 119, 129. The Admiralty Court of Paris freed nearly a hundred slaves during the eighteenth century.

Prophecy, Revolt, & Emancipation, 1787–1794

was Diderot: the *Histoire philosophique et politique des établissements et du commerce des Européens dans les deux Indes* (1782). This monumental work, which presented a universal history of European colonization in the Americas and in Asia, also examined the effects of the colonial venture on metropolitan culture. Diderot railed against the devastation and depopulation brought about by the slave trade in Africa and the brutality against slaves in the Americas.[47] In a much-quoted passage, he delivered an urgent and prophetic warning about the potential of slave revolution that carried with it echoes of the Last Judgment:

> Your slaves do not need your generosity or your advice to shatter the sacrilegious yoke that oppresses them. Nature speaks louder than philosophy or interest. Already two colonies of fugitive negroes have been established, and they are protected from your attacks by treaties and by force. These flashes announce the lightning, and all that the negroes lack is a leader courageous enough to carry them to vengeance and carnage. Where is he, this great man, that nature owes to its vexed, oppressed, tormented children? Where is he? He will appear, do not doubt it. He will show himself and will raise the sacred banner of liberty. This venerable leader will gather around him his comrades in misfortune. More impetuous than torrents, they will leave ineffaceable traces of their just anger everywhere. All their tyrants—Spanish, Portuguese, English, French, Dutch—will fall prey to iron and flame. The American fields will be transported to drunkenness from drinking the blood that they have been awaiting for so long. And the bones of innumerable unfortunates, piled up over three centuries, will shake with joy. The Old World will join its applause to that of the New. Everywhere people will bless the name of the hero who reestablished the rights of the human species, everywhere monuments will be erected to his glory. Then the Code noir will disappear, and the Code blanc will be terrible, if the victors consult only the law of revenge![48]

47. According to Anthony Pagden, Diderot knew that "the metropolis could never be fully insulated from the consequences of the processes of overseas expansion that it had itself initiated" and saw slavery as "a potential moral danger to the metropolitan French" (Pagden, "The Effacement of Difference: Colonialism and the Origins of Nationalism in Diderot and Herder," in Gyan Prakash, ed., *After Colonialism: Imperial Histories and Postcolonial Displacements* [Princeton, N.J., 1995], 129–152, 138–139). For a discussion of Diderot's participation in the Raynal work, see Duchet, *Diderot et l'histoire des deux Indes; ou, L'Ecriture fragmentaire* (Paris, 1978).

48. The exact text of this quotation varies between the different editions of Ray-

L'Ouverture might have read, and been inspired by, this passage, as C. L. R. James has famously claimed. But, if the *Histoire des deux Indes* prophesied insurrection, it could do so because certain slaves had already, as the passage notes, created communities of freedom in the midst of slavery. This resistance was the context for Raynal's prophecy, and certainly L'Ouverture did not need the *Histoire des deux Indes* to teach him that important leaders had emerged from among the slaves of Saint-Domingue to fight for freedom. Yet the invocation of the possible link between Raynal and L'Ouverture suggests the potency of the layered encounter between the fight for liberty that emerged from the Caribbean and the longing for escape from the brutality of the past expressed by the European philosopher.

After the promised insurrection in Saint-Domingue had brought about emancipation, the painter Anne-Louis Girodet reflected on the relationship between Raynal's prophecy and its historical materialization in his famous portrait of the black deputy Jean-Baptiste Belley. Elected to represent Saint-Domingue in the parliament in 1793, Belley was among a group of three who spoke to the National Convention in February 1794, celebrating the abolition of slavery that had been decreed in Saint-Domingue a few months before. Their intervention spurred the Convention to decree abolition in all the French colonies. Afterward, Belley continued to serve as Saint-Domingue's representative for several years. In the painting, he leans comfortably on a bust of Raynal; perhaps Girodet depicted him in this way to portray him as the embodiment of Raynal's prophecy or even as the direct product of the thinker's work. Yet Belley looks upward and away from Raynal, suggesting that the cold white stone is less important than what lies ahead and that the violent colonial history recounted in the *Histoire des deux Indes* might now be, thanks to the figure that turns its back on Raynal, consigned to the past. In the background lies the sea, and, barely visible, smoke rises from the plain, reminding viewers of the burning of Le Cap during battles be-

---

nal's work; here I have translated directly from the version that is most extreme in its bloody imagery and praising of black revolt, *Histoire philosophique et politique des établissements et du commerce des Européens dans les deux Indes*, 4 vols. (Geneva, 1780), III, 204–205. This section of Raynal's text was in fact heavily drawn from Louis-Sébastien Mercier, *L'An deux mille quatre cent quarante, rêve s'il ne fut jamais* (Amsterdam, 1771), in which the author imagined a future in which statues of the "avenger of the New World" would decorate plazas all over Europe; see Dorigny and Gainot, *La Société des amis des noirs*, 18.

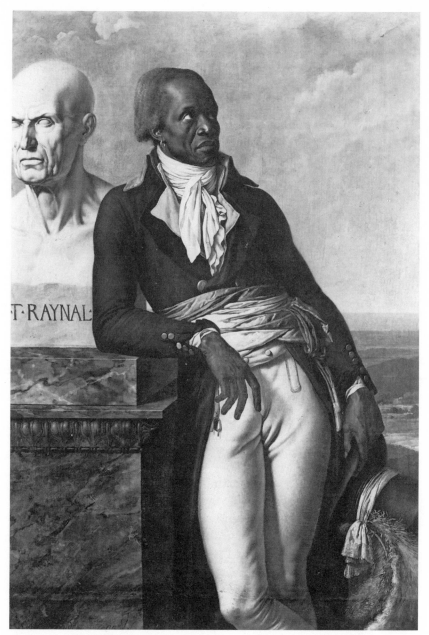

FIGURE 7. Jean-Baptiste Belley. 1798. Painting by Anne-Louis Girodet.
Alinari/Art Resource, N.Y.

tween insurgents and whites in 1793. Out of the irredeemable past of slavery that had been the source of corruption for Europeans emerged the force that eliminated the loathsome stain of slavery from the French Empire.[49]

Long before Belley sat for his portrait, of course, French abolitionists had already imagined how, short of revolution, the evils of slavery might be peacefully undone. Most saw moderate reform and a slow-paced transformation toward emancipation as a means of avoiding the conflagration of colonial society. Many critics of slavery, unwilling to advocate the dismantling of the institution, proposed the improvement of the conditions of slavery — which often boiled down simply to an enforcement of the Code noir, which had in theory been in application since 1685 but whose stipulations on the rights of slaves were consistently ignored by planters. Observers noted the low birth rates within slave communities and made various suggestions about how to improve the situation of women in order to encourage them to have children. Planters had good reasons to encourage enslaved women to give birth, since the result would increase their property and work force. For reformers, however, pronatalist policies were also a way of improving the conditions of the enslaved who, they argued, could become a self-reproducing population if they were treated less harshly, which in turn would make phasing out the slave trade possible. Some suggested various rewards for mothers, whether material, such as additional clothing or small sums of money to be granted for each child born, or symbolic, in the form of public gatherings celebrating fertile women and excluding those who did not have children. In the mid-1780s, regulations about the management of properties whose owners were absent required shorter workdays for pregnant women and decreed that women who were working on the plantations and had six children would be granted one free day a week each year until they were entirely free from plantation labor. If any of their children died, however, this privilege was to be taken away. There was also increasing attention to supplying health care to pregnant women and children on plantations. Pronatalist impulses, of course, could also lead to the physical punishment of women accused of having abortions. In Saint-

49. I draw here on Pagden, "Effacement of Difference," in Prakash, ed., *After Colonialism*, 129–152, esp. 140–141; on the painting, see Helen Weston, "Representing the Right to Represent: The Portrait of Citizen Belley, Ex-representative of the Colonies, by A. L. Girodet," *Res*, XXVI (Autumn 1994), 83–109; for James's description of L'Ouverture's encounter with Raynal, see *Black Jacobins*, 25.

Domingue, one master forced a slave he suspected of killing her child to wear a small wooden sculpture of a human being around her neck.[50]

Whereas some reformers focused on ways of improving the lives of women in order to ensure higher birth rates, others envisioned a general amelioration of slavery meant to lead to a more productive and humane system. Influenced in part by his encounter with black soldiers during the American Revolution, the marquis de Lafayette suggested to George Washington that, together, they could conduct an experiment in the gradual improvement and elimination of slavery. Washington, though impressed with the idea, had other things on his mind. But Lafayette eventually put his idea into practice during the late 1780s, when he acquired two plantations and a few hundred slaves in Guiana and hired a plantation manager to institute a new kind of labor regime there. There was to be no corporal punishment on the plantations, and the slaves were to be paid a salary; furthermore, they would be subject to the same laws that governed whites. Madame de Lafayette corresponded with the plantation manager's wife, who took on the task of giving religious education to the slaves and placed an older enslaved woman in charge of the children's education. After the first manager died in 1787, Lafayette hired another named Geneste, who wrote extensively to Lafayette about his failures and successes on the plantation and claimed that he was able to make the slaves work with little recourse to corporal punishment, as long as his instructions were clear and his orders consistent. Geneste found, however, that the slaves remained wary of him and refused to talk to him when he visited their houses in the evening. Lafayette considered it a measure of his success that, in 1791, when revolts swept through nearby plantations, his slaves did not rise up; afterward Geneste publicly defended the slaves of the plantation against accusations that they had participated. Just as Victor Hugues would do a few years later, however, Geneste expressed his "disappointment" with the blacks, writing, "When you know them well, all you can say about the general perversity of this unfortunate race can only give you a feeble idea of the truth." Frustrated by the failures of his timid reforms, Geneste pointed to the seemingly innate characteristics of the enslaved.[51]

50. See Gautier, *Les Soeurs de Solitude*, chap. 4, esp. 107–114.

51. Liliane Willens, "Lafayette's Emancipation Experiment in French Guiana, 1786-1792," *Studies in Voltaire and the Eighteenth Century*, CCXLII (1986), 345–362, esp. 357–359. On colonial reformism more broadly, see Tarrade, "L'Esclavage est-il réformable? Les Projets des administrateurs coloniaux à la fin de l'ancien

The tracks of reform crossed continents and affected policy in complicated ways. If Lafayette's experiences in North America had sensitized him to slavery, his plan for the Guiana plantations in turn caught the attention of Louis XVI. In fact, Lafayette's influence in part might well have encouraged a series of royal decrees for the improvement of slave conditions that were sent out from 1784 to 1786, in response to reports of incidents of particularly shocking brutality on the part of masters. The ordinances reiterated and expanded on the well-established, but constantly ignored, stipulations of the Code noir and insisted that masters provide slaves with both food and a plot of land for their own use. They placed new regulations on corporal punishment, providing for penalties against masters who gave more than fifty whiplashes and declaring that a master who murdered a slave could be punished with the death penalty, as with other homicides. Though planter resistance thwarted the application of the decrees in the colonies, the actions taken by Louis XVI helped set the stage for later rumors that the king had freed the slaves—rumors that animated many revolts of the early 1790s. His actions also, however, highlighted the prerevolutionary government's willingness to take only very small steps on the issue of slavery.[52]

On the eve of the French Revolution, the results of Lafayette's experiment in Guiana were publicized by a friend and supporter of the plan, Daniel Lescallier, who had worked as a colonial administrator since the 1780s in Grenada and later in Guiana. In 1789, Lescallier published his *Refléxions sur le sort des noirs dans nos colonies*, which argued, based on the experience of the Lafayette plantation, that, the more slaves were treated reasonably and kindly, the more the plantation owner profited

régime," in Dorigny, ed., *Les Abolitions de l'esclavage*, 133-141; Ghachem, "Sovereignty and Slavery." Projects for reform could, of course, veer toward the ridiculous. In the 1770s, the French traveler Jean-Betrand Bossu recommended placing *affranchis* (freedmen) who spoke "the languages of Guinée" on slave ships to explain to the slaves that the whites did not plan to eat them and that they were being brought to a land where they would find many "compatriots and relatives." Bossu also suggested that affranchi musicians—there were many in the French regiments, who would be put to better use on the slave ships—could animate the Middle Passage with music to distract the slaves from their melancholy. Africans, Bossu wrote, were singularly attuned to harmony, and the music would help make the Middle Passage more bearable *(Nouveaux voyages dans l'Amérique septentrionale* ... [Amsterdam, 1777], 372-374, 379-380).

52. Willens, "Lafayette's Emancipation Experiment," *Studies in Voltaire and the Eighteenth Century*, CCXLII (1986), 345-362; Gisler, *L'Esclavage*, 46-47.

from their labor. He further suggested that a system of free labor would be more profitable and humane than slavery ever could be. Wary of the dangers of immediate emancipation and the difficulty for ex-slaves to adjust to free society, he outlined a plan leading to general emancipation in which the slave trade would be abolished, slaves working as domestics, artisans, or skilled workers would be freed—along with mulâtres and *métises* (half-castes)—and field slaves would spend a nine-year period of apprenticeship that would transform their juridical status from one determined by the Code noir to one determined by a new *Code colonial* that would legislate their labor and their rights. In 1791, as Saint-Domingue erupted in revolt, Lescallier published another work that imagined the successful development of the colony of Guiana through the application of these kinds of humane approaches to slavery.[53]

A similar case was made in another 1789 antislavery text, *Le More-Lack*. Lecointe-Marsillac claimed that he was inspired to write the work by a chance meeting with an ex-slave on the island of Guernsey, off the coast of England. The man had been born a slave, son of a white master and an African mother, but had been emancipated at a young age and had traveled to West Africa, where he had witnessed the horrors of the slave trade. Fearing that he would become its victim, he came to Europe to find sanctuary and settled alone on the isolated island. He had written an account of his life, which he showed Lecointe-Marsillac, who copied parts of it and made them the basis for his antislavery text. After telling the story of the ex-slave and drawing on his own experiences in the Americas to recount the horrors of slavery, Lecointe-Marsillac argued for a gradual elimination of the institution. "Giving freedom suddenly to all the negro slaves," he wrote, "would be an act of arbitrary authority that would destroy the colonies and would excite a dangerous revolution in hearts ulcerated by pain and hopelessness." Agriculture would suffer, and the slaves themselves, with no means of subsistence, would become "brigands always ready to devour us." What was necessary, then, was finding a way the government might "slowly snuff out slavery, through gentle means . . . which assure the cultivation of the land, the existence of the negroes, and the fortunes of the planters." The institution of labor

53. Tarrade, "L'Esclavage est-il réformable?" in Dorigny, ed., *Les Abolitions de l'esclavage*, 133–141, esp. 140–141. Lescallier's *Refléxions sur le sort des noirs dans nos colonies* (Paris, 1789), is rpt. in *La Révolution française et l'abolition de l'esclavage* (Paris, 1968), I; see also his *Exposé des moyens de mettre en valeur et d'administrer la Guiane* . . . (Paris, 1791). For more on Lescallier, see Part III, below.

laws would further improve the condition of slaves. One out of twenty slaves should be emancipated each year and given small parcels of land; children born of legitimately married slaves would be freed at the age of twenty-five. Slowly, free workers would be forged out of slaves.[54]

In order to facilitate this transition, however, the reproduction of workers had to be assured after the abolition of the slave trade. Pronatalist reformers had earlier argued that better conditions and incentives for enslaved women could help to do this, but Lecointe-Marsillac had another plan: the importation of women from Africa should be encouraged by philanthropic societies that would reward slave traders who brought the most women into the colonies. When he offered a copy of his book to the University at Montpellier a few years after its publication, however, Lecointe-Marsillac retracted this proposition. He noted in the margin, "It is unjust and useless, since it has been proved that there exist enough black women in the colony to marry the hommes de couleur." He was probably reacting to the changed attitudes of the early 1790s, when the slave trade was coming under increasing attack. He had altered his language, using the term *femmes noires* instead of *nègresses*, and he added defensively, fearful perhaps of being seen as a friend of the slave trade, "If I dared make this suggestion, it was because I considered it a method less barbarous than that of tearing twenty-five thousand inhabitants each year from Africa in order to have them perish through the most cruel of treatments." Lecointe-Marsillac's attack on the immorality of slavery had become more general in the years since 1789, but his plans for gradual emancipation were rapidly becoming irrelevant. In the introduction to his work, he had called on the "sensible souls" of Europe and argued that it was they who could bring an end to slavery. And he had called on the slaves and ex-slaves who had provided him with his story to "remain faithful to your masters, and prove to them by your conduct that you deserve our admiration"; in the end, "the Great Spirit who protects you will set you free." Lecointe-Marsillac used—or perhaps invented— the story of a man who had been enslaved and could therefore testify to the horrors of slavery; but this man, though described, remained unnamed, excluded from the authorship of his own struggle for freedom.

54. Lecointe-Marsillac, *Le More-Lack; ou, Essai sur les moyens les plus doux et les plus équitables d'abolir la traite et l'esclavage des nègres d'Afrique, en conservant aux colonies tous les avantages d'une population agricole* (Paris, 1789), rpt. in *La Révolution française et l'abolition de l'esclavage*, III, 279–283, xij–xiij. A similar argument was made by Condorcet; see Chapter 6, below.

Yet, a few years later, when Lecointe-Marsillac found himself retracting some of his earlier proposals, the slaves of the Antilles had become the authors of their own script of liberation.[55]

Scripting Emancipation

The emancipation of individual slaves, not by the Great Spirit, but by the masters who owned them, took many guises in the French Caribbean. It was a practice as old as the colonies themselves. In the seventeenth and early eighteenth centuries, masters wishing to reward individual slaves for loyal services, or to free children they had fathered with enslaved women, did so in private acts with no intervention on the part of state authorities. The 1685 Code noir did not provide any specific process for granting liberty, although it did include three articles defining the legal rights acquired by the newly free. The *affranchis* (emancipated) were in principle released from all services that a master might demand of them, although in practice masters often emancipated under the condition that the slave remain a servant until the master's death. Additionally, affranchis were ordered to show particular respect to their former masters and the masters' families. Still, freedom granted them "the same rights, privileges, and immunities enjoyed by those who are born free; and we hope that acquired liberty will produce in them, as much for their persons as for their property, the same effects that natural liberty brings to our other subjects." Emancipation was considered equivalent to naturalization and so gave freed slaves rights denied to foreign-born whites: "We declare that an emancipation that takes place in our islands will replace birth in our said islands, and that the emancipated slaves will not need our *lettres de naturalité* to enjoy the advantages of our natural subjects . . . even if they were born in foreign countries." People of African descent were, according to this article, legal and political equals of French whites in the colony.[56]

Over the course of the eighteenth century, the fairly liberal provisions of the Code noir were systematically dismantled by legislation that lim-

55. Lecointe-Marsillac, *Le More-Lack*, rpt. in *La Révolution française*, III, xxxi–xxxii; the marginal notations are from the copy presented to the University at Montpellier. It is now in a private collection in Paris.

56. See Gisler, *L'Esclavage*, 25–26; Sala-Moulins, *Le Code noir*. See also Garrigus, "A Struggle for Respect: The Free-Coloreds of Pre-Revolutionary St. Domingue, 1760–69" (Ph.D. diss., Johns Hopkins University, 1988).

ited the rights of gens de couleur. A first discriminatory act took shape when gens de couleur were excluded from a clause that exempted whites from poll taxes. Various administrators throughout the eighteenth century made attempts to restrict mixed marriages and instituted decrees forbidding gens de couleur to take the names of whites. A systematic attack on the economic rights of gens de couleur occurred through a series of provisos, including a 1726 royal edict that made it illegal for them to receive bequests from whites. A 1764 royal decree banned gens de couleur from the professions of medicine, surgery, and pharmacy, and another in 1765 extended this to legal professions. Ordinances such as these, issued by the central authority of France, coexisted with a complicated variety of local statutes, decisions, and court judgments that restricted the rights of gens de couleur. During periods of intensified attempts to catch maroons in all the colonies, gens de couleur who did not have proof of their liberty were also in danger of being reenslaved.[57]

Starting early in the eighteenth century, colonial administrators also sought to limit the size of the gens de couleur population, whose expansion was deemed a threat to order in the colony. A local law requiring administrative approval for emancipations was passed in 1711 in Guadeloupe, and in 1713 a royal decree applicable to all the French colonies required that permission from the governor be granted before any slave could be freed in the colonies. The governor, and sometimes local courts, retained the right to deny masters' requests for manumission throughout the eighteenth century. The liberty taxes levied starting midcentury were meant to make passages to liberty more difficult and less frequent. When they didn't dissuade, they at least put money into the state's always-needy coffers.[58]

Although these tactics ultimately had little effect on the growth of the gens de couleur population, they did pose new challenges to the enslaved who hoped for freedom. Granting liberty now involved more than the time and small fee it took to draw up a private act. Masters had to balance their humanitarian impulses with their pocketbooks, and they

57. See Elisabeth, "The French Antilles," in David W. Cohen and Jack P. Greene, eds., *Neither Slave nor Free: The Freedman of African Descent in the Slave Societies of the New World* (Baltimore, 1972), 135-171, esp. 159-162; see also Peabody, *"There Are No Slaves in France."* The 1724 rewriting of the Code noir applied to Louisiana included stipulations outlawing bequests from whites to gens de couleur as well, although Saint-Domingue residents resisted this provision; see Sala-Moulins, *Le Code noir*, 197; King, *Blue Coat*, 130.

58. Debien, *Les Esclaves*, 372-373.

Prophecy, Revolt, & Emancipation, 1787-1794

often cherished the latter more. Various solutions developed in response to this problem. Some masters were able to get exemptions from the tax by declaring that the enslaved person in question foiled a rebel plot or nursed them through illness. More prevalent was the practice of enrolling an enslaved man in the militia or the maréchaussée, which gave the master a tax exemption. For women or men for whom this was not an option, there was another solution: self-purchase. A traditional right granted to the enslaved in societies going back to the Roman Empire, self-purchase could take many different forms. In the eighteenth-century French Caribbean, it seems generally to have entailed enslaved persons' compensating their masters for the cost of freeing them. Entrepreneurial individuals enslaved to willing masters could, by selling goods they grew on their provision grounds or working for pay in one capacity or another, essentially pay their own liberty taxes. Even masters who had no charitable reason to free slaves might be willing to do so if the slaves could meet their price—and indeed might take advantage of such a deal to rid themselves of slaves whom, because of age or infirmity, they could no longer profit from. While working to buy their freedom, many slaves received a *liberté de savane*, a provisional and unofficial liberty that exempted them from plantation labor and allowed them to circulate with relative freedom.[59]

In each of the French islands, the population of gens de couleur developed differently. In Saint-Domingue in 1789, there were 75 percent as many gens de couleur as whites. Gens de couleur were undercounted, however, and the communities were more likely roughly equal in size. In Martinique, the gens de couleur comprised a population 50 percent as large as that of the whites; in Guiana, 40 percent. In sharp contrast, Guadeloupe's population of gens de couleur was a substantial minority, only 20 percent the size of the white population. At the same time, the number of enslaved with mixed European and African ancestry was much higher in Guadeloupe, where they comprised 14 percent of the slave population, than in Saint-Domingue, where they never comprised more than 4 percent. Perhaps because of the difficulty of purchasing slaves in Guadeloupe, having European ancestry was much less likely in that colony to lead to emancipation than in Saint-Domingue.[60]

In all the colonies, even as the granting of freedom undid the master-

<hr>

59. On liberté de savane, see Debien, *Les Esclaves*, 380–387.
60. King, *Blue Coat*, xv–xvi; Vanony-Frisch, "Les Esclaves," *Bulletin de la Société d'histoire de la Guadeloupe*, LXIII–LXIV (1985), 3–165, esp. 154–157.

slave relationship in individual cases, it helped to define the larger social web that bound slaves to masters. The passages slaves followed to their *affranchissement* influenced the terms of their freedom in a thoroughly stratified society. Who had the right to grant freedom? It was the master, who renewed his power as he relinquished it. The documents that granted freedom defined the continuing relationship between ex-slave and ex-master by presenting emancipation as a reward bestowed by the master in return for good services on the part of the slave. And so freedom awarded to exceptional individuals reinforced the larger legitimacy of slavery as it elided some of the ways in which the slaves themselves brought about their own freedom. Acts of affranchissement framed the master-slave relation in a romantic light of service, reward, and sentiment.

Whites gave names to the enslaved, often those of saints, historical figures, or mythological characters—such as Charlemagne, César, Hercule, Radegonde, and Vénus. The idealization represented by these names clashed sharply, of course, with the brutal conditions of life on slave ships and plantations. It illustrates the kind of sentimentality that imbued masters' visions of their slaves, seeking to erase the brutality through a paternalistic "care" for the slaves. The use of names referring back to European religion and mythology also suggests a desire to reinvent the enslaved individual not only as a worker but also as a kind of sculpted personality invested with attributes selected by masters. Many African-born slaves, meanwhile, seem to have resisted the imposition of new names by continuing to use their original, African names in their daily lives on the plantation.[61]

The documents that granted slaves freedom similarly perpetuated the fiction that the freed slave was invented by the master. These documents, in turn, depended on a legal context in which such freedom was recorded and respected. Notary acts registered emancipation and in so doing made it real; promises, conditions, and reasons for the granted freedom were signed into law through the oath of a notary and the surrounding witnesses. In this way, the precarious situation of a freed slave could be stabilized; the state, through the hand of the notary, ensured this new freedom. These acts were meant to transform the very terms of personhood

61. On slave naming, see Debien, *Les Esclaves*, 71–73; Vanony-Frisch, "Les Esclaves," *Bulletin de la Société d'histoire de la Guadeloupe*, LXIII–LXIV (1985), 3–165, esp. 139–143.

for the slaves. At the same time, they emphasized the legal power of the state to determine and police who was free and who was not.

When, in the late 1780s and early 1790s, revolutionary changes began undermining the royal state on both sides of the Atlantic, the practices and regulations surrounding the emancipation of the enslaved began to crumble as well. By 1789, a Colonial Assembly sat in Guadeloupe and the colony's administration lay in disarray. Dispatches from a Paris in turmoil gave no specific instructions regarding legal aspects of colonial administration. The traditional rules governing manumission were effectively suspended, and, with no administration supervising them or collecting liberty taxes, masters could suddenly grant freedom for free. Some masters rushed to take advantage of the new situation, but they confronted difficult questions: who was in charge? Who might remain in charge long enough to ensure that freedom granted today would remain legitimate tomorrow? The French state was going through a radical restructuring, with the colonies several months behind because of the time it took for news to arrive there. So promises were registered along with doubts about how or when they would be fulfilled. This uncertainty highlighted some of the contradictions involved in granting personhood to the enslaved; it also provided certain slaves with new possibilities through which to bring about their freedom. The notarial documents created during this period registered the confusion of slaveowners as well as the transformation of the relationships between the state, slave masters, and the enslaved. They were harbingers of a much greater transformation that was to come.[62]

On July 15, 1791, Pierre Gollelin, the military captain and mayor of the tiny community of Terre-de-Bas in Les Saintes—a group of sparsely populated islands south of Guadeloupe, possibly the farthest periphery of the French nation—sailed to Trois-Rivières to register his intention to emancipate the *mulâtresse* Christonne. He pronounced that he was "happy and satisfied with the good conduct and services rendered him by the mulâtresse Christonne" and that he wished to "recognize, with the gift of liberty, all the good service she has given him." He declared her "truly free and subject to her own will, intending and understanding that, from this day on, she will enjoy all the privileges of liberty and profit from the fruit of her own labor and industry." No one was to prevent Christonne from enjoying this liberty, which would be confirmed

62. Pérotin-Dumon, *La Ville*, 679.

when "the French nation, the king, and the colony have agreed on and prescribed the process, the forms, and the laws through which liberty can be permanently and inexorably granted to deserving slaves." At that time, she would be "permitted to procure, cement, and consolidate her liberty in conformity with the laws and regulations declared on this issue, and no one shall have the right to oppose or prevent her from doing so." In an era of legal flux and uncertainty, the declaration of freedom could provide only a promise, seeking to insinuate itself into a future in which Christonne's liberty could become legally ensured. Christonne most likely returned to Terre-de-Bas with Gollelin, her situation on one level unchanged. Yet the inscription of the promise of liberty obviously meant enough to warrant the trip and the fee required.[63]

The uncertainty about when a clear set of laws governing emancipation would be instituted was just as present in the town of Basse-Terre. In January 1791, Claude Faure, a resident of Basse-Terre, registered his intention to free the mulâtresse Solie and her daughter Marguerite. Referring to the era in which "the nation, the king, or the colony" would determine the process of emancipation, the act originally stated that at that time the Faure family would take responsibility for confirming the liberty of Solie. This phrase, however, was crossed out, as if, at the moment of registering the act, Claude Faure changed his mind about wanting to take responsibility for that future. Perhaps promising to confirm a slave's liberty in a context where everything might change seemed too much. The phrase was replaced in a note at the bottom of the page by a line that transferred the responsibility, interestingly, from the owner to Solie herself: "She obliges herself to use everything within her to work for and prove her own liberty in whatever manner she deems appropriate, in the manner prescribed either by the General Colonial Assembly, the General Assembly of France, or by His Majesty." In effect, the very promise made in the act was undermined as it was being written, so that, although her master surrendered his ownership of her, it was left up to

63. CAOM, Notariat Guadeloupe, Barbier, 52, Jul. 15, 1791. Pierre Guichard, an acquaintance of Gollelin's, similarly registered his intention to free his two slaves, promising to take care of them and allow their exercise of free will "until the French nation, the king of the French, or the general colonial assembly, or some other legislative body have determined and regulated" the mechanisms for their formal emancipation. Barbier, the notary who oversaw these acts, developed a fairly standardized—but still shifting—way of referring to the future laws. See CAOM, Notariat Guadeloupe, Barbier, 52, Aug. 21, 1791.

Solie to provide "proof" of her freedom to whatever state the uncertain future ultimately produced.[64]

Certain acts made clear that the slaves being emancipated already had created for themselves a somewhat independent existence. In Trois-Rivières, François Lafitte declared his intention to free "the négresse Scholastique" and her five children, of whom he was likely the father. In freeing Scholastique, he granted her and her children a small piece of land. Lafitte declared that this land "belongs to Scholastique, who bought it with her money, money which she earned in her 'petit commerce' which he had allowed her to undertake independently as a reward for her good conduct." Lafitte's grant of the land was made ambiguously, for it is noted as a gift to Scholastique, despite the fact that it is also presented as something she earned through her own work. In the notary acts that undoubtedly distorted the complicated relations between particular masters and slaves, freedom might have been earned by the work of the slave; but freedom was always allowed and granted by the owner.[65]

An earlier emancipation act, inscribed in 1789 as part of a will, was more explicit in describing the economic basis for the passage from slavery to freedom. In this document, Marie-Anne Lamy made clear the profound dependence she had upon her slave in the functioning of her business. She freed the mulâtresse Quinette "in consideration of the distinguished services she gave me in all occasions, and particularly in my sale of dry goods, where by her care, her loyalty, her activity and her intelligence I procured myself a comfortable existence." She wished for Quinette "to be emancipated from all slavery and servitude, though not before she has paid all of the sums she owes me, from the profits she has made off the merchandise she sold on my account." The sums owed would be easy to calculate following the technique Lamy had always used with Quinette, who, on her return from her rounds in the countryside, provided a list of all the names of the purchasers and how much they bought. Lamy stipulated that, after her death, Quinette be charged with collecting and handing over any payments due to Lamy. In addition, she asked that one thousand livres be given to Quinette so she would be able "to work and procure herself, through the wise saving and talent that I know well, the means of subsistence, without depending on anyone." Lamy made it clear that her prosperity was the work of Quinette,

64. CAOM, Notariat Guadeloupe, Barbier, 52, Jan. 20, 1791.
65. Ibid., Oct. 29, 1791.

which had involved independent traveling through the countryside as well as keeping accounts. In thanking Quinette for this Lamy interestingly undermines the usual sense of freedom as a gift from the master. The act also gives us an example of the forms of economic independence and mobility that existed for the slaves who played a central part in the internal market economy of Guadeloupe.[66]

The profusion of this kind of "petit commerce" is marked in a startling notary act of the sale of a slave from a white Creole, Louis Cointre, to a mulâtre libre of Trois-Rivières, Jean Baptiste Mouesse. In February 1791, Mouesse completed a two-year payment for a "nègre créole named Louis, twenty-one years old," who had been worth two thousand livres. The payment had taken two years because Mouesse had paid not in money but in small amounts of a variety of commodities, which are listed over a few pages in the notary acts. They included "cups of manioc flour, cod, beef, barrels of candles, handkerchiefs, pieces of cloth, wine, tobacco. . . ." Each payment was noted in detail with its corresponding worth, and, on February 13, 1791, the total came to the worth of Louis. Why did Mouesse want Louis? It seems unlikely that it was to own him as a slave. Mouesse was probably related to Louis and had scraped together the products that made up his price so that he could be liberated from his stingy master. The life that Louis led once he was purchased by Mouesse remains unmarked, but in the long list of goods that Mouesse used to purchase Louis lay a map of the products that circulated through the hands of slaves or mulâtres libres and symbolized their often uncertain economic power and the possibilities for freedom that lay within it.[67]

Taking Freedom

The scripts through which freedom was granted to individuals paralleled the nationalized script of Republican emancipation that took place in 1794. This emancipation was presented by Republican administrators as an action taken in France, by French delegates, for the benefit of the slaves. Yet, as in the larger movement toward freedom, there were other routes toward emancipation, created by slaves who manipu-

66. ADG, Damaret 2E2/11, Aug. 26, 1789. My thanks to Fréderic Régent for pointing out this act to me.

67. CAOM, Notariat Guadeloupe, Barbier, 52, Feb. 14, Apr. 11, 1791. Soon after this purchase, Mouesse purchased a baby born in the Saintes from a sailor named Jean-Baptiste Léger and in doing so maintained a stipulation that he was to be free when he was six years old (ibid., Apr. 11, 1791).

lated juridical structures in the production of their own personhood. In late 1793, following the revolt at Trois-Rivières and with the possibility of a general emancipation of slaves looming on the horizon, a flurry of manumissions took place in Guadeloupe. Meanwhile, one slaveowner— Marcel, an homme de couleur and a wigmaker who lived in Basse-Terre —stepped forward to declare that his apparent ownership of one slave was in fact a legal lie. In 1792, he had purchased from the citizen Marette Rousseau a slave, "la nommée Marthe dite Majou," along with her child, Rosalie, then nine months old. The price had been 2,640 livres, the standard rate for a slave and a small child. It was declared at the time that Marcel had paid the full amount. However, as a notary act dated 1793 stated,

> The truth is that the sum of 2,640 livres paid to Marette Rousseau at the time of the said sale had actually been given to him by the said Marthe dite Majou, to whom it belonged, having been earned through her work and savings. . . . In making the present declaration, Marcel stands witness to the truth and, by this present act, surrenders all rights to property that he had seemed to hold through the said sale, over the person of Marthe dite Majou and her daughter Rosalie, and that he consents that she and her children and descendants enjoy liberty, and all the privileges granted to free people in accordance with the laws and regulations. He places them outside of his power and releases her from all slavery and servitude as well as from all services that he could have demanded of her based on the said sale, which he dispenses her of, along with all of her descendants now and forever; it is up to her to procure the registration of her freedom as she sees fit, and Marcel has given her, in the presence of the notaries, the above-mentioned sale which she releases him of.[68]

This document presents us with a remarkable legal contradiction. It retroactively admits that Marthe dite Majou had bought herself and her daughter from Marette Rousseau with her own money, with the aid of

68. ADG, Notariat, Castet 2E2/208, Sept. 28, 1793. Marcel was also one of the signers of the "Adresse des nouveaux citoyens" (see below); a "new citizen" was a free person of color who, by the law declared in the National Assembly on April 4, 1792, was proclaimed a citizen with full political rights. On this case and the increase in emancipations, see Pérotin-Dumon, *La Ville*, 680, 685; registers of the notary Jaille, in ADG, 2E3/7, which include thirty-six such affranchissements dating from a few weeks in October and November of 1793, many of them in Capesterre.

Marcel as a false purchaser. It therefore legally grants Marthe dite Majou the right she has already taken for herself: to make contracts as a free legal subject. At the beginning of the act, she is not free, since Marcel has to release her; by the last line, she is the one actively releasing Marcel of the conditions of the sale.

Why was this subterfuge necessary? No explanation is provided in the document. Perhaps Rousseau was unwilling for some reason to free Marthe and her daughter, even with monetary compensation from the enslaved woman, but was willing to sell her as a slave. Refusing their freedom could have been a way of punishing them. Or perhaps Marthe had wished to hide the fact that she had saved up enough money to purchase herself and preferred to seek a tentative freedom by working with Marcel. Given the state of flux of the legal process of emancipation, this act that presented itself as the unveiling of the truth could easily have hidden other operations. The same state of flux provided an opening in which Marcel and Marthe dite Majou felt that the truth could be asserted in a document that therefore freed both of the contractors from a lie. The question remains how, exactly, Marcel and Marthe—were they a couple, friends, or father and daughter, or was this primarily a business agreement?—related to each other during the time she was officially his slave.

This same question was raised by a later act that unmasked a similar, but older, legal lie. On February 7, 1794, an homme de couleur and carpenter named Germain, "employed in the service of the Republic," declared that when, on December 8, 1783, he had purchased the slave Désirée and her children Jeannette and Jean-Baptiste he had done so with their own money. Germain was in fact reiterating something he had already declared in front of a notary in 1787: "The money that he had paid for the three slaves was actually that of the slaves themselves and was part of their savings that they had gathered through their work in industry." "If they appeared to be his," Germain declared in 1794, "it was only because he was acting for the slaves, who could not do so themselves." Therefore he once again declared that Désirée and her children, "whom he has never considered to be his slaves, should enjoy all the rights of the free and should never be bothered with regards to their status" and that he had "given up . . . all rights of property and all other useful rights that he appeared to have over them."[69]

What was the history of this legal lie? And what was the relationship between Germain and Désirée? The notarial declaration stated that

69. ADG, Vauchelet 2E2/163, Feb. 7, 1794.

she had been unable to purchase herself. As with Marthe dite Majou, one possibility is that the owner of Désirée and her children had refused outright to allow them to purchase their freedom but had consented to selling them. Another possibility, however, was that the local administration turned down the master's wish to free his slave and her children, something that would have been unlikely in the early 1790s but could well have occurred in 1783. In this scenario, Désirée's master would have colluded in the sale so that Désirée could live with Germain. In any case, it is probable that Germain was the father of Désirée's children and that his repeated attempts to register her official freedom were steps toward legitimizing their relationship. The declaration that she and her children were free was the first step to a new life.[70]

A similar situation involving a white woman lasted almost as long as Germain's. On January 8, 1784, Esther Marsan, who lived in the plantation area above Basse-Terre, bought a mulâtresse named Marie-Thérèse from Marie Anne La Fontaine for two thousand livres. However, as Marsan declared in 1793, "the truth is that the said sum had been given to her by the said Marie-Thérèse and that she had only lent her name for the said sale, and that she had included her on her list of slaves until Marie-Thérèse could register her freedom." Therefore, Marsan, "wanting to return to Marie-Thérèse what is her right, has by this present act freed and granted liberty to the said mulâtresse Marie-Thérèse, her children and her descendants, in the state of privilege granted to free persons." Once again, freedom was granted officially in a case in which the true agent of the original sale, Marie-Thérèse, simply could not oversee the exchange; Esther Marsan "lent" her name for the action that Marie-Thérèse was conducting and saw in the moment of legal chaos and openness the proper time to unveil a legal disjuncture that had been going on for nearly a decade. In all three cases, freedom was granted not only to those who originally bought themselves but also to their children and descendants, specifically mentioned, asserting the power of this decision. How had Marsan and Marie-Thérèse negotiated their relationship for the previous ten years? Where had Marie-Thérèse lived and worked? Had the truth of the matter been kept secret—and how?[71]

70. Ibid. In his declaration, Germain was careful to note his compliance with a regulation requiring he register his act with the local government and titled the act a "declaration of the legal status" of his ex-slaves.

71. ADG, Notariat, Castet 2E2/208, Jul. 21, 1793; in the original act, "mademoiselle" is originally written in front of Marsan, then crossed out and replaced by

These are difficult questions on which the documents remain silent. What is significant, however, is the way in which three enslaved women, by earning money and by making connections, were able to contract their own freedom. Within the limits placed on them by plantation society, these slaves first bought themselves and ultimately managed to get the truth inscribed in official documents, freeing them and their descendants.

These enslaved individuals, like those who ran away from the plantations into the mountains or overturned rocks to divert water from the state's canals into their gardens, left scattered traces in the archives. Such testimonies make possible a social cartography of eighteenth-century Guadeloupe. Within the official geography of plantations and ports, with its economic ordering based on production for export to France and its social ordering based on racial hierarchy, lay another geography. It was made up of the complex interconnections and hidden networks that existed among gens de couleur, whites, and the enslaved who struggled for survival, autonomy, and liberty. It was rich with suffering and with possibility. For from it emerged, in the early 1790s, a dramatic challenge to slavery, one that transformed the meaning of rights in the Atlantic world. Enslaved women like Marthe dite Majou and Désirée, excluded from making contracts, nevertheless acted as legal agents in order to turn themselves into free citizens. Their actions presaged and paralleled the process through which enslaved insurgents acted as Republican citizens in defending the nation—and ultimately forced national authorities to inscribe the official truth of the citizenship they had already claimed for themselves.

"citoyenne"—another mark of the uncertainty of official terminology at the time. Marsan had owned other slaves, which makes her participation in the legal trick even more interesting; see EC, Basse-Terre, 8, no. 56, 30 Prairial, An III (June 18, 1795); EC, Basse-Terre, 11, no. 67, 12 Pluviôse, An VI (Jan. 31, 1798).

Chapter 3

PROPHETIC RUMOR

In August 1789, groups of slaves began gathering on the waterfront of the town of Saint-Pierre, Martinique. Many of these slaves were employed in the town in various trades, but, on Sunday, August 30, they headed out of town for a large meeting held in a valley between two plantations, where they were joined by others from the surrounding region. They were inspired to action by the news—spread by what some insurgents later described as "black doctors"—that the king of France, encouraged by some of the slaves' distinguished friends in Paris, had abolished slavery. Local slaveowners, according to the same report, were determined to resist the decision, so the enslaved would have to rise up and force them to accept the decree of emancipation. As Governor Vioménil described it, the rebellious blacks, "armed with the instruments they use to cut the sugarcane, refused to work, saying loudly that they were free." Warned of the meeting outside Saint-Pierre, however, the militia quickly dispersed the rebels. Troops captured two hundred maroons who were suspected of having aided them. During the course of September, twenty-three slaves were punished for their participation in the revolt, and eight of them were executed.[1]

This revolt took place before the news of the revolutionary events of Paris in July 1789 reached Martinique. Still, word had arrived of the calling of the Estates-General as well as of the marquis de Condorcet's early 1789 attempt to put slave emancipation on the agenda of that body. The

1. David Geggus, "The Slaves and Free Coloreds of Martinique during the Age of the French and Haitian Revolutions: Three Moments of Resistance," in Robert L. Paquette and Stanley L. Engerman, eds., *The Lesser Antilles in the Age of European Expansion* (Gainesville, Fla., 1996), 280–301, esp. 282–283; "Lettre du Gouverneur Vioménil au ministre de la marine et des colonies," Sept. 14, 1789, in CAOM, C 8A, fol. 57, rpt. in Marie-Hélène Leotin, ed., *La Martinique au temps de la Révolution française, 1789-1794* (Fort-de-France, Martinique, 1989), 27.

existence of the Société des amis des noirs, founded the year before, was also known. Indeed, some of its publications had arrived in the colony, and blacks were seen gathering in the towns to hear them read aloud. When the new governor of the island, the comte de Vioménil, arrived in July 1789 and, following the spirit of recent royal edicts on the colonies, sought to gather information about excessive cruelties committed against slaves, he was seen by some as an envoy of the société. There were among the enslaved those who expected him to announce emancipation at a ceremony honoring his arrival, and, when he didn't, a rumor circulated that he was in complicity with local slaveowners determined to resist the order of the king. The governor himself, so tightly caught up in the web of rumor and expectation, blamed the revolt of August on slaves in metropolitan France for passing on this information. "The slave no longer ignores that his revolt has found supporters, that many no longer even dispute his choice of methods. Their fathers, their brothers . . . instruct him through their correspondence about the maxims with which all the societies resound, and which tend to do no less than to bring iron and poison into the hearts of the inhabitants of the colonies." Indeed, rumors about the king's decisions circulated as well in Saint-Domingue, where one observer noted in 1789: "Many imagine that the king has granted them their freedom and that it is their master who does not want to consent to it."[2]

Even if they were inspired by the news of the debates in Paris, though, the rebels in Martinique claimed as reality a transformation more radical than even the abolitionists of Paris envisioned: the sudden emancipation of the enslaved by the king himself. Two anonymous letters sent to local officials in Saint-Pierre powerfully stated what they were willing to do if the king's orders were ignored. The first of these, signed "nous, Nègres," claimed, "We know that we are free and that you accept that rebellious people resist the orders of the king. . . . We will die for this liberty; we want it and will gain it at whatever price, even through the use of mortars, cannons, and rifles." The letter attacked the inhumanity of slavery but added that there was little point in making claims to the humanity of the readers, since they had none, and ended by saying, "If this prejudice

2. Geggus, "Slaves and Free Coloreds of Martinique," in Paquette and Engerman, eds., *Lesser Antilles*, 280–301, esp. 284–285; "Lettre du Gouverneur Vioménil," Sept. 14, 1789, in CAOM, C 8A, fol. 57, rpt. in Leotin, ed., *La Martinique*, 27; Carolyn E. Fick, *The Making of Haiti: The Saint Domingue Revolution from Below* (Knoxville, Tenn., 1990), 83.

is not entirely annihilated, there will be torrents of blood as powerful as the gutters that flow along the roads." The second of the two letters read:

> The entire nation of the black slaves united together has only one wish, one desire for independence, and all slaves with one unanimous voice articulate only one cry, the demand for a liberty that they have justly won through centuries of suffering and ignominious servitude. This is no longer a nation that is blinded by ignorance and that trembles at the threat of the lightest punishments; its suffering has enlightened it and has determined it to spill to its last drop of blood rather than support the yoke of slavery, a horrible yoke attacked by the laws, by humanity, and by all of nature, by the divinity and by our good king Louis XVI. We hope it will be condemned by the illustrious Vioménil. Your response, great general, will decide our destiny and that of the colony.[3]

The letter drew on the possibilities opened up by political transformations across the Atlantic in calling on a variety of authorities—from nature and law to God and king—to condemn slavery. It also drew on another complex web of symbols by presenting its demand as emanating from "the entire nation of the black slaves."

The term "nation" had multiple meanings in the Caribbean. Newly imported slaves were often identified by slave traders and planters as being of a particular nation of African origin. These categories, usually applied according to the port from which the enslaved were taken across

3. "Copie d'une lettre anonyme adréssée B. M. Mollerat, de St. Pierre, le 28 août 1789," "Copie de la lettre des esclaves de la Martinique, le 29 août 1789," both in CAOM, C 8A, 68–69, rpt. in Leotin, ed., *La Martinique*, 19–21. Geggus and Léo Elisabeth suggest that the author of the letters was a "noir libre" named Aléxis Casimir, or Aléxis Réné, who was an actor and had recently returned from France; Yves Bénot argues that the authors took their inspiration from the writings of Raynal. See Geggus, "Slaves and Free Coloreds of Martinique," in Paquette and Engerman, eds., *Lesser Antilles*, 280–301, esp. 286; Elisabeth, "Résistances des esclaves aux XVIIe et XVIIIe siècles dans les colonies françaises d'Amérique, principalement aux îles du Vent," Bénot, "La Chaîne des insurrections d'esclaves dans les Caraïbes de 1789 à 1791," both in Marcel Dorigny, ed., *Les Abolitions de l'esclavage de L. F. Sonthonax à V. Schoelcher, 1793, 1794, 1848 . . .* (Paris, 1995), 78–86, 179–186. On the religious overtones of the letter and its connections to the activities of a Catholic priest of Saint-Pierre, see Sue Peabody, "'A Dangerous Zeal': Catholic Missions to Slaves in the French Antilles, 1635–1800," *French Historical Studies*, XXV (2002), 53–90, esp. 89.

the Atlantic, were imperfect representations of the actual origins of slaves. But the preferences of planters for slaves from certain nations, the vagaries of the slave trade, and the practice of helping newly arrived Africans integrate by placing them under the tutelage of an individual of the same background all contributed to the formation of communities that shared a particular African language and culture. The enslaved who were united in these cultural communities helped one another survive by gathering for events (particularly burials for one of their group) where they told stories, played music, and danced. In the French Caribbean, such gatherings were not facilitated by the creation of black confraternities as they were in the Spanish colonies, notably Cuba—an attempt by Jesuits to create a confraternity devoted to the Virgin Mary in Guadeloupe in the 1750s was blocked by colonial administrators—but they occurred regularly nonetheless. During these gatherings, groups of Africans sometimes identified themselves as members of a particular nation, as was the case during the wedding witnessed in Basse-Terre by Nicolas Léonard in the 1780s (see Chapter 2, above) and in gatherings of members of the Igbo and Caplaou nations in Martinique in 1793.[4]

Such groups could also be the basis for resistance, as they were in the 1730s in Antigua, when the Coromantee slave Court was apparently crowned king in a widely attended coronation as a prelude to insurrection. His nobility, however, was not conferred as it would have been in Africa but rather through an election, and he appointed two Creole slaves as his lieutenants, which suggests that alliances based on certain nations were not exclusive.[5]

In the 1789 letter, the naming of a "nation of black slaves" represented the merging of different traditions of identification. It evoked the continuing presence of certain African nations even as it spoke for a coalition of enslaved blacks ready to fight for their freedom. And it did so in a context where conflicts were breaking out on both sides of the Atlantic over who should represent the French nation.

The events of 1789 in Martinique provide an example of how, during

4. John K. Thornton, *Africa and Africans in the Making of the Atlantic World, 1400–1800* (New York, 1998), 320–332; Peabody, "'A Dangerous Zeal,'" *French Historical Studies*, XXV (2002), 53–90, esp. 79–80. On Martinique, see Josette Fallope, "Contribution de Grand Lahou au peuplement Afro-Caribéen," in Serge Daget, ed., *De la traite à l'esclavage: Actes du colloque internationale sur la traite des noirs, Nantes 1985* (Paris, 1988), 9–24, esp. 17.

5. On the Antigua conspiracy, see David Barry Gaspar, *Bondmen and Rebels: A Study of Master-Slave Relations in Antigua* (Baltimore, 1985).

Prophecy, Revolt, & Emancipation, 1787–1794

the last decade of the eighteenth century, enslaved rebels expanded the realm of the possible, mobilizing around prophetic rumors, successfully carrying out large-scale insurrections, and ultimately bringing about general emancipation. Soon, however, slaves began calling, not on the king, but on the nascent French Republic to bring them freedom. The history of this period, both in Saint-Domingue and in Guadeloupe, was shaped by the actions of slaves who took the news of the French Revolution and reinterpreted it to express their demands. The circulation of rumors of impending freedom, part of a long tradition in the Americas, helped coalesce and organize revolts. In a moment of political effervescence and transformation, these revolts gave new content to the ideologies and symbols of republicanism.

Like revolutionaries in France, black insurgents expressed themselves by speaking and acting—uninvited—in the name of the French nation, and in so doing they brought about the declarations that officially made them part of that nation. The bearing of revolutionary symbols and the assimilation of the vocabulary of Republican citizenship and patriotism became part of the conflicts over public space and political institutions that grew increasingly violent and radical, both in the colonies and the metropole, as the democratic revolution of 1789 moved toward the more extreme republicanism of 1793. Gens de couleur and slaves alike watched whites' reactions to news from France, as soldiers rose up and demanded new rights and political conflicts exploded between white colonists. The language of rights and the public demonstrations that manifested the power of this language became part of the political culture through which insurgents could claim improved conditions, social equality, and ultimately emancipation. Gens de couleur and slave insurgents, rooted in the social terrain of Guadeloupe, would reconfigure narratives, political symbols, and Republican ideals, ultimately bringing about emancipation in 1794.

News of Revolution

If material contraband presented a threat to metropolitan authority throughout the eighteenth century, there were other goods in circulation that were even more difficult to track and potentially more dangerous. In the era of the Haitian Revolution the movement of information between the Caribbean islands, North and South America, Europe, and Africa tied the Atlantic together. Whereas official information traveled along uncertain and restricted routes, African-American communities had their own networks of travel and information that allowed for political mobilization. Sailors—often ex-slaves—brought news from a variety of sources to the docks of the islands, passing it on to the slaves who worked unloading the ships. Newspapers and pamphlets also provided information about events elsewhere in the Americas or across the Atlantic to free people of African descent as well as to the enslaved. It took only one literate individual to read aloud from the printed page to the groups of eager listeners, who could quickly spread what they heard from the towns to the plantations. Received with great interest and circulated with enormous speed, rumors of events in Europe could present a serious threat to the order of slave colonies in the Caribbean. This was especially true toward the end of the eighteenth century, as this news increasingly included the progress of abolitionist movements in England and France. Communities of slaves, freed slaves, and maroons understood that in certain cases metropolitan authorities might be a source of support against local administrators. This dynamic, which is central in understanding the developments in the French Caribbean from 1789 to 1794, was a constant presence in the struggles around slavery earlier in the eighteenth century. Rumors that emancipation had been (or would soon be) decreed in the metropole, but that local authorities or inhabitants were resisting and silencing this fact, often stirred up revolts. Through these rumors and the mobilization they afforded, slaves inserted themselves into the political conflicts between metropole and colony, accelerating the movement toward freedom.[6]

6. The pioneering work in this regard is Julius Sherrard Scott III, "The Common Wind: Currents of Afro-American Communication in the Era of the Haitian Revolution" (Ph.D. diss., Duke University, 1987); see also Scott, "Crisscrossing Empires: Ships, Sailors, and Resistance in the Lesser Antilles in the Eighteenth Century," in Paquette and Engerman, eds., Lesser Antilles, 128-143. The widespread importance of rumor in slave mobilization is also explored in Geggus, "Slavery, War, and Revolution in the Greater Caribbean, 1789-1815," in Gaspar and Geggus, eds., A Turbulent Time: The French Revolution and the Greater Caribbean (Bloomington, Ind., 1997), 1-50; Michael Craton, "Slave Culture, Resistance, and the Achievement of Emancipation in the British West Indies, 1783-1838," in James Walvin, ed., Slavery and British Society, 1776-1838 (London, 1982), 100-122. The role of black sailors in transmitting news is explored in Jeffrey Bolster, Black Jacks: African-American Seamen in the Age of Sail (Cambridge, Mass., 1997). On the importance of Haiti in the creation of a diasporic identity among such sailors in the early nineteenth century, see Bolster, "An Inner Diaspora: Black Sailors Making Selves," in Ronald Hoffman, Mechal Sobel, and Fred-

Slave resistance was present from the earliest days of slavery, but the eighteenth century saw its acceleration and consolidation. In the 1730s, a series of conspiracies and revolts in Saint-Domingue, Antigua, Jamaica, Dutch Guiana, and the Danish colony of Saint John terrified the Greater Caribbean. In the 1750s, insurgents in Saint-Domingue led by Makandal poisoned a number of whites and spread fear throughout the colony. By the late 1700s, the maroon communities in Jamaica and Saint-Domingue —as well as the Black Carib group on Saint Vincent—had signed treaties guaranteeing their freedom. Governors in the Caribbean understood the profound threat slave uprisings represented to all the plantation societies in the region, and they sometimes put aside their rivalries in order to repress them. In 1734, for instance, after both the Danish and a troop of English soldiers were roundly defeated during the insurrection in Saint John, the governors of the island went to the French for help in putting down the revolt. The governor of the French West Indies wrote to the minister: "I could not imagine refusing my assistance in a matter of such importance for all the nations of the Americas. . . . It is necessary to eliminate to the last these wretches." The company that he formed included nègres libres and mulâtres who were "appropriate for a war in the woods," and his intervention saved slavery in Saint John. The governor claimed he stilled a wind of fear that had spread through the entire Caribbean. It was a moment of imperial cooperation that contrasted sharply with what happened six decades later.[7]

Throughout the century, the possibility of freedom declared from elsewhere inspired resistance among slaves. In 1749, slaves organized a revolt in Caracas, Venezuela, around rumors spread by Juan de Cádiz, "a free black recently arrived from Spain, who circulated news that the king had decreed that all the Spanish slaves in the Indies be liberated." In Martinique in 1768, a number of slaves were punished for circulating a rumor that "a powerful African king had arrived, had purchased from the colonial government all the slaves on the island, and that they could

rika J. Teute, eds., *Through a Glass Darkly: Reflections on Personal Identity in Early America* (Chapel Hill, N.C., 1997), 419-448, esp. 441-446.

7. Marquis de Champigny to the minister of the colonies, Apr. 12, 16, 1734, in CAOM, F 3, 58; on Saint-Domingue, see Fick, *Making of Haiti*. For the British islands, see Gaspar, *Bondmen and Rebels*; Michael Craton, *Testing the Chains: Resistance to Slavery in the British West Indies* (Ithaca, N.Y., 1982); on Guiana, see Richard Price, *First-Time: The Historical Vision of an Afro-American People* (Baltimore, 1983).

soon expect to board vessels to return to Africa." By the late 1780s, the spread of abolitionist rhetoric in Europe accelerated rumors and conflicts over an always-impending freedom. In Venezuela in 1789, the arrival of the Spanish king's cédula, whose contents were in principle to be kept secret, sparked "powerful rumors heralding an impending end to slavery." Slaves discussed the cédula and "asserted—quite accurately —that the new regulations called for a short workday with 'hours of rest.'" The continuing official silence about the reforms contained in the cédula prompted menacing posters that demanded an end to the document's suppression, accompanying text with "a rough drawing of a dark-skinned man wielding a raised machete apparently about to cut the throat of a white man." One group of slaves, convinced that the new document had granted them freedom, killed their overseer. News of the English debates around abolition spread through slave communities by means of oral accounts of domestic slaves who had traveled to England, antislavery pamphlets, and the engravings and other graphic representations of the suffering of slaves. In 1780, in Tortola, slaves mobilized around a rumor that abolition had been declared in England but that its application had been "suppressed at the Instance of the Inhabitants." Such events confirmed for planters the dangerous power news of antislavery activity could have in the Caribbean.[8]

Starting in 1789, this news included the dramatic developments of the French Revolution. The whirlwind of debate in Paris raised profound questions: What institutions could legitimately represent the national will? Who would be granted the right to shape these institutions? In a French Caribbean constructed around plantation slavery, such conflicts over the meaning of citizenship took on a particular inflection. The response of various groups in the colonies to the events in France was made more complicated by the fact that news—and therefore new laws, constitutions, and symbols—could take more than three months to arrive in the Antilles. Political struggles in the colonies, therefore, were often based on conjectures about the state of things in France. Rumor, then—important in earlier slave insurrections—took on an even more pivotal role. As has been suggested, notaries attempting to register emancipation during this period confronted uncertainty about appropriate legal forms and the legitimacy of existing political institutions. This uncertainty incited confusion, but it also provided opportunities. Free people of color, as well as the enslaved, made the arriving Republican symbols and ideals their

8. Scott, "Common Wind," 21–23, 117–118, 133–134, 153–155.

Prophecy, Revolt, & Emancipation, 1787–1794

own and infused them with the hope of an imminent emancipation from racial exclusion and bondage.

On September 18, 1789, the first of the symbols of the French Revolution arrived in Guadeloupe on a ship called *La Jeune bayonnaise*. The sailors from this merchant ship entered Pointe-à-Pitre and displayed and distributed *cocardes*—the tricolor symbols that had come to stand for the popular revolution and the new National Assembly. These symbols immediately caused a commotion as the young people of the town began not only to wear them but to insist that local authorities wear them as well. The captain of the regiment at Pointe-à-Pitre refused at first, awaiting orders from above, but he soon realized that he should submit to the people's request in order to avoid a riot. In the next days, all those who traveled to the city were asked, upon entering, to don cocardes. On his way to Pointe-à-Pitre, Governor Clugny encountered a crowd of men and women in Sainte-Anne who were wearing the cocarde and demanded that he wear one. He eventually acquiesced, giving a speech in which he said that the cocarde was nothing more than a "symbol of the reunion of all the French, and of their loyalty to their sovereign." The crowd applauded and cried, "Vive le Roy!" The symbol also quickly became a vehicle for the aspirations of the gens de couleur. "The gens de couleur libres requested, as subjects of His Majesty and French citizens, the permission to carry the cocarde," reported Clugny. "The whites delivered this request in their name." "I thought it was the best policy to grant them this favor," he continued, "especially considering how the minds of the slaves must be working given what is going on in Martinique and in Europe." The slaves of Martinique had indeed recently made clear their intention to participate in the changes they understood were in the air, and Clugny made clear he would not countenance any ill behavior in Guadeloupe. "I ordered it announced everywhere, at the sound of the drum, that any slave who wore the cocarde would be whipped on the public square." So the tricolor symbol of the Revolution, from its first appearance in Guadeloupe, highlighted the problems that would wrack the colony in the next years: the conflict between different groups of whites, the problem of the citizenship of gens de couleur, and the danger of insurrection among the slaves.[9]

9. See Governor Clugny to the minister, Sept. 29, 1789, in CAOM, C7A, 45, rpt. in Anne Pérotin-Dumon, *Etre patriote sous les tropiques: La Guadeloupe, la colonisation, et la revolution (1789–1794)* (Basse-Terre, Guadeloupe, 1985), 262–263, esp. 121. See also Pérotin-Dumon's summaries of the political struggles in

During the next year, the question of trade with foreign merchants and economic conflicts between Pointe-à-Pitre and Basse-Terre would drive the political struggles within the new island assembly. The onset of the Revolution allowed plantation owners to accelerate their attacks on the exclusif system and demand a more open trade system whose advantages had been made clear through years of contraband. The issue of free trade was immediately brought to the fore because, during the fall of 1789, in the wake of the Great Fear in France, imports of food into Guadeloupe nearly stopped, and the colonies gained permission to get supplies from foreign merchants. Yet both Basse-Terre and Pointe-à-Pitre wanted to be the exclusive port for trade with foreign merchants. In December 1789, an islandwide Colonial Assembly met at Petit-Bourg and resolved the problem by granting both cities the right to greet foreign ships. The architect of some of the first compromises within the assemblies was Jacques Coquille Dugommier, the representative for the town of Trois-Rivières, who soon became the president of the assembly and a leading Republican figure on the island.[10]

Dugommier was a planter who had owned property in the area of Trois-Rivières since the late 1770s and also a navy officer and a veteran of the American War of Independence, by virtue of which he had been named a chevalier of the Order of Saint-Louis. In addition to playing a role in the local assemblies, Dugommier was at the heart of a 1791 insurrection among French soldiers stationed in Basse-Terre. That event illustrates well how the public performance of political allegiance could express demands and interests against existing hierarchies. Although reports describe mainly the actions of white soldiers, the days of insurrection involved the entire area and were certainly observed by gens de couleur and slaves within the city and beyond. In this sense the insurrection was an event that set the tone for later revolts that more directly implicated slaves. It also signals the beginning of the schism between patriots

---

Guadeloupe during this period in "The Emergence of Politics among Free-Coloreds and Slaves in Revolutionary Guadeloupe," *Journal of Caribbean History*, XXV, nos. 1, 2 (1991), 100–135, and "Free Coloreds and Slaves in Revolutionary Guadeloupe: Politics and Political Consciousness," in Paquette and Engerman, eds., *Lesser Antilles*, 259–279. Bénot has also emphasized that the slaves in the Antilles "immediately saw the deep importance of the new slogans arriving from France"; see "La Chaîne des insurrections," in Dorigny, ed., *Les Abolitions de l'esclavage*, 13–35.

10. Pérotin-Dumon, *Etre patriote*, 119–126. The Great Fear was a period during which peasant uprisings paralyzed much of France's countryside.

FIGURE 8. Jacques Coquille Dugommier. c. 1850. This was probably rendered during Dugommier's service as a general in France. Engraving by Couché fils. *Cliché Bibliothèque nationale de France, Paris*

and royalists that was at the center of the Trois-Rivières insurrection of 1793.

According to an official report from 1791, the problems began when, on the feast day of Saint-Louis, Dugommier asked the governor of the island for wine for the soldiers. Military authorities refused Dugommier's request and ordered the soldiers to stay stationed in Fort Saint-Charles of Basse-Terre, "to amuse themselves quietly in their own company and not to march through the streets." Soon, however, under the leadership of a sergeant named Duprat, the troops left the fort and lined up to march through the town. The drum major refused to participate and was quickly replaced; following the drums, the soldiers marched across Basse-Terre to the Saint-François neighborhood. Dugommier joined the soldiers, carrying the new national tricolor flag, and delivered a speech praising their patriotism. Duprat asked one of the colonels in the regiment whether he was "a patriot in his soul"—a question he would repeatedly pose to a series of those officers he, and others in the company, considered aristocrats. For most of the day, the soldiers paraded through the streets of Basse-Terre, particularly near the government buildings of the town center. At one point they entered the building of the *Comité colonial* and performed a Federation Act. Citizens from the town milled about and watched the events, and at night many went to the fort to drink with the soldiers, some of whom were overheard saying that they should hang all the aristocrat officers from tamarind trees. Witnesses heard Duprat telling groups of soldiers "that they were all free, that they were all soldier-citizens and citizen-soldiers." The disorder continued for days as soldiers refused to report to duty, ignored the orders of officers who had refused to join them, and even promoted themselves as replacements for these aristocrats. The hierarchy of the regiment had been completely undermined by the popular insurrection of the soldiers, which also forced local officials of the town to take sides and, in some cases, respond to accusations that they, too, lacked patriotism.[11]

11. "Détail des événements arrivés au régiment de la Guadeloupe depuis le premier septembre dernier, époque de l'insurrection de ce corps, jusqu'au premier de ce mois," in CAOM, Dêpot des fortifications des colonies (hereafter cited as DFC), Guadeloupe, carton 29, no. 444. The celebration of Saint-Louis—the thirteenth-century crusading French king Louis IX—may seem an ironic date for an insurrection against aristocrats. But France was as yet a constitutional monarchy, not a republic, and principles of equality were seen as compatible with a continuing respect for the king. The Federation Acts were statements of loyalty made to the new republic through public ceremony, which became common after the first cele-

Prophecy, Revolt, & Emancipation, 1787–1794

The official report on the event noted hostilely that Duprat "is a native of Savoy, and therefore is not French." The significance of this procession, however, and the generalized insubordination by patriot troops against their aristocrat officers, was in bringing into practice new political distinctions on which the emerging French nation was based. The question posed by the foreigner Duprat—"Are you a patriot in your soul?"—suggested that the definition of the nation, and who could be part of it, was subjective. As Duprat said to one of the officers: "It is not enough to assert that you are a patriot, you have to be one in your soul. We will see whether you are." Aristocratic officers could be questioned, their pretensions to power and superiority interpreted as attacks on the Republican ideals of citizenship and equality. By breaking the orders of these officers and processing through the streets with the Republican flag, the soldiers were asserting themselves as the true defenders of the Republic, taunting those whom they saw as enemies of the nation by drawing the battle lines and appropriating the flag for themselves. This symbolic choreography of patriotism carried with it the threatening overtones that existed in metropolitan France, propelled by the fact that counterrevolutionaries throughout Europe were planning to fight the revolutionary changes.[12]

During the early years of the Revolution, the divide between patriots and royalists in the French Caribbean quickly led to open conflict. Under Dugommier's leadership, a number of the soldiers and volunteers

---

bration of Bastille Day took place in Paris in July 1790 with a massive Festival of the Federation. See Mona Ozouf, *Festivals and the French Revolution*, trans. Alan Sheridan (Cambridge, Mass., 1988), 33–60.

12. The events of 1791 were the first in a long series of such townwide riots in Basse-Terre. Late that year, after the departure of Dugommier and after a number of troublesome soldiers from Basse-Terre had been sent back to France, a curious incident set off another round of disorders. Some soldiers and officers claimed that, even if rebellious soldiers were sent away, "le noyau"—the core—of the rebellion remained. As he was walking past a house, a soldier heard someone exclaim "Ah, le f . . . Noyau!" and saw the *noyau* (pit) of a mango thrown on the road in front of him. Soon armed soldiers paraded through the streets demanding an apology for the insult, and they beat up its supposed author. The symbolism of accusation and insult was ubiquitous enough that a mango pit could be read as a symbol of a "core" group of political subversives in such a way as to lead to an upheaval. See the report of the envoy Lacoste, in CAOM, C 7A, 45, 15–43; see also the letters written to the Comité colonial during 1791, in AN, D XXV, 120, 939; Louis Bovis, *Historique des événemens qui se sont passés à la Basse-Terre, ville capitale de l'île Guadeloupe, depuis la révolution* (Basse-Terre, Guadeloupe, 1791).

from Basse-Terre went on two expeditions to help the besieged patriots of Martinique, who starting in 1789 had come into conflict with a royalist group. The altercation there eventually pitted the countryside against the cities and quickly involved the gens de couleur of the island and even the slaves themselves in the mobilization on both sides of the divide. In Guadeloupe, the schism between patriots and royalists also quickly deepened, with Dugommier at its center. In June 1791, Dugommier left the island of Guadeloupe, declaring that he was under constant threat by conspirators who resisted the new French constitution and sought to murder him for his support of the new Republican order. He felt especially at risk in Trois-Rivières, "where the thick woods can hide any enemy who wishes to commit his crime." He left his property in the hands of a local manager, who was to be paid a yearly salary in order to maintain the plantations and send the profits to France. Once in France, Dugommier became a Republican hero, as an officer who fought at Toulon alongside Napoléon Bonaparte in 1793 and later as a general in the Pyrenees, where he was killed in 1794. Meanwhile, Dugommier's legacy in Guadeloupe would continue, since it was on his recently sold plantation and through the actions of his ex-slaves that the Trois-Rivières insurrection unfolded in April 1793.[13]

Insurrections of soldiers continued in Guadeloupe and throughout the Antilles, just as they did throughout metropolitan France. They show how, within the army, citizenship and equality could motivate complaints about treatment, hierarchy, and even the right to celebrate the feast of Saint-Louis. But the questioning of the officers for their patriotism presaged a much more serious conflict in Guadeloupe that would pit Republicans against those they saw as conspirators against the Revolution. As the increasingly radical course of the Revolution caused splits among the whites on the islands, gens de couleur and then slaves would also use and transform that language of republicanism in formulating and acting on their demands for rights.

The Political Rights of the Gens de Couleur

In metropolitan France, the period from 1789 through 1791 brought debates about the administration of the colonies into the National As-

13. CAOM, Notariat Guadeloupe, Barbier, 52, June 20, 27, 1791; on Dugommier and the expeditions to Martinique, see also Auguste Lacour, *Histoire de la Guadeloupe*, 4 vols. (Basse-Terre, Guadeloupe, 1855-1858), II, chaps. 2, 3.

sembly. The problem of slavery loomed behind these discussions, even when it was not explicitly discussed. At the heart of the colonial question lay a contradiction: the Declaration of the Rights of Man and Citizen had been declared universally applicable, and yet its application in the colonies seemed unimaginable. Was the blatant transgression of the rights of man embodied in slavery justifiable? Were the economic interests of the nation, deeply tied to colonial commerce, more important than the universal application of rights? The first article of the declaration proclaimed, "Men are born and live free and equal in their rights; social distinctions can only be based on common good." Was enslavement of human beings useful for the common good? Article 17 declared property an "inviolable and sacred right," begging the question of which right was more important—the right of a slave to equality, or the right of a master to his human property.

Representatives in the National Assembly confronted these questions as they sought to define the administrative identity of the colonies within the emerging Republican order. The debates around the colonies brought together a complicated mix of interests and social positions; many representatives had colonial property, and others were tied to the merchant interests of the port towns that profited from the colonial trade—including Antoine Barnave, who played a leading role in the National Assembly. During the early and less radical years of the Revolution, the question raised by the Société des amis des noirs in conjunction with gens de couleur in Paris was, not the problem of slavery itself, but rather the (seemingly) more manageable question of the rights of the already free gens de couleur. Uninvited, white delegates from Saint-Domingue had traveled to the meeting of the Estates-General in June 1789; there, they participated in the Tennis Court Oath, during which the representatives of the Third Estate proclaimed themselves a National Assembly. In early June, members of the Société des amis des noirs raised an objection to the integration of the white Saint-Domingue delegates into the Assembly. These delegates had requested that the number of seats granted them be proportional to the total number of inhabitants in the colonies. The comte de Mirabeau responded pointedly:

> You claim representation proportionate to the number of inhabitants. The free blacks are proprietors and taxpayers, and yet they have not been allowed to vote. And as for the slaves, either they are men or they are not; if the colonists consider them men, let them free them and make them electors and eligible for seats; if the contrary is the

case, have we, in apportioning deputies according to the population of France, taken into consideration the number of our horses and mules?

This debate produced a compromise, granting six delegates to Saint-Domingue and one each to Guadeloupe and Martinique. Yet the problem of representation for the gens de couleur remained unresolved, and throughout 1789 members of the société, particularly Abbé Grégoire, and gens de couleur representatives who demanded to be seated in the Assembly repeatedly raised the issue. Two hommes de couleur from Saint-Domingue, Julien Raimond and Vincent Ogé, were among those who argued that, as propertyowners who were fully capable of paying the necessary taxes, they should be given full political rights. One petition written by gens de couleur in Paris powerfully put forth the claim that the gens de couleur in the colonies understood and were ready to exercise these rights: "Instructed by the Declaration of the Rights of Man and Citizen, colored colonists have realized who they are; they have risen up to the dignity you have bestowed upon them; they have learned what their rights are, and they have used them." The question remained unresolved through 1789 and the beginning of 1790.[14]

In Paris, white colonial interests—led by a planter lobby group with a number of prominent members, the Club Massiac—successfully undermined the claims of the gens de couleur. An anonymous pamphlet, purportedly written by the "Nègres Libres, Colons Americains" but actually published by planter interests, attacked the claims of the gens de couleur and claimed that, unlike the free blacks, who were of a pure race, mulâtres were mixed and, therefore, like gold alloy, less valuable. Echoing a supposed offer by the gens de couleur to make a massive contribution into the state coffers as a show of their patriotism, the pamphlet made a similar offer on the part of the free blacks. It cleverly hinted that the

14. Geggus, "Racial Equality, Slavery, and Colonial Secession during the Constituent Assembly," *American Historical Review*, XCIV (1990), 1290-1308; Robin Blackburn, *The Overthrow of Colonial Slavery, 1776-1848* (London, 1988), 163-211, esp. 174 for the Mirabeau quote; David Brion Davis, *The Problem of Slavery in the Age of Revolution, 1770-1823* (Ithaca, N.Y., 1975), 137-148; Bénot, *La Révolution française et la fin des colonies: Essai* (Paris, 1989). For statements made by the citoyens de couleur, notably Ogé and Raimond, to the National Assembly during January through March 1790, see AN, AD VII, 21 A, 6, 7, 11; the 1789 petition, from Oct. 18, 1789, is in AN, D XXV, 110, 876, and is quoted in Pérotin-Dumon, "Free Coloreds and Slaves," in Paquette and Engerman, eds., *Lesser Antilles*, 259-279, esp. 259.

demands of the gens de couleur might open the way for those of other segments of society, such as the free blacks and perhaps even the enslaved. At the same time, the pamphlet sought to highlight and encourage divisions within the population of gens de couleur. Preserving racial hierarchy among the free was, in the eyes of most planters, the only way to preserve slavery in the colonies. The slaves, they believed, could only be contained through the constant assertion of the racial superiority of whites. If people of African descent gained equality with white colonists, the enslaved would come to believe that they too could, and should, be equal and free. It was therefore vital to keep the class of gens de couleur in a legally and politically inferior position to humiliate and exclude them. Any other course would open the door to revolution.[15]

To justify a perspective that went so openly against the ideas of political equality that were at the heart of the French Revolution, those who resisted granting gens de couleur rights argued that the colonies were crucially different from the metropole and therefore required different laws. Such laws, they asserted, could only be created by the inhabitants of the colonies themselves. Unlike metropolitan abolitionists and administrators, these inhabitants understood from experience the complexities of maintaining peace and order in these societies. Monsieur de Cocherel, one of the deputies representing Saint-Domingue, argued that the local assemblies should have the right to form a constitution "appropriate for our customs, our traditions, our products and our climate" and that this constitution would necessarily have to be different from that of France. "France is inhabited and can only be inhabited by a free people; the colonies, in contrast, are inhabited by a mixture of Africans and Europeans. Their system is not and cannot be the same as that of the Metropole." Co-

15. "Observations sur un pamphlet ayant pour titre: Réclamation des nègres libres, colons ameriquains [sic]," in AN, AD VII, 21 B. This includes the original text and a refutation by a writer sympathetic to the gens de couleur, who argued that men were all equal in their rights and that the gens de couleur—who had already shown their patriotism by fighting for France during the American War of Independence—would ultimately show their worth. Lacour, *Histoire*, II, 8–9, notes the planter origin of the pamphlet. The distinction between "free black" and "mulatto" was one of a broad set of complicated racial terminologies used in the colonies; see Médéric-Louis Élie Moreau de Saint-Méry, *Description topographique, physique, civile, politique, et historique de la partie française de l'isle Saint-Domingue . . .* (Philadelphia, 1797), I, 83–111, for a description of the gens de couleur that includes an extensive (and certainly at least partially phantasmagoric) racial typology.

cherel felt that the constitution of the colonies should be decided in local assemblies that would have the advantage of "local knowledge" in crafting the new laws. Dutrône de la Couture similarly argued that, although an integral part of France, the colonies needed—because of the contrast in climate, agricultural production, and the Africans themselves—a different, racially defined administration. The well-respected Martinique-born jurist Médéric-Louis Élie Moreau de Saint-Méry, who had worked as a lawyer and judge in Saint-Domingue in the 1780s and, as president of the Assembly of Paris, presented the keys of the city to Louis XVI in 1789, also defended this viewpoint.[16]

In October 1789, a representative from Guadeloupe, Louis de Curt, suggested the formation of a commission to write particular constitutions for the colonies. Such a committee was set up, and, on March 8, 1790, the National Assembly passed a law that granted the colonial assemblies, "freely elected by the citizens," the right to form laws particularly suited to the administration of the colonies. Yet, as the gens de couleur representatives argued in a pamphlet responding to the law, it failed to define who was a citizen in the colonies and therefore allowed for the continuing exclusion of the gens de couleur from elections and political life. Whereas in France the title "active citizen" might include all men who had fulfilled the property and age requirements of the law, the whites of the colonies would certainly exclude gens de couleur from the category. By not specifying their inclusion in "citizen"—through a stipulation such as "all free people, without exception"—the law cynically avoided judgment on the question of the rights of gens de couleur. Taking advantage of the seman-

16. "Opinion de M. de Cocherel, député de Saint-Domingue, sur l'admission des nègres et mulâtres libres aux assemblées provinciales," in AN, AD VII, 21 B; Jacques-François Dutrône la Couture, *Vues générales sur l'importance du commerce des colonies, sur le caractère du peuple qui les cultive et sur les moyens de faire la constitution qui leur convient* (Paris, 1790). On Moreau's life and political stances during the Revolution, see Étienne Taillemite's introduction to the reprint edition of *Description topographique*, I (Paris, 1958). On Moreau and the broader legal tradition of which he was a part, see Malick Walid Ghachem, "Sovereignty and Slavery in the Age of Revolution: Haitian Variations on a Metropolitan Theme" (Ph.D. diss., Stanford University, 2001), esp. chap. 4. For analyses of the planters' political stances during this period, see Florence Gauthier, "Qu'est-ce que c'est la terreur? Terreur et abolition de l'esclavage, 1793-1794," in Germain Sicard, ed., *Justice et politique: La Terreur sous la Révolution française* (Toulouse, France, 1997), 47–58, esp. 48–52; see also the detailed study of Gabriel Debien, *Les Colons de Saint-Domingue et la révolution: Essai sur le Club Massiac (août 1789–août 1792)* (Paris, 1953).

Prophecy, Revolt, & Emancipation, 1787–1794

FIGURE 9. "Les Mortels sont égaux. . . ." 1791. This is an allegory celebrating reason and nature together, showing the equality of black and white. The black man holds the Rights of Man and the decree of May 15, 1791, as demons leave to wreak havoc in the colonies. *Cliché Bibliothèque nationale de France, Paris*

tic vagueness of the term "citizen," the law encased a policy of inequality in a Republican language of equality.[17]

When a group of planter representatives from Guadeloupe proposed a detailed colonial constitution to the Comité colonial in Paris in late 1790, they openly argued that the white planters were the only ones capable of creating the laws for "lands so far away and so morally and physically different" from the rest of France. Their proposal defended slavery by declaring that the nation must respect the "property of all types" of the planters. The exclusion of gens de couleur from political rights was implicit, as it was in the regulations that had created municipal assemblies for Pointe-à-Pitre and Basse-Terre in March 1790. "To be an active citizen," these regulations read, "one must be French or have become

17. Blackburn, *Overthrow*, 178–179; "Réclamation des citoyens de couleur des isles et colonies françaises sur le décret du 8 Mars 1790," in AN, AD VII, 21 A, 11.

French." Gens de couleur were excluded on the basis that they were not "French," referred to as subjects who would be policed by the municipalities but never as members of the body of citizens. Although the Code noir of 1685 had made emancipation equivalent to naturalization, assuring at least in principle that freed slaves had the same rights as other subjects of the king, in 1790 the planters made "French" racially exclusive.[18]

The gens de couleur representatives in Paris continued to contest this exclusionary understanding of French nationality during 1790 but made little headway. In the middle of that year, the homme de couleur Vincent Ogé, disgusted with the unwillingness of the National Assembly to confront the planters of Saint-Domingue, left France, traveling to England and the United States before arriving in Saint-Domingue in October. There, joined by Jean-Baptiste Chavannes, a veteran of the American War of Independence, and two hundred supporters, he incited a revolt in the town of Grande-Rivière. Routed by local soldiers, the group fled to the Spanish part of the island; the French secured their extradition in January 1791. Ogé and Chavannes were broken on the wheel and then killed, their heads placed on stakes at the crossroads along the two roads leading out of Le Cap. Ultimately, Ogé's martyrdom and the scandal it caused in France brought about the May 1791 granting of political rights to those gens de couleur who were born of two free parents. Despite this decision's limitations, its symbolism still enraged the planters of Saint-Domingue. Through 1791, the relative impasse regarding colonial issues continued in Paris. It would be broken when a massive slave revolt erupted in Saint-Domingue in August of that year, transforming the political landscape of the Caribbean and recasting the very possibilities of antislavery action on both sides of the Atlantic.[19]

18. The project for a constitution, from Oct. 5, 1790, is in AN, D XXV, 120, 940; for the *réglement* (regulation) for Basse-Terre and Pointe-à-Pitre, Mar. 31, 1790, see AN, AD VII, 21 C, 2. The notion that the citizenry should be composed of the propertyowning colons—and should exclude poor whites as well as gens de couleur—was a clear assumption among the planter groups in Basse-Terre, who dismissed their white political enemies as "young people" who "owned nothing" and asserted their right to full citizenship by adding descriptions of their property after their signatures. See AN, D XXV, 120, 939; see also Louis Sala-Moulins, *Le Code noir; ou, Le Calvaire de Canaan* (Paris, 1988), and Chapter 2, above.

19. Fick, *Making of Haiti*, 82–83; Bénot, *La Révolution*. Thomas Clarkson, who had met Ogé through Lafayette in 1789, hosted Ogé when he was in London, although he later denied accusations that he had helped him pay for and organize

Rumor and Revolt

In *Soirées bermudiennes*, the exiled planter Félix Carteau claimed that one of the roots of the 1791 revolt in Saint-Domingue was the communication to the slaves of insurrectionary ideals—through pamphlets, engravings, and conversations between slaves and sailors working together on the docks. He had seen abolitionist texts, such as the work of Raynal, "among the hands of some Negroes." And, though few of them could read, "all it took among the slaves of a plantation was one who could read to the others, as the plots were being formed, to give them proof of how much they were pitied in France, and how much people wanted them to free themselves of the terrible yoke of their pitiless masters." The Société des amis des noirs was particularly guilty, in his view, of disseminating "among the negroes of the colony many books that showed pity for their fate, and many similar engravings." These last were particularly dangerous, since slaves had only to open their eyes "and listen to the interpretation of the subject, which was repeated from mouth to mouth," in order to understand that people across the Atlantic would support them if they revolted.[20]

Carteau provides a window into how slaves heard about, and interpreted, the news coming from France as they imagined and planned out their own revolution. During 1790 and 1791, the information about political changes in France—and notably the debates over the rights of gens de couleur—increasingly made emancipation issuing from France the subject of hearsay in the French colonies. Passing on rumors was a way of spreading news but also of intervening by suggesting the possibility of an alliance between the slaves and the metropolitan French government. Impressions about the intentions of various imperial metropoles had helped stir up insurrection throughout the early to mid-eighteenth century; during the 1790s, such talk, again mobilizing slaves, produced a real alliance between slaves and metropolitan authorities that brought the institution of slavery crumbling down in the French Caribbean.

The power of rumors only deepened as the pace of political transformation in metropolitan France accelerated. In the months following

---

the revolt. See his letters in the appendix of Charles Mackenzie, *Notes on Haiti, Made during a Residence in That Republic* (London, 1830), II, 246–258.

20. J. Félix Carteau, *Soirées bermudiennes; ou, Entretiens sur les événements qui ont opéré la ruine de la partie française de l'île Saint-Domingue* . . . (Bordeaux, France, 1802); see also Scott's discussion of this text in "Common Wind," 170–171.

the August 1789 insurrection, news from the summer events in Paris arrived in Martinique, and revolts spread through the colony. Slaves continued to assert that the king had made them free, refusing to work, escaping to the mountains, sometimes killing plantation managers. When one master offered to give his slaves three days a week for themselves, they refused, saying they wanted "all or nothing." When the Declaration of the Rights of Man arrived in the colony in early 1790, one plantation manager wrote to the minister of the colonies about the anxieties of the whites:

> Since we have learned here of the Declaration . . . there are none among us that do not want to participate in the great benefits it promises us, but there is also no one who does not shudder at the idea that a slave or even a free homme de couleur might say, "I am a man as well, so I also have rights, and those rights are equal for all." This declaration is certainly something very dangerous to promulgate in the colonies.[21]

Throughout the French colonies, meanwhile, slaves mobilized around rumors that France had fulfilled the promise of the Declaration of the Rights of Man. On a plantation in Guiana, "all the slaves gathered and told their master that they knew that they had been declared free in France and that they wanted to take advantage of their freedom." In Guadeloupe in April 1790, authorities dispersed gatherings of slaves in the neighboring areas of Capesterre, Goyave, and Petit-Bourg, north of Trois-Rivières. Six gens de couleur were hanged for having "excited the slaves to revolt." According to Governor Clugny, however, domestic slaves started the revolt by suggesting to field slaves that, "since the French had dethroned their king, they too should throw off their yoke and defend themselves against their masters." The organization of the revolt was quite extensive, involving the lighting of fires throughout the area, which signaled the beginning of the uprising, and contact with maroons, who sheltered one insurgent afterward. Rebellion was not limited to the islands under direct French control: in Dominica, at the same time the governor received news that the slaves of Martinique were determined to gain their emancipation, slaves returning from the capital of the island to the plantations spread the word that the governor had issued

21. Deposition of Hayot Baucage, Nov. 11, 1789, in CAOM, C 8A, 89, fol. 62; M. De Laumoy to the minister of the colonies, Jan. 18, 1790, rpt. in Leotin, *La Martinique*, 35–39, 43.

Prophecy, Revolt, & Emancipation, 1787–1794

a decree giving them three days per week free and declaring that they were to be paid for their work. Many of the enslaved refused to work or deserted their plantations.[22]

In May 1791, a rumor similar to the one in Martinique in 1789 circulated among the prosperous sugar plantations of Sainte-Anne, Guadeloupe. This time, however, the benevolent authority overseas was no longer the king but the National Assembly. According to the governor of the island, a "mulâtre slave who lived in Sainte-Anne" had recruited "a number of blacks by telling them that I had received a declaration from the National Assembly declaring all slaves free, but that I was refusing to proclaim it until I was able to sell all my property, which would take a long time." "Since they were the stronger party, he suggested, they should claim their freedom themselves." One slave, however, reported the plan to local officials; the small group that gathered on the night of May 15, 1791, to start the revolt was quickly disarmed by a troop of local whites, and eighteen slaves were interrogated. The governor noted, "This conspiracy was formed before the arrival" of some troops recently from France, and therefore they could not have been the source of the explosive rumor. He insisted, though, that "the basis for the uprising makes it all too apparent that such a train of thought could not come from a negro." Whatever its origin, this train of thought evoked a stirring prospect: the revolutionary changes in France that produced the Declaration of the Rights of Man might well lead to the logical next step, the abolition of slavery.[23]

The Revolt in Saint-Domingue

In Saint-Domingue, during the months leading up to the massive slave uprising of 1791 in Le Cap, rumors from France also inspired the organizers. The ongoing discussions in Paris of the rights of gens de couleur—news of which was, as always, slow in coming and often distorted—spread fear among whites and hope among the slaves. One observer wrote, "It was said that, according to a number of letters arriving from France, liberty was going to be granted to the slaves, and the whites

22. "Lettre de Clugny au ministre," May 30, 1790, in CAOM, C 7A, 44; see also Pérotin-Dumon, *Etre patriote*, 137–138. For the Guiana revolt, see Bénot, "La Chaîne des insurrections," in Dorigny, ed., *Les Abolitions de l'esclavage*, 182–183.

23. Governor Clugny to the minister, May 21, 1791, in CAOM, C 7A, 45, 5; Bénot, "La Chaîne des insurrections," in Dorigny, ed., *Les Abolitions de l'esclavage*, 179–186, esp. 185.

FIGURE 10. "Revolte des nègres à St. Domingue." c. 1796.
Cliché Bibliothèque nationale de France, Paris

---

were very worried about this." Several months later, the slaves of Saint-Domingue carried out the largest slave revolt in history, transforming the feared possibility of insurrection into an immediate and overwhelming reality, precipitating the events that ultimately sent the "good news" of emancipation from the Caribbean to France.[24]

Accounts of the August insurrection are—like the competing accounts of the 1793 Trois-Rivières insurrection—packed with accusations against various groups about the roots of the rebellion. The colony of Saint-Domingue, like that of Guadeloupe, was by 1791 in the throes of a com-

24. Catin Dubois, "Certificat relatif au décret des gens de couleur, déposé entre les mains d'un député de l'Assemblée nationale," *Le Patriote français*, Sept. 22, 1791, 355–356.

plex political conflict pitting whites against one another and against various groups of gens de couleur. In the wake of the August insurrection, these opposing groups traded blame for setting it in motion, with Republicans accusing royalists of starting it as part of their counterrevolution and many whites claiming abolitionist operatives from the metropole were responsible. Whether outsiders encouraged the enslaved to revolt, the insurrection took a course unimagined and unexpected, even for the insurgents themselves. The initial demands of the rebels were not for full emancipation: according to one captured slave's testimony, at a meeting called to organize the revolt "a statement was read by an unknown mulatto or quadroon to the effect that the king and the National Assembly in France had decreed three free days a week for every slave, as well as the abolition of the whip as a form of punishment." Insurgents frequently repeated demands for "three days" during the early months of the revolt. Only through the insurrection was the goal of complete emancipation imagined and then solidified as a project. That uprising, which emerged from within highly developed sugar plantations in the north of Saint-Domingue, brought together African and European military tactics and political philosophy and ultimately forced a transformation in the meaning of liberty and citizenship in the French Empire.[25]

Slaves rose up on plantations throughout the northern part of Saint-Domingue, attacking estate homes, killing their masters, torching cane fields, and systematically destroying the tools of sugar production. The slaves burned huge tracts of cane fields, so that the northern province of Saint-Domingue was covered by a cloud of smoke for days; they took full control of a large section of the province, and their numbers quickly grew as slaves from burned plantations joined the bands of rebels.[26]

The fury, speed, and organization of the revolt astounded those whites who were its victims. In September 1791, a plantation manager working for the marquis de Gallifet, absentee owner of some of the largest and most prosperous sugar plantations in Saint-Domingue, wrote to his employer:

> There is a motor that powers them and that keeps powering them and that we cannot come to know. All experienced colons know that this

25. Fick, *Making of Haiti*, 91; Michel-Rolph Trouillot, *Silencing the Past: Power and the Production of History* (Boston, 1995), 89.

26. Fick, *Making of Haiti*, chap. 4, esp. 97; C. L. R. James, *The Black Jacobins: Toussaint L'Ouverture and the San Domingo Revolution* (New York, 1963), chap. 4.

class of men has neither the energy nor the combination of ideas necessary for the execution of this project, whose realization they nevertheless are marching toward with perseverance. . . . We have executed many slaves, among them ten from your plantation; all have observed an obstinate silence when questioned about who armed them and incited this odious trance, though they admit to being guilty and having participated in it.[27]

In organizing their revolt, the enslaved drew inspiration from the religious practices they had maintained and developed. Religious ceremonies, which had long provided the opportunity for slaves from different plantations to gather, also provided a context for both organization and mobilization during the weeks leading up to the August 1791 uprising. During the now legendary Bois-Caïman ceremony that preceded the revolt, the leader Boukman called on the slaves to "listen to the voice of liberty that speaks in all of us." The potent combination of religious inspiration with political organization that drove the revolt is made clear in the objects that were found on one rebel who was captured, then executed: "pamphlets printed in France [claiming] the rights of man; in his vest pocket was a large packet of tinder and phosphate and lime. On his chest he had a little sack full of hair, herbs, and bits of bone, which they call a fetish." The report added, "It was, no doubt, because of this amulet, that our man had the intrepidity which the philosophers call Stoicism."[28]

If African-based religion inspired and protected the insurgents, the military experience many slaves had gained before their enslavement was also essential to the success of the insurrection. Many among the 60–70 percent of the African-born enslaved of Saint-Domingue had direct military experience from the wars that wracked West Africa and the regions of the Kongo and Angola during the eighteenth century. The tactics of the insurgents of Saint-Domingue, which involved attacking in small groups and advancing and retreating repeatedly, paralleled the tactics developed in these African wars. The differences between Africans and Creole blacks, who drew on different experiences in developing their strategies, emerged during this early phase of the Haitian Revolution

27. Pierre Mossut to marquis de Gallifet, Sept. 19, 1791, in AN, 107, AP, 127, dossier 3.

28. Fick, *Making of Haiti*, 111. There has been much debate about the fragmented historical evidence regarding the Bois-Caïman ceremony. The best examination of the evidence is in David Patrick Geggus, *Haitian Revolutionary Studies* (Bloomington, Ind., 2002), chap. 6.

Prophecy, Revolt, & Emancipation, 1787–1794

and would continue to be a crucial dynamic in the following decade of military and political struggles. Enslaved Africans also drew on political ideology from struggles over the meaning of kingship, notably those of the Kongo people, as they mobilized for insurrection and debated their goals and tactics. The profound influence of a variety of African cultures on the conflict highlights the transcultural nature of the political revolution that emerged from Saint-Domingue, transforming the order of the French Empire. As insurgents advanced to the tune of African music or amid a silence broken only by the "incantations of their sorcerers," as one French soldier reported, they confronted the existing order with their own vision of social transcendence. In so doing, they expanded the idea of rights in the colony and beyond.[29]

The insurgents were extremely resourceful in finding weapons—material and ideological—in the pursuit of their liberation. At one point, a group took control of a battery along the coast, and, when a French ship fired on the battery to dislodge them, they braved a barrage of 250 cannon shots. They then used the cannonballs that had landed around them to fire back at the boat, which was seriously damaged and fled. Insurgents also phrased their demands in the language of Republican rights on numerous occasions. When a small group of slaves were questioned about the meetings they had held just before the August insurrection began, they responded "that they wanted to enjoy the liberty they are entitled to by the rights of man." Several months later, after an engagement with the French, some insurgents requested a parley with the general, and, when asked what they wanted, replied, "Perfect liberty" for all the slaves. The insurgents also made, on at least one occasion, an unequivocal response to what they considered unacceptable compromises. In late 1791, a group of rebels told a French officer that they would be willing to surrender "on the condition that all the slaves should be made free." The group of whites who were sent with the official French response—which rejected emancipation but offered amnesty to those who would return to the plantation and denounce their leaders—were nearly all killed by the disgusted insurgents.[30]

29. John K. Thornton, "African Soldiers in the Haitian Revolution," *Journal of Caribbean History*, XXV, nos. 1, 2 (1991), 58–80; on the incantations of the sorcerers, quoted by Thornton, see Michel-Étienne Descourtilz, *Histoire des désastres de Saint-Domingue* (Paris, 1795), 192. See also Thornton, "'I Am the Subject of the King of Kongo': African Political Ideology and the Haitian Revolution," *Journal of World History*, IV (1993), 181–214; Trouillot, *Silencing the Past*, chap. 3.

30. *General Advertiser* (Philadelphia), Oct. 11, Nov. 11, 1791.

In the immediate wake of the insurrection, some whites and gens de couleur—who had up until then often fought one another with staggering violence—formed alliances. With renegade slaves organizing in the mountains, the gens de couleur, who were as numerous as whites in the colony and therefore represented a serious military threat and potential resource, were able to gain previously unimaginable concessions. In the western province of Saint-Domingue in October 1791, a concordat signed between representatives of the two groups proposed the erasure of racial distinctions such as *le nommé, nègre libre, mulâtre libre, quarteron libre*, and *citoyens de couleur* so that free people would simply be referred to as citizens. A procession and a mass were organized to unite the groups in their vow to fight for "the nation, the law, and the king." This local initiative augured the direction of colonial policies that would soon be decreed from the metropole.[31]

The news of the insurrection in Saint-Domingue arrived slowly in France, with early accounts of an "army of fifty thousand blacks" dismissed as late as November by the *Patriote français* as a "convenient rumor" spread by speculators in colonial commodities. In the same month, the marquis de Gallifet wrote from Paris to Saint-Domingue anxiously seeking news from his plantation manager Odeluq. The response came from another planter of Saint-Domingue, who announced: "Your plantations, *monsieur le marquis*, have disappeared, your manager is no more! The insurrection has spread the horrors of devastation and carnage on our property. . . . All is shattered."[32]

When the evidence of the revolt finally became irrefutable, the seriousness of the event ushered in a drastic change in colonial policy. The promised insurrection had come, and arguing about how to avoid it was now pointless. The debates about the rights of gens de couleur took on a new urgency and a new dimension. Some free-colored representatives, drawing on the long history of their community's service in the battles against maroons, argued that they were the only bulwark against the slave insurrection; in the new situation, many in the metropole were

31. *Concordat; ou, Traité de paix entre les citoyens blancs et les citoyens de couleur des quatorze paroisses de la province de l'ouest de la partie françoise de Saint-Domingue*, Oct. 19, 1791, BN; see also Blackburn, *Overthrow*, 194.

32. *Le Patriote français*, Nov. 3, 1791, 519. For a similar statement, see Nov. 5, 1791, 528. This paper was edited by Jacques-Pierre Brissot de Warville, founder of the Société des amis des noirs, who definitely had an interest in minimizing the news of a revolt that his opponents had consistently said he would bring on through his antislavery stance; for Gallifet, see AN, 107, AP, 128, dossier 1.

receptive to the argument. The blossoming revolutionary war against the British was radicalizing the political climate in France, and Jacques-Pierre Brissot, along with some of his political allies, was placed in control of the colonial ministry. As news of the gestures made by certain white planters toward the British filtered to Paris, these new forgers of colonial policy became convinced that there was a severe danger of counterrevolution among the whites of the Caribbean. Granting political rights to the gens de couleur, he believed, would both consolidate the reaction to the slave insurrection and strengthen the Republic in the face of defecting whites.[33]

On March 28, 1792, the National Assembly declared, "The hommes de couleur and the nègres libres must enjoy, along with the white colons, the equality of political rights." They would be allowed to vote in all local elections and also would be eligible for all positions, as long as they had fulfilled the national requirements for "active" citizenship—which were still based on the ability to pay a certain level of taxes. The decree explicitly presented this decision as a way of confronting the "enemies of the public good" who had "profited from the discord that has developed in the colonies, and have placed them in danger of total subversion, by encouraging the uprising of the slaves, by disorganizing the forces of public order, and by dividing the citizens, whose unity is the only thing that can preserve their property from pillage and fire." This "odious conspiracy," continued the decree, was "linked to the projects of conspiracy against the nation of France . . . which are about to explode simultaneously in the two hemispheres." The Republic would triumph against the enemies that were poised to attack it by granting equality to those who had been excluded and integrating these new citizens into the nation. In order to administer this transition in the colonies, Republican authorities chose commissioners—for Saint-Domingue, they included Étienne Polverel and Léger Félicité Sonthonax—and gave them the power to dissolve the existing colonial assemblies and to form new ones through the inclusion of gens de couleur as voters and as candidates. They were sent to the Caribbean with convoys of troops to help suppress the slave insurrections in Saint-Domingue and elsewhere.[34]

Signed by the king on April 4, the new law created only two categories of people within the colonies: free and enslaved. The legal racial barriers

33. Blackburn, *Overthrow*, 196, 206.

34. "Loi relative aux colonies et aux moyens d'y apaiser les troubles, donnée à Paris, le 4 avril 1792," in AN, AD VII, 20 A; Blackburn, *Overthrow*, 196–198.

among the free were, in principle, to be abandoned in order to maintain the distinction between the slave and the citizen. The slave insurgents had suddenly expanded the political horizon of the colonial debate, forcing the elimination of racial divisions among the free as it solidified that category as something besieged and endangered. The revolt radicalized the situation and forced the Republic to grant political rights to the gens de couleur, new citizens who would increasingly become the main allies of the Republican commissioners in Saint-Domingue against the counterrevolutionary planters. At the same time, many whites turned against a republic that they blamed for the violence they had endured. Already, in the wake of the insurrection in Saint-Domingue, some planters had appealed for help from the British governor of Jamaica; a British warship that was received enthusiastically by whites in Le Cap in September 1791. The Creole sugar planter Paul Cadusch sent a letter to William Pitt requesting an English occupation of the island, along with a memoir defending slavery, claiming that Saint-Domingue was the source of French wealth and that France and Saint-Domingue were two "federated" societies that had the right to pursue independently their own well-being. In Cadusch's plan, autonomy for Saint-Domingue under the protection of the British would guarantee the continuation of slavery. The movement for autonomy deepened during 1792, when planters from Saint-Domingue again appealed for help directly to London in reaction to the granting of political rights to the gens de couleur. In the next years, representatives from the colonies, including the Guadeloupean Curt, would travel to London to negotiate with the British government. In 1793, they would sign a pact forging an alliance with the British and handing over the colonies to them. The cycle leading ultimately to emancipation was underway, as the Republic expanded citizenship in order to preserve its hold on the colonies and many white planters increasingly distanced themselves from the Republic, becoming traitors to the nation in an attempt to save their rapidly disintegrating world.[35]

35. Geggus, *Slavery, War, and Revolution: The British Occupation of Saint Domingue, 1793–1798* (Oxford, 1982), 53, n. 51, and chap. 3; Blackburn, *Overthrow*, 193–204; see also Michael Duffy, "The French Revolution and British Attitudes to the West India Colonies," in Gaspar and Geggus, eds., *A Turbulent Time*, 78–101; request by chevalier de Sance to serve in the British army in the West Indies, in CO, 110/3, Public Record Office.

Three Wars

The disruptions in France's pearl had an immediate effect on the other French islands. There was a rapid boom in exports from Guadeloupe, which were needed to compensate for the losses caused by the chaos. There was also a sharp increase in slave imports into Guadeloupe, as ships bound for Saint-Domingue rerouted toward ports more secure than a besieged Le Cap. In fact, 1792 saw more slave imports to Guadeloupe from ships coming from Africa—a total of 3,571 slaves arrived on eight ships operating out of Nantes—than any year since the British occupation of the island. Another 1,006 slaves arrived in 1793 on two ships from Nantes. Planters might have been pleased that they were finally receiving their share of slaves, but the reason for their good fortune must have given them pause. Governor Clugny wrote in late 1791 that officials on the island worried, in the wake of the "disasters" of Saint-Domingue, that "the free would form a party among the slaves, and that this colony would become in its turn the theater for a massacre." He claimed, "In general, the negroes here are more gentle, more submissive, and better treated than those of Saint-Domingue" and hoped that, because they were "mostly Creoles . . . who think and reason" and "calculate well," they would realize "even if they held the advantage during the first moments of a revolt, they would soon lose it, and would be submerged by troops arriving from France." Nevertheless, he ordered increased patrols among the slaves. On Guadeloupe's dependency of Marie-Galante, a man named Bonhomme, who was originally from Saint-Domingue and had lived in France, planned a conspiracy for Christmas Day 1791, only to be arrested and hanged. He had allegedly told an English colonist that Raynal's prophecy of a black Spartacus had come true and that the blacks in Saint-Domingue were going to take power from the whites.[36]

The fear of slave insurrection pushed the various political constituencies of whites in Guadeloupe to reposition themselves in relation to both the gens de couleur and the enslaved. Planters formed and dominated local federations. Guadeloupe's representatives in Paris, who were forced to defend these federations against those who saw them as anti-Republican, gave justification by evoking "the danger that coursed

36. Clugny to Comité colonial, Dec. 21, 1791, in AN, D XXV, 120, 941; on the slave imports, see *The Transatlantic Slave Trade: A Database on CD-ROM* (Cambridge, 1999). On Bonhomme, see Pérotin-Dumon, "Free Coloreds and Slaves," in Paquette and Engerman, eds., *Lesser Antilles*, 259–279, esp. 269.

through Guadeloupe after the plot formed in Sainte-Anne" and by arguing that they were "a way of preventing the horrible misfortunes that have ruined the best part of the richest colony of France." These federations, along with the Colonial Assembly, soon became a focal point for political activity of the royalist planters who sought to gain control of the colony. Meanwhile, a group who called themselves patriots (and, later, Jacobins) formed political clubs such as the *Société des amis de la République française* in Basse-Terre. This group was composed mostly of white artisans, shopkeepers, and professionals centered in the towns, who for a variety of reasons—notably, different interests in trade policy with France—coalesced in opposition to the planters who supported the islandwide Colonial Assembly. The two groups vied for control of local decisions in ways that also identified them with the larger political schism in metropolitan France between differing visions of the Revolution. For the royalist planters, the increasingly firm hold on local power by the patriots provided a dangerous source of egalitarian propaganda; for the patriots, the planters represented a defense of the ancien régime. Both of these groups sought advantage by making alliances with the gens de couleur, who despite being outnumbered by whites four to one still constituted a political entity on the island. In recruiting gens de couleur to help them, the opposing white political groups took actions that paralleled the National Assembly's decision to grant citizenship to the gens de couleurs, at a time when that law was already being discussed in France but was unknown in the Caribbean. The planters of Guadeloupe went a step further than their patriot enemies by using their armed slaves in the battle for political power.[37]

The conflict between the planters and patriots exploded in Basse-Terre in April 1792, when the Colonial Assembly ordered the dissolution of the patriot-dominated municipal government. At a town meeting, the local officials and many inhabitants repudiated the order: they would wait for the new laws on the colonies from the National Assembly before accepting any changes in the structures of local government. Soon after the decision, however, a group of about fifty soldiers—including officers and a number of hommes de couleur—burst into the meeting and violently broke it up. Patriots armed themselves to fight back, but they were unable to stop the planters, who had mobilized both gens de couleur and slaves to help them dissolve the municipality by force. These recruits

---

37. Députés de la Guadeloupe to Comité colonial, Dec. 2, 1791, in AN, D XXV, 120, 941; see also generally Pérotin-Dumon, *Etre patriote*.

helped the planters take over the administrative buildings of the town, where, in a ceremony, they named three new commissioners. For most of the day, the town was in "effervescence," as those in the planter camp ripped Republican cocardes off the jackets of local citizens, and gens de couleur insulted and attacked white patriots until the planters took firm control of the town. Elie Dupuch, a local notary and author of the official report on the incident, wrote, "Everyone is sure that money was distributed to the [free people of] color and that freedom was promised to the slaves." Whatever the terms of the alliance made by the planters with gens de couleur and slaves—for slaves led by their masters, there was perhaps little choice in the matter—the coalition made clear that these groups were a political force on the island. The planters' actions incited an equivalent response among the patriots, who also recruited slaves in responding to the attack; Fort Saint-Charles, abandoned by soldiers who took part in the street battles, was left guarded by a few soldiers joined by "slaves who were coming in from all parts." It was the first time slaves participated on such a scale in the political battles of Basse-Terre, but it was not the last. The family of Eloy de Vermont, one of the planters who led armed slaves into the town on that day, was attacked by the insurgents of Trois-Rivières a year later. And Pierre Brindeau, one of the three new commissioners named to take charge of Basse-Terre after the planter takeover, was the first person killed in the Trois-Rivières insurrection.[38]

When, in late May 1792, the law of April 4 arrived in Guadeloupe, the alliance between the planters and certain gens de couleur was still in place, and the planters accepted the new decree. In the next months, news from France about the increasing conflicts between the radicalizing revolution and the king pushed many planters to take sides with the royalty. When (false) rumors announced the triumph of the king in Paris, planters determined to take over the colony, once again by arming and mobilizing gens de couleur and slaves. By August 1792, they controlled the entire island, and the white flag of the royalty had replaced the tricolor. Royalists also took control of Martinique, and Republicans from both islands fled into exile, many of them to the British island of Domin-

38. "Précis des événements qui se sont passés à la Basse-Terre, Guadeloupe, le 30 avril et le 1er mai 1792, présenté par Dupuch, député de Basse-Terre," in CAOM, C 7A, 45, 181–185; see also Elie-Louis Dupuch's more detailed *Précis historique des troubles survenus à la Guadeloupe, depuis l'arrivée des commissaires du roi à la Martinique* (Paris, 1792); see also Pérotin-Dumon, *Etre patriote*, 152–157; Pérotin-Dumon, "The Emergence of Politics," *Journal of Caribbean History*, XXV, nos. 1, 2 (1991), 100–135, esp. 114–115.

ica. The new governor of Guadeloupe sent out the new regulations for the postal system of the island. The mail was to be transported from town to town by slaves, each of whom was to wear a fleur-de-lis. The slaves were to be watched carefully, however, to make sure they did not deliver anything other than the letters they were carrying.[39]

Only a few months later, in Paris, January 21, 1793, would mark the revolutionary rejection of the fleur-de-lis as a symbol for the French nation. Both in the metropole and the colonies, the execution of the king hardened the political conflicts of the previous years into an all-out war between Republicans and royalists. In the Caribbean, the increasing involvement of slaves and gens de couleur in this war soon brought about a profound, and unexpected, transformation in the order of colonial society. In the next year, groups of gens de couleur and slaves would become the key players in overcoming a political impasse that the *maréchal de camp* Ricard described as an irresolvable complex of three wars: the war between gens de couleur and whites, the war between whites of different political persuasions, and finally the war against slave insurgents.

Each conflict, Ricard argued, made the resolution of the others impossible. If a serious campaign were undertaken to reclaim Martinique from the royalists, there would be no way to assure that "in the midst of the disorders one hundred thousand slaves will be contained." In Saint-Domingue, the conflicts between whites made a sustained campaign against the slave insurgents impossible. These rebels "established camps" and dug in the paths leading to them "deep ditches and hidden traps." A quarter-million slaves had left their plantations, among whom fifty thousand were armed; their chiefs had "shown some intelligence in the distribution and the choice of the posts they are occupying" by establishing camps "on lower hills and on the slopes of high mountains to be well situated for their incursions into the plains." Furthermore, they had "established a system of communication between camps so that whenever one has been attacked others have come to their aid, and they have hidden surveillance and meeting points." Ricard believed that the elimination of the sixty important chiefs among them would end the conflict, but he noted that they were hard to catch because they were often mounted on prime horses taken from the plantations and skillfully escaped into inaccessible hideouts when discovered. Though Ricard expressed confidence that the whites could, if they mobilized enough sol-

39. Pérotin-Dumon, *Etre patriote*, 147–157; Blackburn, *Overthrow*, 201. The postal regulations are in CAOM, C 7A, 45, 227–232.

Prophecy, Revolt, & Emancipation, 1787–1794

diers and took the right approach, defeat the insurgents, his descriptions suggest that such a defeat was far from imminent. Indeed, in their mountain camps, the leaders Ricard identified as the heart of the revolt were consolidating their positions, their armies, and their tactics, among them a little-known figure named François Dominique Toussaint L'Ouverture.[40]

New Citizens

In mid-1792, the National Assembly called on all regions of France, including the colonies, to hold elections. By the time the news arrived in Guadeloupe and Martinique, however, the royalists were in power. In October, a group of Republicans who had fled to the British island of Dominica decided to remedy this situation. Gathering together in an electoral assembly, they declared that they were the true "French of the islands of Guadeloupe and Martinique" and were "the only ones who were loyal to the metropole." Therefore, "only their wishes could legitimately be heard by the National Assembly." Among them were gens de couleur who had recently become French citizens; they found in exile their first opportunity to exercise their new political rights. Of the electors present, 36 of 209, or 15 percent, identified themselves as citoyens de couleur when they signed. (In 1790, gens de couleur made up 22 percent of the free population of Guadeloupe.) Among them was Louis Delgrès, who would lead the resistance against the reestablishment of slavery in Guadeloupe in 1802; he described himself as a citoyen de couleur and a propertyowner. Most of the citoyens de couleur signed in groups on the page, as if they walked up together—not mixed in with the other electors. In this Republican election in exile, the citoyens de couleur asserted and enacted their newfound role in the political life of the French nation. Their participation was a watershed in French history. The racially integrated electoral assembly elected, for the first time, a citoyen de couleur as a representative, a Martinican named Jean Littée.[41]

40. See letters from November 1791 and October 1792 in "Mémoires de M. Ricard, maréchal de camp," in CAOM, C 7A, 45, 119–147.
41. "Procès verbal de l'élection de l'assemblée électorale des députés pour la Martinique et la Guadeloupe," Oct. 28, 1792, in AN, C 181, 86. My statistics about the representation of citoyens de couleur are taken from analyzing the signatures. For population percentages, see "Recensement général de la colonie," in CAOM, DFC, Guadeloupe, carton 29, no. 443. For Jean Littée in the National Convention, see his 1793 note to the Société des amis de la République of Basse-Terre, in

A deputation soon left for Paris, consisting of Littée and two other representatives, one of whom was the notary Elie Dupuch of Basse-Terre, in the future to become a Jacobin. The group finally arrived in February 1793 and presented themselves to the National Convention, which by then had replaced the National Assembly. They contended that, although their election had not taken place in French territory, it was legitimate because it had united the only true Republicans of the islands. The election of Littée, argued the white representatives who accompanied him, was proof of the virtue of the electors and their loyalty to the Republic that had proclaimed the political rights of the gens de couleur. "He is an homme de couleur, he is our colleague," they declared, "and this is the first homage the whites have given to the virtues of this class that has until now been so unjustly forgotten." In accepting the petition, the National Convention reemphasized the value of having a racially integrated group of representatives: "Nothing better proves the respect of the electors for equality than the nomination of the Citoyen Littée." They predicted that "his admission into the Convention" would have "great effects" not only among the Republican gens de couleur who elected him "but also among those who have been misled by the counterrevolutionaries and who will quickly abandon them as soon as they hear of the great welcome their brothers have received from us." "This is perhaps all that will be necessary to reestablish our two colonies to their legitimate dependence," they concluded.[42]

Their confidence was well placed. Across the Atlantic, the royalist control of the island of Guadeloupe had been broken, thanks in part to the actions of gens de couleur. In early December 1792, a French convoy sailed into the eastern Caribbean, carrying Republican troops led by Admiral Jean-Baptiste Raymond de Lacrosse, who had been named governor of Martinique and Guadeloupe by the National Convention. Its arrival also had a symbolic importance, for it undermined royalist claims that the king was victorious in France and so gave succor to the besieged Republicans on the island. On December 20, a large crowd of "nègres and mulâtres" gathered in Pointe-à-Pitre and joined up with a group of

AN, D XXV, 123, 935, rpt. in Pérotin-Dumon, *Etre patriote*, 289; for Dupuch, see Marcel Dorigny and Bernard Gainot, *La Société des amis des noirs, 1788–1789: Contribution à l'histoire de l'abolition de l'esclavage* (Paris, 1998), 344.

42. See the "Pétition des députés des îles Guadeloupe et Martinique," Feb. 26, 1793, in AN, AD VII, 21 C, no. 37, which includes the response of the National Convention.

soldiers who were carrying a tricolor flag. They demanded that local officials fly it over the city in place of the white flag of the royalists. Similar movements occurred elsewhere on the island, and when Lacrosse heard of the events he quickly took over governance of the colony, putting it once again under the control of the French Republic.[43]

The many gens de couleur who participated in this action had become a decisive pro-Republican force. In March 1793, a group of signatories describing themselves as "new citizens" of Basse-Terre printed a declaration addressed to Lacrosse that asserted—in the face of the recent treason of many whites—their attachment to the Republic and their intention of asserting their new political rights:

> An odious faction, enemy of the French Revolution, had plunged us into error (which was criminal if it was voluntary) that made us forget even the exercise of our rights; this faction debased us, degraded us, disdained us, forced us into the most outrageous humiliations; this faction misled us, tricked us, and frustrated us. Your voice was heard, and you have brought us, in the name of the French Revolution, words of peace. You have enlightened us as to the benefits that the mother country lavishes on us; you have given us consciousness of our rights and obligations: our tyrants have fled. . . . What satisfaction for us to be able to show our joy, and to participate in the glory of our ancestors: their joy seems complete, but ours sweeps it away. We have the advantage over them of being able to transmit to future generations this event as memorable as it is important for the colonies. We will immortalize it for our sons; we will become fathers and our wives mothers; our children, taught of this era that brought glory to them, will be flattered to owe their political existence to the wise legislators that regenerated France. Accept, governor, our gratitude for your good acts, by transmitting to the French Republic . . . our thanks, and our firm resolution . . . to spill, if necessary, to the last drop of our blood to force the respect of the laws of liberty and equality, which are the foundation of our political existence.[44]

Who were these new citizens? The proclamation was followed by a printed list of 147 signatories—all men, residents of Basse-Terre. Some

43. Lacour, *Histoire*, II, 126.

44. "Adresse des nouveaux citoyens de la Basse-Terre, au citoyen Lacrosse, gouverneur provisoire de la Guadeloupe," Mar. 3, 1793, in CAOM, C 7A, 46, 190–192.

signed simply with one name, such as Coco or Dieudonné. Some marked these single names with a familial descriptor, such as "Claude aîné [elder]," or the mention of a profession, such as "Silvestre, maçon." Others had both a first and a last name; many of these surnames were also those of local white families. There was one Noël Lesueur, for instance, whose last name was the same as that of a white family that had been present in Guadeloupe since the seventeenth century. There was also a Nicolas Dugommier, who might have been the son of one of the Dugommier planters who owned property in Trois-Rivières. Two of the signatories, the brothers Louis and François Gripon, were tailors who lived in the Saint-François section of Basse-Terre. They were the sons of Françoise dite Gripon, who was described in a notary record as a "nègresse libre" and lived on a small parcel of land that ran up against the Capuchin convent on the northern edge of town. They were not alone among the tailors signing the declaration. Jean-Georges was a tailor practicing in Basse-Terre, living with his wife Isabelle and their three children. He thrived during the decade following the declaration, coming to own a number of properties in Basse-Terre, including a shop that he rented to a white jeweler. François Hamel worked as a tailor in Basse-Terre, where in 1796 he lived with his wife Magdeleine Pierrot. Another of the signers, Raimond Isaac, was, in 1801, described as a shoemaker. Indeed, the new citizens must have been an important force in the fashion world of Basse-Terre: one of the signers of the declaration was Marcel, the wigmaker who had helped Marthe dite Majou buy her freedom in 1792 and who a month later spread rumors of impending freedom that were part of the Trois-Rivières insurrection.[45]

Another signer of the declaration was Germain, the carpenter who, on behalf of his slave Desirée, had participated in a similar legal trick to Marcel's. Joachim Boudet worked for the postal system at Basse-Terre and also owned three canoes and three slaves who worked as fishermen. He had his own house, located on rented land in the town, and two young daughters; in the summer of 1794, he married their mother, the citoyenne Judith. His friend Joachim Bouis, a witness at the wedding, also signed the declaration, as did Charlemagne Bouis, who was probably Joachim's brother. Canut Robinson, who was to play an important political role in

45. CAOM, Notariat Guadeloupe, Barbier, 52, Oct. 22, 1791; "Etat nominatif . . . de Basse-Terre," in CAOM, G 1, 500, no. 5; ADG, Vauchelet 2E2/166, 21 Pluviôse, An VII (Feb. 9, 1799), 2E2/165, 18 Thermidor, An VI (Aug. 5, 1798); ADG, Dupuch 2E2/26, 23 Prairial, An IX (June 12, 1801).

Prophecy, Revolt, & Emancipation, 1787–1794

the coming years, was another witness at Boudet's wedding. The signer Boromé lived in the neighboring town of Baillif, where, in 1796, he and his wife Nicole lived on a small piece of land worked by one Thélémaque, then their ex-slave.[46]

These signatures presented and united a disparate social group as a political presence within the terms of the new law of the colonies. The declaration of the new citizens used the celebration of the French Revolution to condemn the royalist whites and so highlight their own connection to the Republic. It also broadcast their intention to use their new rights to participate in and defend the changes brought by the Republic. The signatures on the declaration represented a charter for a new political force; for, in the next year, many of these new citizens would play key roles in the various comités, commissions, and sociétés that would set the political agenda for the island in the wake of the Trois-Rivières insurrection. Perhaps, too, their example was present in the minds of the slaves who, a month and a half later, also proclaimed themselves citizens and defenders of the Republic in a more radical, and violent, manner.

46. ADG, Castet 2E2/208, Sept. 28, 1793; ADG, Vauchelet 2E2/163, Feb. 7, 1794; ADG, Serane 2E2/157, Apr. 6, 1794; "Etat nominatif . . . Baillif," in CAOM, G 1, 500, no. 4.

THE INSURGENT REPUBLIC

In 1993, Carlomann Bassette, a teacher, poet, and activist from the town of Trois-Rivières, organized a series of tours of the sites where the insurrection of 1793 took place. Following the path the slaves took that night is easy enough, since the town is still laid out along the topography defined during the eighteenth century. The Brindeau plantation, where the insurrection began, sits along the road that heads eastward toward Basse-Terre, winding its way around steep hills and by a series of waterfalls. The first floor of the house where Brindeau was killed still stands. A plaque placed there in 1994 commemorates the two hundredth anniversary of the death of the celebrated Republican general Jacques Coquille Dugommier, who lived in the house before leaving for France in 1793. Farther along the road, down the hill, lies the site of the Fougas plantation, the second one hit during the insurrection. No buildings remain, only the reminder of what happened there in a metal cross placed on a rock outcropping amid the banana trees. According to Bassette, it was placed there long ago to chase away the ghosts that people kept encountering in the area at night—the disturbed spirits of those killed in 1793. Next along the road is the site of the Jarre plantation, the third one attacked by the insurgents. The structure of the old plantation house and its gardens has been partially preserved in the renovated building, owned by the municipality that now stands on the site.

Between the Dugommier plantation and the center of the town is the one large plantation the renegades left entirely untouched during the uprising—that of the Republican Jean-Baptiste Thyrus de Pautrizel. Beyond it, near the schools and shops of the town, are the ruins of the Roussel plantation, which include little besides a *cachot* (a tiny stone prison where unruly slaves were locked up) and a tomb that houses the bones of Catherine Roussel, killed in 1793. At the opposite end of town from the Brindeau plantation are the remnants of the plantations of Gondrecourt and Vermont, both of whom escaped, although their families were

FIGURE II. Plantation in Trois-Rivières. Early nineteenth century. Engraving by Joseph Coussin. ©*Arch. dép. de la Guadeloupe, G 68*

killed. Surrounded by a stone wall, near the remaining buildings of the Gondrecourt plantation—now a small hotel—lie the bones of Gondrecourt's wife and daughters. Nearby, in a place called Bambou, Gondrecourt hid during the revolt and heard the killings. This is a place that Bassette remembers, as a child, avoiding scrupulously during the night, for it, like the ex-Fougas plantation, was haunted by spirits.

Despite Bassette's efforts, the Trois-Rivières insurrection remains a little-known event in the town and in Guadeloupe generally. No one since the nineteenth-century Guadeloupean historian Auguste Lacour has devoted much attention to the uprising, which was treated by the major historians of the period as a footnote to the larger conflict between royalists and patriots. In a modern survey of slave revolts in Guadeloupe during the revolutionary period, the event was briefly mentioned as a case involving "slaves under the command of political forces they did not understand." Yet, as a moment of bloody conflict that pitted slaves against masters and blacks against whites, its presence still lingers in the town. What role can the stories of these mostly forgotten deaths, of un-expected allegiances and betrayals, play in a Guadeloupe whose simultaneous assimilation and exclusion from the French nation remains a constant cultural and political concern?[1]

Near the Jarre plantation, Bassette has constructed his monument to the uprising. It consists of a large stone on a pedestal; on the stone is written a fragment from one of Bassette's poems: "1793-1993: Each event, tragic, epic, heroic, is the sap of memory." The base of the monument remains empty, as does a nearby wall that is meant to contain a local painter's mural of the insurrection. But Bassette hopes one day to inscribe there the names of both the victims and the participants of the insurrection. The names of the whites who died that night were well documented by Lacour, as were the names of a few slaves who apparently died defending their masters. But the archives contain the names of a small fraction of those who participated. The only one commonly known is the slave Jean-Baptiste, leader of the revolt, manager of the Brindeau plantation, and commandeur of the slaves when the plantation was in the hands of Dugommier. In France, the name of General Dugommier is widely known, commemorated by a metro stop in Paris and a major boulevard in Marseille. For now, the name of his onetime slave Jean-Baptiste, who mobilized the language of citizenship in the struggle for the rights of slaves, remains on the edges of historical memory even in Guadeloupe.

Insurrection

On April 24, 1793, the *Journal républicain de la Guadeloupe*, a short-lived Jacobin newspaper, celebrated the recent miracle that had occurred on the island. A few days before, according to the newspaper, the "enemies of the nation" had hatched "the most horrible of plots"—"in one

1. Lucien-Réné Abénon, "Les Révoltes serviles à la Guadeloupe au début de la révolution," in Marcel Dorigny, ed., *Esclavage, résistances, et abolitions* (Paris, 1999), 209-215, esp. 213. Some analysis of the revolt is provided in Anne Pérotin-Dumon, *Etre patriote sous les tropiques: La Guadeloupe, la colonisation, et la revolution (1789-1794)* (Basse-Terre, Guadeloupe, 1984), which first alerted me to the event. Hitherto unknown sources about the insurrection have been uncovered by Fréderic Régent in his thesis "Entre esclavage et liberté: Esclaves, libres, et citoyens de couleur en Guadeloupe de 1789 à 1802, une population en Révolution" (Ph.D. diss., Université Paris I, 2002), 756-761. I am grateful to him for sharing this passage of the thesis with me as he was writing it.

FIGURE 12. Carlomann Bassette's monument to the Trois-Rivières uprising.
Photograph by Laurent Dubois

night all of the friends of equality were to fall under the blades of hired assassins." These "bloody men" had decided to use "the most dangerous means imaginable" in pursuit of their goal. "It is by inciting the slaves against the patriots, and by distributing money and arms to the slaves, that they hoped to execute their vile project. But, by some effect of Providence, the daggers that they sharpened were turned against them."[2]

On April 20, three soldiers doing rounds in Basse-Terre encountered "negroes armed with rifles and pistols," who punched one of the officers and then fled. An infantry detachment and some cavalry gathered to pursue this armed troop, but, just as they were about to leave, "the citizen Cardonnet arrived from Dos-D'Ane and announced that a large gathering of negroes was under way in Trois-Rivières. Immediately the drum sounded the general alarm; all the citizens gathered their weapons, and in a few minutes thirteen companies from the town were ready to march." The order was given to a "few companies to march immediately to the site of the assembly of the slaves," and at dawn the first companies arrived on the heights known as Valcanard.

> Soon afterward we saw a column of about two hundred men armed with rifles, pistols, sabers, and axes. This column advanced in silence and in fairly good order; their movements did not seem hostile; they were allowed to approach to within rifle range. Then the advance sentinel called out, "Who goes there?"; the negroes responded, "Citizens and friends!"

After the insurgents explained that they had risen up to stop a royalist plot, they were escorted to town by the white troops, crying, "Vive la République!" along the way. Meanwhile, in Basse-Terre, local police took control of the streets "with orders to keep all slaves from coming and going."[3]

According to the *Journal*, "on the basis of the depositions and the answers to the various questions we have asked of them ourselves," it was clear that the rebels had defused a major royalist conspiracy that aimed to hand the colony over to the English. The insurgents identified Brindeau as one of the chiefs of this plot and testified that on his plantation they had found sabers, rifles, bullets, and barrels of powder.

2. *Journal républicain de la Guadeloupe*, Apr. 24, 1793, in CAOM, C 7A, 47, 124.

3. Ibid.

The conduct of the slaves in this insurrection is surprising and almost unbelievable. After using their weapons against those who had armed them in order to sacrifice the patriots, they committed no additional thefts; they barricaded the doors they had kicked in, posted sentinels, and outlawed everyone from touching anything in the houses, under penalty of death. It is true, nonetheless, that they took three trunks and one bag full of money; but they put these, on their arrival, in the hands of the commissioners who, at this moment, are working around the clock to stop the movements that have been incited throughout the entire colony.[4]

Twenty-three whites from six of the eight largest plantations in the bourg of Trois-Rivières were killed that night: Pierre Brindeau, along with his wife and brother-in-law; Julie-Marie Fougas; Jean Gabriel Marre; the elderly widow Catherine Roussel and her sons Duroc and Désir, along with Désir's wife and child; the wife and three daughters of Hurault de Gondrecourt; and the wife, mother, and two sisters of Eloy de Vermont. Vermont and Gondrecourt were on a neighboring planta-tion during the revolt; Gondrecourt later admitted he heard the screams of his family but assumed they were the result of arrests rather than kill-ings. Once he heard the news of the death of his family, "thinking that it was a general massacre in the colony," he escaped into the woods. In May, Governor Victor Collot ordered him, along with Vermont, arrested for their involvement in the royalist conspiracy. Gondrecourt escaped from the colony soon afterward, taking refuge in Saint Christopher and then Saint Eustatius. Vermont was imprisoned, to be released by the British when they took over the island in early 1794.[5]

The only group of identifiable insurgents, other than Jean-Baptiste, came from the Gondrecourt plantation, where most of the male slaves— ranging in age from fifteen to sixty—participated in the revolt: Mars, Pierre Ibo, Étienne, Charles Boriqui, Grec, Gabriel, Thélémaque, An-

4. Ibid.

5. Auguste Lacour, *Histoire de la Guadeloupe*, 4 vols. (Basse-Terre, Guade-loupe, 1855–1858), II, 183–185; ADG, Dupuch 2E2/28, 19 Pluviôse, An XI (Feb. 8, 1803); Collot to Lafolie, May 13, 1793, in AN, D XXV, 120, 954, no. 33; Cooper Willyams, *An Account of the Campaign in the West Indies, in the Year 1794 . . .* (London, 1796), 136. The names and birth dates of Vermont's wife, mother, and sisters were unknown at the time of burial because the papers on their plantation disappeared during the insurrection.

toine (identified as a mulâtre), Hillarion, Girau, Léveillé, Apollon, Bouqui, Laurent, Aura Saint Francisque, and Ouanoua. That so many of Gondrecourt's slaves were involved testifies to the effective organization of the revolt. The Brindeau plantation was on the opposite side of the bourg, yet all the slaves on these plantations acted as a group and, it seems, according to a plan.[6]

The insurrection was the largest massacre of whites to occur on the island during the eighteenth century. News of it spread far beyond the Caribbean: in May 1793, a North American ship arriving from Guadeloupe brought news to Baltimore that "the negroes had killed a number of whites of that island a few days before the brig [left] that place." And yet the slaves were not punished. Instead, their revolt incited a massive investigation of the conspiracy they claimed to have defused. The white officials of Basse-Terre put forth the explanation provided by the slaves themselves for their actions: pushed by their masters to massacre Republicans, they had instead risen up against the royalists in order to protect the Republic.[7]

Any examination of a revolt must take into consideration the complex path evidence can take from the insurgents themselves to reports and memoirs now available as documents. Certainly slave testimony was often dictated or disturbed by whites and shaped by prisoners seeking to save themselves or protect other conspirators. Yet the brilliance and uniqueness of the Trois-Rivières insurgents was that they unpredictably intervened in the conflict between Republicans and royalists in Guadeloupe, ultimately preempting the mechanisms of justice among the fragmented white population. In a world where slave testimony had little weight, these slaves, as a group, accused their masters of treason and carried out the punishment, then presented the completed act to the local officials. They held their own trial, delivered their own accusations, and enforced their own sentence. Their revolt set the agenda for the investigation that followed, which accused those the slaves had already tried and convicted as traitors against the Republic. The enslaved evinced their innocence and even heroism through their assertions of the guilt of the whites they had killed. Though the Republicans knew that the royal-

6. See ADG, Jaille 2E3/7, June 14, 1793; these slaves were listed as "au parc d'artillerie," which is the way the insurgents were described in other documents (see Lacour, *Histoire*, II, 173).

7. *General Advertiser* (Philadelphia), May 31, 1793.

Prophecy, Revolt, & Emancipation, 1787–1794

ists of the island were organizing against them, it was the slave uprising that exposed the plot and made possible a Republican counterattack.[8]

The institution that took up the task of interrogating and judging the rebel slaves was the Comité de sûreté générale of Guadeloupe, located in Basse-Terre and modeled on the increasingly powerful Jacobin committees of France. Its members included Thyrus Pautrizel, who a few years before had been the mayor of Trois-Rivières and by 1793 was one of the few Republicans in the town. Pautrizel was a close friend of Dugommier and shared with him the distinction of being a member of the Order of Saint-Louis. That the insurgents, many of whom were until recently Dugommier's slaves, bypassed Pautrizel's plantation suggests they either spared him because of his political opinions or else were actually in league with him—as many of the accused royalists probably suspected. He and the other members of the comité were indeed dedicated to destroying the royalists, whom they portrayed as "cannibals who breathe only blood" who had been "maneuvering silently on the plantations . . . luring the slaves with a freedom they had never imagined." But their claims about the danger posed by their enemies were based in reality; after all, the royalists had successfully taken over the island, as well as Martinique, the year before. And they had done so in part by leading armed slaves into battle. It was perfectly believable that royalists of Trois-Rivières such as Pierre Brindeau had again planned to mobilize their slaves to fight the patriots during early 1793.[9]

Brindeau, however, put too much confidence in his slaves. Auguste Lacour described indignantly how Jean-Baptiste—who he claimed was a favored and well-treated slave of Pierre Brindeau—eagerly cut down his master. Lacour's version of the events, however, seriously misrepresents Brindeau's relationship to Jean-Baptiste and to the larger population of

8. For detailed studies that deal extensively with the problems posed by slave testimony about conspiracies, see David Barry Gaspar, *Bondmen and Rebels: A Study of Master-Slave Relations in Antigua* (Baltimore, 1985); João José Reis, *Slave Rebellion in Brazil: The Muslim Uprising of 1835 in Bahia*, trans. Arthur Brakel (Baltimore, 1993); Winthrop D. Jordan, *Tumult and Silence at Second Creek: An Inquiry into a Civil War Slave Conspiracy* (Baton Rouge, La., 1993).

9. "Rapport du Comité de sûreté générale à la Commission générale et extraordinaire de la Guadeloupe," May 8, 1793, in AN, D XXV, 129, 1008, nos. 5–6. On Pautrizel, see CAOM, Notariat Guadeloupe, Barbier, 52, Jan. 25, June 27, 1791. In addition to his sugar plantation near the town, Pautrizel owned land in the *quartier des zombis*, a wooded area on the heights above the town (Barbier, 53, Dec. 1, 1791).

slaves on the plantation. In fact, Brindeau had owned the plantation for less than a year, and his acquisition of it, previously owned by the Republican Dugommier, was a part of the larger political conflict between royalists and Republicans on the island. Dugommier fled Guadeloupe in June 1791, fearing he would be killed by royalists. In April 1792, Brindeau was one of the royalist commissioners placed in charge of Basse-Terre after the takeover. Brindeau also happened to be a lawyer for the *Conseil souverain* of the island, and in this capacity he represented Marie Lauriol, a member of the family from whom Dugommier had purchased his property in Trois-Rivières seventeen years earlier. Since Dugommier had left the island with large and unresolved debts to the Lauriol family, the court of Basse-Terre empowered Brindeau to take an inventory of the Dugommier property. A few months later, the man Dugommier had placed in charge of his land arranged a deal by which Brindeau received Dugommier's sugar and coffee plantations and in return took over a portion of his extensive debts.[10]

The slaves of the Dugommier plantation were not indifferent to these transactions. When Brindeau came to take the inventory, accompanied by three other men whose plantations would be attacked in 1793 — Gondrecourt, Joseph Mondésir Roussel, and Fougas — he found a plantation entirely devoid of slaves. They had abandoned it as a group at dawn, taking with them the four best mules. The manager of the plantation nevertheless provided Brindeau with a list of the 170 slaves, of whom 70 were men, 66 women, and 34 children under fourteen. Thirteen of the slaves had already fallen prey to the struggles over Dugommier's debts and were in the hands of a merchant in Basse-Terre. Among the remaining slaves, a few clearly had a particular connection to Dugommier. He had made sure that the mulâtresse Luce, along with her four métisse children (whose father was likely Dugommier himself) would not be sold to service his debts. And one of the most highly valued slaves in the inventory was a thirty-eight-year-old man whose name was Jean-Baptiste Gommier. Though he was not commandeur of the plantation in 1792, his

10. Lacour, *Histoire*, II, 162–164; ADG, Damaret 2E2/14, Feb. 27, May 6, 1792; see also the discussion of the earlier sale by Dugommier's widow in ADG, Dupuch 2E2/26 (2Mi178), 14 Fructidor, An IX (Sept. 1, 1801); and the original purchase, in CAOM, Notariat Guadeloupe, Le Coeur, 1656, Apr. 19, 1778. One pro-Republican declaration that defended the actions of the insurgents described Brindeau as a "lawyer" who was the "acquirer of Dugommier's property"; see declaration of Jean-Baptiste Lange, in AN, D XXV, 123, 976, no. 2.

name suggests that he had held some managerial role among the slaves. So the Jean-Baptiste who led the revolt and, according to Lacour, killed Brindeau was the second of the important Republicans on the island to carry the name "Gommier."[11]

The Republicans investigating the activities of Brindeau and other royalists after the revolt depended on the insurgents' testimony. One white celebrated the slaves' prevention of a royalist plot aimed at "killing all the patriots, their wives, and their children," noting that he "knew of these facts because of the interrogation of these same slaves, who all made uniform declarations about this event." Jean-Baptiste, as well as another slave of Brindeau's named Pierre, had testified that the inhabitants of Trois-Rivières were waiting for an expedition of royalists that was to come to the island. The insurgents also provided details that specifically incriminated Brindeau, who had, according to the comité's report, bought sabers to arm them and "told them a thousand horrible stories about the patriots," whose "triumph would be short-lived." The royalists, he added, already had eight hundred armed slaves ready to attack Basse-Terre. The comité also learned—again probably from the rebels—how the older Vermont, whose son's plantation was attacked in Trois-Rivières, had stockpiled weapons and ammunition, including cannon, "excited his slaves against the patriots," and even proclaimed that he wanted to "roast a new citizen alive." Similar accusations were directed against royalist planters who had not been attacked in Trois-Rivières but who had participated in the 1792 takeover. It was reported that Sieur Beaupein Beauvalon had recruited his slaves to attack Basse-Terre, and Romain Lacaze and Cezaire Billery had armed their slaves with shipments from nearby British colonies and were in contact both with French émigrés and British officials who were planning to attack Guadeloupe. A new citizen who was a soldier and a guard at Fort Saint-Charles testified that Billery had asked him to open the doors of the fort to the royalists; in the days before the insurrection, Billery had also fired on a local patrol composed of slaves and gens de couleur. The Société des amis de la République of Basse-Terre declared that they had heard that Dame Le-Blond had bought ten barrels of powder and many swords and had forced her slaves to swear loyalty to the king, sealing the deal by giving them

11. ADG, Damaret 2E2/14, Feb. 27, May 6, 1792. There were two other slaves named Jean-Baptiste on the plantation, but the age and position of Jean-Baptiste Gommier suggest he was the insurrection's leader. The name "Gommier" came from a region close to Trois-Rivières.

beef. One resident of Trois-Rivières later testified that, the week before the April insurrection, several people started refusing to carry out their assigned night patrols among the plantations. Furthermore, the men assigned to patrol on April 21, all royalists, were suspiciously absent that night, presumably to allow the slaves to rise up and attack the patriots.[12]

While royalist whites prepared for their attack, familiar talk of impending freedom spread among the slaves. According to the comité's report, "An unknown . . . circulated the rumor that, once the tree of liberty had been planted, there should no longer be any slaves." Some claimed that the revolt had been inspired by "the demand that the slaves wanted to make, to the general, for *the rights that had arrived for them*," and a Portuguese slave declared that "one of his country," perhaps a sailor, "talked to him of the grouping of six hundred armed slaves." Just before the insurrection, an "unknown mulâtre" had approached a slave in Basse-Terre and had hired him "to open his master's door at night." Some slaves had traded in weapons, notably Jean-François, who gave the "négresse Anne" a knife disguised in a cane that she later deposited with the comité as evidence. And, on the night of the insurrection, one slave had said to another, "If I do not come at midnight, tell yourself that I am dead." Two maroons arrested near Trois-Rivières after the insurrection— one of whom had escaped ten months earlier—might have played a part in spreading the news of insurrection. As far as Baillif and Habitants, on the other side of Basse-Terre, two slaves, the brothers Maximin and Denis, apparently planned to "kill all the whites, take their freedom, and establish a camp in the woods to defend themselves." When he was interrogated, Maximin insisted that he had been tricked by a "nègre libre" who had told him that "there were five thousand freedoms signed to give to negroes who would come to fight against the English."[13]

These facts offer some of the outlines of the organization of the revolt, albeit no conclusive evidence. Though the center of the insurrection was Trois-Rivières, plans for revolt seem to have circulated quite widely in Basse-Terre. Links between plantations of different regions and between slaves and the free provided the channels through which plans, ideas, and rumors could travel. Some slaves and gens de couleur in

12. Testimony of Jean-Baptiste Lange, in AN, D XXV, 123, 976, no. 2; "Rapport du comité," May 8, 1793, in AN, D XXV, 129, 1008, nos. 6–7, 15–19; "La Société des amis de la République au . . . Citoyen Collot," Apr. 25, 1793, in AN, D XXV, 120, 954; declaration of Étienne Soulés, in AN, D XXV, 123, 976, no. 2.

13. "Rapport du comité," May 8, 1793, in AN, D XXV, 129, 1008, nos. 7–13.

Prophecy, Revolt, & Emancipation, 1787–1794

Basse-Terre—notably those who attacked the police patrol on the night of the insurrection—were clearly aware in advance of what was to occur in Trois-Rivières. The slaves on a plantation near Basse-Terre who, after the arrival of the insurgents at the fort, sent a delegation to the local officials offering their assistance, and who impressed the whites with their "tranquillity," also might have known in advance about the revolt.[14]

One account from the period explained that the insurgents had "little confidence in the promises of their masters" and were "more disposed to support the patriots." In the broader context of suspicion and conflict, Jean-Baptiste probably played a central role in cultivating and channeling the distrust toward royalists, like his own master Brindeau, and therefore in giving form to the uprising. But the fact that he was able to mobilize so much support shows that many slaves had a strong sense that their actions would be received well by the Republicans. If they had wanted to, they could have fled up to the inaccessible mountains, where there had long been communities of maroons, but, instead, they surrendered, placing their fate in the hands of the Republican officials. The slaves made a correct calculation based on observation of the political conflicts in the region in the previous years. They effectively intervened in this conflict, resisting slavery as they resisted enemies of the Republic. In so doing, they linked their fate to that of a nation that still excluded them.[15]

The comité made clear that the pursuit of conspirators on the island should continue, and Governor Collot ordered the arrest of many royalists during the next months. On the other hand, the comité concluded that there was insufficient information to prosecute the slave insurgents and that nothing was to be decided in Trois-Rivières until further investigation provided "full and perfect instruction" on the case. The Republicans of the comité were impressed, and grateful, for the insurgents' actions and protected them from punishment. But they could not, at least at first, bring themselves to exonerate them or—despite the suggestion—to turn them into soldiers for the Republic. This impasse, which continued for nearly a year, reflects the deep ambiguity that whites, even radical Republicans, felt when faced with the slaves as a political force. The members of the comité were unprepared to confront the extent to which the

14. Ibid., 11; *Journal républicain de la Guadeloupe*, Apr. 24, 1793, in CAOM, C 7A, 47, 124.

15. Declaration of Michel Gaudin, in AN, D XXV, 123, 976, no. 2.

slaves, in entering uninvited into the conflict between Republicans and royalists, had altered the political landscape of the island.

According to the *Journal républicain de la Guadeloupe*, in the days after the insurrection slaves throughout the colony came forward, representing to local officials the views of the slaves on various plantations. They came "to offer their arms to the Republic." At the same time, "they complained that their masters were not giving them enough food." In response, the Commission générale extraordinaire decreed on April 22 that all slaves had to stay on their plantations and could not leave under any pretext. A few days later, Governor Collot, worried about the possibility of further revolt, ordered officials in the towns of Saint-François and Moule to search slave cabins for weapons and to confiscate any they found.[16]

That plantation workers were sending representatives with complaints and offers to local Republican administrators suggests that the insurrection, and the success of the insurgents in presenting their case, provided an opening for other slaves to think differently about their potential political power. The insurgents had paralyzed the judicial power of the island because they had stepped into the center of the conflict over that power. In so doing, the enslaved had seriously deepened the conflict—in no earlier incident had so many whites been killed—and redefined it as they redefined their role within it.

The Wake of Insurrection

On May 22, 1793, Saint-Germain Roussel, accompanied by local officials, drew up an inventory of the plantation where his mother and two brothers had died "in the terrible event of the night of the 20th to the 21st of April." The house had been locked since the insurrection, and when the party entered they found "a number of pieces of furniture smashed and the papers in complete disorder." They picked up the papers and put them "in a large Carib basket that we left in the room, and had all the linen, which was in a frightening state, picked up and placed in piles on the billiard table, along with many household utensils, so that they would not be taken away." In other rooms, the group found a shattered mirror, three broken wardrobes, and a small chest of drawers broken into

16. *Journal républicain de la Guadeloupe*, Apr. 24, 1793, 66–67; Collot to Lafolie, Apr. 25, 1793, in AN, D XXV, 120, 945; see also Pérotin-Dumon, *Etre patriote*, 186–191.

pieces. Elsewhere, little had been disturbed; the bed still had its mosquito netting above it, and the drugs on the shelves were untouched. The cane manufacturing buildings and the fields were also in normal condition. The inventory listed nearly two hundred slaves present on the plantation—and there is no indication that any were part of the group imprisoned in Basse-Terre. This suggests that the attackers were slaves from the Gondrecourt and Brindeau plantations, although some of Roussel's slaves might well have participated and then chosen not to march to Basse-Terre with the rest of the troop. The insurgents had taken a trunk of valuables, but afterward they had handed it over to local officials who returned it to Roussel. In the trunk were jewelry and plates of silver and gold, a teapot, silver spoons, two golden watches, and money. Fearing further theft, perhaps, Roussel requested that the municipality place new locks on all the doors and windows of the house.[17]

A few weeks later, the same group oversaw the inventory of the plantation of Hurault de Gondrecourt, who had just emigrated from the colony. The house had been locked and uninhabited for nearly two months; when the officials entered, they found the women's rooms in disorder. They listed all the objects on the plantation, most of which were intact; they also listed all the slaves, including five who were maroons and seventeen who, having joined the march to Basse-Terre, were imprisoned. Because Gondrecourt had not left behind a surviving relative, they and his plantation became the property of the state, to be overseen by an appointed manager. For those connected to the victims of the revolt, the government claim placed on the destroyed plantation must have seemed particularly cynical: among those overseeing the transfer was Pautrizel, mayor of Trois-Rivières and a member of the same Comité de sûreté générale that had exonerated the slaves who drove Gondrecourt out of Guadeloupe.[18]

Meanwhile, the actions of the Trois-Rivières insurgents reverberated throughout the colony. In August 1793, a revolt erupted near the town of Sainte-Anne. It was triggered by the actions of two citoyens de couleur from the town, Auguste dit Bonretour and André Mane. While in Pointe-à-Pitre as part of a delegation meeting with Governor Collot, the

17. ADG, Jaille 2E3/7, May 22, 1793. The description "terrible event" was added afterward.

18. ADG, Jaille 2E3/7, June 14, 1793. The sequestration took place according to a law passed by the National Convention in August 1792, which was applied in Guadeloupe starting in April 1793.

two heard some exciting news: a new law had recently arrived in the colony. It granted illegitimate children the same inheritance rights as legitimate children. The news was rooted in truth—a few months before, the National Convention had in fact decreed that in principle legitimate and illegitimate children were to have equal inheritance rights—but it was also an exaggeration. The Convention had not applied this decision to France in any concrete way and had not sent orders to apply it to the colonies. But, for gens de couleur, many of whom were the illegitimate children of white planters and as such denied any inheritance, such a law would have had immense importance. Mane and Bonretour also believed a disappointing report that accompanied the news: the governor had decided not to apply the law in the colony and was in fact seeking to stifle any news of its existence.[19]

Two years before, in May 1791, a "mulatto" had spread a rumor among the slaves of Sainte-Anne that emancipation had been decreed in Paris but that the governor was refusing to enforce it. Officials had quickly crushed the revolt that was brewing at the time, but Mane and Bonretour would certainly have remembered the event. Having decided to organize and put pressure on Collot, they understood that they needed more support than the gens de couleur community could give them and managed to rally slaves. On August 26, "1000 to 1200 Africans" attacked several houses, taking weapons and ammunition and demanding "The law! The law!" They also attacked Sainte-Anne, but a local detachment of the National Guard repulsed them.[20]

Despite this union, gens de couleur and slaves had very different positions and very different interests in Guadeloupe. The granting of equal inheritance rights, pressing for the former, would have been irrelevant to the enslaved unless preceded by a grant of liberty. Why did several hundred slaves join with Mane and Bonretour? What did they think they were fighting for? What law were they calling for as they attacked? According to Collot, Bonretour and Mane had roused the slaves by declaring, "March with us. All the negroes are free." Although the two might

19. Victor Collot, "Insurrection de St. Anne," in *Précis d'événements qui se sont passés à la Guadeloupe pendant l'administration de Georges Henri Victor Collot*, in CAOM, C 7A, 46, 15–40. On the inheritance laws in Paris, see Laurence Boudouard and Florence Bellivier, "Des droits pour les bâtards, l'enfant naturel dans les débats révolutionnaires," in Irène Théry and Christian Biet, eds., *La Famille, la loi, l'état de la révolution au Code civil* (Paris, 1989), 122–144, esp. 129.

20. Collot, "Insurrection de St. Anne," in *Précis d'événements*, in CAOM, C 7A, 46, 15–40.

Prophecy, Revolt, & Emancipation, 1787–1794

have used the promise of freedom to recruit followers from the beginning, the course of the insurrection suggests that there was in fact a complex struggle between enslaved and free insurgents over what demands should be issued. Slave participants made clear what they wanted. At one point, hearing of a plan to compromise with the whites, some stated, "This is not what we want; we want freedom for all right now." Others, who had received promises of eventual emancipation from their masters, demanded that these promises be fulfilled immediately. Once the insurrection was under way, the leaders who set it in motion seem to have panicked. Bonretour entered Sainte-Anne on August 27 and told the mayor, "All is lost, these people will no longer listen to reason; I am no longer their master. . . . They want liberty and are setting up their camps. Soon there will be more than three thousand of them." Bonretour proposed offering some insurgents their freedom and forcing the rest to "go back to their duty." When the whites of the town, joined by troops from nearby Abymes, went into the countryside, they found enslaved insurgents on the sugar plantations trying to recruit other slaves. Bonretour and Mane had imagined they could mobilize the enslaved without taking into consideration their own political projects. They had been sorely mistaken.[21]

On the second day of the insurrection, Governor Collot led his own attack, capturing some insurgents and dispersing the rest. The whites in Sainte-Anne lynched the leaders before a trial could take place, and afterward Collot pursued the remaining rebels. In the weeks following the uprising, seventy-nine slaves were tried: twenty-nine were shot, ten were put in prison, five were whipped, and thirty-five were absolved. Writing in defense of his actions in 1796, Collot claimed that, without a violent suppression of the insurrection, "all of the plantations of Grande-Terre would have risen up," followed by those of the rest of the island, "and the destruction of the colony would have been the result."[22]

The contrast between the insurrection at Sainte-Anne and that of

21. "Procès-verbal dressé par la municipalité de Sainte-Anne du soulèvement d'esclaves, survenu sur son territoire le 26 août 1793," in AN, D XXV, 121, dossier 959, rpt. in Pérotin-Dumon, *Etre patriote*, 278–282; Pérotin-Dumon, "Free Coloreds and Slaves in Revolutionary Guadeloupe: Politics and Political Consciousness," in Robert L. Paquette and Stanley L. Engerman, eds., *The Lesser Antilles in the Age of European Expansion* (Gainesville, Fla., 1996), 259–279, esp. 275.

22. Collot, "Insurrection de St. Anne," in *Précis d'événements*, in CAOM, C 7A, 46, 15–40; "Etat des esclaves jugés et exécutés depuis le 31 août 1792 au 12 septembre courant," in AN, D XXV, 121, dossier 958; Pérotin-Dumon, *Etre patriote*, 278.

Trois-Rivières is striking. In Sainte-Anne, no whites were killed, yet the repression of the revolt was brutal, leaving thirty-two dead. Unlike the insurgents of Trois-Rivières, those of Sainte-Anne were unable to undermine the legal and military structures organized against them. That citoyens de couleur led the revolt in Sainte-Anne—and that tensions between them and slave insurgents apparently surfaced—must have diminished the strength of the rebellion. In Trois-Rivières and Basse-Terre, meanwhile, alliances between whites, gens de couleur, and slaves were strong and indeed grew stronger in late 1793 and 1794. As one of the whites who had participated in the repression of the revolt at Sainte-Anne had understood, the defeat of insurrection there did not signal the end of revolutionary transformations on the island. When some soldiers boasted about their victory by saying, "We made them dance the Carmagnole" (a revolutionary dance), this white citizen responded "mockingly": "Yes, but this is only the beginning, and soon you will all dance the *Grande carmagnole*."[23]

Friends of the Republic

Throughout 1793 and early 1794, the fate of the imprisoned slave rebels of Trois-Rivières remained unresolved. They were camped in an "artillery park" near Basse-Terre, guarded by sentries, and Jean-Baptiste circulated freely in the town. The example and presence of the insurgents drove the discussions that took shape in a rapidly changing political context. As the threat of an English attack increased, and with the Colonial Assembly discredited by its association with the royalists, the politically moderate Governor Collot sought to consolidate the strength of the Republic by allying himself with Jacobin clubs such as the Société des amis de la République of Basse-Terre. Among the Republican administrators who ruled with Collot were a number of prominent and politically active gens de couleur, who by early 1794 pressed for the same policy that Sonthonax was putting into practice in Saint-Domingue—the transformation of slaves into citizen-soldiers.[24]

23. "Procès-verbal . . . de Sainte-Anne," in AN, D XXV, 121, dossier 959.

24. See Lacour, *Histoire*, II, 175–176. Victor Collot noted that immediately after the insurrection up to twenty insurgents were allowed to leave Fort Saint-Charles per day, and Jean-Baptiste had total freedom of movement; it is likely that similar stipulations were maintained through late 1793 and early 1794. See Collot, "Insurrection de St. Anne," in *Précis d'événements*, in CAOM, C 7A, 46, 15–40.

FIGURE 13. "Le Nègre armé." 1794. In a reflection of the event at Trois-Rivières, this man walks out the door, which is decorated with a paper—referring either to the 1792 decree or the 1794 abolition of slavery—that mentions the freedom granted to hommes de couleur. In keeping with the gendered Republican tropes of the time, the engraver has portrayed a virile father and son as political actors in part by contrasting them with a frightened, weeping woman and curiously feminized child. Engraving by Fougea.
Private collection

Through the application of the decree that granted them citizenship, their participation in the election-in-exile in Dominica, and their alliance with Lacrosse, the new citizens of Guadeloupe had played an increasingly important part in the public life of the colony. Their political integration, however, posed complicated problems that surfaced a few months before the Trois-Rivières insurrection. In February 1793, a rumor circulated that the new citizens meant to brand the faces and cut the hair of all those still enslaved. Slaves in Trois-Rivières took the rumor seriously, and local officials had to use force to disperse a group of several thousand that gathered at the town church to resist. In Baillif, a town west of Basse-Terre, a similar rumor was put to rest by the public declarations of several new citizens. The anxiety among slaves about the possibility of having their faces branded pointed to the larger question— repeatedly raised by planter enemies of gens de couleur rights—of how a plantation society could function once racial distinctions between the free were illegal. Branding presumably would have been a way for the free new citizens to be immediately distinguishable from those still enslaved, a marking of the body that could somehow help with the integration of the ideally markless new citizens in the body politic.[25]

The rumors addressed the contradictions involved in a colonial policy that meant to abolish racial distinctions without abolishing slavery. The intricate connections that had long existed between freed people and slaves only complicated this new order; the rumors might have been an attempt on the part of whites to encourage conflict between slaves and gens de couleur. However, there was solidarity to be found between the two groups. In the comité's report on the Trois-Rivières insurrection, "a young mulatto, an apprentice wigmaker," had said that, if he were in the place of the slaves, "he would cut the heads off of all the whites." At least

25. "Rapport du comité," May 8, 1793, in AN, D XXV, 129, 1008, 6; declaration of Michel Gaudin, in AN, D XXV, 123, 976, 2. The Code noir had stipulated that captured maroons were to be punished by having their ears cut off and a fleur-de-lis branded on their backs; for a description of this practice, see "Lettre du P. Fauque au P. Allart," Cayenne, May 10, 1751, in M. L. Aimé-Martin, ed., Lettres édifiantes et curieuses concernant l'Asie, l'Afrique, et l'Amérique (Paris, 1851), 51–57; see also Louis Sala-Moulins, Le Code noir; ou, Le Calvaire de Canaan (Paris, 1988); Yvan Debbasch, "Le Marronage: Essai sur la désertion de l'esclave antillais," in L'Année sociologique (1961), 1–112. "Vagabonds" and criminals in France were also sometimes punished by having their faces branded; see Robert M. Schwartz, Policing the Poor in Eighteenth Century France (Chapel Hill, N.C., 1988), 156.

in his case, then, a new citizen linked his own freedom with that of those still enslaved.[26]

In the wake of the Trois-Rivières insurrection, local officials in Basse-Terre became even more preoccupied with the political assimilation of the gens de couleur. In July 1793, the homme de couleur citizen Segouny-Fortemaison, speaking to the Société des amis de la République of Basse-Terre, celebrated the fact that all free men in the colony were equal under the law; he proclaimed that the nation was "our common mother" and that "even the slightest nuance of demarcation between us has been forever abolished." He also, however, suggested that, now that "sovereignty" lay "within them," the gens de couleur had to learn to follow the laws and take responsibility for the governance of the island. Soon afterward, the Commission générale extraordinaire encouraged their political participation by granting new citizens an exception from the general policy that required all who served in public office to prove that they had remained loyal to the Republic during the royalist takeovers of the previous years. Many of "the citizens our new brothers," the commission declared, had been "wickedly excited" by false information spread by royalists, but, after the reconquest of the island, their eyes had been opened, "and in general their behavior in the path of the law has been constant, firm, and worthy of French Republicans." Therefore, unlike white citizens, the new citizens would be exempted from providing *certificats de civisme* regarding their behavior between September and December 1792. This law solidified the alliance between the local administration and the gens de couleur that had begun with Lacrosse's arrival on the island following the royalist takeover.[27]

The revolt in Sainte-Anne had brought to the fore the desire of gens de couleur to secure their right to property and economic standing in Guadeloupe. Shortly afterward, Collot gave a doubled response to their demands in the form of a law that encouraged their social and political integration even as it limited their access to economic power. The law noted that, since April 1792, "the prejudice of color has been destroyed, and all free men have been united under the quality of *citizen*." Unfor-

26. "Rapport du comité," May 8, 1793, in AN, D XXV, 129, 1008, 6; see also Chapter 2, above.

27. "Discours prononcé par le citoyen Segouny-Fortemaison à la Société des amis de la République," Jul. 22, 1793, in AN, D XXV, 123, 975, 153; "Extrait des régistres de la Commission générale et extraordinaire," Aug. 10, 1793, AD, VII, 21 C, no. 36.

tunately, Collot noted, this change was not always reflected in the language used by the local authorities, who out of necessity continued to distinguish the new citizens as a separate group. Since any speech that indicated "some nuance or distinction among citizens goes against the spirit of the law," Collot followed the lead of the Jacobin clubs of Basse-Terre, in which gens de couleur were well represented, and declared that terms such as "citoyen nouveau," "citoyen de couleur," "and others which mark the distinction between free men" were to be eliminated in all public speeches and laws. Such terms would yield to the undivided denomination of "citizen."[28]

This decree was meant to create social and political unity, yet it actually asserted a new basis for exclusion. Although the "law of the 4th of April" had "called on all free men to exercise the same rights," Collot's proclamation found "those who have been deprived of their rights until now" in no state to do so, the result of years of oppression. "Debased by unjust prejudice" and "deprived of all political rights, and even civil rights," the gens de couleur had experienced "only the shadow of liberty, and not its effects." "This degradation," he added, "produced discouragement and inertia" among them: "What was the point in educating and enlightening their children, when all the positions and advantages of society were barred to them!" The result was "an unformed chaos" and a lack of social order; the gens de couleur were plagued by "the indifference of each individual, the dismemberment of families, the carefree behavior of both sexes, and the paucity of their fortunes." "The free man limited himself to his physical existence and worried little of a future that promised nothing." For Collot, this chaos could be eliminated only if the gens de couleur were granted a future. As public careers opened up to them, they would bury the marks of their past through the "emulation" of the "virtues and behavior" of whites. As the state established primary schools where children of all colors could learn the "lessons of the spirit, the heart, and the soul that will one day form true and good citizens," equality would acquire "its ultimate perfection." But the first and most crucial step in granting "this class of individuals" the "characteristics that will place them in society and establish the relationships

28. "Extrait des régistres de la Commission générale et extraordinaire," Sept. 5, 1793, in AN, D XXV, 123, 973; see also "Extrait des régistres de la Société des amis de la République française," 21 Pluviôse, An II (Feb. 2, 1794), in AN, AD VII, 21 C, no. 46, discussed below.

that unite individuals" was the creation of "legitimate" families. And, in order to do so, gens de couleur had to take on family names.[29]

Collot's law adroitly dovetailed with the issues of inheritance that had precipitated the revolt of Sainte-Anne. Responding to the broad demands of the insurgents, the law controlled the economic ramifications of political integration by expanding on previous segregationist legislation. In 1773, a law for the colonies had outlawed affranchis from taking the names of their masters and required mothers to choose a name from an "African language," although the continuation of interracial marriage meant that many gens de couleur did use their former masters' names. In 1793, Collot explicitly eliminated the potential for legal claims by gens de couleur to the property of their white parents by reiterating that they could not use their former masters' names, or names granted by masters at the time of emancipation, as "proper and characteristic" names for themselves. Instead, they were ordered to devise new names for themselves. In large families, the eldest member—whether male or female—was to determine the name of the family in order to establish the "division of the branches that spring from the same free trunk." The children of a free mother were also to gather together and choose a common name that would assure their inheritance rights. Collot was particularly preoccupied with the identification of a "legitimate trunk" within matrifocal families, a fact made clear by the grammatical slippage from masculine to feminine in one article of his law: "In order to give to free individuals and families a civil existence like that of all citizens, all free people, of all sexes, freed recently or long ago, will take, if they have not already, a proper name that will characterize her and the children that she bears, if she marries." By gaining a legitimate name that could assert the "links of blood," gens de couleur would, in Collot's moral universe, receive the legal existence necessary for the orderly transfer of property within families. The acquisition of new names was to be a public and official act, documented by a notary who would draw up an *acte de famille* and supplemented by official declarations that were to contain "the exact name of each of the individuals that compose the family, the degree of kinship, and the relationships between them from the trunk to the last branches . . . as well as the surnames assigned to different branches to distinguish among them." These acts were to be posted at the municipal buildings

29. "Extrait des régistres de la Commission générale et extraordinaire," in AN, D XXV, 123, 973.

and copies sent to all family members in the declaration, who were to post them on their doors for all to see.[30]

Collot's project, and the arguments he used for its necessity, likely drew to some extent on the projects of gradual abolitionists as well as on the writings of hommes de couleur such as Julien Raimond who examined in detail prejudice and its effects on gens de couleur. Indeed, the concern with legitimizing the families of gens de couleur paralleled the way in which gens de couleur in Saint-Domingue and Paris challenged "stereotypes of racial pollution and effeminate vice" by highlighting their civic virtue, specifically their long history of service in the local militias.[31]

And yet, just as Victor Hugues would do a few years later, Collot sought both to apply policies of racial equality and to contain their effects. For both Collot and Hugues, eliminating distinctions depended on as-

30. "Extrait des régistres de la Commission générale et extraordinaire," in AN, D XXV, 123, 973. On the 1773 law, see Debbasch, *Couleur et liberté: Le Jeu du critère ethnique dans un ordre juridique esclavagiste* (Paris, 1967), 69–70. At least two hommes de couleur seem to have taken seriously Collot's program for the creation of new names, appearing in the Société des amis de la République with hyphenated names—the citoyen Segouny-Fortemaison, discussed above, and the citoyen Lacharrière-Larery, discussed below. I have not come across any records explicitly designated as actes de famille among the notary registers I have examined for Basse-Terre and Trois-Rivières, which suggests that new citizens generally ignored Collot's instructions. In at least one case, however, a new citizen made an effort to legitimize an existing family through official channels. In April 1794, the homme de couleur Joachim Boudet married the citoyenne Judith, with whom he had two children; the couple planned to recognize their children "as legitimate" through a religious wedding (ADG, Serane 2E2/157, Apr. 6, 1794). During the same period, the citoyen Germain came forth and declared the legal trick through which he had helped Désirée, Jeannette, and Jean-Baptiste buy their freedom (see Chapter 2, above); it is conceivable that Désirée and her children were actually Germain's family and that this notarial act of affirming their freedom was intended to legitimize the relationship through an acte de famille. For a discussion of similar questions raised in Martinique after the 1848 emancipation, see Myriam Cottias, "'L'Oubli du passé' contre la 'citoyenneté': Troc et ressentiment à la Martinique (1848–1946)," in Fred Constant and Justin Daniel, eds., *1946–1996: Cinquante ans de départementalisation outre-mer* (Paris, 1997), 293–314.

31. Julien Raimond, *Observations sur l'origine et les progrès du préjugé des colons blancs contre les hommes de couleur* . . . (Paris, 1791). On Saint-Domingue's gens de couleur, see John Garrigus, "Redrawing the Colour Line: Gender and the Social Construction of Race in Prerevolutionary Haiti," *Journal of Caribbean History*, XXX, nos. 1, 2 (1996), 28–50, esp. 41; see also generally Yves Bénot, *La Révolution française et la fin des colonies: Essai* (Paris, 1989).

serting a difference in capacity between those who were simply citizens and those who were new to political participation. The new citizens required, according to these projects, a moral transformation, an apprenticeship in legitimacy, before they could truly fulfill the responsibilities of citizens of the Republic. The political exclusions that were a part of Collot's project had their counterpart in the economic exclusion the project solidified. By counteracting gens de couleur claims on the property of their white fathers by forcing them to form themselves as families distinct from those of the whites, he was seeking to prevent an explosive conflict over land that could have changed the balance of power between the two groups. Of course, as would occur under the regime of Hugues, those for whom Collot had mapped out a complex route toward legitimate political participation were already busy participating in, and transforming, the terrain of citizenship. The gens de couleur had already taken on the duties of active, and activist, citizenship and were allying themselves with whites and slaves to propose a much more radical broadening of citizenship than Collot, or the metropolitan France he sought to represent, was ready to realize.

Slaves into Soldiers

By early 1794, the political forums of Basse-Terre had become vibrantly integrated. Many among the ranks of the new citizens who had signed the declaration to Lacrosse became members of the ruling governing body of the island, the Commission générale extraordinaire. In May 1793, the new citizens Joseph Hays, Lacharrière-Larery, Joseph Icard, and Canut Robinson were members of the commission; Icard was also an active member of the Jacobin Société des amis de la République, delivering a published speech to the société, and Robinson was a member of the Comité de sûreté générale. By October 1793, the tailor François Gripon of Basse-Terre was a member of the Commission générale extraordinaire, as were St. Priest, Jean Charles, and the wigmaker Pierre Laurent. J. B. Maillard, also a member of the commission, seems to have been especially zealous in his political activities—he was accused by some whites of tricking them into signing one petition. In early 1794, Hays, Gripon, Icard, Laurent, and Robinson were among 24 gens de couleur who joined 103 whites in a call to all the "loyal Republicans" of the French Antilles. The wigmaker Marcel, along with Joachim Boudet and Joachim Bouis, also signed the call; so did a number of men who had not appeared in the public documents of the town since the 1793 declaration of the new citizens.

As these new citizens increasingly participated in Basse-Terre's political forums, they put forward ever-more-radical responses to the looming issues represented by the Trois-Rivières insurgents and their challenge to slavery. The slaves' heroism against the enemies of the Republic, who were so vigorously attacked in the speeches of the Jacobin clubs and by Governor Collot himself, brought the contradictions of the fragile order of slavery to the surface. As royalist strength increased through 1793 and early 1794 and the menace of a British alliance with the anti-Republican French became manifest, the slaves' claim that the Republic needed them became harder and harder to ignore.[32]

In August 1793, Governor Collot made the homme de couleur Louis Gripon a captain in the army, and at some point during the year he also made Izaac Jacques a sublieutenant. In Martinique, General Donatien Marie Joseph Rochambeau had taken a similar course, promoting Antoine Zamore, an homme de couleur who had served in the local militia since 1785, to captain and making Magloire Pélage a lieutenant. By doing so, both Collot and Rochambeau reversed a long trend of excluding men of African descent from the higher ranks of the military. They were responding to the political demands of the gens de couleur, but they were also addressing the urgent military problem of maintaining a strong army on the island in the face of the widespread defection of whites to the royalist camp. In early January 1794, as a British attack became more and more likely, Collot went a step further, requisitioning slaves from different areas to help build fortifications and prepare the defense of the island. A small number were working at Fort Fleur d'Epée, the central defen-

32. All of the hommes de couleur mentioned here signed the 1793 "Adresse des nouveaux citoyens," Mar. 3, 1793, in CAOM, C 7A, 46, 190–191. Among those who signed were J. B. Canon, Étienne Mechin, Jean-Pierre-Gérard, Benoît dit Choco, Jean Salvator, and Jean Baptiste dit Esprit. For Robinson and Hays, see the "Extrait des régistres de la Commission générale et extraordinaire de la Guadeloupe," May 15, 1793, in AN, AD VII, 21 C, no. 33; for members of the commission in October 1793, see the names attached to the *profession de foi* (declaration of faith) in the "Extrait," Oct. 18, 1793, in AN, AD VII, 21 C, no. 41; for Joseph Icard's membership in the commission, see the "Extrait," May 15, 1793, in AN, AD VII, 21 C, no. 33. For his speech to the Jacobin club, see AN, D XXV, 123, 975, 156. Jean-Charles owned land in Basse-Terre, which he sold in August 1794; see CAOM, Castet, 572, 5 Germinal, An XII (Mar. 26, 1804); Pierre Laurent's profession is noted in the 1796 "Etat nominatif . . . de Basse-Terre," in CAOM, G 1, 500, no. 5. For J. B. Maillard's political zealousness, see ADG, Serane 2E2/157, Jan. 21, 1794. See also "Eveil aux français de toutes les Antilles fidèles à la république," in AN, AD VII, 21 C, no. 44.

Prophecy, Revolt, & Emancipation, 1787–1794

sive fort of the Pointe-à-Pitre area; in the nearby town of Anse-Bertrand, officials were using slaves to build ammunition depots. Some planters refused to supply the requested slaves, and Collot attacked them for being "bad citizens."[33]

By February, Collot was forced to deal with a more extreme proposal for the defense of the colony. He noted that "the most important object being discussed in the colony" was the debate over "the formation of an infantry corps composed of five hundred slaves." "Citizen delegates" from the different regions of Guadeloupe had decided to defer any decision on the matter to their constituents, and Collot agreed that this was the best policy. But he tentatively gave his support to the arming of slaves, writing, "It certainly might be necessary and indispensable to do it," but it was a "delicate matter" that had to do both "with the methods necessary to save the colony and with a very delicate issue that affects the properties." He responded "in advance to the denigrators of this operation" by sending the delegates a proclamation, to be attached to their public declarations. Such denigrators of the recruitment of slaves, Collot concluded, likely did not "know its necessity or its urgency." And they also might "pretend to ignore that this measure was provoked by the mass of the people of Basse-Terre, as the only way to avoid the worst, an armament that would happen indiscriminately and forcibly, at the moment of final danger." In timidly advocating the arming of slaves for the Republic, Collot was responding to a popular movement in the aftermath of the Trois-Rivières insurrection. By presenting the measure as a way of preempting the armament of slaves in the midst of the conflict, citizens registered their understanding that the slaves were already, and unavoidably, a potential military force on the island. Even Collot understood that the only reasonable solution in the midst of the crisis in Guadeloupe was to appropriate that force so as to be able to control it when the storm came. It is an opinion Collot later erased from his own history, marking the extent to which the choice was forced on him by the slaves' pro-Republican organizing.[34]

33. On the promotions of hommes de couleur, see the "Formation de la compagnie des hommes de couleur," the "Etat des officers des différents grades," and the list written by Alexis Dumeny, all from 1798, in AHAT, X i, 80; on the slave recruitment, see the January letters from Collot to Lafolie, in AN, D XXV, 120, 946; "Extrait des régistres de l'assemblée provisoirement adminstrative de la Guadeloupe," 15 Pluviôse, An II (Feb. 3, 1794), in AN, D XXV, 120, 942.

34. "Extrait des régistres de l'assemblée provisoirement administrative de la Guadeloupe," 13 Pluviôse, An II (Feb. 1, 1794), in AN, D XXV, 120, 942.

On 17 Pluviôse, year II (February 5, 1794)—coincidentally, the day after slavery was abolished by the National Assembly, though the population of Guadeloupe had no way of knowing this—the citoyen Lacharrière-Larery mounted the stand at the Société des amis de la République to argue that arming the slaves was the only way to save the Republic. "Let us create new defenders of liberty," he commanded, dismissing those who feared that "as soon as they are released from slavery" these armed men would attack their new companions. These fears arose from the greed of the propertyowners, for, if they offered their best slaves ("those who through their services have shown they deserve their reward") to fight for the Republic, "then far from troubling the order of the colony, they will consolidate it by adding to the numbers and force of the free." Furthermore, service to the nation would transform worthy slaves into valuable citizens:

> We cannot give political rights to people who have done nothing to deserve it, it will be said; perhaps not, but we can show them what is expected and give them the means to achieve it. May he who can show three wounds be freed immediately . . . may he who has saved the life of a citizen be immediately declared a citizen himself. The recompense for actions and virtues will awaken honor in the souls of these new men, and will prepare them by degrees to be admitted into the class of free men. . . . to make war you need two things, men and money; men we can make.[35]

Joseph Hays of the Commission générale extraordinaire seconded these arguments when he spoke to the same société four days later, calling on all to unite behind the Republic and support the arming of the slaves. Hays thanked the nation for the gift it had given him and his fellow new citizens and argued that, if the enemy took back the colony, they would all be plunged back into "the degradation of slavery" at the hands of the white émigrés. "May the voice of the true Republican support this levy of slave troops, from one end of the colony to the other; may a firm and imposing attitude show them that our resolution is to save the colony or be buried under its ruins." Hearing this speech, the members

35. "Extrait des régistres de la Société de amis de la République française," 17 Pluviôse, An II (Feb. 5, 1794), in AN, AD VII, 21 C, no. 45. Lacharrière-Larery continued to use this hyphenated name, likely an application of Collot's law of the previous year, during the decade to come; see ADG, Vauchelet 164, 2E2, 21 Brumaire, An VI (Nov. 11, 1797); CAOM, EC, Basse-Terre, 21, 11, 28 Ventôse, An XI (Mar. 18, 1803).

of the société loudly applauded, and "many spoke in favor of the suppression of the word *citoyen de couleur*, arguing that this denomination—already proscribed by the société—seemed to maintain a line of demarcation insulting to equality." "There should not among citizens be even the shadow of distinction." The société members, both whites and gens de couleur, determined that when the speech was published it should not be specifically marked as being given by and for the citoyens de couleur. Instead, the société would "take in its name the address given by Hays," which would be "signed not only by the members, but also by all those in the galleries."[36]

This gesture, through which a racially mixed audience—of both members of the société and participants from the galleries—publicly supported the elimination of any distinction between an homme de couleur and a white citizen, marked a powerful moment of political cohesion. One hundred six people signed the declaration. Among them were whites such as the surgeon Antoine Fontelliau, who had owned and sold slaves in the preceding years, and twenty men who had signed the 1793 declaration of the new citizens of Basse-Terre. These new citizens included members of the the Commission générale extraordinaire as well as those who had signed "Éveil" of the Société des amis de la République a few weeks before. A few were present who had not penned their names to any public documents since March 1793, namely Maurice, the tailor Jean-Georges, and the carpenter Hypolite Debort. One man who had not signed in March but who was later described as "de couleur" added his name to the declaration: Ciprien Dugommier, a carpenter from Trois-Rivières who was perhaps related to Jacques Coquille Dugommier. Also among the names was one Jean-Baptiste. This was quite a common name, and he might have been an homme de couleur from Basse-Terre. Or he might have been the Trois-Rivières insurrection leader, who had provided an example and created the conditions for the armament of slaves as Republican soldiers. Held in custody in Basse-Terre, he could well have attended Hays's speech and had perhaps even discussed the possibility of arming slaves with him or other members of the société. And, if it was he who signed the declaration, he did so boldly, as if he were a free citizen.[37]

36. "Extrait des régistres de la Société des amis de la République française," 21 Pluviôse, An II (Feb. 9, 1794), in AN, AD VII, 21 C, no. 46.

37. On Fontelliau, see CAOM, Notariat Guadeloupe, Barbier, 53, Jan. 23, 1792; on Dugommier, see CAOM, EC, Basse-Terre, 6, nos. 41, 58.

In the weeks following the speeches given by Lacharrière-Larery and Hays, Collot agreed to create a battalion of three hundred *chasseurs noirs* to help defend the colony from attack. The slaves who joined were promised the prize of "indefinite liberty." Recruiters were sent to plantations throughout the colony, and a "mulâtre libre" named Louison was placed in command of the slave battalion. The effort was, however, too little, too late. When the British attacked Guadeloupe in late March, many royalist whites joined them, and others sabotaged the Republicans' defense. As the enemy troops approached Basse-Terre, the slave battalion retreated from its position above the town; their fate is unknown. Most white Republicans—including all the officials of Basse-Terre—were taken prisoner by the British and deported from the island, eventually arriving in France. Several dozen gave testimonies about the events in Guadeloupe, often celebrating the actions of the insurgents at Trois-Rivières. One group noted in 1796 that the Republicans had been saved from a royalist conspiracy when "some of the negroes who had been armed to carry it out turned the weapons against the conspirators, crying that they were Republicans" and in so doing "pulled the patriots out of their lethargy," only to see the incompetence of Collot and the inaction of the planters pave the way for a British takeover.[38]

By then, of course, the political conclusion arrived at by Joseph Hays and other Republicans of Guadeloupe had become foundation for a new form of colonial governance. Even as Hays and Lacharrière-Larery had spoken, the principle of transforming slaves into citizens, already a fact in Saint-Domingue, had been consecrated as the law of the French Republic. Guadeloupe's representatives to the National Assembly celebrated what had happened in their colony, exaggerating its novelty: "Never before had those who are governed by the Code noir been entrusted with weapons." Some of the exiled Republicans from Guadeloupe, meanwhile, lambasted the planters who had refused to offer up their slaves to serve in the chasseurs noirs, putting their property interests over that of the Re-

---

38. Pérotin-Dumon, *Etre patriote*, 217; declarations of Étienne Soulés, Jean-Baptiste Delannay, in AN, D XXV, 123, 976, 2; declaration of Michel Gaudin, in AN, D XXV, 123, 976, 1; municipality of Basse-Terre to National Convention, in AN, D XXV, 125, 991, 12; on the takeover of Guadeloupe, see Michael Duffy, *Soldiers, Sugar, and Seapower: The British Expeditions to the West Indies and the War against Revolutionary France* (Oxford, 1987), chaps. 2–6, esp. 93–97; "Les Patriotes déportés de la Guadeloupe par les Anglais aux membres de la Convention nationale composant la Commission des colonies," 20 Brumaire, An III (Nov. 10, 1796), in AN, AD VII, 21 C, no. 44.

public. And the royalists soon lost their hold over Guadeloupe. In June 1794, a mission under the command of Victor Hugues would arrive in the colony, bringing news of the emancipation decree and putting into practice the suggestion made by the insurgents of Trois-Rivières, sending waves of slaves-turned-citizen-soldiers against the British in the eastern Caribbean.[39]

What happened to Jean-Baptiste and the other insurgents who had so transformed the political situation on the island? When the British attacked Guadeloupe, these rebels were transferred to Fort Saint-Charles and locked up, though it is unclear why, and under whose orders, this was done. According to one report, as the British approached Basse-Terre, the prisoners managed to break free of their chains and the two doors that locked them in. They then "escaped over the ramparts" and ran away under fire. Where did they go from there? None of the British accounts of the takeover mentions them at all. General Charles Grey noted that in their conquest of Martinique and Guadeloupe the British had discovered "dangerous spirits" who were "not well disposed to our government" and described the deportation of some "free mulattoes," but no slave insurgents. A British naval officer who described the taking of Basse-Terre in detail also made no mention of rebel slaves, though he did note that, as they attacked, "some incendiaries who had plundered the town set it on fire and got off on an armed schooner." Perhaps some of the Trois-Rivières insurgents who escaped the fort were among them.[40]

After the British takeover, Hurault de Gondrecourt was named commissioner of Trois-Rivières and returned to the town. He found his plantation devastated, the instruments of sugarcane processing "com-

39. Declaration of Representatives Dupuch and Lion to Comité du salut public, 15 Floréal, An II (May 4, 1794), in AN, D XXV, 125, 989, cited in Pérotin-Dumon, "Free Coloreds and Slaves," in Paquette and Engerman, eds., *Lesser Antilles*, 259–279, esp. 275–276; municipality of Basse-Terre to National Convention, in AN, D XXV, 125, 991, 12.

40. See "Rapport des faits passé dans le Fort St. Charles," in AN, D XXV, 125, 993, 11; see also Régent, "Entre esclavage et liberté," 756–761 (my thanks to Fréderic for generously sharing his discovery of this important source with me); Lacour, *Histoire*, II, 175–176; Jean Barreau, "La Perte et la reconquête de la Guadeloupe en 1794," *Bulletin de la Société d'histoire de la Guadeloupe*, XXVIII (1976), 13–48, 27–29. For British accounts of the taking of Guadeloupe, see Willyams, *Account*, 85–98, 136; for Grey's report, see Jul. 17, 28, 1794, HO 30/1, 336, Public Record Office. For navy officer Boyne's account, see Apr. 23, 29, 1794, Adm. 1/316; see also the accounts in WO 1/82, 25, 49, 111–149.

pletely crushed," and thirty-eight of the plantation slaves—likely some of whom had participated in the 1793 insurrection—either dead or escaped. Soon afterward, when Hugues brought emancipation to Guadeloupe, Gondrecourt left for England with some of his slaves, entering into what would ultimately become a permanent exile. Two years later, none of the slave insurgents from the Gondrecourt plantation had returned to Trois-Rivières; they had either been killed in 1794 or left the plantation, and perhaps the island, permanently. Yet, in that year, the *chef d'atelier* (overseer) of Brindeau's plantation was none other than the Jean-Baptiste who led the insurrection. Perhaps his freedom of movement and his connections in the town of Basse-Terre allowed him to escape vengeance. He had managed not only to avoid punishment for leading an insurrection that killed his former master but also to return as a manager of the plantation. It was now called the "Habitation nationale Brindeau," run by the state, for the profit of a republic that had as one of its most powerful weapons a declaration that made all slaves citizens, equal under law.[41]

41. Declaration of Étienne Soulés, in AN, D XXV, 123, 976, no. 2; ADG, Dupuch 2E2/28 (2Mi180), 19 Pluviôse, An XI (Feb. 8, 1803); "Etat nominatif des citoyens . . . de Trois-Rivières," in CAOM, G 1, 502, no. 2. My conjecture that the manager of the plantation in 1796 was the same rebel leader is based both on his previous experience in this capacity and the broader politics of Hugues's regime. It could be, of course, that there is simply a coincidence in names.

Chapter 5

THE ARRIVAL OF EMANCIPATION

In Saint-Domingue, two months after the insurrection in Trois-Rivières, the civil commissioner Léger Félicité Sonthonax granted freedom and citizenship to those slaves who would fight for the Republic. As a representative in the colony for Republican France, Sonthonax was besieged not only by insurgent slaves but also by the English, the Spanish, and, perhaps most seriously, anti-Republican whites. His call to the slaves was a last-ditch effort to defeat the new royalist governor François-Thomas Galbaud, who on his arrival from France had rallied sailors and other whites in the town to take over the government from the commissioners. Although Sonthonax had previously garnered the support of the new citizens of the town, his defeat was imminent. Then, on June 21, the commissioners declared that slaves who volunteered to fight France's external and internal enemies would be granted liberty and citizenship. Several thousand insurgents who were camped outside Le Cap, under the command of a leader named Pierrot, responded immediately. Having taken an oath of allegiance to France in front of the commissioners, they attacked the capital and forced Galbaud and his royalist followers to retreat.[1]

During the fighting, much of Le Cap was burned to the ground—by the retreating and vindictive royalists, according to some accounts, and by the barbaric slaves, according to others. In the aftermath, Pierrot became the first black general of France's Republican army. One group of white refugees later wrote that they saw Sonthonax, in his house, "seize and pass in his arms the chief of the brigands, to call them his preserves, and to testify to them their gratitude." Thousands of refugees from Saint-Domingue sailed to other islands in the Caribbean. Many ended up in the United States, congregating in towns such as Charleston and Phila-

---

1. Carolyn E. Fick, *The Making of Haiti: The Saint Domingue Revolution from Below* (Knoxville, Tenn., 1990), 159.

delphia. Some in the United States blamed them—and more particularly their black slaves—for bringing yellow fever to Philadelphia, and the presence of slaves who had seen the insurrection in Saint-Domingue frightened whites, who feared a contagion of such ideals among their own enslaved population. In Richmond, Virginia, as rumors of imminent slave insurrection circulated in June 1793, one slave confronted another who was skeptical of plans to "kill the white people" by reminding him "how the blacks had kill'd the whites in the French island . . . a little while ago."[2]

The most enticing offer the commissioners had extended to the slaves in return for their service was not the plunder of the city—though plunder certainly might have been a motivation—but the promise of liberty and citizenship. Such a promise was more dangerous to the plantation society of Saint-Domingue than the razing of Le Cap: it would shatter the colony's foundation. In the months following the attack, the offer of freedom broadened and inexorably consolidated the strength of the Republic in Saint-Domingue. After June 21, Sonthonax left open his offer for freedom and citizenship to any enslaved who would fight for the Republic. Yet most insurgents did not respond, and the Republic was still threatened not only by remaining royalists but also by the Spanish and British armies, eagerly anticipating a conquest of the "pearl of the Antilles." On July 11, Sonthonax extended his offer to the wives and children of those who fought for the Republic. A multitude of slave insurgents then came to Sonthonax's aid, receiving in turn freedom for themselves and their families; in some areas, the slave populations of entire plantations were freed. Independently, a group of insurgents made a pact in which three of the leaders, Biassou, Jean-François, and Guyambois, would rule Saint-Domingue in a new order. Emancipation would be declared for all slaves and property distributed to them. Whites called to a local meeting supported the plan. A planter in the north told Sonthonax "what his own slaves had made clear to him: only universal freedom

2. Deposition of citizens from Le Cap, Charleston, S.C., Oct. 25, 1799, William L. Clements Library, University of Michigan, Ann Arbor. See AN, D XXV, 23, 231, for the correspondence of the insurgents recruited to the cause of the Republic, esp. nos. 66, 67, 69–76, written by Pierrot during late 1793. On the incident in Richmond, see James Sidbury, *Ploughshares into Swords: Race, Rebellion, and Identity in Gabriel's Virginia, 1730–1810* (Cambridge, 1998), 39–48; see also generally Julius Sherrard Scott III, "The Common Wind: Currents of Afro-American Communication in the Era of the Haitian Revolution" (Ph.D. diss., Duke University, 1987).

Prophecy, Revolt, & Emancipation, 1787–1794

could spare the whites from total annihilation." On August 24, fifteen thousand "souls" voted—unanimously, according to Jacques Garnier, a local official—for the emancipation of all the slaves in the northern province. Garnier recognized that the slaves "had become defenders of the land of liberty: we had to finally return their natural rights to them." Meanwhile, the increasingly powerful insurgent leader François Dominique Toussaint L'Ouverture also seems to have pushed for emancipation, perhaps spurring on the decisions of Republican commissioners.[3]

On August 29, Sonthonax declared slavery abolished in the northern province of Saint-Domingue. By the same pronouncement, he put into effect the Declaration of the Rights of Man and Citizen. Commissioner Étienne Polverel soon followed suit in the southern and western provinces. Within a few months, the edifice of slavery had crumbled in the Americas' most profitable slave colony, and the insurgents had saved Saint-Domingue for the Republic.[4]

The slave revolution of Saint-Domingue had created a military force to which the Republic turned in its moment of need. From the beginning, certain insurgents had deployed the language of rights in pursuit of liberty, and through their military strength they ultimately forced the Republican administration to make good on the promises embodied in this language. By acting as protectors of the French nation, they ultimately forced administrators to embrace their cause. What had taken place in microcosm in Trois-Rivières had played itself out on the broader stage of Saint-Domingue.

In the wake of the August 29 declaration, the Republican commissioners continued to struggle for insurgents' allegiance, confronting their suspicion and complicated loyalties. The insurgent leader Macaya, who had participated in the attack on Le Cap, had retreated to his camp soon afterward and responded to Polverel's entreaty: "I am the subject of

3. Fick, *Making of Haiti*, 161; for Garnier's quotes, see Florence Gauthier, "Le Rôle de la députation de Saint-Domingue dans l'abolition de l'esclavage," in Marcel Dorigny, ed., *Les Abolitions de l'esclavage de L. F. Sonthonax à V. Schoelcher, 1793, 1794, 1848* (Paris, 1995), 200–211, esp. 203. On L'Ouverture's complicated maneuvering during this period, see the detailed examination presented in David Patrick Geggus, *Haitian Revolutionary Studies* (Bloomington, Ind., 2002), chap. 8.

4. As Fick notes, "By a twist of historical irony, if the existence of the colony for the metropolis had previously depended upon the absolute maintenance of slavery, its salvation for revolutionary France now depended precisely upon freeing those very slaves and making them into French citizens" *(Making of Haiti*, 163).

three kings: of the King of Congo, master of all the blacks; of the King of France, who represents my father; of the King of Spain, who represents my mother. These three Kings are the descendants of those who, led by a star, came to adore God made Man." His words reflect a complex political ideology that drew on kingship and authority within the Kongo; the Christian imagery of the three Magi—already widely known in the Kongo because of Portuguese missionaries—powerfully suggests the transcultural nature of the political ideology among insurgents in Saint-Domingue. Today, *serviteurs* of the lwa of Haitian Vodou still celebrate the feast of the three kings with a ceremony devoted to spirits from the Kongo.[5]

Macaya was not the only one who refused allegiance to the Republic. Wary of French intentions toward a general emancipation on the island, L'Ouverture kept fighting them with Spanish support. Other insurgents, however, rallied to the Republic and argued that it was the truest defender of the slaves' liberty. In late August 1793 a rebel named Bramante Lazzary wrote to L'Ouverture, whom he referred to as "my brother," pleading with him to come to the French side. Lazzary told L'Ouverture that the fight against slavery was the cause of twenty-five million French co-citizens who "annihilated tyranny and persecution." "There are no more slaves in Saint-Domingue, all men of all colors are free and equal. . . . What have you received from the time of kings for centuries, for your work and your natural virtues? Shame and disdain. . . . You know as I do how much we suffered." Lazzary wrote a similar letter to other insurgent camps who were still fighting alongside the Spanish, incorporating the idea of the tricolor with the idea of the racially equal society in Saint-Domingue: "Our flag makes clear that our liberty depends on three colors: black, mulatto, and white; we are fighting for these three colors." Lazzary's adapted Republican flag had its analogue in a flag carried into the National Convention in May 1793 by a delegation of gens de couleur headed by the 114-year-old Jeanne Odo. A black man was superimposed on the blue, a mulâtre on the red, and a white man on the white, and all were armed with pikes topped with liberty caps. The motto on the flag was "Notre union fera notre force"—a precursor of the motto of indepen-

5. See John K. Thornton, "'I Am the Subject of the King of Kongo': African Political Ideology and the Haitian Revolution," *Journal of World History*, IV, no. 2 (Fall 1993), 181–214; Macaya's quote can be found in Pamphile de Lacroix, *Mémoires pour servir à l'histoire de la révolution de Saint-Domingue*, 2 vols. (Paris, 1819) (republ. in Paris, 1995, as Lacroix and Pierre Pluchon, *La Révolution de Haïti*), I, 25.

dent Haiti, "L'Union fait la force." The equality of all citizens, regardless of color, was meant to be the foundation for the radical transformation of the colonial society into a Republican society.[6]

Lazzary's evocation of the new order brought about by the French commissioners did not convince L'Ouverture at the time; throughout late 1793 and early 1794, however, black citizens buttressed the Republic's position for general emancipation through their continued military loyalty and resistance to pro-slavery forces. L'Ouverture's ultimate turn to the Republic was the result of complicated circumstances, not the least of which was a dampening of his relationship with the Spanish over their intentions to reestablish slavery in the occupied sections of Saint-Domingue. Although his reasons and choices remain largely undocumented, the most thorough examination of his volte-face concludes that he avoided full allegiance to the Republic until June 1794, when he received official word that the National Convention had ratified Sonthonax's local emancipation decree. L'Ouverture's cautious relationship toward Sonthonax and the Republic was transformed at that point; turning against the Spanish, he achieved a series of brilliant military victories for France that began his rise toward the leadership of the new, emancipated, but still colonial, Saint-Domingue.[7]

The ratification of Sonthonax's decree was rooted in the events in Saint-Domingue, but the radical political climate of France at the time also made it possible. Indeed, an assembly other than the National Convention of year II (1793–1794) might well have seen emancipation as impossible and unacceptable. But the word from Saint-Domingue arrived at the right time, carried by representatives who argued convincingly for the role of emancipation in the larger epic battle of Republican France against its enemies. On September 23, 1793, Sonthonax had presided over a unique election in the northern province of Saint-Domingue, and the result was a "tricolor" slate of three blancs, three

6. For Lazzary's letters, see AN, D XXV, 23, 231, letters 96, 98; see also Fick, *Making of Haiti*, 159. For the flag in Paris, see Gauthier, "Le Rôle de la députation," in Dorigny, ed., *Les Abolitions*, 200–211, esp. 200–201. The presentation of this flag was part of a larger campaign by gens de couleur in France. Under the leadership of Julien Raimond, a corps of soldiers called the *Légion des Américains* formed in August 1792; later, in May 1793, the *Société des citoyens de couleur de Paris* appeared in the National Convention, arguing for the abolition of slavery. Whether this society originated in Paris or Saint-Domingue is not clear.

7. Geggus, "From His Most Catholic Majesty," *Revue française d'histoire d'outre-mer*, XLV (1978), 481–499.

mulâtres, and three noirs to represent Saint-Domingue in the National Assembly. Three of those elected were alternates; five of the six delegates soon departed for France via Philadelphia. There, émigré colons harassed them, offended that Jean-Baptiste Belley, a noir who had been born in Gorée, West Africa, and enslaved as a child, was wearing the uniform of a deputy. From Philadelphia, only three of the delegates made it to France: Louis Dufay, a French-born official from Saint-Domingue, Jean-Baptiste Mills, a mulâtre, and Belley, who had been freed before 1789. Detained on their arrival in France, they were ultimately admitted to the National Convention on 15 Pluviôse, year II (February 15, 1794).[8]

The next day, Dufay gave a long speech describing how the royalists had nearly taken over Saint-Domingue, eulogizing the behavior of the slaves who saved the colony for the Republic. As he told it, in June 1793, slaves, indignant at Galbaud's impending victory over the Republican commissioners from France, gave their support to the mulattoes who were fighting the royalists. Later, insurgents from the countryside came to the town, armed, and presented themselves to the commissioners: "'We are negroes, and French. . . . We will fight for France, but in return we want our freedom.' They even added: our *Droits de l'Homme.*" Dufay argued that there was no other choice for the commissioners, that it was sound policy "to create new citizens for the Republic in order to oppose our enemies." Moved by his speech, one deputy followed it up by asking that the National Convention decree the immediate abolition of slavery throughout the Republic. Seconded by other representatives—who quickly argued that further discussion on the question would dishonor the Convention—the law was drawn up: "The National Convention declares that slavery is abolished throughout the territory of the Republic; in consequence, all men, without distinction of color, will enjoy the rights of French citizens." A short discussion ensued about whether the use of the term "slavery" would soil the law; but Abbé Grégoire insisted that, if slavery were not named, it would not disappear. The law was passed by the Convention to thousands of cries of "Vive la Répu-

8. Gauthier, "Le Rôle de la députation," in Dorigny, ed., *Les Abolitions*, 200–211, esp. 204. Gauthier claims that newly freed slaves participated in this election. This could have been the case, but there is no proof for this assertion in the declaration of the electoral assembly. There were, however, among the electors as well as among the candidates, a number of gens de couleur. See "Procès verbal de l'assemblée électorale des deputés du nord de St. Domingue," Sept. 23, 1793, in AN, C 181, 84.

FIGURE 14. "Allegorie de l'abolition de l'esclavage décrété par la Convention, le 16 Pluviôse, An II." 1794. The engraving emphasizes the unanimous support of the French people and the Supreme Being for the decree, though some shadowy figures in the left corner do not seem so pleased. Note the presence of the black soldier in the foreground, perhaps meant to stress the military importance of the decree, and the two women next to him—one black and one white—with their arms around each other. *Cliché Bibliothèque nationale de France, Paris*

blique!" Belley and Mills were hugged by other members of the Convention and gave witness of their deep gratitude, in the name of "all of their brothers of the colonies." A citoyenne de couleur who regularly attended the debates of the convention—perhaps Jeanne Odo—fainted out of joy on hearing the law pronounced; the deputies voted that this incident should be written into the register of the debates.[9]

That women were written into the history of emancipation as passive and overwhelmed recipients of the good news is not insignificant. Despite the important participation of women in the insurrection of 1791 and the events that had followed in Saint-Domingue, the 1794 decree focused on the passage from slavery to manhood. Indeed, Dufay had described the insurgent slaves as Republican husbands and soldiers and argued that their wives deserved liberty despite the fact that the "weakness of their sex" made it impossible for them to take up arms for France. In a sense, Dufay's speech represented an older strain of thought in gens de couleur activism that had been important since the 1780s, wherein military service proved a virtuous masculinity and therefore merited political equality. The figure of the male slave-turned-soldier was crucial to the shaping of emancipation in the French Caribbean, where military service would be the realm in which freedom was most accessible to ex-slaves. In a context where the soldier became the central symbol of Republican citizenship—and where those who were not soldiers were meant to serve as cultivateurs—the possibilities for women's experiencing freedom were profoundly limited.[10]

9. J. Mavidal and E. Laurent, eds., *Archives parlementaires de 1787 à 1860, première série (1787-1799)*, LXXXIV (Paris, 1962), 276-285. The elaboration of the Declaration of the Rights of Man and Citizen and of the constitution passed by the National Convention on June 24, 1793, in which Article 18 specified that no person could be bought or sold or buy or sell himself, to some extent had paved the way for the abolition of slavery. Nevertheless, this in and of itself would clearly have not brought on abolition without the events in Saint-Domingue and the intervention of the delegates sent to France. See Gauthier, "Le Rôle de la députation," in Dorigny, ed., *Les Abolitions*, 200-211, esp. 203. A few weeks later, the National Convention, following the suggestion of the deputies from Saint-Domingue, ordered the arrest of several important planters in Paris and the seizure of their papers; see Gauthier, "La Convention thermidorienne et le problème coloniale, septembre 1794-septembre 1795," in Michel Vovelle, ed., *Le Tournant de l'An III: Réaction et terreur blanche dans la France révolutionnaire* (Paris, 1997), 109-119, esp. 110.

10. See Elizabeth Colwill, "Sex, Savagery, and Slavery in the Shaping of the French Body Politic," in Sara E. Melzer and Kathryn Norberg, eds., *From the*

Nevertheless, the 1794 decree heralded a dramatic transformation, and thousands of Parisians gathered in the Temple of Reason—the once and future Cathedral of Notre Dame—to hear speeches and sing songs greeting the arrival of a new era of liberation. Representatives from the Convention, including the three *montagnards américains* representing Saint-Domingue, presided over the celebration. Other festivities followed throughout France: in Bordeaux, the capital of the eighteenth-century slave trade, two hundred hommes de couleur celebrated abolition; in Le Havre, another port that profited from the slave trade, a woman representing the "Goddess of Liberty" embraced the hommes de couleur to the acclamation of the crowd. Nearby, in the town of Barnay, hommes de couleur arrived bound as part of the parade, and the Goddess of Liberty smashed their chains. The "freed slaves" "expressed their gratefulness with expressive movements and their kind of dances." "One spoke and painted a touching picture of what they had endured . . . another sang couplets inspired by the joy that such a rapid and unexpected change gave him." The whites in the crowd then rushed forth and hugged their "new brothers." Far from Paris and the coast, in Bourg-sur-Rhône, whites dressed up as blacks were placed in chains on an island in the Rhône (representing the sugar islands) and then liberated by the people of the town. In many smaller, rural towns, a huge portion of the population attended such celebrations, suggesting the symbolic importance of these events to the Republican fight against the "slavery" of political oppression and tyranny even in areas distant from Paris and the slave ports. In the following years, several plays in Paris lauded abolition, notably one in which a French slave trader, upon receiving news of the French decree of emancipation, freed his cargo.[11]

Royal to the Republican Body: Incorporating the Political in Seventeenth- and Eighteenth-Century France (Berkeley, Calif., 1998), 198–223, esp. 210–215; see also Joan Wallach Scott, *Only Paradoxes to Offer: French Feminists and the Rights of Man* (Cambridge, Mass., 1996). On the gens de couleur tradition, see John Garrigus, "Redrawing the Colour Line: Gender and the Social Construction of Race in Pre-revolutionary Haiti," *Journal of Caribbean History*, XXX, nos. 1, 2 (1996), 28–50, esp. 41–42.

11. Jean-Claude Helpern, "Les Fêtes révolutionnaires et l'abolition de l'esclavage en l'An II," in Dorigny, ed., *Les Abolitions*, 187–198; on the plays, see Edward Derbyshire Seeber, *Anti-slavery Opinion in France during the Second Half of the Eighteenth Century* (Baltimore, 1937), 183. The representatives from Saint-Domingue were called "montagnards américains" because they had joined Robes-

MOI LIBRE

A Paris, chez Basset, M.ᵈ d'Estampes, rue Jacques, au coin de celle des Mathurins.

FIGURE 15. "Moi libre" (above), "En liberté comme toi" (right). 1794. These illustrations were part of a series produced in the wake of emancipation: a black man or woman is presented as a citizen, bearing a caption ("I am free"; "I am equal to you") in what is supposed to be Creolized French. "En liberté comme toi" engraved by François Bonneville. *Cliché Bibliothèque nationale de France, Paris*

F. Bonneville del et Sculp.

En Liberté comme toi
La République fran.ᵉ d'accord avec la Nature
l'ont voulu: ne suis-je pas ta Sœur?

At the Temple of Reason celebration, Pierre-Gaspard Chaumette attacked the brutality of the slave trade and hailed the new dawn emancipation had brought, but he ended his speech with a plea for moderation in the application of freedom. In the Convention, too, the enthusiasm of the decision had been followed by caution. Dufay had noted that the ex-slaves needed enlightened guides to help them move from slavery to freedom. And, although some representatives had asked that the law immediately be dispatched to the colonies, Georges-Jacques Danton recommended that the matter be forwarded to the *Comité de salut public* and the *Comité des colonies* "to bring together the means to make this law useful for humanity without endangering it." Continuing with his famous claim, "Today is the death of the English," Danton warned that, although the law's defeat of all tyrants would help make France great again, the Republic's generosity should not "exceed the boundaries of wisdom." The Convention sent the matter on to the Comité de salut public, which elaborated only slightly on the decisions already taken, noting that the English would not be able to protect themselves from the effects of French abolition and that the "inevitable revolution" would spread through the Antilles.[12]

Before abolition was decreed, the comité had drawn up detailed instructions for the commissioners they were then preparing to send to the colonies. They did not alter these instructions or add to them any concrete suggestions about how to administer emancipation, leaving it up to the "wise firmness and revolutionary declarations" of the commissioners they had chosen. So the new administration of freedom ultimately took shape in the Antilles, at the hands of Republican representatives who often operated in isolation. In Saint-Domingue Sonthonax and Polverel, who in 1793 and 1794 found themselves in charge of a war-ravaged country inhabited suddenly by hundreds of thousands of freed slaves, took

pierre and his radical followers, who occupied high seats called the "mountain" in the Convention.

12. Mavidal and Laurent, eds., *Archives parlementaires*, LXXXIV, 276–285; Colwill, "Sex, Savagery, and Slavery," in Melzer and Norberg, eds., *From the Royal to the Republican Body*, 198–233, esp. 213. The speech given in the Temple of Reason by Chaumette is reprinted in *La Révolution française et l'abolition de l'esclavage* (Paris, 1968), V. For Danton's cautions, see Mavidal and Laurent, eds., *Archives parlementaires*, LXXXIV, 284; "Extrait des régistres du Comité de salut public de la Convention nationale," 25 Pluviôse, An II (Feb. 13, 1794), in CAOM, C 7A, 47, 126. The comité's earlier instructions are discussed in Chapter 7, below.

Prophecy, Revolt, & Emancipation, 1787–1794

foundational steps in setting up the new regime of freedom. Following their lead, Republican administrators carried out a unique experiment in freedom that transformed the Caribbean. The legal order established in Saint-Domingue by Sonthonax and Polverel, followed by L'Ouverture, and then in Guadeloupe by Victor Hugues (whose regime is the focus of Part II), combined liberation with new forms of coercion. The slaves were freed but forced to keep working. Administrators instituted certain kinds of democracy on plantations, but the new citizens remained under severe restrictions even though they now composed the majority of the colonial population. New forms of racial exclusion became interwoven with the language of rights, forming a Republican racism that initiated a long French engagement with the problem of organizing colonial relationships within a universalist framework. The struggle for emancipation was, ultimately, only the first step in a broader struggle for freedom and full citizenship.

The enslaved of the French Caribbean had gained their freedom because they had acted, uninvited, as citizens. This is a point Sonthonax repeatedly made in Paris, where he had been recalled to face charges that he had destroyed Saint-Domingue through his actions. Sonthonax went so far as to suggest that it was the ex-slaves who were the only true patriots in the Antilles:

> Nothing can prevent me from granting justice to the people of Saint-Domingue, or from shouting from the rooftops that, if France abandoned the colony to itself, without weapons or ammunition, the last place where the flag of the Republic would fly would be that defended by an army of blacks. The blacks are the true sans-culottes of the colonies, they are the people, and only they are capable of defending the country.[13]

From being enslaved to being the only citizens truly capable of defending the Republic, the insurgents of the French Antilles had taken an impressive journey. Through their actions, they broadened the idea of citizenship as they applied it to their own world. This radicalization of the Declaration of the Rights of Man and Citizen, a major moment in

13. "Sonthonax, ci-devant commissaire civil, délegué de St. Domingue, à la Convention nationale," 2 Fructidor, An II (Aug. 19, 1794), in AN, AD VII, 20 A. Ironically, the order that recalled Sonthonax to Paris arrived on the same ship that brought the news of emancipation to the colony.

the development of modern political culture, depended on the concerted action of slaves within the Antilles. In the midst of a volatile social climate, these insurgents reconfigured the meaning of Republican citizenship by giving new content to the language of rights, and in so doing they transformed the compass of universalism itself.

Part Two

THE
MEANING OF
CITIZENSHIP,
1794-1798

MAKING SLAVES CITIZENS

What Is the Citizen?

Are we born into citizenship? Can we be naturalized into it? Does citizenship reside in our blood, or must it be learned? Is it a territorial concept, based on borders? Is it a political concept, based on an abstract "cité"—an "imagined community"? Is it beautiful?[1]

The French Revolution played a crucial part in shaping the ideas and practices surrounding national citizenship. As the political theorist Étienne Balibar has suggested, the key document of the Revolution, the 1789 Declaration of the Rights of Man and Citizen, brought about the "constitution of citizenship—in a radically new sense." The power of the Declaration, and therefore of citizenship itself, is that it is a "hyperbolic proposition": *"The wording of the statement always exceeds the act of its enunciation."* Citizenship represents "the opening of a possibility" through which any configuration of political representation can be challenged and even destroyed "by a struggle for equality and thus for civil rights." So, although revolutionaries at first described the ancien régime as a state of "slavery" even as they accepted true slavery in the colonies, "the insurrection for the immediate abolition" of it quickly took place "in the name of the equality of rights."[2]

1. Benedict R. O'G. Anderson, *Imagined Communities: Reflections on the Origin and Spread of Nationalism* (London, 1983).

2. See Rogers Brubaker, *Citizenship and Nationhood in France and Germany* (Cambridge, Mass., 1992), 35; Étienne Balibar, "Citizen Subject," in Eduardo Cadava, Peter Connor, and Jean-Luc Nancy, eds., *Who Comes after the Subject?* (London, 1991), 33–57, esp. 44, 52–53. For a discussion of the development of the 1789 Declaration and of its antecedents on both sides of the Atlantic, see Keith Michael Baker, "The Idea of a Declaration of Rights," in Dale Van Kley, ed., *The French Idea of Freedom: The Old Regime and the Declaration of Rights of 1789* (Stanford, Calif., 1994), 154–198, as well as Van Kley, "Introduction," 5–20. See

In the first part of this study, slaves and gens de couleur took advantage of the language of rights to infuse new and unforeseen content into the idea of citizenship, expanding the imagination of Republican political culture. The slave emancipation in Saint-Domingue in 1793, ratified and applied to all the French colonies in 1794, established a new juridical order in the French colonies. The people and territory of these colonies were to be integrated equally into a nation with no distinctions between colonial and metropolitan law; France and its colonies had become one, legally consistent, a nation-state. Once this radical experiment was reversed in the early nineteenth century, it would not be repeated to the same extreme until the departmentalization of French colonies in 1946. Because of the extent of these transformations, and because of the lasting impact of their reversal, the 1790s left a deep mark on the French Empire. The second part of this study examines how emancipation transformed the French Caribbean after 1794 and how the administration of freedom brought with it both liberation and forms of Republican racism that excluded former slaves from full citizenship.

The transformation of citizenship by slave insurgents brought major challenges for Republican administrators. After slavery, what should freedom mean? What kinds of citizens would the ex-slaves be, and what would be the terms of their political participation? What would be their rights as citizens? What rights would the state have over them as citizens? The transformation of slaves into citizens in the Caribbean sharply illuminates the complex responses that emerged to what Balibar identifies as the central problem of Republican governance: "Which citizens are 'representable,' and under which conditions? Above all: Who should the citizens be in order to be able to represent themselves and be represented?" In metropolitan France as in the Caribbean, the early years of the French Revolution were marked by conflicts over the question of who should be able to exercise fully their political rights. The idea that only the wealthy could be capable and disinterested political actors motivated many of those who supported the creation of a distinction between "active" and "passive" citizens. The former could participate in politics by voting and being elected; the latter, including women, children, servants, and men unable to pay a standard poll tax, were protected by the laws of the Republic but deemed incapable of voting or being representatives. Though the particular terms of exclusion and in-

also Shanti Marie Singham, "Betwixt Cattle and Men: Jews, Blacks, and Women and the Declaration of the Rights of Man," 114–153.

clusion shifted radically during 1793 and 1794, the virtue of citizens continued to be a central concern, with the difference that, whereas previously wealth had been the basis for responsible political action, it became something that potentially divided a person from the nation. When the distinction between active and passive citizenship was destroyed, allowing (in principle) high political participation, accusations of treason and antirepublicanism increasingly became the basis for severing the accused citizen from the political body. Though foreigners had originally been the beneficiaries of a hospitality inspired by universalist Republican ideals, they soon became subject to policies of identification and exclusion. Indeed, by the late 1790s, some writers were attacking slave emancipation in the Caribbean by suggesting that it was dangerous to assimilate foreigners—that is, those of African descent, and in particular those who were African-born—into the French Republic.[3]

During the French Revolution, the Republicans distinguished between the universal and natural rights of man and the capacities necessary for the representation of those rights through citizenship. This distinction upset the equation between "people" and "citizens," between those who had natural rights and those who could protect and legislate those rights, between those subject to the "general will" and those fit to express it. The creation of differences between citizens depended upon "an anthropology of the subject" that defined the criteria for such distinctions and in so doing justified the paradox of a citizenship at once universal and exclusionary. Universalist citizenship therefore presented a double contract, founded on a set of universal claims that were inexorably entwined with the existence of qualifications that limited these claims' application.[4]

One of the key contributors to the debate about the meaning of rep-

---

3. Balibar, "Citizen Subject," in Cadava, Connor, and Nancy, eds., *Who Comes after the Subject?* 47; Olivier Le Cour Grandmaison, *Les Citoyennetés en révolution, 1789-1794* (Paris, 1992); Pierre Rosanvallon, *Le Sacre du citoyen: Histoire du suffrage universel en France* (Paris, 1972); Sophie Wanich, *L'Impossible citoyen: L'Etranger dans le discours de la Révolution française* (Paris, 1996).

4. Balibar, "Citizen Subject," in Cadava, Connor, and Nancy, eds., *Who Comes after the Subject?* 47–49. In his examination of the contradictions within the writings of Locke and Mill, Uday Mehta has similarly noted that it is through a disjuncture between the description of "anthropological capacities" natural to all humans and "the necessary conditions for their political actualization" that exclusionary rhetoric manifests itself; see Mehta, "Liberal Strategies of Exclusion," *Politics and Society*, XVIII (1990), 427–454.

resentation and citizenship was the Abbé Sieyès. In his influential 1789 pamphlet, *What Is the Third Estate?* Sieyès asked, "Where do we find the nation?" He responded, "Where it is; in the forty thousand parishes that embrace all the territory, all the inhabitants, and all that pertains to the public good." His pamphlet invoked labor as the foundation for political belonging and excluded the "parasitic" nobility from the citizenry, thereby preparing the ground for the Third Estate to assert their legitimacy as representatives of the nation. The people were the heart of the nation, and only political equality could create a legitimate and representative government. Sieyès accepted the existence of social inequality among the citizens of the nation, but he insisted that fundamental political equality should override differences in status and in wealth. His pamphlet presented a powerful argument in favor of universal citizenship. Nevertheless, Sieyès also argued that certain people should be excluded from political participation: "It is unquestionable that vagabonds and beggars cannot be charged with the political confidence of nations. Would a servant, or any person under the domination of a master, or a nonnaturalized foreigner, be permitted to serve as a representative of the nation? Political liberty, thus, has its limits, just as civil liberty has." And he contradicted his idea that productive workers were the only true members of the nation by suggesting that the best representatives for the Third Estate were those with "some sort of affluence," who had the economic independence, education, and leisure to develop the abilities necessary for political participation. Sieyès's pamphlet, like the revolution it helped set in motion, pushed for political equality and universal citizenship even as it created new hierarchies and exclusions.[5]

In a series of private notes written in parallel with his published works, Sieyès went further in his discussion of the question of who was fit to practice citizenship. He argued that there were "two nations" within France: one made up of the wealthy classes, who had the education and ability to shape the government, and the other made up of the laboring classes, who would have the legal rights of citizens but were to play a passive role in the political sphere. Here Sieyès was sketching out the distinction between active and passive citizens, which he presented in detail in *Reasoned Exposition of the Rights of Man and Citizen*, a July

5. Emmanuel Joseph Sieyès, *What Is the Third Estate?* ed. S. E. Finer (New York, 1963), 74–75, 78; William H. Sewell, Jr., *A Rhetoric of Bourgeois Revolution* (Durham, N.C., 1994), 145–152.

1789 pamphlet that was essential in establishing these as legal categories. His argument was that laborers, although they did the work that was the foundation for the nation's existence, were also degraded by the difficult life they led. The weight of labor itself made it hard for them to develop the capacities necessary for shaping the nation's policies. In his private notes, Sieyès did express some uneasiness about a distinction that excluded those who were, according to the criteria he himself had put forth in *What Is the Third Estate?* the soul of the nation. In confronting this contradiction, he was driven to propose a surreal racial solution. Through the interbreeding of "negroes" and different "species of monkeys," he envisaged new species of laborers, "a strong race (six to eight feet tall) for hard labor . . . a middle-sized race (three to four feet tall) for domestic details . . . a small race (from twelve to fifteen inches) for petty services and amusement." These new laborers would be trained and commanded by "negroes," and the "heads of production" would be the whites. "However extraordinary, however immoral this idea may be at first glance," he wrote, "I have meditated on it for a long time, and you will find no other means, in a large nation especially in very warm and very cold countries, to reconcile the directors of work with the simple instruments of labor." The creation of a series of new races would make it possible for all citizens to be active citizens while their engineered servants took care of the nation's production. The existence of slaves would make possible the proper functioning of egalitarian political culture.[6]

Sieyès did not explicitly write about France's Caribbean colonies in either his published or unpublished works. Yet the bizarre utopian solution to the political problem that preoccupied him in fact reflected the actual relationship between the French metropole and its colonies. Two nations did exist, one central and the other marginal, the latter a place where society was indeed organized along a labor-based racial hierarchy. The legal structures of the two nations differed profoundly, and this difference was justified by the colonies' providing an economic base for the metropole—exactly mirroring Sieyès's argument that slave races could provide the foundation for governance by the elite classes. What Sieyès imagined was rooted in the reality of his time: he defended and justified his ideas in terms that clearly echoed the defenses put forth by pro-

6. Sieyès, *Ecrits politiques*, ed. Roberto Zapperi (Paris, 1985), 75, esp. "Notes et fragments inédits"; I draw on the interpretation and English translation in Sewell, *Rhetoric of Bourgeois Revolution*, 152–154, 176–177.

slavery advocates, adding the twist of creating a series of new races but basing his argument on a mindset that was not new at all.[7]

Sieyès was never directly involved in the administration of the colonies, nor was he an active participant in the revolutionary debates about slavery and emancipation. But the private writings of this central theorist of Republican citizenship provide an important illustration of how a discourse founded on political equality could accommodate the existence of laborers who were to serve as auxiliaries to the true citizens. In the Caribbean, the administrators who oversaw emancipation would use similar arguments in limiting the political participation of those who had formerly been enslaved. Without the benefit of genetic engineering, these administrators—notably Victor Hugues—sought to achieve feats of social engineering by transforming slaves into free citizens who were nevertheless loyal and submissive plantation laborers. Demands to preserve a profitable economic system drove Hugues to do everything possible to maintain the production of sugar and other essential commodities in the wake of emancipation. In order to accomplish this, he found ways to force ex-slaves to keep working on plantations. Because of the terms of emancipation, however, Hugues had to justify the limitations he placed on the freedom he granted in the language of Republican rights. And so, like Sieyès, he created a system based on the principle of political equality that nevertheless enabled the exclusion of those who worked productively for the good of the nation. He justified his regime of labor coercion by invoking the economic needs of the Republic and the responsibilities owed to it by the men and women whom it had transformed from objects to citizens. The ex-slaves, like Sieyès's laborers, were asked to take a passive role in the political life of the nation. And, like Sieyès's engineered "races," they were given the responsibility of working for the nation while others governed it.

In the decade before the Revolution, French abolitionists had critiqued slavery and reflected on the question of how plantation production could be maintained without it. Like the abolitionists who followed them in the early nineteenth century, they confronted a tension within the emerging liberal political and economic theory of the day—the same tension that had driven Sieyès to his fantasy of producing new races. They argued against slavery on the basis of the idea that society would be better served

7. See Sewell's different interpretation in *Rhetoric of Bourgeois Revolution*, 156–157.

if all individuals were free and equal before the law. In place of a world where state-sanctioned violence maintained a population in forced servitude, they imagined a society that would flourish as all members pursued their own economic interests. But, despite their faith in the principles of liberal economic theory, many were concerned about the dislocations and disruptions that would come with emancipation. What if the former slaves, used to coercion and violence, refused to work once they were free? What if they used their freedom for revenge and idleness rather than became productive workers and citizens? Like abolitionists elsewhere in the Atlantic world at the time, French abolitionists concluded that a gradual transition from slavery to freedom was necessary in order to avoid violent disruptions in the colonial economic system. A carefully calibrated process would be necessary to inculcate the former slaves with the habits and reasoning that were a prerequisite for participating in a liberal economic and political system. Liberty was to be granted, but also limited, as those debased by slavery were transformed into individuals fit for society.[8]

One of the central figures in French abolitionism was the marquis de Condorcet, who, in 1781, published *Réflexions sur l'esclavage des negroes* under the pseudonym M. Schwartz. In 1788, the newly founded Société des amis des noirs issued a revised version of the work. Condorcet's writing influenced the abolitionist thinking of the Revolution and the Republicans' vision of slave emancipation. His opening "Epître dédicatoire aux nègres esclaves" lamented that the slaves, whom he had always considered his brothers and his equals, would never read the work. Just as Sonthonax would do over a decade later, Condorcet asserted the superiority of the slaves to the violent and decadent colons: "If you were to search for a man in the American islands, you would not find him among the whites." Like Montesquieu before him, Condorcet systematically and satirically undermined pro-slavery arguments. "The reasoning of the politicians who believe that the slavery of the nègres is neces-

8. My thinking here, and my approach to Hugues's regime in general, has been shaped by Thomas C. Holt, *The Problem of Freedom: Race, Labor, and Politics in Jamaica and Britain, 1832–1938* (Baltimore, 1992). The classic work on abolitionism and liberal economic ideology is David Brion Davis, *The Problem of Slavery in the Age of Revolution, 1770–1823* (Ithaca, N.Y., 1975); on antislavery in the British Caribbean, see also Gordon K. Lewis, *Main Currents in Caribbean Thought: The Historical Evolution of Caribbean Society in Its Ideological Aspects, 1492–1900* (Baltimore, 1983), chap. 4.

sary reduces itself to this: *Whites are miserly, drunken, and sordid, so the blacks must be enslaved.*"⁹

Condorcet's work emerged from a broader analysis of and attack on slavery made by the Physiocrats, who developed their thoughts in dialogue with parallel currents in North America and had a broad impact on French intellectual life during the 1760s and 1770s. In a 1756 work entitled *L'Ami des hommes; ou, Traité de la population*, the marquis de Mirabeau (father of the comte de Mirabeau) anticipated many of the critiques of slavery that would become standard among Physiocrats, arguing that slavery undermined the creation of a productive population of laborers. In the *Ephémerides du citoyen* which in 1767 became the Physiocrats' official organ, this argument was developed more fully by authors such as Pierre-Samuel Dupont de Nemours and Anne-Robert-Jacques Turgot. Slavery, the Physiocrats argued (drawing in part on the ideas of Benjamin Franklin), was fundamentally inefficient because slaves had no incentive to work for their masters, and coercion and violence became the only means to assure continued labor. Some Physiocrats suggested that, rather than enslave Africans and bring them to the Caribbean to grow certain crops, with all the violence and waste this entailed, the French should find ways to cultivate these crops in Africa itself. The Abbé Nicholas Bauleau, founder of the *Ephémerides du citoyen*, wrote in the journal in 1766 that the best way to settle the colony of Louisiana would be to purchase slaves in Africa (as well as Asia), "not in order to keep them in their chains and crush them with forced labor," but rather to "transform them into free men, industrious cultivateurs, true citizens of Louisiana." He envisioned multicultural villages, created by placing European families alongside Africans and native Americans, spreading across a thriving colony.¹⁰

Condorcet's arguments about slavery were part of his broader theorization on creating citizens fit for a new republic. Other thinkers had previously suggested that slave vices were the result of slavery rather than innate nature, but for Condorcet that theory pointed to his more general vision of the way oppressive institutions created vices that only politi-

9. Marie Jean Antoine Nicolas Caritat, marquis de Condorcet, *Réflexions sur l'esclavage des negroes. Par M. Schwartz . . . [pseud.]* ([1781]; Paris, 1788), esp. i, 17.

10. "Des colonies françoises aux Indes occidentales," *Ephémerides du citoyen*, V (1766), 65–80, esp. 68, 75; Edward Derbyshire Seeber, *Antislavery Opinion in France during the Second Half of the Eighteenth Century* (Baltimore, 1937), 99, 114–115.

cal equality could undo. His arguments about the human equality of the enslaved were very similar to those arguments he presented regarding the rights of women in a July 1790 speech, wherein he suggested that the very reasons for excluding women from the enjoyment of rights in fact resulted from their exclusion: any perceived inferiority on the part of women would disappear once they were given equality.[11]

Olympe de Gouges, who argued famously in a riposte to the Declaration of the Rights of Man (entitled *The Declaration of the Rights of Women and Citizenesses*) that women had a natural right to citizenship and political equality, also argued in favor of the rights of the people of African descent. Her declaration ended with an endorsement of free-colored rights. And in 1789 her antislavery play had a brief run at Paris's leading theatre, the Comedie Française, under the title *L'Esclavage des noirs; ou, L'Heureux naufrage (The Slavery of the Blacks; or, The Happy Shipwreck)*. The play celebrated the resistance of the enslaved as well as solidarity across racial lines. The heroine of the play, Mizra, refuses the advances of her master's white employee, who takes revenge by ordering her lover Zamore, also a slave, to execute her. Rather than follow the order, Zamore kills Mizra's persecutor, and the two escape to a desert island, where they come to the aid of a French couple whose ship has sunk nearby. The grateful French couple becomes friends with the enslaved fugitives and ultimately—along with rebellious slaves—manage to win both forgiveness and liberty for Mizra and Zamore. Throughout the play, various characters attack the inhumanity of slavery. Mizra wonders why there is such a "difference" between Europeans and themselves when they are all human beings; Zamore asks God to give the enslaved back their lost rights; the shipwrecked Frenchman announces to the slaves that the French people abhor slavery, and that when they are free themselves they will work to improve the slaves' lot. Indeed, the play represents the metropolitan French as unambiguously humane toward the enslaved and therefore at odds with the cruel local slave-owners. Still, de Gouges, who had uncompromisingly demanded immediate rights for women, was less radical in her vision of how slavery should be ended. In the last lines of the play, the enslaved are told by the colonial governor that, if, as he hopes, they are freed one day, they should avoid "reprehensible excesses" and await "everything" from an

---

11. Condorcet, "On the Admission of Women to the Rights of Citizenship," in Baker, ed., *Condorcet: Selected Writings* (Indianapolis, 1976), 97–104; see also Baker, *Condorcet: From Natural Philosophy to Social Mathematics* (Chicago, 1975).

"enlightened and benevolent Government." And Zamore repeatedly emphasizes his loyalty to his master and his willingness to continue serving him even after he has been freed. Despite her sympathetic portrayal of black revolt, de Gouges imagined a slow and peaceful transition from slavery to freedom carried out by generous and enlightened white governors. Indeed, in her 1791 preface to the published version of the play, she attacked the insurgents of Saint-Domingue for their violence against whites.[12]

The question of how, precisely, slaves were to be transformed into free individuals was a preoccupation of many abolitionists. Among the multiple tracts that attacked slavery during the eighteenth century, Condorcet's work stood out for its sustained discussion of the means through which slavery could be abolished without causing a "revolution" in the colonies. He proposed the gradual abolition of slavery and incremental integration of slaves into political and economic freedom. This, he argued, could be achieved by a policy that would force masters to emancipate all slaves born after a certain date once they reached thirty-five. These slaves, starting at eighteen, would be granted a modicum of legal subjecthood: they could file complaints against their masters for ill-treatment, and judges could transfer an abused slave to a hostel run by the state. Condorcet claimed that, if his plan were followed, slavery would be abolished in sixty-six years, and most slaves would be freed within thirty or forty; meanwhile, the colonial economy would continue functioning as before, since the ex-slaves would be gradually incorporated as free workers without a sudden shock to the social system.[13]

Blaming the barbarity of slavery for degrading blacks and depriving them of their reason, Condorcet argued for withholding their rights for a time. He justified his scheme:

12. Olympe de Gouges, *L'Esclavage des noirs; ou, L'Heureux naufrage* ([1792]; Paris, 1989), 32–33, 44, 46, 56, 133–134; see also the introduction by Eléni Varikas. An English version of the play and its preface, translated by Maryann DeJulio and Sylvie Molta, along with a translation of the relevant portion of *The Declaration of the Rights of Women*, trans. Maryann DeJulio, are presented in Doris Y. Kadish and Françoise Massardier-Kenney, eds., *Translating Slavery: Gender and Race in French Women's Writing, 1783–1823* (Kent, Ohio, 1994), 84–120; on de Gouges's moderation, see Doris Kadish, "Translation in Context," Marie Pierre Le Hir, "Feminism, Theatre, Race: L'Esclavage des noirs," in Kadish and Massardier-Kenney, eds., *Translating Slavery*, 26–64, esp. 35–42, and 65–83, esp. 76–77.

13. Condorcet, *Réflexions sur l'esclavage*, 32; for the description of the plan for emancipation, see 33–45.

If, because of their lack of education and the stupidity contracted through slavery by the corruption of their morals (the necessary result of their masters' influence), the slaves of the European colonies have become incapable of fulfilling the duties of free men, we can (at least until the experience of liberty has returned to them what slavery has taken away) treat them as men who have been deprived by misery or sickness of a portion of their faculties. We cannot, therefore, grant them the full exercise of their rights without exposing them to the risk of hurting others or harming themselves.

Though the natural rights unjustly taken from the slaves had to be returned to them, it would be "incompatible with justice" to grant "to all nègres at once the enjoyment of their rights," in particular their political rights. What the legislator owed the slaves, argued Condorcet, was "less their rights than the assurance of their well-being." The true challenge of emancipation would be confronting the economic problem created when men who owned nothing were suddenly granted freedom. For slaves (as for serfs), Condorcet suggested, freedom accompanied by a larger set of rights would lead to disaster, since there would be no way to maintain the preexisting economic order.

In granting them their liberty too suddenly, we would reduce them to misery. If a man owes the fulfillment of his material needs to the loss of his political rights and if, in giving him his rights, we expose him to a lack of what he needs, then the humane legislator must reconcile his security with his rights. In such circumstances, it is not a violation of men's rights or a protection of those who have violated them to show restraint in the granting of rights. It is simply a way of making sure that the destruction of the abuses takes place in such a way as to assure that freedom will more certainly be the foundation for happiness.

The legislator also had a responsibility to protect the larger society from the violence and chaos that could be unleashed by those who were emerging from slavery: "The right to be protected by the police against violence is one of the rights that man acquires in entering society; therefore, the legislator has a duty to exclude men who are strangers to society and who could disturb it. . . . Before placing the slaves in the ranks of free men, the law must assure itself that in this new quality they will not trouble the security of the citizens."[14]

14. See "De l'injustice de l'esclavage des nègres, considérée par rapport au législateur," chap. 5 in Condorcet, *Réflexions sur l'esclavage*, 11–16.

Condorcet noted, as other abolitionists would after him, that the elimination of slavery must also change the moral identities of the masters themselves. Yet his plan ultimately focused on the need to reform the slaves. Condorcet envisioned a shift in plantation economy, a diversification of industry that would include separating cane cultivation from cane processing—an innovation never attempted by Republican officials and rarely reiterated by later abolitionists. However, Condorcet's ideas about the need for gradual emancipation would become part of the platform of the Société des amis des noirs as well as in other texts of the period, such as the later editions of the Abbé Raynal's *Histoire des deux Indes*. Indeed, a 1786 edition of Raynal's influential work repeated Condorcet's arguments:

> We should not, according to the opinion of one enlightened man, shatter the chains of the unfortunates who are born into slavery and have grown old in it. These stupid men, who will not have been prepared for this change of status, will be incapable of conducting themselves well. Their life would be nothing more than a habitual laziness or a tissue of crime. The great boon of liberty should be reserved for their posterity, and with certain modifications.[15]

Condorcet's vision of the history of enslavement undermined the common argument that slavery civilized the slaves. Yet it shared with pro-slavery advocates a determination that the enslaved and Africans in general needed to be uplifted and taught to live in a society governed by laws. Condorcet read the history of slavery as separating slaves from social existence and thus from social rights. They had never learned the meaning of those rights and could not exercise them; their moral condition, formed by violence and abuse, would carry that debasement into society. Thus Condorcet's work gives us insight into what can be termed Republican racism: an abolitionist version of the history of slavery became a vehicle for justifying continued racial exclusion.

As it happened, abolitionist projects did not dictate the terms of emancipation. The decree of 1794, propelled by slave revolution, provided for no period of transition from slavery to freedom, granting all slaves im-

15. The passage went on to propose a plan of gradual emancipation similar to Condorcet's, with an additional element: "We will give to the new citizens a cabin, with enough land to create a small garden . . . and no regulation will prevent these men, now free, from expanding the property they received." See Abbé Guillaume-Thomas-François Raynal, *Histoire philosophique et politique des établissements et du commerce des Européens dans les deux Indes* (Avignon, 1786), book VI, chap. 24.

mediate and unconditional liberty. The abolitionism of the enslaved in the Caribbean had outrun that of reformers in Paris. The administrators sent to colonies were given a difficult task: to apply universal emancipation while containing its economic, social, and political effects. In a context defined by a radical and uncompromising Republican project, they were to maintain economic continuity even as they instituted political and social discontinuity, to maintain the forms of labor and modes of production of plantation slavery while governing according to the egalitarianism of Republican citizenship. As they struggled to confront this challenge, they drew on the abolitionist theories that had preceded emancipation. As Condorcet had done before them, they insisted on equality and liberty but also argued that the ex-slaves were incapable of fulfilling the responsibilities that came with freedom. Faced with a sudden de facto emancipation, the administrators strove to apply the principles of gradual emancipation to the Antillean societies over which they took control. Condorcet's suggestions presaged Hugues's approach:

> As it is to be feared that the nègres, accustomed to obeying only force and whim, will not in the beginning be contained by the same laws as the whites—that they will form mobs and give themselves over to theft, to individual vengeance, and to a vagabond life in the forests and the mountains; that disorders will be fomented by the blancs, who will try to use them as a pretext to reestablish slavery—it will be necessary to subject the nègres in the beginning to a severe discipline, regulated by laws; it will be necessary to entrust the exercise of power to a man who is human, firm, enlightened, and incorruptible, who will be indulgent toward the rapture into which this change of status will plunge the nègres yet not leave them with the hope of impunity, and who will disdain the gold of the whites as well as their intrigues and their threats.[16]

Hugues might have read this passage and modeled his behavior on it, for, as the chief administrator in Guadeloupe between 1794 and 1798, he certainly followed its suggestions. Texts like Condorcet's provided the foundation for Hugues's arguments about the incapacity of ex-slaves for immediate citizenship. Hugues's regime also drew on the Jacobin emphasis upon virtue and sacrifice to the nation that was so powerful in France during 1793 and 1794. A 1793 pamphlet written by the homme de couleur lawyer Julien Raimond highlights the particular inflection

16. Condorcet, *Réflexions sur l'esclavage*, 29–30.

this ideology took when engaging with slavery and emancipation. Even more than Condorcet's text, its language directly anticipated that used by Hugues. Raimond's pamphlet probably directly influenced Hugues, who was in Paris when it was published and circulated; some of Raimond's exact wording reappears in Hugues's decrees and speeches.

In the late 1780s, Raimond wrote several memoirs to the minister of the colonies in Versailles demanding reforms for the gens de couleur in Saint-Domingue, and early in the Revolution he emerged as one of the more important representatives of the gens de couleur, sometimes attacking slavery itself. In his 1793 pamphlet, Raimond argued, like Condorcet, that gradual emancipation was the only way to transform slaves into citizens. Part of his pamphlet addressed the slave insurgents, by then gaining strength in Saint-Domingue: "Your souls, long oppressed by the debasement of vigorous punishment, have been degraded; slavery has snuffed out the divine fire that produces and maintains the virtues that are necessary for man and are indispensable for the state of sociability." If the slaves compared their moral habits to those of free men, Raimond suggested, they themselves would soon recognize "that you lack morals." Echoing Montesquieu, that bad laws make bad subjects, he argued, "It was impossible for you to acquire morals under the defective laws that have reigned over you until now." But different laws would produce different subjects. The slaves had been kept from having property and so had not learned to respect the property of others; but the laws would allow them, slowly, to acquire property, starting with their own bodies. Raimond recommended gradual self-purchase, where the slaves, with the money they made during their one free day of the week, could buy an additional day of freedom from their masters. With these two free days, the slave could then make more money and purchase additional days until entirely free. According to Raimond, this system would allow those who worked hard and developed the virtues necessary for freedom to be the first to buy themselves free, setting an example for the other slaves. In this way, society would slowly be transformed as the slaves became responsible, hard-working, independent citizens.[17]

17. Julien Raimond, *Réflexions sur les véritables causes des troubles et des désastres de nos colonies . . . adresses à la Convention nationale* (Paris, 1790), 19–21, 24–25. I am indebted to Carlo Celius for having pointed out this text to me. He explores the influence of Raimond's thinking on Toussaint L'Ouverture in "Le Contrat social haïtien," *Pouvoirs dans la Caraïbe* (1998), X, 27–70. Despite his major importance, Raimond has not received the detailed attention of scholars until recently, and little is published on his life; I draw here on John Garrigus, "The Free

Unlike Condorcet, Raimond did not have the luxury of suggesting the slaves would wait quietly as the evils of slavery were slowly undone. He himself spoke to the insurgent slaves of Saint-Domingue, seeking to persuade them to participate in a gradual elimination of the system they were already tearing apart. It was a remarkable move, one that presaged what the French National Convention would do with its 1794 decree. Although the enslaved in Saint-Domingue had effectively freed themselves through their revolt, Raimond asserted that it was up to the French state to decide when and how freedom would come and to determine what it would mean once it was granted. "This powerful and generous nation extends its hand to you in order to dry up the source of your misfortunes." Yet, he added, "To attain this goal, the French nation must first take care to plant within your souls the seed of virtue necessary for the new state destined for you." The nation demanded "submission to the laws, and to the order that must result from them," and Raimond commanded: "Come promptly to order, lost men, and wait in silence for the laws that will bring about your regeneration." The laws of the nation would "uproot the vices from your souls and replace them with virtues," but, "for this, it is necessary that you stay for a certain time under the tutelage of those who are responsible for improving your condition; for it is only by developing the habit of practicing what the law requires of you that you will show yourselves worthy of the happiness it will bring to you."[18]

Raimond outlined the "qualities necessary for the state of liberty and equality" that the slaves must begin to develop: absolute respect for the property of others, moral conduct, love for work—"Those who do not work, either to procure their needs or to conserve their property, soon become a charge to society." Again echoing Condorcet, he argued, "It is necessary that you continue to work after acquiring your liberty not only to procure all the things necessary for your new state but further

---

Colored Elite of Saint Domingue: The Case of Julien Raimond, 1744-1801," MS, and Florence Gauthier, "Julien Raimond; ou, La Triple critique du système colonial, esclavagiste et ségrégationniste," paper presented at the Western Society for French History, Los Angeles, November 2000. On Raimond's political involvement in the struggle for gens de couleur rights, see *Réflexions*, chaps. 2, 3; Yves Bénot, *La Révolution française et la fin des colonies: Essai* (Paris, 1989). Several decades later, an emancipation plan nearly identical to Raimond's was put forth by the French abolitionist Comte Agénor-Étienne de Gasparin, who suggested that this system would, "before creating citizens, create workers, fathers, Christians"; see Gasparin, *De l'affranchissement des esclaves . . .* (Paris, 1839), 15.

18. Raimond, *Réflexions sur les véritables causes*, 19-21.

to acquire property that will protect you in your later years from want and misery." The slaves must also learn how to be consumers "of certain commodities" as a way of gaining the secondary virtues necessary to the "state of sociability." They would find "that in order to be equal to the free, you will have to work . . . to procure all the objects of luxury and convenience that distinguish the free from the slave." Additionally, they would have to learn to be sexually virtuous. "Decency, that necessary virtue, must also be the privilege of your wives and daughters; for if they continue to show themselves in public without being decently clothed or dressed in such a way as to inflame desire, then, inevitably, they will be pursued and will succumb."[19]

Raimond skillfully deployed a language of nationalism to justify limitations on liberty. Once the slaves had become free citizens, they should always remember "the boons you have received from the nation." They would have a responsibility to pay back the nation for the gifts it had granted them.

> And there is no better way to prove your gratefulness than by always continuing to make, through your work, the soil of the colonies productive, in order to obtain a large quantity of commodities, whose production will always turn to your advantage. By showing your gratefulness to the nation in this way, you will also bring happiness to yourselves. For, if you neglect, after your emancipation, to cultivate the rich commodities of the colony, then the nation will have nothing to exchange with you and will no longer bring to these countries all the necessary objects that can give you the joys to which you aspire.

After freedom, Raimond insinuated, the ex-slaves would be subject to a particular kind of social contract, in which their role within the nation was to work to produce the commodities around which the colonial economy had been organized: sugar, coffee, and cotton. Through his nationalist language of responsibility, Raimond countered the appropriation of Republican discourse by the slave insurgents and the expansion of the possibilities of citizenship that had resulted from it.

19. Ibid., 24–28. In *Observations sur l'origine et les progrès du préjugé des colons blancs contre les hommes de couleur* . . . (Paris, 1791), Raimond had argued that in gaining their freedom gens de couleur had shown themselves worthy of it. Raimond's argument, rooted in the emerging liberal economic thinking of the times, is remarkably similar to those arguments that became the centerpiece of the post-emancipation policies in Jamaica during the mid-nineteenth century; see Holt, *Problem of Freedom*, esp. 13–79, 263–309.

He did so by arguing that freedom was, in effect, not an inherent quality but rather something that had to be earned. Seeking, as thinkers like Condorcet had done before him, a way to justify offering a conditional and limited freedom, he fixed upon the idea that slaves would effectively owe a debt to the Republic that had freed them. Given back their natural rights by the French state, they would have certain responsibilities to it. These would not be common to all the citizens of the French nation but peculiar to those citizens who had recently been property and had, as property, helped produce vital commodities for the nation. Their old condition would determine the meaning of their new rights; they would be free, but they would have to pay for their freedom through the limitation of their liberty. And, as they paid their debt, they would transform themselves into virtuous citizens driven by economic self-interest. A circumscribed freedom would guide them slowly along the path to a fully realized humanity. In Raimond's argument, there remained a tenuousness in the freedom that was to be granted; the nation implicitly reserved the right to retract what it had given. This is what being a new citizen would mean: to be free and to be a part of the nation like all other citizens but to have a particular role tied to a past condition. As new converts to the nation, the ex-slaves would carry the mark of the generosity that freed them, and they would be responsible for not disappointing the needy Republic.

These arguments became the foundation for Hugues's regime and its restrictive labor policies. Hugues would repeatedly refer to what he called the "price of liberty." Convinced that the ex-slaves should recognize their national duty to work on the plantations, Hugues would be disappointed by the new citizens, many of whom struggled for a more profound freedom by leaving the plantations. They perhaps recognized that, in Hugues's system, they would never be able to pay the "price of liberty." If they were incapable of exercising full citizenship because they had always been forcibly contained on the plantations and had never had the experience of freedom necessary to cultivate the habits of free men, Hugues's system condemned them to a permanent political incapacity as it prevented them from becoming anything other than plantation laborers. For adult male slaves, there was another option—service in the Republican army—which was a powerful counterpoint precisely because it provided a foundation for claims toward the citizenship denied them on the basis of their past enslavement. For women, escape from the plantations necessitated breaking the draconian laws of the new regime.

Raimond ended his 1793 speech to the slaves demanding that they return to their plantations and wait, quietly and obediently, for the nation to oversee their transformation into free citizens, noting that the nation, "like a tender mother, will punish those who refuse her concern." He reiterated:

> Since until now, because of the degradation in which you have been kept, you have not been able to obtain the required qualities and the habits of the free, it will therefore be necessary to obtain them through education, which will be for you a kind of minority, during which you will occupy yourselves earning your liberty through your work and your good conduct. . . . We have indicated to you the virtues and the qualities that you must acquire to become French citizens; we have shown you the means through which you can achieve this, proving to you that this was within your power. Work, therefore, with courage, in order to deserve the blessings of the nation.[20]

Meanwhile, across the ocean, immediate emancipation was being declared as a direct result of the slaves' refusal to associate themselves with the Republic until they had been declared unconditionally free. And, if Victor Hugues spent the next years attempting to apply the principles of gradual emancipation to a population that was already free, the struggles of the freed people on the plantations and in the towns of Guadeloupe showed that they knew very well the value of social rights and political citizenship—and were ready to mobilize them. The disjuncture between the social reality of the Antilles and the contorted arguments of republicanism would propel the strange freedom that took hold in the Caribbean for the next decade. The contradictions of abolitionist thought haunted this period of emancipation and sowed the seeds for the reversal of freedom.

20. Raimond, *Réflexions sur les véritables causes*, 28–29.

WORTHY OF THE NATION

In 1955, the Cuban writer Alejo Carpentier was traveling from Cuba to Paris when his plane broke down and made a forced landing in Guadeloupe. There, Carpentier learned about a historical figure who fascinated him: Victor Hugues. Over the next years, Carpentier searched for accounts of Hugues's life and the history of the period in libraries and archives in France, Mexico, Guadeloupe, Barbados, and Cuba. In Mexico, he chanced upon a copy of Auguste Lacour's nineteenth-century *Histoire de la Guadeloupe*. With its detailed descriptions of Guadeloupe under Hugues's rule, it became Carpentier's key source. The result was Carpentier's novel *El siglo de las luces (Explosion in a Cathedral)*, which remains the longest treatment of the fascinating and contradictory "Victor Hugues of History."[1]

Hugues, the son of a baker from Marseilles, became a sailor and traveled to the Americas, working as a merchant throughout the Caribbean before acquiring a shop in Port-au-Prince. Sometime during 1791 or 1792, his shop was burned down and his brother was killed. In October 1792, Hugues arrived in Paris, where he made connections among the Jacobins and was named revolutionary tribunal judge of the port town of Rochefort. His revolutionary credentials and his experience in the colonies made him an ideal candidate as an administrator in the Antilles, and in February 1794 the Comité de salut public appointed him one of three commissioners to carry the emancipation decree to Guadeloupe. Hugues led the Republican troops in the June 1794 assault on the British-held island and quickly became its most powerful adminis-

---

1. This quote is the title given by Alejo Carpentier to the epilogue of *Explosion in a Cathedral* (New York, 1963); on the writing of the work, see Florence Delay, "La Fabrication du siècle," Carmen Vasquez, "Dans le sillage de Victor Hugues et de son temps," in Jacqueline Baldran, ed., *Quinze études autour de El siglo de las luces* (Paris, 1983).

trator. Between 1794 and 1798, he turned Guadeloupe into the Republican stronghold of the eastern Caribbean, sending armies of French sansculottes and slaves-turned-citizens against the British. Yet, despite its "considerable military significance and social interest," Hugues's regime has received little attention from historians. Lacour's classic *Histoire de la Guadeloupe* drew on the accounts of white planter families who suffered during Hugues's regime to depict him as a tyrannical and brutal Jacobin. Lacour's work served as the basis for the only existing biography of Hugues, published in 1932 by the comte de Sainte Croix de La Roncière, which celebrated Hugues's military accomplishments even as it reiterated Lacour's negative portrayal. It is in fact *El siglo de las luces* that offers the most powerful account of Hugues's story as it illustrates the spiraling contradictions of the Revolution itself.[2]

Hugues's political career did not end in Guadeloupe; his ideals changed with the times, and he adapted enough for Napoléon Bonaparte to send him, a few years later, to Guiana as a governor. There, he presided over the 1802 reestablishment of slavery. Once again, he carried the news from France—this time the decision of Napoléon—to the Americas, ending eight years of freedom. His treason against the ideals of liberty, a sign of a more general failure of the Revolution, forms one of the key issues in Carpentier's novel. Yet Carpentier claims that Hugues's political heritage in a sense outlived his own treason: "In the end it was from Guadeloupe under the governorship of Victor Hugues that all the propaganda came that served to light the great burst of flame of the South American Wars of Independence." Carpentier powerfully evokes the ambivalences

2. See Auguste Lacour, *Histoire de la Guadeloupe*, 4 vols. (Basse-Terre, Guadeloupe, 1855–1858), II, 280–281; see also Georges, comte de Sainte-Croix de La Roncière, *Victor Hughes, le conventionnel* (Paris, 1932), vol. I of *Grandes figures coloniales*. The quote is from Robin Blackburn, *The Overthrow of Colonial Slavery, 1776–1848* (London, 1988), 262. On Carpentier's use of Lacour, see Vasquez, "Dans le sillage," in Baldran, ed., *Quinze études*, 85–97. For analyses of Hugues's regime as an extension of the Jacobin terror, see Edith Géraud-Llorca, "Victor Hugues: La Terreur en Guadeloupe," in Germain Sicard, ed., *Justice et politique: La Terreur sous la Révolution française* (Toulouse, France, 1997), 317–326; William S. Cormack, "Victor Hugues and the Reign of Terror on Guadeloupe, 1794–1798," in A. J. B. Johnston, ed., *Essays in French Colonial History: Proceedings of the Twenty-first Annual Meeting of the French Colonial Historical Society* (East Lansing, Mich., 1997), 31–41. I have presented a condensed version of the material presented in this chapter in "'The Price of Liberty': Victor Hugues and the Administration of Freedom in Guadeloupe, 1794–1798," *William and Mary Quarterly*, 3d Ser., LVI (1999), 363–392.

of the Republican project's Antillean "arrival" in the opening scene of his novel, which describes the flotilla of French ships bearing Hugues and his sans-culottes, along with their two central weapons: the abolition of slavery and the guillotine. By no means was Hugues the one who brought the language of rights to the Antilles, as I have shown; what he did bring, along with the official decree of emancipation, was repressive power the state deemed necessary for the construction of a new political order. Carpentier dramatizes the encounter between the Republican search for purity, embodied in the guillotine, and the social topography created by slavery. Hugues saw himself as a warrior on a mission for the Republic and exercised an often merciless justice against those he declared enemies of the French nation. He was harsh in his discipline of those ex-slaves who did not follow his plan for the new order of the island. Resistance to directives for work and cultivation were considered treason during war with the British, and malefactors were punished severely. These aspects of Hugues's character pushed Lacour to grant him an oft-repeated nickname: "the Robespierre of the Antilles."[3]

But any interpretation of Hugues's legacy is complicated by his presiding over a precocious, radical, and in many ways admirable project of ending slavery and creating a new order in its place. He oversaw the transformation of Guadeloupe from a slave society to one at least theoretically based on universal citizenship and social equality. He mobilized huge numbers of black soldiers in the imperial conflict with Britain, and these armies were at least partially successful in taking over other islands and temporarily ending slavery there. The presence of black soldiers and sailors throughout the Caribbean during the late 1790s sent a radical message that rocked slave societies throughout the Americas.

In this chapter, I follow Alejo Carpentier's insight by reading Hugues's story as the broader tale of a revolution and its limits, of the ways the Enlightenment project sought to heal the wounds Europe had created by transforming, without ever escaping, the racial inequality that resulted from colonial expansion. Hugues's actions and writings provide us with a fascinating glimpse of the Republican project in its encounter with an order based on racial exclusion and plantation labor. As Carpentier's work suggests, Hugues's story illustrates how the metropolitan project of revolution, which celebrated both political equality and the virtues of individual labor, confronted the limits of its own imagination in the Antilles.

3. Donald Shaw, *Alejo Carpentier* (Boston, 1985), 74; Carpentier, *Explosion*, 7.

FIGURE 16. "Reprise de la Guadeloupe." 1802. Hugues's takeover of
Guadeloupe is celebrated in this engraving. *Cliché Bibliothèque nationale
de France, Paris*

Black Citizens

When Victor Hugues's flotilla of Republican soldiers arrived off the
coast of Guadeloupe in June 1794, they faced a well-fortified island
manned by the British troops who occupied it with the help of royalist French. Nevertheless, in a military action that was to be touted in
France as an example of the sans-culottes' almost superhuman qualities,
the French soldiers—joined by the slaves they freed—managed to rout
the British forces and take back Grande-Terre. One of the commissioners
who served with Hugues wrote shortly afterward, "Never have Republicans been more intrepid when equipped with such feeble means." With
such bravery and with the help of military reinforcements, he claimed,
the French could capture all of the British colonies in the area. His opti-
mism was premature: although the Republicans were able to regain most
of Grande-Terre and the city of Pointe-à-Pitre, including the Fort Fleur

d'Epée, the British kept their hold on Basse-Terre and occupied positions above Pointe-à-Pitre, from which they could shell the city. So the French conquerors settled into a state of siege as they continued their assault against the British.[4]

In celebrating the taking of Pointe-à-Pitre two months later, Hugues compared the military feat of the Republicans in Guadeloupe to those of the Romans. "All of humanity will thank you and pass on your actions and your names to posterity; your enemies will become infamous and will be objects of horror for future generations. . . . Those who fight for liberty will always be victorious." He went on to praise the "citoyens colons who, always firm in their principles, resisted the perfidious maneuvers of our enemies" and the "citoyens noirs who, thankful for the blessings granted them by the French nation, have shared in our victories by fighting for liberty." He counseled these new citizens to follow the example of their brothers the sans-culottes, "who will always show you the path to victory and will consolidate with you your liberty and your children's." All of them, concluded Hugues, using a Jacobin formulation that filled the speeches and declarations of the National Convention at the time, had shown themselves "WORTHY OF THE NATION."[5]

The early Republican victory had depended on the key weapon of war they had brought: the abolition of slavery. Outnumbered, the French troops quickly augmented their fighting force by inviting slaves to join them. After the taking of Pointe-à-Pitre, the commissioners made this haphazard policy official; they asked for volunteers to join in the fight against the British, who had made the citizens of Guadeloupe "without distinction" into a "people of slaves." The Republicans had shattered those chains, but with this liberation also came the responsibility of all good citizens to participate in the struggle against the British. "Citizens of all colors" were invited to register at the municipality so they could be called as national volunteers to the battalions being organized. In recruiting men of "all colors" into the army, Hugues was filling a desperate need for troops. But he was also laying the ground rules for liberty, sug-

4. "Les Commissaires délégués aux îles du Vent par la Convention nationale aux représentants du peuple composant le Comité de salut public," 18 Prairial, An II (June 6, 1794), in CAOM, C 7A, 47, 5–6. See also the report by the navy commander Pierre Villegegu, in CAOM, C 7A, 47, 95–101.

5. "Le Commissaire délégué . . . aux Républicains des armées de terre et de mer de la République, actuellement à la Guadeloupe," 1 Thermidor, An II (Jul. 19, 1794), in CAOM, C 7A, 47, 18.

gesting that the formerly enslaved needed to earn the freedom granted to them by picking up arms in the service of the Republic.[6]

Hugues reported to the Comité de salut public about the former slaves: "Many have taken up arms and shown themselves worthy of the fight for liberty." His decision to create battalions composed of sans-culottes of all colors, he wrote, was a success. "This mix has had the best possible effect on the former slaves. I have granted them the same pay as the troops from France. They exercise twice a day and are flattered to be treated like our brothers the sans-culottes, who, thanks to my constant fraternal exhortations, respect the former slaves as much as is possible." Hugues praised their behavior in battle: "The black citizens, our new brothers, have shown on this occasion what the spirit of Liberty can accomplish; out of men previously brutalized by slavery, she made heroes." With the arrival of emancipation, the freed slaves were finally accepted as Republican soldiers who could help in the crucial battle for the preservation and expansion of the Revolution. The suggestion made for the Trois-Rivières insurgents and carried out by Sonthonax in Saint-Domingue had become official French policy. Yet, within the new order predicated on equal treatment, a hierarchy of value remained. Hugues was skeptical of what could be expected of the black soldiers; he tempered his praise of them by adding, at the end of his report, "The blacks alone, without Europeans, will never fight well."[7]

The transformation of slaves into soldiers provided a simple and edifying way for Hugues to apply the decree of emancipation. By fighting the British and showing courage on the battlefield, newly freed men demonstrated their capacity to fulfill the duties of freedom. But what of those men and women who remained on the plantations? When Hugues and the other commissioners published the National Convention's emancipation decree in Guadeloupe, they attached the following explanation of what the law would demand of both whites and new citizens:

6. "Les Commissaires délégués . . . à tous les citoyens de la Pointe-à-Pitre," 20 Prairial, An II (June 8, 1794), in CAOM, C 7A, 47, 9.

7. Hugues to the Comité de salut public, 4 Thermidor, An II (Jul. 22, 1794), in CAOM, C 7A, 47, 20–25. Hugues had praised the blacks' military participation from the first, noting that "the actions of our brothers the blacks have consistently deserved praise." See "Les Commissaires délégués . . . au . . . Comité de salut public," 18 Prairial, An II (June 6, 1794), in CAOM, C 7A, 47, 5–6. His more benevolent opinion was seconded by Pierre Villegegu, who wrote: "In all our diverse attacks the citoyens nègres behaved themselves well and we can praise them for their courage." See CAOM, C 7A, 47, 103–104.

The Meaning of Citizenship, 1794–1798

CITIZENS,

A Republican government accepts neither chains nor slavery, and therefore the National Convention has just solemnly proclaimed the liberty of the negroes and confided the execution of this law to the commissioners it has delegated for the colonies; the result of this natural repayment and its civic organization must be (1) the benevolent equality without which the political machine is like a clock whose pendulum loses its equilibrium and its perpetual action; (2) an administration both generally and individually committed to guaranteeing the property already held by some, and the product of the work and industry of others.

CITIZENS of all colors, your happiness depends on this law . . . but the white citizens must kindly offer, in fraternity, and with reasonable wages, work to their black and colored brothers; and the latter must also learn and never forget that those who have no property must provide, through their work, for their own subsistence and that of their family, as well as to the support of their nation. CITIZENS, you have become equal in order to enjoy happiness and to share it with all others; the person who oppresses his co-citizen is a monster who must be banished from the social world.[8]

The proclamation presented an idealized picture of how ex-masters and ex-slaves would relate to one another in the new order, but it did so by granting little, and demanding much, of the new citizens. As freedom was declared throughout Grande-Terre and ex-slaves celebrated their freedom, their actions suggested they had a different vision of the rewards that were to come from liberty. Many probably doubted that the co-citizens who just days before were masters would in fact offer them "reasonable wages." Some took food from the plantations, believing that they now had a right to take what they had worked to produce. But the commissioners reacted by forcefully declaring that the end of slavery did not signify an alteration in property rights. Six days after the initial proclamation, they reminded the ex-slaves, "The National Convention, through its decree of 16 Pluviôse, has granted you the highest of blessings: LIBERTY," and "her intention, in smashing your chains, was to grant you greater happiness by allowing you to enjoy your rights." The commissioners would be "responsible to the nation and humanity if we do not prevent the disorders that the enemies of the public interest hope

8. "Extrait du procès-verbal de la Convention nationale," 19 Prairial, An II (June 7, 1794), in CAOM, C 7A, 47, 8.

to make you the victims of." They had therefore been "pained to learn that depredations have been committed in the countryside, that manioc plants have been cut and bananas removed, for no reason, with the simple intention of hurting the owners." "It is hard for us to believe these accusations," they added diplomatically but insisted that, given the circumstances, it was "vital to provide for the conservation of the property of each individual, and especially of the provisions of all kinds." Therefore, "all citizens of whatever color" were forbidden "to touch the provisions of the habitations, such as manioc, bananas, corn, etc., without the express permission of the owner." Furthermore, those who broke this law would be "pursued to the full extent of the law; and in those cases where they take the said provisions with malevolence, they will be declared outlaws and punished with death as traitors who have consorted with the enemies of the Republic."[9]

This declaration asserted the continuing rights of the ex-masters over their land and went further by making "stealing" from these properties not only a crime against the owner but an act of treason against the nation. Since the provisions grown on plantations were declared fundamental to the nation's security, the realms of agriculture and labor were to be administered by the new state for the benefit of the nation's expansionist Republican project. The claim on the part of the commissioners to control production on the island had particular salience, since many plantations had become state property under Republican laws that sequestered the holdings of émigrés or counterrevolutionaries. Yet it also had a broader significance: the state was laying claim to the economic and social possibilities of the new citizens themselves.

The new citizens' behavior apparently continued to dissatisfy Hugues, who wrote a "Proclamation to the Black Citizens" seven days later. In it, he again cast as treason the slaves' refusal to fulfill the roles he demanded of them. "The Republic, in recognizing the rights that nature gave you, did not intend to release you from the obligation of working for what you need to live," he opined. "He who does not work deserves only disdain and must not profit from the blessings of our regeneration; we must assume, with good reason, that the lazy survive only through pillaging."

9. "Les Commissaires délégués . . . aux habitants des campagnes de toutes les couleurs," 25 Prairial, An II (June 13, 1794), in CAOM, C 7A, 47, 10. The proclamation was to be read and posted on all the plantations, and the response of the ex-slaves was, when possible, to be reported back to the commissioners.

All citizens could not be "employed in the defense of the colony," but it was just as important for the island's survival that "those who are not incorporated into the armed forces go to work cultivating the land and planting food as quickly as possible."

> In fact, citizens, he who sacrifices his pain and his sweat to provide food to his co-citizens deserves just as much a reward as he who sacrifices to defend them. In consequence, citizens, we invite and require those of you who are not incorporated into the army to return to the plantations where you previously lived, and to work there without interruption planting potatoes, yams, and other edible roots. We promise to protect you and to pay you for your work; but, if, against our will, some of you refuse to respond to our invitation, we will declare you traitors in the name of the Republic and punish you to the full extent of the law.

Many plantation dwellers took advantage of freedom to travel away from home, perhaps to visit family members elsewhere or simply to savor the liberty of movement they assumed came with emancipation. Such movement and the gathering of ex-slaves throughout the colony alarmed the commissioners, who commanded the municipal government of Pointe-à-Pitre to use soldiers to "break up the mobs and force the black citizens to return to their respective plantations and plant provisions."[10]

Hugues, like Raimond, believed that the ex-slaves owed a debt to the nation that freed them. Those who fought for the Republic had in a sense paid that debt, as he made clear when he celebrated the war against the English in July 1794. "The benevolent decree of 16 Pluviôse, in assuring our hold over our colonies, assures the destruction of the colonies of our enemies," he wrote, "and those men who were degraded in days past have learned the price of liberty by fighting for it, and they have found victory." "They will do more," he bragged; "they will carry this liberty to the British colonies; already terror precedes them and assures their success; the weapons of the Republic have been victorious in Europe—how could they not be in America!" Hugues also felt, however, that many ex-slaves, particularly those who he believed should be working on the plantations, had not learned this lesson. "The black citizens don't yet know the price

10. "Proclamation: Le Commissaire délégué . . . aux citoyens noirs, à qui la Convention nationale a accordé la liberté, par son décret du 16 Pluviôse," 2 Messidor, An II (June 20, 1794), in CAOM, C 7A, 47, 14.

of liberty and are using it only to steal and destroy," he complained in June 1794. Instead of "providing us with resources," the decree of liberty "steals them from us, because of the lack of education of our brothers in the colonies." "Nevertheless," he added, "it is to be hoped that careful and severe measures will make them feel the price of liberty." Pursuing this goal would become the cornerstone of his regime.[11]

For Hugues, there were essentially two roles open for the citoyens noirs in the new order: soldier and cultivateur. In the Republican political culture of the day, the occupations of soldier and farmer were commonly celebrated as ideal ways for citizens to fulfill their responsibilities as virtuous Republicans. The new citizens' place in the new society was to be circumscribed by what Hugues saw as their duty toward the nation: to defend the new order and to assure the continuing functioning of the plantations. The ex-slaves' labor was to be mobilized and controlled from above once again; now, however, the benefactor of that labor was, not individual masters, but the nation itself.

Hugues's vision of the ex-slaves was a complex one, rooted both in his past as a slaveowning white and in his passionate (though short-lived) belief in Jacobin ideology. His writings on the behavior of the new citizens of Guadeloupe are full of vacillations between praising the possibilities of their uplift and lamenting their inability to fulfill these possibilities. In interpreting the failures he saw, he quickly turned to racialized characterizations of the limited capacities of Africans, repeating the arguments of pro-slavery advocates. Yet he also consistently returned to the theory that education and social reform could transform the ex-slaves into citizens. His uncertainty suffused a report he wrote to the Comité du

11. "Proclamation de Victor Hugues," 29 Messidor, An II (Jul. 17, 1794), in CAOM, C 7A, 47, 16; "Nous commissaires délégués ... au ... Comité de salut public," 26 Prairial, An II (June 14, 1794), in CAOM, C 7A, 47, 12–13. The letterhead, which read, "We the commissioners delegated by the National Convention," had been given to the commissioners on their departure from France; Hugues crossed out the "we" and the "s" in "commissioners," pointedly transmitting that he had, by that time, essentially become the sole governor of the island. Perhaps because of pressure from Hugues himself, Commissioner Lebas seems to have retreated from official duties, although he remained somewhat involved and occasionally signed proclamations and wrote letters. Pierre Chrétien died soon after their arrival and, according to a letter by Hugues, had ceded all power over the administration of the colony to him before his death. See "Nous commissaires délégués," 26 Prairial, An II (June 14, 1794), in CAOM, C 7A, 47, 11.

salut public in July. "The blacks who, by ignorance, never think about tomorrow consume all the provisions but refuse to plant," he complained. Still, "it is not that they would keep doing so if we could talk to them on all the plantations; but there are too few of us to send the kind of preachers they can trust; there is no way they can grant their trust to the people of this land." In a pessimistic vein, he noted, "Having spent twenty years in the colonies and having always owned negroes, I had always feared what would happen if they were to be set free." But he admitted that in general the ex-slaves had "shown themselves deserving of liberty by their behavior, avoiding thievery and laziness—vices innate among those enslaved by the degradation in which they are kept—and they have not carried themselves to extremes against their former masters." Although they had pillaged a great deal, he added, they had "limited themselves to that."[12]

Hugues believed the symbols and ideals of republicanism could help transform the ex-slaves into productive citizens. In a note added to the above letter, he asked for thousands of cocardes to replace the expensive locally made ones he had been using, as well as new banners for the black troops: "These are little stimulants that produce great effects," he wrote. Yet, even if he meant to dress the ex-slaves in the colors of the Republic, he had a restricted vision of how far their rights as citizens would go. He constantly invoked the dangerous possibilities of undisciplined freedom and the need to harness that freedom to profit the nation. Hugues justified his administration through a peculiar logic in which the responsibilities of the new citizens were defined by the very tasks to which they had been limited by the slave system that emancipation had in principle shattered.[13]

A new order was emerging. A month after his arrival, Hugues, in

12. In the Caribbean, of course, being a cultivateur meant something quite specific. It meant being a worker in a labor-intensive system on a plantation owned and managed by someone else, often men who, until recently, had claimed you as their human property. Although the benefactor of the ex-slaves' labor had changed, the plantation workers would remain subjugated within a hierarchy hauntingly similar to what had come before. See Hugues to Comité de salut public, 4 Thermidor, An II (July 22, 1794), in CAOM, C 7A, 47, 20–25. Note that Hugues vacillates between using the term *noir* (black) when talking about his mission in Guadeloupe and *nègre* (negro) when talking about his own slaveowning past.

13. Hugues to Comité de salut public, 5 Thermidor, An II (Jul. 23, 1794), in CAOM, C 7A, 47, 31.

celebration of the Republican victory, had Pointe-à-Pitre renamed Port de la Liberté—a name it would keep until the early nineteenth century. Months later, when the French had taken back all of Guadeloupe, Hugues had a peculiar monument erected. It was built on the site of the grave of the British general Thomas Dundas, who had died of fever three days before the arrival of the French troops. Under Hugues's orders, Dundas's bones were dug up and "thrown to the wind." The "lofty monument" to be erected in place of the grave would bear (in both French and English) an epigraph declaring that "public indignation" had caused the Republic's enemy to be "disinterred." The British, according to this inscription, had violated "the rights of humanity, of men, of war, and of nations," and the monument would transmit the memory of these "crimes" to "posterity." Whereas the date of the monument's construction was inscribed using the Republican calendar, the date of Dundas's death was written in the Gregorian calendar, followed, in parentheses, by the note "style esclave" (in the style of slaves). The British lived by the old calendar, enslaved in a different temporality, a different history, outside of the liberation of the French Revolution. Over Dundas's empty grave, the monument was to proclaim forever the absence of his bones, standing as a reminder of an erased past. As he had done with the monument, Hugues stamped his new order with the old structures and vocabularies of style esclave. The productive role given the slaves in the old colonial system would be adapted to, rather than eliminated from, the new Republican system, and as a result the freed men and women of the Caribbean would be made to carry the mark of their past as slaves. Slavery had been wounded and ultimately buried by the slave revolts of the early 1790s, and France's decree of emancipation meant to throw its remnants to the wind and replace them with a new Republican society. In fact, though, the past of slavery would not be erased—not from the economic order Hugues inherited and sought to transform or from the minds of the men and women whose labor he sought to command and control.[14]

14. On Port de la Liberté, see "Arrêté . . . du commissaire délégué," 28 Messidor, An II (Jul. 16, 1794), in CAOM, C 7A, 47, 15; on the monument, see "Les Commissaires délégués aux isles du Vent, au peuple de la Guadeloupe," 20 Frimaire, An III (Dec. 10, 1794), in CAOM, C 7A, 47, 38. The Republican calendar that replaced the Gregorian calendar was set up in October 1793, and year I was declared to have begun retroactively on Sept. 22, with the declaration of the French Republic. See Mona Ozouf, *Festivals and the French Revolution*, trans. Alan Sheridan (Cambridge, Mass., 1988).

The Meaning of Citizenship, 1794–1798

On 16 Frimaire, An III (December 6, 1794), six months after the arrival of the Republican troops in Guadeloupe, the British surrendered, and all of the island fell once again into the hands of the French. Commissioner Pierre Lebas compared the French victory to that of the North American revolutionaries when he wrote, "General Graham, fighting liberty in Guadeloupe as his compatriots had at Saratoga, laid down his arms and surrendered at Camp Berville." The British who surrendered were allowed to leave the island, but many of the 865 French who had fought with them faced the darker fate reserved for "traitors of the nation": execution. One hundred forty were guillotined and 363 were killed by firing squad. Those who were deemed less culpable—including 36 "women, all black, who served the British army in the camp"—were condemned "to the chain" and to forced labor.[15]

After the British defeat, the Republican administration took control of the entire island. They faced the task of rebuilding political and juridical institutions that had been shattered both by conflict between political parties during 1792–1793 and by the British occupation that followed. One of the major questions facing them was how to manage the massive amount of property that had been owned by "traitors" or émigrés who had either been killed or left the colony. The commissioners had published initial regulations for identifying such property within Pointe-à-Pitre early during the occupation: houses were to be marked as "national property" when the owner was a known émigré; if the owners were absent and it was not known whether they were émigrés or simply gone because of the war, the property would be labeled with the less permanent "sequestered property." Commissions were set up to oversee the renting of these plantations. Many abandoned properties had been looted during the fighting, and Hugues ordered all "furniture and personal" effects that had been "gathered by patriots" to be returned to local

15. "Contrerévolutionnaires armés, servant dans l'armée anglaise," in CAOM, C 7A, 49, 94. Among those killed were a number of citoyens de couleur, many of whom had been singled out for harsh criticism (and treatment) by Hugues since his arrival in Guadeloupe. When the Republicans had taken Pointe-à-Pitre, for instance, they had captured the brother of Jean Littée, the homme de couleur who had been elected as a representative for the Antilles in Dominica in 1792. According to the commissioners, "He suffered the punishment due traitors." See "Les Commissaires délégués . . . au . . . Comité de salut public," 18 Prairial, An II (June 6, 1794), in CAOM, C 7A, 46, 5-6.

authorities. Among this property, Hugues noted, "there are objects precious for the sciences and arts that create the genius of liberty" that he planned to gather in a public house "to serve for public instruction and to widen the sphere of knowledge that all free men must have." Those who held on to such property, then, were not only guilty of stealing from the state; "those guilty of this conduct also testify to the desire to keep their co-citizens in the shadows of ignorance, the sad fruit of the prejudices and the slavery the Republic just abolished." All horses belonging to émigrés (including those traitors who had been executed or killed in the fighting) were also to be brought to local officials, who would distribute them to the state's plantations to help cultivate the land. The proclamation was to be posted in the cities—but also read and explained to the black citizens working on the plantations.[16]

Hugues also sought to rebuild the juridical institutions of the island. He created a police force composed of approximately one hundred members for the entire island, distributed between all the communes (there were to be three in Trois-Rivières) with larger concentrations in Basse-Terre and Port de la Liberté. This institution drew recruits from various parts of the island and distributed them where needed. Fabien Belaire, for instance, a resident of Moule, was brought to work as a gendarme in Basse-Terre. Of course, police—and judges—had to deal with many new issues, since the role of the new citizens in the army, on the plantations, and in political institutions had to be determined. The very terms of legality had been transformed by emancipation, as Hugues had noted soon after the taking of Pointe-à-Pitre when he had set up new tribunals on the island. "It is not enough to take possession of the territory of the Republic and to bear arms against our enemy," he proclaimed. "We must also purge it of the various monsters that have soiled it and the vices that afflict it . . . we must finally assure the reign of law and introduce the public spirit that has been exiled from these lands for too long. The LAW is indivisible; it must strike all citizens equally, just as all are equally entitled to its protection. Under its reign tranquillity and happiness will be reborn." Hugues had created two sets of tribunals; on the municipal level, the institutions were to continue functioning as they had before, punishing minor crimes with the "moderation that corresponds to the institution." The entire island, however, was to fall under the power of the military tribunal that would deal with "national crimes," whose expan-

16. "Le Commissaires délégué . . . arrêté," 3 Frimaire, 1 Nivôse, An III (Nov. 23, Dec. 21, 1794), both in CAOM, C 7A, 47, 37, 43–44.

The Meaning of Citizenship, 1794–1798

sive definition included "treason, communication with the enemies of the Republic, crime and cowardice, devastation, arson, destruction, stealing and pillaging provisions, etc." The municipalities were to refer all cases dealing with such crimes to the military tribunal composed by Hugues. This system solidified once Hugues took control of the entire island, and it remained a crucial pillar of his regime.[17]

Making crimes against property synonymous with crimes against the state and creating tribunals to convict those found guilty of such crimes were Hugues's way of dealing with the huge number of plantations that had come directly under his control. This problem was greatly augmented after the surrender at Camp Berville, since the vast majority of those killed by Hugues were planters. Coupled with the fact that large numbers of propertyowners had already left Guadeloupe during the previous years, these executions left nearly half of the plantations in Guadeloupe—over one thousand in total—in government hands. The island was full of masterless, state-owned plantations without official managers. Many ex-slaves simply left these plantations, joining the Republican army or settling in the towns. Those that stayed on their plantations often refused to work in their traditional roles, instead tending to their own gardens.[18]

In establishing new state institutions such as tribunals and hospitals, Hugues drew on the Republican institution building that was sweeping metropolitan France. He also had at his disposal a set of instructions that had been prepared in January 1794 for the commissioners assigned to the eastern Caribbean colonies. The document declared that the "principal object" of the commissioners' mission was to "solidly establish the

17. "Arrêté sur la police de l'île," 29 Frimaire, An III (Dec. 19, 1794), in CAOM, C 7A, 47, 42. For Belaire, see CAOM, Etat civil Basse-Terre, 6, 24 Ventôse, An III (Mar. 14, 1795); "Proclamation de Victor Hugues . . . aux citoyens de l'île de Guadeloupe," 29 Messidor, An II (Jul. 17, 1794), in CAOM, C 7A, 47, 16. The term "commune" replaced the older, church-based "parish" during the Revolution.

18. In Grande-Terre alone, there were 638 plantations, among them 288 sugar plantations, under government control. The former number doubled when the French captured Basse-Terre from the British (Lacour, *Histoire*, II, 381–394). In 1796, a majority of the sugar plantations of the commune of Basse-Terre were in the hands of the state, and 1,346 citizens (mostly noirs) lived on these "habitations nationales." A smaller number (444) lived on nationalized coffee plantations. Most of the noirs over twenty-one—58 percent of the men and 65 percent of the women—worked as cultivateurs; another 23 percent of the men and 27 percent of the women worked as domestics. See the 1796 "Etat nominatif . . . de Basse-Terre," in CAOM, G 1, 500, no. 5.

principles of the Revolution and the French Republic" in the colonies, destroy the roots of monarchism, and defend the colonies from internal and external enemies. The commissioners were to use whatever force was necessary and to set up tribunals under their command. They were also given the right to determine which of the Republic's laws would be applied in the colonies under their control. In addition, they were sternly ordered not in any way to encourage "distinctions" between the "free men of the colony," notably in the armed forces.[19]

These instructions, however, were written before the emancipation decree was passed in Paris, and they were never supplemented by guidelines on applying emancipation. They provided no concrete guidance for Hugues as he confronted the main quandary of abolition—how to keep free men and women working on the plantations. Hugues had been granted far-reaching powers, but he was on his own when it came to figuring out exactly how to exercise those powers in governing the transition to freedom.

Nonetheless, he did have one model to draw on: the post-emancipation administration of Sonthonax and Polverel in Saint-Domingue. Though Hugues had left France before either commissioner had arrived to explain his actions in detail, and therefore what Hugues knew had been filtered by rumor and accusation, Saint-Domingue likely provided Hugues with some guidance. The regime Sonthonax and Polverel put into place required ex-slaves to continue working on plantations in return for a salary. The commissioners ultimately settled on a system by which the workers would receive one-quarter of the plantation's yearly production, to be divided among them. Under Polverel's regulations, which were applied in the southern and western parts of Saint-Domingue and were more detailed than Sonthonax's, workers were also given the right to transfer to other plantations during a period of six months. They did not, therefore, have to continue working where they had been slaves, although they were required to fix themselves on a plantation somewhere. They were also given a say in the choice of *conducteurs* (drivers) and managers on the plantations.[20]

19. "Extrait des régistres du Comité de salut public," 3 Pluviôse, An II (Jan. 22, 1794), in AN, Marine, AA, 2, 3. I am indebted to Fabien Marius-Hatchi for providing me with a copy of his mémoire, which alerted me to the existence of this document; see his "Libèté oswa lanmò!: La Guadeloupe dans le cadre des révolutions caribéennes, 1789–1804" (mémoire de D.E.A., Université Paris VII, 2000), 98.

20. See proclamations of Sonthonax (Aug. 29, 1793) and Polverel (Oct. 31,

The Meaning of Citizenship, 1794–1798

In late August 1793, days before Sonthonax decreed general emancipation in the north, Polverel had freed those slaves on plantations that had been abandoned by their owners and therefore had become the property of the Republic. In this decree he had actually promised that these freed slaves, along with those who fought for the Republic, would be granted portions of land from these plantations in return for their service. Polverel's promise was deferred at the time, and ultimately it found no place in future decrees. But the formerly enslaved on many plantations clearly believed that they had a right to occupy portions of land and claim them as their own. During the months after emancipation was mandated, many extended their individual gardens and sold harvests from the plantation provision grounds in the markets. Many also sought to gain more time for the work they did for themselves, pushing for three free days a week. Women, who received less of the plantation products than men, also protested this policy. Such actions led Polverel to issue a new set of regulations in February 1794 that sought to contain and channel the plantation workers' demands. Contradicting his August proclamation from the year before, he announced that the ex-slaves had no claim to the land. He also insisted that it was right for women to be paid less than men and encouraged male plantation workers to contest the "pretensions" of the women. He responded to the demands for more free time by offering plantation workers a choice: they could choose, as a community, to work only four days a week, but they would receive a substantially smaller salary. The decrease was quite out of proportion with the amount of labor they would still perform. Nevertheless, on several plantations, the workers decided they would rather take the pay cut and have more time for themselves. Women often led their communities to such decisions: paid less then men, and often comprising the majority on plantations left behind by those who enlisted in the army, they had good cause to be suspicious of the new system and to seek as much autonomy as they could.[21]

1793), in Gabriel Debien, ed., "Aux origines de l'abolition de l'esclavage," *Revue d'histoire des colonies*, XXXVI (1949), 348–423, esp. 348–356, 372–387.

21. Proclamation of Étienne Polverel, Aug. 27, 1793, in Debien, "Aux origines," *Revue d'histoire des colonies*, XXXVI (1949), 24–55, esp. 45–48; Carolyn E. Fick, *The Making of Haiti: The Saint-Domingue Revolution from Below* (Knoxville, Tenn., 1990), 168–170; Judith Kafka, "Action, Reaction, and Interaction: Slave Women in Resistance in the South of Saint-Domingue, 1793–94," *Slavery and Abolition: A Journal of Comparative Studies*, XVIII (1997), 48–72.

Sonthonax and Polverel's system was maintained and perfected by those who followed them, notably Toussaint L'Ouverture. The challenge faced by L'Ouverture was a daunting one, for the slave insurrection of 1791 and the years of war that had followed it had left many plantations, and the colonial economy as a whole, in ruins. As L'Ouverture complained in July 1794, although he fully intended to pay the cultivateurs, he could not do so until something had actually been produced there to pay them with. But L'Ouverture, along with the French administrators he worked with, concluded that rebuilding the plantation economy was vital in order to feed the population and sustain the war against the British. In many parts of the colony, L'Ouverture did manage a partial economic recovery as early as late 1794, notably by helping ex-masters return to their plantations to oversee the labor of their former slaves. In the southern province, which was under the command of André Rigaud, the many abandoned plantations were rented out to new tenants who took charge of managing and paying the plantation laborers. This system was instituted in the north as well by 1796 and became a cornerstone of the plantation economy. Often it was black and gens de couleur officers in the military who rented these plantations, so that a new elite invested in maintaining order and productivity on the plantations was born. Plantation laborers, meanwhile, continued to contest the system, sometimes through violent uprisings that L'Ouverture and his officers steadfastly repressed.[22]

The situation in Guadeloupe was similar in many ways to that in Saint-Domingue. Hugues, like his administrators and officers in Saint-Domingue, believed that productivity was fundamental to the war effort against the British. In both colonies, the Republic had taken over a large number of plantations, and both were almost completely isolated from the metropole and had to sustain the war effort using local troops and resources. At the same time, the situation in Guadeloupe also differed from that in Saint-Domingue. Because slave revolt had been relatively limited and contained in Guadeloupe, most of the slaves had never left their plantations, whereas in many parts of Saint-Domingue, notably the northern plain, this was not the case. In addition, little of the equipment or

22. Gérard M. Laurent, *Toussaint L'Ouverture à travers sa correspondance, 1794-1798* (Madrid, 1953), 121-124; Mats Lundahl, "Toussaint L'Ouverture and the War Economy of Saint-Domingue, 1796-1802," *Slavery and Abolition*, VI (1985), 122-138, esp. 124-125.

cane fields were destroyed during the uprisings—the insurgents at Trois-Rivières had specifically avoided this—or during the battles against the British. It was in fact Hugues's arrival that set in motion the disruptions of the plantation system. His challenge would be to keep the formerly enslaved on plantations rather than entice them back, as leaders in Saint-Domingue often had to do.

During the first months after the reconquest, Hugues seems to have been too busy with other administrative details to set forth a consistent policy on labor. In October 1794, however, he consolidated his original, disparate orders into an islandwide proclamation on the labor question, which took the form of an urgent call for the new citizens to report to plantations in order to harvest coffee. Hugues noted that there was "a huge quantity of coffee plantations seized from the émigrés, which promise a huge harvest," and that, though the coffee was ready to be reaped, much of it was "lost each day due to the negligence or the bad faith of those destined to harvest them." The income was vital, since "the Republic needs funds in this part of its empire in order to subsidize the war it is forced to sustain against its enemies." Coffee cultivation was less labor-intensive than sugar production, and Hugues hoped that this crop could quickly be sold and converted into money for the administration. The coffee beans were hanging on the trees, and all that was needed were hands to pick and process them. But, Hugues declared, "most of the citizens of the countryside have deserted their plantations to take refuge in the city, where, unconcerned about the public good, they wallow in laziness, hide from the public authorities, and give themselves up to all kinds of secret banditry to survive." Several local ordinances that had directed men and women to return to their plantations, furthermore, had failed to end such "disorders." More serious measures were needed. The law therefore summoned those "who usually work during the harvest" to complete the next harvest, adding, in what almost seems an afterthought, "The council unanimously decrees that all citizens not employed for the public good are once again and definitively required to return to the plantations where they previously lived." Those who worked on sugar plantations were ordered to help with the coffee harvests, as were those on both private and state-owned plantations. They would all receive a salary that was "reasonable and proportional to their work," and they would all be punished as counterrevolutionaries if they refused. Hugues understood that the promise of salaries was not enough to entice the formerly enslaved, who had good reasons to be skeptical. Indeed, his fragile administration had little money and would have been hard-pressed to provide any immediate payment to reward those who obeyed his orders and began picking coffee.[23]

Hugues did not follow the Saint-Domingue administrations' path—that of promising the cultivateurs a share of what the plantations produced. This system had the advantage of providing a motivation for the workers, since their gain would be greater the more they produced. It also would have seemed more realistic than Hugues's vague assurance of salaries. Why did Hugues not make the same promise as his Saint-Domingue counterparts? He assumed that force would be sufficient to bring the formerly enslaved back to the plantations and that, given the costs of upholding the army and the administration in general, he simply could not afford to divert any of these valuable commodities to pay the plantation workers.

Unable to fulfill his promise of salaries, Hugues looked to less material forms of encouragement. He sent a document to the state-appointed managers on sequestered plantations, describing how plantation labor should be overseen. At five o'clock, all the cultivateurs were to be woken up and gathered together; they were to be led in singing the "Marseillaise," followed by cries of "Vive la République!" The cultivateurs would then be led to work, "still singing, with that naive and lively happiness that must animate the good child of the nation." The manager was to visit the houses and demand explanations from those who were not working, then determine whether their excuses were legitimate. Working hours were set with specified meal breaks and cessation at dusk. If, "when the good of the plantation requires it," additional work was needed for the mills or for other reasons, the assumption was that all would "work like true Republicans." The managers would report regularly to Hugues and take note of those cultivateurs who were particularly hardworking. A new version of the "Marseillaise" was written with words hailing the Republican war against slavery. It thanked "that infinite being that men adore / Under different names and through different religions" for "shattering the chains of captivity everywhere." "In making man in your image," one of the choruses began, "you made him free like you; / Trying to enslave him / Is therefore to attack the law." With its echoes of the rituals of worship dedicated to the "Supreme Being," which Robespierre sought

23. "Extrait du régistre des délibérations du Conseil général de la commune du Port de la Liberté," 29 Vendémiaire, An III (Oct. 20, 1794), in CAOM, C 7A, 47, 117.

to put into place in metropolitan France, the song's focus on gratitude was meant to inculcate a deference to the Republic that was doing God's will through the benevolent authoritarianism of its representative, Victor Hugues.[24]

How did plantation workers respond to Hugues's directives and the propaganda that went with them? Did they sing his "Marseillaise" or perhaps parody it? Many simply ignored the orders to return to their former homes, whereas others left their plantations altogether. In early March 1795, the frustrated commissioner of Anse-Bertrand, a town near Port de la Liberté, wrote: "No matter what I do to secure all citizens on their respective plantations, nothing works." He noted of the cultivateurs from one plantation: "Yesterday, again, five or six from this plantation left without permission, carrying baggage and weapons and heading for Port de la Liberté or the bourg of Abymes. All of the *ateliers* [work gangs] disperse when we talk to them of work, and each day a considerable number are missing." If Hugues did not give some clue as to how to remedy this situation, the official wrote, soon "all the plantations will be abandoned." A survey of the change in populations on certain plantations between 1793 and 1796 indeed indicates that the period saw a massive exodus by the ex-slaves.[25]

Meanwhile, plantation managers and the formerly enslaved had to negotiate their relationships in a context defined both by emancipation and by the threat of punishment against those who refused to work. There are frustratingly few indications of the reactions and attitudes of the plantation residents during this period. There is, however, some in-

24. Lacour, *Histoire*, II, 384–386. The exact date of the order is unknown, but it probably dates from late 1794. See also Lucien-Réné Abénon, "L'Ordre révolutionnaire sur en Guadeloupe: Travail et liberté, 1794–1802," in Michel L. Martin and Alain Yacou, eds., *De la Révolution française aux révolutions créoles et nègres* (Paris, 1989), 97–104.

25. Commissioner of Anse-Bertrand to president of the Comité de surveillance révolutionnaire, Mar. 22, 1795, in Lacour, *Histoire*, II, 384–386. In Trois-Rivières in 1796, the Duquerey plantation had 75 percent of the working population it had had in 1793, whereas the Gondrecourt plantation had 55 percent. Furthermore, this population actually included new arrivals, probably taken from captured slave ships; see ADG, Jaille 2E3/7, June 14, 18, 1793, in comparison with the 1796 "Etat nominatif des citoyens . . . de Trois-Rivières," in CAOM, G 1, 502, no. 2. A detailed and sustained study of demographic changes in Guadeloupe during the revolutionary period is provided in Fréderic Régent, "Entre esclavage et liberté: Esclaves, libres, et citoyens de couleur en Guadeloupe de 1789 à 1802, une population en Révolution" (Ph.D. diss., Université Paris I, 2002).

dication that they expressed dissatisfaction with the number of days they were expected to work and demanded to be given more free time. In March 1795, Hugues issued a proclamation that declared: "For agricultural work to be pursued with exactitude and perseverance, it is necessary to consecrate certain days to rest and relaxation so that the cultivateurs can recover from their fatigue and recuperate their strength." The practice among different plantations was inconsistent. In some parts of the colony, the cultivateurs had "conserved the habit of keeping their Sundays as days of rest, as was the practice under the ancien régime." Cultivateurs in other areas, however, had adopted the Republican calendar and observed "the *décadi* as a day of rest." In order to unify the practice in different areas, Hugues declared that, throughout the colony, "the cultivateurs attached to the plantations either of the Republic or of individuals will dispose of the *nonedi* for taking care of their personal affairs and of the décadi as a day of rest." This change gave the "free citizens" a means "to provide for their needs and their personal affairs" as well as helped them "forget everything that reminds them of their time of servitude."[26]

The granting of two free days during the ten-day Republican week was an improvement for plantation workers, who now would have more time to work their gardens or travel to market. Though this was a response to complaints, it also might well have been an attempt by Hugues to stop the exodus from the plantations. Still, though Hugues's proclamation asserted the need to erase the past of slavery, his system was in many ways little different from what had come before: the cultivateurs still labored without the promised pay and only had limited time to work for themselves. Hugues, however, proudly defended his policies. He wrote to General Étienne Laveaux in July 1795, criticizing the general's policies, which he claimed had led to a total disintegration of the plantations there. "Saint-Domingue," Hugues wrote immodestly, "only lacked a man of genius and a friend of equality" to do what he had achieved in Guadeloupe: "All the citizens have been treated equally, and they all carry a love of the good, of the nation, and of the work that we have seeded within their hearts; but the lazy of all colors have been punished, for in a laboring society how can we accept that some men live at the expense of others?" As with ineffective or libertine soldiers, Hugues had

26. "Arrêté sur les journées de travail," 23 Ventôse, An III (Mar. 13, 1795), in CAOM, C 7A, 48, 8. The décadi was the tenth day of the week in the Republican calendar and the replacement for Sunday; the nonedi was the ninth day.

The Meaning of Citizenship, 1794–1798

punished "the cultivateur who abandons his work in order to vagabond" about the island. By this measure, he declared, he had managed to pay all the soldiers and the civil servants with the profits that came from the plantations. By using coercion to force plantation laborers to work, he had been able to pay for his battles against the British and to prop up his administration in the colony.[27]

Still, Hugues seemed to have some doubts about the prospects for his regime. Sometime in mid-1795, he sent three commissioners from Guadeloupe to Paris to report on the situation in the colony, hoping they might send or bring back some official guidance for him. Already in December 1794, he had said in frustration that, through the incompetence of the "maritime agents in the ports of Brest and Rochefort," he did not have a complete printed set of laws, "which paralyzes the authorities and makes it impossible for them to organize themselves and forces them to go astray in the most important of matters." How could he represent the Republic in Guadeloupe if he did not have access to its laws?[28]

In the report they presented to Paris's Comité de salut public in August 1795, Hugues's agents reiterated this complaint. "None of the laws emanating from the National Convention was known here, other than the abolition of slavery," they wrote. The authorities, "having no rules to follow, were forced either to stay inactive or to exercise over the citizens an arbitrariness, which is always dangerous." This had led to an impasse in the colony, one in which the transformation from slavery to freedom had been only half achieved. "At the time of the publication of the benevolent decree that welcomed into humankind the precious class of man that had been driven out of it by European greed and Creole vanity," Hugues's representatives wrote, "many plantations—especially those still owned by individuals—were abandoned by the black citizens who were attached to them." "It was," they consented, "natural that men who were used to seeing their sweat and their energy absorbed by a greedy master might, at first, associate the ideas of liberty to those of rest and be swept away by the enthusiasm produced by the spectacle of their broken chains and the fall of their tyrants." The commissioners recounted how Hugues called on the ex-slaves to return to their plantations and reported that he had been for the most part successful in this project, "even though the cultiva-

27. "Les Commissaires délégués . . . au citoyen Etienne Laveaux," 19 Messidor, An III (Jul. 7, 1795), in CAOM, C 7A, 48, 17–18.

28. Hugues to Comité de salut public, 20 Frimaire, An III (Dec. 10, 1794), in CAOM, C 7A, 47, 37.

teurs receive for their labor no indemnity other than the fruit of their own gardens, which they can only cultivate two days per décade." But this lack of a salary was, the report noted, "a huge vice," since it "separated the interest of the cultivateur from that of the propertyowner." With no salary, "the black citizen will always neglect the work of the plantation in order to spend more time working for his garden, which is the only place where he will receive compensation for his pains." It was therefore vital to "combine the two interests, and to attach the cultivateur to the prosperity of the whole plantation, so that he will work harder and with more care for the plantation in the hopes of drawing some advantage from his labor." This was "the opinion of those who are the most devoted to agriculture in the colonies and who have for many years studied the behavior and the character of the blacks." The ex-slaves were "generally good and simple" but "therefore easy to seduce," and it was essential to send intelligent teachers to the colonies so that the "blacks" would learn "to know their rights, to use them with moderation, to defend them with passion." Once properly paid and educated, they would "soon contract the virtuous habits extinguished in them by slavery and barbarism."[29]

The report presented the Comité de salut public with a powerful argument that only through the deployment of free labor could the colony be prosperous. It imagined a transformation of the social relations between propertyowners and laborers, which the collaboration of free labor and just payment would create and which would also uplift and educate the blacks. This was a compelling vision. But, receiving no military or financial support from the metropole, Hugues did not have the resources to apply it in Guadeloupe. Probably in reaction to continued flight and refusal on the part of the ex-slaves, he made some attempts to pay the cultivateurs. On August 28, 1795, with coffee in much of the colony ready to be picked, Hugues issued a new declaration regarding plantation labor. He noted that his administration's "care and surveillance" of plantation work had enabled it to pay for the war it had been fighting for the previous year and that, with the war continuing, making sure the plantations continued to produce their commodities was vital. But, he admitted, the cultivateurs had received no recompense for their work other than "the advantage of seeing the liberty they have been called to consolidated." It was time to enable them to "more efficiently" enjoy this liberty by assur-

29. "Les Envoyés des commissaires délégués aux îles du Vent auprès du Comité de salut public," 22 Thermidor, An III (Aug. 9, 1795), in CAOM, C 7A, 48, 72–76.

The Meaning of Citizenship, 1794–1798

ing them some payment for their work. Seeking once again, as he had in late 1794, to assure that the island's coffee crop would be collected, he promised that those who picked coffee would be paid a "demi-gourde" for each barrel collected. Those who were "attached to cultivation" on the coffee plantations would be supplemented by requisitions among the cultivateurs on sugar plantations. And Hugues also invited other citizens to join in the coffee harvest in return for the task-based salary he proposed. He also promised in the same declaration that "a decision will be made without delay on a proportional salary for those working in the cultivation and fabrication of sugar and cotton."[30]

Hugues had realized that, in order to assure that coffee was picked, he had to offer more than threats and words. But, just as he had put off the payment of salaries he had promised in late 1794, he continued to put off any system of payment to workers on sugar and cotton plantations. Many cultivateurs, therefore, received no more than what they had received during slavery—food, clothing, and the right to cultivate their own plots of land. Still, with emancipation had come change, or at least the promise of change. On plantations throughout the island, ex-slaves, ex-masters, and the new local administrators appointed by Hugues remained in a complex struggle to define exactly what the new freedom should mean.[31]

Life on the Plantations

Traveling in 1799 in Saint-Domingue, Michel-Étienne Descourtilz dined with a planter in the region of Saint-Marc. The planter's property had been taken over by the state and was managed by one of his slaves, who in a startling reversal had granted his ex-master "asylum on his property." The planter—"once opulent, now humiliated by his subjects, suffering their continual and outrageous refusals"—was embarrassed at his inability to provide Descourtilz and the other travelers a decent meal. His request for a glass of milk and some potatoes for his guests was at first refused by his former slaves. This (perhaps exaggerated) picture of a world turned upside down, of ex-masters begging their ex-slaves for food, suggests the profound transformations in daily interactions that followed emancipation in the French Caribbean. The relations between

30. Proclamation of the commissioners, Aug. 28, 1795, printed in Lacour, *Histoire*, II, 393–394.

31. Lacour, *Histoire*, II, 392–394.

ex-masters and ex-slaves, mediated on many levels by the local Republican administration, varied widely, but a picture can be drawn from the broad outlines of the new and contradictory order that took shape on the plantations of Guadeloupe during Hugues's rule.[32]

Following emancipation, plantation production in Guadeloupe dropped substantially, despite Hugues's efforts. Between 1790 and 1799 (the two years for which islandwide statistics exist), the number of sugar plantations decreased from 397 to 363. During the same period, however, the number of small plantations—those growing coffee or cotton— actually increased; there were 787 coffee plantations in 1790 and 1,323 in 1799; and there were 652 cotton plantations in 1790 and 825 in 1799. In a crisis, these smaller and less capital-intensive plantations seem to have been more viable. Yet many of these plantations barely functioned during this period. Between 1790 and 1799, the total surface farmed on the island of Guadeloupe decreased dramatically, from 51,279 hectares to 18,469. Here, cotton was hardest hit, despite the increase in the number of plantations: after a rapid expansion in the 1780s, there were 8,766 hectares in 1790 and only 2,214 in 1799, a drop of 75 percent. Overall production of coffee decreased as well, though not as markedly: the number of hectares dropped from 8,607 in 1790 to 5,281 in 1799 (61 percent). And the amount of land cultivated in sugar decreased from 22,620 hectares in 1790 to 7,288 in 1799 (68 percent). Statistics on the amount of sugar actually produced are difficult to come by because its distribution was not very well controlled, but the available numbers note a drop from 18,300 metric tons of sugar produced in 1784 to only 3,900 in 1799. These calculations probably underestimated the total output on the island because they did not account for commodities that were stolen from plantations and sold in the active underground economy described below. They do, however, suggest that, even as land defined by the administration as coffee and cotton plantations multiplied in number, cultivateurs focused on growing provisions rather than on producing crops for export.[33]

Plantations varied widely between the different regions of the island,

32. Michel-Étienne Descourtilz, *Voyages d'un naturaliste et ses observations* . . . (Paris, 1809), II, 12.

33. See Christian Schnakenbourg, "Statistiques pour l'histoire de l'économie de plantation en Guadeloupe et en Martinique, 1635–1835," *Bulletin de la Société d'histoire de la Guadeloupe*, XXXI (1977), 1–121, esp. 55–57, 87, 107–108. These official statistics did not account for the commodities stolen from plantations and sold in the active underground economy, described below.

particularly between those that were still privately owned and those that had become the property of the nation, where Hugues's regime had complete control. A picture of the profound conflicts that surrounded the new order on state-owned plantations is provided in a 1799 memoir by one of Hugues's former local administrators, the citoyen Jastram. Jastram, though not himself an ex-slave, used a potent metaphor in asserting his independence from Hugues. He believed that "blind and passive obedience is the condition of the slave" and therefore had resisted many of Hugues's orders. Because of this and the fact that Jastram had publicly celebrated when news of the fall of Robespierre reached Guadeloupe, Hugues had accused Jastram of stealing from the state plantations. Jastram was eventually convicted by a military tribunal and briefly imprisoned for having "tolerated stealing on the plantations of the Republic." Jastram's trial and his description of it in his memoir provide a window into the struggles that arose when ex-slaves sought to take advantage of their new roles as plantation laborers and, in some cases, managers.[34]

As a representative for Hugues, Jastram was in charge of selling the productions of the state plantations and was responsible for depositing all the profits into the island's treasury, where they would serve for public expenditures. He hired and fired "all public *fonctionnaires*" and oversaw the sequestration of émigré properties and the appointment of sequestrators to manage them. He was also to "call on the authorities and the armed forces when appropriate for the good and interest of the Republic" and "to keep all suspicious people under surveillance," arresting them and bringing them to Port de la Liberté when necessary. Jastram monitored the activities of the managers, among them a majority of ex-slaves, who essentially ran the plantations. The managers' important economic and administrative role was highlighted by their central place in the trial against Jastram. Whereas before emancipation the testimony of a slave had had no legal weight, Hugues's judges now based their decisions against Jastram heavily on the testimony of ex-slaves; they coaxed

34. "Le Citoyen Jastram, député de la Guadeloupe au Conseil des cinq cents, à ses concitoyens," in AN, AD VII, 21 C, no. 57 (hereafter cited as "Le Citoyen Jastram"). Jastram was elected in Guadeloupe as a representative to the *Conseil des cinq cents*, one of the parliamentary bodies put in place under the Directory regime, in April 1799 and traveled to Paris soon afterward. There, he wrote his memoir on Hugues, who had already been removed from the colony. For his election, see the "Procès verbal de l'assemblée électorale du département de la Guadeloupe," 20 Germinal, An VII (Apr. 9, 1799), in AN, C 577, no. 102. For another attack on Hugues, see AN, C 591, no. 212.

one into testifying by calling him "a black citizen" and "a patriot." The trial also made clear Hugues's profound difficulty in controlling the production and distribution of sugar in the colony of citizens, especially on plantations owned by the Republic. Hugues's plan sought to channel plantation production into the coffers of the state, and this required disciplining the workers' independent economic activities. On state plantations where their masters had since been killed or fled, ex-slaves, often former commandeurs like Jean-Baptiste, the leader of the Trois-Rivières insurrection, had become managers in charge of the state's sugar production. They were therefore also in a position to take control over the underground sale and distribution of the commodity so central to France's colonial project.[35]

By setting up night patrols to police the plantations and visit private warehouses, Jastram caught managers and workers stealing sugar. A number of barrels of sugar were in the warehouse of one "citoyenne" who had purchased them from managers in the area. These included the high-ranking *commissaire de campagne* Marcel and the manager of a sugar plantation in the neighboring commune. Thanks to the denunciation delivered by one citoyenne de couleur, Jastram discovered that another manager had also put aside sugar for his own profit. And Jastram caught and punished one man who, in order to maintain the functioning of his *guildivrerie* (rum distillery), encouraged cultivateurs to steal syrup from their plantations and sell it to him at very low prices. Producing convincing proof that these barrels of sugar had been sold illegally, however, was difficult for Jastram. The delegate called on one barrelmaker named Jean-Charles to identify the origin of the barrels, but he was unable to do so because there was no distinctive sign that identified the sugar as coming from state plantations rather than private ones. When Jastram was under investigation, the judge also called on Jean-Charles as well as other ex-slave barrelmakers. These men, who put distinctive marks on barrels and could also recognize the styles of different artisans, were vital for tracking who bought and sold the state's sugar.[36]

35. "Le Citoyen Jastram," 11–16. In Trois-Rivières in 1796 there were twenty noir managers on national plantations—including Jean-Baptiste; there was also one noir, André, who was the *séquestre* of a small, state-owned coffee plantation ("Etat nominatif des citoyens . . . de Trois-Rivières," 1 Vendémiaire, An V [22 September 1796], in CAOM, G 1, 502).

36. "Le Citoyen Jastram," 13–23. Hugues's successor, Étienne Desfourneaux, would also recognize the importance of being able to identify the origins of bar-

Jastram wrote in 1799 that, if the diversion of products from state plantations was so common and difficult to control, it was because of "these miserable *séquestres* [managers] who for three years had as their only salary nothing but work and more work and, as their only repayment, repeated promises and the violation of the most respectable of property rights—that to one's own work and industry." Hugues was firm in repressing any séquestres who complained about their lack of pay; when one of them did, Hugues stripped him of his functions and shouted in the street, "Any noir or mulâtre may hang him from the first tree." Despite many promises by Hugues, including a memo noting that the question of the sequestres' payment would be resolved, a series of séquestres from Baie-Mahault wrote a petition asking for their pay—and were all imprisoned and deported. Hugues, wrote Jastram, had left these men, "whose labor is the source of the subsistence of the colony, with the cruel choice of either paying themselves or perishing of misery."[37]

Despite their hardships, those who worked on state-owned plantations had at least experienced a change in their daily work relations, and some had achieved positions from which they could exploit the system as never before. But, on many other plantations, the white masters were now managers, still overseeing the labor of their former slaves-turned-cultivateurs. Substantial numbers of ex-slaves had abandoned these private plantations for the army or for the anonymity of the towns. In 1796, for instance, on the coffee plantation of Gabriel Pinau, only two of nineteen of those who had been slaves in 1791 remained. Pinau's widow, Robertine Rabès, noted that her coffee plants were in poor condition and that production was at a standstill. Although Pinau had been one of the staunch Republicans in Trois-Rivières before and after the 1793 insurrection, Hugues's regime had brought his family little advantage—as Rabès suggested pointedly when she noted that it was impossible for her to estimate the value of her land until the Republic's laws clarified the plantation laborers' situation.[38]

According to a 1797 report, the overall level of production on private plantations was 63 percent of what it had been in 1789, and, of

rels of sugar; see "Extrait des régistres de l'agent du directoire executif," in AN, AF III, 208, no. 8.

37. "Le Citoyen Jastram," 20–21.

38. ADG, Serane 2E2/157, 26 Thermidor, An IV (Aug. 13, 1796); CAOM, Notariat Guadeloupe, Barbier, 52, Feb. 28, 1791; "Etat nominatif des citoyens . . . de Trois-Rivières," in CAOM, G 1, 502, no. 2.

704 privately owned plantations in Guadeloupe, 77 had been abandoned "for lack of cultivateurs." When placed in the context of the broader drop in production on the island, however, these statistics highlight the relative success of the privately owned plantations at maintaining the rhythm of production. In the wake of emancipation, then, even as production decreased overall, many ex-masters and ex-slaves throughout the island continued to work and produce commodities as they had before. How had their relationship changed? Was it possible, for instance, for a propertyowner who died to leave his cultivateurs to someone else? These questions were subject to complex negotiations exemplified in the stories of two plantations during this period.[39]

In 1796, a dying planter named Joseph Bourgade of the commune of Pointe-Noire called two friends, Antoine Raymond and Pierre Beaujean, to his bed and asked them to be the executors of his will. Like the administrators of the island, Bourgade was uncertain of the French laws at the time, though he had heard that the National Convention had outlawed testaments. Hoping to avoid having the Republic take over his property, Bourgade maintained the cultivateurs on his plantation as part of the property without ever explicitly mentioning his ownership over them. When he died, Raymond and Beaujean took over, and the cultivateurs were not given any say in the transfer. The larger legal order of equality, however, did make the relationship between workers and owners somewhat different than it might have been under slavery. During the four months that local officials investigated the succession, the plantation was left "under the care and guardianship of the citoyennes Nanou and Anne-Rose." Anne-Rose was Nanou's daughter, and her father might well have been Bourgade himself. Indeed, Bourgade had asked Raymond and Beaujean to give Anne-Rose and Nanou each six thousand livres out of his inheritance and to take over feeding and lodging Anne-Rose and Nanou from the time of his death until his inheritors came to claim his property. Furthermore, Bourgade stipulated that during this time, if the two citoyennes wished to "leave my plantation and live elsewhere," Raymond and Beaujean were to provide them with a pension drawn from the profits of the plantation. The forms of this agreement echoed the provisions for emancipation left in testaments during the time of slavery. Even though Anne-Rose and Nanou, for a time, were assigned management of

39. See the "Etat comparatif par apperçu du produit des habitations des émigrés des différentes communes d'une année commune antérieure à 1789 avec celui de l'An 5," in CAOM, C 7A, 49, 176.

The Meaning of Citizenship, 1794–1798

the property, their right to food and lodging from the property's official administrators was granted by their former owner.[40]

Bourgade left Raymond and Beaujean with instructions to "make the citoyens cultivateurs work, treat them with fraternity, and give them everything the existing authorities grant them." They were to use an unspecified amount of the profits to procure some *douceurs* (comforts) for the cultivateurs and to keep the rest. The notary act that officialized Bourgade's request reiterated that all the property would go to Raymond and Beaujean's care, along with "the administration and conduct of the twenty cultivateurs and their children who live on the said plantation." Among the buildings, twelve *"cazes* [shacks] for the lodging of the citoyens noirs" were forgotten in the main inventory and added in a footnote as an afterthought. Did the cultivateurs own their cazes? Did they have any right to the fruit of their labor? It seems clear that such rights were very contingent. When in 1796 Beaujean and Raymond later rented part of the plantation to Charles Mathieu, who in that year oversaw the gathering of census data in the region, the agreement stipulated that the cultivateurs were allowed to harvest what they had already planted in their gardens but could not plant anything more. Though technically free, they were treated as unfree laborers tied to the land on which they had worked as slaves, and even their own gardens were not left under their control.[41]

So were the cultivateurs property or not? This was an open question that certain planters clearly exploited. In 1797, the members of an established Creole family were forced to address this question when their father died. Nicolas Capbert was a former militia captain who was part of a well-ensconced Creole family in Basse-Terre and owned a coffee plantation on the heights above the town at the Montagne de l'Espérance. At the time of his death, twenty-five cultivateurs lived on the plantation—including one named "Marie Louise dite la Misère"—who were described in an inventory, as had been the case under slavery, as "Creole" or as being of specific African nations. In addition to those actually on the plantation, some who were absent whose names were listed nevertheless were noted for "mémoire," as things with no economic value traditionally were. By marking the names of all those who had once been slaves, including those who were no longer present, the Capbert family was explicitly laying a claim on these bodies that had once been theirs

40. ADG, Serane 2E2/158, 14 Brumaire, An V (Nov. 4, 1796).
41. Ibid.

and that, they suspected, might be theirs once again. By the time the family conflicts were resolved and the division of the property was legalized by a notary in 1798, the reign of Victor Hugues was increasingly coming under attack. Rumors of an indemnity for planters was in the air. The Capberts made even more explicit than before that they wished to maintain legally their potential rights over their cultivateurs:

> As for the cultivateurs, given that the parties have declared that they have no knowledge of what has been done by the laws of the Republic, to which they wish to conform themselves on this subject, they have decided that until these laws are known and proclaimed, the said cultivateurs, except for those who are serving in the army or are dead, will continue to live attached to the cultivation of the said plantation, as they have remained until now under the laws of the existing authorities. However, by this act they expressly reserve all their rights, names, reasons, actions, and pretensions that could result in their favor by the promulgation of new laws for the Republic, whether in terms of an indemnity or otherwise, and to divide equally among them the profit.[42]

In the next years, as talk of a possible reversal of emancipation increased on both sides of the Atlantic, planters prepared for a return to slavery, articulating continuing claims over the human property they had lost through emancipation. Ex-slaves, too, watched for signs of a possible return to the old order, and, as time went on, they prepared to resist the retraction of the citizenship they had gained from the Republic. For, despite the many restrictions and ambiguities of life on the plantations, freedom did bring possibilities for ex-slaves as it transformed emancipation into a powerful weapon of war. Indeed, at the heart of Hugues's regime was a structural contradiction. As Republican administrators and ex-masters sought to maintain the productivity of plantations and control the movement of ex-slaves on the island, they also mobilized large numbers of them in a massive war effort that drew laborers from the plantations and powerfully undermined the social hierarchies that had existed within slavery. Hugues had envisioned a society in which the formerly enslaved would fulfill their Republican duties as both soldiers and cultivateurs. But his recruitment of ex-slaves as soldiers in fact undermined his attempt to rebuild the plantations. Military service and the wartime economy provided opportunities for men and women to leave

42. ADG, Serane 2E2/158, 4 Germinal, An V (Mar. 24, 1797), and 2E2/159, 28 Thermidor, An VI (Aug. 15, 1798).

the plantations and test the boundaries of freedom. As the Capbert family attempted to keep hold over the men and women they had owned for years, their ex-slaves used the networks and the aspirations they had developed within slavery as they left in pursuit of a better life. The movement from the plantation had started early: thirty-year-old Michel "Ibo" and fourteen-year-old Isaac "Congo" had "absented themselves from the plantation" at the time of the British occupation; as the French under Hugues took back the island a few months later, twelve-year-old Benjamin "Congo" and the thirty-year-old "négresse créole" Henriette had also "escaped from the plantation." Five men from the plantation, all Creole, had left and were "employed in the armed forces in the service of the Republic." Two "mulâtres"—who had worked as a cook and a domestic—had been killed in the army. Freedom offered possibility and danger as the troops of the French Republic struck against the British and against slavery, spreading war and insurrection throughout the eastern Caribbean.[43]

43. See ADG, Serane 2E2/158, 4 Germinal, An V (Mar. 24, 1797).

WAR AND EMANCIPATION

In the middle of 1794, as British troops attacked Pointe-à-Pitre in a failed attempt to wrest it from the control of Hugues's Republican troops, a captain leading a troop of grenadiers into the town was severely wounded by an exploding ammunition depot. His "brother officers" pulled off his burning clothes, but his "face and hands were rendered entirely black by the explosion." In the confusion, a group of his own grenadiers, "taking him for one of the French blacks, attacked him with charged bayonets and wounded him in three places before he could make himself known to them. The instant they discovered their mistake they expressed the utmost horror and contrition and brought off this excellent officer in their arms." At the time of this incident, emancipation had only recently been decreed, and the British in the eastern Caribbean had not been confronting ex-slave Republican troops for very long. Yet "blackness" had in some sense become the primary uniform of the French, a military "color" that could incite immediate attack.[1]

A few years before, in 1791, rumors had circulated in Saint-Domingue that there were some whites among the slave insurgents who "have been seen leading them with blackened faces, who were discovered by their hair." At that time, of course, blackness was associated with an insurrection against the very existence of Saint-Domingue, and the idea that whites were participating in the revolt was stunning and execrable to their opponents. By 1794, insurrection had been transformed into military assimilation as part of the Republic's war, and the concept of whites, blacks, and gens de couleur joined together in a struggle for liberty was

1. Cooper Willyams, *An Account of the Campaign in the West Indies, in the Year 1794* . . . (1796; rpt., Basse-Terre, Guadeloupe, 1990), 125. Another British officer, one Lieutenant Colonel Gomm, was not so lucky. A veteran of the "American war," he was killed in the July 2 "storming" of Pointe-à-Pitre. His body probably stayed in Guadeloupe, but his death was commemorated in a tablet erected in the Bath Cathedral at the time of his daughter's death in 1817.

FIGURE 17. "La Liberté des côlon." 1794. Africans are dressed in military uniforms by whites. *Cliché Bibliothèque nationale de France, Paris*

the foundation of France's colonial policy. In a contemporary engraving celebrating the "liberty of the colonies," two black figures dressed in what is intended to be African costume are shown under the heading "Rights of Man." One of the figures has his arm around a uniformed white soldier, and a white woman holds out a similar uniform to another slave. The engraving, with its suggestion that Republican civilization covered up African primitivism, is perhaps a parody and a critique, but it stands for the radical transformation promised by the incorporation of ex-slaves into the military units of the Republic.[2]

2. For the white insurgents in blackface, see "St. Domingo Disturbances," *General Advertiser* (Philadelphia), Oct. 10, 1791; for the engraving—which is generally

During the 1790s, the Caribbean became a central theater in the global conflict that raged between France and Britain. The 1794 French decree of emancipation transformed this conflict into a war over slavery itself. By mobilizing large numbers of ex-slaves into the Republican army, as well as by creating alliances with insurgent slaves on British islands, the French changed the nature and impact of warfare in the region. For a time, these new tactics gave the French a strong military advantage. Although the British had managed to capture both Martinique and Guadeloupe in late 1793 and early 1794, the emancipation decree made it possible for the French to take back Guadeloupe, which became the base for attacks on other islands in the eastern Caribbean. The British soon lost Saint Lucia to Hugues's armies and struggled to defeat insurrections and French incursions into Grenada and Saint Vincent. Though they held Martinique until 1802, their attempt to conquer Saint-Domingue, which began with important victories in 1793, turned into a costly failure. In Saint-Domingue as in the eastern Caribbean, the French fought with locally recruited armies of ex-slaves. The British, meanwhile, sent large and expensive expeditions across the Atlantic to invade Saint-Domingue and counter French advances in Saint Lucia, Saint Vincent, and Grenada. By the end of the 1790s, the British had lost an estimated sixty thousand soldiers to disease and battle in the Caribbean. The campaigns that took place in the region were an essential, though often unacknowledged, part of the global Franco-British conflict.[3]

The French transformation of slaves into citizen-soldiers was not without precedent, of course, since slaves had been incorporated into the military in a variety of situations throughout the eighteenth century. Lord Dunmore's 1775 invitation to the slaves of Virginia to leave their patriot masters and join the British forces ultimately brought twenty-five thousand slaves into military service on both sides of the American Revolution. In fact, throughout the Caribbean, military service had long

---

dated 1791 but which was probably printed in 1794—see Helen Weston, "Representing the Right to Represent: The Portrait of Citizen Belley, Ex-representative of the Colonies, by A. L. Girodet," *Res*, XXVI (Autumn 1994), 83–109, esp. 89.

3. See Michael Duffy, *Soldiers, Sugar, and Seapower: The British Expeditions to the West Indies and the War against Revolutionary France* (Oxford, 1987), for a detailed examination of the British campaigns during the period; see also Michael Craton, *Testing the Chains: Resistance to Slavery in the British West Indies* (Ithaca, N.Y., 1982), chaps. 15, 16; on Saint-Domingue, see David Patrick Geggus, *Slavery, War, and Revolution: The British Occupation of Saint Domingue, 1793–1798* (Oxford, 1982).

been a route for slaves to gain their freedom, since masters could avoid the taxes associated with emancipation by enlisting a slave. In other instances—such as militia regiments in Antigua, as well as more generally on the British islands during the Seven Years' War—slaves were occasionally incorporated into the armed forces without such services' leading to freedom. Military roles were generally restricted for slaves, who often worked as laborers and auxiliaries rather than as soldiers. And in many cases slaves who served in pursuit of their own freedom did so by protecting the slave system, carrying out the policing of other slaves and campaigns against maroons. Nevertheless, the arming of slaves was often controversial. This was especially true when, as in times of crisis and war such as the American Revolution and the 1790s, administrators and officers found it necessary to arm large numbers of slaves. Many whites feared, with good reason, that the presence of men of African descent in the military undermined and threatened racial hierarchy. Indeed, the central role enslaved men played in the British campaigns of the 1790s, and the courage they demonstrated in battle, helped invigorate abolitionist arguments in the early nineteenth century. Still, the leap toward a blanket emancipation of all slaves never became a possibility in the British Caribbean.[4]

In a few historical instances, arming slaves actually led to overturning plantation slavery: during the revolutions in the French Caribbean in 1793 and 1794, in the Spanish colonies during the early-nineteenth-century wars for independence, in the multiple insurrections that led to Cuba's 1898 independence, and with the Emancipation Proclamation of 1863 that helped turn the tide of the American Civil War. Indeed, in 1861, an anonymous pamphlet published in Boston argued that Sonthonax's 1793 actions in Saint-Domingue provided an example that the Union should follow. Although for many the Saint-Domingue insurrection represented fearful barbarism, throughout the antebellum period it inspired abolitionists. By emphasizing that the French Republic had

4. Sylvia R. Frey, *Water from the Rock: Black Resistance in a Revolutionary Age* (Princeton, N.J., 1991); David Barry Gaspar, *Bondmen and Rebels: A Study of Master-Slave Relations in Antigua* (Baltimore, 1985), 119–124; Andrew O'Shaughnessy, *An Empire Divided: The American Revolution and the British Caribbean* (Philadelphia, 2000), 45–46, 174–181; Duffy, "The French Revolution and British Attitudes to the West India Colonies," in Geggus and Gaspar, eds., *A Turbulent Time: The French Revolution and the Greater Caribbean* (Bloomington, Ind., 1997), 78–101; Roger Norman Buckley, *Slaves in Red Coats: The British West India Regiments, 1795–1815* (New Haven, Conn., 1979).

saved its colonies by emancipating and recruiting slaves, the pamphlet made a powerful historical connection that marked the role of black military service in contributing to the destruction of slavery in the Americas.[5]

Throughout Europe as in the Caribbean, the mobilization of citizen-soldier armies was at the heart of the political and social transformations brought about by the revolutionary period of the 1790s. Military service became a crucial arena for the definition and demonstration of citizenship and national loyalty, and the figure of the soldier became the embodiment of a true republicanism that brought virtue, sacrifice, and commitment to the Revolution. The military also provided opportunities for quick social mobility based on performance rather than background. In the French Caribbean, military action had been the vehicle through which slaves had most clearly expressed their demands for citizenship, and it became the vehicle through which the national service demanded of them could be unambiguously combined with the meritocratic advancement touted by Republicans. The post-emancipation recruitment of the formerly enslaved into the army represented a break with the long tradition of arming slaves in the Americas. Rather than promise liberty in return for military service, French administrators, having proclaimed a general emancipation, used military service as a model of what citizenship was to mean in the Caribbean. The creation of soldiers out of slaves served as a template for the complicated work of turning slaves into citizens. Administrators often drew parallels between the work of soldiers in the army and cultivateurs on the plantations, insisting on both as necessary and valued forms of service to the nation. In fact, however, the principles of equality announced by the abolition of slavery were applied more fully in the military than in other realms of post-emancipation society.[6]

5. See the anonymous *Lesson of Santo Domingo: How to Make the War Short and the Peace Righteous* (Boston, 1861), which was first published in the *New York Tribune*. On Cuba, see Ada Ferrer, *Insurgent Cuba: Race, Nation, and Revolution, 1868–1898* (Chapel Hill, N.C., 1999); see also Alfred N. Hunt, *Haiti's Influence on Antebellum America: Slumbering Volcano in the Caribbean* (Baton Rouge, La., 1988); James Theodore Holly and J. Dennis Harris, *Black Separatism and the Caribbean, 1860* (Ann Arbor, Mich., 1970).

6. On the revolutionary armies in France, see Richard Cobb, *The People's Armies* (New Haven, Conn., 1987); see also Lynn Hunt, *The Family Romance of the French Revolution* (Berkeley, Calif., 1992), chap. 3, esp. 68–70. The correlation between military service and republicanism was a common feature of other revolutionary contexts, notably the American Revolution; see Paul A. Rahe, *Repub-*

Military service also provided economic opportunities for soldiers and sailors on the Republican corsairs, who received part of the loot from the captures in which they participated. In Saint-Domingue, military service additionally became a route toward landownership as Toussaint L'Ouverture created a regime in which officers were given abandoned plantations to manage, allowing them in some cases to amass fortunes. This level of economic gain was never made available to the officers of Hugues's Guadeloupe, but the new military order on the island nevertheless transformed the economic and political possibilities of ex-slaves there and throughout the eastern Caribbean.[7]

The Contagious Republic

In 1796, Victor Hugues boasted that noirs made up "seven-eighths of the soldiers, sergeants, and corporals" and "a third of the officers" in his army. "We have nothing but praise for their wisdom," he continued; their presence and their discipline "is the despair of our enemies." At the time, of the approximately 4,600 soldiers in the garrison of Guadeloupe, only 20 percent had arrived from France, and more than 50 percent were ex-slaves. A report from the next year estimated about 3,600 soldiers, with similar proportions of Europeans and ex-slaves. These figures did not include the substantial number of soldiers, both from Guadeloupe and Martinique and from the British islands, who fought in the service of the French Republic elsewhere in the region. There might have been as many as eleven thousand such soldiers at the height of the campaigns, during 1795 and 1796, when for a moment it seemed as if the French Republic were about to gain control of some of the most valuable British colonies in the eastern Caribbean.[8]

lics Ancient and Modern: Classical Republicanism and the American Revolution (Chapel Hill, N.C., 1992).

7. Mats Lundahl, "Toussaint L'Ouverture and the War Economy of Saint-Domingue, 1796–1802," Slavery and Abolition: A Journal of Comparative Studies, VI (1985), 122–138, esp. 130.

8. "Les Commissaires délégués au ministre de la marine et des colonies," 22 Thermidor, An IV (Aug. 9, 1796), in CAOM, C 7A, 49, 43–45; for the numbers of soldiers, see Jacques Adélaïde-Mérlande, Delgrès; ou, La Guadeloupe en 1802 (Paris, 1986), 37–48; Louis-François Tigrane, "Histoire méconnue, histoire oubliée que celle de la Guadeloupe et son armée pendant la période révolutionnaire," Revue historique, DLXXI (1989), 167–186.

Saint Lucia, Grenada, and Saint Vincent all had been settled by French inhabitants during the seventeenth and early eighteenth centuries, and many of these stayed on the islands after they were ceded to the British in 1763, at the end of the Seven Years' War. The presence of French Catholics on these islands posed delicate juridical and social issues, just as it did in Canada. In Grenada during the 1760s and 1770s, local administrators had initiated a unique experiment through which French Catholics were incorporated into the island's juridical and political structures. During the American Revolution, when the French occupied Grenada, they received support from many French residents, including free coloreds serving in the British militia who deserted their posts as the attack came. After the return of the islands to Britain in 1784, many British inhabitants attacked the policies of tolerance toward the French, and hostilities between the two groups increased, culminating in the 1792 retraction of the rights granted to French inhabitants. Grenadian administrators were particularly concerned with the possibility of sedition among the free coloreds, the vast majority of whom were of French extraction. Subject to the racial discrimination common to all the British Caribbean colonies, they were specifically targeted by the local administration in the 1780s. Free coloreds were ordered to provide information about where they lived and proof of their status as free people; regulations outlawed them from holding nighttime meetings without official permission and even limited their freedom to circulate in public. Chafing under such regulations, the free coloreds of Grenada watched intently as the nearby French colonies instituted policies of racial equality. Among them was a man named Julien Fedon, who had probably migrated to Grenada during the occupation by France a decade before and who by 1794 owned a substantial plantation worked by nearly a hundred slaves.[9]

In Saint Vincent, the conflict between British and French inhabitants was made more complicated by the presence of the Black Caribs, who were descended from Caribs and African maroons. During the seventeenth century, although Saint Vincent was in principle a reserve island for the Caribs, small numbers of French settlers began to populate the coast, living and trading with the Black Caribs. One British visitor described in 1723 how he met a Black Carib chief who "spoke excellent

9. O'Shaugnessy, *Empire Divided*, 124–125; Edward L. Cox, *Free Coloreds in the Slave Societies of St. Kitt's and Grenada, 1763–1833* (Knoxville, Tenn., 1984), 80–87.

French and gave answers with the French compliments" and declared that his group was "under the protection of the French." After the cession of Saint Vincent to the British in 1763, the French assisted the Black Caribs as they fought against British settlement. In 1779, the French took over the island, supported by six hundred Black Caribs, and, in the articles of capitulation, the British went to great lengths to restrict the rights of this group. The island was returned to the British in 1783 and remained in their hands for the next decade, and conflicts continued between Black Caribs and settlers who wanted to take over their land. The British proposed numerous plans to defeat the Black Caribs and sell them as slaves, but continued military resistance, maintained with the support of the French, thwarted such plans. An exasperated William Young, publicist and organizer of British settlement on the island, complained in 1795 "that the Charaib will ever be French," noting that many of the Black Caribs had taken on French names: "A spiritual consanguinity was thus vamped up [sic] between Jean Baptiste the Frenchman, and Jean Baptiste the Charaib," with the result that French influence was "deeply rooted." By then, Young was convinced "that the British planters *or* the Black Charaibs, must be removed from off the island of St. Vincent's."[10]

In Saint Lucia, also home to a significant number of French inhabitants, the British confronted a particularly bold pro-French onslaught during the early 1790s. On January 1, 1791, a group of slaves revolted and demanded their freedom, claiming that the Republicans of Martinique had freed their slaves. During 1791 and 1792, a group of French Republicans managed to get control of Saint Lucia, deposing the isolated British governor and his French royalist allies. In 1793, Lacrosse's arrival in the Antilles strengthened the Republicans' position in Saint Lucia. As in Guadeloupe, slaves began mobilizing, deserting plantations in large numbers. In early 1794, the "Great Push"—a massive British military campaign meant to shore up the occupation of Saint-Domingue and roll

10. Philip P. Boucher, *Cannibal Encounters: Europeans and Island Caribs, 1492–1763* (Baltimore, 1992), 31, 106; see also Peter Hulme, *Colonial Encounters: Europe and the Native Caribbean, 1492–1797* (London, 1986), chap. 6; Bryan Edwards, *The History, Civil and Commercial, of the British Colonies in the West Indies* (London, 1793), I, 384–385; "Articles of Capitulation," *St. Vincent Gazette and General Advertiser*, June 19, 1779; Sir William Young, *An Account of the Black Charaibs in the Island of St. Vincent's . . .* (1795; rpt., London, 1971), 17–18, 122–125.

back the alarming advances of the French in the eastern Caribbean—put Saint Lucia, along with Martinique and Guadeloupe, in British hands. Many French Republicans eluded capture, however, escaping to the interior of the island and fighting a guerilla war against the British. A special corps of "Island Rangers" was created to combat these "brigands," but it met with little success. General Grey, the chief of the British occupying force, advocated the deportation of all free coloreds from the island as potential subversives.[11]

By the time of Victor Hugues's arrival in Guadeloupe in June 1794, then, all three British colonies were ripe for insurrection. The French emancipation decree provided the necessary spark, spreading waves of revolt—and paranoia—through the British islands. In early 1795, the British in Saint Vincent, convinced the Black Caribs were mobilizing for an assault, decided to strike preemptively by attacking a group of their chiefs who were gathered at the house of a French woman. The Black Carib leaders fought back successfully, however, and the conflict spread quickly, as slaves on many plantations joined in generalized attacks against the British. Slaves killed one overseer "by inhumanely passing his body between the cylinders of the sugarmill." Soon the island was in the midst of an all-out war in which Black Caribs, local slaves, deserters from the British army, and Republican troops sent from Guadeloupe fought together for control.[12]

It was only the beginning of the problems for the British. In March 1795, a large insurrection exploded among the slaves and gens de couleur in Grenada. Led by the French homme de couleur Julien Fedon, it quickly engulfed the island. Doubting the loyalty of the free coloreds and French whites who composed more than half of the militia on the island, local officials withheld arms from them—and in so doing seriously undermined their own cause. Many whites were killed, and forty prisoners, including the governor, were brought to the insurgents' headquarters. Fedon demanded the surrender of the island's forts and ordered all residents to rally to the French flag. British officials proclaimed martial law and placed a bounty on any insurgent, whether dead or alive, brought in by soldiers or residents. Fedon threatened to kill his prisoners, and

11. Gaspar, "La Guerre des Bois: Revolution, War, and Slavery in Saint Lucia, 1793-1838," in Gaspar and Geggus, eds., *A Turbulent Time*, 102-130; Duffy, *Soldiers, Sugar, and Seapower*, 89-91.

12. Charles Shephard, *An Historical Account of the Island of Saint Vincent* (1831; rpt., London, 1971), 52-63, 101-148.

The Meaning of Citizenship, 1794-1798

the British broke off negotiations with him. Both sides prepared for an extended military campaign.[13]

From Guadeloupe, meanwhile, Hugues issued a declaration of all-out war against the British. They had trampled over the "rights of humanity" by placing a bounty on the heads "of our brave and loyal Republicans" in Grenada and by attacking "our friends and loyal allies the Caribs" in Saint Vincent. "The Carib nation has always had treaties with the French nation, to which it has always been attached," he noted, and he therefore named their chief, the citoyen Duvalay, an officer in the Republican army. He also sent two French representatives to Saint Vincent to join in the attack. All the officers of the Republic "on islands conquered or to conquer" were to "observe the laws of war" and, "in cases where a Republican is intentionally killed," to destroy those who had been responsible, then "erase their name and their memory from the country where the crime was committed."[14]

Hugues also sent an agent to Grenada to publicize this proclamation. Fedon, however, seemed to need little help. Already by the end of March, there were 7,200 people in his camp, including a fighting force of 4,000 to 6,000 slaves and 600 whites and free coloreds. The British forces, meanwhile, included only 500 soldiers and fewer than 400 militiamen. After reinforcements, including troops sent by the Spanish governor of Trinidad, arrived in March 1795, the British mounted an attack against Fedon's camp. They were repulsed, and, as he had threatened, Fedon executed nearly all of his British prisoners, including the governor. The British retreated to the capital of Saint George, where they managed to hold out against Fedon while his troops pillaged and destroyed the abandoned plantations on the rest of the island. Republican calls for emancipation had quickly brought about a complete shift in Grenada's military situation, leaving the British regular soldiers facing a massive and growing army of determined ex-slaves. As a result, the British, too, decided to recruit slaves as soldiers, creating a corps of Black Rangers, who were promised freedom in return for service fighting the insurgents in Grenada and Saint Vincent. Although members of the rangers some-

13. Edward L. Cox, "Fedon's Rebellion, 1795–1796: Causes and Consequences," *Journal of Negro History*, LXVII (1982), 7–19. For a contemporary account of the insurrection, see Gordon Turnbull, *A Narrative of the Revolt and Insurrection of the French Inhabitants in the Island of Grenada* (Edinburgh, 1795).

14. "Les Commissaires délégués . . . arrêté," 11 Germinal, An III (Mar. 31, 1795), in CAOM, C 7A, 48, 10.

times defected to the other side, attracted perhaps by the French promise of universal emancipation, they were crucial in averting a total British defeat on both islands. However, through the middle of 1796, Republicans managed to keep control over much of Grenada.[15]

The greatest victory of the Republican campaign against the British islands came in Saint Lucia, where the French took over and briefly abolished slavery. In the wake of Hugues's June 1794 attack on Guadeloupe, the British in Saint Lucia—still battling the French Republicans entrenched in the center of the island—were, according to General Grey, "ever apprehensive of an Insurrection among the Negroes, in consequence of the Note of Emancipation of the French Government." General Vaughan, who replaced Grey, declared that the best solution to thwart such rebellion would be "to arm and train a regiment of negroes, obtaining men either from the various islands, if the local government would grant them, or if that were not practicable, to import them." He was unable to implement this plan but did deploy the Black Carolina Corps—slaves and free blacks who had fought with the British during the American Revolution—against the insurgents of Saint Lucia, hoping this would stave off insurrection.[16]

In January 1795, Hugues sent a man named Jean-Joseph Lambert on a scouting mission to Saint Lucia. Lambert had been a captain in the National Guard in Saint Lucia in the 1790s and joined the *Gens des bois* before fleeing to Guadeloupe upon the arrival of Hugues. He therefore knew Saint Lucia well and on his scouting mission made contact with French patriots, telling them to prepare to turn against the British occupiers. On Lambert's return, Hugues gave him a commission as a representative of the French Republic and sent him back to organize the war against the British. He made contact with the Gens des bois, who were led by a man named Marinier, and took command of this group of Republicans in order to strengthen their war against the British. In his memoir, Lambert later described how he had announced to the "black citizens" that they were free and how the slaves cried "vive la République" and "fanned out into the countryside, with tears of joy flowing from their eyes." Black citizens from the plantations played vital roles in the conflict with the British, at one point bringing boats owned by local

15. Cox, "Fedon's Rebellion," *Journal of Negro History*, LXVII (1982), 7–19, esp. 8, 13; Shephard, *An Historical Account*, 149–175.

16. Gaspar, "La Guerre des Bois," in Gaspar and Geggus, eds., *A Turbulent Time*, 104–107.

The Meaning of Citizenship, 1794–1798

residents in order to ferry troops to a surprise attack. Slaves in British-held areas heard about the emancipation decree, and increasing numbers ran away from their plantations to join the French. Lambert preached Hugues's doctrine to those ex-slaves on the plantations in the regions under his control. He told "the black cultivateurs" that, since the Republic had given them "one of the greatest gifts, *liberty*," they had to respond with the "love of work" in order to provide sustenance for those who were fighting. It was, he noted, only by producing colonial commodities that they were able to trade with the neutral ships bringing them provisions.[17]

In April, Hugues sent another agent, Commissioner Goyrand, to the island, this time accompanied by soldiers and weapons. Guided by a Saint Lucian slave named Eustache, Goyrand joined up with the insurgents under Lambert's command, and together they managed to secure Republican control. The British made several counterattacks, but they made little progress against the rebels, who rarely committed themselves to large battles and instead continued a low-level harassment from posts scattered throughout the island's inaccessible interior. Meanwhile, the Republican forces continued to expand with slave recruits, growing to nearly six thousand men. In June, a small group of Republicans crying "Vive la République" managed to send the British in a disorderly retreat from their last stronghold on the island. It was an impressive victory that echoed Hugues's success in Guadeloupe, for, as Goyrand described it, 300 volunteers armed with guns, along with 300 pike-toting slaves, had defeated 2,400 British soldiers. The event was "one of the most disgraceful events that ever happened," according to one British witness, "for we had more Regular troops in Garrison there, than the whole Brigand army, and which mostly consisted of Color'd People," and yet the British had retreated precipitously without a shot fired. Saint Lucia was now in the hands of the French Republic.[18]

Pursuing the work Lambert had started, Goyrand set about applying the principles of administration Hugues had developed in Guade-

17. "Mémoire de Jean-Joseph Lambert" (Paris, 1799), in AN, AD VII, 34 A, no. 13, 7, 10, 12.

18. Duffy, *Soldiers, Sugar, and Seapower*, 142; Gaspar, "La Guerre des Bois," in Gaspar and Geggus, eds., *A Turbulent Time*, 108-109; Goyrand, "Dépêche du commissaire de la Convention nationale," 16 Vendémiaire, An IV (Oct. 8, 1795), in CAOM, C 7A, 49, 110; Goyrand, "Compte rendu par le Sr. Goyrand," 6 Thermidor, An VII (Jul. 24, 1799), in CAOM, C 7A, 49, 67-109, esp. 73-74; on Lambert, see the "Etat des mouvements . . . des hommes noirs et de couleur . . . embarqués," in AHAT, X i, carton 80.

loupe to the newly conquered island. Years later, in 1799, he submitted a detailed account of his mission in Saint Lucia to the French government. In the memoir, he described how he had repressed "disorders" in the wake of his 1795 capture of the island by organizing his volunteers into a police force to patrol the towns and arrest anyone found pillaging. "In this way," Goyrand wrote, "order was restored; persons and property were respected," and as a result "the sudden transition from slavery to freedom" went smoothly. The next day Goyrand sent out a proclamation ordering people "of whatever color" on the island to return to their domiciles and to "take up their old occupations." The proclamation, he noted, "was executed with joy in the six municipalities I formed in the colony, whose administrations were composed of brave Africans and hommes de couleur who could read and write." "In this way I proved that everyone would enjoy civil liberty, and political equality, according to the French constitution." The plantations were in terrible shape, noted Goyrand, having "suffered the ravages of the Africans who wished, rightfully, to be free," but he sought to rebuild them. Like Hugues, he confiscated the émigrés' estates and put them under the control of the state, naming inspectors to oversee their functioning. Since Goyrand had no "organic laws," he issued individual orders to the local administrations, who reported to him periodically on events and the "behavior of the Africans." He also toured the municipalities, where he was satisfied with the local administrations and with the "tranquillity and obedience of the African citizens." "I recommended to the mayors to be gentle with them," he wrote, "to keep them under tutelage, like big children, and to attribute their faults to the lack of education and enlightenment." Goyrand also regularly spoke to the ex-slaves. On their day off, he gathered them and "defined in accessible speech civil liberty, political equality, the respect of persons and property required by the law." He assured them that "they would be treated well, if they doubled their love of work, which was the only thing that could consolidate their new existence."[19]

At the time of his triumph in 1795, Goyrand declared, "We have shattered the chains of the Africans in two beautiful colonies, Guadeloupe and Saint Lucia." As Hugues did, Goyrand sought to use this stronghold to continue the expansion of the Republic and its gospel of emancipation. A few months after taking Saint Lucia, he organized "one hundred

19. Goyrand, "Compte rendu," 6 Thermidor, An VII (Jul. 24, 1799), in CAOM, C 7A, 49, 74–77.

Africans who had long taken refuge in the woods and had successfully resisted the British tyranny" into the First Battalion and sent them to Saint Vincent under the command of two Saint Lucians who had been leaders among the insurgents. Two refugees from Martinique brought Goyrand a list of partisans who would fight with him against the British, and he made plans to organize a nucleus of insurrection against what had become the command center for the British campaign in the eastern Caribbean. Elsewhere in the Greater Caribbean, other attempts to spread insurrection were made. In 1795, six black men apparently disembarked in Saint Christopher from a French ship carrying tricolor cocardes to distribute to local slaves in the hopes that this would spark revolt. In the same year, in the Venezuelan port town of Coro, a runaway slave from Curaçao started a large slave rebellion with the aim of creating a republic under French law and free of slavery.[20]

Goyrand later reported of the ex-slaves of Saint Lucia: "These men, who for so long have been oppressed, have a natural sense of justice and injustice." When he wrote this in 1799, emancipation and the mobilization of ex-slaves into the armies of the Republic were increasingly coming under attack from planters and metropolitan officials. These officials, most important among them Napoléon Bonaparte, viewed with distaste the transformation of the Caribbean through the Republican policies of racial equality and imagined that they could restore the colonies to what they had been before 1789. Having overseen the formation of this army and profited from its successes, the French administrators of the late 1790s sought to contain and ultimately reverse the changes they had set in motion. They were in for a rude awakening.[21]

In France as in the Antilles, Republican leaders had created a popular army, idealizing soldiers and encouraging them to think of themselves as active citizens and virtuous defenders of the nation. The campaigns in the Caribbean had created a proud and well-trained army made up primarily of men of African descent who had risked their lives fighting the British and spreading emancipation. The French government would

20. Goyrand, "Dépêche du commissaire," 16 Vendémiaire, An IV (Oct. 8, 1795), "Compte rendu," 6 Thermidor, An VII (Jul. 24, 1799), in CAOM, C 7A, 49, 67–114, esp. 77–80; Julius S. Scott, "Crisscrossing Empires: Ships, Sailors, and Resistance in the Lesser Antilles in the Eighteenth Century," in Robert L. Paquette and Stanley L. Engerman, eds., *The Lesser Antilles in the Age of European Expansion* (Gainesville, Fla., 1996), 128–143, esp. 137.

21. Goyrand, "Compte rendu," 6 Thermidor, An VII (Jul. 24, 1799), in CAOM, C 7A, 49, 77.

find that these Republican veterans of the Antilles were committed to defending their hard-won rights, even if it meant turning against France. Among those who had risen through the ranks in the campaigns in Saint Lucia and fought in Saint Vincent was a free-colored man from Martinique named Louis Delgrès. Another veteran of the Saint Lucia campaign was a man named Palerme, who was perhaps an ex-slave. Within a few years, both of them would use the tactics they had perfected fighting for the Republicans, this time against French troops who had come to reestablish metropolitan control—and ultimately slavery—in Guadeloupe.

Citizen-Soldiers

In 1802, General Antoine Richepance blamed the "ignorance" of the Republican black soldiers for the insurrection he had just defeated. The island of Guadeloupe, he complained, had been "under the influence of an army made up almost entirely of men with no education, who had not been prepared by any principle for the noble profession of the soldier" and "whose passions, needs, and ideas did not go beyond the most vulgar." Several years before, a Guadeloupean planter griped to the minister: "The spirit of license that Hugues has excited and fomented among the blacks against the whites is gaining the strength of habit. The blacks compose almost all of the army, and they take advantage of the rarity of whites, although most of them, or nearly all of them, preserve a certain respect for whites, which is a good sign." The next year he noted that the multiple mutinies among the troops were the result of having only a "small number of whites" in an army "almost completely composed of blacks."[22]

Like the "people's armies," which had been defending France at the time Victor Hugues left for Guadeloupe, the Republican army of the Caribbean was notable for the rapid promotions it provided soldiers of all social classes. Indeed, military service in the Caribbean opened up social mobility beyond that available in metropolitan France, since slaves who had always been kept outside the legal order were now transformed into the ultimate defenders of a new legal order. The army units formed by Hugues in the mid-1790s, furthermore, were racially integrated and

22. For Richepance's proclamation, 25 Messidor, An X (Jul. 14, 1802), see Auguste Lacour, *Histoire de la Guadeloupe*, 4 vols. (Basse-Terre, Guadeloupe, 1855–1858), III, 352–353; Thouluyre Mahé to the minister, 2 Ventôse, An IV (Feb. 21, 1796), "Coup d'oeil," in CAOM, C 7A, 49, 133, 138–143.

The Meaning of Citizenship, 1794–1798

so provided a context for the emergence of new social networks that connected whites and blacks.

Unfortunately, there are few existing sources that provide information about the composition of eastern Caribbean Republican armies. État civil records from the period, however, provide a window into the lives of soldiers and the diversity of the military units in which they served. From such records we can garner details about the Bataillon des sans-culottes, the first Guadeloupean unit formed by Hugues, which was garrisoned in Basse-Terre in 1795. The captains of the companies included Noël Corbet and Pierre Gédéon—two men who would play important roles in the insurrection of 1802—along with a leper named Jean-Baptiste Vulcain. Vulcain had become an officer thanks to a provision, promulgated by Hugues, through which any man who brought more than twenty recruits to join the army would automatically be named a sergeant. Within a few months he had already risen to the rank of captain and commanded both gens de couleur such as Pierre Boudet and ex-slaves such as Thimothé and Jean-Louis. A native of Basse-Terre, Jean-Louis decided to use his newfound right to documentation to marry another ex-slave named Magdelaine, who lived on a local plantation. His comrade Thimothé, as well as another ex-slave who had become part of the town's National Guard, were witnesses at the wedding. During January and February 1795, many other members of the Bataillon des sans-culottes similarly rushed to legitimize long-term relationships, and many appeared with a combination of ex-slave and French metropolitan witnesses. At the wedding of Civil and Jeanne, for instance, the witnesses were Pierre Blondeau and Bangou as well as Civil's captain, Noël Corbet. At the wedding of Gérôme and Christine, the witnesses were Pierre Desfontaine and Jean-François. When Lindon married Frogine, the witnesses were the officers of his company—Jean-Baptiste, the lieutenant, and Chaumont, the sub-lieutenant. Many of these ex-slave soldiers had come to Basse-Terre from other parts of the island, and their partners had followed them, likely contributing to the maintenance of the army. Although groups of ex-slaves had often enlisted together, once they enlisted they developed connections with metropolitan whites. The Bataillon des sans-culottes and the relationships that grew out of it therefore demonstrated potent enaction of the possibilities for social integration embodied in the Republican decree of emancipation.[23]

23. CAOM, EC, Basse-Terre, 6, nos. 4–6, 13, 14; races were not noted in these acts, but I have inferred from the names and other details which soldiers were

As Hugues established himself more firmly in Guadeloupe and began sending missions against the British colonies, the battalions on the island multiplied, with ex-slaves continuing to enlist. The former slave Charles, who joined the army sometime during 1795, was garrisoned in Basse-Terre. He was able to stay close to his companion Léonide and his new-born son Désir, who still lived on the nearby Bisdary plantation, where all three would have been slaves but for the decree of emancipation. By the middle of 1796, one company in the Second Battalion included the "black citizens" Alex Cocu, Joachim, Paul, Charles, and Hypolite —the last two of whom had been born in Africa. Some ex-slaves enlisted in various artillery corps, probably at Fort Saint-Charles, including Étienne, Jean-Pierre, Gilles François, and Pierre. Pierre had a child with an ex-slave named Eugenie, who named it Sans-Culottes.[24]

Many soldiers from Guadeloupe were sent to fight in Saint Lucia and Saint Vincent. When the tide turned against the French in 1796, most of these soldiers were captured by the British and sent to Europe, where they were traded to France in prisoner exchanges. In 1798, these Caribbean veterans were organized into a military unit by the French government. The unit itself was short-lived, but thankfully lists of the soldiers in it have survived to provide us with valuable information. Among the veterans in Saint Lucia and Saint Vincent whose names appear in these documents were a number of ex-slaves from Grande-Terre, including Briste, Guillaume, and Jean-Charles from Sainte-Anne, Félix and Branche d'Or from Moule, Jean-Romain from Gosier, and Philibert Coup d'Air from Sainte-Rose. Hypolite Yeyete, Honoré Ambroise, and Maximin Baugé, who had likely joined the army soon after Hugues took over their hometown of Pointe-à-Pitre, also participated in the attack against the British colonies. Basse-Terre sent Louis Hilaire and Jean Eugène as well as Claude Theodore and Pierre Denis, who had signed the 1793 declaration of the new citizens. Among the Martinicans who fought against the British were also a number of ex-slaves who probably escaped the British-controlled island to find freedom in Guadeloupe after Hugues brought emancipation to the Caribbean. And among local recruits who joined the French in Grenada and Saint Lucia were slaves

---

likely ex-slaves and which were whites—the vast majority of whom had recently arrived from the metropole. On Vulcain, see also Lacour, *Histoire*, II, 314; Cobb, *People's Armies*.

24. CAOM, EC, Basse-Terre, 7, no. 146; 6, nos. 36, 45. For the artillery troops, see EC, Basse-Terre, 6, no. 42; 9, no. 136; 10, nos. 40, 69, 107.

who left their plantations to join the war for emancipation. This was the case in Saint Vincent as well, where the French Republic gained the services of a ten-year-old slave named Augustin Miston. There was, indeed, a startling range of ages among the volunteers who joined the French. One man named Louis Jason, though he was sixty-two years old in 1794, had escaped from the British island of Dominica to join the Republicans. A number of the recruits had been born in Africa and survived the Middle Passage, factors that perhaps shaped their decision to join the armies fighting for emancipation. Remarkably, when they were captured by the British, many—if not all—of the soldiers in the French camp, including a number who had until recently been slaves on the British islands, were treated as prisoners of war and traded back to France. Their enemies respected the status these soldiers had gained by taking up arms in support of the French, which must have provided an important lesson for the veterans. Their experiences of battle, imprisonment, and transatlantic travel certainly gave them new perspectives on the Caribbean societies in which they lived.[25]

The unconventional warfare practiced by the French Republicans in Grenada, Saint Vincent, and particularly Saint Lucia, in which battlefield promotion took on a particular importance, opened up opportunities for such new recruits to rise through the ranks of the army. As he battled the British in Saint Lucia, for instance, Commissioner Goyrand rewarded officers Palerme and Pierre Lebrun with promotions to the rank of captain and also made André Laura a lieutenant and Guillaume Arbousset a sublieutenant. After his victory against the British, Goyrand rewarded at least twelve officers with promotions, making Sainte-Foix and François Xavier lieutenants and Louis Delgrès and Tade Bonny captains. He also appointed Magloire Pélage the head of a battalion, citing "his bravery" and making him one of the highest ranking officers in Saint Lucia. All of these officers could read and write and seem to have been gens de couleur from either Guadeloupe or Saint Lucia. During the remainder of 1795, Goyrand promoted several other officers, including

25. These details are garnered from the two "Etats des mouvements," in AHAT, X i, 80. I discuss the formation of this unit, and the controversy it engendered, in Chapter 10, below. Among the recruits born in Africa were Jean-Louis, François Firmin, Lubin Gaoulé, Augustin Nicolas, Hiacinte, Léonard, Samsine, and Isidor-Fort. Martinican ex-slave recruits included Alou and Romain; Grenadian recruits included Jean-Joseph; and Saint Lucian recruits included Jean Hippolite, Jacques Angélique, Silvestre, Jean-Charles, and Vincent. Their French names suggest that their masters were French residents of the islands.

Jacques Rose de l'Isle, who was literate and would later be reputed as a good instructor for other officers. Among this group were also a number of men who could not read or write, including Lieutenants Saint-Aimé and Martial Joyeux and Sergeant Séraphin, who might well have been former slaves. Séraphin was sent to Saint Lucia from Guadeloupe in October 1795, where soon afterward Goyrand made him a sublieutenant. During the course of 1796, Goyrand promoted another nine officers, such as Captains Marcel and Laurent Daniel, who were also illiterate and perhaps ex-slaves. In addition, Goyrand selected two men who had been leaders of the Republican insurgents before his arrival—Marinier and Jean-Louis Marin Pèdre—to lead the troops he sent to Saint Vincent. Marin Pèdre was a native of Saint Lucia who was either a free colored or a slave before joining the French, and his seventeen-year-old son also joined the Republican army. Once in Saint Vincent, Marin Pèdre—like another of Goyrand's agents on the island, Audibert, and Hugues's agent in Grenada, Josset—began promoting men, making Charles Patience and Joseph Carascot lieutenants. In this way, the power of selecting who would rise through the ranks of the Republican army was transferred to the new officers of African descent.[26]

Of course, military service could carry with it serious costs—and left many recruits from the Antilles permanently crippled. In the unit formed in France in 1798, there were seventy-one who carried serious wounds with them. Many had been maimed by gunshot and cannon and had lost arms, legs, and eyes to battle. But nearly half had been crippled during imprisonment in Europe, having lost toes—sometimes, like the former slaves Pita and Scarpin, all of them—to the frost. Beyond all those who were wounded were those who died in battle or in prisons, to be buried far from home. And then there were those who died of illness, like Claude Theodore of Basse-Terre, who was twenty-two when he was emancipated in 1794 and, after fighting and being captured by the British, died at the age of twenty-seven in a hospital in France.[27]

Soldiers who faced such dangers were justifiably proud of their service to the Republic and were ready to defend the rights they believed such service granted them. One of the benefits was, of course, the sal-

26. "Formation de la compagnie des hommes de couleur," "Etat des officiers des différents grades," "Etat des sous officiers à la suite," all in AHAT, X i, 80; for Séraphin, see CAOM, EC, Basse-Terre, 6, no. 66.

27. "Etat des hommes blessés," "Etat des mouvements" (Claude Thedore), in AHAT, X i, 80.

The Meaning of Citizenship, 1794–1798

aries granted to soldiers and officers, which especially for ex-slaves would have provided economic power. In 1801, when a number of soldiers in Basse-Terre felt that they were being overcharged by local merchants, they did not hesitate to use their social power to confront the injustice. Though the value of the various forms of currency used in Guadeloupe during this period was in principle fixed, merchants often granted less than the official amount. Soldiers demanded the full value of their currency from merchants; when shop owners refused, soldiers sometimes took the amount of merchandise they believed they were entitled to. Fights often ensued in the streets. Conflicts over the value of money coexisted, and were perhaps intertwined, with conflicts that came out of the lack of respect shown by white merchants to black soldiers. After the grenadier Michel fought with the merchant Descombes in the streets of Basse-Terre, officials declared that Descombes had started the fight by saying "things that were infuriating to this grenadier." Perhaps to still the wrath of Michel and other black soldiers who were increasingly angry with the officials of the island, authorities sentenced Descombes to eight days' imprisonment in Fort Saint-Charles. Whatever he said to infuriate Michel—there is a good chance it was a racial slur—he learned that it was dangerous to disrespect a soldier.[28]

The Republican Corsairs

Military service in the armies of the Republic coexisted with another form of potentially lucrative military service: that of the sailors who manned the Republican corsairs. These small, quick ships were specially equipped and manned to capture enemy ships or neutral ships going to enemy islands and bring their confiscated cargo into the nearest French port. Beginning in January 1793, when the National Convention passed a decree inviting citizens to arm corsairs and attack enemy shipping, many French merchants and sailors privateered in the Atlantic, regularly striking at ships coming to and going from British ports. In Bordeaux and Nantes, merchants who had lost much of their colonial business as a result of the Revolution or who could no longer legally outfit slave-trading vessels turned to privateering. In doing so they did not necessarily disregard their previous habits; when they caught slave ships off the coast of Africa, they sold the human cargo in the nearest foreign port

28. Lacour, *Histoire*, III, 231–232; arrest of Descombes, 8 Messidor, An IX (June 27, 1801), in CAOM, C 7A, 55, 62.

and divided the profits among themselves, as they were entitled by the practices of privateering. A 1795 article published in a Nantes newspaper defended those practices by arguing that it was a better fate to be sold as a slave in the Americas than to be returned, free, to a dangerous Africa. Although slavery and slave trading had been outlawed in France, the government seems to have made little effort to punish such actions on the high seas, willing to support privateering against the British even if it meant violating the principles of the 1794 decree of emancipation.[29]

Meanwhile, Hugues turned Guadeloupe into the main base for French privateering in the eastern Caribbean. He began arming corsairs soon after his arrival, and, by late 1795, 25 such ships were operating in the waters around Guadeloupe. Corsairs proliferated in the following years, reaching a peak of 121 by the end of Hugues's regime. Over these four years, 1,800 enemy and merchant vessels suspected of trading with the British were destroyed or captured by corsairs operating out of Guadeloupe.[30]

Manning the corsairs (and sometimes capturing slave-trading vessels) were many ex-slaves. As with the Republican army, there are few records documenting these sailors, though one historian has estimated at 3,500 the number of former slaves working in such a capacity during Hugues's regime. One 1800 crew list for a privateer armed in Cayenne, in French Guiana, included twenty-one men who were listed with only one name and were likely former slaves, along with two men described as "Indians," out of a crew of sixty-one. Since Guiana had a smaller population of slaves than Guadeloupe, the percentage of former slaves on ships armed in Guadeloupe might well have been higher. Other evidence also suggests that men of African descent were a significant presence on these ships. In 1797, a British officer wrote that sailors on the French privateers were "chiefly blacks and Mulattoes." In the same year, a French corsair

29. Eric Saugera, *Bordeaux, port négrier: Chronologie, économie, idéologie, XVIIe–XIXe siècles* (Paris, 1995), 117–122; Yves Bénot, *La Démence coloniale sous Napoléon: Essai* (Paris, 1992), 17.

30. Anne Pérotin-Dumon, *La Ville aux Iles, la ville dans l'île: Basse-Terre et Pointe-à-Pitre, Guadeloupe, 1650–1820* (Paris, 2000), 229; see also H. J. K. Jenkins, "Guadeloupe's Commerce Raiding, 1796–98: Perspectives and Contexts," *Mariner's Mirror*, LXXXIII (1997), 303–309. The captains of the captured ships were given a trial, during which they could present evidence showing they were not guilty of trading with the enemy; not all captures were condemned. The register of these trials from 1794 to 1798, from which Pérotin-Dumon's numbers are drawn, is located in CAOM, C 7A, 48, 80–157.

captain described how, in order to approach a U.S. merchant ship without inciting suspicion, he had hidden all the cocardes and ordered all men of color below deck. Just as the blackened skin of a British officer had incited an attack from his own men in 1794, sailors on the high seas seemingly recognized in a multiracial crew a symbol as clear as the Republican tricolor. If they were captured, meanwhile, ex-slave sailors sometimes found themselves put below deck in chains. When the British managed to capture corsairs, they often sold the blacks on board as slaves rather than treat them as prisoners of war, as they did with white prisoners. In 1795, a court in Barbados denounced the practice, which blatantly disregarded the French abolition of slavery, but it nevertheless continued.[31]

Although, unlike the pirates who had once been a major force in the Caribbean, the corsairs operated with official sanction from the French government, they drew on the style of warfare that had been perfected by earlier outlaws on the high seas. In 1799, after Hugues had been deposed, the new administrators discovered that he had maintained a secret store of weapons specifically for the crews of corsairs. Among them were rifles "cut down to ten or twelve inches" to make *pistolets d'abordage* (boarding guns). In addition, there were bayonets cut in half to make daggers and straps for ammunition boxes turned into belts for swords. The method of warfare was not the only unconventional thing about these corsairs. Although many such ships in Guadeloupe—indeed, the majority between 1794 and 1796—were armed directly by the Republican administration, which therefore drew a direct profit from their plunder, Hugues also granted privateering commissions to individual citizens. In return for the investment such individuals put into their ship and their crews, they gained the right to dispose of the loot. This policy did not require any investment on the part of the state administration, which meanwhile benefited directly from the fees associated with these commissions as well as profited indirectly from the harm inflicted on the British and from the infusion of goods into the economy of Guadeloupe. Hugues's dependence on privateering increased dramatically as time went on, and by the half

31. Louis-François Tigrane, "Histoire méconnue, histoire oubliée que celle de la Guadeloupe et son armée pendant la période révolutionnaire," *Revue historique*, DLXXI (1989), 167–186, esp. 180–181; "Repartition des prises," 9 Brumaire, An VIII, ADGn, X, 16. For the account of the French captain, see Pérotin-Dumon, *La Ville*, 234; on British policies toward captured sailors, see Jenkins, "Slavery and French Privateering in the 1790s," *Mariner's Mirror*, LXXII (1986), 359–360; Jenkins, "The Heydey of French Privateering from Guadeloupe, 1796–98," *Mariner's Mirror*, LXIV (1978), 245–250, esp. 249.

of his reign in Guadeloupe, the vast majority of corsairs operating out of the colony were privately owned. In the year VI, the peak of privateering, there were 114 such ships, as opposed to only 7 armed directly by the Republican administration.[32]

Among the corsair captains were a significant number—according to one estimate, at least fifteen in Guadeloupe between 1793 and 1801—of men of African descent drawn from the class of free coloreds. But most of those who were able to invest in the arming of ships were probably white. Indeed, Hugues himself took advantage of the policies he implemented, investing privately in the arming of at least one corsair, *La Légère*, and entering into a number of deals with merchants involved in privateering. Another resident of Basse-Terre who seems to have amassed a significant fortune either through arming or serving on corsairs was the sailor Joseph Leogane. In 1797, Leogane, a Dominica native married to a descendant of the Caribs of Les Saintes, paid twenty thousand livres for a luxurious house—which included two "boutiques," a separate kitchen, a living room, and an interior courtyard—in Basse-Terre. In 1800, he joined three other sailors in making Marie Dupré from Les Saintes his *procureur* (attorney) to oversee the distribution of property he likely gained from the capture of a ship. Privateers flying the French flag did not necessarily operate out of French colonies, and their crews were drawn in part from the broad international community of sailors present in the Caribbean. In 1795, a visitor to Saint Thomas noted that several privateers were operating out of the Danish island under the French flag, but on their crews were only fifteen to twenty Frenchmen, the rest being Italians and Danes together with sailors he described as "people without a fixed placed of residence."[33]

The exact mechanism through which the loot was distributed to shipowners and crew members probably varied extensively, but in some cases

32. Report of General Pélardy, 18 Vendémiaire, An X (Oct. 10, 1801), in CAOM, C 7A, 5, 209; Pérotin-Dumon, *La Ville*, 229.

33. Pérotin-Dumon, *La Ville*, 235, 242–243. On the ownership of *La Légère*, see ADG, Serane 2E2/157, 13 Fructidor, An IV (Aug. 30, 1796); see also the relationship between Hugues and another wealthy merchant, Barthelemi Salager, in ADG, Bonnet 2E2/41, 8 Thermidor, An VI (Jul. 26, 1798); on Leogane, see ADG, Vauchelet 164/2E2, 7 Thermidor, An V (Jul. 25, 1797), Castet 2E2/208, 30 Fructidor, An VI (Sept. 16, 1798), and 2E2/209, 3 Frimaire, An VIII (Nov. 24, 1799); CAOM, EC, Basse-Terre, 6, no. 2. On Saint Thomas, see Scott, "Crisscrossing Empires," in Paquette and Engerman, eds., *Lesser Antilles*, 128–143, esp. 132.

The Meaning of Citizenship, 1794–1798

it was carefully overseen by the authorities of the state. When in 1800 *La Bergère* captured the *Betsy*, a ship from Salem, Massachusetts, and brought it into Cayenne, the capital of French Guiana, the local tribunal drew up careful accounts noting how much each crew member was to receive from the capture. The profit from the sale of the ship's cargo totaled the impressive sum of 281,147 francs. The private investors who had armed the ship took two-thirds of the profit, leaving the remainder to the crew members, who were rewarded according to their rank. The *matelots* (seamen) received a portion worth about 340 francs; the captain received five times this, and the lowest ranked *mousses* (cabin-boys), such as "Simon, noir," received a half portion. What they owed from the voyage was assiduously subtracted from these sums; Simon might well have wondered whether the sixty-three francs he finally received for his efforts had been worthwhile. Comparatively, Simon was lucky, since, in another case where the *Bergère* participated with two other vessels in a capture, mousses such as Augustin, Armand dit Dejoie, and Salvador were awarded only about twenty francs—before deductions—for their efforts. In these cases the distribution of the loot was carefully overseen by the tribunal of Cayenne, which set aside the portions for those who were "dead or absent" as well as received claims from various parties who were owed money by the sailors; Pistache, Magloire, and Izidor, for instance, all owed the citoyenne Gaulthier of Cayenne for shirts she had made for them.[34]

Even if the spoils were sometimes meager, the corsair trade did create new sources of money for at least some ex-slaves. This wealth benefited not only the sailors themselves but others living in port towns as well: sailors often left before they could receive their share of their ship's latest haul and named citizens of the port towns to collect, in their absence, the amounts due to them. Often, rather than being paid in cash from the proceeds of the sale of the looted cargo, crew members were actually given a portion of the cargo itself. If they were leaving on another journey, they had to contract with others to oversee the receipt and sale of this cargo. After a 1797 capture that was brought into the port of Basse-Terre, the sailors of *La Légère* appointed the merchant Borès to oversee the sales of the plunder and distribute their share back to them. Other sailors, like Joseph Leogane, left women in charge of selling the loot. In 1797 and 1798, two sailors from the corsair *La Prosepine*, Jean-Louis and Louison

34. "Répartition des prises," 15 Messidor, An VIII, 1 Thermidor, An IX, in ADGn, X, 16.

(a Martinican), directed Martine Command to dispose of the booty from their recent captures. In 1798, Janvier Delivré, a black sailor from Saint-Domingue, was aboard the *Bonne Mère* when it captured an American ship. The ship was brought to the harbor of Basse-Terre, but it, and its cargo, had not been sold before Janvier was to leave on another corsair. Having been a prisoner of the British before, and uncertain of his return to Guadeloupe, he placed Lali dite Lacharière, a new citizen of Basse-Terre, in charge of collecting his portion. As a compensation for such services, some sailors declared that, if they died on the seas and did not return, those in charge of their affairs during their absence were to inherit their cut. When François, a Martinican who was also part of the crew of the *Bonne Mère*, found himself on his deathbed in Basse-Terre, he revoked all his previous wills and left everything he owned—his portion of the ship's capture—to Véronique, who was also from Martinique. During the same period, the sailor Saint-Jean from Basse-Terre gave Clairon Cornu, a new citizen of the town, the responsibility of collecting his portion of the captures made by the *Bonaparte* and declared that she would inherit his allotment if he did not return. All these men and women were probably linked by personal liaisons that went beyond these business transactions. Sailors who worked on the corsairs, then, found ways to make sure the wealth they gained from their service supported the economic improvement of friends and family.[35]

Women played important roles in the wartime economy of Guadeloupe, taking advantage of the conflict with the British and exercising economic freedom they had gained with emancipation. But their opportunities for social and economic advancement in the new order were limited by their exclusion from military service. Whereas men could escape the plantations of Guadeloupe through service as soldiers and sailors, this option was closed off to women, most of whom therefore found their rights circumscribed by their status as plantation laborers, whose role was marked by continuities with the regimes of slavery. Military service, in contrast, provided formerly enslaved men with possibilities for both social advancement and political participation that were denied to women. Bearing arms in the service of the nation allowed formerly enslaved men to assert a manhood that had been denied in slavery, and it en-

35. ADG, Serane 2E2/157, 7–28 Fructidor, An IV (Aug. 24.–Sept. 14, 1796); Vauchelet 2E2/164, 7 Nivôse, An VI (Dec. 27, 1797), and 2E2/165, 12 Ventôse, An VI (Mar. 1, 1798); Bonnet 2E2/41, 30 Prairial, 11 Messidor, 11 Thermidor, An VI (June 18, 29, Jul. 29, 1798).

abled free coloreds to counter stereotypes that had characterized them as weak and effeminate. Occupying a role that was consistently celebrated as the epitome of Republican virtue and sacrifice, soldiers and officers were in a position to actively define and reshape the models of citizenship they were defending. Having been, like all the enslaved in the French Caribbean, granted liberty, those who served in the military were also freed in many ways from the social and racial hierarchies of the past.[36]

In early 1795, when the soldier Cazimir married Marie-Noël, they were joined by fellow soldiers Nicholas and Thimothé (a drummer), who served as witnesses. Although all of those present were, it seems, black, only Marie-Noël was marked as such when she was described as a "citoyenne noire." During the same period, when the ex-slave Anastazie married the soldier Pierre Louis Labiche, a native of metropolitan France who had recently arrived in the colony as a grenadier in the army, the only person among the interracial group who was described according to her race was Anastazie's mother, the citoyenne noire Marie. Anastazie's father, who was perhaps white or free colored, was not present at the wedding. In these marriage acts, military service allowed male ex-slaves to escape racial ascription while underscoring the racial difference of certain women. In the past regime of slavery, in Guadeloupe as in other plantation societies, children had inherited the legal status of their mothers. In the Republican regime, women were no longer the bearers of slavery, but they remained in some sense bearers of racial difference. Constrained to the plantations, they were also fixed in ways that male ex-slaves, at least those who served in the military, were not.[37]

Many women militated against the limitations placed on them by Hugues's regime, testing their freedom by insisting on their right to movement and economic independence. In May 1795, on the Champ

36. On the importance of military service for free-colored men in Saint-Domingue, see John David Garrigus, "Redrawing the Colour Line: Gender and the Social Construction of Race in Pre-revolutionary Haiti," *Journal of Caribbean History*, XXX, nos. 1, 2 (1996), 28–50. For an examination of women's exclusion through the construction of an ideal of citizen-soldiers in the American Revolution, see Linda K. Kerber, "'May All Our Citizens Be Soldiers, and All Our Soldiers Citizens': The Ambiguities of Female Citizenship in the New Nation," in Joan R. Challinor and Robert L. Beisner, eds., *Arms at Rest: Peacemaking and Peacekeeping in American History* (New York, 1987), 1–21.

37. See CAOM, EC, Basse-Terre, 6, 6 Ventôse, 6 Germinal, An III (Feb. 24, Mar. 26, 1795), no. 30. I examine the complexities of racial terminology in post-emancipation Guadeloupe in Chapter 9, below.

d'Arbaud—the park at the center of Basse-Terre—Hugues's officials stopped "a mass of citoyennes who were watching the troops march." Another group of thirty women was found the same day in Fort Saint-Charles, having followed a battalion of soldiers who had recently been transferred from Port de la Liberté. By watching and mingling with Republican troops as well as by living among them, as some partners of soldiers probably did, women took part in a sphere of citizenship that was, in principle, closed to them. Indeed, administrators saw their presence as a threat. They were all brought back to their respective plantations, which they once again immediately abandoned. Some women also insisted on their right to choose the kinds of work they were to do. Former domestic slaves, for instance, protested demands that they work in the fields. Hugues explicitly responded to this claim in an April 1795 circular to the mayors of the towns, in which he declared that there was "a class of citoyennes" who were not following the principle that all individuals, especially Republicans, owed their work to the society of which they were members. "The citoyennes noires living on the plantations refuse to work the land on the pretext that they were formerly only employed in purely domestic occupations." If these women insisted on this refusal and continued to "model themselves on their nonchalant and lazy mistresses," they were to be deported to Saint Martin or Désirade (a prison island and leper colony) to "receive the treatment they deserve."[38]

Although women were not granted many of the basic rights they expected from emancipation, they were able to take advantage of the newly available forms of documentation as they sought to solidify and expand their economic freedom. Building on practices of resistance developed within slavery, women struggled to maintain family ties, secure their hold over property, and guarantee its transfer to the next generation. The documents through which they did so provide a window into the ways in which new citizens used their rights to change their communities. While armies of ex-slaves spread the gospel of Republican rights to other islands in the eastern Caribbean, in Guadeloupe a different kind of struggle over the meaning of rights was under way.

38. Lacour, *Histoire*, II, 391–392.

Chapter 9

THE MARK OF FREEDOM

In December 1783, the holy father of the Capuchin order at Basse-Terre granted three women a ninety-nine-year lease on land bordering his monastery. Marie-Anne, a métisse libre, organized the contract and took the largest portion of land for herself. The two other women, Fatime and Hedezie, both nègresses libres, received slightly smaller portions of land. At the time, Hedezie was still a slave, though she was to be freed "at any moment," so Fatime stood in for her as the actual subject of the act, which stipulated that Hedezie would gain her right to the land once her master officially declared her freedom. The properties lay along a path that led from the Rue du Sable, one of the main roads of Basse-Terre, down to the Rivière aux Herbes, one of two rivers that cut through the town. To the south and west were lands designated to become the garden for the Capuchin house, and the three women were obligated to build a wall between their property and that used by the monks. The women were also required to build houses on the property and to maintain them in good condition throughout the term of their lease.[1]

Marie-Anne, Fatime, and Hedezie were not the only women to gain rights over the land bordering the Capuchin house. In 1785, the nègresse libre Marie-Françoise, wife of Benoit, nègre libre, rented a nearby portion of land. In 1787, another nègresse libre, Françoise dite Gripon, took over the rent granted a few months earlier by the Capuchins on a neighboring piece of land. In 1791, she granted this land to her two sons, François Gripon and Louis Gripon. Both were tailors, and, unlike their mother, they could write. When they took over the land, she kept part of the property in the back, leaving the facade to them—perhaps so that they could create a workshop on what was an increasingly well-used path. Altogether, during the 1780s, the Capuchins gave five portions of land, possibly more, to freed women of Basse-Terre. Though the Capu-

1. CAOM, Notariat Guadeloupe, Mimerel, 2099, Dec. 13, 1783.

chins' intentions are unclear, their actions helped create a new neighborhood in Basse-Terre. In the vicinity, which was not too far from the commercial center, freed women created a foothold and a foundation for the social and economic improvement of themselves and their families. This may be why the area is still called "Petite Guinée" by some in Basse-Terre today. Out of leases ultimately came permanence; the presence of these women's descendants on the land outlasted the Capuchin house itself. In 1793, a decade after the first leases were signed, the Capuchin landholdings were liquidated, and the ninety-nine-year leases became de facto ownership.[2]

In that same year, both of Françoise dite Gripon's sons, as well as Hypolite Debort, the son of her neighbor Marie-Anne, signed the "Adresse des nouveaux citoyens." François Gripon also became a member of the Commission générale extraordinaire of the island, and Hypolite Debort continued his political activity by signing the 1794 call for the levy of slave troops. Hypolite used the name of his father, the white merchant Pierre Debort, in signing these documents. His mother eventually followed suit; although she had simply presented herself as Marie-Anne at the time she rented her land in 1783, when she sold it for a handsome profit in 1799 she called herself Marie-Anne Debort. She also demonstrated one aspect of the social improvement she had gone through in the intervening years: she signed her name.[3]

Marie-Anne died in 1799, just before her daughter Sophie-Angélique

2. For Marie-Françoise, see ADG, Castet 2E2/202, Jan. 15, 1793, in which her husband ceded the land; for the Gripon family, see CAOM, Notariat Guadeloupe, Barbier, 52, Oct. 22, 1791; on the liquidation of the Capuchin properties in Basse-Terre, see CAOM, C 7A, 45, 99. See also Anne Pérotin-Dumon, *La Ville aux Iles, la ville dans l'île: Basse-Terre et Pointe-à-Pitre, Guadeloupe, 1650–1820* (Paris, 2000), 481–482. The Capuchins were not the only religious group to rent land to women of color; in 1789, the Religieux de la charité granted one woman the right to live on a parcel of land neighboring their convent for the rest of her life. See "Copie des actes et des délibérations du gouvernement," in CAOM, C 7A, 58, 52–127, esp. 99–100.

3. For the "Adresse," see CAOM, C 7A, 46, 190–191; for François Gripon's political involvement, see also AN, AD VII, 21 C, nos. 33, 44. For Hypolite's political career, see CAOM, C 7A, 46, 190–191; AN, AD VII, 21 C, no. 46, discussed in Part I, above. Hypolite was present years later at Gripon's wedding; see ADG, Vauchelet 2E2/166, 11 Pluviôse, An VII (Jan. 30, 1799). Pierre Debort left two of his daughters an inheritance in the form of a slave when he died; see CAOM, Notariat Guadeloupe, Barbier, 53, Nov. 18, 1791. For Marie-Anne's sale of the land, see ADG, Bonnet 2E2/41, 29 Germinal, An VII (Apr. 18, 1799).

Debort married a tailor from France. One of those present at the wedding was Marie-Anne's old neighbor, Jean-Baptiste Seignoret, who had served as a public official in Basse-Terre and who had recently augmented his library with a series of books, including the works of Rousseau and *L'Esprit de l'Abbé Raynal (The Spirit of the Abbé Raynal)*. Seignoret, then, seems to have been familiar with some of the antislavery currents of Enlightenment thought. Indeed, the spirit of the Abbé Raynal—or at least that of Dénis Diderot, who wrote the famous passages in Raynal's history of European colonialism—would probably have been pleased at Seignoret's involvement in Sophie-Angélique's wedding, where the participants carried out to its fullest the vision of a body of citizens undivided by racial distinctions. Although the wedding brought together some who in previous times would have been described as "métisse" and others whose "natural" whiteness had required no racial ascription, no one was described according to race. During the service, Sophie-Angélique referred to her deceased mother as Marie-Anne Bourseau. Though where the name Bourseau came from is impossible to track—it was used by a white family in Trois-Rivières as well as others in the region of Basse-Terre—Sophie-Angélique's use of what was likely her mother's unacknowledged maiden name represents a significant claim to legitimacy and equality. In using this name, the daughter documented her mother's ancestry and registered it officially.[4]

She was among many who took advantage of the new racial equality to publicly declare family histories that had previously been hidden. Another example is the 1799 wedding of the ex-slaves Jean-Baptiste and Luce. Jean-Baptiste was the son of Magdeleine and Pierre Angeron, a local white merchant who, in 1792, oversaw the sale of nearly three hundred slaves brought by a trader to Basse-Terre. Luce was the daughter of Felicité and Louis Laflute, who had likely been Felicité's former master. Neither Luce nor Jean-Baptiste took on the last name of a father. Sev-

4. For the wedding, see CAOM, Notariat Guadeloupe, Dupuch, 902, 4 Floréal, An VII (Apr. 23, 1799). On Seignoret's position as the *agent national* of Basse-Terre, see ADG, Serane 2E2/159, 3 Vendémiaire, An VI (Oct. 16, 1797); for his book purchase, see ADG, Serane 2E2/158, 25 Ventôse, An V (Mar. 14, 1797). For the white Bourseau family in Trois-Rivières, see CAOM, Notariat Guadeloupe, Barbier, 52, May 2, 1791; "Etat nominatif des citoyens . . . de Trois-Rivières," in CAOM, G 1, 502. See also the documents pertaining to Martine dite Bourseau, who married the mulâtre libre Joseph Guillard—who like Hypolite Debort signed the 1794 slave troop petition—in ADG, Vauchelet, 164, 2E2, 21 Brumaire, An VI (Nov. 11, 1797).

eral years earlier, the ex-slave Anastazie publicly declared at her wedding that her father was Charles Auffray, the first husband of her ex-master's wife. She, too, did not use her father's name as her own. The contrast between these ex-slaves' decisions and the story of Marie-Anne's daughter highlights the complicated decisions individuals made in embracing or rejecting a certain paternity.[5]

The elision of racial descriptions in official documents was not a uniform policy in post-emancipation Guadeloupe. Individual notaries seem to have taken different approaches to the vexing problem of marking race in a society that was meant to assure racial equality. The notary Elie Dupuch, who drew up Sophie-Angélique Debort's wedding document, consistently avoided the use of racial markers in his acts. In 1799, for instance, when François Gripon was a witness at the wedding of Jean-Baptiste Duparquet and Anne-Nanette, none in the diverse group of participants, including former slaves and white soldiers, was described according to race. This was probably an ideological stance—Dupuch, a committed Republican in Basse-Terre during the early 1790s, was elected to represent the Antilles in October 1792 and became a committed Jacobin in the National Convention; in 1798, he was part of the Société des amis des noirs in Paris. He even maintained a policy of drawing up notary documents for certain ex-slaves, including the participants of the Duparquet wedding, free of charge. Yet not all representatives of the state followed Dupuch's assiduous application of such principles. Other notaries often included racial markers either for all involved or for certain individuals, thereby illustrating the complicated intersection of racial identification with other social categories.[6]

The creation of état civil and notary records became a terrain where previous forms of social silencing and racial identification were contested and negotiated, as many ex-slaves participated in wedding, birth, and death declarations. In a society where racial difference was at once being

5. See CAOM, Notariat Guadeloupe, Dupuch, 902, 21 Prairial, An VII (June 9, 1799); on Angeron's slave trading, see ADG, Castet 2E2/208, Feb. 28, 1792, May 31, 1792; for Anastazie, see CAOM, EC, Basse-Terre, 6, no. 30, 6 Germinal, An III (Mar. 26, 1795). Auffray had been deported by the English in 1794 and seems not to have returned; see "Le Patriotes déportés de la Guadeloupe," 20 Brumaire, An III (Nov. 10, 1794), in AN, AD VII, 21 C, no. 54.

6. See CAOM, Notariat Guadeloupe, Dupuch, 902, 23 Prairial, An VII (June 11, 1799); on Dupuch's political career, see Marcel Dorigny and Bernard Gainot, *La Société des amis des noirs, 1788–1799: Contribution à l'histoire de l'abolition de l'esclavage* (Paris, 1998), 344.

erased and reinscribed, the naming of race was at the heart of the shaping of the post-emancipation order, which was forged in part through these very documents. In the wake of freedom, many gens de couleur developed new connections and solidarities with ex-slaves, whereas others marked their difference, using their history of freedom as a social distinction. At the same time, some new forms of naming began to appear in the documents, such as "de la Côte" ("from the coast of Africa"), which described the origin of many ex-slaves in Guadeloupe. It is hard to determine exactly how the use of this particular term emerged. Although it could have been self-applied by certain African-born individuals, it also might have been used by local officials to mark race in a new way, one that pointed to the difference of the African-born by referring to place of origin rather than color. Over time, however, the term, along with other variants of the descriptor "African," was embraced by former slaves in Guadeloupe. Such new methods of naming were part of a move by many new citizens to cement links of kinship and ownership over land and property through documentation. Even as formerly enslaved individuals sought, through those practices, to overcome the effects of racist subordination they had experienced in the past, however, Hugues's administration governed on the basis of social distinctions that depended on racial hierarchies. Indeed, his regime initiated a massive census project that demanded the explicit categorization of the island's population according to race.

The documents produced out of a struggle over the meaning of freedom highlight the continuities between before and after emancipation. Older histories of resistance, through which towns such as Basse-Terre had been shaped, formed the foundation for the new demands of freedom. Though Hugues, drawing on abolitionist thinking, saw the period of slavery as one in which slaves had lost all notion of their rights, the actions of the Guadeloupean ex-slaves show that their experience of slavery and resistance provided them with a foundation for pursuing the vision of liberty once they were free. Ultimately, by mobilizing their new rights, they helped transform the island in ways that outlasted their short-lived time of freedom.

African Citizens

In April 1794, just after the British occupied Guadeloupe, Jean Hubert, the manager of a sugar plantation in Baillif, bought two slaves from the owner of the plantation. The next day, he drew up an act of emancipation for the two slaves, Jeannette, a nègresse, and her five-year-old daughter Nina, a *câpresse*. Two years later, Jean Hubert married Jeannette and declared that Nina, as well as her two older sisters, was his child. Though he worked as a sugar refiner at the time of his wedding, by the next year he had amassed enough money to rent some land for his own use in Baillif and Basse-Terre. He was clearly an important person, for the two witnesses at his wedding were the prominent gens de couleur Canut Robinson, a municipal officer, and Jean-Georges, a wealthy tailor. In what was perhaps an assertion of Hubert's prominence and of the difference between his family and those who had been freed by the 1794 decree, the wedding act used the racial designation *câpresse* for Hubert's daughter, maintaining a term based on racial hierarchies that by then had in principle been abandoned. Yet Hubert's actions, first in freeing Jeannette and then in legitimizing their relationship and so assuring his daughters' inheritance of his property, were part of the larger movement through which the ex-slaves of Guadeloupe took advantage of their new rights to documentation.[7]

During the era of freedom, as many ex-slaves migrated from the plantations to the cities, another form of migration occurred: that of new citizens into the état civil registers, which were kept by the local administration to keep track of births, deaths, and marriages in the community. Although in the ancien régime some parishes had recorded slave baptisms and, occasionally, marriages, these records were kept in separate registers only for slaves. Furthermore, the master's permission was generally required for such ceremonies. In the new order, all people had an equal right to legal documentation, and the distinctions between categories of people were eliminated. One of the major privileges that previously had been accessible only to the free—the right to draw up notary documents such as wills, marriage contracts, or property transfers—became available to ex-slaves, although the costs associated with hiring a notary made this opportunity inaccessible to most of them. Having a birth, marriage, or death recorded in the état civil, in contrast, was free; it was also required. Both of these factors likely played a role in encouraging large numbers of ex-slaves to make the effort to be registered. Pre-

7. See the emancipation act in ADG, Vauchelet 2E2/163, Apr. 16, 1794, and the wedding in CAOM, EC, Basse-Terre, 6, no. 16. For Hubert's rented land, see ADG, Vauchelet 2E2/166, 16 Germinal, An VII (Apr. 5, 1799), 15 Brumaire, An VII (Nov. 5, 1798). The terms *câpre* and *câpresse* were used to describe the child of a mulâtre and a nègre.

cisely what motivated them is obviously difficult to know, but ex-slaves had many reasons to participate actively in the forms of legal documentation that were made available to them. Having had firsthand experience of the costs of exclusion from legal recourse, the formerly enslaved probably well understood its value as a mechanism for asserting and preserving their rights. They saw that being legally married and declaring and legitimizing one's children could help solidify a family's new, and fragile, hold on property. Registering births and marriages was also a way of asserting another fragile right: the right to liberty itself. The recently freed presumably did not take their freedom for granted and turned to the very system that had once been used to deny them their rights—the law—in building a legal bulwark to bolster their freedom and protect it should it ever come under attack. Ex-slaves' large-scale use of the right to documentation is a testament both to their comprehension of the social rituals of citizenship and their determination to keep hold of the rights they had won.[8]

Legal documentation in the colonies had always depended on the standard of whiteness. Those who deviated from this norm—whether freed people of African descent or slaves—had their races noted in documents. Yet this assumption of whiteness was undermined, at least for a while, with the onset of emancipation. After the arrival of the Hugues mission in Pointe-à-Pitre, while Basse-Terre was still under the control of the British, local officials there sporadically introduced a new form of racial categorization in certain état civil records. In late July 1794, the father of twins born in Basse-Terre was described as "European." On the same day, a man from Marseilles was described as "European," though his wife, also from Marseilles, was not. The next week, "European" was applied to both members of a married couple. Local officials were likely responding to the legal confusion in the colony, particularly the imminent arrival of emancipation, by reaching for terms that designated racial difference without depending on references to skin color itself. The experiment might also have been an attempt to mark the difference between locally born, or Creole, whites and those who had been born in or recently arrived from France. Soon, however, the use of the term faded, and women who had been born in Europe were buried without such designation. In one baptism, the mother was described, as had been the tradition within slavery, as a "femme de couleur libre." So, despite the appearance

8. On slave baptisms and weddings, see Gabriel Debien, *Les Esclaves des Antilles françaises* (Basse-Terre, Guadeloupe, 1974), chap. 14, esp. 268.

of the new description "European" during a two-week period, it ultimately disappeared for the most part—although in 1794 one child was
described as "white," and, in the 1796 census of Basse-Terre, one manager of a private plantation was labeled as "European." As the policies
of emancipation settled on the island, some of the old habits returned,
and whites regained the privilege of being raceless in the documents.
Yet these documents make clear that the advent—or the threat—of an
order of racial equality challenged the documentary forms that had previously existed and pushed local officials to experiment with new kinds
of designations. Of course, racial terms had always been fluid, both on
the individual level for prerevolutionary gens de couleur who sometimes
escaped racial identifiers and on the level of censuses whose racial terminology changed over the years. But the post-emancipation use of new
racial designations was the beginning of a long series of experiments
through which, during the next years, the legal representatives of the
state and those who registered themselves with them collaborated in the
creation of new terms of racial ascription.[9]

The term *noir* was first used in the post-emancipation Basse-Terre
état civil to describe two female plantation laborers named Marie and
Marie-Noël. As I mentioned in the previous chapter, they were listed as
such in wedding acts in which several black soldiers were given no racial
designations. *Noir* became shorthand to identify plantation laborers in
a context where other ex-slaves who were skilled craftsmen or served
the Republic as soldiers tended to be left free of any racial description.
By 1795–1796, the use of racial terminology in the état civil had spread
more randomly to people in a variety of social situations, although *noir*
continued to be applied most commonly to plantation workers. The use
of racial markers did not, however, become completely consistent. Although the terms *noir, blanc,* and *de couleur* were the most commonly

9. See CAOM, EC, Basse-Terre, 5, cahier 5, 51–60, Jul. 28–Aug. 12, 1794. The
use of the term "European" did not correlate to any particular class status; among
those who were not marked as Europeans were military officers and merchants as
well as a woman who, in baptizing her child, could not declare the father's name
and could not sign. For the white child, see EC, Basse-Terre, 7, no. 27; for the census, see the 1796 "Etat nominatif . . . de Basse-Terre," in CAOM, G 1, 500, no. 5.
Before emancipation, the état civil highlighted the difference between whites and
gens de couleur by the use of terms such as "sieur" or "madame" only for whites
and the use of terms such as "le nommé"—"so-called"—before the last names of
gens de couleur; see Yvan Debbasch, *Couleur et liberté: Le Jeu de critère ethnique
dans un ordre juridique esclavagiste* (Paris, 1967), 71.

used, terms such as *mulâtre, métis*, and *câpresse* also sporadically appeared. And whites, though they were involved in a large portion of the acts, were still rarely given a racial marker. Gens de couleur found ways of distinguishing themselves from those freed in 1794 not only through the use of old racial terms such as *câpre* but through the new term "free before the decree." The new designation *de la Côte* appeared and solidified.[10]

Through the ritual of inscription, ex-slaves joined whites in being registered as citizens rather than as objects, as individuals whose gender, name, and age were documented and filed away in the offices of the local administration. Deploying the symbolic power of the trips to the municipal offices, in which social existence was documented, names and filiations were written down, was a key assertion of citizenship. Inequalities remained between those who could sign and those who could not, between those who could mobilize well-respected witnesses and those who could not. Yet even the most marginalized in the society, the cultivateurs of the plantations, actively used and reshaped documentation, in particular the registration of births.

10. In the Basse-Terre birth registers from the year IV (1796–1797), I have calculated that approximately 70 percent of the acts involved ex-slaves. In the death registers from the year III (1795–1796), approximately 42 percent of the acts involved ex-slaves; in the first half of the year IV, 54 percent involved ex-slaves, whereas in the second half the percentage dropped to 45 percent. Not all ex-slaves were described as "noir," so these approximate figures depend on the assumption that those who presented themselves with only a first name were ex-slaves. Of 177 birth acts registered in 1795–1796, 66 percent involved racial ascriptions of one kind or another (for example, *noir, de couleur, câpre*, etc.): 54 percent of these involved persons described as "noir," and 11 percent involved people described either as "de couleur" or with similar terms. Of 155 deceased, 68 (43 percent) were given a racial ascription. Of these, 36 were described as "noir," 21 as "de couleur" and 5 with similar terms, and 6 as "blancs." By the first half of year IV, 48 percent of 150 deaths registered involved people who were given racial ascriptions, but none of these were whites; 39 percent were marked "noirs," and 10 percent were described as "de couleur." In a register of deaths for the second half of the year IV, 51 percent of 197 acts involved people who were given racial ascriptions, and once again none of these was white. Thirty-six percent were "noir," and 16 percent were "de couleur" (or similar terms). For the data above, see "Naissances An 4," "Décès An 3," "Décès An 4," all in CAOM, EC, Basse-Terre, 9–10. For examples of the use of the term "free before the decree," see the 1796 weddings in CAOM, EC, Basse-Terre, 6, nos. 26, 29, 34; see also the 1797 birth decree in CAOM, EC, Basse-Terre, 10, no. 332.

The Mark of Freedom

During the course of 1797 and 1798, a series of workers from the Lasalle plantation, which was located on the hills above Basse-Terre, traveled to the town to declare the births of various children. Often groups of men and women from the plantations traveled there together, declaring several births on the same occasion. Following the traditional forms of godparenting, two people, sometimes a man and a woman, sometimes two women, always made the presentation. Whereas the older children generally had names, some of the younger children did not and were noted simply as "Ursule's child" or "Véronique's child." Where did the volition for traveling to Basse-Terre to make such declarations come from? Did the manager of the plantation send the laborers, or was it something that they decided to do on their own? The manager of the Lasalle plantation was never present at these occasions, and race was never mentioned in these acts. The decision on the part of Lasalle's cultivateurs to declare the births of children spawned a broader move on the plantations, so that after the initial declarations all of the plantation's recent mothers took the trip to Basse-Terre. The decision to register the births of the children seems to have come from the laborers themselves; it may well have been an expression of their desire to show that the children were citizens rather than property.[11]

A series of fascinating baptisms that took place between 1797 and 1799 demonstrates the significance of registration in the état civil for plantation workers. In 1795, the recently married Sophie Mondésir and Fabien Bellair, a twenty-two-year-old policeman in Basse-Terre, presented to the municipal officer of Basse-Terre "a little girl who is a native of Guinée and who has recently arrived in this colony." Acting just as new parents did in the register's other birth declarations, they gave her a new name—Zaide. As usual, the municipal officer "exhorted" Sophie and Fabien on their obligations toward the child. No other acts of this kind appeared for almost two years, but from December 1796 into 1798 they became almost standard as forty-six new arrivals from Africa were given French names, sometimes by plantation managers but more often by a variety of ex-slaves who were soldiers, cultivateurs, or residents of Basse-Terre.[12]

These new arrivals were men and women captured on slave ships by French corsairs and brought to Guadeloupe as free men and women.

11. See the acts from November and December 1797, in CAOM, EC, Basse-Terre, 11, nos. 28, 29, 39, 40, 43–45, 48, 49.

12. The act, from March 1795, is in CAOM, EC, Basse-Terre, 7, no. 68.

The Meaning of Citizenship, 1794–1798

British documents recorded 817 such slaves in 1795 alone and another 750 during the next four years. Once on the island, these individuals, now free, were placed on specific plantations by the government, where they were to serve as cultivateurs. In most cases, workers from these same plantations took them to Basse-Terre to give them new names. Yet the re-namings also brought together people from different plantations or from plantations and the town, which suggests that the baptisms were orga-nized through a variety of social connections and were not carried out under orders from plantation managers. In the first of the series of acts, Louison, a twenty-five-year-old noir plantation worker, and Marie-Anne brought a sixteen-year-old "nouveaux citoyen de la Côte," to whom they gave the name Modeste. On the same day, a man and a woman from dif-ferent plantations gave a citoyenne nouvelle de la Côte the name Fanny. Six days later, two workers from the Patriat plantation gave a citoyenne nouvelle who was living on the same plantation the name Magdelaine; here, for the first time, the description "de la Côte" was dropped. Being a new citizen now meant having just arrived from Africa. A few days later, when workers from two neighboring plantations gave a fourteen-year-old girl the name of Anne-Rose, she was described as a "citoyenne noire nouvelle"—a "black new citizeness." In a few cases, those doing the naming were not listed as being attached to a plantation or to the army; Louison, described as "de couleur," and Bernadine, who gave a sixteen-year-old citoyenne nouvelle the name Charlotte, were likely residents of the town.[13]

Certain plantations—notably the Patriat plantation—seem to have been singled out to receive a large number of the captured Africans as cultivateurs, and these new arrivals were named by a combination of plantation workers and former slaves who had since left. In one case, a woman from the plantation was aided by Alexis, a volunteer soldier in the Fourth Battalion, which was garrisoned in Basse-Terre, in naming a new citizeness. Alexis had perhaps worked on the Patriat plantation before emancipation, and perhaps he was the one who recruited other soldiers from his battalion—Laurent Lagarde (who named one new citizen Lau-rent) and André Cicard—to join women from the plantations in naming "citoyens noirs de la Côte." Rozette, a de couleur former slave of Patriat,

13. See the acts from December 1796, in CAOM, EC, Basse-Terre, 10, nos. 19, 20, 38, 44, 50. The distribution of the captured slaves is documented in CAOM, C 7A, 81; for the numbers of slaves captured as recorded in British documents, see *The Transatlantic Slave Trade: A Database on CD-ROM* (Cambridge, 1999).

helped name a number of new citizens on the Patriat plantation. A month after the first renamings, one new citizen, Jean-Baptiste, was explicitly identified as being "from the Patriat habitation." Soon afterward, four new citizens from the Patriat plantation were all brought to Basse-Terre and given new names on the same day, and the manager participated in naming a young citoyenne nouvelle.[14]

Workers and new citizens from other plantations in the region also went to Basse-Terre to conduct such naming ceremonies. The manager of the Galean plantation, along with workers from other plantations, gave names to a number of new arrivals. A mason named Modeste helped name a new citizeness placed on the Miraude national plantation. Networks of citizens from the towns also mobilized to name some new arrivals, who seemed not to have been assigned to particular plantations. On one day, three new arrivals were named by an interconnected group of townspeople that included Barthélemy Lecoudray, a de couleur tailor, Charles, a worker at the port, and his wife Marie. Though the use of the terms "new citizen" and "de la Côte" for such new arrivals remained for the most part consistent through 1797–1798, in three cases—all involving residents of Basse-Terre—a different terminology was used. When Michel, a "garde de la municipalité" (town policeman), and Théotiste Gaguet gave a fourteen-year-old the name of Amélie, she was described in the act as a "jeune citoyenne africaine"—a "young African citizeness." When the married couple César and Marie-Catherine gave an eighteen-year-old the name Joseph, he was noted as a "citoyen africain," as was Jean, who was named the same day by two women who were probably domestic servants.[15]

That ex-slaves took it upon themselves to give French names, and in so doing to integrate the new arrivals into the society of Guadeloupe, gives us a fascinating glimpse of one moment in the history of African acculturation in the Americas. It also shows how the diversity of ethnicities among these arrivals from Africa could be transformed—through the actions of plantation laborers themselves—into the term "de la Côte" or "africain." "De la Côte" was, during the same years, used in the état civil to describe men and women who had been slaves in Guadeloupe before emancipation but who had been born in Africa. So it was not a marker of

14. See CAOM, EC, Basse-Terre, 10, nos. 45, 46, 52, 60–62, 64, 67, 74, 106, 136, 146, 183.

15. CAOM, EC, Basse-Terre, 10, nos. 122–124, 128, 129, 146, 183; EC, Basse-Terre, 11, nos. 56, 122.

The Meaning of Citizenship, 1794–1798

difference between those who were already acculturated to live in Guadeloupe and the new arrivals. In contrast to slave traders' terms describing the nations of their slaves, it was a distinction based, not on ethnicity or specific place of birth, but on their origin in a continent. Why did the individuals who registered these "rebirths" embrace this generalizing term? Why was it used rather than ethnic markers that had been common in slavery, such as "Ibo" or "Congo"? Since the coast of Africa was, for most of the slaves, not a home but rather the site of their transfer from local slave traders to European vessels, the term might have functioned in some cases as a reminder of the experience of capture and deportation that had brought them to the Caribbean. It also served, however, to craft a broad identity, based on a common origin in Africa, out of an enormous diversity of origins. The application of terms linked to Africa during the namings in Basse-Terre transformed the origins of these arrivals into a new community of meaning. This process was therefore part of the ways in which individuals in the Americas began to imagine an African identity, one made possible through an uprooting from particular communities within the continent.[16]

The impetus for these renamings appears to have come from ex-slaves who clearly understood the importance of official documentation. Traveling to the town in order to give new names to these citoyens de la Côte, and in so doing register them as free people in Guadeloupe, was one way these laborers struggled against the continuing subjection they were experiencing as cultivateurs forced to stay on the plantations. The new arrivals from Africa were, at least in many cases, given few rights; but their ex-slave coworkers took the initiative to assert a right they could act upon—the right to documentation.

Their story has a bitter conclusion. The mark of citizenship so powerfully asserted in 1797 would ultimately be reversed for these new arrivals baptized into the Republic. In 1802, after the reestablishment of slavery, those plantation managers or owners who had received cultivateurs on their plantations "from the captures" were invited to come and register them as slaves. Once again these men and women were brought in front of the local officials of Basse-Terre to be described and registered,

16. For broader discussions of the ways in which slaves and ex-slaves came to see themselves as African, see James Sidbury, *Ploughshares into Swords: Race, Rebellion, and Identity in Gabriel's Virginia* (Cambridge, 1998); Michael A. Gomez, *Exchanging Our Country Marks: The Transformation of African Identities in the Colonial and Antebellum South* (Chapel Hill, N.C., 1998).

but now they were documented as objects, given prices, and identified by particular African ethnicities. Their place of origin was described according to the old categories of slave traders, and their bodies and the marks they carried—either from rituals of scarification or from acts of brutality—were described in detail. They were no longer de la Côte, and they were certainly no longer citoyens africains. They were enslaved, as they would have been had they never had the fortune to land on an island of emancipation a few years before.[17]

The difference between the rituals that took place in the time of freedom and those in the time of slavery suggests the power that the registration of individuals as citizens could hold. But, even within freedom, ex-slaves confronted the attempt by Hugues's regime to categorize them racially and so control their labor. Documentation could represent a certain freedom and an assertion of rights. But it could also—as the enslavement of the African arrivals in 1802 showed all too well—serve as a mechanism for control. Hugues clearly believed that disciplining the recalcitrant cultivateurs of Guadeloupe required informing them of who they were and where he felt they were meant to be.

White, Black, and Red

Already in the ancien régime, control of slaves' movement between plantations and towns was a central concern in the colony's administration. After emancipation, the entire functioning of Hugues's regime, in its attempt to force cultivateurs to stay on their plantations, depended on the repression of one of the ex-slaves' key assertions of freedom: movement. But freedom transformed surveillance, since it was a different matter to police slaves than it was to police men and women who, at least in principle, were free citizens. The exigencies of the administration of freedom led Hugues to embark, in 1796 and 1797, on a massive project of documenting the population of the island. In place of the plantation registers of the previous decades, islandwide censuses listed names, ages, races, and professions by commune.

In metropolitan France before the Revolution, officials had drawn up lists of noirs and issued identity cards to them as part of the attempt to control the movement and the growth of that group. During the same period, an endeavor to reform Saint-Domingue's plantation system and to curb abuses on the part of masters included a demand for more care-

17. See CAOM, C 7A, 81, 22 Frimaire, An XI (Dec. 13, 1802).

The Meaning of Citizenship, 1794–1798

ful record-keeping regarding the enslaved. But these reforms were never applied; they incited a storm of controversy because planters saw them as an unacceptable and dangerous intervention on the part of the state into their private affairs. In May 1793, however, as Sonthonax and Polverel prepared the terrain for abolition, they drew on these earlier plans for reform and ordered all propertyowners and plantation managers to provide a list of "all free men, all slaves of all ages and sexes that make up their house, plantation, or workshop, by names, surnames, and ages." Once emancipation was decreed, more provisions followed regarding the counting and surveillance of the formerly enslaved population.[18]

In Guadeloupe, this type of documentation was taken to a higher, more rigorous level. On the first day of the Republican years V and VI (September 1796 and September 1797), the administration of each commune delivered a complete list of all its inhabitants. These censuses were most likely ordered by Hugues himself, since there is no indication that the metropolitan government requested them. Indeed, these censuses are the only ones known to have been produced in the French Caribbean during the 1790s. They divided the free population of Guadeloupe into three categories based on color: black, white, and red. The term "red" identified those individuals of mixed European and African ancestry, who in other contexts were described as "mulâtre" or "câpre." Though "red" had occasionally surfaced in the Caribbean, along with "yellow," to describe such individuals, its use as an official, state-sanctioned term was unique to Guadeloupe. Nowhere in the archives is the choice of the term explained. Its use as a middle category between black and white, however, was probably tied to Paris and Saint-Domingue's "tricolor" flag of 1793 that featured the black, white, and mulatto figures placed respectively over the blue, white, and red. From this symbol that asserted racial equality even as it represented racial difference, Hugues and his administration could well have drawn the symbolic terms necessary for the creation of a census that brought together the entire population of the island in one document—even as it maintained the separation between the races as a practical way of identifying and controlling the labor necessary for the nation.[19]

18. On the uniqueness of the census, see Pérotin-Dumon, *La Ville*, 21; see also her extensive use of the censuses' demographic data in chap. 6.

19. On metropolitan France, see Sue Peabody, *"There Are No Slaves in France"*: *The Political Culture of Race and Slavery in the Ancien Régime* (Oxford, 1996), chap. 5; for Saint-Domingue, see Debien, *Les Esclaves des Antilles françaises* (Basse-Terre, Guadeloupe, 1974), 485–487; Debien, ed., "Documents: Aux orig-

Local administrators completed the censuses with forms that were standardized throughout the island. In most communes, the list began with the population of the towns, followed by the plantations, which were divided into "habitations nationales" (state-owned plantations) and "habitations particulières" (privately owned plantations) and further divided by the kind of plantation (sugar, coffee, cotton, or provisions). The census seems to have been put together based on the declarations of the citizens themselves; it grouped families together, but it also contained unstated affiliations such as those between ex-masters and ex-domestic servants. Frequently, the names of whites were followed by the names of women and men listed as "noir" or "rouge" and described as "femmes" or "hommes de confiance" (domestic servants). Each commune's census included a table that listed population according to a variety of categories, notably those of race.[20]

Though identical forms were sent to all local representatives, there was a place in which particular strategies of notation could be used: the column made available for "observations." Placed in this column were descriptions of the cultivateurs on the plantations, transforming the censuses into documents that evaluated and noted the laborers' behavior. The Basse-Terre census described those who were absent for the only legal reason they could be—military service—as "in the armed forces." For those cultivateurs who were not on the plantations or in the army, the term "divaguant" was added in the observations column. "Divaguant," then, was the new term for an old practice that, ironically, was still a meaningful assertion of freedom: marronnage. This term, which literally meant "rambler," turned an action into a characteristic. Officials in neighboring Baillif used a different terminology, one that simply marked the

ines de l'abolition de l'esclavage," in *Revue d'histoire des colonies*, XXXVI (1949), 24-55, 348-423, esp. 35-43.

20. On the left of the census forms was a column for names, then a set of three columns for ages—over twenty-one, between fourteen and twenty-one, and under fourteen—in which the corresponding category was checked. The next column listed professions, although a large number of people listed were not given any profession. Next were two groups of three rows: one for "masculin," divided into "blancs," "rouges," and "noirs," and the second for "feminin," divided the same way. Here, again, the appropriate categories were checked. Finally, there was a column for observations. The 1796 Basse-Terre census noted that certain citizens had not provided the names of their children in the declarations; see "Etat nominatif . . . de Basse-Terre," 1 Vendémiaire, An V (Sept. 22, 1796), in CAOM, G 1, 500, no. 5 (hereafter cited as "Etat nominatif de Basse-Terre").

action; they described certain cultivateurs as "absent." Other character-istics were noted only in the case of the plantation laborers: some were described as "surâgé" ("overaged"), others as "infirme" ("disabled"). In addition, on the national plantations, certain cultivateurs were set apart with the description "ancien libre," which marked them as freed before the decree of 1794.[21]

How were people categorized as black, white, and red? To a large extent, the classification seems to have depended on the census takers' evaluations of color and phenotypical characteristics. A comparison of demographics from before and after emancipation shows that approxi-mately twelve thousand formerly enslaved individuals were listed as "red." Guadeloupe's slave population had included a large number of men and women of mixed European and African descent who, removed from the legal category of the slave, were now placed in a category based on race. They joined individuals who had been free before emancipation and had been described as "métisse," "mulâtre," or "de couleur" in other documents such as notary records or the état civil.[22]

Some cases, however, suggest flexibility in how these terms were ap-plied and negotiation over who ended up in which column in the cen-suses. The wife of Charles Latour, a blanc, was noted as "rouge" in 1796, but in a 1792 document she had not been given a racial ascription—an absence that was usually the privilege only of whites at that time. In the 1796 census, the widow Truc, owner of a small plantation in Trois-Rivières, was first marked as "blanc" before ending up with a check in the "rouge" box next to her name. Mont Louis, a ten-year-old new ar-rival from Africa who was described as "noir" in one document, appeared

21. Ibid.; "Etat nominatif . . . Baillif," Dernier jour complémentaire, An IV (Sept. 21, 1796), in CAOM, G 1, 500, no. 4.

22. Pérotin-Dumon, *La Ville*, 333–334; "Etat nominatif de Basse-Terre"; "Etat nominatif des citoyens . . . de Trois-Rivières," 1 Vendémiaire, An V (Sept. 22, 1796), in CAOM, G 1, 502, no. 2 (hereafter cited as "Etat nominatif de Trois-Rivières"). In Basse-Terre, the tailor and signer of the 1793 declaration of the new citizens, Jean-Georges, was described as "rouge," as was the tailor Barthelemi, who, along with his family, was described as "de couleur" when he was married in 1796; see CAOM, EC, Basse-Terre, 9, no. 6. Also described as "rouge" was Sophie Coupri, who was elsewhere described as "de couleur"; see the 1796 decla-rations in CAOM, EC, Basse-Terre, 7, nos. 7, 140. Additionally, the mason Jean-Baptiste Desange was noted as "rouge" in the census and as "de couleur" in an-other document; see CAOM, EC, Basse-Terre, 9, no. 131. See also CAOM, Barbier, 51, Nov. 25, 1790, 53, Jan. 11, 1792.

The Mark of Freedom

in the census as "rouge." In the Basse-Terre census, a woman named Marie Icard—probably a relative of the Joseph Icard who was a prominent homme de couleur in 1793—was described as "rouge," whereas her brother (or perhaps half-brother), Baptiste Icard, was described as "blanc." And one Angélique, who in the census was noted as "blanc," seems to have been the same woman who in 1804 was described as a "métisse libre."[23]

The process through which race was named—and the particular roles administrators and the individuals so described played in this naming—is ultimately difficult to capture through the documents. The preceding examples do suggest that census takers did not always simply evaluate a person's color but rather responded to the assertions of those they sought to categorize. Indeed, some individuals seem to have successfully laid claim on the category of "red" or "white," perhaps in a bid to assert a higher status or else present themselves as part of a particular community. These negotiations, which occasionally impacted the production of censuses, were also a crucial part of the more individually focused état civil and notary registers through which women and men attempted to define themselves, even as they were defined by the officials who oversaw the creation of these documents.

Freedom and Land

In the late 1790s, Marie-Jeanne, a woman from Trois-Rivières, lived in a house "behind the Capuchins" in Basse-Terre, in the neighborhood where Marie-Anne Bourseau, Françoise dite Gripon, and other women had first established themselves in the 1780s. Marie-Jeanne had once been a slave of Thyrus Pautrizel, and she had probably lived on his plantation at the time of the 1793 insurrection. After emancipation, she had chosen to stay on Pautrizel's plantation, where in 1796 she was listed as a cultivateur. But, at some point during the next year, she decided to move with her son, François dit Chocot, to Basse-Terre. There, however, her son died after being shot—according to her declaration—"imprudently and without premeditated design." Marie-Jeanne's movement from the

23. For Latour's wife, see CAOM, Barbier, 53, Feb. 14, 1792; for both her and the widow Truc, see the 1796 "Etat nominatif de Trois-Rivières." For Mont Louis, see CAOM, EC, Basse-Terre, 10, no. 106, 27 Germinal, An V (Apr. 16, 1797); for Angélique, see CAOM, Castet, 472, 16 Thermidor, An XII (Aug. 4, 1804). The latter three examples are in the 1796 "Etat nominatif de Basse-Terre."

plantation to the town suggests the larger set of possibilities and dangers that existed for the ex-slaves of Guadeloupe.[24]

During the time of slavery, free and enslaved people in Guadeloupe had continually struggled for control over land. Slaves sought water for their small gardens on plantations and sold their products in the markets to earn a bit of money. Some freed people were able to buy parcels of land in the towns or small plantations. Sometimes they entered into conditional contracts, as did the mulâtre Jean-Baptiste when, in 1791, he rented, from Marie-Claire Bontemps, land in Trois-Rivières—which, however, he would have to give up if he married. With the upheavals of the 1790s and the emigration or death of a substantial number of landowners, more land became available to the new citizens.[25]

In 1798, the citoyenne noire Bijoux entered into a contract with the local administration to rent a piece of land in the center of town. The municipality had declared that this land would be used for the assistance of indigents, so the rent Bijoux paid went to the "indigent's fund" of Basse-Terre. In fact, however, the contract signed between the municipality and Bijoux simply officialized an arrangement that had gone on for some time. On the property stood already a fairly valuable house built collaboratively by Bijoux with another woman, Marie Questel. After making her use of the land official through the contract with the local administration, Bijoux also officialized the informal agreement she had made with Questel, by which they split the costs of the property. The contracts made in that year—between the municipality and Bijoux and between Bijoux and Questel—solidified an acquisition resulting from the independent initiative of these two women. They had taken over property and built a house for themselves in the heart of Basse-Terre. Both women were originally from Trois-Rivières, where Questel was the owner of a plantation worked by thirty-three laborers. In 1791, Bijoux had been owned by Gabriel Pinau, who died during the British occupation of the island in 1794. Though his widow had remained on their coffee plantation, cultivation had essentially ceased by 1796. Bijoux left for Basse-Terre, where she was able to work and gain enough money to build a house. That a few years later she could enter into a contract with a former slaveowner from her town on equal terms, sharing costs and responsibilities in the con-

24. CAOM, EC, Basse-Terre, 9, no. 87, 26 Ventôse, An V (Mar. 16, 1797); "Etat nominatif de Trois-Rivières."

25. CAOM, Notariat Guadeloupe, Barbier, 52, Sept. 18, 1791; "Etat nominatif de . . . Basse-Terre."

struction of a house, was a powerful measure of the possibilities opened up by emancipation.[26]

Another woman, the citoyenne Béatrix, also built a house for herself on the Republic's land. Béatrix had five children, though three of them— André, Philippe, and Joseph—were "absent from the colony" when she died in 1800. To her children still in Guadeloupe, she left a few possessions, including handkerchiefs, cooking utensils, and clothes as well as a small house built on a "plot of land belonging to the Republic." Béatrix might have supported herself in part by having boarders in her house; in 1797 the sailor Thomas died there. She probably had been free before 1794, and in this sense her activities can be seen as continuation of the prerevolutionary practices of free women of color such as those who had rented land from the Capuchins in the 1780s. The revolutionary context, however, did provide her with new opportunities, since the state-owned land on which she built her house was probably a plot abandoned as the result of the turmoil of the period.[27]

Some new citizens built structures on private land. In 1800 in Basse-Terre, Zouzou and Jean-Louis Baffa signed a lease renting land in the Bas-du-Bourg, near the ocean. Zouzou and Baffa, it was noted, were already in possession of the land and in fact had already constructed some buildings on it, which they promised to maintain through the lease. If the owners decided to sell the property, Zouzou and Baffa would have the first option on its purchase. Other men who had built themselves a home on private land in Basse-Terre had less luck preserving their rights over the structures they had built. In 1798, two citoyens noirs named Frontin and Zéphir were forced off of a piece of land in the center of Basse-Terre where they had lived during the previous years. The owner of the land, Jean Certain, had allowed Frontin and Zéphir to build a shed on his property. In 1798, however, he rented the land to the merchant citoyen Cloud, who demanded that Frontin and Zéphir leave the property and

26. See ADG, Serane 2E2/159, 6 Germinal, An VI (Mar. 26, 1798), which describes the contract made by Bijoux with the municipality on 27 Nivôse, An VI (Jan. 16, 1798). For Questel's plantation, see "Etat nominatif des citoyens . . . de Trois-Rivières," in CAOM, G 1, 502, no. 2. For Bijoux and Pinau's property, see CAOM, Barbier, 52, Feb. 28, 1791; ADG, Serane 2E2/157, 26 Thermidor, An IV (Aug. 13, 1796).

27. ADG, Castet 2E2/209, 2 Fructidor, An VIII (Aug. 20, 1800). For Thomas's death, see CAOM, EC, Basse-Terre, 9, no. 71. Béatrix's three sons had left the colony sometime after 1791, but they had a legal representative since then, a fact that suggests Béatrix was free before 1794.

either take apart the shed or sell it to Cloud at a price that was "agreeable to him." In their own act, which was appended to the rental contract between Cloud and Certain, Frontin and Zéphir noted that, given the option of either destroying the shed or selling it, they preferred "the latter option, which is more in line with their interests," and sold the structure to Cloud.[28]

The extent to which the new citizens of Basse-Terre occupied and used plots of abandoned land is made clear by the force with which the local administration attempted to reverse this situation after the reestablishment of slavery in 1802. During this period, those who had been reenslaved were stripped of any property they might have gained while emancipated. But the administration compounded this policy with a directive aimed at men and women of African descent—including those who had been free before the Revolution—who had expanded their property holdings in the towns. In a decree "concerning the illicit use of plots belonging to the government," administrators noted that "individuals, with no legal title, have usurped other plots of land belonging to the government . . . and have permitted themselves to build on them and use them in a variety of ways for their personal profit." A number of people had also made use of land along the waterfront, encroaching on the fifty meters that had always been reserved for the government. This was the case of the water seller François, who owned a series of *appentis* (sheds) along Pointe-à-Pitre's beach. He rented them out for profit and had been able to afford their construction by building them with boards pulled up from the main dock of the nearby port. Or so it was reported when he was caught one night stealing a board and was killed during a struggle with a soldier.[29]

Those who had lived on the series of national properties that had "once belonged to the former religious orders established in Basse-Terre," the decree continued, had not paid rent in years. To rectify this situation, the administrators ordered all those who were in possession of lands previously owned by religious orders to present titles justifying their possession of these lands. They had to declare how much they had formerly paid for the properties and deliver to the government all the back pay for

28. ADG, Castet 2E2/209, 11 Vendémiaire, An VIII (Oct. 3, 1799); ADG, Serane 2E2/159, 1 Prairial, An VI (May 20, 1798).

29. Lacrosse and Lescallier, decree, 23 Brumaire, An XI (Nov. 14, 1802), in CAOM, C 7A, 58, 33; *Gazette politique et commerciale de la Guadeloupe*, 9 Floréal, An X (Apr. 29, 1802), in CAOM, C 7A, 56, 252–253.

the years they had not paid rent. Furthermore, those who were occupying government land without permission or with "irregular, verbal permission" would have to make similar declarations and offer the government a certain amount of money for their previous use of the land as well as for their continued right to live there. If they were unable to justify their presence on these lands and to pay the necessary fees, they would be evicted, and everything they had built would become government property. So, after a decade, the land that had been the property of the Republic yet used by slaves-turned-citizens in pursuit of a better life was placed firmly back in the hands of the government. The land rented by the Capuchins to women such as Marie-Anne and Françoise dite Gripon, which for a moment had become a kind of property for their children, once again became something held tenuously, something that had to be paid for. The new policy forced those like Anne-Joseph Yoyo La Grenade, who in 1799 had taken over a lease originally granted by the Religieux de la Charité a decade before, to pay years of back rent to the state. This probably seriously undermined the small independence she had gained by owning a plot of land bordering her husband's and cultivated with coffee trees.[30]

As part of a program meant to reassert the social hierarchies swept away by emancipation, the prefect Lescallier passed a law dividing the towns of Pointe-à-Pitre and Basse-Terre into six sections, with each street named and each house numbered. The state attempted to gain control over towns and the unnumbered structures new citizens had taken possession of within them. Yet many of the structures that had been built on these lands by the new citizens certainly remained, just as some of those who had been free before 1794 and who had profited from the time of freedom were able to hold on to the new property they had acquired. Ex-slaves had transformed the topography of the capital of Guadeloupe as they created a better life for themselves.[31]

30. Lacrosse and Lescallier, decree, 23 Brumaire, An XI (Nov. 14, 1802), in CAOM, C 7A, 58, 33; for La Grenade, see ADG, Vauchelet 2E2/164, 10 Messidor, An V (June 28, 1799).

31. Lescallier, arrêté, 21 Vendémiaire, An XI (Oct. 13, 1802), in CAOM, C 7A, 58, 26.

The Meaning of Citizenship, 1794–1798

The right to the products of one's labor was, of course, a fundamental sign that slavery had been left behind. The exception was the cultivateurs, whose work remained for the most part unrewarded. As I have already mentioned, soldiers and sailors were paid for their labor, but many other profitable work options existed, especially in the towns. In Basse-Terre in 1796, whites, ex-slaves, and gens de couleur were present in roughly equal numbers—out of a population of 2,774, there were 864 blancs (31 percent), 954 rouges (35 percent), and 956 noirs (34 percent). Not all of the noirs were listed with a profession in the census, but among the group, 6 percent—45 women and 12 men—were described as merchants. Another 70 noir men (7 percent) worked as masons and carpenters, 49 (5 percent) worked as fishermen, and a small number worked in other trades. Ex-slaves also formed the majority of the 79 domestic servants in Basse-Terre after 1794.[32]

Many ex-slaves were employed by the Republic itself in Basse-Terre, providing labor for a variety of enterprises that the state had taken over. Paul Laporte dit Languedoc, for instance, was a noir who in 1796 was employed by the Republic as a mason, while his wife Veronique worked as a domestic. The ex-slave Chalot also worked for the Republic as a mason, as did the noir François Legros. In 1795, the citizen Charles, whose wife Catherine lived on a nearby plantation where he, too, had perhaps lived before emancipation, was a "carpenter working for the Republic." The sixty-year-old noir carpenter Jacques Pierret was similarly employed, as was Jean Catherine, also a noir, who worked as a carpenter "at the fort." One de couleur carpenter named Alexis was working for the Republic when he married Catharine, who lived on a plantation outside the town, in 1795. The next year, he became a carpenter attached to the Scheffer plantation, and, as if the change in employer brought with it a change in racial status, he was described as "noir." In their line of work, these carpenter ex-slaves worked with men who were free before 1794, such as the citoyen Germain who had helped free Désirée and her children. They also worked with whites, such as Bertrand Rodney, a native of the Bayonne region of France.[33]

32. "Etat nominatif . . . de Basse-Terre," in CAOM, G 1, 500, no. 5. The population of the town comprised 43 percent of the total population of 6,446 in the commune of Basse-Terre, which included 1,208 blancs (18 percent), 1,786 rouges (28 percent), and 3,452 noirs (54 percent).

33. For Paul Laporte dit Languedoc, see ADG, Castet 2E2/210, 3 Messidor,

There was other state employment open to ex-slaves as well. Grégoire, for instance, worked in the provisions warehouse, along with the eighteen-year-old Marzile. Jacques worked as a barrelmaker, as did Joseph and Nicolas, a noir who was originally from Martinique. The forty-year-old Claude had the interesting job of mattressmaker. Romain and Alexis, both noirs, were working in the coffee mill when they declared the death of their forty-year-old coworker Africain, who died at the mill, presumably as the result of an accident. A number of ex-slaves worked on the *acons*—the small barges that were used for loading and unloading the ships in the harbor. Bape, a noir who was registered at his wedding as "de la Côte," worked in this capacity, as did his friend Marcel, also a noir, who was a witness at this wedding. Jean, who was described in his son's birth declaration as a câpre, was also employed in the acons. The loading and unloading of ships was likely tied into the corsair trade that brought a great deal of merchandise into harbors such as that of Basse-Terre.[34]

The thriving trade in Basse-Terre, in turn, opened up many opportunities for independent merchants. A set of agreements made in the early 1800s between a merchant and a woman named Agnès Corbet indicates how some women were able to establish themselves in the mercantile world. Corbet, a widow, owned a few plots of land in Basse-Terre. In 1800, she borrowed 3,700 francs from Pierre Chequey to be paid back in six months. The money was to be used specifically to set up a business in the "buying and selling of dry merchandise and comestibles of all kinds." The profits made by Agnès were to be split equally with Chequey, as were any losses she might incur. Another woman of Basse-Terre, the citoyenne Bonne, incurred a debt with the merchant Jean Baptiste Rousseau, perhaps through a similar agreement.[35]

In certain professions, the ownership of the instruments of labor was fundamental in determining who worked for whom. In Basse-Terre, sev-

---

An IX (June 22, 1801). See also CAOM, EC, Basse-Terre, 6, no. 23 (Charles); 7, no. 104 (Jean Catherine); 9, nos. 7, 26 (Alexis), no. 27 (Legros), no. 35 (Chalot). For Jacques Pierret, see EC, Basse-Terre, 6, 20 Pluviôse, An IV (Feb. 9, 1796). For Germain, see Chapter 2, above. For Rodney, see ADG, Serane 2E2/158, 4 Brumaire, An V (Oct. 25, 1796).

34. See CAOM, EC, Basse-Terre, 7, no. 6 (Grégoire), no. 60 (Jacques); 9, nos. 10, 36 (acon workers), nos. 25, 27 (Nicolas), no. 30 (Claude), no. 125 (coffee mill workers); 10, no. 55 (Marzile); 11, no. 46 (Joseph).

35. See ADG, Dupuch 2E2/25, 7 Pluviôse, An VIII (Jan. 27, 1800); ADG, Serane 2E2, 12 Germinal, An XI (Apr. 2, 1803). For Bonne, see ADG, Dupuch 2E2/24, 11 Prairial, An VII (May 30, 1799).

eral men and women who owned *seines* (nets) hired fishermen to work for them. "Master" Baptiste, for instance, had four fisherman working for him in 1797: two men in their fifties, Ignace and Charles, a younger man also named Charles, and François. The citizen Lacour, a *senneur* who lived near the water, employed at least one man, Colas. Marie Fauconnier, a widow who owned a plantation and numerous plots of land in Basse-Terre, employed Moyse, a noir de la Côte, along with Jean, Louis, and Romain, also noirs, on her seine. When Moyse was married in 1796, his two coworkers Louis and Romain were witnesses. Perhaps all of these men were the ex-slaves of Fauconnier or her deceased husband Michineau. But if they were, they seem to have freely chosen to continue working for her, given that the senneur Jean-Pierre, whom Michineau specifically noted in 1795 as his ex-slave, had chosen to work independently after emancipation. When Fauconnier died in 1799, her seine was part of her succession, and at least one of her senneurs, Romain, continued working for her descendants. Louis, meanwhile, found work at another seine. Other ex-slaves worked independently as fisherman, such as Jean Edouard and Benoît of Basse-Terre, Antoine of Vieux-Fort, and Jacques of Trois-Rivières. So the fishermen of Basse-Terre, including ex-slaves, worked in a variety of circumstances, including that of managing a seine owned by someone else, as the senneur André dit Allocor did.[36]

Other skills were put to use by one woman from Vieux-Fort, the *sage-femme* (midwife) Rosette. Seeking care from her, two women from Capesterre traveled separately to Vieux-Fort in the year IX (1800). Both of them died, perhaps during childbirth, and so their presence away from home was noted in the état civil. That these women had traveled from Capesterre suggests that Rosette was a well-established and widely known midwife, just as it suggests some of the reasons women from the plantations might have had for asserting their freedom to move about the

36. See CAOM, EC, Basse-Terre, 9, no. 13 (Charles), no. 30 (Ignace); 10, no. 160 (François). For the declaration of the death of François's child, where he was joined by his coworker the younger Charles, see 9, no. 159. For Lacour, 8, no. 92, and 6, no. 45. On Fauconnier's workers, see 9, no. 92. For Moyse, see 9, no. 92; for Jean, see 10, no. 315; for Jean-Pierre, see 6, no. 53. For Romain's work after Fauconnier's death, see 11, no. 166; for Louis, see 11, no. 206. For the independent fishermen, see Jean Edouard's participation in the declaration of the death of the interestingly named Vieux Corps ("Old Body"), in 9, no. 179; for Benoît, see 11, no. 14. For Antoine, see EC, Trois-Rivières (5Mi378), 9; for the sixty-two-year-old Jacques, see EC, Trois-Rivières (5Mi378), 4, 7. For Allocor, see EC, Basse-Terre, 6, no. 46, and 10, no. 105.

island. Other, more official, institutions of health care provided ex-slaves with employment. A cook named Joseph, who had previously worked at a hospital outside Basse-Terre, participated in the wedding of a man named Joseph, who still worked in the apothecary there. The hospital also employed the noir Victor, Constance, Pierre, the nurse Thimothé, and Ursule in the dispensary. These workers had connections with the numerous cultivateurs who worked on the plantation attached to the hospital, as well as with fishermen and soldiers who lived in Basse-Terre. Another employee at the hospital, Louis, had connections with a particularly diverse group of people in Basse-Terre. With his longtime companion Medecis, he had raised two children—Baptiste, a carpenter, and Étienne, a drummer in the army. When the couple married in 1795, the witnesses at the wedding were two soldiers, a carpenter, and a wigmaker from Basse-Terre and Louis's ex-master, the *officier de santé* Jacques Code, who, along with the surgeon Antoine Fontelliau, ran the Basse-Terre hospital.[37]

Another institution in Basse-Terre that employed new citizens was the municipal administration itself. Most notable was the employment of twenty-eight-year-old Joseph Gérard as a municipal officer who oversaw the drawing up of acts in the état civil. Because of his position, Gérard participated as a witness in a large number of wedding, birth, and death declarations, many of which involved ex-slaves. Other new citizens found positions as "guards of the municipality," such as Ismaël and the citoyens Pierre and Bernadet. Though all of these municipal workers were either noir or de couleur, their races were rarely mentioned, probably as a result of their privileged status as members of the local administration. Another municipal guard involved in a series of declarations was Michel, the twenty-five-year-old who had given the name Amélie to a young African citoyenne. In 1797, he participated in the birth declaration of Jacques, who lived in his house at the time and practiced another profession that had opened itself up to the new citizens: that of the *boulangers*.[38]

37. For Rosette, see CAOM, EC, Trois-Rivières (5Mi378), 7, 8. For the cook Joseph, whose wife was described as the daughter of a noir and a *caraïbesse*, see CAOM, EC, Basse-Terre, 6, 20 Vendémiaire, An IV (Oct. 12, 1795); for the Joseph who worked at the apothecary, see EC, Basse-Terre, 7, no. 16, and 9, no. 7; see also 7, no. 12 (Victor); 9, nos. 13, 39, 160 (Thimothé and Ursule); 10, no. 295 (Constance); 11, no. 22 (Pierre). For Louis, see 6, no. 50. On Code and Fontelliau, see ADG, Serane 2E2/157, 9 Fructidor, An IV (Aug. 26, 1796).

38. Usually Gérard was not given a racial ascription, but twice he was described as "noir"; among many examples of his appearance as a witness, see CAOM, EC,

Jacques was only one out of twenty-four noir bakers who, in 1796, were listed in the census of Basse-Terre, along with men such as Amadis, Paschal, Rémy, Hector, Lafortune, Thélémaque, Baptiste Capiard, Fosil le Sot, and Louis Manonda. The bakers Jean and Jean-Paul were both de la Côte and ex-slaves of the citoyen Arnoux. Probably purchased off slave ships by Arnoux, once emancipated they continued working together in their profession. They were married within a week of each other in the same municipality. Two other noir bakers—Jean-Baptiste and Gaspard —were ex-slaves of a merchant from Basse-Terre named André Négré. The bakeries of Arnoux and Négré, staffed by black bakers drawn from their ex-slaves, were the most important producers of bread in Basse-Terre between 1794 and 1802, providing the population, including the troops and sailors, with their daily bread. Arnoux grew rich from the labor of black bakers, both during slavery and the emancipation period, buying a large, luxurious, walled-in house in the center of Basse-Terre in 1798. Some ex-slave bakers possibly operated independently, though it might have been difficult for them to acquire the ovens and the space necessary for baking and selling their goods. A baker named Joseph Michel, who might have been an ex-slave, amassed enough money to buy a house in 1800.[39]

Despite all its limitations, emancipation in Guadeloupe brought with it important opportunities for former slaves living in busy towns such as Basse-Terre. The institution of a Republican regime provided men and women—once treated primarily as objects by the law—the right to act as legal subjects and created documents aimed at securing their hold on property and even on freedom itself. Some also found work within the new administration, which brought them both economic and social advantages. At the same time, many blacks came to occupy important economic niches in the port towns, taking advantage of new patterns of trade driven by war and fed partly by the loot from Republican corsairs. All of

Basse-Terre, 6, nos. 38, 54. For his description as a noir, see EC, Basse-Terre, 6, no. 33, and 8, no. 105. See also 7, nos. 10 (Pierre), 11 (Bernadet). For Ismaël, see his appearances in 1796–1797, in EC, Basse-Terre, 9, nos. 15, 16, 22, 27, 41, 48, 57; for Michel, see 11, nos. 19, 122.

39. For the list of bakers in the town, see the "Etat nominatif de Basse-Terre." See also CAOM, EC, Basse-Terre, 9, nos. 46 (Jean), 47 (Jean-Paul); for Jean-Baptiste, see EC, Basse-Terre, 10, no. 189, and 11, no. 53; for Gaspard, see EC, Basse-Terre, 11, no. 31; for Arnoux's house, see ADG, Serane 2E2/159, 9 Frimaire, An VI (Nov. 29, 1797); see also CAOM, EC, Basse-Terre, no. 21, 10; for Joseph Michel, see ADG, Castet 2E2/210, 3 Messidor, An IX (June 22, 1801).

these changes led to more interdependence between whites and blacks, to new collusions as well as new tensions: in 1802, the administrator Lacrosse would complain that the white merchants of Guadeloupe had contracted the habit of ignoring the "color of those who govern them" as long as they could still make a profit. When, during the late 1790s and early 1800s, French administrators sought to contain, and then reverse, the effects of liberation, many of the new connections born of emancipation began to unravel. And some of the competition between different social groups, developed during the time of freedom, exploded into open conflict. Meanwhile, those who resisted Guadeloupe's increasingly repressive administrations, demanding instead an even greater share of liberty, founded their vision of the future on the advantages they had wrested out of the regime of emancipation.[40]

---

40. Lacrosse to minister, 15 Vendémiaire, An XI (Oct. 7, 1802), in CAOM, C 7A, 56, 173-174.

THE REVOLUTION'S SPIRAL

In Alejo Carpentier's *Explosion in a Cathedral*, the Cuban character Esteban, disappointed with the excesses of Victor Hugues's regime, leaves Guadeloupe to serve as a sailor on a corsair. Traveling the seas in the service of the Republic, Esteban and the rest of the crew—led by a first mate who is "a mixture of Carib and negro, born in Marie-Galante"— often spend days harbored along abandoned stretches of coast, where he confronts various forms cast up by the Caribbean Sea: pieces of European glass perfected by the water and the indigenous spiral snail shells that speak to him of a temporal logic profoundly different from the linear progress envisioned by the Revolution. His corsair runs across a Spanish slave ship on which the slaves have mutinied, killed the crew, and taken over. "All along the African coast they knew that the Republic had abolished slavery in its American colonies and that the negroes there were now free citizens." The French captain promises those on the ship that they will be freed once they have arrived in Guadeloupe and "complied with the legal requirements of naming and registering, which turned former slaves into French citizens." In fact, however, the captain, following Hugues's orders, brings the ship to a Dutch island to sell them as slaves. To Esteban's quotation of the abolition decree, the captain replies, "We live in an illogical world. Before the Revolution a slave trader sailed these seas, owned by a *philosophe* and a friend of Jean-Jacques. And do you know what she was called? The *Contrat social*." Traveling the waters, Esteban comes face-to-face with the reversals and contradictions of a revolution in retreat.[1]

During 1797 and 1798, there was increasing conflict in Paris about

---

1. Alejo Carpentier, *Explosion in a Cathedral* (New York, 1963), 184, 189; see also Simon Gikandi, *Writing in Limbo: Modernism and Caribbean Literature* (Ithaca, N.Y., 1992).

the wisdom and results of the slave emancipation project inaugurated in 1794. Its supporters managed to consolidate its institutional and symbolic foundations: the juridical and political assimilation of metropole and colony, the celebration of former slaves-turned–citizen-soldiers, and the belief that plantation agriculture could be maintained without slavery. At the same time, however, opponents of emancipation gathered strength on both sides of the Atlantic, arguing that the end of slavery had opened the door to the innate wildness of Africans and destroyed the once-thriving colonial economy.

At the heart of the debate over emancipation lay questions about the nature of the ex-slaves and their capacity to be free laborers and citizens. The portrayals of brutalized slaves put forth by gradual abolitionists like Condorcet had helped lay the foundation for the Republican racism of Hugues's regime in the mid-1790s. Meanwhile, the arguments made by Hugues and other administrators that ex-slaves needed strict guidance in their move from bondage to freedom were taken up by those who asserted it was necessary to severely contain, and even reverse, emancipation's effects. Hugues's transformation of Republican liberation into coercion became a model for some critics of abolition, who promulgated racist discourses in a push that would ultimately unravel the egalitarian project of 1794.

In his prerevolutionary writings, Condorcet had imagined what society would look like, and what the former slaves would do, after slavery. Unlike him, writers in the late 1790s could claim the advantage of having observed and evaluated what emancipation had actually wrought in the Caribbean. Many pointed to the years of economic and social disruption, particularly in Saint-Domingue, as proof that the slaves had not been ready for sudden freedom, which they claimed had done little more than let loose their inherent laziness and barbarism. Of course, such critics presented a highly selective portrait of the situation in the French Caribbean, emphasizing images of chaos over more balanced evaluations that took into account the military and occasional economic successes of administrations such as Hugues's in Guadeloupe and L'Ouverture's in Saint-Domingue. Having been primed on the dangers of emancipation before 1794, they interpreted the complexities of the present according to the scripts of the past, often concluding from afar, blind to the nuances of the colonial situation, that sudden freedom had been an unmitigated disaster. There was, in fact, a striking continuity between the arguments in favor of gradual abolition proposed in the 1780s, the arguments used by Hugues in justifying his coercive labor policies during his regime, and the arguments that began as early as 1797 in favor of a reversal of emancipation.

This chapter explores the progress of antiabolitionist arguments during the late 1790s and the defense mounted against them on the part of friends of emancipation. It begins, however, by examining the evolution of Hugues's ideas as he adapted and responded to the changing political landscape. Seeking to justify his actions in Guadeloupe, Hugues meditated in detail on the difficulties—and failures—of his mission in the colony, producing an archive that illustrates both his own frustrations with manumission and the spiraling contradictions embedded in the antislavery and Republican thought that had been the foundation for his regime.

The Republic's Retreat

By 1795, the radical Republic of the previous years was in retreat in the Antilles as in metropolitan France. In the summer of 1794, Robespierre had been guillotined and the Jacobin control of the state had been broken. Subsequently, the clubs, tribunals, and institutions of direct democracy that had been the hallmark of the Jacobin regime were dismantled. The new 1795 constitution decreased and diffused the power of elected representatives by replacing the National Convention with a *Corps législatif* composed of two bodies, the *Conseil des cinq cents* and the *Conseil des anciens*, overseen by an executive council, the Directory. But Jacobin policies of emancipation remained. Although the representatives of the Saint-Domingue planters had succeeded in staging Sonthonax and Polverel's public trial, in which they accused the two commissioners of destroying the colony, it ultimately ended with the public vindication of the defendants and of the abolition they had decreed in 1793. Attempts on the part of deputies from the Indian Ocean colonies to exempt them from the decree of 1794 also failed. The 1795 constitution cemented the 1794 emancipation decree in crucial ways. It declared the colonies an "integral part" of France and made them departments within the nation, thus confirming their full integration into the political and legal sphere of the Republic. There was to be, in principle, no distinctions between the forms of administration applied in metropole and colony. In specifying its colonial policy, the Convention explicitly stated that the commissioners it sent could not deviate from this principle or undo any of the provisions of the 1794 emancipation regarding the legal status of the colonial policy.[2]

If the bold confirmation of the political implications of emancipation was a defeat for exiled planters, the new regime did improve their situation in another respect. With the Jacobin government destroyed and the Terror ended, French policies regarding the émigrés who had fled—because they were actively being pursued as traitors to the Republic or simply feared falling prey to its guillotines—was considerably softened. Many (though by no means all) refugees began to return to metropolitan France. Many of those exiled from the Caribbean colonies, often in nearby British colonies or in the United States, also took advantage of the new French policy to return home. Their arrival in the colonies, of course, raised many complicated issues. Their abandoned plantations had, after all, been taken over by the state and were under the control of state-appointed managers or else individuals renting the properties from the state. Former owners had to petition the local administrators to take back control over their property and sometimes found significant obstacles placed in their way. When they did get their plantations back, they once again gained control—though not, of course, ownership—of those of their former slaves who remained there. Understandably, many of the formerly enslaved in Guadeloupe, as well as in Saint-Domingue, watched the return of their old masters with suspicion and worry about what was to come.

Victor Hugues put the new French policies of émigrés into effect in November 1795 with a proclamation inviting residents of Guadeloupe who had fled to the United States to come home. Although the point of his administration, he wrote, had been to "erase the miseries of our co-citizens in Guadeloupe"—that is, the former slaves—"by drawing a curtain across all that had happened" before his arrival in 1794, Hugues emphasized that the "blacks" had only been given "that portion of liberty that could be accorded to unfortunates who have barely surpassed the limits of instinct." "We have never believed," he wrote, "that a rascal was the equal of an honest man, that a brute, or a drunk, thanks to

2. Florence Gauthier, "La Convention thermidorienne et le problème coloniale, septembre 1794–septembre 1795," in Michel Vovelle, ed., *Le Tournant de l'An III: Réaction et terreur blanche dans la France révolutionnaire* (Paris, 1997), 109–119, esp. 113–115. Transcripts of the debates between Sonthonax and Polverel and their attackers were published in *Débats entre les accusateurs et les accusés dans l'affaire des colonies* . . . (Paris, 1795).

equality can enter and sit at the patriarchal banquet of an honest family; that the wife of a virtuous citizen could be compared to a prostitute." As a result, "people have been protected. . . . Property has been respected. . . . The agriculture is just as it was three years ago: there are no idlers, no vagabonds."[3]

By declaring publicly that he had maintained agriculture just as it had been before emancipation, Hugues was attempting conciliation with the planter class he had so ferociously attacked a few years before. In a letter to the Comité de salut public a few days after this proclamation, Hugues wrote in a similar, patronizing vein: "The blacks of Guadeloupe are good, they have no seed of corruption, they are easy to control, happy thanks to the fertility of the soil, and they are working as they did in the ancien régime." He had, he was suggesting, succeeded in extracting as much labor from the people he had freed as their owners once had. At the same time, however, he noted with sympathy that some ex-slaves were anxious about the return of their "ex-masters and executors." Many new citizens, furthermore, were aware of the increasing power of exiled planters in government circles in Paris and were concerned about their danger to emancipation. As Hugues understood, returning masters and rumors of impending assaults on freedom were an explosive combination. The new political situation threatened to destroy his administration's balancing act, which had at least partially succeeded (as those who had appointed him in 1794 had requested) in applying emancipation while avoiding the collapse of the colonial economy.[4]

Hugues dealt with the problem, characteristically, by solidifying his authoritarian regime. To do so, however, he had to openly resist the central tenet of the 1795 constitution's colonial policy: that the colonies were an "integral" part of the French Republic, and therefore their residents had the right to elect representatives to the parliament in Paris. In letters written to the minister of the colonies in Paris in late 1796, Hugues sought to justify his rejection of this and other provisions of the nation's new constitution. There he provided, more forthrightly and honestly than he ever had before, an ideological justification for his enforcement of Republican liberation through a dictatorial and coercive system.

"The constitution that offers so many advantages in France," Hugues

3. "Proclamation aux citoyens français des isles du Vent actuellement aux Etats-Unis," 27 Brumaire, An IV (Nov. 18, 1795), in CAOM, C 7A, 48, 34.
4. "Les Commissaires délégués . . . au Comité de salut public," 29 Brumaire, An IV (Nov. 20, 1795), in CAOM, C 7A, 48, 37-38.

announced, "presents only difficulties in these lands; apply it here, and tomorrow there will be no more colonies." By making the colonies departments of France, the constitution asserted the residents' rights to vote. Suffrage was not universal—voters were required to make an "electoral contribution" that would have been beyond the means of most of the colonial population—but the constitution also declared that all those who had participated in military campaigns for the "establishment of the Republic" were automatically citizens with full political rights. Many men of African descent, whether because of their ability to meet economic requirements or because they were veterans, were thereby assured the right to vote. Hugues, however, announced clearly that he had no intention of allowing their democratic participation. "The government alone can create the happiness of the noirs," he wrote late in December 1796 to the minister. "They are incapable of doing it themselves." The "will" of the blacks was "none other than that of those vile instruments who have constantly manipulated them." Although Hugues accepted they might one day be ready for political participation, that time was not yet at hand. "It is only by degrees," he explained in August 1796, "through education, through the needs and even the vices of society that we can bring these unfortunates to the state the government calls them toward." He advocated placing "the most intelligent of the blacks" in "civil and military positions," where they could learn to "enjoy the liberty that will turn to their advantage and to that of the government." He kept this selective granting of administrative positions to blacks entirely in his hands, however, and did not address broader political participation by the black population.[5]

Hugues pointed to recent events in Saint-Domingue, where he claimed black voters had been manipulated into casting ballots for candidates favored by local leaders. He insisted that black electoral participation, far from strengthening democracy, instead opened the door to anti-Republican and antimetropolitan activity. Indeed, Saint-Domingue

5. Hugues to minister, 22 Thermidor, An IV (Aug. 9, 1796), 20 Frimaire, An V (Dec. 10, 1796), in CAOM, C 7A, 49, 43–45, 61–63; on the 1795 constitution, see Bernard Gainot, "La Constitutionnalisation de la liberté générale sous le Directoire," in Marcel Dorigny, ed., *Les Abolitions de l'esclavage: De L. F. Sonthonax à V. Schoelcher, 1793, 1794, 1848* . . . (Paris, 1995), 213–229, esp. 222; on Hugues, see also William S. Cormack, "Victor Hugues and the Reign of Terror on Guadeloupe, 1794–1798," in A. J. B. Johnston, ed., *Essays in French Colonial History: Proceedings of the 21st Annual Meeting of the French Colonial Historical Society* (East Lansing, Mich., 1997), 31–41, esp. 37–38.

The Meaning of Citizenship, 1794–1798

under L'Ouverture's regime was already "lost for all the powers of Europe," and "the greatest folly our government can commit is to try and reestablish control over it; to do that, we would have to sacrifice a huge number of men and almost all of the existing population," and "three centuries of prosperity would not compensate" for the "expense" of such a war. He was determined not to allow a similar situation in Guadeloupe and was convinced that doing so required closing the door entirely to black voters. In August 1796, he threatened the minister with the specter of the massacres should his control over the colony be loosened: "Who will be able to contain ninety thousand strong and robust individuals, embittered by long suffering, terrible tortures, and horrible punishments? Who will be able to contain the natural ferocity of the Africans when it is compounded with their desire for vengeance?"[6]

To prevent black rampages against whites as well as the rise of dangerous local dictators seeking autonomy from France, they must be ruled through his own brand of dictatorship. As he put it forcefully in a personal letter in December 1796:

> I have not felt it necessary to assemble the *peuple noir* to name representatives, I will never do it; honor and my conscience will not permit me to. I will not play games with what is most sacred to society. No. Show my letter to the minister, to the directors, tell them that he who reestablished order, ... who maintained the work of the manufacturers will never burn this all down under the *vain* word of liberty. I will not sacrifice the blood of Europeans, only that of the British. The noirs are freer here than in Saint-Domingue, they suffer no bad treatment, *they depend only on the government* and not on their former masters; they are fat and happy, and they love and cherish the whites because the leaders of the colony are men who deserve to be *cherished*.[7]

Yet, if the blacks in Guadeloupe indeed "cherished the whites" thanks to his regime, he did not share their sentiments. In fact, he saw white political participation as extremely dangerous as well, though for reasons different from those that encouraged him to suppress black voting. The colonial whites were hopelessly corrupt and hostile to the Repub-

---

6. Hugues to minister, 22 Thermidor, An IV (Aug. 9, 1796), 20 Frimaire, An V (Dec. 10, 1796), in CAOM, C 7A, 49, 43–45, 61–63.

7. "Extrait d'une lettre de Hugues à Fourniols," 26 Frimaire, An V (Dec. 16, 1796), in CAOM, C 7A, 49, 65–66. Fourniols was one of the deputies in exile from Martinique who lived in Paris.

lic and to emancipation. They did "nothing but sigh after the arrival of the British or of some other order that will allow them to enjoy and dispose of their slaves." "It is impossible," he added, "to persuade them that slavery has been abolished and that they must lose all hope of seeing it reestablished." Reviving the old portrait, favored by Sonthonax among others, that painted white planters as traitors loyal to nothing but slavery, Hugues argued that allowing such individuals to have political power could just as easily lead to the end of the colony for France as black political participation might. And, just as allowing free rein to the blacks would lead to the killing of whites, allowing too much power to the whites would also incite violence. With the exception of two or three hundred "men of principle" who had come from the metropole, all the whites in the colony were "the sworn enemies of the blacks, as much as the blacks are the sworn enemies of the whites." Only strict control over the population could prevent civil war between the different groups.[8]

Not only the democratic institutions promised by the 1795 constitution were, according to Hugues, inapplicable to the colonies. The constitution, as Hugues wrote in August 1796, made it illegal to "subject a man, through regulations, to work for others." But such subjection was fundamental to the colony's labor regime. If he followed the "spirit" of the constitution, he would have to give complete liberty to "a man who only needs ten days out of the year to procure himself all he needs to live for a year." In the Caribbean, he wrote in December 1796, a man "has no needs, clothes are useless to him, indolence and laziness are his ultimate happiness, and he is inspired by none of the passions that can motivate men to work." Mimicking old arguments regarding the necessity of slavery, Hugues stated that the alternative to forced plantation labor—the distribution of land—was not viable for the same reason: "We must tell you with assurance that, if the government decided to distribute the national properties, even to the Africans, the Republic would lose a great deal of capital owing to the natural laziness of all inhabitants of countries where life's basic needs can be procured for nothing." Even money could not inspire laborers in such a climate: "There is nothing more painful than agricultural work in the colonies, there is no wealth in the world that can recompense the cultivateur for his pains under this burning sun." Without the threat of force, the ex-slaves would simply

8. Hugues and Lebas to minister, 22 Thermidor, An IV (Aug. 9, 1796), in CAOM, C 7A, 49, 43–45. See also Cormack, "Victor Hugues and the Reign of Terror," in Johnston, ed., *Essays in French Colonial History*, 31–41, esp. 37–38.

The Meaning of Citizenship, 1794–1798

choose other means of survival, and the colonial economy would crumble. And it would be impossible for him to fulfill the orders from the government that expected him to maintain the colony's productivity. "How can I, Minister, reconcile the constitution with the orders you have given: *make severe regulations for cultivation?*" Referring to the methods he was forced to use to maintain production, he asked provocatively: *"Is this the spirit of the constitution?"*[9]

The answer was no, as Hugues admitted. Ironically, he was openly advocating the position that had been the mainstay of planter politics during the early 1790s: that the governance of the colonies required a set of particular laws to be developed by those familiar with their climate and customs. The argument came with a twist. Having contended both that blacks were incapable of democratic participation and that colonial whites could not be trusted to support the Republic, he himself was the only "expert," and the regime he had constructed was the only effective model for colonial administration. He insisted he was a supporter of abolition: "We are far from thinking of a recall of the decree of 16 Pluviôse, we are not friends of slavery," he wrote to the minister in August, but his regime provided an effective middle road between too much and too little freedom. In December, he asserted that it was as dangerous "to submit [ex-slaves] to a rigorous slavery" as it was to allow them "to enjoy a great liberty."[10]

During the next year, Hugues governed Guadeloupe as he had since 1794, essentially ignoring the provisions of the 1795 constitution. He kept careful control over the whites who returned to Guadeloupe, as L'Ouverture did for those who returned to Saint-Domingue during the same period. The formerly enslaved, meanwhile, found no relief from plantation labor—and no opportunity for political participation.

Hugues was lucid enough to see that his outright refusal to apply the government's orders was dangerous, and he knew that exiles from the colony were campaigning in Paris for his removal. In December 1797, therefore, he wrote new justifications for his behavior to the minister of the colonies. His letters, now somewhat desperate, fervently condemned the Caribbean society he was seeking to govern, arguing that its history made its residents incapable of living according to Republican principles.

9. Hugues and Lebas to minister, 22 Thermidor, An IV (Aug. 9, 1796), in CAOM, C 7A, 49, 43–45.

10. Hugues to minister, 22 Thermidor, An IV (Aug. 9, 1796), 20 Frimaire, An V (Dec. 10, 1796), in CAOM, C 7A, 49, 43–45, 61–63.

"The preferences, the injustice, and the dangerous and destructive pleasures" of slavery's "corrupted regime" had given the colony a degraded population whose "contrary elements" made it virtually ungovernable. He reiterated that the principles of the Republic, "excellent in theory," were simply "inapplicable to the colonies and to the men of all colors who inhabit them." Whites were interested only in money and in regaining their former power. "The devouring ambition to command, the desire to enslave the African and slit the throats of the whites" possessed the gens de couleur, and only a campaign of public education could prevent them from passing on "their vices and their corruption" to their children. "As for the miserable blacks," Hugues continued, "they demand all the interest and the attention of the government; there is no time to lose if we wish to call them to liberty by gentle and gradual means." They had to be persuaded to "no longer see Europeans as executioners, as they did before," or—he wrote with what might have been a tinge of self-criticism— as men who were "sent from the metropole . . . to torture their painful lives." In the meantime, he added with more characteristic firmness, they needed guidance from wise Europeans "to bring them true happiness, as opposed to some chimerical happiness that in making them free delivers them to the passions, the stupidity, and the ferocity so natural to the climate from which they come."[11]

Never shy about criticizing the white planters, Hugues nevertheless turned to the seductive language of racism at the center of planter ideology in illustrating the difficulties he had faced in Guadeloupe. In late 1796, he had focused primarily on the climate of the Caribbean as the main cause of "indolence"; by late 1797 he increasingly concentrated on the African background of the formerly enslaved in emphasizing their "barbarism." He invoked the danger that Guadeloupe might become "a theater of carnage and blood, like the coast of Africa that is inhabited by the most barbarous of peoples." And he argued that the mixing of so many of Africa's "opposed and diverse peoples" in Guadeloupe was itself a source of conflict. There were a "great number of different nations that can never sympathize with one another" among the Africans on the island. Five or six hundred different nations were represented, "some holding on to religious practices, others to political practices, all enemies of one another." "The Mandinques disinter cadavers to eat them, and others have customs that are less cruel but as repugnant for their

11. Hugues and Lebas to minister, 7 Nivôse, An VI (Dec. 27, 1797), in CAOM, C 7A, 49, 240-243.

extraordinary filth, and from which they cannot abstain in the colonies, even though they are under surveillance. Infanticide is a religious sacrifice for some of them." Their cultural differences were a danger to the tranquillity of the island. "All these different customs form the pretext for a thousand particular quarrels between them that would become general if it were not for the attentive eye of the government." These African ex-slaves were uncontrolled in their violence. "Since the decree of general liberty we have been unable to prevent them from buying sabers," and, where quarrels and wife beatings had occurred before with fists and sticks, they had now become lethal. "We have seen them next to their mutilated victims, crying and lamenting and asking for death, and cursing the inanimate metal to whom they attributed their crimes." Furthermore, they settled their romantic quarrels with poison. Hugues went so far as to blame the Africans in the colony for the worst qualities among the "whites born in the colonies," who were just as immoral, subject to drunkenness and excess and "the most inconceivable superstitions." "There are few among the rich planters, who were raised by the former slaves, who do not carry the traces of the first impressions they received, and all believe in *revenants* [ghosts] and *enchanteurs* [magicians]."[12]

Hugues's late 1797 writings paint a portrait of a culture tainted both by "barbaric" African culture and the conflicts it brought to the New World and by the brutality of slavery and the corruption it induced in blacks and whites alike. He had sought to replace it with his own magic, his own cause for ultimate sacrifice: the Republic. But within a few short years he was openly expressing his disillusionment with transforming the colonies. The letters of 1796 and 1797 were of course shaped by his desire to justify his actions to the French government and in no small part to protect the authoritarian regime he had crafted for himself in Guadeloupe. Still, they reflect a broader trend then taking shape in the French Atlantic, where many once-passionate defenders of slave liberation a few years before increasingly decried the period of emancipation as a failure and suggested, as the defeated planters of 1794 once had, that the laws of the metropole could not effectively be applied to the colonies.

As he strained to resolve the contradictions between Republican rights and official determination to salvage the colonial economy, Hugues ex-

12. Hugues and Lebas to minister, 4 Brumaire, 7 Nivôse, An VI (Oct. 25, Dec. 27, 1797), in CAOM, C 7A, 49, 228–229, 240–243. For a contemporary description of African religions in Saint-Domingue, see Michel-Étienne Descourtilz, *Voyages d'un naturaliste et ses observations . . .* , 3 vols. (Paris, 1809), III, 109–234.

plained the failures of his reign by focusing on the colonial population's incapacity. Burying any reflection on the courses not taken (for instance, that of distributing land and creating a new economy based on small-scale agriculture), Hugues accounted for the disappointing outcome of the project of liberation by lashing out against the sloth and savagery of the ex-slaves. Within a few years, in Saint-Domingue, L'Ouverture would make similar claims as he set up a militarized and dictatorial regime emphasizing the maintenance of a plantation economy. Unlike L'Ouverture, Hugues had also, at least by 1797, begun to blame the faults of the colonial laborers on their origin in Africa, albeit while attacking white planters. Many critics of emancipation, meanwhile, ultimately came to depend entirely on racist portrayals of the formerly enslaved in explaining what had gone wrong in the Caribbean. Some in fact contrasted Hugues's white-run regime, presented as successfully containing the violence and laziness of the ex-slaves, to the black-run government of Saint-Domingue, portrayed as both bloody and despotic, overlooking how the similarities between the two regimes far outweighed their differences. Buttressed by the power of a racism that the strident egalitarianism of the Revolution had sought to dull but had instead found new outlets in the form of Hugues's Republican racism, advocates of the old order began, quietly at first, arguing that the best solution was to restore the colonies to their situation before 1789, before the upheavals of the Revolution had thrown the vital production of colonial commodities—and the racially ordered society that maintained it—into disorder.[13]

Defending the Past

In 1797, the former planter Thouluyre Mahé found himself in exile in Paris, far from his home in Guadeloupe. Mahé had been deported by Victor Hugues, and he was unsparing in his attacks against the commissioner. Because it was at a "distance from the protective power" of the metropole, Guadeloupe had long suffered under Hugues's abusive rule,

13. Hugues's turn to racism in explaining the failures of his regime presages the broader development of racist thought in post-emancipation Jamaica; see Thomas C. Holt, *The Problem of Freedom: Race, Labor, and Politics in Jamaica and Britain, 1832–1938* (Baltimore, 1992); Holt, "The Essence of the Contract: The Articulation of Race, Gender, and Political Economy in British Emancipation Policy, 1838–1866," in Frederick Cooper, Thomas C. Holt, and Rebecca J. Scott, eds., *Beyond Slavery: Explorations of Race, Labor, and Citizenship in Postemancipation Societies* (Chapel Hill, N.C., 2000), 33–60.

The Meaning of Citizenship, 1794–1798

wrote Mahé, and it was time for the Directory regime to replace him. The white population in Guadeloupe had decreased from 13,000 before the Revolution to only 3,000 in 1797, to some extent because of the emigration of those "attached to royalism" but more important because of "fear of the horrible scenes that the extreme license among the blacks would lead to after the proclamation of their liberty." The blacks, Mahé claimed, had also suffered from the preceding years. Of the 110,000 that were in the colony in 1790, only 80,000 were left; the number had diminished both from emigration of whites who took slaves with them and from the "ravages of all kinds of sicknesses and the losses in combat." According to Mahé, "the black cultivateurs of the countryside, after two years of the ordeal of their new state of liberty, after abandoning themselves to pillage and devastation in the first excesses of their enthusiasm and the license," were miserable, hungry and sick and ready to return to their masters. In fact, most of them had already "confessed their faults" and had "once again, on their own and with heartfelt feeling, begun calling the whites their masters and fathers."[14]

Mahé was one of many planters from the Caribbean who took refuge in metropolitan France. Some had arrived in Bordeaux throughout the 1790s, taking advantage of previous contacts they had with merchants to set up residences for what they hoped would be short periods of exile. Before the Revolution and during its early years, planters had often been in conflict with merchants who controlled colonial commerce and supported the monopoly regulations that protected their share in it. By the late 1790s, however, these two groups were increasingly united behind the argument for a return to the old economic order. In June 1797, when nearly a hundred merchants from the town of Bordeaux produced a memoir about the colonies, they presented the planters as innocent victims of savage slave insurgents and the Republican policies that had supported them, declaring that it was time for "all good citizens to speak of the colonies, to sigh over their ruins, and to invoke justice and humanity" for the persecuted planters. Unlike Mahé, however, these merchants approved of Hugues's regime. Although most of the pre-

14. Thouluyre Mahé, "Coup d'oeil sur la Guadeloupe et dépendances en 1797," in CAOM, C 7A, 49, 138-143. According to a 1796 census, the population of whites had indeed dropped sharply, though not as much as Mahé claimed, from the 14,000 or so in 1790 to 7,006. His claim about the number of blacks was more accurate; there were 79,445 people on the island who were described either as "noirs" or "rouges" in 1796. See the "Etat sommaire des citoyens," in CAOM, G 1, 502, no. 9.

Revolutionary colonial commerce that was "indispensable to France"—in part because of "tastes that had become needs"—had been destroyed by careless projects of emancipation in Guadeloupe, they wrote, "the sequestered habitations are cultivated to a certain extent, and the captures made in its waters are the primary resource that feeds the population." The planters there, haunted by the events in Saint-Domingue, were afraid to ask too much of their cultivateurs, but they were alive under the power and protection of "a man who, like others, believed that one could not accelerate the application of the constitution to the French colonies"—Victor Hugues. Hugues, the merchants noted, understood what administrators in Saint-Domingue ("where terror and death reign, where the blind wander aimlessly," contained through fear by "cruel leaders who themselves are tormented by the crimes they have committed") had not: that the colonies had to be ruled by a separate regime of laws from metropolitan France.[15]

The "new" colonies of the Americas, the merchants argued, were not like the colonies of past times, which were founded "under the same skies, where the same customs and habits could be propagated." The majority of their population was composed of "men born under the burning skies of Africa" whom nature had carefully distinguished "from Europeans." Given this, could the "regime" of metropole and colony "be the same?" The policy of emancipation had argued that they could, in the belief that Republican laws could transform slaves into citizens. But "the exercise of political rights can only belong to a civilized population," and it was obvious that, on the "bloody island" of Saint-Domingue, there was "a majority of savages." "It is a great error to think that the Africans see liberty with the same eyes as the Republicans," the merchants wrote. "The majority do not understand it; many disdain it." In fact, the Africans, "called to the exercise of their rights without having been enlightened on their duties," were "far from happy." The precipitous emancipation decree had completely neglected the "care and management" necessary for the modification of "the primitive races," and, as those who had opposed it had predicted, the result was misery for Africans and Europeans alike. Instead of equality, the domination of whites over blacks had been exchanged for the domination of blacks over whites. In Saint-

15. "Mémoire des négociants de Bordeaux sur les colonies," 1 Messidor, An V (June 19, 1797), in AN, AF III, 208, dossier 947, no. 26. On Bordeaux, see Eric Saugera, *Bordeaux, port négrier: Chronologie, économie, idéologie, XVIIe–XIXe siècles* (Paris, 1995).

Domingue, only a "regime of force" could bring the cultivateurs back to work and give the planters security. Inspired, perhaps, by Hugues's example, the merchants noted that, even within the existing laws of the Republic, the ex-slaves' liberty could be restricted. A distinction could be made "within the black," between "his person and his work." "May his person be free," proposed the merchants, "but may his work belong to the person who feeds him and promises to take care of him in his old age."[16]

In its appeals and demands, the memoir of the merchants of Bordeaux was typical of the documents produced during this period by individuals in the metropole—both among the merchant classes who had been involved in the Atlantic economy and the community of exiled planters from the Caribbean—who had been affected by the dramatic transformations in the colonial economy set in motion by slave revolt and slave emancipation. Emboldened by the increasing conservatism in France, seeking redress for the injuries they felt they had received as the result of abolition, such individuals came to form an important political community that revived the old activism of the Paris planters, which had been defeated in 1794. They would ultimately have a profound impact on French colonial policy, shaping attempts at reform that had dramatic, and unintended, consequences when they were applied in the Caribbean.

One particularly illustrative document from the time was issued by a representative of the planters of Cayenne, in French Guiana, Marie St. Elaire, who echoed and expanded on the suggestions made by the merchants of Bordeaux in presenting a detailed plan for a new labor regime meant to reestablish order and prosperity in the Caribbean colonies. St. Elaire's plan is fascinating for the way it brought together various approaches, blending pro-slavery and abolitionist arguments from before the Revolution with new arguments shaped by observations about the recent course of emancipation in the French Caribbean. Africans were the only ones who could do the labor necessary in the sugar colonies, St. Elaire argued, since "nature has organized each species according to the temperature under which she placed it at its birth." Even if a mixed race that combined the characteristics of white and black might ultimately provide the ideal population for the colonies, a solution had to be found in the meantime. Given this, all had come to agree upon the "reality of the evil" of what had happened in the Antilles since the Revolution, and even "if opinions are divided on the possibility for remedying the situation, all

16. "Mémoire des négociants de Bordeaux," in AN, AF III, 208, dossier 947, no. 26.

agree that it would have been better to arrive at the stated goal through a more gradual and measured process." Presenting a plan for self-purchase similar to that put forth by Raimond in 1793, St. Elaire argued that this would have prevented all of the horrors that had flowed from immediate, large-scale emancipation. But what was to be done? Like the merchants of Bordeaux, St. Elaire was careful to distinguish between the different colonies of the Antilles and noted that the situation was the worst in Saint-Domingue. Martinique, because it had fallen into the hands of the British and slavery had never been abolished, would present no problem since once it came back into French hands gradual abolition could be instituted there with a clean slate. Guadeloupe, although it had seen "a part of the horrors that ravaged Saint-Domingue," had been preserved to some degree because Hugues "had been able to hold blacks in total submission to his will," keeping them "in fact, in slavery." The slavery of the cultivateurs of Guadeloupe was "the kind of slavery that is the most unbearable for them" because they were under the command of managers who had no personal interest in taking care of them, and it would therefore be easy to rebuild the old links between ex-masters and ex-slaves, who would be relieved to find themselves under responsible care again.[17]

Like Hugues and the merchants of Bordeaux, St. Elaire suggested that it was a folly to attempt to assimilate the colonies as departments of France without making modifications to the constitution. "For example," he asked, "shouldn't the right to citizenship be more difficult to acquire in these countries than in France? The easy attribution of this right degrades it and takes away the force that makes it the basis of public order. The exercise of this right requires great discernment, acquired knowledge, and many moral qualities." Soldiers, sailors, and servants were all restricted to a state of bondage; why shouldn't the blacks be, "at least until they have shown themselves worthy of escaping from it?" Practically speaking, immediately removing the rights of citizenship from all of the noirs (whose vanity had been flattered by this status) might cause problems. The solution was "to leave them the right to become a citizen but to make its acquisition difficult, basing this difficulty on the wider good." Only those with property or commercial establishments should be granted citizenship. In the meantime, plantations should be returned to their previous owners, and ex-slaves—with the exception of

17. Marie St. Elaire, "Mémoire sur les moyens de rétablir l'ordre, la culture et l'industrie dans les colonies françaises," 14 Messidor, An V (Jul. 2, 1797), in AN, AF III, 208, dossier 947, no. 29.

The Meaning of Citizenship, 1794–1798

those couples who had been married as a result of migrations during the previous years—forced to return to where they had lived at the moment of the "general decree of liberty." The ex-slaves were to sign contracts of at least six years with their ex-masters, with salaries based on the usefulness of the labor and the availability of capital in the region. Slowly, a new world would be born, one in which prosperity would be brought to the colonies through a regulated and just system of servitude that would reverse the chaos of the preceding years.[18]

St. Elaire, however, refrained from advocating the legal reestablishment of slavery, just as the Bordeaux merchants had done. Indeed, both texts suggested that such a legal reversal was unnecessary. But another text published in 1797 went a step further and argued that, although in the past slavery had been contrary to justice, a well-organized and rational system of slavery could be established that would not be a transgression of the rights of man. Using a critique of the "enslavement" of the free market, in which men were dependent "on a multitude of individuals who would employ them according to their whims," the text argued that to be enslaved under a set of rational laws and institutions was actually an advantage. In fact, slavery, according to the author, should be reestablished not only in the colonies but in metropolitan France as punishment for criminals and as an option for the indigent. Although emancipation in the Caribbean had been a disaster, entirely reversing its effects was impossible. "The time in which a crowd of nègres trembled in front of a single blanc is passed." So the author proposed a combination of slavery and freedom in which land would be distributed to those who were willing to cultivate it, but heavy taxes would be levied to force cultivateurs to produce a certain amount. Those who failed would be placed in slavery.[19]

The writings of Mahé, the merchants of Bordeaux, St. Elaire, and the anonymous advocate of slavery were assaults, issued by an increasingly vocal minority, on the reigning colonial policies of the French government. Since the 1795 constitution had declared the colonies to be departments, officials in Paris had continued to pronounce support for emancipation, and sympathetic portrayals of ex-slaves and gens de couleur as the saviors of the Republic in the Antilles were commonplace. In 1797, a major government report on the colonies again defended the ex-slaves and the gens de couleur as the heroic defenders of Saint-Domingue. In

18. St. Elaire, "Mémoire sur les moyens de rétablir l'ordre," 14 Messidor, An V (Jul. 2, 1797), in AN, AF III, 208, dossier 947, no. 29.

19. De la nécessité d'adopter l'esclavage en France . . . (Paris, 1797), 6–22.

the same year, a public report presented in the name of the Comité de salut public argued that the abolition of slavery was vital to the maintenance of the Republic in the Antilles and that the continuing labor of the free cultivateurs proved that slavery was not necessary in the colonies. On the stage in Paris in 1796, a play called *Sélico; ou, Les Nègres généreux* represented insurgent slaves who, joined in revolt by their master's son, showed their generosity by sparing their master's life. In 1798, another play entitled *Adonis; ou, Le Bon nègre*, told the story of a plantation owner who was taken prisoner by insurgent slaves under the command of Biassou (the name of an actual insurgent in 1791); eventually, the owner chose to free his slaves. During the same period, however, Bernardin de St. Pierre, the author of the 1788 *Paul et Virginie*, wrote a play that presented its attack on slavery by telling the story of white characters enslaved by blacks in Africa—a gesture that perhaps revealed growing anxieties about the power of ex-slaves over former masters in the Caribbean.[20]

Despite the widespread official support and artistic celebration of emancipation, its opponents had never been completely silent. In July 1795, during a heated debate in the National Convention, Jean Jacques Serres, a deputy from Île-de-France (a colony in the Indian Ocean), protested that "French blood" was being spilled so "Africans" would triumph in the colonies. When an angry black deputy from the colonies responded by shouting, "Am I a dog?" an anonymous voice responded, "No, but you are not French." During the same year, planter sympathizers continued to publicly denounce Sonthonax and Polverel, as well as Thyrus Pautrizel, the Republican from Trois-Rivières who had survived the 1793 insurrection to serve as a representative for Guadeloupe in the National Convention. The basic tenets of the planter ideology— that blacks were unworthy of liberty and citizenship and that the colonial economy could only function through forced labor—were no different in the late 1790s than they had been earlier in the decade. What changed was the political context into which their critiques were issued. Under the Directory regime, conservative policies regarding property rights and citizenship gradually gained popularity. Planters such as Son-

20. Gainot, "La Constitutionnalisation," in Dorigny, ed., *Les Abolitions*, 213–229, esp. 215–217; Jean-Philippe Garran de Coulon, *Rapport sur les troubles de Saint-Domingue* (Paris, 1797–1798); on the plays, see Edward Derbyshire Seeber, *Anti-slavery Opinion in France during the Second Half of the Eighteenth Century* (Baltimore, 1937), 183–187.

The Meaning of Citizenship, 1794–1798

thonax's attacker Jean Augustin Brulley and Serres gained clout, finding a sympathetic ear among conservatives in the government, notably those who gathered in the *Société de Clichy*, a body that had an important influence on shaping laws at the time and came to include attacks on colonial policy as part of a larger reactionary push.[21]

Opponents of colonial policy in Paris exploited the political conflicts occurring in Saint-Domingue in justifying their arguments against emancipation. One of the major targets of their attacks was General Étienne Laveaux, who had taken charge of Saint-Domingue when Sonthonax departed in 1794 and who had consolidated the alliance between Republican officials and the ex-slaves. In March 1796, Laveaux had made Toussaint L'Ouverture lieutenant governor of the island, a position he maintained after the arrival in May 1796 of the new commissioners, among them Sonthonax, sent by the Directory regime. Laveaux and L'Ouverture, however, alienated sectors of the gens de couleur population, many of whom saw themselves as the rightful inheritors of political power in the colony. The stronghold of this group was in the southern province, where General André Rigaud, even as he fought for the French Republic, carved out a local regime that operated with near autonomy. When the 1795 constitution arrived in the colony, L'Ouverture organized elections in the north to fill the seats allotted for Saint-Domingue in the Paris conseils. Among those chosen was Laveaux, whom L'Ouverture encouraged to travel to Paris in order to defend emancipation. Rigaud, however, also organized a set of elections. Two competing groups of delegates therefore left for Paris, where they both claimed the same seats in the Corps législatif. Planters astutely took advantage of the conflict, espousing the cause of the representatives from Rigaud's domain, arguing that the regime in the northern province was nothing more than a tyranny enforced by L'Ouverture's barbarous black troops. They succeeded in having the elections in the north declared null and void, removing key defenders of emancipation, notably Laveaux, from power. Clashes between various delegates from Saint-Domingue would continue throughout the following year. During the same period, news arrived in Paris that the two commissioners who had been sent to abolish slavery in the Indian Ocean colonies had been unceremoniously expelled by local whites, an event hailed by some planter representatives

21. Gauthier, "La Convention thermidorienne," in Vovelle, ed., *Le Tournant de l'An III*, 109–119, esp. 109; Gainot, "La Constitutionnalisation," in Dorigny, ed., *Les Abolitions*, 213–229, esp. 215–217.

as the triumph of reason over the dangerous law of emancipation. Daniel Lescallier, then head of the Bureau of the Colonies in the ministry in Paris, wrote a report defending the conduct of the whites in the Indian Ocean. In June 1797, responding to memoirs such as those written by Jastram and Mahé, the Directory recalled Hugues from his post in Guadeloupe. For a moment, it seemed the tide was beginning to turn against the policies of emancipation and racial equality that had transformed the Caribbean during the previous years.[22]

Across the Atlantic, French military gains were being rolled back dramatically. In Grenada, the arrival of massive reinforcements in the Caribbean enabled the British to defeat Fedon's rebellion in mid-1796. Although Fedon escaped the island, many of the captured insurgents were executed and the remainder deported to Honduras. The British mission also recaptured Saint Lucia, defeating the now-outnumbered French under Commissioner Goyrand. One British officer noted the courage of the French soldiers who "behaved, altho black, so well that they stood firing at half Pistol shot with the head of our attack, and only yielded, I verily believe, one Inch of ground, in the hopes of getting round us." Some of these soldiers escaped to the interior of the island and kept fighting a guerilla campaign, as they had in 1794. But the British offered amnesty to all those who surrendered, and increasing numbers responded. Additionally, in Saint Vincent, the British reestablished control and decided to rid the island of the Black Caribs who had resisted them for so long. On March 11, 1797, eleven ships carrying approximately two thousand mem-

22. See Gainot, "La Constitutionnalisation," in Dorigny, ed., *Les Abolitions*, 213–229, esp. 217–220; Dorigny and Gainot, *La Société des amis des noirs, 1788–1799: Contribution à l'histoire de l'abolition de l'esclavage* (Paris, 1998), 304–307; on Saint-Domingue, see Carolyn E. Fick, *The Making of Haiti: The Saint Domingue Revolution from Below* (Knoxville, Tenn., 1990), 190–194; C. L. R. James, *The Black Jacobins: Toussaint L'Ouverture and the San Domingo Revolution* (New York, 1963), 163–173; Robert Louis Stein, *Léger Félicité Sonthonax: The Lost Sentinel of the Republic* (London, 1985), chap. 10. The relationship between Laveaux and L'Ouverture during the years 1794–1796 is well documented in the correspondence between the two; see Bibliothèque nationale, Manuscrits occidentaux, Nouvelles acquisitions, 12102, T. 1–3. On the Indian Ocean situation, see Claude Wanquet, *La France et la première abolition de l'esclavage, 1794–1802: Le Cas des colonies orientales, Ile de France (Maurice) et la Réunion* (Paris, 1998); on Hugues, see H. J. K. Jenkins, "Controversial Legislation at Guadeloupe regarding Trade and Piracy, 1797," *Revue française d'histoire d'outre-mer*, LXXVI (1989), 97–106, esp. 104.

bers of this group sailed away from the eastern Caribbean. The successful campaigns Victor Hugues had carried out from his base in Guadeloupe had come to a close, and the French Republic had little to show for its bold moves against the British.[23]

"This System of Absolute Unity"

"I, too, will speak of the colonies," the author J. Rey-Delmas, a representative to the Corps législatif from Saint-Domingue, announced exuberantly in 1797. "I will open the register, where, by the light of the torches of the Eumenides, the steel chisel of truth will trace, in characters of blood, the horrors of the revolution of Saint-Domingue." The truth, proclaimed Rey-Delmas, was that the royalist white planters themselves, through their furious "detestation of French principles" and "hatred of liberty and equality," had caused the horrors of the revolution. They had incited the insurrection of 1791, but they could not contain it, and the "slave" of the north, "abandoning his hoe," pursued, "dagger in hand, the rash men who had armed him." Rey-Delmas defended the actions of Sonthonax and Polverel, arguing that, against the alliance between the planters and the British, "the colony would have been lost without the courage and patriotism of a few Europeans and natives of all colors who stayed loyal to the laws of the Republic, and without the firm resolution among the newly emancipated to defend their liberty to the death." The colony was indebted to these ex-slaves; "in the end it is to the Africans, the nouveaux libres, that Saint-Domingue owes the brilliant perspective that promised the healing of all its calamities." And the Republic had a duty to educate "a people born sober, gentle, and intelligent but corrupted by the vices and the depravity of Europeans, and to give them a

23. Edward L. Cox, "Fedon's Rebellion, 1795–1796: Causes and Consequences," *Journal of Negro History*, LXVII (1982), 7–19, esp. 9, 16; David Barry Gaspar, "La Guerre des Bois: Revolution, War, and Slavery in Saint Lucia, 1793–1838," in David Barry Gaspar and David Patrick Geggus, eds., *A Turbulent Time: The French Revolution and the Greater Caribbean* (Bloomington, Ind., 1997), 102–130; Charles Shephard, *An Historical Account of the Island of Saint Vincent* (London, 1831), 175. The deportees from Saint Vincent were left on an island off the coast of Honduras. Aided by a reputation as fierce fighters (being both maroon and Carib), they worked as mercenaries during the Central American civil wars of the early nineteenth century before settling in Guatemala and Belize, calling themselves the Garifuna. See Nancie L. Gonzalez, *Sojourners of the Caribbean: Ethnogenesis and Ethnohistory of the Garifuna* (Chicago, Ill., 1988).

taste for virtue that, no matter what their enemies say, is foreign neither to the Creole nor to the African."[24]

Eight days after the publication of this text in August, a coup d'état in Paris annulled the parliamentary elections in which many royalists had been chosen and purged the Directory of two of its members. The Abbé Sieyès, who had managed to survive the revolutionary turmoil and rise to power, was one of the architects and chief beneficiaries of the coup. The effect on colonial policy was ultimately to stall the progress of the anti-emancipation forces in metropolitan politics. The decision to recall Hugues was reversed, prolonging his militarily successful if insubordinate regime in Guadeloupe. Étienne Laveaux took up his seat and mounted a spirited defense of the besieged colonial policy, arguing for the need to complete the integration of the colonies into the national body by making the new citizens fully participating citizens. A number of fellow travelers joined Laveaux, notably representatives from Saint-Domingue who were serving in the conseils in Paris as well as the notary Elie Dupuch from Guadeloupe, to relaunch the defunct Société des amis des noirs, which they renamed the *Société des amis des noirs et des colonies*. The changes initiated with Sonthonax's abolition of slavery in 1793 and the National Convention's ratification of this act in 1794 was to continue as the Republic solidified its political assimilation of both the colonies and the ex-slaves.[25]

Laveaux's efforts led to the "Law on the Organization of the Colonies," which sought to create a juridical basis for the full assimilation of the colonies and contained a number of stipulations on the citizenship of the ex-slaves. Building on the provisions of the 1795 constitution, the law explicitly asserted that Caribbean veterans would have full political

24. J. Rey-Delmas, *Exposé rapide de la révolution de Saint-Domingue, depuis 1789, jusqu'en 1797* (Cherbourg, France, 1797). The Eumenides (Furies) were Greek goddesses who exposed and punished insolent mortals; see Robert Graves, *The Greek Myths* (New York, 1955), I, 122.

25. The representatives from Saint-Domingue serving in the parliament were Pierre Thomany, Jean-Louis Annecy (the secretary of the Conseil des anciens), and Étienne Mentor. On the little-known activities of the Société des amis des noirs et des colonies, see Dorigny and Gainot, *La Société des amis des noirs*, 301–396; see also Gainot, "La Constitutionnalisation," in Dorigny, ed., *Les Abolitions*, 213–229, esp. 221–225. Thomany, Annecy, and Mentor, along with Laveaux, were among the eleven representatives elected for the north province of Saint-Domingue in 1798; on Hugues, see Jenkins, "Controversial Legislation," *Revue française d'histoire d'outre-mer*, LXXVI (1989), 97–106, esp. 104.

The Meaning of Citizenship, 1794–1798

rights. A citizen who wanted to vote in a primary assembly could either pay an electoral contribution or present a certificate attesting that he had been part of "one or more campaigns against the enemies of the Republic." The law therefore insisted on the right—which Hugues had steadfastly refused a few years before—to political participation on the part of large numbers of formerly enslaved soldiers in the Caribbean. The law also reasserted the radical and internationalist significance of the French emancipation. "All black individuals, born in Africa or in foreign colonies, brought to the French islands, will be free as soon as they set foot on the territory of the Republic." Furthermore, "individuals who are black or de couleur [and] who were abducted from their homeland [patrie] and transported to the colonies will not be considered foreigners; they enjoy the same rights as a person born of the French territory, if they are attached to cultivation, serve in the army, or exercise a profession or trade." The law also made particular provisions that would make it easier for those born into slavery to access forms of documentation such as the état civil and the possibilities that flowed from them. For those "for whom the birth was not recorded in the public registers that serve to certify the state of citizens," the declaration of four citizens from the commune could serve as a substitute for a birth act.[26]

During the debates leading to promulgation of the law on the colonies, Laveaux argued for the need to expand the rights of citizenship even further. A strict reading of the stipulation that those who fought for the Republic should be citizens would mean that "the black cultivateurs were not French citizens." Yet the cultivateurs were equally vital to the military campaigns of the Republic, and their citizenship would be a crucial foundation for the establishment of "peace and internal tranquility" in the colonies. Laveaux asked, "Hasn't the cultivateur made himself as useful as the noir who has carried weapons? How would we have fed the army, if they had not wanted to cultivate the soil? France sent nothing to the colony of Saint-Domingue." Citizenship, Laveaux concluded, should be granted them as a reward: "If we agree that the state of the cultivateur is pernicious for Europeans, let us honor this state to encourage the noirs to continue."[27]

26. "Loi concernant l'organisation constitutionnelle des colonies," 12 Nivôse, An VI (Jan. 1, 1798), titre III, "Sur l'état des citoyens," Bulletin des lois, nos. 177, 178, in AN, AD VII, 20 A. See also Gainot, "La Constitutionnalisation," in Dorigny, ed., Les Abolitions, 213–229, esp. 222–223.

27. Quoted in Gainot, "La Constitutionnalisation," in Dorigny, ed., Les Abolitions, 213–229, esp. 223.

This radical vision of ex-slaves' profound contribution to the Republic informed Laveaux's public statements during the next years. In a speech celebrating the fifth anniversary of the 1794 abolition of slavery, Laveaux proclaimed: "On 16 Pluviôse, the Republic achieved a conquest of a kind that until then was unknown. She conquered, or rather created, for the *human race*, through a single powerful idea, a million new beings, and so expanded the family of man." This radical action made the vote for emancipation "one of the illustrious days of our Revolution." "In our colonies, *everything is French. This system of absolute unity* makes our disconcerted enemies go pale with rage, and from it the signal for colonial prosperity will be sent; you will soon hear it repeated by our brothers in the colonies, who will shout 'love for the law, the union, and for work!'" The British had expended huge amounts of money and human life trying to take over Saint-Domingue, "but all paled in front of the loyalty of those men that 16 Pluviôse made French citizens." The chief architect of the preservation of the colonies was, Laveaux claimed, Toussaint L'Ouverture, who was "intimately linked to the Republic" and "penetrated" with the principle that the colonies were an integral part of that Republic. The people of Saint-Domingue "never have lost and never will lose sight of the glorious title of the French citizens," and they had proved that, through their liberty, the colonies could be preserved and commerce could prosper. The deputy Pierre Thomany similarly declared on the anniversary—"a holiday for all friends of humanity"—that the National Convention's decision had brought together humanity and good politics. He argued, "Without this benevolent law that, in giving the nation new children, gave it new defenders, the avid Britishman would reign in the Antilles, and the tricolor flag would not float in the New World." The history of the Caribbean had shown that "the French have no friends more impassioned, the Republic has no citizen more zealous, than he who has become free."[28]

The powerful assertions of black citizenship rights made in the 1798 law on the colonies and in such public pronouncements were countered by the actions of some powerful political figures. In May 1798, the minister of the colonies, a planter from Saint-Domingue named Baron de

28. "Discours prononcé par Laveaux, sur l'anniversaire du 16 Pluviôse, An II," Corps législatif, Conseil des anciens, "Motion d'ordre, faite par P. Thomany, député du Département du nord, sur l'anniversaire de la liberté des noirs dans les colonies françaises," 16 Pluviôse, An VII (Feb. 4, 1799), Corps législatif, Conseil des cinq cents, both in the Bibliothèque nationale.

Bruix, ordered the creation of a segregated military unit that was to re-group all the "black or colored" soldiers then in metropolitan France. It was a direct assault on the institution that had most clearly come to define the racial egalitarianism of the Republic during the previous years; men who were serving alongside whites in French units were, solely on the basis of the color of their skin, to be reassigned to a unit composed only of men of African descent. Included in the order were soldiers who were not from the French colonies, such as the fifty-one-year-old Barbot, who was born in Chambéry, and Henry Fruchon, who was from Philadelphia. Throughout Europe, soldiers left their units and traveled to Île d'Aix, where the new unit was to reassemble. Once there, the soldiers, some of whom were accompanied by families, were poorly housed and fed; many illnesses and a few deaths occurred among the troop. They were sub-jected to various indignities, notably a prohibition against leaving the island and visiting nearby La Rochelle. One of the white officers physi-cally abused black soldiers. To make matters worse, a number of officers were demoted with the justification that their promotions on the Carib-bean battlefield were not legitimate—despite the fact that the homme de couleur captain of the new company, Marin Pèdre, had in fact pro-moted many of them himself when he led the Republican mission in Saint Vincent and was willing to vouch for them. Some blacks voted with their feet: the day after he was demoted from the rank of sergeant to that of a common soldier, Peper Sejourna deserted with another soldier from his home town of Saint-Pierre, Martinique. Others would follow in the succeeding months. But still others sought redress from the Repub-lic they had served loyally during the previous years. Through August and September, officers and soldiers from the Île d'Aix wrote more than thirty letters to the deputy Étienne Mentor, who like many of them was from Martinique, asking him to intervene on their behalf to end "their humiliating separation from the whites" and request that they be em-ployed "without distinction, like their comrades-in-arms, in the Repub-lican armies."[29]

29. See the order, from 3 Prairial, An VI (May 22, 1798), in AN, AD VII, 20 B; for the soldiers at the Île d'Aix, see "Formation de la compagnie des hommes de couleur," "Etat des sous-officiers," "Etat des officiers des différents grades," "Con-trôles des femmes et enfants," and "Etat des mouvements," in AHAT, X i, carton 80; on the letters sent by the soldiers, see Mentor's angry letter to Baron de Bruix, 21 Ventôse, An VII (March 10, 1799), rpt. in Dorigny and Gainot, *La Société des amis des noirs*, 385–392.

FIGURE 18. Etienne Mentor. 1802. Engraving by François Bonneville.
Cliché Bibliothèque nationale de France, Paris

The open resistance of these soldiers and officers, both in the form of petitions and desertion, was a powerful assertion of the right to racial equality. The soldiers of African descent who demanded fair treatment found an ally in Mentor. An homme de couleur, Mentor was one of these elected in 1797 as a representative for the northern province of Saint-Domingue and was serving in the Corps législatif in Paris. He sharply attacked the formation of the battalion, arguing that it set up a situation in which these soldiers were "isolated from their European comrades,

The Meaning of Citizenship, 1794–1798

so that it seems they are being punished for having supported, in the New World, the principles of the Republic." How could governors dare "to reestablish such insulting distinctions"? "The time has come to right all wrongs, to redress all grievances. Show yourselves once again to be the defenders of the Republicans of the Antilles, pursued by their old tyrants, by ending the exile that degrades them and that isolates them from the rest of the French. These courageous soldiers wish only to die fighting for the French Republic." Mentor's intervention convinced the other representatives; his proposition to retract the order was "unanimously adopted." Soon afterward, Bruix was relieved of his duties.[30]

As the conflicts over colonial policy raged in metropolitan France, agents dispatched to the Antilles by the Directory in March 1798 were encountering their own difficulties across the Atlantic. Among them was General Edme Étienne Borne Desfourneaux, who had been chosen to finally replace Victor Hugues as the governor of Guadeloupe. With him was Elie Dupuch, who had joined others in criticizing Hugues's arbitrary ways. Having survived years of attacks, Hugues finally fell prey, not to the machinations of his committed enemies the planters, but to those who wished to expand the assimilation of the colonies into the French Republic. His control over the legal institutions of the island, as well as his consistent refusal to apply the constitution of France to the colonies, clearly went against the agenda of Laveaux and his colleagues of the Société des amis des noirs et des colonies.[31]

Desfourneaux, like his Saint-Domingue colleagues, had the responsibility of applying the new colonial law to Guadeloupe. The law as it finally passed fell well short of Laveaux's radical vision. The more conservative members of the conseils had managed to water down much of its language, notably by granting the dispensation from the electoral contribution only to military veterans and not to plantation laborers. So the cultivateurs, who when they were paid at all were usually paid in commodities rather than money, were essentially excluded from voting. In the colonies, the possibilities for expanded electoral participation opened up by this law were incompletely applied, in part because one

30. "Motion d'ordre faite par Mentor," in AN, AD VII, 21 A, no. 52; see also the list of soldiers (including Magloire Pélage and Louis Delgrès) transferred on 29 Thermidor, An VII (Aug. 16, 1799), to the control of the Department of War, in AHAT, X i, carton 80. On Mentor's career, see Gaétan Mentor, *Histoire d'un crime politique: Le Général Etienne Victor Mentor* (Port-au-Prince, Haiti, 1999), esp. 49–53.

31. Dorigny and Gainot, *La Société des amis des noirs*, 320.

crucial loophole compromised the unity between metropolitan and colonial juridical structures. Although all laws decreed for the "continental departments" were applicable to the colonies, the government and their representatives could selectively apply them. The majority of the ex-slaves of the Caribbean essentially experienced only the more oppressive aspects of the law, which tied their citizenship to their continuing labor on the plantations. Indeed, the law repeated the regulations on labor that had become the hallmark of Hugues's regime, declaring that those without "a known domicile and condition" would be considered vagabonds, and those guilty of this crime would be denied the rights of citizenship until they returned to work on plantations or at their trades. The law also facilitated the return of certain émigrés and so accelerated the return of ex-masters to their plantations. Although Laveaux had originally envisioned a law meant to tighten the bonds of metropole and colony into a "system of absolute unity," the version that was ultimately sent to the colonies did the opposite, propelling the centripetal forces that brought the ex-slaves of the Caribbean into a violent conflict with metropolitan forces.[32]

The agent who left France to apply the new law in Saint-Domingue, General Gabriel Marie Theodore Joseph d'Hédouville, was given explicit orders to limit L'Ouverture's power, which was causing growing anxiety in the metropole. Indeed, after expelling Sonthonax from the island, and now commanding the deference of Julien Raimond, the last of the commissioners, to his authority, L'Ouverture had become the de facto ruler of the colony. On arriving, Hédouville pushed L'Ouverture to resign and gave his support to L'Ouverture's main rival, André Rigaud. He also replaced black troops with white ones in strategic locations, antagonized cultivateurs by issuing a decree that required them to sign contracts on their plantations for six to nine years, and ordered the punishment of all "vagabonds." In this Hédouville was perhaps following the suggestions made by Marie St. Elaire in his 1797 memoir. Far from being accepted by the cultivateurs, as St. Elaire had promised they would be, these measures incited revolt, particularly in the south province, where Hédouville put them down with the help of Rigaud. In the north province, Hédou-

32. See the "Loi concernant l'organisation constitutionnelle des colonies," 12 Nivôse, An VI (Jan. 1, 1798), in AN, AD VII, 20 A; for Laveaux's intervention in the debates, see "Opinion de Laveaux sur les colonies," 12 Nivôse, An VI (Jan. 1, 1798), in AN, AD XVIII, quoted in Gainot, "La Constitutionnalisation," in Dorigny, ed., *Les Abolitions*, 213–229, esp. 223.

FIGURE 19. Toussaint L'Ouverture. 1805. From Marcus Rainsford, *An Historical Account of the Black Empire of Hayti Comprehending a View of the Principal Transactions in the Revolution of Saint Domingo, with Its Ancient and Modern State* (London, 1805). *Cliché Bibliothèque nationale de France, Paris*

ville arrested Moïse, L'Ouverture's adopted nephew and a commander who was popular among cultivateurs. Moïse escaped and mobilized an army of cultivateurs to resist Hédouville, and L'Ouverture gave his general Jean-Jacques Dessalines orders to arrest and expel the French agent. Hédouville's mission deepened the conflict between Rigaud and L'Ouverture.[33]

In order to defeat Rigaud, L'Ouverture turned to Britain and the United States for supplies and weapons, operating autonomously and against the current of metropolitan policy. In 1798, tensions over the actions of French corsairs led to a break of relations between the United States and France, inciting a period of conflict that was to be called the "Quasi War." But, in November, L'Ouverture, dependent on external suppliers, wrote to John Adams requesting that trade be reestablished between Saint-Domingue and the United States. It was a bold move that signaled the leader of Saint-Domingue was willing to chart his own diplomatic course. Adams saw the advantages of such an agreement, and ammunition and weapons from the U.S. continued to flow into the colony during the remaining years of the Adams administration. By 1800, a French official estimated that thirty thousand muskets and large quantities of ammunition had been imported to the colonies from Britain and the U.S. At the time of his death, L'Ouverture left behind more than six million francs of deposits in Philadelphia banks, meant for the purchase of weaponry. In the eastern Caribbean, too, North American merchants would supply insurgents with weapons. In 1802, administrators involved in a struggle with the dissidents in Guadeloupe would attack such merchants for contributing to the "state of rebellion" against metropolitan authorities in the Caribbean. One had shocked them by declaring that "it didn't matter to him whether he was trading with blacks, yellows, or whites, as long as they had business, and that it was in troubled water that one caught the best fish."[34]

In 1798, U.S. naval forces actually intervened on behalf of L'Ouverture and Dessalines by blockading the port of Jacmel in order to help isolate Rigaud's army in the south. When a U.S. ship mistakenly captured and detained a white officer who was fighting with Dessalines, the latter an-

33. Fick, *Making of Haiti*, 196–203; see also James, *Black Jacobins*, 188–208.

34. Mats Lundahl, "Toussaint Louverture and the War Economy of St. Domingue, 1796–1802," *Slavery and Abolition: A Journal of Comparative Studies*, VI (September 1985), 122–138, esp. 123–124; Lacrosse and Lescallier to minister, 7 Floréal, An X (Apr. 27, 1802), in CAOM, C 7A, 56, 5–7.

grily wrote to the ship's captain that he should remember he had made a "treaty with an open and frank nation." L'Ouverture, in the concil- iatory letters he soon wrote apologizing for Dessalines's inflammatory words, noted that he wished to avoid anything that would "tend to dis- turb the good understanding between our two nations." Although he expressed no intention of separating from the Republic, L'Ouverture's establishing his own local laws and dealing directly with foreign repre- sentatives alarmed French metropolitan authorities. The increasingly au- tonomous regime in Saint-Domingue also prepared the terrain for the re- sistance that would explode against the French in 1802. In Guadeloupe, L'Ouverture's regime became a symbol for ex-slaves and those gens de couleur who sought to achieve greater equality and representation in the colony. In both Saint-Domingue and Guadeloupe, new citizens were be- ginning to see that, to preserve the Republic in the Antilles, they might have to defend it against France itself.[35]

35. The correspondence between Dessalines, L'Ouverture, and Captain Perry is in Perry Papers, I, William L. Clements Library, University of Michigan. I have examined the influence of Saint-Domingue on the conflict in Guadeloupe during this period in "The Promise of Revolution: Saint-Domingue and the Struggle for Autonomy in Guadeloupe, 1797–1802," in David Geggus, ed., *The Impact of the Haitian Revolution in the Atlantic World* (Columbia, S.C., 2001), 112–134.

Chapter 11

THE PROMISE OF REVOLUTION

In March 1797, a revolt erupted against the regime of Victor Hugues. The insurgents, most of them cultivateurs working on plantations in the region of Lamentin, responded to leaders who traveled from plantation to plantation. According to Hugues, these men evoked the example of Saint-Domingue, where "all those in command are blacks," saying:

> Aren't you tired of being poor? If you are free, why are you working on the land of the whites? Why doesn't all the fruit of your labor belong to you? . . . Where does the money of the colony come from? From the sugar and the coffee that the blacks produce, since the whites have never worked the land. In one hour everything will be finished. The army is ours; we have to kill all the whites and the blacks and the hommes de couleur who hold positions of authority and who have received undue advantages from them; then you will have all the money of the colony, all the sugar, the coffee, the cotton, and the merchandise to dress yourselves in.

The insurgents planned to spare for exile only the Republic's agents, the generals, and "a few Europeans for whom the blacks have a great deal of veneration." Hugues identified the leaders as four "formerly free men of color" named Eugène Rugne, Noël, Damiens, and Sansan. According to the testimonies of three cultivateurs who participated in the uprising, these men represented only a portion of the major leaders — who also included the ex-slave Bazile, who had been a "volunteer" in the army, and Drozin, the chef d'atelier of a state-owned sugar plantation.[1]

The insurgent leaders planned the mutiny for the day of rest in the Republican calendar and used a variety of strategies to convince cultivateurs to join. Noël, a manager on a state-owned plantation, simply gathered

1. Hugues and Lebas to minister, 24 Nivôse, An VI (Jan. 13, 1798), in CAOM, C 7A, 50, 4–11 (hereafter cited as Hugues and Lebas to minister).

the cultivateurs he commanded daily into an armed troop. The carpenter Eugène Rugne, meanwhile, stole a horse from the coffee plantation where he lived and rode from plantation to plantation speaking to cultivateurs. On one such visit, he offered the cultivateur Benjamin some food and told him: "We have to slit the throats of all the whites and make ourselves masters of the country." Benjamin asked where the weapons were, and Rugne responded that there were "many blacks with guns and sticks," enough to overcome the cannon and seize victory. Rugne visited other plantations as well, claiming falsely that Petit-Bourg "was in arms" and that "already all the whites had been vanquished." A number of cultivateurs spoke of Rugne as the "representative of all the blacks."[2]

Streaming from their plantations, the insurgents assembled at a state-owned coffee plantation called Lestier Ravine Chaude, whose isolated position and lack of a government manager made it an ideal location for such an event. When Benjamin and fellow cultivateur Moco arrived there, they saw an "infinite number of blacks." The leaders organized three companies and set out to attack local plantations. Most of the whites in the area had heard news of the insurrection and fled to Lamentin, but the rebels found one family in its house. The family managed to hold the rebels at bay by firing from the windows, then threw a bag of money down the stairs, hoping this would satisfy the cultivateurs, who ultimately retreated. An insurgent named Gros Jacques took advantage of the event to track down and kill the local commander of the national guard, the citizen Raphin, who, according to his murderer, "had finally got what he deserved." One group killed the citoyen Hubert, who owned the plantation where Eugène Rugne lived. According to Hugues's report, the cultivateurs killed a total of four whites during the night.[3]

Next, the insurgents regrouped and prepared to assault the town, where frightened whites had taken refuge. A small troop led by the citoyen Modeste (an old homme de couleur "whose boldness," Hugues wrote, "was so fatal to the British during the last war") was, by chance, in Lamentin. He led a defense against the four or five hundred insurgents and managed to hold them off, and soon he was joined by citizens from the town. As the insurgents retreated, some of their leaders chas-

2. See the testimonies of Benjamin, Moco, Augustin, and an anonymous fragment in CAOM, C 7A, 50, 223–230.

3. Testimonies of Benjamin and Moco, in CAOM, C 7A, 223–226; Hugues and Lebas to minister. On the Lestier Ravine Chaude plantation, see "Etat nominatif . . . Lamentin," 1 Vendémiaire, An V (Sept. 21, 1796), in G 1, 500, no. 12.

tised them, asking, "Since when are blacks afraid of whites?" A speech by two cultivateurs who had come from nearby Baie-Mahault to join the insurrection inspired one group of cultivateurs to attack again. But, by the time the insurgents organized their second assault, soldiers had arrived from Pointe-à-Pitre. The general in charge of this troop approached the rebels to negotiate, and one of them said that he wanted "the head of the agent." Two other insurgents fired at the general and missed, and the rest of the soldiers then opened fire and charged, killing many revolters. The cultivateur Augustin, fleeing into the cane fields, was cut seven times with a sword by the mounted soldiers.[4]

What did the insurgents of Lamentin want? Most of the leaders of the insurrection were men who occupied positions of some power on state-run plantations in the Lamentin region. The cultivateurs who had joined up also seem to have come in large numbers from state plantations where, despite repeated promises by Hugues, they were working without the pay promised to them at the time of emancipation. Their actions made clear that many of the aspirations of the ex-slaves—even those who held managerial positions on the plantations—had been frustrated by a regime that promised much but delivered little in the way of political or economic rights. The insurrection was a powerful indictment of Hugues's labor policies and an effort to create a different kind of system in which the potential of emancipation could be fulfilled.[5]

In voicing their grievances against Hugues's regime, the insurgents were inspired by news from Saint-Domingue and used their sister island as an example of what could happen in Guadeloupe. This had already occurred in early 1797, when a few hommes de couleur in Guadeloupe publicly attacked Hugues's regime and lauded the increasing power of blacks and citoyens de couleur in Saint-Domingue. According to Hugues, the "pretensions" of these men—who included Charlemagne Bouis, a signer of the 1793 proclamation of the new citizens of Basse-Terre—had been instigated by letters describing L'Ouverture's regime. "'Only in Saint-Domingue,' they say, 'do liberty and equality reign, men do what they wish, the agents are de couleur or publicly live with femmes de couleur, and all the generals and the chiefs are de couleur; they dominate and the whites can do nothing about it.'" One man told Hugues that, until there were hommes de couleur among the generals and the highest ranks

4. Testimonies of Moco and Augustin, in CAOM, C 7A, 50, 225–230, esp. 229–230; Hugues and Lebas to minister.
5. Hugues and Lebas to minister.

of the administration, power would not be truly shared. In the hopes of silencing the dissent, Hugues deported three men, including Louis Roche, who had fought in Grenada and because of this ("without any authority," according to Hugues) claimed he was a captain in the French infantry, and the noir Maillard, who had traveled the countryside talking about the need for elections. Several months later, American merchants brought to Marie-Galante the news of L'Ouverture's expulsion of Sonthonax, starting a "general murmur" among the cultivateurs. A crowd descended on the town of Réunion; their "war cries" were "that they should cut the throats of all the whites and do what was done in Saint-Domingue, where all the leaders were blacks or de couleur." The insurrection was quickly suppressed, but the demands would soon resurface at Lamentin.[6]

News of L'Ouverture's growing independence served as a catalyst for Guadeloupeans who, in early 1797, were increasingly aware that the pro-slavery lobby (whose setback at the hands of Laveaux and his partisans was still months away) was gaining ground in metropolitan France. Before the Lamentin insurrection, pro-slavery speeches that had been given in the Corps législatif in Paris were circulated, along with pamphlets that claimed whites were doomed to leave their "heads on the scaffold" for applying the decree of emancipation in 1794. This, according to Hugues, spread "worry among the blacks that the government had resolved that they would lose their liberty." The former slaves saw clearly what he saw—that, despite all his efforts, the planters still viewed their former slaves "as prey that has escaped them" and were ready to "seize with eagerness and greed any opportunity they have to get them between their hands." Furthermore, with loosened metropolitan legislation, many émigrés were returning to Guadeloupe, making claims on their property and on the labor of their ex-slaves–turned-cultivateurs. It was therefore difficult, wrote Hugues, "to contain the passions, the justifiable hatred, and the severity of the miserable black Africans against their former tyrants" that had propelled the insurrections at Lamentin. In fact, if the generally obedient ex-slaves were up in arms, it was due largely to the inflammatory talk of their former masters, "particularly that of the wives of émigrés, of which there are many in this colony."[7]

6. "Les Agents particuliers . . . au ministre de la marine et des colonies," 17 Ventôse, An V (Mar. 6, 1797), in AN, AF III, 209, dossier 954, no. 8; Hugues and Lebas to minister.

7. Hugues and Lebas to minister.

Despite the provocations of ex-masters, Hugues claimed he still had the support of the black soldiers of Guadeloupe. He might well have been exaggerating the strength of their loyalty; he knew, after all, that his domain was coming under steady attack in Paris and certainly wanted to present the news of the insurrection in as flattering a light as possible. And his are the only extant descriptions of their actions during the revolt. Still, given that black troops made up a majority of the soldiers in the colony, Hugues probably would not have been able to suppress them if they had been unwilling to support him. The "government and all citizens," he announced, owed "a great deal to these men." The revolt had tested the loyalty of this "army composed entirely of ex-slaves," but the "brave soldiers" responded with "extreme indignation" and were "the first to convince their co-citizens that they were being trapped and misled." In Capesterre just before the insurrection, the artillery officer Pierre Gédéon had arrested five leaders of the conspiracy who asked him to join them. And, in the company that defeated the insurgents at Lamentin— "the elite of the army of the Antilles," according to Hugues—nine-tenths of the soldiers were "blacks and former slaves, unequaled in their boldness and in their wise and exemplary behavior." In fact, Hugues suggested, the whites left alone would likely have fled rather than confront the insurgents. "They scorn the blacks," he wrote, "and nevertheless in all the insurrections of the Africans they are the first to run and hide. He who holds the key to the human heart seems to tell us that, in this country as in all others, tyrants, though used to commanding their slaves, always tremble in front of them."[8]

The conflict at Lamentin, then, was primarily played out between opposing groups of new citizens; it showed that Hugues's regime had produced both a sense of continuing dissatisfaction among cultivateurs— which the rebels tapped into—and a sense of loyalty to the regime among those who constituted its new army. Thanks to the fidelity of the black soldiers, Hugues had been able to stop the progress of the insurrection and preserve his regime, at least for a time. The story of what the insurgents had demanded at Lamentin, and of how the black soldiers of Guadeloupe had stood by the French administration, made its way to Paris through Hugues's correspondence as well, perhaps, as in other forms. Indeed, this news might have encouraged Laveaux to fight for new colonial legislation that was voted into law in early 1798, which was meant precisely to appease and control the cultivateurs and assure the

8. Ibid.

The Meaning of Citizenship, 1794–1798

loyalty of the black soldiers. Within a few months, a new administrator would arrive in Guadeloupe to apply this law, ending Hugues's tenure in the colony.

"We have had to fight the despotism of the former masters and the exaggerated pretensions of the former slaves," Hugues had written a few months before the Lamentin insurrection, seeking to evaluate his reign. "If we have been unable to change the hearts of men," he concluded, "we have at least contained their passions." If Hugues had not changed the hearts of men, his regime had transformed the social and economic world of Guadeloupe. Ex-slaves–turned-citizen-soldiers had left the island in droves to fight in the battles against the British in Saint Lucia, Saint Vincent, and Grenada or on the corsairs that ranged far and wide through the region, while war transformed the social and economic life of the port towns of Guadeloupe. If his regime failed to bring a meaningful freedom to the vast majority of Guadeloupe's former slaves, it had created a new sense of possibility and a group armed and ready to defend that possibility. Finding themselves increasingly alone in the face of hostile metropolitan governments, they would again draw on the example of Saint-Domingue, and on older traditions of resistance, as they continued to struggle for liberty.[9]

When they battled the French in 1802, insurgents would take refuge in the old haunts of maroons, joining communities that had in fact grown after emancipation with the elimination of the maréchaussée that had continually harassed them. These maroons had been joined by some "nègres nouveaux" captured by corsairs from British ships; like newly arrived Africans for generations, they had fled the plantations and opted for a life in the woods. One such community—which was large enough that in 1801 an unsuccessful mission was sent to destroy it—called itself the Mondongs, and its members had established themselves "in the most inaccessible regions" in the woods of Basse-Terre. They had "houses, plantations, and the means of existence," wrote General Gobert. "It was a kind of little independent republic."[10]

The possibility of independence—invoked by the Lamentin insurgents and enacted by the Mondong maroons—would become increasingly important to many of the new citizens of Guadeloupe as the larger

9. Hugues and Lebas to minister, 4 Brumaire, An VI (Oct. 25, 1797), in CAOM, C 7A, 49, 228–229.

10. Gobert to minister, 21 Vendémiaire, An XI (Oct. 13, 1802), in CAOM, C 7A, 57, 63–69.

Republic began to dismantle the gains of liberty. From out of isolated pockets the idea of independence gathered steam and converts. The groups that had faced off at Lamentin would find they had an interest in joining together against a common enemy. Gédéon, who had fought the insurgents of Lamentin, three years later fought against the French army that sought to reestablish control on the island. And the black captain Fourne, who led the 1801 incursions against the Mondong maroons, in 1802 used the maroons' techniques as he himself battled the French. Other soldiers, who had fought for the Republic in Saint Lucia or Saint Vincent, later mobilized the same tactics in fighting for the ideals that the French government had rejected, battling for the unfulfilled promise of Republican emancipation.[11]

11. Ibid.

Part Three

THE

BOUNDARIES

OF THE

REPUBLIC,

1798–1804

Chapter 12

THE ROAD TO MATOUBA

The road curves over a narrow ravine, and, on the other side, at a fork, lies a small, inconspicuous marble plaque mounted on a stone. It commemorates the May 1802 defeat and suicide of Louis Delgrès. Off to the left you can head along fields that once composed the D'Anglemont plantation, which Delgrès and his troops mined and blew up in their last, resounding gesture. To the right a road goes higher in the mountains toward the town of Matouba. The plaque reads simply, "À la mémoire de Delgrès et de ses compagnons, 28 mai 1802"—"To the memory of Delgrès and his comrades."

In 1802, a civil war exploded in Guadeloupe as segments of the army and the population fought against metropolitan troops and their colonial allies. The central protagonists in this insurrection, which had been presaged in numerous conflicts during the previous years, were soldiers in Guadeloupe, a majority of whom were ex-slaves. As in 1793 in both Saint-Domingue and Guadeloupe, the issue of fighting for the Republic largely defined the terms of citizenship in the Antilles. By the late 1790s, however, the political context had changed radically. Exiled planters, colonial administrators, and even former abolitionists had increasingly joined in an attack on the policies of emancipation that had transformed the Caribbean. After 1799, with Bonaparte's rise to power, the developments of the early 1790s—when slave insurrections smashed juridical and political separation between metropole and colony—were reversed as new laws declared that, once again, the colonies would be subjected to different laws from those of the metropole, dictated from Paris.

The confusing changes placed the people of the Antilles in a difficult position. As they heard about the new direction of colonial policy—and about the metropolitan political context out of which it emerged—they had to make choices about how they would respond to the new authorities sent to the island. Emancipation had been administered by Republican regimes in the previous years as part of a larger, national struggle against the British. Service to the nation, both as laborers and as soldiers, became the template for responsible citizenship, and despite its limitations this template provided economic and social mobility outside the lines set forth by the administrations. The Republic had been the guarantor of emancipation, even as the defense of the Republic was used to justify freedom's limits. What, then, were the Republicans of the Antilles to do as metropolitan authorities retreated from their previous Republican principles? To whom did the people of Guadeloupe owe allegiance? If they were loyal to the Republic that had overseen the transformations on the island, where should their loyalty lie when metropolitan authorities began to dismantle that Republic? From the moment of its first appearance in Guadeloupe, the possibility of reversing emancipation was hotly contested by the forces created out of the Republican project. As it had in earlier periods, the disjuncture between the metropole and the colonies created contrasting visions of the meaning of citizenship and the reality of freedom. In the Antilles, new citizens made difficult choices between national loyalty and Republican principles. They drew on their experience of freedom and of its complex material and social possibilities in deciding how to act toward a republic that was abandoning manumission and racial equality.

In the conflicts of 1801–1802, however, the fissures created within the population of Guadeloupe through the years of emancipation manifested themselves in a variety of ways. In the middle of 1801, a new group of administrators arrived in Guadeloupe, among them Admiral Lacrosse (who had served on the island in 1793). During the next months, Lacrosse angered many soldiers and officers, particularly when he passed up the popular high-ranking officer Magloire Pélage for a promotion. After a series of small uprisings, Lacrosse tried to arrest Pélage and several other officers. The plan backfired, however, setting off a revolt in Pointe-à-Pitre among the soldiers, who expelled Lacrosse from the island. Pélage formed a provisional government that maintained and enforced the labor regime in place at the time while insisting to Bonaparte on his continued loyalty to France, explaining that his actions were simply directed against Lacrosse himself. In the meantime, however, Bonaparte had dispatched two major military missions to the Caribbean, one to Saint-Domingue and a later one to Guadeloupe, with orders to reassert metropolitan control and crush the autonomous regimes of L'Ouverture and Pélage. The Guadeloupe mission, led by General Richepance, was welcomed by Pélage's administration. Once Richepance's men began to disarm the black troops in Pointe-à-Pitre, however, a segment of the army led by the officer Louis Delgrès rose up in revolt. After several weeks of fighting, the French defeated the rebels in a final battle on the heights of Matouba.[1]

As these events unfolded, the people of Guadeloupe were sharply divided in their attitude toward the metropole and toward violent resistance. This was clear in the army itself. Although a majority of soldiers were willing to mobilize against acts they saw as racial discrimination, they took different approaches to confronting and negotiating with metropolitan administrators. At the center of these differences was a question of trust. There was widespread sentiment in the army in 1801 about the need to attack certain local representatives, but, once the army had created a semiautonomous regime in Guadeloupe, its members granted very different levels of trust to the metropole itself. Whereas some officers and soldiers trusted that the central administration would ultimately see the justice of their cause, others were suspicious of the motives of Napoléon Bonaparte and his envoys. These rifts were of profound importance in Guadeloupe as well as Saint-Domingue. Indeed, in Guadeloupe, the rallying of many local troops to General Richepance's mission was essential to his victory over the insurgents and the subsequent reestablishment of slavery.

Among those who took up arms against the Richepance mission in 1802, there were other discrepancies, notably surrounding the types of tactics used against the French troops. Whereas Delgrès and his troops chose to fight a fairly conventional series of battles, holding Fort Saint-Charles before retreating to other positions in the mountains—and avoiding and punishing attacks against civilians—many plantation laborers, in some cases led by army officers, decided instead to attack and burn plantations and take white civilians prisoner. We have little information about the debates among the insurgents, although one of the few descriptions of their practices identifies a woman named Solitude as one of the most fervent advocates for an all-out war against the whites of the island.

It is indeed legitimate to wonder whether the various insurgents in 1802 were in fact fighting for the same things. Because the Guadeloupe insurrection, in contrast to that of Saint-Domingue, was crushed, there is no way to know how Delgrès, for instance, might have acted toward

1. The most important documents relating to this period are reproduced, with essays providing a good account of the events, in Jacques Adélaïde-Mérlande, René Bélénus, and Fréderic Régent, eds., *La Rébellion de la Guadeloupe, 1801–1802* (Basse-Terre, Guadeloupe, 2002).

the cultivateurs or what his approach to plantation production might have been. Delgrès's proclamation of 1802, the only written document he seems to have left behind, did clearly reject slavery, though its most powerful attack was on racial inequality. Certainly the visions of freedom of different groups on the island—women and men, soldiers and cultivateurs, gens de couleur and the formerly enslaved, city dwellers and those living on the plantations—were different, and, just as these divergences played a role during the insurrections of 1801–1802, they likely would have animated continuing conflicts if the French mission had not successfully taken control of Guadeloupe and established its own political vision: a return to slavery. Even if the end of the colonial relationship with France would have transformed the possibilities on the island, the basic economic and political problems faced by Hugues and other French administrators who followed him would have dogged the regime of an independent Guadeloupe, just as they precipitated continuing conflicts in Haiti after 1804.

Even after Delgrès's death in 1802, resistance continued in Guadeloupe. The French army hunted down insurgents in the mountains, and in Sainte-Anne whites and blacks joined together in a final revolt in favor of freedom. Indeed, only in 1804, with the independence of Haiti, did the last rebel leaders in Guadeloupe agree to French demands to leave, perhaps with the goal of traveling to their now-independent sister island. The struggles in Guadeloupe and Saint-Domingue were connected in other ways as well. At Matouba in 1802, the insurgents flew a tricolor flag from which the white had been removed. Dessalines, two years later, would make the same gesture in creating the Haitian flag, whose colors were the blue and red of a purified tricolor. The news of the events that took place in Guadeloupe after Delgrès's defeat in fact propelled resistance against the French reestablishment of slavery in Saint-Domingue. Between 1802 and 1804, the creation of a new nation, the Republic of Haiti, buried colonial Saint-Domingue. United for years in a Republican project of slave emancipation and all-out war against the British, the islands of Haiti and Guadeloupe would follow two completely different paths during the next centuries. Where Haiti charted a difficult course as an independent nation, Guadeloupe remained—as it remains today—part of France.

The reconstruction of slavery in Guadeloupe after 1802 was a unique historical event. In combination with what occurred in the smaller colony French Guiana during the same years, it is the only case in which the majority of a population of freed people was actually reenslaved. This proce-

FIGURE 20. General Antoine Richepance. c. 1840.
Cliché Bibliothèque nationale de France, Paris

dure itself took several years, because French administrators continually put off official decrees mentioning slavery for fear of inciting new revolts on an island that was still not entirely pacified. In addition to the legal and economic challenges of reenslavement and the dismantling of the institutions created during the Republican regime on the island, this program also entailed actively suppressing the political possibilities opened up through emancipation and rendering continuing struggles for free-dom and independence unimaginable. After the defeat of Delgrès, his comrade Joseph Ignace, and their followers, the fort they held against the French in Basse-Terre was renamed Fort Richepance. It would keep this name for more than a century and a half.

Of all the events of the revolutionary period in Guadeloupe, it is the events of 1802 that have received the most sustained treatment by Antil-lean historians and novelists. Delgrès's struggle and the reenslavement of the Guadeloupean people took on a particular significance in the sec-ond half of the twentieth century. In 1946, as part of a sweeping post-war reform of colonial policy, Guadeloupe, along with Martinique and French Guiana, became (once again) a department of France. Two years later, the plaque to Delgrès was placed at Matouba. But over the next decades many, including some like Aimé Césaire who had advocated departmentalization, became disenchanted with the effects of political assimilation. By the 1970s and 1980s, independence movements in the Caribbean gained steam. For advocates of independence, 1802 gained significance as a moment when separation from France had briefly ap-peared possible, when Guadeloupe could have become a free nation like Haiti. Through intertwined historical and literary efforts, the story of Delgrès and the struggles of 1802 became a way of exploring the silenced histories of Guadeloupe. Two novels—André Schwartz-Bart's 1971 dra-matization of the life of *La Mulâtresse Solitude* and Daniel Maximin's 1981 *Lone Sun (L'Isolé soleil)*—played a central role in making this period of Guadeloupe's history the subject of discussion and research. As I de-scribe in the conclusion of this book, the remembrance of Delgrès has ex-panded in recent years, in a reconfiguration of the memory of the period in both the Caribbean and metropolitan France.[2]

2. André Schwarz-Bart, *La Mulâtresse Solitude* (Paris, 1972). The influence of the novel on discussions of slavery in Guadeloupe can be seen in the fact that, in 1985, the historian Arlette Gautier in her study (one of the first devoted to the history of enslaved women in the French Caribbean) referred to Schwarz-Bart's work in her title; see Gautier, *Les Soeurs de Solitude: La Condition féminine dans l'esclave aux Antilles du XVII au XIX siècle* (Paris, 1985). See also Daniel Maximin, *Lone Sun*, trans. Clarisse Zimra (Charlottesville, Va., 1989). A series of works by Guadeloupean historians have taken up the story of 1802; in 1977, Ger-main Saint-Ruf wrote *L'Epopée Delgrès*, the first full-length study devoted to the struggle against the reestablishment of slavery, presenting an argument for Guade-loupean independence. Examining the resistance of Guadeloupeans in 1802, he suggested, was a way to overcome the ambiguities of an Antillean history in which

The next chapters build on the work of those who have revived the memory of 1802 to tell the story of the reestablishment of slavery; they also seek to explain why Bonaparte's France embarked on such a disastrous and radical attempt to reverse emancipation. To answer this question requires moving away from a focus on Bonaparte, or even on 1802 itself, and toward an exploration of how and why powerful forces attacked and undermined the 1794 policies of emancipation. Rather than see Bonaparte as the motor of the reversals of the early 1800s, I argue that his policies in fact emerged from a general consensus that emancipation had led to chaos and barbarism and that the metropole needed to assert firmer control over the ex-slaves in their colonies. This vision of the failures of manumission was itself rooted in many ways in the principles of gradual emancipation, which had predicted that immediate emancipation would lead to the disintegration of colonial society. The profound violence of the reestablishment of slavery, an event with few parallels in history, highlights both the radical changes brought about by emancipation and the abysmal failure of the French administrators to effectively respond to or negotiate with the ex-slaves' increasing demands for political power and autonomy. The brutal repression that struck Guadeloupe in 1802—and the ultimate victory symbolized by the creation of Haiti in 1804—marked the disintegration of the radical Republican project that had been created through the dramatic events of the early 1790s. The wars of this period were also the climax of efforts by the ex-slaves of the French Caribbean to craft a meaningful freedom, one in which the Republican rights promised by emancipation were fully applied. The challenge of understanding how the promise of 1794 ultimately led to the signal brutality of 1802 forces us to retrace the road to Matouba.

---

emancipation had been decreed, in 1848, from the metropole and to recover the "role of the blacks" who "wrote, in their own various ways, the history of the Antilles, in their lacerated skin" (*L'Epopée Delgrès: La Guadeloupe sous la Révolution française (1789-1802)* [Paris, 1977], 150-154). This was followed in 1986 by Jacques Adélaïde-Mérlande, *Delgrès: La Guadeloupe en 1802* (Paris, 1986); Henri Bangou, *La Révolution et l'esclavage à la Guadeloupe, 1789-1802: Epopée noire et génocide* (Paris, 1989); Lucien-Réné Abénon, Jacques Cauna, Liliane Chauleau, and Bernard Lehembre, *Antilles 1789: La Révolution aux Caraïbes* (Paris, 1989); Roland Anduse, *Joseph Ignace, le premier rebelle: 1802, la révolution antiesclavagiste guadeloupéenne* (Paris, 1989), 299. See also André Nègre, *La Rébellion de la Guadeloupe (1801-1802)* (Paris, 1987); Michel L. Martin and Alain Yacou, eds., *Mourir pour les Antilles: Indépendance nègre ou esclavage, 1802-1804* (Paris, 1991), which features discussions on both Guadeloupe and Saint-Domingue.

Chapter 13

DEFENDING THE REPUBLIC

"I am a friend of liberty, though I once owned slaves," declared the colonial administrator Daniel Lescallier in 1798. A decade before, Lescallier had been a manager on Lafayette's experimental Guiana plantation and drew on this experience to argue for gradual emancipation in the colonies. He had remained on Lafayette's plantation through most of the 1790s, experiencing firsthand the changes brought on by an emancipation very different from what he had advocated. "Since the revolution that made France a Republic" had abolished slavery and given back to the oppressed the "enjoyment of the Rights of Man and Citizen," he wrote, everything in Guiana had changed. Slaves had suddenly been "given mastery of their persons and left free to contract or not with their former masters." Emancipation was the just course of action, Lescallier argued, staying true to the ideas he had defended in 1789. "France was the first, and so far the only, European nation to abolish this scandalous institution." He noted with satisfaction that many of his former slaves stayed on the plantation with him after they were freed—a testament, he considered, to their appreciation for what he had done for them.[1]

Still, Lescallier was not uncritical of the results of emancipation. "Almost all of the plantations" in the region where he lived, the Aprouague, had been "abandoned" or had at least "diminished substantially" in their levels of production, and no new ones had been constructed. This made Lescallier wonder whether plantation agriculture could in fact be reconciled with the freedom of the "nègres cultivateurs" and whether all the beneficial economic progress brought about in and by the colonies of the eighteenth century could have occurred without slavery. He concluded,

---

1. Daniel Lescallier, *Notions sur la culture des terres basses dans la Guiane et sur la cessation de l'esclavage dans ces contrées* . . . (Paris, 1798), 74–78. On Lescallier's *Réflexions sur le sort des noirs dans nos colonies* (Paris, 1789), rpt. in *La Révolution française et l'abolition de l'esclavage* (Paris, 1968), I, see Chapter 2, above.

however, that, if the effects of emancipation had been "disastrous," it was primarily because of the way things were handled. The National Assembly had done nothing to apply the rights of man to Saint-Domingue, and, once insurrections began, reversing the cycle of violence proved impossible. Then, under the "system of Robespierre," wrote Lescallier, "we launched liberty into the colonies, not as a good deed, but as a method for defense against the opponents of the Revolution and the enemies of the Republic." "Anarchy and license took control, and all the vices and passions were unchained." It was of course impossible, Lescallier asserted, that liberation would not lead to a "crazy joy" on the part of the ex-slaves and to a momentary avoidance of work. That this celebration of freedom had turned into a general abandonment of the plantations, however, was due to errors on the part of administrators. Well-meaning officials had moved cultivateurs away from the plantations where they had been slaves, but this disrupted their lives and the functioning of the plantations. Too many ex-slaves were placed in the army, and official positions, money, and authority were given to "men who could neither read nor write and who were taken away from plantation labor for no reason"— in part to staff administrations for areas "where there are no inhabitants but monkeys and parrots."[2]

The French decree of 1794 would necessarily, according to Lescallier, bring on the eventual elimination of slavery throughout the Americas. "The nègres [in other colonies] are not ignorant—or at least they will not be for long—of the very different condition of those like them in the neighboring French colonies. How could we hide this from them? Do we really imagine that they ever were ignorant of their rights and that the voice of nature has gone to sleep inside of them, as their possessors wish?" Echoing Raynal, but carefully avoiding any evocation of the slave insurrections that had in fact brought about the French emancipation, Lescallier added: "Although their detractors represent them as stupid, they have shown themselves capable of a great energy. . . . In Dutch Guiana, as in Jamaica, there is the example of a number of the men of their race, who through their courage have taken their liberty and whose former masters are forced to deal with their independent existence."[3]

The experience of French emancipation, suggested Lescallier, pro-

2. Lescallier, *Notions sur la culture*, 76–78, 99–102; on Guiana during the Revolution, see Yves Bénot, *La Guyane sous la Révolution française; ou, L'Impasse de la révolution pacifique* (Kourou, French Guiana, 1997).

3. Lescallier, *Notions sur la culture*, 80–81.

vided an important lesson for the future: "The projects of humanity in favor of the noirs should have been, and should be, executed through a good policy, through time and gradation." Only gradual emancipation could assure that freedom would arrive "without a shock, without disturbing individual property, and especially without the effusion of blood." Repeating his own earlier arguments as well as those of Condorcet, Lescallier declared that, as a result of "the prejudice that creates their situation" and "the way in which they are treated," slaves were incapable of immediately exercising the rights of citizenship. Only under a "humane and reasonable regime" could their vices gradually disappear. Lescallier had attempted to incite such a gradual transformation on Lafayette's plantation in the 1780s, and in 1798 he again emphasized that this was the best way to destroy slavery in those places where it still existed. The slave trade should be eliminated and plantation conditions improved, and then the name "slavery" itself would be eliminated—"It would be in vain that we would reform the thing, it would still seem odious, and would tend to return, if we did not change the name." The Code noir would be replaced by a Code colonial in which "wise regulations" would protect the slaves from arbitrary and barbarous rule, making their right "perfectly known, through written laws." They would therefore "no longer exactly be slaves," even if they were constrained to the plantations as workers. The entire work force of each plantation would be given the right to receive one-tenth of the plantation profits, and, if they worked hard and were able to increase production, they would then receive one-ninth of the profits. As long as productivity escalated, they would be granted larger and larger shares of the profits, up to one-third—all without, according to Lescallier, ever causing the plantation owner to lose money. Meanwhile, individual families who saved up enough money to buy themselves plots of land and move off the plantations would slowly consolidate the class of the free. Over time, there would be fewer and fewer slaves and more and more free workers.[4]

But what of the French colonies where slavery had already been abolished? For these, Lescallier had few concrete suggestions. He did, however, argue for one crucial restriction—the limitation of the rights of the nègres nouveaux who arrived from Africa. "It must be admitted that the nègres nouveaux, those who are not yet accustomed to the language and the customs of Europeans, cannot, without endangering the plantations and without causing problems for themselves, be given liberty instantly

4. Ibid., 78-84, 93-97.

and without precautions." Reiterating his vision of a gradual path to citizenship, Lescallier wrote: "In the same way eyes weakened by a long obscurity cannot suddenly see the light without being blinded: one has to give it to them carefully and by degrees."[5]

Lescallier's similar viewpoints before and after emancipation highlight the larger continuity between prerevolutionary proposals for gradual abolition, the arguments of administrators like Hugues in favor of restrictive policies on plantation labor, and finally the arguments used by Bonaparte to reestablish slavery in the Antilles in the early 1800s. Stances such as Lescallier's, combined with those of more virulent enemies of emancipation, were slowly eating away at the consensus that had until then protected the Republican policy of emancipation. The threat of a reversal was already quite clear to some in Guadeloupe, where the struggles over the meaning of Republican citizenship that eventually exploded into full-scale war in 1802 were already beginning. Within a few years, the onetime abolitionist and reformer Lescallier would find himself once again in charge of a unique experiment in colonial governance: the transformation of citizens back into slaves.

Walking on Volcanoes

In November 1798, after four transformative years of rule, Victor Hugues was finally relieved of his position as the commissioner of Guadeloupe. His departure, however, did not go uncontested. General Desfourneaux, who had been sent to replace Hugues and apply the 1798 law on the organization of the colonies, wrote that, as soon as he arrived, small-scale insurrection spread throughout the island; this was spurred on by "agitators," who claimed that "the counterrevolution had taken place in France, that the royalists were dividing up the jobs, and that I had been sent to reestablish slavery and to remove the patriot administrators from all civil and military posts." In reaction, he arrested rebellious soldiers, sailors, and many ordinary "black citizens." Believing that Hugues himself was behind the unrest, Desfourneaux invited him to a meeting on his ship in the harbor of Basse-Terre and then arrested him, confining him to the hold and spiriting him away to France without his family or his belongings. As the boat sailed away, Hugues hurled a string of insults at Desfourneaux in his native Provençale.[6]

5. Ibid., 84.
6. Desfourneaux to minister, 23 Frimaire, 25 Frimaire, An VII (Dec. 13, 15,

Another of those deported by Desfourneaux was one of Hugues's assistants, the citizen Liard, who wrote that Desfourneaux had, upon his arrival, followed the advice of "all the secret partisans of the English, all the men Victor Hugues had destituted or chased from the colony . . . this class of men most of whom have no nation, so well painted by Raynal!—the white planters." The sense that the new mission represented the counterrevolution and the interest of émigré planters paralleled the sentiment of many in Saint-Domingue. There, L'Ouverture had already expelled Desfourneaux's analogue, General Hédouville. News of this, brought by passengers on a ship that, Desfourneaux lamented, "arrived and landed before I was warned," encouraged some on the island to compare the two missions, "predicting that the same disasters would happen in Guadeloupe." One witness heard a merchant cry "with indignation that Saint-Domingue had been completely destroyed only because of the actions of similar men, and that in truth they were all *chouans*." The use of this term—which had been used by Jacobins during 1793 and 1794 to describe royalist insurgents from the Vendée—was a clear indication that these individuals saw themselves as defenders of a republic imperiled by counterrevolutionaries.[7]

Unlike Hédouville, Desfourneaux successfully repressed the movement against him, in part because of the help of key gens de couleur administrators in Guadeloupe, notably Canut Robinson. He arrested three men named Morin, Trinchard, and Menet, charging that they had "formed a plot to use force and the most atrocious means to oppose the establishment in the colony of the new order conforming to the constitution of the year 3." Although who these men were is unclear, Menet had been involved in arming corsairs in Basse-Terre during the previous years and so would have been directly affected by Desfourneaux's new policies on the island, which included a repression of privateering. But the depositions gathered to support the charge against these three men are a window into the general worry among the new citizens about what

---

1798), An VII, in AN, AF III, 209, dossier 954, nos. 10, 22; Auguste Lacour, *Histoire de la Guadeloupe*, 4 vols. (Basse-Terre, Guadeloupe, 1855-1858), III, 3-7.

7. Citoyen Liard to minister, 6 Thermidor, An VII (Jul. 24, 1799), in CAOM, C 7A, 51, 201; Desfourneaux to minister, 25 Frimaire, An VII (Dec. 15, 1798), in AN, AF III, 209, dossier 954, no. 22; deposition of Fizeller, 14 Frimaire, An VII (Dec. 4, 1798), in AN, AF III, 209, dossier 954, no. 57. The merchant who said this, Pierre Linard, had signed the "Eveil" to the Republicans in 1794; see AN, AD VII, 21 C, no. 44, and Chapter 4, above.

the change of regimes meant for slave emancipation, and they give a hint of some of the plans for the future circulating among the ex-slaves.[8]

A few days after Desfourneaux's arrival, a merchant from Port de la Liberté, Duvergé, was walking on the main square of the town when he was "attracted by curiosity to a group of black and colored citizens who seemed to press around two individuals whom he could not identify in the darkness but who he was told were named 'Gaugnet and Pignon'; he was struck by the audacity with which [the two speakers] sought to mislead these ignorant men by painting the leaders who had recently arrived in the colony as chouans and counterrevolutionaries, agents of a faction that was the enemy of the patriots." "In their frenzy," he continued, "these crazed men called on all true Republicans to join with those in whom the citizen Hugues had always invested his confidence as the only supporters of the general emancipation he had brought to the negroes." The speakers called on the crowd to fight against the departure of their liberator and to expel the one who came to replace him in order to bring the Republic triumph in Guadeloupe and all of France.[9]

The next night, outside Port de la Liberté, in Abymes, another witness saw the same men giving a speech to a "crowd of negroes and gens de couleur," claiming that Hugues, "who had brought liberty . . . was the only one who could conserve it." All the good patriots were preparing to "chase away these chouans who talked only in terms of 'mon-

8. For the trial, see "Extrait des régistres des arrêtés de l'agent particulier," 18 Nivôse, An VII (Jan. 7, 1799), in AN, AF III, 209, dossier 954, no. 53. For Robinson in the early 1790s, see Chapter 4, above. Under Hugues, he became a municipal officer in Basse-Terre and was the witness for the weddings of a number of ex-slaves; see CAOM, EC, Basse-Terre, 6, nos. 16, 45; 9, nos. 6, 27, 45. Desfourneaux made him president of the municipality of Basse-Terre; see the *Rédacteur colonial*, no. 1, 23 Nivôse, An VII (Jan. 12, 1799), 3, in AN, AF III, 209, dossier 954, no. 72. On Menet's involvement in the corsair trade, see Anne Pérotin-Dumon, *La Ville aux Iles, la ville dans l'île: Basse-Terre et Pointe-à-Pitre, Guadeloupe, 1650–1820* (Paris, 2000), 758. A man named Morin was part of a company of merchants in Pointe-à-Pitre in 1788, though this might have been a different person (Pérotin-Dumon, *La Ville*, 746). I have found no information on Trinchard, and nowhere are any of the three men given racial ascriptions.

9. Deposition of Duvergé, 12 Frimaire, An VII (Dec. 2, 1798), in AN, AF III, 209, dossier 954, no. 54. The same speech was witnessed by another man, who noted that the speakers declared the new arrivals' aim was "to take freedom away from the negroes and to put them back in the state they were in before the arrival of Citizen Hugues." See the deposition of Duchamps, 13 Frimaire, An VII (Dec. 3, 1798), in AN, AF III, 209, dossier 954, no. 55.

sieur' and 'madame'" and, if they followed Trinchard and Morin, the Republic would be preserved "here as well as in France." Trinchard himself was seen elsewhere speaking to a "considerable crowd," advising them to join him in repulsing these new arrivals, whose sole mission was to "rob the blacks of their liberty and return them to the state of slavery." Interestingly, he referred to the members of the Desfourneaux mission as "chouans with *cadenettes* [tresses] and *habits quarrés*"—the latter being flashy clothes worn as an explicit rejection of Jacobin aesthetics. L'Ouverture had similarly criticized some members of the Hédouville mission for wearing habits quarrés, which suggests both the wide circulation and cultural complexities of the contemporary politics in the Caribbean.[10]

During the same period, the black fisherman Ignace overheard Trinchard talking to some friends on a state-owned plantation, saying with "a great deal of fire" that the new arrivals were "chouans" who had come "to put us back into slavery." An officer responded that, if they were chouans, "we will release the army against them," and Trinchard added, if they had come to "return us to slavery, well to hell with them." Noticing Ignace, they gave him a glass of rum, and he heard no more.[11]

In an anonymous letter that Desfourneaux claimed Trinchard—or one of his collaborators—had written, the colonies were represented as the last refuge of the Republic. "We can no longer doubt that republicanism, harassed and attacked everywhere in France, is speaking the last words of its expiring voice, which has been suffocated by despotism." The émigrés and the priests were taking over the government—"all is counterrevolution, only the name is lacking." "A few Republican forms are observed, and vain ghosts of liberty still wander without eyes among a people abused, waiting for the chains they carry to be permanently attached. Liberty has fled this country and has taken with it the Republican virtues that inflamed hearts in 1793." "Love of the nation has been replaced by love of gold," the letter continued, and "the men in whom this corrupt government placed its confidence" had already caused the loss of

10. Deposition of Duchesne, 13 Frimaire, An VII (Dec. 3, 1798), in AN, AF III, 209, dossier 954, no. 55; deposition of Lambert Mauther, Frimaire An VII (December 1798), in AN, AF III, 209, dossier 954, no. 58; on L'Ouverture, see Claude B. Auguste, "Independantisme Louverturien et révolution française," in Michel Hector, ed., *La Révolution française et Haïti: Filiations, ruptures, nouvelles dimensions* (Port-au-Prince, Haiti, 1995), 234–257, esp. 239.

11. Deposition of Ignace, in AN, AF III, 209, dossier 954, no. 61.

The Boundaries of the Republic, 1798–1804

Saint-Domingue. Guadeloupe would be next thanks to "these chouans, these *vendéens* [Vendeans], these men vomited on our shores" whose actions would destroy the prosperity of the island and lose "this rich possession" for France. "AUX ARMES CITOYENS," the letter called: "Loyal to the sacred oath we took at the foot of the tree of liberty, will we allow another conqueror of the colony to govern?"[12]

In the turmoil surrounding Hugues's removal, some put forward the idea that an even more radical uprising might be necessary to preserve liberty. A Guadeloupean homme de couleur named Pierre Miller, who was in exile after Hugues deported him in 1797, was heard saying that "the reign of the whites was over, that he was surprised Guadeloupe was still in their hands and that it had not suffered the fate of Saint-Domingue." After Desfourneaux's arrival, Miller boarded a ship for Guadeloupe with two other "mulattoes who are also bad subjects," but once they landed he was quickly noticed by the new authorities and deported from the island.[13]

Some plantation laborers—perhaps encouraged by an increase, after Hugues's departure, in the return of émigré plantation owners, which, as one administrator wrote, "made the citizens anxious"—rallied around a similar idea. The merchant Pierre Metro stated that, one afternoon along the port in Basse-Terre, he had seen a crowd gathered around "a black citizen who was giving an incendiary speech, saying that all whites were *scélérats* and that they had come to impose laws and that it was time to fall upon them." Around the same time, a white plantation owner, Le Vanier, who had been part of the group Ignace had seen talking to Trinchard, was accused of being aware of similar plans for revolution among the cultivateurs. According to one informant, "the blacks" visited Le Vanier during the night and told him what was happening on the plantations, received advice from him, and promised him "that if they cut the necks of the whites his would be preserved, because he had been able to inspire their confidence." The thirdhand information delivered here was certainly refracted through the fears and, perhaps, personal conflicts between those mentioned. Yet the sense that whites might be positioning themselves in relation to a future insurrection among the cultivateurs spoke volumes about the sense of danger and volatility on the island.[14]

12. See the copy of the letter sent to the publisher Cabre of Basse-Terre and intercepted, in AN, AF III, 209, dossier 954, no. 62.

13. See the various letters about the case in CAOM, C 7A, 51, 77–80.

14. Lacour, *Histoire*, III, 118; deposition of Pierre Metro, 5 Nivôse, An VII

After Desfourneaux and his *Conseil de guerre* (Council of War) ex-pelled Trinchard, Menet, and Morin from the island, they carried out a series of trials against other suspected enemies of the new regime. A group of soldiers garrisoned in Basse-Terre was accused of planning to march to Port de la Liberté to capture Desfourneaux and drive him from the island. The accused included both ex-slaves, such as Azor (who had been born in Africa), Mequi, Eustache, and Bassine, and metropolitan whites, such as Jacques Michel, who had developed connections with ex-slaves in Basse-Terre. Two whites were executed as the leaders of the conspiracy, whereas the rest of the soldiers were acquitted because, the council determined, they had only been caught up in the moment.[15]

In another trial, the central figure was Pierre Victor, a tailor who ac-cused his former master of having "attacked liberty and the rights of man" by writing Victor a letter in which he offered to "send him his liberty in return for a payment of thirty *noeudes*." Victor, however, was himself accused of falsifying the letter in order to prove that his master "doubted that liberty was a sacred right" and "in order to inflame spirits and push them toward a sedition against the authorities of the colony." Victor was found guilty of attempting to stir up insurrection in the colony and was unanimously condemned to death, though his punishment was commuted to permanent exile. Some of Victor's accomplices were also brought to trial. Noel Piron, a merchant who was originally from Saint Lucia, was accused of encouraging Victor to forge the letter and then publicly reading it in order to "attack the public tranquillity." And the grenadier Yoyo Delgresse had apparently "advised" Victor to fabricate this letter and "pushed him to make it public" because he believed "that would indubitably lead to general discontent and convince the noir and

(Dec. 25, 1798), in AN, AF III, 209, dossier 954, no. 59; deposition of Citoyen Beaugendre, 15 Nivôse, An VII (Jan. 4, 1799), in AN, AF III, 209, dossier 954, no. 60. The term *scélérat* means "rogue" or "wicked person."

15. "Jugement rendu au Conseil de guerre," Basse-Terre, 4 Germinal, An VII (Mar. 24, 1799), in CAOM, C 7A, 51, 46–48. For Azor, see CAOM, EC, Basse-Terre, 9, no. 60, 5 Floréal, An V (Apr. 24, 1797); for Jacques Michel, see his role as a witness in the weddings of ex-slaves in CAOM, EC, Basse-Terre, 9, nos. 41, 95. The accused soldiers were part of the battalion that Hugues had originally formed to bring together metropolitan and colonial soldiers; for a history of this battalion, see Roland Anduse, "L'Histoire singulière du 1er bataillon de l'armée de la Guade-loupe: Loyalisme révolutionnaire et révoltes militaires," in Michel L. Martin and Alain Yacou, eds., *Mourir pour les Antilles: Indépendance nègre ou esclavage, 1802–1804* (Paris, 1991), 57–64.

The Boundaries of the Republic, 1798–1804

de couleur citizens to undo themselves of Citizen Desfourneaux." Both of these men were also deported.[16]

That such punishment could flow from the act of forgery was a mark of how tenuous was the sense of faith in the metropolitan authorities and how dangerous even the intimation of a return to slavery could be. If the council's account of the actions of Pierre Victor and his conspirators is true, it shows a knowledge on their part that evoking a return to the ties of slavery—even through a private letter presented as an offer of a personal transaction—could present a political danger in the colony. Shortly after this trial, Desfourneaux wrote to the minister in Paris, "The public administrators of the colonies all walk on volcanoes, whose explosions constantly menace the national authority and their security." Indeed, the new administrator found himself in a simmering conflict that would soon make him its next victim.[17]

Integrating the Colony

"I insist on assuring you that I will always maintain the sacred right of liberty," Desfourneaux declared, with perhaps too much insistence, in December 1790, as his battle against those opposed to his new regime was just beginning. His first public proclamation was addressed to the "citizens of all colors" who lived in a "colony that is an integral part of the French Republic" and who had proved themselves "worthy of the nation" by "reconquering and preserving" the island under the leadership of his predecessor. The new government, he declared, had as its "unshakable foundation" the "ruins of slavery and of despotism" and guaranteed "liberty, equality, security, and property." He called on "all citizens" to join in working for prosperity and, as Hugues had before him, specified how they should contribute: *"Cultivateurs!* Go by your diligence and work, fertilize a land that would never be ungrateful for your care that you will lavish upon it. All means will be used to improve your situation and encourage you." He made clear that there was little choice in the matter: "Laziness and vagabondage will be severely repressed; for our principles reject from society all lazy men, who are the enemies of good citizens, just as a careful cultivateur weeds parasitic plants out of his fields." Several

16. "Jugement rendu par le Conseil de guerre," Basse-Terre, 15 Germinal, An VII (Apr. 4, 1799), in CAOM, C 7A, 51, 49–54.

17. Desfourneaux to minister, 21 Germinal, An VII (Apr. 10, 1799), in CAOM, C 7A, 51, 42–43.

months later, he gave teeth to this measure by ordering each local administrator to post a list of the divaguants and to announce that they had ten days to return to their respective plantations, "after which they will be arrested, brought before the Conseil de guerre, and punished by death." When he eventually published the French constitution of the year III, declaring that it had become "the fundamental law of the French Republic" and therefore of "the entirety of the individuals who compose it," he simultaneously announced that, since the French colonies were in a state of war, the island would remain in "a state of siege," and therefore the constitution could be applied only partially according to his decisions. Very little of the democratic and egalitarian impulse that had initially been part of Laveaux's 1798 law was to find expression in Guadeloupe.[18]

One of Desfourneaux's first actions in the colony was to dismantle the network of corsairs that had flourished under Hugues. The persistent corsair attacks against U.S. ships traveling to British islands had led in 1798 to the severing of diplomatic relations between France and the United States in the so-called Quasi War. From Guadeloupe in 1799, Desfourneaux attempted to patch up differences with the U.S. by writing to President John Adams and announcing that, although the French corsairs would still pursue the "enemies of the Republic," they would no longer harass neutral ships as they had in the past. Furthermore, the ports of Guadeloupe would be open to trade with U.S. merchants. A few months later, L'Ouverture, in his negotiations with the U.S. and the British, also agreed to limit the number of corsairs by channeling their authorization through a very specific set of officials. Yet there were internal reasons for restricting the corsairs as well. Desfourneaux noted that, in addition to deserters from the army and navy, "citizens employed in cultivation" were "constantly hired to serve on corsairs." This, he noted, posed a danger to "the source of profit and public prosperity," which would be "dried up by the corruption of the cultivateurs." He therefore passed a law stipulating punishments for all sailors, soldiers, or cultivateurs who were found working on corsairs, as well as for all those who hired them. Further, "any soldier, sailor, or cultivateur who has not returned on his ship, to his corps, or to his place of work within twenty-four hours after the publication of this present act will be considered guilty

18. "Proclamation aux citoyens de toutes les couleurs," 14 Frimaire, An VII (Dec. 4, 1798), in AN, AF III, 209, dossier 954, no. 40; Lacour, *Histoire*, III, 18; "Proclamation pour accompagner la publication de la constitution de l'An 3," 7 Ventôse, An VII (Feb. 25, 1799), in AN, AF III, 209, 115–116.

The Boundaries of the Republic, 1798–1804

of desertion." The law obviously had little effect, for a month later Desfourneaux reiterated it and noted in particular that French sailors continued to desert to the corsairs, and others were "hidden in the countryside, where they are causing, through their perfidious insinuations, a relaxation in cultivation." Clearly, the lucrative corsair trade was deeply entrenched, for subsequent agents once again sent out similar orders in 1800.[19]

In February 1799, Desfourneaux issued a detailed law governing the labor of the cultivateurs. He lamented that, under Hugues, "men previously reduced to slavery by despotism, freed by the just laws of the Republic, learned they were free without being instructed as to their responsibilities toward society, without being told by what means they would procure their existence or what fruit they would gather from their work and their pains." Nevertheless, he noted, certain individual "propertyowners," guided by "principles of justice and humanity, and in fact more enlightened as to their own true interests," had given the cultivateurs "remuneration for their work," which had allowed them to "take advantage of their properties and keep them in good condition." "It is time," he concluded, "to give ourselves over to the evidence offered by their conduct"—paying the laborers was the best way to ensure continued plantation production.[20]

Through resistance to the labor regime instituted by Hugues, both individual and collective, ex-slaves had expressed their desire for a different kind of order on the island. During the early days of Desfourneaux's regime, some had apparently circulated the idea that the point of the Revolution was to eliminate the differences between workers and propertyowners and had called on the cultivateurs to refuse to work until they were given ownership of the land. Desfourneaux made clear in his proclamation that this idea "must be forever dispelled." "The cultivateurs are not propertyowners," he declared, "but they must fertilize the

19. Desfourneaux's letter to John Adams is reprinted in *Le Rédacteur colonial*, no. 1, 23 Nivôse, An VII (Jan. 12, 1799), 2, in AN, AF III, 209, dossier 954, no. 72. On Saint-Domingue, see "Letters of Toussaint Louverture and of Edward Stevens, 1798-1800," *American Historical Review*, XVI (1910), 64-101, esp. 68. For the laws against corsairs, see "Extrait des régistres des arrêtés de l'Agence du Directoire exécutif aux îles du Vent," 7 Frimaire, An VII (Nov. 27, 1798), 3 Nivôse, An VII (Dec. 23, 1798), in AN, AF III, 209, dossier 954, nos. 18, 21; "Agents particuliers," 20 Nivôse, An VIII (Jan. 10, 1800), in CAOM, C 7A, 51, 95.

20. "Proclamation de l'agent particulier . . . aux citoyens de toutes les couleurs," 22 Pluviôse, An VII (Feb. 10, 1799), in AN, AF III, 208, dossier 951, no. 9.

countryside; they must be paid for their work" and given "a treatment that will increase in relation to their intelligence and work and therefore offer the double advantage of improving the situation of the cultivateurs and the situation of the properties." Desfourneaux put into place a system similar to that Sonthonax had instituted in 1793, in which "all cultivateurs, skilled workers, and others" of a given plantation would divide among themselves one-quarter of what remained of the plantation's revenues after deducting maintenance costs, notably managers' salaries. On coffee and cotton plantations, where the harvest occurred only once a year, advances would be given to the workers and deducted at the time of the harvest. The salaries for domestic workers throughout the island were fixed by Desfourneaux. This plan granted a smaller portion of production to the cultivateurs than Sonthonax had, but, in further contrast to Sonthonax, Desfourneaux gave the same salary to men and women, a factor of key importance given that women were the majority on many plantations. Pregnant women would be paid for the five *décades* (fifty days) of rest they received before and after giving birth, and the Republic would pay a bonus to women for each child born.[21]

Rather than appoint managers, Desfourneaux planned to rent out the state-owned plantations to private citizens, a measure he believed would reduce corruption and increase productivity. Although he did not have the chance to fully carry this out, he did organize a number of auctions, such as one held on a sugar plantation in the presence of the cultivateurs attached to the plantation who watched their "free" labor being sold to the highest bidder. Desfourneaux reported a few months after instituting his new system that "the cultivateurs who had left the countryside are returning daily to the plantations and all the signs promise the return of cultivation." In September 1799, he reported that "eleven thousand cultivateurs, brigands, thieves, and divaguants had returned to the plantations" out of what he later reported were fifteen thousand divaguants in the colony as a whole. Desfourneaux's policies on payment were put into effect on a number of the Basse-Terre area's private plantations, including one where, once the *quart des cultivateurs* was divided up, each received twenty-three livres for one year of work producing coffee, manioc, and bananas and another where each received a total of thirteen livres for two coffee harvests.[22]

21. Lacour, *Histoire*, III, 19; "Proclamation de l'agent particulier," 22 Pluviôse, An VII (Feb. 10, 1799), in AN, AF III, 208, dossier 951, no. 9.

22. For the auction, see the adjudication, 7 Thermidor, An VII (Jul. 25, 1799),

Desfourneaux's stabilization of the plantation regime in Guadeloupe in many ways paralleled L'Ouverture's efforts in Saint-Domingue during the same period, although there were important differences. Under L'Ouverture, state-owned plantations were also distributed to managers, but most of those who profited from this were army officers of African descent. In 1799, for instance, the ex-slave generals Henri Christophe and Jean-Jacques Dessalines both had made enormous profits from the plantations under their control; Dessalines was renting some thirty plantations. This management by officers was only one part of the militarization of agricultural work. During L'Ouverture's regime, military officials governed the various districts in the colony and oversaw the administration of the state-owned plantations. As in Guadeloupe under Hugues and Desfourneaux, and as in Saint-Domingue under Sonthonax and Polverel, L'Ouverture issued laws requiring former slaves to return to their plantations. A decree on agricultural work from October 1800, for instance, gave those who were away from their plantations eight days to return, and a police force was organized to catch vagabonds who did not comply. Recalcitrant workers were judged by military tribunals and punished according to military law. Plantations were frequently inspected by military officers, even Dessalines and L'Ouverture, and, although whips were outlawed, other forms of corporal punishment continued. The regime was meant to reverse the increasing move on the part of ex-slaves to farm small plots of land on the estates, which they sometimes purchased individually or in groups, for their own subsistence and profit.[23]

L'Ouverture announced to the citizens of Saint-Domingue in his 1800 decree on cultivation that agriculture was "the most important support of governments." His harsh policies seem to have been driven by a sense that only plantation agriculture, rather than small-scale farming, could

in CAOM, C 7A, 52, 5; for Desfourneaux's reports, see his letters to the minister, 2 Germinal, An VII (Mar. 22, 1799), 13 Thermidor, An VII (Jul. 31, 1799), 19 Fructidor, An VII (Sept. 5, 1799), in CAOM, C 7A, 51, 27, 62–63, 68–69; for the payment of cultivateurs, see the inventories in ADG, Dupuch 2E2/25, 13 Fructidor, An VIII (Aug. 31, 1800), and ADG, Bonnet 2E2/41, 11 Nivôse, An VIII (Jan. 1, 1800). For other inventories that noted the quart des cultivateurs, see ADG, Dupuch 2E2/26, 3 Brumaire, An IX (Oct. 25, 1800), 25 Vendémiaire, An IX (Oct. 17, 1800); ADG, Castet 2E2/210, 18–29 Nivôse, An IX (Jan. 8–19, 1801).

23. Mats Lundahl, "Toussaint L'Ouverture and the War Economy of Saint Domingue, 1796–1802," *Slavery and Abolition: A Journal of Comparative Studies,* VI (1985), 122–138, esp. 126–132.

provide the colony with the export commodities necessary to continue trade with his new allies. The United States, in particular, was an important supplier of various goods, especially the arms crucial to victory over Rigaud. Facing a dilemma that leaders in the Caribbean would face again and again, L'Ouverture chose to pursue repressive tactics within Saint-Domingue in order to be able to trade and negotiate with other powers. The policies developed in 1799 and 1800 were eventually consolidated with L'Ouverture's 1801 constitution, which went so far as to authorize the recruitment of slaves from Africa who, again as in Hugues's Guadeloupe, were to be put to work on state-owned plantations. They were remarkably effective: by 1801, exports in sugar had risen to 13 percent of what they were in 1789, from only 1.2 percent in 1795; coffee exports, at only 2.8 percent of their 1789 level in 1795, had risen to 57 percent by 1801, and cotton was at 35 percent. By the next year, when coffee exports had dropped to 45 percent of the 1789 level, sugar had jumped to 38 percent and cotton to 58 percent.[24]

As administrators in both Saint-Domingue and Guadeloupe reshaped policies regarding the plantations, ex-slaves and ex-masters continued to renegotiate their relations with one another. The case of the Joseph Langlois plantation, in the area of Basse-Terre, shows some of the possibilities available to ex-slaves during this period. A 1799 inventory of the plantation, which did not include a list of cultivateurs, noted that, "with regard to the industry and the work of the cultivateurs attached to the plantations," the parties would make "arrangements in conformity with the laws to assure that the said plantations continue to be cultivated." The next year, however, the names of the thirty cultivateurs of the plantation were listed, including eleven who were "absent," among these one extended family and the former commandeur, Charles. Charles had left the plantation after emancipation and worked for the Republic as a carpenter. By 1801, he had taken on his former master's name and was rich enough to rent a piece of land in Basse-Terre and build a house there. Nevertheless, along with another former slave who was a soldier in the army, he was listed as a "reminder" in the inventory, which suggests that his former master's family felt that he was somehow still attached to the plantation. Langlois, however, had accepted Charles's departure, and on his plantation he independently set up a system of wage labor in order to get his cultivateurs to work. Over the course of fourteen

24. Lundahl, "Toussaint L'Ouverture and the War Economy," *Slavery and Abolition*, VI (1985), 122–138, esp. 132, 135.

The Boundaries of the Republic, 1798–1804

months, Langlois made a profit of 2,370 francs selling fruit, paying 443 francs, probably to some of his cultivateurs, for "their harvest and sale." The exact arrangement made between Langlois and those who worked for him is not explained, although Langlois's use of paid labor in fruit harvesting seems to have been more profitable than the cultivation of manioc and coffee on his lands. The work of such fruit gatherers gives us a glimpse of some of the new economic relationships that had developed on the plantations in parallel with those that had developed in the towns. These new configurations of labor opened up options for autonomy and movement not available to those paid with the quart des cultivateurs. Such possibilities, despite their limitations, perhaps provided ex-slaves with glimpses of what fuller freedom might mean. Yet, ultimately, Desfourneaux's regime, like that of Hugues and that of L'Ouverture, gave the emancipated citizens little more than the right to work.[25]

The Tail of Hugues

In April 1799, nearly five years after emancipation had arrived in Guadeloupe, the island's citizens finally participated in an election. Where Hugues had refused outright to allow ex-slaves to vote, Desfourneaux assured their exclusion more quietly simply by applying the laws passed by the Directory, which limited voting rights to those who could pay a poll tax. Desfourneaux had already, it seems, shown some opposition to integrated electoral assemblies when he tried to shut down one in Le Cap in 1797. Still, the law on the colonies that guided his regime had stipulated that soldiers who had fought for the Republic would be exempted from the poll tax, and many of them did vote in Guadeloupe in 1799. The electors chosen represented 16,600 men—a number substantially larger than the population of 3,989 white and "red" adult males listed in the 1796 census of the island. Even if we account for errors in the census and the probability that several hundred gens de couleur from Martinique were present in the Guadeloupean army, in 1799 several thousand ex-slaves finally experienced the political enfranchisement the Republican decree of 1794 had promised.[26]

25. ADG, Bonnet 2E2/41, 9 Brumaire, An VIII (Oct. 31, 1799); ADG, Dupuch 2E2/25, 13 Fructidor, An VIII (Aug. 31, 1800). On Charles Langlois's land purchase, see ADG, Castet 2E2/212, 9 Germinal, An XI (Mar. 30, 1803).

26. "Procès verbal de l'assemblée électorale du département de la Guadeloupe," 20 Germinal, An VII (Apr. 9, 1799), in AN, C 577, no. 102. There were eighty-three electors chosen, and each in principle represented two hundred people. Un-

The eligibility requirements for electors were even more exclusive than those for voters, but the electors' political trajectories over the preceding decade covered a wide range. Most of those elected were wealthy whites, and many of them had been involved in the island's administration in one form or another in the previous years. One of the few electors who was not white was the homme de couleur Canut Robinson, who represented Basse-Terre. Like Robinson, the notaries Joseph Serane and Maximilien Vauchelet, other electors for Basse-Terre, had been active Republicans in the town in 1793, serving as members of the Commission générale extraordinaire. The same was true of the president of the electoral assembly, Laurent Masseguin. Vauchelet and Serane had signed the 1794 petition in favor of slave troops, as had another elector, Jean-Baptiste Lagarde. One of those from Trois-Rivières, Joseph Redaud, had been a royal official as late as 1791 and likely left the island not long afterward to return with the softening of émigré policies in the late 1790s. Within a few years, he would oversee the return of plantations to émigrés and the transformation of Africans captured on slave ships during Hugues's regime from free citizens into slaves. Pierre Romain, who was also a representative from Trois-Rivières, was part of a family that had lived in the area since the seventeenth century and had stayed out of politics but remained on his plantation through Hugues's regime. Another elector from the town, the surgeon Antoine Roubaud, had in 1793 helped sequester the habitations abandoned in the wake of the insurrection.[27]

Those chosen by the electors to represent Guadeloupe also were drawn from across the political spectrum. One, Clauzel, had served in the heavily Jacobin National Convention. Another was the citizen Jastram, who

fortunately, the only local report in the archives about the selection of the electors is a brief letter from Port de la Liberté, so more detailed information on who voted is unavailable. For Desfourneaux's intervention in Saint-Domingue, see the "Procès verbal de l'assemblée électorale de la colonie de St. Domingue," 20 Germinal, An V (Apr. 9, 1797), in AN, C 513, no. 99. For the 1796 census, see the "Etat sommaire des citoyens," 1 Vendémiaire, An V (Sept. 26, 1796), in CAOM, G 1, 502, no. 9.

27. On the commission and the petition, see AN, AD VII, 21 C, nos. 33, 46, and Chapter 4, above. Serane was married to Brousse, who was a femme de couleur; see CAOM, EC, Basse-Terre, 7, no. 33, 26 Pluviôse, An III (Feb. 14, 1795); on Redaud, see CAOM, Barbier, 52, Jan. 1, 1791; ADG, Dupuch 2E2/26, 14 Fructidor, An IX (Sept. 1, 1801), in CAOM, C 7A, 81, 5 Pluviôse, An XI (Jan. 25, 1803). For Romain, see CAOM, Barbier, 52, Mar. 8, Aug. 21, 1791; CAOM, G 1, 502, no. 2. For Roubaud, see ADG, Jaille 2E3/7, June 14, 1793.

The Boundaries of the Republic, 1798–1804

once in Paris wrote his memoir criticizing Hugues's regime. In a gesture of political expediency, the electors also chose as one of their representatives the minister of the colonies himself, Baron de Bruix, who had recently sought to create a segregated unit for black soldiers in France. The notary Roydot, working as Desfourneaux's assistant, wrote that, despite Hugues's repeated fears that the gathering of electoral assemblies would lead to disruptions in the colony, the elections had gone perfectly smoothly. A few months later, General Pélardy, who had taken part in the 1794 attack on Guadeloupe before being expelled by Hugues and then returning with Desfourneaux, wrote to the minister that the new regime had restored order on the island and that "soon Guadeloupe will have no more of these misfortunes, only the memory of them."[28]

In fact, however, Desfourneaux's hold on power was exceedingly fragile. In October 1799, news about the fall of the Directory began circulating in the colony. At a dinner, when someone mentioned that this might bring about the return of the Terror, Desfourneaux declared, if this were the case, he would attempt to preserve the colony from such a regime, with force if necessary. A number of his subordinates quickly branded him a traitor to the metropole. Soon, crowds in Port de la Liberté and Basse-Terre, composed of "all the classes of the colony," demanded his departure. The revolt was so generalized that Desfourneaux quickly gave up on the idea of using force against it and instead called a meeting to negotiate with the insurgents. During the packed meeting, "a considerable crowd of men, women, and children of all colors preceded by the municipal officers" arrived, "shouting and demanding the embarkation of 'the traitor Desfourneaux.'" He was placed in custody on a ship called, ironically, the *Desfourneaux* and sent by the insurgents to the metropole, along with reports defending their actions and proclaiming their loyalty to the constitution of the year III—which had already been abrogated by the Consulate at the time.[29]

28. Roydot to minister, 8 Floréal, An VII (Apr. 27, 1799), Pélardy to minister, 25 Fructidor, An VII (Sept. 11, 1799), in CAOM, C 7A, 51, 136, 129; see also Chapters 7, 10, above.

29. See the mémoire of General Paris, 18 Fructidor, An IX (Sept. 5, 1801), in CAOM, C 7A, 51, 115–119, and the attached documents in 120–127; see also CAOM, C 7A, 51, 111–114. The incidents are also described in Lacour, *Histoire*, III, 39–48. For the official accusation made against Desfourneaux, see "Extrait des régistres de la municipalité de Port Liberté," 11 Vendémiaire, An VIII, in CAOM, C 7A, 53, 185–195.

Exactly what were the roots of the insurrection against Étienne Desfourneaux? He considered it the nefarious handiwork of "throat cutters in the pay of Victor Hugues." General Pélardy also described the leaders of the deportation as "partisans of Hugues," noting that an anonymous letter intercepted after the insurrection declared: "Finally the tail of Hugues has crushed the head of Desfourneaux." Yet some of those who joined the uprising—notably Canut Robinson—had, less than a year before, rallied to the new agent upon his arrival rather than defend Hugues. Robinson shared a background in the Republican organizing of the early 1790s with other participants in the expulsion, such as Masseguin. Other army officers figured prominently in the insurrection. Two battalion leaders named Dandieu and Frontin, the latter of whom was an homme de couleur, were the first to publicly denounce Desfourneaux and headed the group that forced him onto the boat for deportation. Another participant was the citoyen Félix, who had been in charge of a depot of the corsairs' weapons that had been discovered and confiscated by Desfourneaux's men. The island's new administrator had managed to alienate a wide section of the population of Guadeloupe, including some of his early allies. They were not the only ones who reacted to him this way: a few years later in Saint-Domingue, General Charles Leclerc described Desfourneaux, who served under him, as an "ignorant" man who was "disdained" in the colony and asked Bonaparte to recall him to Paris.[30]

One resident of the island, the citizen Raboteau, wrote to his nephew in Bordeaux celebrating Desfourneaux's expulsion. The new agent, he noted, had tried to fool the people of the island with his proclamations while arresting and deporting many "patriots." With him gone, the people of Guadeloupe were determined to fight against anyone else who would seek to trick them with "false news from France," wrote Raboteau. He ended his letter by asking his nephew to send him newspapers and write to him about what was actually happening in France. Confused about the political developments in the metropole and seeking to stay true to a vision of the Republic they themselves had helped create, many of the leaders in Guadeloupe were ready to defend that vision when they felt it was threatened.[31]

30. Desfourneaux to minister, 19 Frimaire, An VIII (Dec. 10, 1799), in CAOM, C 7A, 51, 71–72; Report of General Pélardy, 18 Vendémiaire, An X (Oct. 10, 1801), in CAOM, C 7A, 55, 207–209; Lacour, *Histoire*, III, 39–48; Leclerc to Bonaparte, 14 Ventôse, An X (Mar. 5, 1802), in Paul Roussier, ed., *Lettres du Général Leclerc, commandant en chef de l'armée de Saint-Domingue en 1802* (Paris, 1937), 116.

31. The letter, from October 1799, is in CAOM, C 7A, 53, 250.

The Boundaries of the Republic, 1798–1804

The insurgents had, coincidentally, been acting in parallel with metropolitan officials. Sensing that Desfourneaux was inexperienced and unable to deal with the complicated situation on the island, Minister Bruix had recommended two months before that he be replaced, and soon three new deputies were named to take charge of Guadeloupe—Étienne Laveaux, René-Gaston Baco, who had failed in his 1796 mission to abolish slavery in Île de France and Réunion, and Nicolas-Georges Jeannet-Oudin, who had served as governor in French Guiana. Roydot, who had accompanied Desfourneaux to Paris after his expulsion, wrote that the constitution of this new commission was a terrible reversal of policy, one that would return the colony to the days of Hugues's terrorist administration. Meanwhile, Hugues wrote from his new position in Spain that he hoped Desfourneaux could "control for as long as I did spirits so worried and turbulent." Hugues was still popular as a hero of the struggle against slavery—in 1799, a pro-emancipation newspaper suggested his name as a replacement for Minister Bruix. Yet what he had achieved in Guadeloupe was also an inspiration for those who wished to reverse emancipation. In his "secret instructions" to Leclerc, Bonaparte noted that, once Leclerc's mission had been completed, "all the blacks will live in Saint-Domingue as they do today in Guadeloupe." Indeed, as Leclerc grew desperate in his struggle against the rebels in 1802, he would plead with Bonaparte to send him an administrator "who was knowledgeable as a military man and as an administrator" and had a "great character." He suggested "a man little known in France but known to the English because of his good conduct in Guadeloupe: Victor Hugues." Hugues would be sent to Guiana, this time with a very different mission from that which he had fulfilled in 1794. In that colony, where the slaves had been freed as they had in Guadeloupe, Hugues reestablished slavery in 1802, facing no large-scale resistance. The Republic was retreating, and Hugues was retreating with it. The failures of his regime in Guadeloupe were a piece of the general failure of French colonial policy during this period: the inability to reconcile the promise of freedom with the economic exigencies deemed necessary for the survival of empire.[32]

32. See the minister's report, from 17 Thermidor, An VII (Aug. 4, 1799), the naming of the new commission, from 14 Fructidor, An VII (Sept. 1, 1799), and the recall of Desfourneaux a few days later, in CAOM, C 7A, 51, 174-179, 181, 186; Roydot to minister, 6 Frimaire, An VIII (Nov. 27, 1799), in CAOM, C 7A, 51, 138-139; Hugues to minister, 25 Pluviôse, An VII (Feb. 13, 1799), in CAOM, C 7A, 51, 134; Marcel Dorigny and Bernard Gainot, *La Société des amis des noirs, 1788-1799: Contribution à l'histoire de l'abolition de l'esclavage* (Paris, 1998), 320;

As metropolitan officials backed away from the emancipation project, many in the Caribbean rallied to defend it. The "partisans of Hugues" who agitated in Guadeloupe in 1798 did so by defending the man who had brought liberty to the island. Their actions suggest that, despite the constraints on most residents' economic roles and freedom of movement during his reign, they still valued the measure of self-possession that had come with their new status. When the French government moved to strip the people of Guadeloupe of their hard-won rights, it found many would rather die than acquiesce. In Guadeloupe, those in revolt would soon no longer be the partisans of Hugues but a large segment of the population who wished to preserve the policies of emancipation that he had sought, unsuccessfully, to limit.[33]

The End of the Republic

"At the moment when we left for this colony," the new agents wrote from Guadeloupe, "the Directory had been dissolved and the Consulate did not yet exist." A few months after their selection but before their departure, Napoléon Bonaparte, aided by the Abbé Sieyès, overthrew the Directory in the coup d'état of 18 Brumaire, An VII (Nov. 8, 1798). Bonaparte's brother-in-law, General Leclerc, commanded the troops that dispersed the Conseil des cinq cents. The agents that had been chosen by the Directory regime left for Guadeloupe despite the coup, and, somewhere in the Atlantic, unbeknownst to them, crossed paths with the deposed Desfourneaux. They arrived to find the colony nominally under the control of General Marie-Auguste Paris and, once they were in charge, continued the progressive softening of the policies on émigrés, handing over many state-owned plantations to their former owners.[34]

"Notes pour servir aux instructions à donner au Capitaine Général Leclerc," and Leclerc to Bonaparte, 29 Fructidor, An X (Sept. 16, 1802), both in Roussier, ed., *Lettres du Général Leclerc*, 235, 269. On Hugues in Guiana, see Bénot, *La Guyane*, 177–183.

33. Report of General Pélardy, 18 Vendémiaire, An X (Oct. 10, 1801), CAOM, C 7A, 55, 207–209.

34. Old grievances surfaced, such as that of Toussaint Rivière, an inhabitant of Port de la Liberté; when he was working to gather the horses of the municipality under the orders of Hugues and Lebas, his own horse was requisitioned and given to an officer. The new agents decided that, since Rivière "had always been faithful to the Republic," he should have his horse returned. See agents to minister, 4–5 Pluviôse, An VIII (Jan. 24–25, 1800), in CAOM, C 7A, 52, 20–23, 4, 12; for

The Boundaries of the Republic, 1798–1804

The agents had been given a clear mission: Bonaparte ordered them to take action so that Guadeloupe would "furnish the Republic with five million [francs] in commodities from the national plantations." Following Desfourneaux's lead, they decided to rent out the national plantations. They believed that this system would encourage responsible work and management and in so doing would be more productive than the state-controlled administrations, which they claimed had led to corruption and made the *agriculteurs* "suspicious, unhappy, and discouraged." The agents sought to bring plantation production under the control of one centralized administration, pursuing managers of state-owned plantations who did not pay their rent, forcing them to stop "thinking of themselves as owners of the property they have rented." Putting pressure on the managers, the agents claimed, would help stop "the scourge of *divagation* [rambling]." As a way of ending the underground trade in sugar that had flourished under Hugues's regime, they ordered all barrels of sugar and coffee stamped with the name of the establishment that produced it. Many barrels that had been sold without such stamps, they noted, contained volcanic rock or manure instead of sugar and coffee.[35]

The agents also took care to suppress opposition in the colony. Shortly after their arrival, in May 1800, they accused seven men of having "hatched a plot tending toward revolt against the authorities." All but one of those accused were "soldiers by profession," and all seem to have been ex-slaves or gens de couleur, most of whom were originally from the commune of Égalité. Jean Charles, the alleged leader, was sentenced to death, whereas the others were deported to Saint Eustatius. Two white men were also deported for aiding the conspirators. Although the documents say little about exactly what the conspirators' plans were, they had some connection to men who would later revolt, more successfully, against metropolitan officials. Leandre Gripon, one of the deportees, was

---

Rivière, see CAOM, C 7A, 52, 47–81, which contains the register of the agents' administrative decisions between 18 Pluviôse and 22 Ventôse, An VIII (Feb. 7, Mar. 13, 1800); for Rivière's horse, see C 7A, 52, 47–81.

35. "Mesures à prendre," "Demande d'un état relatif aux cultures," 9 Germinal, An VIII (Mar. 30, 1800), in CAOM, C 7A, 52, 219, 223; agents to minister, 7 Messidor, An VIII (June 28, 1800), 12 Thermidor, An VIII (Jul. 31, 1800), in CAOM, C 7A, 52, 101–106, 121–127; "Circulaire," 1 Brumaire, An IX (Oct. 23, 1800), in CAOM, C 7A, 52, 208. The agents also set about building a canal through Port de la Liberté in order to supply water to the large number of "poor" in the town, including, presumably, the many ex-slaves who now lived there. See arrêté, 9 Vendémiaire, An IX (Oct. 1, 1800), in CAOM, C 7A, 52, 204.

likely related to François Mondésir Gripon, who would play an important role in 1802 in Basse-Terre. And Pierre Desfontaines, one of the accused white soldiers, had served under a black captain named Jean-Baptiste and knew Pierre Frontin, another of those who would soon rise up against the authorities again. Among those who sentenced these men, however, was Joseph Ignace, who would soon become one of the most radical leaders of the insurrections against the French government. The game of allegiances between local soldiers and metropolitan administrators was indeed a complicated one.[36]

As the agent Baco noted in one letter, he and his colleagues were in a difficult situation, since they depended on the same black soldiers who they felt represented a danger to their regime. "Without them or the fear they inspire, you would have no colonies in the Antilles, your agents would have been embarked, and a flood of blood would fertilize the deserted savannas of Guadeloupe." The agents clearly understood the importance of co-opting potential insurgents from the army. Shortly after their arrival in the island, the agents promoted Pierre Frontin, who had been involved in the coup against Desfourneaux, to the position of *chef de bataillon*. When they asked for confirmation of this promotion, they wrote: "The citizen Frontin is métis, and the encouragement he will receive from the approval of his promotion can only produce the best of effects on the citizens of color, and bring them to follow the excellent conduct of this officer."[37]

Such measures were, they recognized, only temporary responses to what Baco described as a "political labyrinth." The French Republic, he argued, preserved no real power in Guadeloupe or the other colonies. "The famous decree of 16 Pluviôse has irrevocably alienated all the

36. "Jugement rendu par le Conseil de guerre permanent," 11 Floréal, An VIII (May 1, 1800), in CAOM, C 7A, 53, 299; for the deportation orders, see 12 Floréal, An VIII (May 2, 1800), 19 Floréal, An IX (May 7, 1800), 19 Messidor, An IX (Jul. 8, 1800), in CAOM, C 7A, 52, 185, 191, 199. For Desfontaines, see EC, Basse-Terre, 6, no. 6, 18 Pluviôse, An III (Feb. 6, 1795), and 1 Messidor, An IV (June 19, 1796), no. 34. Two months after this incident, another plot aiming to deport the agents from Guadeloupe was discovered; one black soldier was executed, and five others were placed in prison. See agents to minister, 7 Messidor, An VIII (June 26, 1800), in CAOM, C 7A, 52, 94.

37. Baco to Consul, 4 Thermidor, An VIII (Jul. 23, 1800), in CAOM, C 7A, 52, 115–118; agents to minister, 3 Vendémiaire, An IX (Sept. 25, 1800), in CAOM, C 7A, 52, 142.

whites and particularly the planters," who were so deeply beholden to their "antique prejudices" that, even when threatened by violence, they would "never voluntarily accept philosophical ideas." No matter what the agents did to bring the "haughty" whites close to the blacks, the whites resisted, murmuring their discontent, muttering "blasphemies against the metropole." The new planters on the island, those who were renting plantations from the Republic, were "just as crazy as their exiled predecessors," and they hated "the nation that feeds them." As Hugues had before him, Baco drew attention to the fine line the administrators trod between slavery and liberty, arguing that, whether the government paid too much attention to the planters or "abandoned them," the result would be the same: the white inhabitants would be "chased away." It was vital, he pleaded, for the consul to select one agent who would be powerful enough to administrate this labyrinth. "An emissary who is too effervescent will ignite passions despite himself . . . the one who thinks of reestablishing slavery will ignore the torches and sharpen the daggers, the *negrophile* will be dragged into actions whose end is unforseeable."[38]

Not long after their arrival in the colony, Baco and Jeannet forced their co-commissioner, Étienne Laveaux, into exile from the colony for being just such a "negrophile." Before they had even left metropolitan France together, Laveaux and Baco had argued about emancipation and L'Ouverture. Once in Guadeloupe, Baco later explained to the minister, Laveaux became a source of inspiration for the mulâtres who, "always worried, always active, spy and watch over us." "They know their numbers," he wrote; "they have tried their courage," and they sought to influence and master the government as they waited for an opportune moment to take control. "Our colleague Laveaux raised their hopes; his direct friendly and active liaisons with them and his indiscreet speeches, his apologies for the murders committed under the orders of Toussaint forced us to the distressing decision to exile him." Laveaux managed to escape at first, and crowds in Basse-Terre gathered to defend him; ultimately, the other commissioners carried out his embarkation by using a group of exclusively white soldiers and ordering the black troops of Basse-Terre to stay in their garrisons during the event. They noted, however, that, since his departure, "his name circulates, his intentions to give favors to the blacks and mulâtres are remembered"; some conspirators

38. Baco to Consul, 4 Thermidor, An VIII (Jul. 23, 1800), in CAOM, C 7A, 52, 115–118.

had planned to arrest and "immolate" the agents. "The blacks had divided up the power, and the whites waited quietly," but the conspiracy was discovered, and the guilty were caught and tried.[39]

The continuing game of conspiracy and repression exposed tensions that spread throughout Guadeloupe, as former slaves braced themselves for the possibility that the days of freedom were numbered. Some began preparing to assert their right to individual freedom if emancipation were reversed. In 1799, the citoyen Albert, a merchant in Basse-Terre, departed from Guadeloupe. Before he left, however, he deposited a sealed packet with Marinette, who remained on the island. The packet was addressed to her, but in a peculiar way—she was described as "Marinette, free girl of Basse-Terre." Why should Marinette be described as "free" on an island where everyone was free? Marinette took the packet to the notary Vauchelet in order to open it in his presence, presumably to assure that it would have legal weight. They found that it contained Albert's testament, which granted Marinette, again described as a "fille de couleur libre," forty thousand livres from his inheritance, along with the property of a large house Albert owned in Basse-Terre. Having learned what the document was, Vauchelet and Marinette went to see the notary Serane, who watched as the testament was resealed. The packet, Vauchelet noted in his declaration of the event, had originally been sealed in red wax imprinted with "Liberty." He resealed the testament with a simple seal, and Serane kept it for Marinette so that, in case of Albert's death, she could collect her inheritance.[40]

The envelope was not opened again until 167 years later, in 1969, when a worker at the National Archives in Paris broke the seal to microfilm what was inside. Marinette had never returned to retrieve the testament from Serane, and it had remained among the yellowing registers until, in the 1960s, the notary who had inherited these documents deposited them in the archives. The message in the unopened envelope tells us that, when the merchant Albert left Guadeloupe in 1799, he seemed to know something few others on the island knew: that, soon enough, it would become necessary for women of African descent like Marinette to prove their freedom with documents—or face reenslavement.

39. Agents to minister, 28 Ventôse, An VIII (Mar. 19, 1800), in CAOM, C 7A, 52, 86–87; Baco to Consul, 4 Thermidor, An VIII (Jul. 23, 1800), in CAOM, C 7A, 52, 115–118; Bénot, *La Démence coloniale sous Napoléon* (Paris, 1992), 36–37.

40. See ADG, Serane 2E2/160, 19 Floréal, An VII (May 8, 1799).

Chapter 14

THE NEW IMPERIAL ORDER

In the middle of 1801, Napoléon Bonaparte received a letter from Guadeloupe. Written by the citizen César-Dominique Duny, it lamented the fate of an island that, since 1790, had seen "a constant war against property, industry, individual liberty, reason, and humanity." The property-owners and merchants of the island—the "most interesting portion of its inhabitants"—had been attacked and either killed or forced to flee, and the remaining whites were languishing in "disorder and anarchy." Duny hoped that the Consulate would soon come and "repair all the evils and heal all the wounds of the French colonies."[1]

Several months earlier, another native of Guadeloupe, Guesnier, had written a long memoir that was published as a pamphlet and forwarded to Bonaparte. "The miseries that have overwhelmed Guadeloupe started the day the decree of general liberty was issued," he wrote.

It is easy to conceive what the sentiments of the blacks must have been when they first heard the flattering words *you are free*. They were told nothing more and were allowed to remain ignorant of the true characteristics of the freedom of man in society and the indispensable duties it imposes. They took the shadow for reality and had only vague and indeterminate ideas about the meaning of their new existence.[2]

From the day the "fatal" word "liberty" was pronounced, the tools "fell from the hands of the cultivateurs," leaving the fields prey to the wandering cows and to the "cultivateurs themselves who, in destroying the products that they had watered with their sweat, annihilated, as if on

1. "Duny au premier consul de la République," 19 Germinal, An IX (Apr. 9, 1801), in CAOM, C 7A, 55, 246.

2. A. M. R. E. Guesnier, *Coup d'oeil rapide sur la colonie de la Guadeloupe*, 3, in CAOM, C 7A, 53, 282–291.

purpose, the people's shared resources. They wished to destroy anything that reminded them of their old condition, and they arrived at such a point of extravagance that for a long time they lived persuaded that the work of cultivation was incompatible with liberty." The ex-slaves were a "people of children who had no understanding of the liberty that had just been offered to them," and the administrators who had made them free without "placing next to the boon the responsibilities that had to be fulfilled to deserve it" had placed a "sharp knife" in their hands. Blacks murdered whites, encouraged by men who traveled through the countryside and told them that "the colony had become for them a patrimony, that they could divide it according to their desire." Reiterating the central arguments of the Hugues regime, even as he criticized Hugues himself, Guesnier wrote that "slaves made free had contracted by this fact obligations to fulfill." "Since each citizen is held to give to the nation the sacrifice of his work and his industry and to use his hands to perpetuate the movement of the political machine, all become, without distinction, its dependents," he concluded. "A civilized people cannot accept idle people in the empire."[3]

The citizen Bourget, who traveled to Guadeloupe during this period, corroborated Guesnier's opinion in his own letter to Bonaparte. The misery on the island was caused by "the abuse of liberty in the hands of the blacks and the hommes de couleur." The solution, suggested Bourget, was to create a "gap" in the Republic's constitution, allowing a "particular regime" for each colony. This would make it possible to keep the cultivateurs on their plantations, following the example set by Desfourneaux of paying them with a share of what they produced. Once paid, "the noir feels the price of work, and in return for the quarter of the productions given to him, he works just as he did before, like a child who has left his father's house." In fact the ex-slaves, wrote Bourget, repeating the words of St. Elaire from the year before, "all sigh after the return of the old propertyowners." The only exception were those "blacks or hommes de couleur who had been on the corsairs" and who therefore had become "accustomed to a lazy and vagabond life" of a "kind of war" that "satisfied at once the greed of the shipowners and the whims of the blacks and the hommes de couleur." Bourget ended his text with a recommendation that, once order was reestablished on the island, administrators should turn to one of the most pressing concerns in the

3. Ibid., 4, 10, 12, in CAOM, C 7A, 53, 282–291.

colony—developing a means to fight the fever that killed so many European soldiers.[4]

Unfortunately for Bonaparte and the soldiers he soon sent in large numbers to the Antilles, he listened selectively to the suggestions he received—but he did not put Bourget's recommendations on the control of disease into effect. He did, however, follow the outlines of the plans proposed by Bourget and Guesnier and in similar writings that multiplied during the early 1800s on both sides of the Atlantic. These writings reflected the growing consensus surrounding colonial policy within the Consulate. After his coup in 1799, Bonaparte staffed the ministry of the colonies with a number of figures who had defended slavery in the early 1790s. They included François Barbé-Marbois, who had been an intendant in Saint-Domingue in 1789 and retained royalist sympathies throughout the Revolution, and Pierre Malouet, a propertyowner from Saint-Domingue who was a member of the pro-slavery Club Massiac in 1791. In 1793, Malouet had led the negotiations through which the planters of Saint-Domingue offered to hand the colony over to the British. Also part of the new ministry was the exiled Moreau de Saint-Méry, who, in Philadelphia in 1796, had published his magisterial *Description* of colonial Saint-Domingue, lamenting that the prosperous colony had been destroyed since 1789. Perhaps, he noted, the details he provided might help change the colony back into what it once had been.[5]

Colonial policy during this period involved many figures with disparate agenda, and there was certainly no unanimous support for a return to slavery at this stage. Some continued to express a principled Republican support of emancipation of the kind that had governed colonial policy immediately after 1794. In late 1799, for instance, Admiral Laurent Jean François Truguet, who had known Bonaparte since they fought together in 1793, wrote several private letters to the consul in which he sharply denounced those who were attacking the policies of emancipation. He

4. "Observations sur la colonie de la Guadeloupe," 27 Vendémiaire, An IX (Oct. 19, 1800), in CAOM, C 7A, 53, 276–281.

5. Yves Bénot, "Bonaparte et la démence coloniale (1799–1804)," in Michel L. Martin and Alain Yacou, eds., *Mourir pour les Antilles: Indépendance nègre ou esclavage, 1802–1804* (Paris, 1991), 13–35, esp. 19; Jacques Adélaïde-Mérlande, *Delgrès; ou, La Guadeloupe en 1802* (Paris, 1986), 15; Étienne Taillemite, "Introduction," in Médéric-Louis Élie Moreau de Saint-Méry, *Description topographique, physique, civile, politique, et historique de la partie française de l'Isle-St.-Domingue* ... ([1797]; Paris, 1958), I, 5–7.

was critical of the Indian Ocean colonies, which "dared call themselves French" even as they continued to practice slavery, and he echoed Sonthonax's 1795 writings in claiming that "the true people, the only people, of our Antilles are the blacks" who had "conquered their liberty themselves" and had "defended it against both the English and the Spanish." He also defended Toussaint L'Ouverture. Two members of the Saint-Domingue delegation of 1794, Louis Dufay and Jean-Baptiste Belley (who had been part of the Hédouville mission and returned bitter about L'Ouverture's actions), though staunch defenders of abolition, did argue that Bonaparte should send a force to Saint-Domingue to prevent moves toward independence on the island. The planter Pierre François Page, who had been Belley and Dufay's enemy in 1794, insisted that there could be no return to slavery in the colonies but, like Bourget, argued for laws forcing all those who did not own property to work for wages. In the ministry of the navy, one bureaucrat in early 1800 proposed a set of laws regarding slavery and the slave trade that, although they did not reverse the abolition decree, would allow for the importation of "people born in slavery in countries where it exists" to the colonies, where they would be free but not citizens.[6]

In response to various suggestions and in the pursuit of his own vision, Bonaparte developed a new colonial policy. In December 1799, he issued a proclamation to the "Brave Blacks of Saint-Domingue" assuring them that the decree of 1794 would be maintained. His proclamation, however, announced the promulgation of the year VIII constitution, which abandoned the integration of metropole and colony and stipulated that a particular set of laws would be created for each colony. This signaled a profound political transformation in the Caribbean: the inhabitants of the colonies would no longer have the same rights as those of the metropole, and the colonies would no longer have representatives in the French parliament. Bonaparte determined that Guadeloupe would be governed by a team of three officials: a *commissaire de justice* would oversee the courts; a *capitaine général* would take over the administration of the army, fortifications, trade, and passports; and the *préfet colonial* would oversee state finances, salary payments, censuses, public education, commerce, and agriculture, including control of the "divagation of the noirs." The position of commissaire de justice was ultimately filled by an obscure individual named Coster. But the other two posts would be occupied by veterans of colonial administration. To fill the position of capitaine géné-

6. Bénot, *La Démence coloniale sous Napoléon: Essai* (Paris, 1992), 47–54.

The Boundaries of the Republic, 1798–1804

ral, Bonaparte selected Admiral Lacrosse, the same man who in 1793 had broken the royalist hold on the Antilles and had been greeted by the new citizens of Basse-Terre as a liberator. The prefect of the new mission was Daniel Lescallier.[7]

Although Bonaparte's colonial policy was in many ways the fruit of pro-slavery planters' return to dominance, it was also defined by certain continuities with Republican administrators' ideals during the 1790s. The central tenets of the arguments proposed in 1801 and 1802 had in fact been powerfully voiced not only by exiled planters but by Republicans like Hugues and Lescallier. Liberty had led to license and an abandonment of work on the part of the ex-slaves, and this situation, combined with the increasingly autonomous black regimes of the Caribbean, threatened to permanently undermine the prosperity France had gained from its colonies. The vision of the chaos that had followed emancipation was also built on the arguments presented before the Revolution by abolitionist thinkers such as Condorcet. The scripts provided by such gradual abolitionists had determined how metropolitan observers interpreted the actions of ex-slaves in the wake of emancipation and helped create a profound disjuncture between metropolitan views of the colonies and the political aspirations of colonial citizens themselves. This disjuncture would become tragically clear once Bonaparte's emissaries arrived in the Caribbean. The first consul and those who supported him would later claim that insurrections against metropolitan authority in the Caribbean made necessary their use of force. Yet it was the consular government itself that initiated open insurrection by breaking with the colonial project of the previous years and denying that the laws of the Republic applied equally to all people in all lands.

The Liberator's Return

On his arrival in Guadeloupe in May 1801, Admiral Lacrosse was welcomed by a populace for whom he was a part of Republican history. It was to him that the new citizens of Basse-Terre had addressed their powerful 1793 declaration of loyalty to the Republic. Lacrosse, however,

---

7. Carolyn E. Fick, *The Making of Haiti: The Saint Domingue Revolution from Below* (Knoxville, Tenn., 1990), 204–205; "Les Consuls de la République," 29 Germinal, An IX (Apr. 19, 1801), in AN, AD VII, 21 C, no. 62; nomination of Lacrosse, 1 Frimaire, An IX (Nov. 22, 1800), in CAOM, C 7A, 52, 217–218; see also Adélaïde-Mérlande, *Delgrès*, 49–54.

discouraged the connection between his past role as a liberator and his new role in 1800. He was invited to a dinner in the major town of the island, which he had just renamed Pointe-à-Pitre. One of the guests was a woman who, in 1793, as a *dame de la nation* of the city's Jacobin club, had placed the red bonnet of liberty on Lacrosse's head during a ceremony. Seeing her, Lacrosse said, "Go, citoyenne; know that the Lacrosse of the year 7 is not the Lacrosse of 1793!" Lacrosse had left metropolitan France ahead of Bonaparte's other administrators. Before they even arrived in Guadeloupe, however, he managed to have himself expelled by an uprising of black and de couleur soldiers.[8]

One of the central protagonists in this uprising was Magloire Pélage, who in seeking to defend his actions afterward had the most detailed extant account of Lacrosse's regime written by one of those who served with him in Guadeloupe. Another of the participants in the revolt was Louis Delgrès. After being allies, Delgrès and Pélage ended up fighting against one another in 1802. The trajectories that brought them to this conflict were, in fact, remarkably parallel; they had spent much of their military careers together. When the Revolution began in 1789, both men were hommes de couleur in Martinique and joined the Republican camp on the island. Delgrès participated in the first racially integrated election in French history, held in exile in Dominica in 1792, whereas Pélage distinguished himself in battle against royalist forces and was promoted in October 1793 to the rank of lieutenant by Rochambeau in Martinique. Delgrès and Pélage were both taken prisoner when the British took over in 1794 and, once freed, became part of the *Bataillon des Antilles* formed with exiles who had ended up in metropolitan France. In October 1794, as this battalion was being consolidated, both men were promoted on the same day, Pélage to captain, Delgrès to lieutenant. After arriving in Guadeloupe in 1795, the two officers were sent to Saint Lucia to serve under Commissioner Goyrand, who again promoted both officers within a few days of each other, making Pélage the chef de bataillon of his army and promoting Delgrès to captain. Delgrès was then sent to fight in Saint Vincent, where he was captured once again by the British, as was Pélage later on in Saint Lucia. Released once again to metropolitan France, they were mobilized in 1798 as part of the *Compagnie des hommes de couleur*

8. Chevalier Hippolyte de Frasans, *Mémoire pour le chef de brigade Magloire Pélage . . .* , 2 vols. (Paris, 1803), I, 60. This larger work drew on two previous texts by Pélage; see Pélage, "Précis des événements," 6 Brumaire, An X (Oct. 28, 1801); Pélage, *Mémoire*, in CAOM, C 7A, 55, 123-138, and 56, 258-265.

The Boundaries of the Republic, 1798–1804

that was eventually disbanded, then spent some time on military leave in Paris. In 1800, they were placed as officers in the missions accompanying Baco, Jeannet, and Laveaux to Guadeloupe. Pélage was named a *chef de brigade* and was the second ranked officer in Guadeloupe. Both he and Delgrès commanded a great deal of respect and loyalty among the troops of Guadeloupe, many of whom had served in various campaigns with them. An officer noted in 1798 that, according to many testimonies, Delgrès was "an excellent soldier" besides being well educated, and Pélage had been promoted in Saint Lucia because of his "bravery." Pélage also carried physical marks of his extensive service: his left arm had considerable scarring on it, stretching up to his skull, as a result of a gunshot wound. According to one officer, this injury meant he could only serve in the army with "a great deal of difficulty." He would soon prove otherwise.[9]

The stories of these two men's rise through the ranks of the Republican army reflect the general experiences of former slaves and gens de couleur in the wars of the 1790s. When the authorities began dismantling Guadeloupe's Republican regime, large numbers of soldiers, along with the cultivateurs, rose up to resist. Propelled by these rebels' actions, Pélage and Delgrès emerged as leaders in the insurrection against Lacrosse.[10]

When Lacrosse arrived in Guadeloupe, he invited all émigrés back, and many of those who had taken refuge on neighboring islands quickly returned. Like his predecessors, he also quickly arrested a number of soldiers and officers he believed were conspiring against him, notably the homme de couleur Pierre Frontin. The arrests were very unpopular, for Frontin and the others were well liked by the soldiers. Forewarned of Lacrosse's decision to seize these men, Pélage had advised

9. See "Etat des hommes blessés" and "Etat des officiers . . . bien constaté par le Délégué Goyrand et le Général Rochambeau," both from 29 Fructidor, An VI (Sept. 15, 1798); "Officiers et sous-officiers . . . des compagnies coloniales," 6 Fructidor, An VII (Aug. 23, 1799), in AHAT, X i, carton 80; Pélage's letter to Bonaparte (and the attached documents), 27 Thermidor, An X (Aug. 15, 1802), in CAOM, C 7A, 56, 258–259. See also Frasans, *Mémoire*, I, 51–55; Adélaïde-Mérlande, *Delgrès*, 9–10, 89–93; André Nègre, *La Rébellion de la Guadeloupe (1801–1802)* (Paris, 1987), 33–37; Germain Saint-Ruf, *L'Epopée Delgrès: La Guadeloupe sous la Révolution française (1789–1802)* (Paris, 1977).

10. For the best analysis of the uprising against Lacrosse, see part I of Adélaïde-Mérlande, René Bélénus, and Fréderic Régent, eds., *La Rébellion de la Guadeloupe, 1801–1802* (Basse-Terre, Guadeloupe, 2002).

General Antoine-Charles de Béthencourt, the commander of the army in Guadeloupe, to send a mix of metropolitan and colonial troops to do the job, presumably in order to undermine the appearance of white troops' disarming black troops. Despite this precaution, in the wake of the arrests Pélage had to quell anger among the soldiers in order to "prevent the murmur among the colonial troops from exploding into an insurrection that would have been difficult to stop." Many officers petitioned Lacrosse to release the prisoners, including General Béthencourt, who vouched for the arrested officers' loyalty. Although Lacrosse relented in a few cases, most of the prisoners, including Frontin, were deported.[11]

On their arrival in France, these officers wrote a report attacking Lacrosse for placing recently returned émigrés, some of whom had served with the British army, in positions of authority. Furthermore, the officers wrote, the admiral had stirred up anger among the cultivateurs on private plantations by appointing administrators to oversee the payment of their salaries. Although this measure was intended to assure the payment of the proper amounts to the laborers, the new administrators took a commission out of the cultivateurs' share as well as decided whether they would be paid in plantation commodities, which was the usual practice, or alternatively in provisions or clothes. This decreased the payments and took away an important right from the cultivateurs. Lacrosse's regime also stepped up attempts to force "vagabonds" back to the plantations. Former masters seem to have received some signal that their old power was returning: one of them commanded a "little black boy" who lived on his plantation to sell some milk and bring him the profit. When the child failed to sell it, his former master, furious, threw him into a coffee processing mill, breaking his arm and legs. Someone placed the child on the doorstep of Béthencourt's house, but he soon died.[12]

Cultivateurs on many plantations experienced the return of former masters who had left the colony before emancipation. In Trois-Rivières, the widow of Jacques Coquille Dugommier returned and took back the property left behind by her husband nearly a decade before. She found many of the cane fields "abandoned" and "ravaged by rats," although

11. Frasans, *Mémoire*, I, 56–62; see also Adélaïde-Mérlande, *Delgrès*, 55–57. Sixteen of the deported soldiers, including Frontin, arrived in France in August 1801; see minister to first consul, 9 Fructidor, An IX (Aug. 27, 1801), in CAOM, C 7A, 55, 264.

12. "Abrégé historique," in CAOM, C 7A, 55, 279–282.

The Boundaries of the Republic, 1798–1804

production had not entirely ceased. Jean-Baptiste, who had led the 1793 insurrection and had in 1796 been the plantation manager, was still there, but many other former slaves had disappeared. Although there were 117 laborers on the plantation in 1796, there were only 49 listed in 1801, and twelve of those were "absent." The African Theresine "dite l'Etat" ("the State")—so named, perhaps, because she had been one of the Africans captured by corsairs and placed on the plantation by the state—was missing. The sixteen-year-old Cézaire had taken refuge in Pointe-à-Pitre. The Africans Isaac and Pierre were living on plantations in nearby Capesterre. Dugommier listed the names of those who were absent in order to "preserve all her rights" over them.[13]

Many cultivateurs were not ready to accept a return to their plantations. A "black citizen named Arselle," who had been a slave before emancipation and had since been part of "the company of the artillery workers," was stopped one day by his former manager, accompanied by a local administrator. They ordered that he return to the plantation. "He responded that he was free and French and had a profession that he had always had the right to pursue." When the plantation manager "grabbed him by the collar," Arselle "pulled a dagger from his pocket and stabbed himself six times, saying that he knew how to die." "Indeed, he died the next day." Some cultivateurs returned to old strategies of resistance by poisoning animals on the plantations. Lacrosse reacted quickly and brutally, declaring that all those "poisoners who have spread in a frightening manner throughout the colony" would be subject to the death penalty. Backing up his declaration, he sent a troop under Pélage's command to Petit-Bourg to round up and execute some cultivateurs who were accused of poisoning animals. The poisonings evoked the classic fears of the eighteenth century, and panic spread far and wide; residents in Guadeloupe later received letters from France asking, "Are you alive or dead?" The cultivateurs perhaps intended to send a signal to émigrés who were considering returning to Guadeloupe: that, contrary to what critics of emancipation had said, the cultivateurs were not eagerly awaiting their return. In Basse-Terre, posters of Lacrosse's new regulations liberalizing émigrés' access to their former properties were ripped down, and some were smeared with excrement.[14]

13. See ADG, Dupuch 2E2/26, 14 Fructidor, An IX (Sept. 1, 1801); "Etat nominatif des citoyens . . . de Trois-Rivières," 1 Vendémiaire, An V (Sept. 22, 1796), in CAOM, G 1, 502.

14. "Abrégé historique," in CAOM, C 7A, 55, 279–282; Frasans, *Mémoire*, I,

One man from Guadeloupe wrote in a letter to a friend that Lacrosse's policies, notably his attacks against an army that was seven-eighths "noirs and hommes de couleur," were sure to incite revolt: "Is it not to be feared that they will repeat in Guadeloupe all the scenes of devastation and carnage for which Saint-Domingue has for so long been the theater?" Lacrosse feared a revolt among the soldiers as well. In addition to arresting officers and punishing cultivateurs, he granted rations and additional pay to the troops "arriving from France" in order to "encourage" them and reward them for their "good behavior," lest they side with their comrades from Guadeloupe in a moment of crisis. Yet this action also sent a clear message that a line was being drawn between the multiracial troops of Guadeloupe and the white troops Lacrosse had brought with him from France.[15]

In September 1801, Lacrosse made another gesture that further marginalized the soldiers of Guadeloupe. When the well-regarded General Béthencourt died of fever, Lacrosse placed himself in command of the army rather than promote Magloire Pélage. He announced his ascension with great fanfare in Basse-Terre, and some soldiers openly protested the decision. Lacrosse's response was swift: he arrested the dissenters and dissolved their company. "Only hommes de couleur participated in this insurrection," Lacrosse noted, and this convinced him it was part of a larger plot against him. He therefore arrested twenty-five other men whom he considered "extremely dangerous" and prepared boats to deport "all the hommes de couleur." Although no evidence of a plot was discovered—and despite the protests of high-ranking officers such as the homme de couleur Alexandre Kirwan—the tribunal found three soldiers guilty of having "broken ranks" and having "made comments tending toward sedition, revolt, and the degradation of the authorities of the colony." Two of these men were sentenced to two years in prison, the third to five years. The rest of the soldiers accused of speaking out against Lacrosse were also kept in prison.[16]

On an evening soon after the sentencing, "a little noir" brought a basket with some food and half a bottle of rum to the imprisoned soldiers.

71–74; Auguste Lacour, *Histoire de la Guadeloupe*, 4 vols. (Basse-Terre, Guadeloupe, 1855–1858), III, 119–126.

15. Lacour, *Histoire*, III, 126; on the troops' pay, see the orders of Lacrosse, 28 Prairial, An IX (June 17, 1801), in CAOM, C 7A, 55, 34.

16. Lacrosse to minister, 14 Fructidor, An IX (Sept. 1, 1801), in CAOM, C 7A, 55, 95–98.

The guard refused to deliver the contents of the basket. One of the soldiers, Joseph Lagarde, cursed the guard and said to the other prisoners, "They had been truly stupid to have controlled the country and to have ceded it to scélérats like that one." Then he waved his fist, bared his teeth, and declared: "We won't stay here forever." The guards reported the incident, and, after a brief trial, Lacrosse's war tribunal determined that Lagarde was guilty of having "soaked in criminal conspiracies" and sentenced him to execution. Lacrosse went even further. Gathering the gens de couleur of the town—many of whom had celebrated him as a liberator in 1793—he declared that "all hommes de couleur" were "enemies of the government." The gens de couleur responded with a variety of claims to citizenship, mentioning the property they owned, describing the services they had given the colony, and showing off "the honorable wounds that they had received defending the nation." Lacrosse threatened them all with permanent deportation, making similar threats in Pointe-à-Pitre soon afterward. He arrested other officers and transferred the soldiers who had been captured with Joseph Lagarde to Marie-Galante.[17]

Lagarde's angry words in the prison were a reflection of the aspirations of the women and men of Guadeloupe toward fuller political participation and greater power on the island. As Lacrosse brutally rooted out such aspirations, he gave them more force and direction. He was attacking a tight web of acquaintances and families who had considerable power and were unwilling to quietly give up their hopes for equality. The twenty-three-year-old Joseph Lagarde was probably the younger brother of Jean-Baptiste Lagarde, a métis who owned a plantation in Baillif and had been both a soldier and a sailor on a corsair ship during the previous years. Jean-Baptiste's wife was Elizabeth Corbet, whose brother was the officer Noël Corbet. He, in turn, had been an acquaintance of the deported Pierre Frontin. Both Corbet and Frontin were acquainted with two other officers who had, like them, been captains in a battalion garrisoned in Basse-Terre during the high tide of Hugues's war against the British. Soon these two officers, Pierre Gédéon and Joseph Ignace, along with Corbet, would be at the head of a movement to take back control of Guadeloupe.[18]

17. Frasans, *Mémoire*, I, 79–87.

18. For Jean-Baptiste Lagarde, see CAOM, EC, Basse-Terre, 6, no. 39, and 9, nos. 6, 30. See also ADG, Castet 2E2/209, 13 Frimaire, An VIII (Dec. 4, 1799). For weddings involving the officers Corbet, Gédéon, and Ignace (as well as Vulcain), see CAOM, EC, Basse-Terre, 6, nos. 34, 50. On Ignace, see EC, Basse-Terre,

In the middle of the night on October 21, 1801, Magloire Pélage was woken up and called to the home of one of Lacrosse's white officers. When he arrived, Pélage was told he was under arrest. Furious, he pushed his way past the officer and walked into the street. White officers also attempted to arrest Gédéon and Ignace, who escaped, woke up their troops, and called them to arms. Quickly, company after company of black troops mobilized; they went on the offensive, arresting all of the white officers who served Lacrosse. Stopped by a black soldier, one of these officers fired three times with his two pistols, missing all his shots, before being disarmed and carried away. As black and de couleur officers and soldiers rallied around the insurrection, they rebuffed Lacrosse's actions by telling the history of their service to the Republic, naming the battles they had fought against the British. Because it was a day of rest for the cultivateurs, large numbers of them had come into town from their nearby plantations, and they joined the soldiers. The crowd attacked the house of the police chief, where they found lists of gens de couleur who were supposed to be arrested and a letter from Lacrosse announcing that those who had already been deported were being sent to Madagascar. News of the uprising spread quickly outside of Pointe-à-Pitre, and hommes de couleur from other towns came into the city. One elderly propertyowner from nearby Petit-Bourg, who almost never left his house, was seen in the streets of Pointe-à-Pitre. When asked what he was doing there, he said, "My caste is being attacked, and all good people must unite to defend it!"[19]

Pélage quickly acted to control the situation. He gathered troops around him, concentrating them in the town's main fort and preventing white and black troops from firing on one another. He also broke up the massing of cultivateurs and encouraged them to return to their plan-

---

6, no. 27; ADG, Vauchelet 164/2E2, 17 Pluviôse, An VI (Feb. 5, 1798); see also Roland Anduse, *Joseph Ignace, le premier rebelle: 1802, la révolution antiesclava-giste guadeloupéene* (Paris, 1989), 137–144; Anduse, "L'Histoire singulière du 1er Bataillon de l'armée de la Guadeloupe: Loyalisme révolutionnaire et révoltes militaires," in Martin and Yacou, eds., *Mourir pour les Antilles*, 57–64.

19. Frasans, *Mémoire*, I, 94–99; Lacour, *Histoire*, III, 129–133, 141. According to Lacrosse, the list of the accused was a fake produced by Savigny, a white judge who had served with Hugues first in the revolutionary tribunal of Rochefort and then in Guadeloupe; see the "Liste des hommes tant blancs que de couleur qui ont le plus figurés dans l'insurrection de la Guadeloupe, arrivée le 29 Vendémiaire, An 10," in CAOM, C 7A, 55, 269–278.

tations. By afternoon, calm had been restored. Pélage called a meeting that brought together most of the wealthy merchants of Pointe-à-Pitre, many of whom had been on Lacrosse's list of suspects. Four of these were elected to help Pélage in administering Pointe-à-Pitre until Lacrosse's arrival, and two others were sent to give a message to Lacrosse. These emissaries did not have to go far to find the admiral, who was at the head of a large troop of soldiers marching from Basse-Terre; the messengers managed to convince him to stop his advance and await further word from Pélage. Meanwhile, black soldiers from Basse-Terre skirted Lacrosse's troops to come to Pointe-à-Pitre, where they announced that, before he had marched out of town, Lacrosse had placed a number of hommes de couleur in chains in the holds of ships. One soldier also tore down a proclamation Lacrosse had posted calling the insurgent soldiers "outlaws" and brought it to Pointe-à-Pitre, where it circulated among the soldiers for a few days before being turned over to Pélage. Some of the black soldiers in Lacrosse's troop deserted to Pointe-à-Pitre; they did not, they said, want to fight "against their own color." In Pointe-à-Pitre, the black troops assembled and proclaimed a hesitant Pélage "general in chief of the army of Guadeloupe."[20]

Pélage arranged for a meeting between Lacrosse and a delegation from the town, which invited Lacrosse to enter alone and take back control of the army on the condition that he grant a general amnesty. Lacrosse refused and, once in Pointe-à-Pitre, openly blamed Pélage for initiating the insurrections and demanded the resignation of the officers who had participated, insulting and threatening the black soldiers. A detachment of black grenadiers attacked Lacrosse, calling, "Vivre libre ou mourir!"—"Live free or die!" Pélage and Gédéon protected Lacrosse from this first assault, but soon afterward, with Pélage absent, a group of soldiers led by Ignace arrested and forced the admiral out into the street at gunpoint, then marched him to the Fort de la Victoire. When they arrived, Pélage was speaking to the soldiers there, and he shouted "Vive la République!" and "Vive le Capitaine-Général Lacrosse!" Some soldiers took up the cry, but others began shouting "Vive la liberté!" "A bas Lacrosse!" ("Down with Lacrosse!") and "Vivre libre ou mourir!" The ranks broke, and Ignace, along with other soldiers, surrounded Lacrosse and locked him and his aides in a room.[21]

At this moment, the officer Louis Delgrès joined the rebellion. Del-

20. Frasans, *Mémoire*, I, 94–110.

21. Ibid., 114–123; see also "Liste des hommes," in CAOM, C 7A, 55, 269–278.

grès had been serving as an aide-de-camp to Lacrosse, and at first he protested the admiral's imprisonment. Ignace and other officers, however, prevented him from freeing Lacrosse and took Delgrès aside to ask him to join their cause. When he eventually agreed, he apparently said: "All right! I am with you, but on the condition that we will defend ourselves to the death, unless we are offered a treaty that covers the past and assures the future!" Fearing that Lacrosse would be executed, Pélage made a decision for which he would later be accused by French authorities of treason: he negotiated with the insurgents and managed to get Lacrosse released a few days after his arrest so that he could get on a Danish boat that happened to be in the harbor. The agent sent by the Consulate to Guadeloupe ended up forcibly expelled at the hands not so much of Pélage himself as of a rebellious army that entered into insurrection to defend its officers and racial equality within the armed forces. Lacrosse himself noted early on after his expulsion that "the insurgent black troops no longer follow any leader, and they refuse to put down their weapons." Guadeloupe was under the control of an autonomous regime, which had been put into power by troops who, having fought for the Republic against the British, were now defending it against a French administrator.[22]

As Lacrosse was leaving Guadeloupe, the British captured him and took him to Dominica. Soon, however, news reached the Caribbean that France and Britain had signed the preliminaries for a peace treaty that was to end the global conflict between the two empires. Lacrosse, no longer a prisoner, became a guest, hosted by Dominica's governor. He was soon joined in his exile by Daniel Lescallier and the third agent named by Bonaparte, Coster, who arrived from France. The "Three Magistrates" of the island declared war on Guadeloupe, setting up a blockade to prevent ships from stopping there and calling on all citizens to resist the "illegal" government of Pélage. The situation that both Lacrosse and Delgrès had experienced in 1792 and 1793—when the royalist takeover in Martinique and Guadeloupe sent Republicans in exile to Dominica—was ironically reversed. The representatives of the metropolitan government, like the Republicans who had escaped the royalists, declared themselves the true representatives of the nation. But the principle upon which they stood was the opposite of what it had been eight years before: in Guadeloupe, Pélage and his conseil defended racial equality,

22. Lacour, *Histoire*, III, 147; Lacrosse to minister, 26 Frimaire, An X (Dec. 17, 1801), in CAOM, C 7A, 55, 102–105.

The Boundaries of the Republic, 1798–1804

whereas Lacrosse and the onetime abolitionist Lescallier sought to destroy the racially integrated army of Guadeloupe.[23]

"The colonies of the Antilles," the Three Magistrates wrote to the Consulate in Paris, "are full of men who are supremely dangerous to the establishment of a reasonable order in these colonies, and even to their very existence." The first of these were "the noirs, who, previously slaves and submitted to masters, suddenly fell into the most extreme license"; a majority of them were "armed" and had "grown accustomed to murder, pillage, and the most fanatical and immoral ideas." The second were "the mulâtres, or *sang-mêlés*, who escaped suddenly from the state of submission and respect toward whites in which they were held" and "made abusive use" of the "benefits the laws of the metropole presented to them." In Guadeloupe in particular, these "instruments of disorder" had been joined by some whites, "the refuse of the nation, covered in crime," and together they had "spread with fervor anarchic ideas" and created "a perpetually revolutionary system." Besides those in Guadeloupe, there were many just as dangerous in Martinique and imprisoned at the hands of the British. It was necessary to "purge the colonies of all those who resemble them, the active instruments of anarchy, the enemies of all government and of all social order," or else lose the colonies. This was, in fact, a problem that both the British and the French had to confront. "Here the interests of the two nations is the same. . . . We must deport all men who, upon examination, are recognized as guilty and dangerous, those who own nothing, have no place to live, and have no honest means to exist." The deportations had to be done with care. If these people were brought to Madagascar or to the Seychelles, places important for the prosperity of France, they would "spread disorder there" as well as in the colonies of Réunion and India. The only reasonable choice would be a completely isolated island, "far from all communication with any European colony."[24]

Lacrosse sent the minister of the colonies, Denis Decrès, a detailed

23. "Manifeste adressé aux gouvernements des puissances amies ou alliées . . . par les Trois magistrats," Dominica, 14 Frimaire, An X (Dec. 5, 1801), "Lescallier, préfet colonial, et Coster, commissaire de justice . . . aux citoyens des dites îles," 8 Nivôse, An X (Dec. 29, 1801), in CAOM, C 7A, 55, 101, 117. Lescallier apparently did seek to soften Lacrosse's stance against the rebels, and Pélage saw him as a potential ally; see Frasans, *Mémoire*, II, 196–197.

24. "Mémoire adressé aux consuls de la République par les Trois magistrats composant le gouvernement de la Guadeloupe et dépendances," 15 Nivôse, An X (Jan. 5, 1802), Roseau, Dominica, in CAOM, C 7A, 56, 1.

list, divided by race, of the men who he claimed had participated in the insurrection against him. Among the whites were some who had rebelled against Desfourneaux. One, Monroux, had claimed that by himself he could arm "thirty thousand negroes." There were others whom he simply described as "anarchists," including a man named Savery who, apparently, worked to "have himself named colonial prefect by the negroes." Among the hommes de couleur were Pélage, Pierre Gédéon ("one of the principle motors of insurrection"), and Ignace ("a ferocious and sanguinary man, one of the hottest partisans and the principle instrument of insurrection"). He noted the names of those who had assumed leadership positions in the wake of the insurrection: "Delgresse," who had accepted the command of Basse-Terre given him by Pélage; Massoteau, who had become the leader of the Fort Saint-Charles; and the noir Palerme, who had been placed in charge of Port de la Liberté. He also mentioned the members of the conseil Pélage had set up to govern Guadeloupe: Danois, who had claimed that "the government did not need to send agents to Guadeloupe, and the colony could govern itself," and Corneille, "a dangerous, immoral anarchist." The list ended with a number of names that do not appear in any other documents of the insurrection. These were most likely soldiers who were ex-slaves and were part of the force behind the radicalization of the movement against Lacrosse. Their names —Nicole, Rémy Dufond, Marcel, Philippe, Jean-Blanc, Monnel, Coupery, Isseris Grand Baton, L. Pelette, Robert, Sabès—stood for the larger army of blacks that was "always disposed toward insurrection and ready to excite the blacks and the mulâtres to all kinds of horrors."[25]

In late 1801, Lacrosse wrote to the minister that the rebels of Guadeloupe had made their sentiments clear: "They want to reign over these islands like the nègres of Saint-Domingue. . . . Their pretensions are such that they say loudly that the island is theirs by right of conquest and that it is up to them alone to govern it." They had, he noted, given "new proof" of their hatred of the consular government by "proclaiming, publishing, and posting the decree of 16 Pluviôse and the Rights of Man, which they carry to all the plantations." His angry response to the governors' publicizing a law decreed by the French Republic in 1794, which was still the law of the land, highlighted the radical change that had taken place in the French administrators' position regarding the colonies. As Lacrosse knew, the force of Bonaparte was behind him, for, during his ill-fated administration in Guadeloupe, a massive expedition had

25. "Liste des hommes," in CAOM, C 7A, 55, 269–278.

been sent out from the metropole with a secret mission: to eliminate the black troops in Saint-Domingue and prepare the terrain for the reestablishment of slavery throughout the French Antilles. The revolutionary project of including the colonies under one law of equality was collapsing as unity turned to conflict throughout a French Caribbean that would soon be the theater for all-out civil war.[26]

Sending Slavery

As the army of Guadeloupe was rising up against Lacrosse, major new developments in colonial policy were taking shape across the Atlantic. Representatives for Britain and France were negotiating a peace settlement that would sap the foundations of the Republican project in the Antilles as it took away the urgency of maintaining a strong army in the region. L'Ouverture, meanwhile, took a bold new step toward autonomy in Saint-Domingue, angering Bonaparte and convincing him that France must reassert its power over its Caribbean colonies.

In 1800, before Lacrosse left for Guadeloupe, Bonaparte dispatched three agents (including Julien Raimond) to Saint-Domingue to apply his new constitution there. Since there was no mention of emancipation in the constitution, Bonaparte gave his envoys a statement making assurances that the freedom of the ex-slaves would not be taken away. L'Ouverture responded to the new constitution's policy of juridical separation between metropole and colony by producing his own constitution for Saint-Domingue: it defined the "territory" of Saint-Domingue as a colony "that is part of the French Empire but is governed by a particular set of laws." The constitution guaranteed "the individual property of people and the liberty of the negroes, the gens de couleur and all people" and declared, "Slaves are not permitted in this territory," "Slavery is forever abolished," and "All men born in this land live and die free, French men." The constitution also, however, made L'Ouverture governor-for-life, proclaimed, "Property is a sacred and inviolable right," and lauded the "union of the propertyowner and the cultivateurs" as necessary for the colony's prosperity. Plantations would be the "tranquil refuge of an industrious and well-regulated family whose father is necessarily the propertyowner of the soil or his representative." "Each cultivateur is a member of this family and must share in its revenues." To protect

26. Lacrosse to minister, 26 Frimaire, An X (Dec. 17, 1801), in CAOM, C 7A, 55, 102–105.

the labor force of the plantations, the cultivateurs' freedom of movement was restricted. In addition, as under Hugues in Guadeloupe, the "introduction of cultivateurs, indispensable for the extension and the reestablishment of agriculture," would be encouraged. So Africans from slave ships would be brought into the colony as "free" men and women, who would nevertheless be placed on plantations to work as laborers. White refugees were invited to return and take over the management of their properties.[27]

Although in many ways simply the "formal embodiment" of the autonomous regime he had been building since at least 1798, L'Ouverture's constitution enraged Bonaparte. In appointing L'Ouverture the governor-for-life of the island, the constitution made him and the colony of Saint-Domingue equal to Bonaparte and France. In declaring that all its citizens would be both "free" and "French," it also posed a challenge to Bonaparte's wish to return the colonial system to what it once had been. Upon learning of L'Ouverture's new constitution, Bonaparte prepared a massive expedition to Saint-Domingue to destroy his power. According to Second Consul Jean-Jacques Régis de Cambacérès, Bonaparte, who until then had been sympathetic to L'Ouverture and had hoped to take advantage of his skills as a governor and military leader, determined that the black general's actions placed him in "a state of rebellion against the Republic." Bonaparte decided that crushing him was the only effective response. The expedition, placed under the command of General Leclerc, left for Saint-Domingue in early December 1801.[28]

By then, the international situation had changed in ways that were to have a heavy impact on the Caribbean. In the fall of 1801, British prime minister Henry Addington and French minister of foreign affairs Charles Talleyrand-Périgord began the negotiations that would lead to the Treaty of Amiens, which in 1802 would end the war between France and Britain. Addington raised the issue of Saint-Domingue, noting that he expected France would send troops to "reestablish completely the au-

27. See "Constitution française des colonies de Saint-Domingue," Cap-Français, 13 Messidor, An IX (Jul. 2, 1801), Bibliothèque nationale; see also Fick, *Making of Haiti*, 204–206.

28. The constitution was brought to Bonaparte in October 1801 by Colonel Vincent, an envoy for L'Ouverture; see Bénot, *La Démence coloniale*, 64; see also C. L. R. James, *The Black Jacobins: Toussaint L'Ouverture and the San Domingo Revolution* (New York, 1963), 263–266, 275–278; Fick, *Making of Haiti*, 206–208; Jean-Jacques Régis de Cambacérès, *Mémoires inédits*, ed. Laurence Chatel de Brancion, 2 vols. (Paris, 1999), I, 587–588.

thority of the metropole." He added that the British might also have to send reinforcements to the Caribbean, and, since the object of the two nations was to maintain order in their "respective possessions," the governments should keep one another informed of their missions. A few weeks later, Addington said: "The interest of the two governments is absolutely the same: the destruction of Jacobinism and above all that of the Blacks." The projected expedition's purpose in Saint-Domingue was cast in terms of the reestablishment of metropolitan power over rebellious black leaders. Talleyrand wrote, "The interest of civilization in general is to destroy the new Alger that is organizing itself in the center of America."[29]

After the preliminaries of the Treaty of Amiens were signed in October 1801, Bonaparte announced that the whites in the French possessions where slavery had not been abolished—those in the Indian Ocean who had refused emancipation and Martinique, which had been in the hands of the British—"did not need to fear the liberation of the slaves." The minister of the colonies informed Lacrosse of this in a private letter, encouraging him to placate the inhabitants of Martinique about the "future state of their negroes." This policy could not be publicly announced for fear of insurrections, but Lacrosse should communicate it to the planters so they would know what was ahead. A few months later, Lacrosse wrote from his exile in Dominica that he had followed these instructions, spreading the message to the white planters of Martinique, and that the "guarantee of their property has produced the best effect." The news of the decision meant something different, of course, for other groups in the colonies. A year earlier, in August 1800, Julien Raimond had written to Bonaparte, insisting Bonaparte not only promise the people of Saint-Domingue that liberty would be maintained where it had been decreed—as in his December 1799 proclamation—but that it would also be instituted in those islands where slavery still existed. Bonaparte's unresponsiveness to this request probably stirred up anxieties. The continuation of slavery in those colonies to be given back to the French would certainly have worried ex-slaves, particularly among the refugees from Martinique who had found freedom in Guadeloupe.[30]

29. Bénot, "Bonaparte et la démence coloniale," in Martin and Yacou, eds., *Mourir pour les Antilles*, 13–35, esp. 20–22. Addington did also mention the need for gradual emancipation and suggested discussing the abolition of the slave trade.

30. Saint-Ruf, *L'Epopée Delgrès*, 88; minister to Lacrosse, 25 Vendémiaire, An X (Oct. 17, 1801), Lacrosse to minister, 26 Frimaire, An X (Dec. 17, 1801), in CAOM, C 7A, 55, 267, 102–105; Bénot, *La Démence coloniale*, 35.

No public decision was made at the time regarding the future of emancipated colonies. When Leclerc left for Saint-Domingue, however, he carried special orders from Bonaparte instructing him to disarm the black armies and force ex-slaves to return to their plantations. He was to start by winning over the black generals such as L'Ouverture and Dessalines, assuring them of his peaceful intentions. Once the French troops had gained control of the port cities and landed their forces, they were to wage war against the black generals. Bonaparte famously commanded: "Do not allow any blacks having held a rank above that of captain to remain on the island." Leclerc's special instructions, like the various memoirs and projects out of which they emerged, did not explicitly mention a return of slavery. But they marked an intention to destroy the important leaders in the colony and the institution out of which they had emerged and from which they drew their power: the colonial army, with its many ex-slave and homme de couleur soldiers and officers.[31]

Several months after Leclerc's departure, news of Pélage's revolt in Guadeloupe arrived in France. One article described Pélage as "one of the greatest scélérats of his century," claiming falsely he had killed his former master, a woman, and was leading the revolt to escape punishment. Minister Decrès noted that according to Lacrosse the insurrection was the result of the "fatal spirit of independence that has spread for many years among the ex-slaves," inspired by "the example of the blacks of Saint-Domingue, which is known in Guadeloupe." The minister made clear his belief that this spirit of revolt was the result of emancipation itself and that it had to be reversed. "The abuse of liberty on the part of the caste of slaves, in all the colonies where this fatal word has been spoken, determines the limits with which it must be circumscribed," declared Decrès. "I reject these supposedly liberal ideas, which, in order to spread my affection to the entire universe, call down misery on my country," he continued. "I am too French to be cosmopolitan . . . I want slaves in our colonies. Liberty is a food for which the stomachs of the negroes are not yet prepared. We must seize any occasion to give them back their natural food, except for the seasonings required by justice and humanity."[32]

31. For the instructions, see Paul Roussier, ed., *Lettres du Général Leclerc, commandant en chef de l'armée de Saint-Domingue en 1802* (Paris, 1937), 264–275; see also Fick, *Making of Haiti*, 210; Claude Bonaparte Auguste and Marcel Bonaparte Auguste, *L'Expédition Leclerc, 1801–1803* (Port-au-Prince, Haiti, 1985).

32. On Pélage, see the *Gazette de France*, 23 Pluviôse, An X (Feb. 12, 1802). The next day, another article was published that described Pélage more accu-

The white troops in the colony were, wrote the minister, vastly outnumbered and "contained" by the others: "1,500 mulâtres, very courageous, owning nothing, and ready for anything" and "15,000 blacks ready to fight," of which "5,000 are armed." It was therefore necessary to send a "considerable force" of up to 6,000 soldiers in order to reduce Guadeloupe, "not to what it was, but to what it must be." He was soon at work mobilizing the troops and supplies necessary for just such a mission, which he placed in the hands of the veteran officer Antoine Richepance. Decrès saw the new mission as a second Leclerc expedition—indeed, he wished to bring ships that had carried the troops to Saint-Domingue back to France and use them for the mission to Guadeloupe. As Leclerc was instructed for Saint-Domingue, Richepance should "positively announce the preservation of the abolition of slavery in Guadeloupe" in order to undermine resistance. This way the "former slaves" would abandon the rebels, since it was "only through the fear of losing their liberty that they have been brought to rebellion." By hiding their true intentions, the French could stall resistance and then reestablish the old order unopposed. To this end, the minister wrote a proclamation for the people of Guadeloupe, which opened with the declaration that France had not forgotten how people "of all ranks and all colors" had reconquered the island in 1794. Based on entreaties written by Pélage, who insisted both on his loyalty to the metropole and on his willingness to maintain order on the plantations, Minister Decrès concluded that Richepance would be welcomed by his regime and would be able to take control without confronting heavy resistance. He was right in his evaluation of Pélage, though wrong in his assumption of a quick victory. Richepance left France with more than three thousand troops on April 1, 1802.[33]

The Leclerc and Richepance missions were dispatched to apply policies that were not officially declared until the fighting in the Caribbean had begun. Only after the Treaty of Amiens was finally signed in March

---

rately; both were reprinted in the *Gazette politique et commerciale de la Guadeloupe*, 4 Floréal, An X (Apr. 24, 1802), in CAOM, C 7A, 56, 250–254. See also Adélaïde-Mérlande, *Delgrès*, 113–114. For Decrès's views, see "Rapport," n.d., in CAOM, C 7A, 55, 248–252; "Série de questions," in CAOM, C 7A, 55, 253–256; Saint-Ruf, *L'Epopée Delgrès*, 89.

33. See the "Rapport" and the "Proclamation au nom du premier consul, le ministre de la marine et des colonies aux habitants de la Guadeloupe," in CAOM, C 7A, 55, 248–252, 256–257; Adélaïde-Mérlande, Bélénus, and Régent, eds., *La Rébellion*, 31.

1802 did the government publicly proclaim its intentions toward slavery in the Caribbean islands that were being returned by the British. In May, a few days before Delgrès and his companions died at Matouba, the consuls signed a decree declaring, "In the colonies returned to France in execution of the Treaty of Amiens . . . slavery will be maintained in conformity with the laws and regulations anterior to 1789." The same law allowed slave trading to resume on French ships. An attachment to the law presented a synthesis of the attacks on emancipation of the previous years. "We know how the illusions of liberty and equality were propagated in these far-off countries, where the remarkable difference between men who are civilized and those who are not, and the difference in climates, colors, and habits, and most importantly the security of European families, inevitably require great differences in the civil and political state of people," it announced. "We also know of the disastrous effects of those innovations so ardently desired by zealots, most of whom, without a doubt, were stimulated only by the honorable desire to serve humanity, but who, in searching to indistinctly make all the men of the colonies equal in their rights, only made them all equally miserable." The "accents of a philanthropy that was falsely applied produced in our colonies the effect of the siren's song: with them came miseries of all kinds, despair, and death." The law ended with a vague reference to the future of Guadeloupe and Saint-Domingue: "In those colonies where the revolutionary laws were executed, we must rush to substitute, for those seductive theories, a healing system, whose combinations will be linked to the circumstances and vary with them and will be placed in the hands of the wisdom of the government."[34]

At the end of May, visits by noir or mulâtre soldiers to Paris or the French port towns were outlawed. Two months later, this policy was extended by a law that recalled the provisions of the 1777 Police des noirs, declaring that "noirs, mulâtres, or other gens de couleur" could not enter the "continental territory of the Republic" without authorization from the tribunals of the colonies or the minister of the colonies himself. All those who illegally entered the territory after the publication of the law would be arrested and imprisoned until their deportation. In early 1803, this law was compounded by one outlawing all mixed marriages in the French Empire. A regime of juridical and political integration had been replaced with an imperial relationship in which metropolitan law

34. "Loi rélative à la traite des noirs et au régime des colonies," 30 Floréal, An X (May 20, 1802), in AN, AD VII, 21 A, no. 54.

The Boundaries of the Republic, 1798–1804

and colonial law were distinct. The changes brought on by emancipation had been swept away in favor of a system in which each colony would be ruled, for the profit of the metropole, with laws decreed from Paris. People of African descent from the Caribbean were no longer equal citizens of France; they no longer had the right to circulate freely within what was now, once again, an empire.[35]

Declaring it to be so was one thing; making it so, another. By the time these laws were made official, the administrators who were sent with "secret" instructions to institute the new colonial order were in the midst of protracted and brutal conflicts on the other side of the Atlantic. The circuits of news that had helped propel the insurrections of the early 1790s once again spread word of the true nature of France's colonial policies. In Guadeloupe, soldiers and cultivateurs had already resisted the dismantling of the most important, hard-won gains of the previous years. In Saint-Domingue, large-scale resistance was taking shape to Leclerc's massive military force. Bonaparte's confident mission there was turning into a desperate, brutal fiasco.

In 1801, in the midst of his negotiations with Britain, Bonaparte and the diplomat Talleyrand had briefly considered what might happen if they opted to ally themselves with L'Ouverture instead of attacking him. If the French government were to "recognize Toussaint" and "constitute French blacks" in Saint-Domingue, Talleyrand mused, commerce would certainly suffer, but the "military force" of France would gain a great advantage. "The government of the blacks recognized in Saint-Domingue and legitimated by the French would be in all times an incredible point for action in the New World." Had Bonaparte followed this course, making the transformation of slaves into citizen-soldiers the center of a policy of French colonial expansion in the Americas, history would have looked very different. Why did Bonaparte decide, instead, to embark on what was ultimately one of the most disastrous campaigns of his career? His racism certainly played a role. Years later, questioned by his friend Truguet about what he had done in Saint-Domingue, an enraged Bonaparte declared that, had he been in Martinique during the Revolution, he would have supported the English rather than accept an end to slavery. "I am for the whites because I am white; I have no other reason, and that one is good," he said. "How is it possible that liberty

35. "Arrêté portant défense aux noirs, mulâtres, ou autres gens de couleur, à entrer sur le territoire continental de la République," 13 Messidor, An X (Jul. 2, 1802), in AN, AD VII, 21 A, no. 55; Bénot, La Démence coloniale, 96.

was given to Africans, to men who had no civilization, who did not even know what the colony was, what France was? It is perfectly clear that those who wanted the freedom of the blacks wanted the slavery of the whites."[36]

Yet just as important in generating this outcome was the limited political imagination of those who administered manumission in the Caribbean. In his 1781 antislavery text, the marquis de Condorcet had advocated the distribution of small plots of land to former slaves as part of his plan for gradual emancipation. They could, he argued, grow sugarcane independently on their plots and bring it to state-run mills for processing. It was a remarkable proposition, and one that would likely have been attractive to many ex-slaves, who dreamed of the independence that would come with owning land. Although it would certainly have entailed a shrinking of the colonial economy, as well as incited profound social change in the colonies, it would also have enabled administrators to create regimes that were not prey to the flagrant contradictions between the rights they promised and the coercion they practiced. A compromise between the exigencies of the colonial economy and the desires for autonomy on the part of the formerly enslaved might have been reached.[37]

Condorcet's proposal never became a reality during the revolutionary years. Instead, colonial authorities considered large-scale plantation agriculture as the only viable economic system for the French Caribbean. When they came up against an understandable resistance on the part of the ex-slaves, they turned to racism to explain the failure of their regimes. What they retained from Condorcet were the arguments that the enslaved were not ready for freedom and the warnings that chaos might ensue if they were freed suddenly. Indeed, according to Second Consul Cambacérès, in 1801—before he learned of L'Ouverture's constitution— Bonaparte made clear that he was not against emancipation in principle, but he believed that the boon of freedom should be granted gradually. In the meantime, "the colonial system had to be maintained as it had existed before the Revolution."[38]

Emancipation had to be reversed so that authorities could put into effect the kind of slow-paced transformation envisioned before the Revo-

36. Marcel Bonaparte Auguste and Claude Bonaparte Auguste, *La Participation étrangère à l'expédition française de Saint-Domingue* (Quebec, 1980), 11, 57–58; Bénot, *La Démence coloniale*, 62, 89.

37. Marquis de Condorcet, *Réflexions sur l'esclavage des nègres* (Paris, 1788), 54–61; see Chapter 6, above, for a discussion of this text.

38. For Cambacérès, see his *Mémoires inédits*, ed. Brancion, I, 587.

lution. The once-radical ideals of gradual abolition were twisted around to justify a brutal withdrawal of freedom. This turnabout was only possible because those who administered emancipation, unwilling to confront and overcome the basic contradictions in their own project, came to think like the old masters who had once reigned in the colonies. Manumission's defeat came in part because its architects were unable to envision a future for the formerly enslaved that truly broke with their past.

The failure of imagination regarding the shape of post-emancipation society was not restricted to white administrators sent from the metropole. In Saint-Domingue, L'Ouverture also opted to maintain the plantation economy rather than explore other alternatives. But, through the distribution of plantations to members of his army, he also integrated the ranks of the economic elite. The second failure of Bonaparte's government was its ultimate inability to accept the implications of this social shift. Had the government been able to compromise with L'Ouverture—and with the leaders who would soon emerge in Guadeloupe—by accepting racial equality within the military and political institutions of the colonies, France would perhaps also have preserved its most important colony, Saint-Domingue. But that was not to be.

The slaves of the Caribbean had, in the early 1790s, expanded the political imagination of the Republic. Their conversion into citizens had been a radical and noble dream, one that changed the very terms of citizenship and identity in the Atlantic world even as it wrought a social revolution in the colonies. Yet the dream ultimately posed too great a threat to the powers that governed France at the dawn of the nineteenth century. In its place they set in motion a remarkably costly and profoundly irrational project: the reversal of history.

"VIVRE LIBRE OU MOURIR!"

In January 1801, Marie Huard and two of her former slaves, Marie-Françoise Sophie and Alexandre, went to visit a notary in the town of Basse-Terre. Huard stated that, "a few years before the Revolution," content with the services of these slaves, she had "renounced all the rights that the laws then accorded her over" them and permitted them to freely dispose of their time and labor for the rest of their lives. Therefore, she noted, "the laws of the Republic, in abolishing slavery in the colonies, only ratified the particular disposition." Responding to the threat against both individual and universal emancipation, Huard declared that she wished to "confirm and renew" these acts.[1]

Two months earlier, Huard had visited the same notary with another of her former slaves, Camille. She said that, "long before the Revolution," she had wanted to free Camille and, using the preabolition legal formula, granted her the freedom to work for her own profit. Camille's twenty-year-old daughter, Marguerite, was also mentioned in the contract as free to work independently. Marguerite's father was the mason Augustin; immediately after the signing of the contract that assured her freedom, and in front of the same notary, Camille married Augustin. Camille, however, had not waited for liberty before she began constructing an independent life for herself. In 1796, when she had appeared with Augustin to declare the death of her daughter, Geneviève, she presented herself as Camille Vatable, taking the name of the man who was likely her father—Joseph Vatable, Marie Huard's deceased husband. Three years later, she again appeared with Augustin, who was described as her husband (though they were not yet legally married), to buy an expensive piece of property in Basse-Terre. That two years later Camille was released by Marie Huard and married Augustin, perhaps for the second time, was a mark

1. See ADG, Dupuch 2E2/26, 21 Frimaire, An IX (Dec. 12, 1800).

of Camille's determination to maintain the status and property that she had gained during the time of freedom.[2]

Why was individual liberty being granted in a colony officially populated by free and equal citizens? By the end of 1800, many in Guadeloupe had begun to realize that the freedom granted by the Republic could well be retracted. The appearance in notarial registers of this new kind of document—renewals of preabolition emancipations—testifies to Guadeloupeans' fears and suggests some of the ways meaning and limits of liberty were being redefined and renegotiated during this period. When individuals drawing up notarial acts stated that the 1794 declaration had "ratified" emancipations previously granted by masters, they were suggesting that, although universal freedom might be temporary, the masters' grants had a longer, more immutable power in the face of a republic unable, it seemed, to make up its mind. Such documents were an assertion of the primacy of the individual relationships between ex-masters and ex-slaves, which might once again come to overshadow the relationship between citizens and the Republic.

Individual acts of "reemancipation" proliferated after the arrival of Lacrosse, who instituted new regulations called the *police des domestiques*; these required servants, like the cultivateurs, to remain with those who had owned them before 1794. In August 1801, the merchant Elie Garrigue, who was a friend of Victor Hugues and had armed corsairs during the 1790s, declared that, "before the decree that pronounced the abolition of slavery in the colonies," he had granted his servant Ursule dite Soussoulle liberty "in the forms then prescribed by the laws and regulations in Martinique, where he lived." The 1794 emancipation grant had therefore "simply ratified" this "particular disposition." Unfortunately, she had lost the act of emancipation. Since, according to the new regulations, she might be "one day disturbed in the right that she has legitimately acquired to dispose of her time and her services for her personal profit and without the obligation to report to anyone," Garrigue reiterated her right, as well as that of her two young children, to liberty. Soon afterward, André Laroche "freed" his former slave Sophie from "all the rights" the new regulations on domestics gave him over her "services, time, and industry" and granted her license to "dispose of them forever" and "for her own personal profit." When a few months later

2. ADG, Dupuch 2E2/24, 13 Messidor, An VII (Jul. 1, 1799), and 2E2/25, 2 Pluviôse, An IX (Jan. 22, 1801); 20 Germinal, An IV (Apr. 9, 1796), in CAOM, EC, Basse-Terre, 8, no. 109.

Julien Langlois wrote up a private act of emancipation, he utilized some of the terms of slavery and ownership: "We renounce all property rights in favor of Anastazie, mulâtresse, forty-eight, who belongs to us, leaving her the mistress of her will and allowing her to enjoy all the rights of a free person, even supposing that things should change." As masters had throughout the eighteenth century, Langlois stipulated that Anastazie must "come take care of us whenever we are sick," assuming it was his prerogative to define the extent of her freedom. In all three of these cases, the contracts were accepted by the women, and Anastazie independently registered the private act with a notary, thereby highlighting their status as free individuals. Yet their forms were startlingly similar to the pre-abolition emancipation acts that had reasserted the rights of masters to grant, or withhold, a claim to their slaves.[3]

Two months later, in the midst of the trials against Joseph Lagarde in Basse-Terre, Geneviève Labothière dite Mayoute and her brother Joseph Labothière appeared in front of the notary Dupuch to reassert Joseph's freedom. Geneviève was a merchant and Joseph a tailor, and both lived in Basse-Terre. In 1794, they had been slaves, but, whereas Geneviève seems to have been in Guadeloupe, Joseph was in Martinique and therefore "did not enjoy the benefit of general liberty pronounced by the laws of the French Republic." In order to free himself, Joseph added to his savings through his "active work" and "honest industry" until he had amassed enough to buy himself. His master, however, was unwilling to sell Joseph his freedom. Desperate, Joseph wrote to his sister to ask for help. She could not, of course, travel to Martinique herself without endangering her own freedom, and so she arranged for a white man named Jacques Dupuy to go to Martinique and buy Joseph. In October 1796, Dupuy found Joseph and purchased him as his own slave. Both men then traveled to Saint Thomas, where two years later Geneviève was able to meet with them. She reimbursed Dupuy and therefore became her brother's legal owner. Soon afterward, Joseph paid back his sister, and they returned to Guadeloupe, both free.[4]

3. For Ursule, see ADG, Dupuch 2E2/26, 17 Thermidor, An IX (Aug. 5, 1801); on Garrigue, see 26 Ventôse, An IV (Mar. 16, 1796), in CAOM, EC, Basse-Terre, 6 (5Mi140), no. 17; ADG, Serane 2E2/157, 15 Ventôse, An V (Mar. 4, 1797). For Sophie, see ADG, Dupuch 2E2/26, 25 Thermidor, An IX (Aug. 13, 1801); for Anastazie, see Castet 2E2/211, 24 Vendémiaire, An X (Oct. 16, 1801). I discuss Anastazie and her wedding in the section "The Republican Corsairs," in Chapter 8, as well as in the opening section of Chapter 9, above.

4. See ADG, Dupuch 2E2/27, 6 Vendémiaire, An X (Sept. 28, 1801).

The Boundaries of the Republic, 1798–1804

All three of these private transactions were registered in an 1801 notary document to record the complicated, trans-Caribbean path Joseph had taken toward his freedom and to defend themselves from the looming possibility of the return to slavery. In drawing up this document, however, Geneviève had to confront a complicated legal problem. Because Joseph was in Martinique, where slavery had not been abolished, buying his freedom was necessary and legal. But Geneviève, as a resident of Guadeloupe and therefore a subject of the laws of the Republic, had broken the law by participating in the purchase of a slave. To justify this transgression, Geneviève invoked both the legal and natural rights she and her brother had as human beings and as citizens of the French Republic. She declared that, although her brother had the right to be "taken out of slavery by the laws of the Republic," he had been "forced by circumstances, because he was in a colony that had been usurped by the enemies of France, to reconquer his liberty with his own money." Therefore, in helping him free himself, she had "purely and simply committed a benevolent and fraternal act, based on the laws of nature, without hurting the laws of the Republic, since her brother himself paid for his liberty and was never sold to her." In order to show she had no ownership over Joseph, she gave up "all the rights that the said documents seemed to give her over his time and his services according to the police regulations currently in force in the colonies." Geneviève and Joseph's declaration, although sensitive to Geneviève's breaking the law by purchasing a human being, claimed that the Republican decree of emancipation—and the natural rights on which it was based—gave all, even those in occupied territory, the right to fight for their freedom in whatever way they found necessary. The care with which these two ex-slaves, who could not sign their names, considered and acted on the legal ramifications of the 1794 Republican decree presents a striking contrast to the actions of the French administrators who soon dismantled emancipation.

Other former slaves delved into their personal archives on their own to reassert the value of the preabolition emancipation grants. In November 1801, the citoyenne Esther, the servant of Jean-Baptiste Maudet, deposited a private document from October 1793. In it, Maudet had stipulated that, in thanks for "good services," Esther was to be free after his death. So that she would not be a "burden to anyone," he granted her "the little house neighboring mine." As an *écrivain public* (one who wrote documents for those who could not themselves write) in post-emancipation Guadeloupe, Maudet participated in a large number of former slaves' weddings. Meanwhile, Esther had probably continued to live in the house next door. Fearing, perhaps, that in the future a document in her own possession, written privately by Maudet, would not be enough to assure her freedom, she decided to deposit the letter with a notary; he would officialize it so that in an uncertain future Esther might invoke the power it had held in 1793.[5]

Former slaveowners were also preparing for a possible return to slavery. In December 1801, François Felet granted his young daughter Françoise "all the rights that the regulations on cultivation give him over Rosillette, câpresse, aged four years, who is part of the list of cultivateurs, cultivatrices, and domestics attached to his plantation," so that Françoise could enjoy these rights during the "life of Rosillette." In return, Françoise was to take on the obligations "the same regulations impose on those who are given rights over the time and services of the cultivateurs or domestics." The previous month, the lawyer Louis Joseph Bovis of Basse-Terre—who was probably well informed about the best way to assure one's future property in men and women who might become slaves once again—registered a series of private acts with Dupuch. The first was the 1793 sale of the mulâtresse Seusine to a man named François. The second was the 1801 transfer from François to Bovis of "the rights that the laws give him over the time and the services of the said Seusine and her child." By registering these transactions, Bovis was likely preparing for a time when they might be used to solidify a more direct relation of property. Times had changed since the moment after Desfourneaux's arrival when the fabricated suggestion that one man might buy another was seen as a severe threat to public security. In Guadeloupe, men and women, faced with deepening uncertainty about the future, attempted to prepare for a change of regime that could completely alter their legal and social worlds. Others, however, prepared to resist such a change with force.[6]

5. See ADG, Castet 2E2/211, 1 Frimaire, An X (Nov. 22, 1801). For some of the twenty-seven weddings I have counted in which Maudet participated, see CAOM, EC, Basse-Terre, 8, nos. 28, 29, 33, 35, 39, and EC, Basse-Terre, 9, nos. 7, 10, 16, 22, 23, 51, 58, 59, 61, 67, 70, 77. For Esther's participation in a birth declaration, see EC, Basse-Terre, 7, no. 101, 10 Floréal, An IV (Apr 29, 1796).

6. ADG, Dupuch 2E2/27, 27 Frimaire, An X (Dec. 18, 1801). The lists of cultivateurs during this period did not, it seems, change in their form, although ethnic terminology such as "créole" and "de guinée" increasingly appeared. See, for instance, ADG, Dupuch 2E2/27, 12 Brumaire, An X (Nov. 3, 1801), 21 Pluviôse, An X (Feb. 10, 1802).

The Boundaries of the Republic, 1798–1804

Blockade

In November 1801, alarming news arrived in Guadeloupe. The preliminaries of the Treaty of Amiens had been signed, which signified, as a newspaper report put it, that the "two powers" of Britain and France had joined together to "establish order and security in their respective colonies." From Guadeloupe, the new alliance between the two former enemies was directly visible, since most of the ships patrolling the waters to enforce the blockade set up by Lacrosse after his exile were British. Many black soldiers, for whom this reversal must have been particularly menacing, openly claimed the news was a "fable" spread by Lacrosse. The British officer sent by Lacrosse to Guadeloupe with copies of the newspaper announcement was insulted by disbelieving soldiers. Some declared that, if such a treaty had been signed, "it would be necessary to reject it as the most fatal of presents, because, for the noir and the homme de couleur, this treaty is slavery." They added that "after wearing a uniform for eight years they would not leave it behind to pick up the hoe under the whip of a commandeur." Others threatened to attack the propertyowners.[7]

For a year since Lacrosse's expulsion, Pélage and his *Conseil provisoire* had kept a tenuous hold over Guadeloupe. Other than Pélage, the key members of this conseil were Danois, a wealthy mulâtre merchant who had served in the municipality of Port de la Liberté under Hugues; Corneille, also a mulâtre who had previously served in the island's administration; and finally Hippolyte Frasans, the only white member of the conseil, a lawyer from Normandy who had been deported to the Antilles. Frasans would later author the *Mémoire pour le chef de brigade Magloire Pélage*, the most detailed source about Pélage's regime; it defended the actions he and his colleagues took as they sought to contain a rebellious army composed of "four thousand and some men, of which fifteen-sixteenths were noirs." In a similar vein, the members of the conseil repeatedly wrote to the administrators in Dominica during 1801, insisting on their loyalty to the metropole and on the continuity they had maintained with the previous French regimes by maintaining order on the plantations and containing violence against whites. They also wrote to Bonaparte directly, assuring him of the same. Ignorant of the consuls' intentions, they celebrated that, on the island, which had been the

7. Auguste Lacour, *Histoire de la Guadeloupe*, 4 vols. (Basse-Terre, Guadeloupe, 1855-1858), III, 169-172, 182. See also "Manifeste," 14 Frimaire, An X (Dec. 5, 1802), in CAOM, C 7A, 55, 101.

"rallying point for the persecuted patriots of the Antilles" throughout the previous years, "liberty had been conquered by all those who enjoy it today." Guadeloupe's new citizens had therefore shown themselves "very deserving of the holy promises of a great nation."[8]

The soldiers who had first precipitated the revolt against Lacrosse, however, were skeptical of Pélage's regime and of its faith that the *mère patrie*, once informed of the truth of what had happened in Guadeloupe, would forgive those Lacrosse called "rebels" and understand that they were loyal to France. As newspapers and personal letters brought news of the Leclerc expedition's departure from France and of a similar mission's preparation for Guadeloupe, these suspicions grew stronger. During the first months of 1802, news of L'Ouverture's resistance against Leclerc arrived in Guadeloupe and inspired some. In April 1802, the conseil declared that dangerous rumors were rampant in the colony and were making a great impression "on spirits so difficult to contain," so that "a great number of negroes deserted their plantations." The rumors took on different forms—some people accused the conseil of wishing to join with the managers of state plantations to "crush the cultivateurs with work," whereas others worried that the hommes de couleur were planning a massacre of all the blacks. Most dangerous of all, however, was the hearsay that "Saint Domingue was resisting with success against the laws and orders of the metropole and that Guadeloupe should follow this example." The rumormongers were "a small number of men who in secret proclaim themselves partisans of Toussaint L'Ouverture and are tempted to imitate his guilty behavior." These ideas had inspired many cultivateurs to abandon their plantations "and take refuge in the woods and in the cane fields." The conseil ordered local officials to find out where the "conciliabules" were taking place and arrest those who were spreading such gossip and planning for insurrection. Some whites had already made reprisals independently, for the conseil asked local administrators to avoid a repeat of such "assaults."[9]

8. On the conseil, see the "Série de questions," in CAOM, C 7A, 55, 253–256; see also the "Etat nominatif de 43 individus . . . prévenus d'être auteurs ou complices de la révolte . . . contre le Capitaine Général Lacrosse," in CAOM, C 7A, 55, 285–286. Frasans himself wrote that he was the "only white" in the conseil, suggesting that this required him to give a "more specific account" of his behavior; see CAOM, C 7A, 56, 255. For the letter to Bonaparte, see "Le Conseil . . . au premier consul," 5 Frimaire, An X (Oct. 27, 1801), in CAOM, C 7A, 55, 139–144.

9. Chevalier Hippolyte de Frasans, *Mémoire pour le chef de brigade Magloire Pélage . . .* , 2 vols. (Paris, 1803), I, 192–194, 252–257; Lacour, *Histoire*, III, 169–

One of those who might have influenced Pélage in his sharp reactions to these rumors was François Rigaud. An homme de couleur, he was the brother of Toussaint L'Ouverture's rival André Rigaud, who had controlled the south province of Saint-Domingue before his defeat in a bloody war that ended in 1800. François Rigaud had taken refuge in Guadeloupe following this war, which had in many ways become a conflict between gens de couleur and former slaves. His account could easily have informed Pélage's attempts to appease metropolitan authorities by maintaining control over the former slaves who made up the majority of the soldiers on the island. Indeed, one of the officers who most strongly opposed Pélage and advocated the expulsion of whites from authority as well as the arming of cultivateurs for the defense of Guadeloupe was a former maroon, Joseph Ignace. Other officers, such as Massoteau, and a large number of rank-and-file soldiers supported this plan. Louis Delgrès took a more moderate position: he was not against the return of metropolitan authority in Guadeloupe but wanted a treaty that would stipulate certain conditions—including the maintenance of racial equality in the armed forces. He was wary of Lacrosse and other metropolitan authorities, and he believed they should prepare for a defense of the island in order to be able to negotiate with metropolitan authorities from a position of strength.[10]

After Lacrosse's expulsion, Pélage had named Delgrès the commander of Fort Saint-Charles. Delgrès used this position to oppose Pélage's conseil, however. As part of the campaign to uphold plantation production, Pélage had ordered Basse-Terre's commissioner to send police after cultivateurs who had taken refuge in the town. But ex-slave soldiers defended the cultivateurs, preventing police from arresting them and forcibly freeing some who had been captured. When the commissioner asked Delgrès to order his soldiers to stop, he refused. By defending the rights of cultivateurs to circulate freely, the soldiers, along with Delgrès, Ignace, and Massoteau, exhibited a different vision of how the island should be governed and resisted the conseil's attempt to appease metropolitan authorities. Joining Delgrès's side was François Mondésir Gripon, the tai-

170; see also "Circulaire," 15 Germinal, An X (Apr. 5, 1802), in CAOM, C 7A, 55, 119–120.

10. Lacour, *Histoire*, III, 153-154, 166-167. I am indebted to David Geggus for suggesting this interpretation of Rigaud's influence, which differs from that of Lacour. On Ignace, see Roland Anduse, *Joseph Ignace: Le Premier rebelle* (Paris, 1989).

lor who had grown up near the Capuchin convent in Basse-Terre. He used his position in the municipality to second Delgrès in defending the cultivateurs and, later, preparing the defense of the town. The matter of the cultivateurs galvanized a group that would soon lead the resistance against Richepance. Throughout the island, plantation workers were anxious about the impending possibility of a return to slavery. Many were skeptical of Pélage's regime and of the surrender he advocated, for, when the time came, rather than follow the orders of the conseil, they presented themselves in huge numbers to Delgrès and demanded weapons to fight the French.[11]

The Cultivateurs Begin

One night in December 1801, cultivateurs on a group of plantations outside Pointe-à-Pitre rose up. Under three leaders—Noel Piron, Fafa, and Ballas—six hundred men and women armed with rifles, swords, and pikes marched into Pointe-à-Pitre. Instead of calling out the majority black troops from the forts, Pélage sent officers to prevent the soldiers from entering the town and joining the revolt. The insurgents had in fact apparently been inspired by army officers to take action, and they expected soldiers to join them. A few troops did, briefly, side with the cultivateurs, but they were dispersed when Pélage led a troop against them. Fearful of stirring up more trouble, Pélage did not execute the leaders of the insurrection and instead had them deported.[12]

This small revolt paralleled the more dramatic events several months before in Saint-Domingue, when a rebellion of plantation laborers who were angered by the provisions in L'Ouverture's constitution broke out in the northern plain. There are contradictory accounts regarding the organization and leadership of the rebellion, but L'Ouverture accused Moïse—one of his highest-ranking officers as well as his adopted nephew —of starting the revolt. Moïse denied the accusation, but he had, in the months before the uprising, spoken out against the rigid forms of discipline instituted by L'Ouverture's administration, refusing to be the "hangman of my own color" in the service of France's interests. He had proposed a variant on L'Ouverture's policies in which the large estates would be broken up and distributed to junior officers and common sol-

11. Lacour, *Histoire*, III, 166–167, 207–208, 210, 228. I discuss Gripon's family in Chapter 9, above.

12. Ibid., 188–189.

The Boundaries of the Republic, 1798–1804

diers rather than managed by higher-ranking officers. Moïse represented a countercurrent within L'Ouverture's regime, one more closely tied to the aspirations of the former plantation slaves who sought the control over land and labor that his regulations denied them. The rank-and-file ex-slave soldiers understood that their future outside the military would be defined by the labor policies of the new order and were unhappy with the hierarchical system they saw emerging around them, where high-ranking officers controlled more and more land. L'Ouverture's response to this resistance was swift and brutal. He had Moïse and many others shot and then issued a proclamation laying out even more draconian regulations on agriculture, requiring workers to carry passports and allowing harsher punishments for those who refused to work. L'Ouverture's actions made clear that he was deeply committed to his new economic vision and was unwilling to suffer any attempt to undermine it.[13]

Beginning with the uprising at Pointe-à-Pitre, Guadeloupe was the theater for similar tensions that pitted the new rulers of the colony against many of its cultivateurs. The conseil had made small reforms in the treatment of the cultivateurs since Lacrosse's expulsion. They reversed his unpopular policy of having state officials oversee the payment of the cultivateurs and instituted a strict schedule to assure the payment of the workers. They also required that the plantation managers' selection of chiefs among the laborers be approved by local officials, who in public ceremonies would give them silver medals decorated with tricolor ribbons. For the most part, however, the new administration maintained the legal stipulations on cultivation established by Desfourneaux. The conseil presented labor as a patriotic duty and maintained the laws on the "repression of divagation," with the addition that one gourd would still be paid to anyone who stopped a vagabond. These labor policies received the approbation of one of Hugues's critics, the planter Thouluyre Mahé. Along with other elected delegates sent to negotiate with Lacrosse later

13. Pamphile de Lacroix and Pierre Pluchon, *La Révolution de Haïti* (Paris, 1995) (orig. publ. Paris, 1819, as Lacroix, *Mémoires pour servir á l'histoire de la révolution de Saint-Domingue*, 2 vols.), 274–276; Mats Lundahl, "Toussaint L'Ouverture and the War Economy of Saint-Domingue, 1796–1802," *Slavery and Abolition: A Journal of Comparative Studies*, VI (September 1985), 122–138, esp. 132–133; C. L. R. James, *The Black Jacobins: Toussaint L'Ouverture and the San Domingo Revolution* (New York, 1963), 263–266, 275–278; Carolyn E. Fick, *The Making of Haiti: The Saint Domingue Revolution from Below* (Knoxville, Tenn., 1990), 206–208; Pierre Pluchon, *Toussaint Louverture: Un Révolutionnaire noir d'ancien régime* (Paris, 1989), 433–438.

"Vivre libre ou mourir!"

in the year, Mahé emphasized how Pélage had repressed divagation by placing a bounty on the head of each recalcitrant cultivateur.[14]

Many cultivateurs were unwilling to accept a regime that seemed more and more like a prelude to slavery. In January 1802, a month after the insurrection in Pointe-à-Pitre, a merchant named Joseph Salager, along with his sister and brother, was killed on the Ducharmoy-Bellevue plantation. Salager was renting and managing this sugar plantation on the heights above Basse-Terre; the original owners had emigrated in the early 1790s. Since then, the plantation had been state-owned and managed by a series of men with Republican credentials—its manager for many years had been a supporter of the levy of slave troops in 1794. The unfortunate Salager, who was hired after the estate had been returned to its original owners, was the brother of a wealthy Basse-Terre merchant who had been a partner with Victor Hugues in arming corsairs. So the sixty-one men and women working on the plantation by late 1800—a remnant of the seventy-four who had been there in 1796—had spent the era of their freedom working under the watchful eyes, not of ex-planters, but of the new class of Republicans who had thrived in the colony. Though the precise reasons why the workers on this plantation rose up are difficult to ascertain—Salager might have been particularly exploitative and unwilling to negotiate with his laborers—their actions make clear that at least some cultivateurs in the colony were ready to challenge the existing order and protest the sharp limits placed on their freedom.[15]

Among these workers was a domestic named Alexis. According to Salager himself, speaking to the police before he died, Alexis had led the attack against him and his family, then fled with a few others into the heights surrounding the Soufrière volcano. Pélage led a group of police to track them down, eventually locating Alexis hiding alone in a cave, under branches and vegetation. He confessed and led the police to the hideout of another of the murderers. Along with these two, three others from the plantation were accused of participating in the murder

14. See the arrêté of the Conseil provisoire, 8 Frimaire, An X (Nov. 29, 1801), rpt. in Frasans, *Mémoire*, II, 113–117; for the declaration of the delegates from 22 Pluviôse, An X (Feb. 11, 1802), see CAOM, C 7A, 56, 3–4.

15. Frasans, *Mémoire*, II, 205–209; Lacour, *Histoire*, III, 214–218. For the plantation in 1796, see the "Etat nominatif . . . de Basse-Terre," in CAOM, G 1, 500, no. 5; see also CAOM, EC, Basse-Terre, 8, no. 52, 75–77, and EC, Basse-Terre, 9, no. 166. For Salager's renting of the plantations, see ADG, Dupuch 2E2/26, 14 Vendémiaire, An IX (Oct. 6, 1800).

The Boundaries of the Republic, 1798–1804

and condemned to death by a court in Basse-Terre. Three others charged with having "known about the project without revealing it" were given prison sentences of ten and twenty years. Those convicted of the murder were a diverse group—born in Guadeloupe, Dominica, Saint Vincent, and Africa—whose connections with the outside world might have been part of what helped them decide to take action against the plantation manager.[16]

The executions took place on the plantation. To be certain the orders were carried out, Pélage gave the mission to a troop of "Europeans and hommes de couleur whose loyalty was considered unquestionable." On the day of the execution, "a multitude of nègres cultivateurs from the neighboring plantations" gathered at the site, along with a number of unarmed soldiers from Basse-Terre. The first four of the rebels were executed without intervention from the crowd. However, at the moment of Alexis's execution, he "raised his force and harangued the nègres in their idiom, and managed to make them pity his fate." The crowd responded: "A universal murmur was heard and was soon followed by an agitation that stilled the detachment of grenadiers. They hesitated and stopped." They were afraid, they later confessed, that, as a "small number of white and de couleur men who were lost in the army," they would be prey to the "infinitely more numerous noirs [who] would throw themselves on them and would avenge, sooner or later, the death of their fellowmen." Pélage intervened, dragging Alexis in front of the firing squad, and the crowd dispersed without violence.[17]

Salager's murder had been avenged, but cultivateurs continued to express their discontent throughout the island. In Sainte-Rose, cultivateurs on one plantation refused to work. Although the local commissioner eventually managed to get them back to the fields, the rumors that were circulating about the imminent reestablishment of slavery worried him: "Spiteful men have spread out through the countryside, tricking the cultivateurs by slandering the brave French of Europe whose arrival is announced, by making them think they are coming to attack their liberty."[18]

Meanwhile, Lacrosse continued relentlessly in his blockade of Guade-

16. See Frasans, *Mémoire*, I, 206–207. An inventory of the plantation offers a slightly different account of what the punishments were; see ADG, Dupuch 2E2/27, 26 Ventôse, An X (Mar. 17, 1802).

17. Frasans, *Mémoire*, I, 207–209.

18. Riffaud to the Conseil provisoire, Sainte-Rose, 22 Ventôse, An X (Mar. 13, 1802), rpt. in Frasans, *Mémoire*, II, 277–278, and see also I, 254.

loupe, awaiting the arrival of the expedition from across the Atlantic. As Frasans's *Mémoire* noted, whereas "a troop of nègres assassinated the miserable Salager . . . on one of the plantations of Guadeloupe," Lacrosse did everything "to assassinate the entire colony." Assemblies were formed in the different communes, and two groups of deputies were elected to present the case of the conseil. One group traveled to Dominica, to meet with Lacrosse, Lescallier, and Coster and entreat Lescallier —whom the conseil thought would be accepted even by the rebellious soldiers—to come to Guadeloupe and take over its administration. Lescallier refused, however. The deputies selected for travel to France left Guadeloupe, only to be brought to Dominica by a ship captain loyal to Lacrosse.[19]

In late January, General Seriziat, sent to replace the deceased Béthencourt, arrived in Dominica with a small number of troops. In Roseau, the capital, a group of black soldiers in the British garrison had recently revolted against their officers, though the insurrection had been crushed before it spread. When six of the insurgents escaped to Guadeloupe, Pélage, perhaps to send a message to the soldiers of Guadeloupe, promptly arrested them and sent them back to Dominica. In the wake of these events, however, tension brewed between the black British troops in Roseau and the recently arrived white French troops, who exchanged heated words. Seriziat sent his soldiers to Marie-Galante, which sat between Dominica and Guadeloupe, to avoid further trouble. The general found the island in the midst of its own conflicts. A mulâtre named Lapoterie, the "captain of the black volunteers," along with his white sublieutenant Baillé led a group of black troops in resisting the "legitimate authorities." According to Bourrée, the former police chief of Guadeloupe who had taken refuge in Marie-Galante, Lapoterie—joined by a recent arrival named Jason—had been arming plantation laborers, some of whom had formed camps in the "less inhabited parts of the island, to create the core of insurrection." Seriziat quickly placed these officers, along with fifteen soldiers, on a boat on the harbor and sent them to Guadeloupe to be "close to their good friends." Bourrée wrote that he had been saved from "the most barbarous of deaths." "I will sleep tonight

---

19. Frasans, *Mémoire*, I, 209, 212–216; Lacour, *Histoire*, III, 189–208; on the delegates, see Three Magistrates to minister, 27 Pluviôse, An X (Feb. 16, 1802), and their declaration from 22 Pluviôse, An X (Feb. 11, 1802), in CAOM, C 7A, 56, 3, 4.

with security and tranquillity," he reported. The attack on the rebels of Guadeloupe had begun.[20]

On the island itself, Pélage's position was extremely weak after the failure of his missions to Dominica and the arrival of Seriziat. In Pointe-à-Pitre, some soldiers apparently planned to take away his power and "declare the colony independent." Meanwhile, some officers were corresponding with Lacrosse in Dominica, including one Pautrizel, a relative of the man who had been spared in 1793 by the rebels of Trois-Rivières and had served in the National Convention as a representative of Guadeloupe. The pro-Lacrosse forces in the army made themselves known when a few officers in Basse-Terre responded joyfully to the (false) news of Lacrosse's imminent arrival and suggested manning Fort Saint-Charles to greet him. But the officers Delgrès and Massoteau sprang into action. They arrested and deported twelve officers who they suspected were partisans of Lacrosse and also took over the fort, preparing its cannons for a battle rather than a welcome. Cultivateurs from the countryside went to Basse-Terre to help prepare the town for an attack, and others gathered in Pointe-à-Pitre. Pélage, fearing that arresting Massoteau and Delgrès would stir up more trouble, negotiated with them and eventually persuaded them to leave the fort.[21]

By the time of the Richepance expedition's arrival, then, the various groups on the island had reached a stalemate. Pélage's policy of loyalty to the metropole still dominated among the political leaders on the island, who were determined to greet the French expedition with open arms. Despite a few attempts by Delgrès and other officers, no solid plan for immediate resistance to the French troops had been put into place. Many soldiers and cultivateurs, however, were prepared for an armed struggle. The arrival of Richepance soon shattered the ambiguities of the situation.

20. Seriziat to Lacrosse, Marie-Galante, 25 Pluviôse, An X (Feb. 14, 1802), Bourée to Lacrosse, 24 Pluviôse, An X (Feb. 13, 1802), in CAOM, C 7A, 56, 55–56. On the revolt in Roseau, see Lacour, *Histoire*, III, 225–227; Coster to minister, 24 Germinal, An X (Apr. 14, 1802), in CAOM, C 7A, 57, 228; Frasans, *Mémoire*, I, 244.

21. Frasans, *Mémoire*, I, 227–233; Yves Bénot, *La Démence coloniale sous Napoléon: Essai* (Paris, 1992), 69.

The Arrival of Richepance

A few weeks after Richepance's arrival in Guadeloupe, as fighting raged in the area surrounding Basse-Terre, the officer Palerme led a group of insurgents against a camp of French troops entrenched on a plantation near the place where, in 1793, the insurgents of Trois-Rivières had met the white troops of Basse-Terre. Palerme's troop managed to close in on the camp because, when the advance sentinel of the camp called out, "Qui vive?" they shouted, "Republicains français!" Palerme's group, many of whom had spent the previous years fighting in the French Republican army against the British, were not lying when they named themselves this way. Palerme himself had been a loyal and successful Republican soldier, promoted to captain by Commissioner Goyrand during the French attack on Saint Lucia in 1795 and later captured by the British and released to metropolitan France. But the arrival of Richepance precipitated a contest over the meaning of the Republican project, splitting the ranks of the colonial army. Many remained loyal to the French nation that had proclaimed emancipation and that they had served during the previous years. Others, however, applied their loyalty to the project of freedom and racial equality that the French Republic had brought to the colony in 1794 but that Bonaparte's regime had now spurned. The split in the army, which developed in the context of confusion and rumor about the metropolitan government's intentions, represented a political and ideological rift about whether accommodation or resistance was the best way to preserve equal rights. The division, though driven by ideals and grievances tied to military service, was connected to a broader conflict within the colony's population of former slaves. For those among them who had left the plantations and taken advantage of the opportunities in the town, the return of the old order threatened to take from them the small gains they had made during the previous years. For those who were still working on the plantations, the specter of slavery's return meant the stalling, and reversal, of their slow move toward autonomy. All of these groups were threatened in different ways by the arrival of Bonaparte's troops, and residents were forced to make difficult choices and calculations about where they stood once the conflict began. But the willingness of a large segment of the population to rise up rather than accept the return of the old order demonstrates that, despite all its limitations, manumission had brought something of value to them— both in terms of what it had delivered and what it promised for the future—that they were unwilling to surrender and were willing to die defending.[22]

Richepance had left Brest in February 1802 with 3,454 soldiers, most of them part of the Fifteenth, Sixty-sixth, and Eighty-second *Démi-Brigades* drawn from the veteran army of the Rhine. By the time the convoy arrived off Guadeloupe, each side had reason to be wary of the other. Both because of what he had heard of events in Saint-Domingue and because of his contact with Lacrosse, Richepance was predisposed against the rebels of Guadeloupe. At the same time, news of the government's decision to maintain slavery in Martinique and the other colonies where it had never been abolished had circulated in Guadeloupe and, according to Richepance, "contributed a great deal to the resistance we found here." Pélage and his administration, however, went to great lengths to reassure Richepance of their loyalty. They even offered envoys as hostages to prove they had no ill intentions. The conseil publicized the signing of the Treaty of Amiens with a proclamation that ended, "Long live our brothers from Europe!" The friendly greeting the French troops in Guadeloupe received contrasted sharply with what had occurred earlier in Saint-Domingue, where Henri Christophe refused to allow General Leclerc to land, then set fire to Le Cap rather than hand it over to the French invaders intact.[23]

As Richepance's troops disembarked, they were greeted by an honor guard of forty men commanded by the officer Joseph Ignace, and a band struck up the "Air de la grande famille." The response was not, however, very familial. The black soldiers were ordered behind the ranks of the European soldiers and the musicians ordered to stop playing. Richepance's troops quickly began investigating the military positions of the town, and as they did so they disarmed many black soldiers, stripped them of their uniforms, and marched them as prisoners to boats in the harbor. General Gobert, who commanded some of these white troops, later asserted that Richepance treated the administrators and officers "with a great deal of disdain, presuming that they were all guilty." Ignace

22. See General Ménard's report ("Récit détaillé des opérations militaires"), in CAOM, C 7A, 57, 21–37, 18; "Etat des officiers," 29 Fructidor, An VI (Sept. 15, 1798), in AHAT, X i, carton 80; see also Chapter 8, above.

23. "Corps d'expédition maritime," Brest, 21 Pluviôse, An X (Feb. 10, 1802), in AHAT, B 9, 2; Lacour, *Histoire*, III, 237–240; Richepance to minister, 11 Prairial, An X (May 31, 1802), in CAOM, C 7A, 57, 1; Frasans, *Mémoire*, I, 258–267. On Saint-Domingue, see Fick, *Making of Haiti*, 210–212.

found Pélage and asked him, "What is going on?" Pélage responded, "We are soldiers and French, we must only know obedience; be certain that justice will be rendered to us." Ignace pressed Pélage but was told he must place his nation first. As Pélage walked away, Ignace apparently murmured, "Traitor!"[24]

Following Richepance's orders, Pélage commanded his troops to leave the forts and gather on the Stiwenson plain outside Pointe-à-Pitre for review, but many soldiers did not respond. When a detachment of French troops entered Fort de la Victoire, where Ignace had gathered his men, he led them out the back entrance and eluded capture. By the time Richepance arrived to review the gathering black troops, night was falling, and he could see that "a large number of soldiers were escaping into the countryside, carrying their weapons." Richepance reviewed the remaining troops and said to them: "The troops I have brought you have conquered the universe with their obedience—obey." He then gave orders for the soldiers to be disarmed and taken to ships in the harbor as prisoners. Among the white officers were Guadeloupean émigrés returning to the island after years of exile who insulted and disarmed black soldiers with particular brutality. Watching this, individual soldiers and entire companies following their officers escaped into the darkness. Among the deserters was a large group of grenadiers, who left with Palerme, Ignace, and Massoteau. Before departing, some of these deserters were heard saying that "Pélage was a traitor."[25]

Richepance posted a proclamation that declared the French Revolution had "finally achieved a degree of power and stability" and his troops had been sent to triumph "over the last resistance that afflicts the authority in these far-off countries." The proclamation invoked the "sympathy" that existed between soldiers who had served France and identified the troops that had arrived as "French like you." But it warned that, if there were still people "insane enough" to resist the legitimate power,

24. Ménard's report, in CAOM, C 7A, 57, 21–27, 3; Gobert, "Particularités non-publiques sur la guerre de la Guadeloupe," 1 Frimaire, An XI (Nov. 22, 1802), in CAOM, C 7A, 57, 70–74; Frasans, *Mémoire*, I, 265–272; Lacour, *Histoire*, III, 241–243.

25. See Richepance's report to the minister, 5 Prairial, An X (May 25, 1802), rpt. in Frasans, *Mémoire*, II, 341–344, as well as the description of the events (I, 271–272); see also Lacour, *Histoire*, III, 243–244. For other eyewitness accounts, see Ménard's report, in CAOM, C 7A, 57, 21–37, 4, and Gobert to minister, 70–74.

The Boundaries of the Republic, 1798–1804

"the national vengeance will immediately fall on them" and "death and shame will become their lot."[26]

Hundreds of rebel soldiers who had escaped from Pointe-à-Pitre were traveling toward Basse-Terre. A femme de couleur reported to Pélage that she had seen 150 soldiers, along with Ignace, Massoteau, and another officer named Eugène Codou, passing through Petit-Bourg the previous night. Meanwhile, in Basse-Terre itself, a soldier who had fled from Pointe-à-Pitre had already arrived and spread the news that Lacrosse had returned and ordered the massacre of the inhabitants. Many refused to believe him, but soon the well-respected officer Noël Corbet arrived and related the news of the mass detentions in Pointe-à-Pitre. Corbet's reports and news that Richepance intended to put Lacrosse back in power in Guadeloupe persuaded Delgrès to fight the French. Cultivateurs, inspired by the rapidly circulating rumors about reestablishment of slavery, marched en masse toward Basse-Terre, demanding weapons from local officials. Soon the deserters from Pointe-à-Pitre arrived in Basse-Terre, led by Ignace and including many women and men who had joined them along the way. They entered Basse-Terre, wrote Auguste Lacour, "like a hurricane." Delgrès assembled all the arriving troops with those from Basse-Terre on the Champ d'Arbaud, in the center of the town, and said to them, "They want to take our liberty, my friends; let us defend it with heart, let us prefer death to slavery." He then told the Europeans among the soldiers that he would not ask them to fight against "your fathers, your brothers" and that they were free to go. François Mondésir Gripon publicly joined the rebel cause at this point. The troops then took over Fort Saint-Charles and prepared for battle.[27]

Some whites chose to join Delgrès, including a young Creole from Martinique named Monnereau, who helped write a proclamation for the rebels signed by Delgrès, "the commander of Basse-Terre," and distributed in the town. It was addressed "TO THE ENTIRE UNIVERSE" as a "CRY OF INNOCENCE AND DESPAIR." "These are the greatest days of a century that will always be famous for the triumph of enlightenment and philosophy," it began. "And yet in the midst of them is a class of unfortunates who are threatened with destruction and find themselves forced

---

26. See Lacour, *Histoire*, II, 245–246; see also Ménard's report, in CAOM, C 7A, 57, 21–37, 5–6.

27. Lacour, *Histoire*, III, 251–253; Frasans, *Mémoire*, I, 274–277.

to raise their voices so that posterity will know, once they have disappeared, of their innocence and misery." General Richepance's declaration, the text noted, was so vague that, "even as he promises protection, he could give us death, without departing from the terms he has used." It clearly carried "the mark of Admiral Lacrosse, who has sworn eternal hatred of us." What were Richepance's intentions? "Are the bayonets of those brave soldiers, whose arrival we have been awaiting and which previously were only directed against enemies of the Republic, to be turned against us?" It seemed, according to what had already occured in Pointe-à-Pitre, that instead those in power had decided to "inflict slow deaths in prison." "Well," the declaration announced defiantly, "we choose to die more quickly."

> Let us dare say it. The maxims of even the most atrocious tyranny have been surpassed today. Our old tyrants permitted a master to emancipate his slave. But it seems that, in this century of philosophy, there exist men, grown powerful thanks to the distance that separates them from those who appointed them, who want only to see men who are black or take their origins from this color in the chains of slavery. To you, first consul of the Republic, warrior-philosopher from whom we expected the justice we deserved, we ask why we have been left to deplore our distance from the home from which the sublime ideas we have so often admired emanate? Ah! Without a doubt one day you will know of our innocence. Then it will be too late. Perverse men will have already used the slander they pour on us to consummate our ruin.
>
> Citizens of Guadeloupe, you for whom a difference in the color of the epidermis is enough of a title for you not to fear the vengeance with which we have been threatened—unless they make it a crime to not carry arms against us—you have heard the motivations that excite our indignation. Resistance to oppression is a natural right. The divinity itself cannot be offended that we are defending our cause, which is that of humanity and justice. We will not dirty it with the shadow of crime. Yes, we are resolved to defend ourselves, but we will not become aggressors. Stay in your homes, and fear nothing from us. We swear solemnly to respect your wives, your children, your properties, and to use all our power to make sure they are respected by others.
>
> And you, posterity! Shed a tear for our sorrows, and we will die satisfied.

The proclamation inspired the rebels of Basse-Terre, who swore to defeat Richepance or "bury themselves in the ashes of the colony." Their rallying cry became "Vivre libre ou mourir"—"To live free or die."[28]

War

On May 10, a fleet of ships appeared off the coast of Basse-Terre and was greeted by cannonfire from "all the batteries of the coast." In the boats were the majority of Richepance's troops, ready to disembark and attack. Accompanying the troops was Magloire Pélage, who sought to avoid a battle by sending his longtime comrade Delgrès a plea for surrender, carried by an homme de couleur officer both of them knew well. As soon as the officer arrived in the port, he was brought to Fort Saint-Charles by an angry crowd shouting, "Vivre libre ou mourir!" Delgrès rejected the entreaty and imprisoned the envoy. He then rallied his soldiers to confront the French troops preparing to disembark on the west side of Basse-Terre.[29]

As soon as the French troops landed, led by Pélage himself, the rebels opened fire, and fierce fighting ensued. Over the course of the afternoon, 120 French soldiers were killed, but the French pushed back the insurgents until, as the sun set, the Rivière des Pères separated the two armies. At dawn the next day Richepance sent his grenadiers into an attack that routed Delgrès's troops. They retreated into Basse-Terre, where the fighting continued in the streets. One soldier took shelter behind a monument of Victor Hugues and fired on the French while, in order to stop the advance, Delgrès sent into the town his most experienced soldiers, who had first fought in Hugues's campaigns in 1795. These seasoned soldiers, however, made up only three thousand of the twelve thousand who took arms against the French. Cultivateurs and inhabitants of the town, women and men who were often armed only with sticks and machetes, threw themselves into the battle. When soldiers fell, these culti-

---

28. Lacour, *Histoire*, III, 253–255. No version of this proclamation exists in the archives; it was first published in an 1848 antislavery work (Félix Longin, *Voyage à la Guadeloupe: Ouvrage posthume* [Paris, 1848]) and then a decade later in Lacour, *Histoire*, III, 253–255, who perhaps drew it from Longin's work or had encountered a copy still in circulation in Guadeloupe. See Bénot, *La Démence*, 71–72, n. 36.

29. Frasans, *Mémoire*, I, 278–280; Lacour, *Histoire*, III, 267–270; Ménard's report, in CAOM, C 7A, 57, 21–37, 6.

vateurs filled in their ranks, dropping their pikes and picking up the precious, fallen guns; it was impossible, wrote General Gobert, to capture an insurgent's weapon until he or she had been killed. From the beginning of the fighting, groups of women carried ammunition to the front lines, singing the "Marseillaise." Many also fought fiercely against the French. Gripon chastised retreating rebel troops: "You do not know how to imitate the women. Follow their example." Lacour described women "animated by a superhuman courage": "When the cannonballs whistled over their heads or a bomb exploded close to them, they held each other's hands, singing and shouting, doing infernal dances that were interrupted by the cry 'Long live death!'"[30]

Nevertheless, by the end of the day Basse-Terre was almost entirely in the hands of the French, and Delgrès's troops had retreated to Fort Saint-Charles or to plantations on the heights above the town. Faced with possible continued resistance and wary of losses among the European troops from both battle and sickness, Richepance attempted to placate the insurgents with a proclamation that promised "not even the slightest attack" would be made against the "liberty that all French citizens enjoy without distinction." The Three Magistrates also issued a proclamation seeking to dispel the rumors that the French forces had been sent to put the cultivateurs "back into chains." Both documents also threatened violent punishment to those who continued to resist. A few days before, an offer of surrender had been delivered to Delgrès, who wrote that he had to respond as a "true Republican, who finds death a thousand times more preferable than slavery." Peace, he noted, could easily be restored by the authorities if they simply withdrew their troops instead of fighting soldiers who were, in fact, loyal to the "motherland" of France. "We are her children, and we will not raise an angry hand against her. But she forces us today to fight against her rights, or rather those who interpret them, against those who disrespect us and go against her noble principles by acting arbitrarily, without the wisdom and justice that she grants her children." A second delegation of gens de couleur from the town failed to persuade Delgrès to surrender. General Ménard later wrote that Delgrès

---

30. Ménard's report, in CAOM, C 7A, 57, 21–37, 7–9; Gobert to minister, 11 Frimaire, An XI (Nov. 22, 1802), in CAOM, C 7A, 57, 70–74; Frasans, *Mémoire*, I, 281–282; see also Richepance to minister, 5 Prairial, An X (May 25, 1802), and Richepance's report, 9 Prairial, An X (May 29, 1802), both rpt. in Frasans, *Mémoire*, II, 341–353. The most detailed account of the battles is in Lacour, *Histoire*, III, 270–277, which draws on interviews with survivors.

"despaired to fight the French but that all those he commanded found death a thousand times more acceptable than the slavery they had come to give them."[31]

The rebels, however, were nearly surrounded. While Richepance was attacking Basse-Terre from the sea, troops under the command of General Seriziat had marched overland almost as far as Trois-Rivières before encountering a group of well-organized insurgents under the command of Palerme. Hearing cannon in Basse-Terre, the first group of French troops overlooked the warnings of experienced soldiers and launched a frontal assault on rebels entrenched in the hilly terrain of Dolé. The insurgents repelled the attack, leaving at least forty-five French soldiers dead. A detachment of the French troops retreated down to Trois-Rivières, left their wounded in a church, and went across Pautrizel's plantation to outflank the insurgents. Meanwhile, the rebels from Dolé went on the offensive, assaulting the outnumbered troops that had been left behind and sending them into a panicked retreat back toward Capesterre. Insurgents began setting fire to the cane fields and plantations and captured the center of Trois-Rivières, killing the wounded soldiers left behind in the church. The situation veered toward total war, as the French, furious at the execution of their wounded, began randomly killing the blacks they encountered. The insurgents continued to ambush troops on the narrow paths and roads in the region. Seriziat's possessions, left in a lightly guarded wagon, were carried off. Eventually, however, the French troops, with the help of a black captain named Anicet who knew the area well, outflanked the various rebel camps and finally pushed them out of the area. Seriziat established himself in a position above Fort Saint-Charles.[32]

The larger conflict played itself out in microcosm among the bakers of Basse-Terre. The bakery of André Négré, which employed many ex-slaves, was close to Fort Saint-Charles. When the fighting began, Négré's workers forced their boss, who did not support the revolt, to provide bread for Delgrès's troops. The arriving French troops, however, also requested bread from his bakery. Some of Négré's workers found out

31. Both proclamations, from 24 Floréal, An X (May 14, 1802), are reprinted in Frasans, *Mémoire*, II, 353–356; Lacour, *Histoire*, III, 277–282; Ménard's report, in CAOM, C 7A, 57, 21–37, 12–13.

32. Lacour, *Histoire*, III, 283–285; Ménard's report, in CAOM, C 7A, 57, 21–37, 13–15; Frasans, *Mémoire*, I, 284; casualty list, Fifteenth Démi-Brigade, 3 Fructidor, An X (Aug. 21, 1802), in AHAT, X i, carton 18.

"Vivre libre ou mourir!"

about the request and, knowing he would likely comply, contacted the insurgents, who sent men to arrest him. Among these men was a former employee, Jacques Ibo, who had been imprisoned after Négré's brother-in-law Peuch accused him of theft. Released at the beginning of the rebellion, Ibo was now determined to take revenge. Négré and Peuch escaped to a nearby house, ultimately managing to avoid capture; a furious Jacques brandished a knife at the house and shouted, "Where is my brigand, so I can settle my account with him!"[33]

Throughout Basse-Terre, small bands of men and women attacked plantations, sometimes killing white propertyowners. A total of twenty-one whites not part of the army were killed by insurgents during the uprising. Among them was M. Pinaud, who was renting a state plantation in Baillif and was murdered along with his family by rebels who then set fire to the plantation. The ranks of the insurgents were split over such tactics: Delgrès and some other officers attempted to stop them, pursuing the strategies of traditional warfare from inside Fort Saint-Charles; others, notably Palerme, sought to incite large-scale insurrection and destroy plantations as a means of driving the French troops from the island. At Dolé, Palerme's camp held a number of prisoners, including civilians, and the question of whether to execute them or to keep them alive was debated in an open assembly—within earshot of the hostages themselves. In this camp was the mulâtresse Solitude, whom Lacour described as the "wicked genius" of the rebels. "She had rabbits," he wrote. "When one of them escaped, she picked up a knife, pursued it, pierced it, and held it up in front of the prisoners. 'Here,' she said, mixing the most injurious epithets into her speech, 'is how I will treat you when the time comes!'" She never had the chance; these prisoners were released by the advancing French troops. Indeed, Solitude was later executed by the French—after giving birth to the child she was carrying. Though its details were perhaps exaggerated by Lacour, Solitude's idea that an all-out attack on whites was the best way to guarantee freedom seems to have represented a broader, preexisting strain of thought among the cultivateurs, which had already surfaced in the wake of Hugues's departure. During the later fighting at Matouba, debates on whites continued among the insurgents. Some commanders—including Sans-Peur, an older man who had served in the army under Victor Hugues—attempted to protect whites living in the area while others attacked and killed plantation owners. The veteran officer Alexandre Kirwan was so pained when one of his white friends,

33. Lacour, *Histoire*, III, 297–298.

the judge Amaury, was killed that he committed suicide. Before doing so, he told Amaury's wife: "It was I who gave the orders to fire the first cannon-shot on the French division! I thought then that I would fight soldiers with soldiers. I was wrong. Today, I see, I command nothing but looters and assassins . . . or, rather, I command nothing . . . I am in the midst of a movement that I cannot follow or stop."[34]

In the face of continuing and widespread insurrection, Richepance's troops turned to systematized tactics of terror, executing anyone they suspected of supporting the insurgents. Richepance felt, however, that the destruction of Delgrès and his soldiers would be the best way to end the war, and he decided to prepare a direct assault on Fort Saint-Charles. Citizens in the town were drafted to help build fortifications from which cannons could bombard the fort. The expedition, however, had to ask the British commander of Dominica, Cochrane Johnson, for shells. In a moment of imperial cooperation, the colonial troops of Guadeloupe were bombarded with English cannonballs fired out of French guns.[35]

To try to break the siege, Delgrès sent out sorties to attack the French positions on the surrounding plantations, and his troops suffered heavy casualties. The French experienced losses as well, however, and many of these recent arrivals also fell prey to fever. Pélage suggested to Richepance that in order to assure victory he should release the black troops he had imprisoned in Pointe-à-Pitre and use them against the insurgents. Richepance agreed, and in the next days the colonial troops were "incorporated into the French battalions." "This measure," wrote one officer, "saved our soldiers much fatigue and was very useful: the black soldiers, wishing to gain the confidence of the army, conducted themselves well." According to the *Mémoire*, as they saw their old comrades eagerly attacking them, many insurgents lost "hope of chasing the French from the colony and making it independent, a hope they had dared conceive of when they were fighting only European soldiers, whom they saw diminished each day by sickness." With the support of the black troops, a number of plantations that had been held by Delgrès's men were taken

34. Ibid., 301–306, 311–312, 319–325; Ménard's report, in CAOM, C 7A, 57, 21–37, 11–12, 18; see also Bernard Moitt, "Slave Resistance in Guadeloupe and Martinique, 1791–1848," *Journal of Caribbean History*, XXV, nos. 1, 2 (1991), 136–159. Solitude's presence in the camp also suggests some of the mostly hidden ways in which women participated in the formulation and application of war strategies.

35. Lacour, *Histoire*, III, 286–288; Lescallier to minister, 12 Messidor, An X (Jul. 1, 1802), in CAOM, C 7A, 57, 135.

over by the French troops, who slowly but surely surrounded Fort Saint-Charles.[36]

On the night of May 19, a fire began in Basse-Terre. Delgrès sent out a message to Richepance offering a truce so that the fire could be extinguished. A detachment of 150 soldiers left the fort and, side by side with French soldiers, put out the fire. The soldiers then saluted one another and returned to their positions. When the bombardment of Fort Saint-Charles resumed, Delgrès was seen tempting fate, playing his violin on the battlements. Two days after the fire, with the aim of the batteries perfected, Richepance's troops began shelling the fort from all sides. The assault continued all day, inflicting heavy casualties in the fort, and Delgrès decided to use the cover of night to escape. He and his troops left out of an entrance that faced away from the main French lines, near the Galion River. A plan to blow up the fort was foiled by a few of Delgrès's officers, who stayed behind instead of retreating and opened the gates for Richepance's troops.[37]

Outside, the insurgents split into two groups, led by Delgrès and Ignace. While Delgrès traveled toward the heights of Matouba, Ignace (accompanied by Palerme) left with four hundred soldiers to go up the coast, in order to encourage the population to rise up against the French and attack Pointe-à-Pitre. Most of the women who had been in the fort went with Ignace, and it was they who recruited laborers from the plantations, forming what Frasans described as "a multitude of nègres armed with pikes." From Basse-Terre, General Gobert left in pursuit and managed to capture some of the insurgents' cannons and ammunition and one of their flags. The mass of the insurgents, however, moved unopposed. From a ship, Daniel Lescallier followed their progress as they "burned the entire coast," so that "from Basse-Terre to Petit-Bourg there were only flames." Ignace's march inspired groups throughout the island, including one as far as Gosier, on the other side of Pointe-à-Pitre, to attack estates and set them on fire. In Lamentin, across from Pointe-à-Pitre, Palerme and his followers separated from Ignace and began assailing plantations, forming a small and mobile army that would outlast both groups under Ignace and Delgrès.[38]

36. Ménard's report, in CAOM, C 7A, 57, 21–37, esp. 19–20; Frasans, *Mémoire*, I, 284–287.

37. Frasans, *Mémoire*, I, 289–290; Ménard's report, in CAOM, C 7A, 21–37, esp. 21–22; Lescallier to minister, 4 Prairial, An X (May 24, 1802), in CAOM, C 7A, 37, 128; Lacour, *Histoire*, III, 289–291.

38. Lacour, *Histoire*, III, 307–318; Lescallier to minister, 4 Prairial, An X (May

The Boundaries of the Republic, 1798–1804

When he arrived outside Pointe-à-Pitre, Ignace published a short proclamation calling on the population "to expel the French brigands who have come to trouble our tranquillity." The proclamation added, "If within twenty-four hours you have not executed this order, your cities and your countryside will be ashes." Ignace took up a position in the unguarded Fort Baimbridge, outside Pointe-à-Pitre, while General Gobert's troops arrived in the region, fighting off repeated ambushes from small groups. On the morning of May 25, with the insurgents' red flag flying above the fort, Gobert's soldiers launched a costly and failed assault. During the fighting, the two sides fired at each other from extremely close range; Ignace recognized and taunted a cousin he saw in the ranks of the enemy. Gobert and Pélage, after heavy losses, retreated and began an artillery barrage that decimated Ignace's followers. By the time the French took the fort, 675 men and women had been killed. Many of those who surrendered were executed on the spot, but Ignace, surrounded by three soldiers who were about to take him prisoner, said, "You will not have the honor of taking me alive," and shot himself. His head was exposed on a pike in Pointe-à-Pitre. Another 250 of the insurgents were taken prisoner, and in the next days they were all executed by firing squads on the Place de la Victoire of Pointe-à-Pitre and along a beach outside the town.[39]

Ignace's march on Pointe-à-Pitre was meant to spur the entire island to insurrection. Its failure helped condemn the troops who had remained in Basse-Terre to defeat. They did not know this, however, as they gathered to hold out on the heights of Matouba, which had been held by insurgents since the beginning of the fighting. Delgrès took up a position in the D'Anglemont plantation, which was flanked by two steep ravines, placing two cannons in front of the house and positioning his troops to guard the approaches. Meanwhile, Lescallier wrote a proclamation promising amnesty to the insurgents—particularly the "black cultivateurs" who had been misled by agitators because of their "lack of instruction and their greater simplicity"—and many responded to the pardon.[40]

As Richepance's troops closed in on Matouba, however, they encountered fierce resistance from fighters who, as Frasans later wrote, "having

---

24, 1802), in CAOM, C 7A, 57, 128. Lescallier wrote, "The revenues of the colony for an entire year have been annihilated" by the rebels.

39. Frasans, *Mémoire*, I, 291–294; Ménard, in CAOM, C 7A, 57, 21–37, 22–24; Lacour, *Histoire*, III, 307–318; Anduse, *Joseph Ignace*, 261–274.

40. Lacour, *Histoire*, III, 325–328.

"Vivre libre ou mourir!"

no alternative but victory or death, deployed, to defend themselves, all the efforts of rage." One troop of French grenadiers, which attempted to reach the D'Anglemont plantation through a narrow ravine, was entirely massacred by insurgents who fired on them from protected positions on all sides. General Ménard wrote that, as the French drew near to Matouba, "the activity, the courage, and the daring of the nègres" increased. "The unanimous cry of 'Vivre libre ou mourir!' that they constantly repeated, the care they took to remove the color white from their flag to represent their independence, all this announced that their position was desperate and that their resistance would be terrible." On the flanks of the Soufrière volcano, the insurgents of Guadeloupe flew the Republican tricolor with the white ripped out of it.[41]

Before the battle, Delgrès and his companions had decided to die rather than surrender and had placed barrels of powder around the plantation house to blow it up on the approach of the French. The word was spread among the insurgents, so that those who wished to could escape. As the enemy closed in, the insurgents, holding each other by the hand, yelled, "No slavery! Long live death!" and when the advance guard of the French troops arrived on the porch, a massive explosion consumed the building, leaving "a vast pyre whose flames were devouring more than five hundred corpses, among which were women and children." "This act of horrible courage," wrote Ménard, "ended the war by destroying at once the leaders of the revolt, their elite soldiers, and their ammunition." After a moment of "stupefaction," the French pursued those who had escaped. With premature satisfaction, Richepance claimed that the explosion had "destroyed the revolt at its source": "The leaders are dead, all the rest are disarmed, submissive, and returning to the work they never should have left." Ménard, however, understood that there were still insurgents ready to fight throughout the island, who added to their "disdain of death that bold bravery inspired by the fanaticism of liberty."[42]

Surrounded, and quickly besieged by indiscriminate attacks on all

41. Ménard's report, in CAOM, C 7A, 21–37, 28; Frasans, *Mémoire*, I, 294–295. The Guadeloupean and Haitian insurgents' use of the same flag suggests that, rather than being an individual act on the part of Dessalines, this symbolic severing of the Republican tricolor was a cultural form that spanned the various islands during these years.

42. Ménard's report, in CAOM, C 7A, 21–37, 28–30; Frasans, *Mémoire*, I, 295–296; for Richepance's account in his report to the minister, see Frasans, *Mémoire*, II, 352; see also Jacques Adélaïde-Mérlande, *Delgrès; ou, La Guadeloupe en 1802* (Paris, 1986), 149.

The Boundaries of the Republic, 1798–1804

those noirs and de couleur who had been part of Guadeloupe's colonial army, adherents of the ideals of Republican emancipation retreated to the mountains, to the holdouts of the maroons. The stories of the dead, meanwhile, crossed the waters to Saint-Domingue, unveiling the fate the French planned for those who resisted them, and helped initiate the last stage of Haiti's war for independence.

Chapter 16

THE EXILED REPUBLIC

In Saint-Domingue, Leclerc had been battling fierce resistance since he disembarked in February 1802, but by May he had secured the surrender of most of the major rebel leaders and their followers, including Henri Christophe, Jean-Jacques Dessalines, and—most important—Toussaint L'Ouverture. Worried that L'Ouverture's submission was only illusory, Leclerc had him arrested and deported in June 1802, and he died the next year in a prison in the Jura mountains. The months of hard campaigning, however, had taken their toll: many thousands of French soldiers had been killed in battle, and an increasing and alarming number were succumbing to yellow fever. And so, as he sought to destroy the continuing resistance of bands of rebels, often led by African-born officers, Leclerc was forced to depend on the very institution he had been sent to destroy: the colonial army, whose black Republican soldiers represented a clear threat to Bonaparte's colonial project.[1]

French control in Saint-Domingue depended on the allegiance and support of the officers and soldiers of African descent. In order to maintain their loyalty, Leclerc continually assured them that Bonaparte's government wished only to restore order and had no intention of restoring racial hierarchy and slavery. But, by the middle of 1802, this deception was increasingly difficult to maintain. When news of what had happened in Guadeloupe spread to Saint-Domingue—traveling quickly along the routes of communication that had always tied the Caribbean together, carried as well by deported prisoners from Guadeloupe who managed to escape from boats docked offshore—it helped trigger a reversal of fortune for the French in Saint-Domingue. The Guadeloupean massacres and deportations helped to unmask the French government's ultimate intentions. Indeed, although Richepance had not reestablished slavery in

---

1. Claude Bonaparte Auguste and Marcel Bonaparte Auguste, *L'Expédition Leclerc, 1801–1803* (Port-au-Prince, Haiti, 1985), chaps. 5–7.

Guadeloupe for fear of inciting a new cycle of revolt, the word in Saint-Domingue was that he had. This belief was so widespread that Leclerc himself shared it: in August 1802, he complained to Bonaparte that the news of Richepance's having just "passed a decree to reestablish slavery in Guadeloupe" had made the consul's plans for the colonies "perfectly known." Richepance's decrees, along with letters from France and the government's law reinstating the slave trade, meant "all the blacks" were convinced that the French intended to "make them slaves again." Because it had been promulgated "three months too early," the return of slavery would cost "many people" for the army and the colony of Saint-Domingue. "If my position has turned from good to critical," Leclerc later wrote, "it is not only because of the yellow fever but, as well, the premature reestablishment of slavery in Guadeloupe and the newspapers and letters from France that speak of nothing but slavery." He proposed a desperate plan: "We must destroy all the blacks of the mountains— men and women—and spare only the children under twelve years of age. We must destroy half of those in the plains and must not leave a single colored person in the colony who has worn an epaulet."[2]

Leclerc's counterproductive response was to strike out against black colonial troops who had remained loyal, and in time the French succumbed to a racist delirium, massacring whole units of black soldiers, gassing them in the holds of ships, drowning them in the harbors, executing officers and their families. This only accelerated the flood of desertions to the rebel side. In mid-October, the key officers still serving Leclerc, including Dessalines and Christophe, switched allegiances and attacked the French. Leclerc succumbed to the yellow fever soon after, to be replaced by General Rochambeau, who initiated even more violent tactics than his predecessor. But, decimated through battle and rampant fever, Bonaparte's troops finally found themselves controlling nothing but the northern capital of Le Cap. The resumption of war with the British sealed the fate of the French mission in Saint-Domingue. The few thousand troops left in the colony—the debris of some eighty thou-

2. Leclerc to minister of the navy, Leclerc to Bonaparte, both 18 Thermidor, An X (Aug. 6, 1802), and Leclerc to Bonaparte, 15 Vendémiaire, An XI (Oct. 7, 1802), all in Paul Roussier, ed., *Lettres du Général Leclerc, commandant en chef de l'armée de Saint-Domingue en 1802* (Paris, 1937), 199–207, 253–259; Carolyn E. Fick, *The Making of Haiti: The Saint Domingue Revolution from Below* (Knoxville, Tenn., 1990), 215–222; C. L. R. James, *The Black Jacobins: Toussaint L'Ouverture and the San Domingo Revolution* (New York, 1963), 344–345; Yves Bénot, *La Démence coloniale sous Napoléon* (Paris, 1991), 77–83.

sand soldiers and sailors sent there since late 1801—sailed away along with many residents of Le Cap in November 1803. In January 1804, Dessalines proclaimed the independence of the island. The flag of the new nation was the same flown by the rebels at Matouba: during the last months of the conflict with the French, he and his officers had torn the white out of their Republican tricolors as a way of emphasizing their intention of breaking with the French. The nation of Haiti preserved liberty in a sea of slavery.[3]

Inoculating Insurrection

United in the radical project of equality and citizenship with Saint-Domingue for the previous decade, Guadeloupe saw the order of emancipation dismantled and the old world of slavery rebuilt. In the wake of the defeat at Matouba in 1802, Richepance ordered mass executions and deportations in order to rid the island of insurrection. A military tribunal hastily sentenced insurgents, placing in prison those who had fought and condemning to death those who had been leaders or had attacked plantations. Among those executed were Monnereau, the white Creole author of the letter that called for revolt; François Rigaud, the refugee from Saint-Domingue; and François Mondésir Gripon. The condemned were hanged from gallows in Basse-Terre and then, after twenty-four hours, taken to the top of a high hill so as to be visible to the whole town. Many of those not put to death were deported from the colony. During the restoration of slavery in Guadeloupe, it seems that more than ten thousand men and women were either executed or deported—nearly a tenth of the population. An 1800 census on the island reported eighty-five thousand ex-slaves, whereas in 1818 there were only sixty-nine thousand, a measure of the harshness of the repression and the group most affected by it.[4]

3. Fick, *Making of Haiti*, 216–236; James, *Black Jacobins*, 289–374; Auguste and Auguste, *L'Expédition Leclerc*, 28–30, chap. 11; Beaubrun Ardouin, *Etudes sur l'histoire d'Haïti: Suivies de la vie du général J.-M. Borgella*, 11 vols. (Port-au-Prince, Haiti, 1958), V, 83–84. For a discussion of the conflicts within the insurgent army, see Michel-Rolph Trouillot, *Silencing the Past: Power and the Production of History* (Boston, 1995), chap. 2; for a compelling description of life in Le Cap during this period, see Joan Dayan, *Haiti, History, and the Gods* (Berkeley, Calif., 1995), chap. 3.

4. Auguste Lacour, *Histoire de la Guadeloupe*, 4 vols. (Basse-Terre, Guadeloupe, 1855–1858), III, 333–341; Jacques Adélaïde-Mérlande, "Lendemains de Baimbridge et Matouba: 'Coureurs de bois et brigands,'" in Michel L. Martin and

FIGURE 21. Fort Saint-Charles. Early nineteenth century.
Engraving by Joseph Coussin. ©*Arch. dép. de la Guadeloupe, G 103*

Like Leclerc in Saint-Domingue, Richepance was convinced that preserving the colony depended on eliminating all men of African descent who had served in the army. "Let us not fall into the error of believing that we can arm blacks and use them in our army," he wrote to the minister, adding that otherwise it would be necessary to "start over each day" in the repression of insurrection. Accordingly, he had more than a thousand hommes de couleur and noirs who had been "part of the armed forces" and were "recognized in the colony as dangerous men" arrested and placed onto a convoy of ships that was to drop them off in New York. Months later, Lacrosse sent out new orders to the commander of this convoy, ordering him, if the previous plan failed, "to use all means pos-

Alain Yacou, eds., *Mourir pour les Antilles: Indépendance nègre ou esclavage, 1802–1804* (Paris, 1991), 203–210; Josette Fallope, *Esclaves et citoyens: Les Noirs à la Guadeloupe au XIXe siècle dans les processus de résistance et d'intégration: 1802–1910* (Basse-Terre, Guadeloupe, 1992), 49–52; Bénot, *La Démence coloniale*, 74.

sible to get rid of the deportees," including leaving them on unpopulated beaches along the U.S. coast. Only after exhausting all other possibilities would he carry them to France. Some of these deportees were eventually brought to Corsica, where they were put to work constructing roads. Magloire Pélage, along with forty-three other officers who had fought with the French in Guadeloupe, was deported, and the minister of the colonies made clear that, notwithstanding their previous military positions, they were to be treated as enemies of the Republic because of the "unsurpassed" crimes that had just "bloodied the American colonies." Apparently, rebellion was deeply contagious: Richepance also imprisoned and deported a group of white French officers whose only crime was being held prisoner briefly by Delgrès and his troops in Fort Saint-Charles. Soldiers and officers of African descent, then, were not only a threat because of their capacity for armed resistance. Having fought for the Republic during the previous years under the banner of emancipation, they represented a profound ideological threat as well, as symbols and defenders of a project of liberty and racial equality that the French government was determined to crush.[5]

The general placed Guadeloupe under military rule, ordering the disarmament of everyone except the French soldiers. All cultivateurs were ordered to return to their plantations within five days and could only go into town with a pass given them by their plantation managers; all inhabitants had to carry a pass that indicated their name, profession, and address. In order to prevent sympathizers from supplying the rebels, all of the livestock in each town was gathered together and guarded by soldiers, and all nonwhites were forbidden from buying provisions, even

5. Richepance to minister, 11 Prairial, An X (May 31, 1802), in CAOM, C 7A, 57, 1; Lacrosse to minister, 1 Vendémiaire, An XI (Sept. 23, 1802), in CAOM, C 7A, 56, 157–158; Francis Arzalier, "Les Déportés guadeloupéens et haïtiens en Corse," in Michel Vovelle, ed., *Révolutions aux colonies*, special issue of *Annales historiques de la Révolution française*, CCXCIII–CCXCIV (July–December 1993), 133–154. On Pélage's deportation, see the état nominatif and the *acte d'accusation* as well as the minister's letter to the prefect of Brest and his report on the insurrection, 25 Thermidor, An X (Aug. 13, 1802), in CAOM, C 7A, 56, 278–288; see also Pélage's letter to the minister of justice, 13 Fructidor, An X (Aug. 31, 1802), in CAOM, B 250, 879, in which he noted, "The crime was committed far from here" and asked: "By whom and how must it be judged?" After a lengthy trial, the accused were eventually freed, and Pélage served in the French army until his death in combat in 1813. See Lacour, *Histoire*, III, 350. For the white officers, see their declaration, 18 Germinal, An XI (Apr. 8, 1803), in AHAT, B 9, 2.

for their masters. Crops were destroyed in areas where insurgents were operating. Municipal administrations, many of which had been staffed in part by new citizens, were replaced with commissioners, such as André Négré. Négré organized a troop to search all the houses of Basse-Terre, where he found and arrested a number of rebels in hiding.[6]

By July 1802, having received news of the official proclamation that maintained slavery in the colonies returned to France by the Treaty of Amiens (notably Martinique), Richepance further restricted the rights of the people of Guadeloupe. "Through a revolution and an extraordinary war," he declared, measures had been taken that were "subversive of the security and prosperity of the colony." "Boons granted by the mother-land" had "undermined the principles" essential for the functioning of the colonies, and in Guadeloupe the "noirs left to their own devices" had been overtaken by vagabondage, laziness, and misery. Colonies were "nothing more than establishments formed by Europeans, who brought noirs as the only individuals appropriate for the exploitation of the land." These whites—and not, he emphasized, the *sang-mêlés* who emerged between the two "fundamental classes of the colons and their noirs"—were "the indigenous people of the French nation" and therefore the only ones who should be allowed to "exercise the privileges of that nation." He concluded: "Until further order, the title of French citizen will be carried throughout this colony and its dependencies by whites. No other individual will be allowed to take this title or to exercise the functions or positions attached to it." The rest of Richepance's decree drew out the logical consequences of this new distinction. All men and women who were noir or de couleur and who did not have titles assuring their freedom were to return to the plantations where they lived "before the war"; the two out of ten days of rest the cultivateurs had enjoyed since 1794 were replaced by the old system of a six-day work week with Sunday off. Cultivateurs would receive only food and clothes and no payment for their labor, and propertyowners once again received the right to use the whip. Without using the word "slavery," Richepance had reinstated the Code noir. In Paris at the same time, the Consulate issued a decree calling for the restoration of slavery in Guadeloupe and Saint-Domingue.[7]

Despite these measures, Richepance's control of Guadeloupe was tenuous. In July 1802, he wrote that "the sicknesses that continue to ravage the troops" were killing up to a third of those in the hospitals and

6. Lacour, *Histoire*, III, 345–350; Bénot, *La Démence coloniale*, 73.
7. The proclamation is reprinted in part in Lacour, *Histoire*, III, 354–356.

FIGURE 22. Richepance's grave in Fort Delgrès (center).
Photograph by Laurent Dubois

were becoming so "malignant" that they compromised "the security of the colony." The Fifteenth Démi-Brigade, which left Brest with 684 soldiers and lost 52 in battles with the insurgents, had lost 513 soldiers to the fever by December 1802. Generals were not immune, and, like Leclerc in Saint-Domingue, Richepance succumbed at Matouba in late July 1802. Lescallier, along with Lacrosse, who had recently been brought back to the colony, took over the colony's administration. Lacrosse had a monument erected over the tomb of General Richepance and requested that "Fort Saint-Charles, where his body has been placed, be named Fort Richepance," a request seconded by the fort's garrison. Six months later, by order of the consuls of France, the fort was given the name it would carry for the next century and a half.[8]

8. Richepance to minister, 8 Thermidor, An X (Jul. 27, 1802), in CAOM, C 7A, 57, 8; "Etat des officiers et soldats morts," 1 Nivôse, An XI (Dec. 22, 1802), in AHAT, X i, carton 18; Lescallier to minister, 19 Fructidor, An X (Sept. 6, 1802),

The Boundaries of the Republic, 1798–1804

Throughout the island, the remaining insurgents watched the French soldiers and officers die. "They are waiting for the moment, after the rainy season, when the sicknesses will have considerably weakened the troops," wrote Lescallier. "They are counting and watching and, even among people who appear submitted, there are many who share their sentiments and their hopes." These insurgents attacked plantations by night to "furtively pillage, devastate, and burn," gaining recruits among the cultivateurs. They often escaped or routed the soldiers sent to hunt them down. "Despite the fact that the insurrection has cost the lives of many thousands of blacks" and "the deaths of the most important leaders during this war," as well as the deportation of "more than 1,500 noirs and mulâtres, including many prisoners of war who are now in floating prisons in Martinique," a spirit still glowed in the "thin debris of this rebellion." "It has one last audacious leader, named Palerme," Lescallier noted, "and the means to increase in size as soon as there is a favorable moment."[9]

Although during the first phase the insurgents had "followed a regulated way of fighting war," wrote General Ménard, after defeats at Matouba and Baimbridge they had dispersed to "nearly inaccessible locations" in the mountains. "Leaders who gained experience with this kind of war in the English colonies became the rallying points—Palerme, Jacquet, Fourne, Xavier, Noël Corbet, Codou, Simeon, Hyppolite Avril, [and] Cazimir all formed their bands," he continued. "Their cause was that of all hommes de couleur, and with the help of this common interest these chiefs received recruits and some help from nearly all plantations, at least at first." If these men had been maroons or divaguants, wrote Ménard, simply to contain and starve them out of their refuges would have been enough. "But this is the debris of an army, the majority were part of the old force of the colony, their chiefs were officers, they are veterans and well armed. Some are fanatics for liberty and avid for the blood of the French." Ménard set up lines of defense around plantations, but they were thinly manned, and the insurgents found openings and continued to attack, sending propertyowners fleeing to the towns. The French troops, according to Lacrosse, were "too weak for the difficult

in CAOM, C 7A, 57, 180–181; Lacrosse to minister, 24 Fructidor, An X (Sept. 11, 1802), 30 Frimaire, An XI (Dec. 21, 1802), in CAOM, C 7A, 56, 100–102, 229–232.

9. Lescallier to minister, 12 Messidor, An X (Jul. 1, 1802), in CAOM, C 7A, 57, 137.

and tiring operations" necessary to "purge this colony of all the brigands who continue to infest it." In order to prevent the arrival of those who might support them, he prohibited all people who were "noir or de couleur" from entering Guadeloupe without an official passport. Meanwhile, the practical Ménard offered safe passage from the island for those insurgent leaders who surrendered, and Noël Corbet and Codou accepted the offer. Palerme, however, pretended to want to negotiate and then used the truce the French offered to gather more ammunition and attack unarmed plantations.[10]

After the defeat of Delgrès, white citizens had attacked blacks throughout the island, and Richepance had sought to stop such extra-legal violence, declaring that his army was in charge of "pardoning and punishing" insurgents. Several months later, as Lacrosse watched fever and war decimate his troops, he ordered the formation of a company of "chasseurs des bois," drawn from Guadeloupean white men, and soon ordered all those who had not volunteered to present themselves and be incorporated into the regular army units. These "indigenous, acclimated men," wrote Lacrosse, were able to withstand "the fatigues of the war against the brigands," surrounding their hideouts and preventing their attacks on plantations. Shortly, he hoped, "the last of the brigands will be destroyed." Lacrosse spoke too soon. Not until 1804, not coincidentally after the independence of Haiti, would the last rebel leaders agree to offers from the French to leave the island.[11]

Some whites were already anticipating victory by mid-1802. In August, Lescallier discovered that a merchant in Basse-Terre had, a month

10. Ménard to minister, 24 Fructidor, An X (Sept. 11, 1802), 14 Vendémiaire, An XI (Oct. 6, 1802), in CAOM, C 7A, 57, 14-17, 58-59; Lacrosse to minister, 25 Fructidor, An X (Sept. 12, 1802), 4 Vendémiaire, An XI (Sept. 26, 1802), in CAOM, C 7A, 56, 109-110, 163; arrêté, 3 Vendémiaire, An XI (Sept. 25, 1802), in CAOM, C 7A, 58, 20. See also General Gobert's report, 21 Vendémiaire, An XI (Oct. 13, 1802), in CAOM, C 7A, 57, 63-69.

11. Chevalier Hippolyte de Frasans, *Mémoire pour le chef de brigade Magloire Pélage . . .* , 2 vols. (Paris, 1803), II, 357; Lacrosse, arrêté, 21 Fructidor, An X (Sept. 8, 1802), in CAOM, C 7A, 58, 12; "Circulaire du Capitaine-Général Lacrosse," 6 Vendémiaire, An XI (Sept. 28, 1802), Lacrosse to minister, 15 Vendémiaire, An XI (Oct. 7, 1802), in CAOM, C 7A, 56, 172-174; see also Adélaïde-Mérlande, "Lendemains," in Martin and Yacou, eds., *Mourir pour les Antilles*, 203-210; Fabien Marius-Hatchi, "Libèté oswa lanmò!: La Guadeloupe dans le cadre des révolutions caribéennes, 1789-1804" (mémoire de D.E.A., Université Paris VII, 2000), 8.

earlier, arranged for a friend to take six Guadeloupeans to one of the Spanish colonies and sell them as slaves. A document of sale had been drawn up for each one, describing age and characteristics—"loyal," "very active," "good seamstress"—just as documents had before emancipation. Lescallier suspected that army officers were involved in this still-illegal trade, which he attempted to stop. This was his last attempt to end a practice he had once railed against in his writings. Lescallier himself would soon be deeply involved in transforming free men and women into slaves.[12]

Citizens into Slaves

In September 1802, a packet of documents arrived in Guadeloupe, addressed to the deceased General Richepance from Denis Decrès, the minister of the colonies. Lacrosse opened the packet, which ordered that slavery was to be officially reinstated in Guadeloupe and Saint-Domingue. The minister warned him, however, not to announce this law until he was certain it would not endanger the security of the colony. Lacrosse wrote back to the minister to reassure him that he would follow this precaution and also expressed his deep commitment to the new order. The rebellions in the Antilles, wrote Lacrosse, provided "the lessons that must illuminate the government more than theories whose unreflected application most often contradicts our hopes." Recapitulating Decrès's own arguments, Lacrosse added, "The true liberty of civilized man was not made for the nègres of the French colonies. This gift was disastrous in its results not only to those to whom it was given but also to the metropole, which wanted to take them out of a state of degradation rejected by the philanthropists. Those times of enthusiasm have ended." He singled out the "affranchis, who dipped their parricidal hands in the blood of their benefactors," as deserving of the punishment they were now receiving at his hands. "These rogues," he wrote a few days later to the minister, "who were placed in the ranks of men by indulgent effervescence, have abused liberty, and I feel true satisfaction knowing that the government, in order to punish them for their crimes and assaults, has condemned them to the austerity of the regime of 1789, which is the only one made to reestablish and maintain the order and prosperity of the colonies." In the face of

12. Lescallier's letter, 8 Fructidor, An X (Aug. 26, 1802), and the attached documents, are in CAOM, C 7A, 58, 175-179.

continued rebellion, however, Lacrosse put off the official declaration of the reestablishment for several months.[13]

In preparation for a return to slavery, Lescallier set about reconstituting the laws assuring liberty for some. "During thirteen years of revolution," he declared, "none of the forms that used to exist to determine and assure the state of free people and of their emancipation from all service, slavery, or domesticity has been followed," with the result that the status of various individuals was often unknown—"a problem that will only partially be resolved by a new census." Lescallier, however, wished to make it possible for the "good and honest people" of the "numerous and industrious class previously known under the title of gens de couleur" to exercise their professions "freely and securely" and "under the protection of a just and benevolent government." All "noir and de couleur individuals" who were born free or emancipated before 1794 were ordered to present "the titles and patents of liberty and emancipation, or other proof of their state," to Lescallier, who would verify them. Those who presented sufficient documentation would be granted a patent assuring their liberty. Those who were freed after 1789, however, would have to pay a heavy tax of 1,200 francs in order to gain this document. This meant that the continuing validity of the emancipations that multiplied during 1792 and 1793, including those confirmed in the early 1800s, depended on the economic status of those freed. All who had not received a patent after three months would be "considered vagabonds" and punished as such.[14]

The onetime abolitionist Lescallier was likely seeking to counteract the policies of Lacrosse, whose deep hatred for the gens de couleur was obvious. Lescallier's law noted explicitly that he wished to make sure the honest gens de couleur would not be confused with "those men, strangers to this land for the most part, who have attracted the national vengeance, caused miseries in this colony, and raised doubts and clouds over the heads of a number of individuals who deserve to be distinguished by their morality and good conduct." Lescallier quickly set himself to the

13. See Lacrosse to Minister Decrès, 1, 4 Vendémiaire, An XI (Sept. 23, 26, 1802), in CAOM, C 7A, 56, 137–138, 155–156, 166–169; see also the letters from 15 Vendémiaire, An XI (Oct. 7, 1802), 30 Frimaire, An XI (Nov. 21, 1802), in CAOM, C 7A, 56, 173–174, 229–332. On Decrès, see Chapter 14, above.

14. "Arrêté concernant l'état des personnes de couleur," 22 Fructidor, An X (Sept. 9, 1802), in CAOM, C 7A, 57, 11; arrêté, 21 Vendémiaire, An XI (Oct. 13, 1802), in CAOM, C 7A, 58, 26; see also Lacour, *Histoire*, III, 367–368.

task of determining the validity of the various emancipations the regimes of Guadeloupe had produced; he delivered a number of *patentes de liberté* in October and November and continued to do so until at least May 1803, extending his original three-month deadline. Those who received patents had to present them when they signed a contract or declared a birth, rights that had once again become restricted to a small minority of the population. As they did so, they were named once again according to racial typologies that had receded during the period of emancipation. Among those who received patents from Lescallier were the *métis libre* Jean Icard, who had signed the 1793 declaration of the new citizens, and the nègre libre Jean-Pierre, who presented his when in 1804 he sold a small piece of land he owned along a ravine in Basse-Terre. Marie-Louise dite Rose presented hers when she purchased a house and stables in the center of Basse-Terre in 1804, whereas Laurance LeSueur used hers in the same year when she "liberated herself" from a debt owed to a white man. The nègresse libre Madelaine used her patent when she sold Sophie and her four children as slaves in 1804—presenting a private act of purchase from January 1794 as proof of her ownership.[15]

These individuals were the lucky ones, able to show proof of their freedom. Although there is no record of Lescallier's decisions, there were likely others whose personal archives were insufficient to assure their liberty in the face of a massive return to enslavement. Lescallier was clearly committed to limiting the number of gens de couleur in the colony. The idea that their population might once again grow gave him insomnia. When he heard in October 1802 that General Ménard had proposed a plan for recruiting cultivateurs to help fight the insurgents, Lescallier wrote to Lacrosse: "I barely slept last night." He added that all too often "those blacks we had the most confidence in were the ones who assassinated their masters." "Once they are free," he wondered, "what will we do with them? They will be vagabonds who from then on will disdain cultivation and will become dangerous to society because of that and the habit of carrying guns." Lescallier saw that the practice of granting freedom for military service, which had helped shatter slavery a few years

15. "Arrêté concernant l'état des personnes de couleur," 22 Fructidor, An X (Sept. 9, 1802), in CAOM, C 7A, 57, 11; for Icard, see CAOM, EC, Basse-Terre, 21, 2; for Jean-Pierre, see ADG, Castet, 472, 28 Messidor, An XII (Jul. 17, 1804); for LeSueur, see ADG, Castet, 472, 23 Thermidor, An XII (Aug. 11, 1804); for Marie-Louise dite Rose, see CAOM, Castet, 472, 5 Germinal, An XII (Mar. 26, 1804); for Madelaine, see ADG, Castet, 472, 8 Messidor, An XII (June 27, 1804).

before and had become one of the key symbols of Republican emancipation, could have no place in the new order.[16]

Several years before, Lescallier had advocated the restriction of the rights of the nègres nouveaux, who were brought to the French colonies from captured slave ships. Now he set about transforming those who had once been citoyens africains into slaves. He issued a law requiring all inhabitants of the island to present to local officials any of "the noir or de couleur individuals" residing with them who did not "belong to them," notably those having come from "the captures" or "from other colonies." The citizens brought by other cultivateurs to be given names and "baptized" into the Republic during the 1790s were brought once again in front of the municipal administration of Basse-Terre, this time by white plantation owners. There, they had their size, the shape of their noses, and the markings on their bodies inscribed in a register, along with a value that, once paid, would make them the property of the whites who brought them to the municipality. The citizen Billery of Basse-Terre, for instance, brought "Victoire, an Ibo nègresse who came from the captures, size four feet, eight inches, ordinary forehead, eyes big and fat, nose short, mouth ordinary, lips medium, face round, having marks from her country on her back, her temples, and her stomach." She was given the worth of 1,630 livres that, once Billery had paid it, made her his property. André Négré, commissioner of Basse-Terre, took advantage of his position to purchase a number of slaves. These men and women were auctioned by the French government for its profit, just as they would have been by slavers in other islands had they never been captured by the French corsairs.[17]

In the face of such measures, many kept up their fight against the new order, and by late 1802 the administration was still confronting large-scale insurrection. The insurgents had large camps throughout Basse-Terre and Grande-Terre and still had support on plantations and in the towns. Among them were remnants of the Republican troops of Guade-

16. Ménard, arrêté, 23 Vendémiaire, An XI (Oct. 15, 1802), in CAOM, C 7A, 57, 202–203; Lescallier to Lacrosse, 30 Vendémiaire, An XI (Oct. 22, 1802), in CAOM, C 7A, 57, 204; see also Ménard's response to Lescallier, 6 Brumaire, An XI (Oct. 28, 1802), and Lescallier's notes from the same day, in CAOM, C 7A, 57, 206–207, 209–210.

17. Lescallier, arrêté, 22 Fructidor, An X (Sept. 9, 1802), in CAOM, C 7A, 58, 15. The list of the slaves is in 22 Frimaire, An XI (Dec. 13, 1802), in CAOM, C 7A, 81; on Négré, see Lacour, *Histoire*, III, 378–380, which reprints a number of these transactions.

loupe, like the small group that attempted an attack on Fort Fleur d'Epée, wearing their old uniforms.[18]

In October 1802, a rebellion began on the plantations surrounding the town of Sainte-Anne, where, in 1791 and 1793, insurgents had risen up against slavery. They killed twenty-three whites and took money and horses, but when they attacked the town they were repulsed by French soldiers. Among the rebels were many plantation laborers. Some were African-born, like the thirty-five-year-old Laizerdon. Others were Creoles, like the fourteen-year-old Petit-Noel, the twenty-five-year-old mulâtresse Jeanne Rose, and the twenty-four-year-old Malborough, who had likely been imported from a British island before emancipation. But there were also individuals of African descent who had been free before 1794, such as the mulâtre Jean-Baptiste Girard, who rented a small property near Gosier. Perhaps most alarming for administrators, there were also several whites involved. One of them, Thomas-Michel Meunier, was a native of Le Havre and had served as a lieutenant in the army but—possibly sympathetic to the rebels or disgusted by the exactions against them—had decided to take a stand against the new order. Although several plantation laborers played leading roles in the uprising, administrators focused their attention on three whites whom they described as its leaders: Pierre Barsse, who had been an administrator in Sainte-Anne under the short regime of Jeannet-Oudin and his colleagues a few years before; the elderly Millet de la Girardière, a Martinican ex-officer who had been a member of the Order of Saint-Louis before the Revolution; and Jean Barbet, a laborer from the Gascogne region of France who had, according to Auguste Lacour, "many friends" and "a great deal of influence" among "the people."[19]

18. Lescallier to minister, 19, 26 Vendémiaire, An XI (Oct. 11, 18, 1802), in CAOM, C 7A, 57, 185-197, esp. 193-194.

19. Details on the participants are presented in Lacour, *Histoire*, III, 402, and in "Arrêt rendu par le tribunal spécial," Pointe-à-Pitre, Nov. 12, 1802, Musée des beaux-arts de Chartres, Collection Bouge, affiches, rpt. in Jacques Adélaïde-Mérlande, René Bélénus, and Fréderic Régent, eds., *La Rébellion de la Guadeloupe, 1801-1802* (Basse-Terre, Guadeloupe, 2002), 291-295. On the course of the insurrection, see Lacrosse to minister, 20 Vendémiaire, 21, 27 Brumaire, An XI (Oct. 12, Nov. 11, Nov. 18, 1802), in CAOM, C 7A, 56, 180-181, 192-193, 217-219; Lescallier to minister, 21 Brumaire, An XI (Nov. 12, 1802), in CAOM, C 7A, 57, 200-201; Ménard to minister, 25 Brumaire, An XI (Nov. 16, 1802), in CAOM, C 7A, 57, 60-62. See also the letters to Lescallier in CAOM, C 7A, 57, 198-199; "Ordres divers . . . et déclarations concernant l'insurrection," Vendémiaire An XI

Ménard referred to these leaders as "traitors to their country and their color." In fact, like Delgrès and those whites who had fought alongside him, they were enemies not of France but of the order Bonaparte wished to impose in France's name. Those who joined the rebellion were animated by individual concerns; men like Barsse and Girard were likely worried that the return of émigrés would push them off the properties they were renting, whereas the plantation laborers who joined them were striking out against a return of their old enslavement. In gathering together, though, they showed themselves to be defenders of the radical universalism represented by the 1794 abolition decree. Their intention, Ménard wrote, was "to start a revolution that would have brought the colony back to the political and agricultural regime that had just been overturned." Aware of the continuing resistance in other parts of the colony and of the decimation of French troops by disease, they perhaps hoped that by taking control of Sainte-Anne they would be able to create a base for a wider resistance. Indeed, they did not burn or destroy any plantations, which suggests they planned to continue to use them once they had established control in the area. And the rebels of Sainte-Anne had support in nearby Gosier, where a former slave named Edouard led other plantation laborers into insurrection.[20]

Lacrosse and the local officials of Sainte-Anne responded rapidly and brutally to the uprising. Between eighty and one hundred rebels were executed, most hanged and some burned alive. The involvement of whites in a last-ditch attempt to preserve manumission and racial equality was a danger to Bonaparte's plans to inculcate solidarity among whites, and the administrators sought to make a "terrible example" meant to threaten "brigands of all colors" through the punishment of the white leaders. Jean Barbet deprived them of the opportunity, hanging himself before his trial. Barsse was broken on the wheel and then burned alive in Pointe-à-Pitre. Millet de la Girardière was condemned to be "exposed in an iron cage" whose floor was equipped with a blade upon which, when he was too exhausted to hold himself up, he would fall; he escaped his punishment and died in prison, perhaps after taking

---

(October 1802), in CAOM, C 7A, 58, 298–304. The military granted freedom to two cultivateurs who had saved their masters during the insurrection; see "Copie des actes et délibérations du gouvernement," 23 Vendémiaire, An XI (Oct. 15, 1802), in CAOM, C 7A, 58, 128–130.

20. Ménard to minister, 25 Brumaire, An XI (Nov. 16, 1802), in CAOM, C 7A, 57, 60–62; Lacour, *Histoire*, III, 403–405, 410.

poison sneaked to him by friends. The former slave Edouard, meanwhile, was to be hanged on his plantation. As he was marched to his execution, however, he managed to escape. He was never found.[21]

Following the Sainte-Anne insurrection, Ménard established strict military regulations and initiated an all-out assault against the rebels. All men who had been part of the army before the arrival of Richepance were ordered arrested, and the houses of cultivateurs were searched for weapons and ammunition. In order to prevent an attack by refugees from Guadeloupe gathered in Saint Barthélemy, unarmed cultivateurs were placed on watch along the coasts to warn officials of any arriving ships. Each plantation was ordered to set up guards to keep the "brigands" from stealing or poisoning animals; if any livestock were lost, two of the guards would be broken on the wheel and the other two burned alive, in front of the assembled plantation. Lacrosse approved of such tactics, placing a bounty on the head of each brigand captured or killed. "The gallows did not frighten the guilty. But the nature of the new tortures makes a powerful impression on them," he wrote to the minister. "The assassins are broken on the wheel, and the arsonists are condemned to the fire."[22]

Throughout the island, the autonomous existences that certain ex-slaves had created for themselves were reversed. Charles Langlois, Julien Langlois's former plantation manager who in 1800 had been working as a carpenter for the Republic, lost his right to rent land, and therefore his right to the house he had built, as he lost his legal freedom. Like Langlois, Joseph had been an enslaved carpenter in 1794, living above Basse-Terre on the Ducharmoy-Bellevue plantation. He remained there after emancipation, traveling with the state-appointed plantation manager to have deaths that had occurred among the cultivateurs inscribed in the état civil. When, during the late 1790s, the old owners reclaimed the plantation, Joseph left, but by the time the plantation was purchased by a new owner in 1805, he was sold with it. The inventory,

21. Lacour, *Histoire*, III, 415–422. See also Daniel Maximin's dramatization of the event, and Millet de la Girardière's suicide—which he portrays as being facilitated by one of his former domestic slaves—in *Lone Sun*, trans. Clarisse Zimra (Charlottesville, Va., 1989), 57–62.

22. See "Ordre général, armée de la Guadeloupe," Sainte-Anne, 29 Vendémiaire, An XI (Oct. 21, 1802), and the earlier order from 23 Vendémiaire, An XI (Oct. 15, 1802), in CAOM, C 7A, 58, 27, 31; Lacrosse to minister, 4 Brumaire, 11 Frimaire, An XI (Nov. 15, Dec. 2, 1802), in CAOM, C 7A, 56, 194–195, 220–221.

however, described him as having no value because of a "sickness of the nerves."[23]

Others found ways to maintain the connections they had made during the era of freedom. In 1803, the mulâtre libre Antoine Petit de Genty purchased his wife, Brigitte, who until 1794 had been a slave and had married him after her liberation. He acquired her as a slave and, following the notarial form of a slave sale, signed a declaration that said he "knew her well, having seen and examined her, and is happy and satisfied to be in possession of her, since he had been married to her for several years." Brigitte, it was further noted, was his "real and actual possession," and he could dispose of her as "property, as a thing owned by him." Genty purchased Brigitte from Jacques Dupuy, the same white man who had helped Geneviève Labothière dite Mayoute purchase her brother from Martinique a few years before. Dupuy, it seems, repeatedly used the rights granted by the color of his skin to help a few families find their way to a tenuous safety. Certain practices of resistance, born before emancipation, persisted through the reimposition of slavery.[24]

Whites who had fled into exile during the previous year, meanwhile, returned to rebuild. In Trois-Rivières, Jacques Coquille Dugommier's widow sought to repossess not only her property but those who lived on it. It was on Dugommier's plantation, of course, that the slave insurrection led by Jean-Baptiste against his master Pierre Brindeau had begun in April 1793. Much had changed in the intervening decade; many former slaves had left the state-run plantation, which Jean-Baptiste himself had managed directly for a time. But its residents had been particularly hard hit during the recent fighting. Fifteen of the cultivateurs died in 1801 "fighting during the revolt," and the "African" Jeanneton had been "killed by the rebels." Louise, another African, had been missing "since the time of the troubles" and was also presumed killed by the rebels. The Creole Barthélemy had been killed among the insurgents fighting with Ignace at Baimbridge. Corachy, caught fighting with the rebels, had been executed. Some fell prey to personal enemies who used the battles as an opportunity to take revenge: Damassin had been "removed from his work at the sugarmill, under the orders of the com-

23. On Langlois, see ADG, Castet 2E2/212, 9 Germinal, An XI (Mar. 30, 1803); on Joseph, see the "Etat nominatif . . . de Basse-Terre," in CAOM, G 1, 500, no. 5; CAOM, EC, Basse-Terre, 8, nos. 75–77; ADG, Dupuch 2E2/26, 14 Vendémiaire, An IX (Oct. 6, 1800); ADG, Serane 2E2/160, 18 Germinal, An XIII (Apr. 8, 1805).

24. See ADG, Castet 2E2/212, 12 Pluviôse, An XI (Feb. 1, 1803).

The Boundaries of the Republic, 1798–1804

mander of Trois-Rivières, Citoyen Perrot, and, without any investigation or trial, he was burned alive on the plantation, on the simple denunciation of someone who was his enemy." Finally, a Jean-Baptiste was "killed by firing squad during the events." This seems indeed to have been the same man who had led the 1793 revolt; thus he died just as the Republican project he had helped produce crumbled throughout the island. The group on the Dugommier plantation might have been particularly politicized, given the area's preemancipation history, and Trois-Rivières was the site of some of the worst violence during the battles of 1802. Nevertheless, the death toll on this plantation, whose population was only 118 in 1801, testifies to how deeply the battles of 1802 scarred Guadeloupe's communities.[25]

Jean-Baptiste's execution was not the only revenge history took on insurgents of 1793. Another victim of that uprising, Eloy de Vermont, also came back to recover the slaves he had once possessed. Vermont became the captain of the chasseurs created by Lacrosse to attack the remaining insurgents and was renowned for his brutal effectiveness. In the next decades—as around him the majority of the population labored on sugar plantations, replenished by new arrivals from Africa—Vermont sat with the eager young historian Lacour, telling him stories of 1802 and 1793, forging his influential vision of the revolt of Trois-Rivières.[26]

Some, however, escaped the return of the past. In Saint Thomas and Saint Barthélemy, a handful of the leaders of the insurrection, including Massoteau, gathered and prepared for an attack against Guadeloupe. They were joined by Bigard and Cottin, two whites who had been deported by Lacrosse to Guiana, where they had been released by their former comrade Victor Hugues. Hugues, having been named governor of Guiana for his success at maintaining order in Guadeloupe, did not openly go against Bonaparte's colonial plans; indeed, he followed orders to reestablish slavery in Guiana in 1802, earning the distinction of proclaiming both emancipation and its reversal in a short administrative career. Nevertheless, he seems to have conserved a personal loyalty to those he had worked with during the period of manumission in Guadeloupe: he complained that among those men deported by Lacrosse in late

25. ADG, Dupuch 2E2/26, 8 Germinal, An XI (Mar. 29, 1803); Adélaïde-Mérlande, "Lendemains," in Martin and Yacou, eds., *Mourir pour les Antilles*, 203–210.

26. Lacour, *Histoire*, III, 383–397; Pierre Lacour, "Auguste Lacour: Sa vie-son oeuvre," introduction to Auguste Lacour, *Histoire de la Guadeloupe*, V (Basse-Terre, Guadeloupe, 1979), 7–76.

1801 were several who had served "with zeal and devotion" under him as he battled for the Republic. And, in boldly releasing Bigard and Cottin, who at least in Lacrosse's eyes were comrades of the African-descended rebels in Guadeloupe, Hugues might have been making a small gesture of support for the old order of racial equality he had once been a part of. Other, less well-connected insurgents also escaped, such as the noir Nabau, who forced a ship captain at knifepoint to drop him off at Saint Barthélemy.[27]

Lacrosse sent envoys to track down these men and destroy the "germ of insurrection" they represented. When the governor of Saint Barthélemy refused to extradite some of them without a proper trial, an infuriated Lacrosse wrote to the minister asking him to contact the embassies of Denmark and Sweden and explain to them the danger these insurgents posed for all colonial powers in the Caribbean. Saint Thomas had long been an international crossroads: one Danish visitor noted the presence of people of "all nations," and in the 1790s it was a haven for Republican corsairs. Lacrosse's envoys discovered a boat owned by Bellegarde and Régis-Acard, "both hommes de couleur," in the harbor. When they searched it, they found a great deal of ammunition, along with traces that more had been thrown overboard. They also found "a large quantity of flags of all nations," which proved, according to the envoys, that these men had a plan to go to the French islands and help the rebels there. The envoys tracked down and arrested Régis-Acard, but he jumped out of a second-story window and escaped "with the help of the night." Perhaps Nabau, Régis-Acard, Bellegarde, and others who escaped the French set sail on the Caribbean Sea, carrying with them the flags of all nations and the possibilities of an exiled Republic.[28]

27. Lacrosse to governor of Saint Thomas, 29 Vendémiaire, An XI (Oct. 21, 1802), in CAOM, C 7A, 56, 184–185; governor of Saint Barthélemy to Lacrosse, 23 Brumaire, An XI (Nov. 14, 1802), in CAOM, C 7A, 56, 198–199; Lacrosse to minister, 24 Brumaire, An XI (Nov. 15, 1802), C 7A, 56, 196–197; Hugues to Lacrosse, 23 Fructidor, An X (Sept. 10, 1803), in CAOM, C 7A, 56, 178–179; Hugues to minister, Cayenne, 11 Germinal, An X (Apr. 1, 1802), in CAOM, C 14A, 80, 82, rpt. in Adélaïde-Mérlande, Bélénus, and Régent, *La Rébellion*, 258; on Hugues in Guiana, see Bénot, *La Guyane sous la Révolution française; ou, L'Impasse de la révolution pacifique* (Kourou, French Guiana, 1997). Nabau had a crippled foot, perhaps having been wounded in battle or punished for marronnage before emancipation.

28. See the report and letter of Lacrosse's envoys, 23 Brumaire, An XI (Nov. 14, 1802), 4 Brumaire, An XI (Oct. 26, 1802), in CAOM, C 7A, 56, 207–213, 215.

Nearly three decades later, an abolitionist visiting Guadeloupe described how the arrival of the Republican flag, "that flag of liberty," sent from France after the revolution of 1830 raised the hopes of slaves and the fears of slaveowners.

> From the depth of his caze the unfortunate negro saluted this banner with its three colors, the source of so many hopes. The elders, gathered on the beach, showed the flag of regeneration to the young. Fathers held their children in their arms, drowning them with tears of joy, certain that they would soon see their chains shattered. . . . "Glorious sign of our emancipation, we salute you!" fifteen or twenty negroes cried one day, as they gathered near the port to see the banner of France. "Hello, benevolent flag, which comes to announce from across the seas the triumph of our friends and the hour of our deliverance."

The group of slaves who pointed to the tricolor flag were soon attacked by their masters. Fearful of the implications of the Republic's return, they beat the slaves into submission and forced them to return to their houses.[29]

Another eighteen years would elapse before the story of the Republic's arrival in the Caribbean would repeat itself, with the passing of the 1848 decree of emancipation. In imagining and fighting for an immediate and universal liberation of the slaves, the abolitionist Victor Schoelcher drew inspiration from the history of antislavery in the late-eighteenth-century French Caribbean. Schoelcher later recounted to Frederick Douglass how, just after the revolution of 1848 in Paris, he met with François Arago, the new minister of the colonies, and told him: "It is now time to emancipate the slaves of our colonies." Arago replied that such an action would lead to insurrection and bloodshed, but Schoelcher responded that the opposite was true: if emancipation were not proclaimed immediately,

---

Saint Thomas became an open port in 1724 and was long a "crossroads of empire," according to Julius S. Scott. The Dane, who visited in 1792, described the population of the island as speaking "almost every language." In 1795, an Italian ship captain who had escaped from prison in Guadeloupe on a Danish boat was taking refuge there, along with several corsairs operating under the French flag. See Scott, "Crisscrossing Empires: Ships, Sailors, and Resistance in the Lesser Antilles in the Eighteenth Century," in Robert L. Paquette and Stanley L. Engerman, eds., *The Lesser Antilles in the Age of European Expansion* (Gainesville, Fla., 1996), 128–143, esp. 129.

29. X. Tanc, *De l'esclavage aux colonies françaises, et spécialement à la Guadeloupe* (Paris, 1832), 7–11.

the slaves would revolt. Schoelcher understood the history of the 1790s and knew that in the Antilles the slaves would demand the freedom of the Second Republic. Indeed, when the flag of the Republic arrived in 1848, it was not so much carrying a message of liberty sent from a distant land as it was coming home, carrying the universal possibilities of liberty and citizenship that had been forged in the Caribbean itself, on the slopes between the clouds and the sea.[30]

30. See Nelly Schmidt, *Victor Schoelcher et l'abolition de l'esclavage* (Paris, 1994), 53–54, 104.

The Boundaries of the Republic, 1798–1804

EPILOGUE

In the Panthéon—the French temple of heroes, in the heart of Paris—
is a crypt containing several graves. Victor Schoelcher, the architect of
the 1848 abolition, lies near Jean Jaurès, the nineteenth-century Socialist political leader and historian who was one of the first to mention the
Caribbean in a history of the French Revolution. The crypt also contains the grave of Félix Eboué, the Guyanese-born colonial administrator. Eboué was one of the first to rally to Charles de Gaulle's call for
resistance during World War II. These graves have lain together for
several decades, but, in 1998, the hallway that leads to them was decorated with two new sets of inscriptions. One side bears the name of Toussaint L'Ouverture; the other bears that of Louis Delgrès, "hero of the
struggle against the reestablishment of slavery in Guadeloupe" who died
"so that liberty could live." In order to reach the tomb of Victor Schoelcher, visitors must now walk past dedications to these two Antillean
heroes who died decades before the 1848 abolition.

Within the Panthéon, these two memorials are unique. Although the
inscriptions note that L'Ouverture died in a prison cell at the French
Fort de Joux in the Jura Mountains and Delgrès died at Matouba in
Guadeloupe, no mention is made that both figures died fighting French
armies. Their opposition to the mother country, however, was certainly
well known among those who campaigned for the placement of these
plaques, and it was tacitly evoked during their unveiling ceremony when
the French minister of justice Elisabeth Guigou described these men as
"precursors of decolonization." Guigou declared: "The French Republic
wishes to honor these heroes of the Republic who faithfully and zealously defended justice and the equality of rights and fought against discrimination and inhumanity." The struggles of Delgrès and L'Ouverture,
then, were presented as struggles for the Republic—a republic that, at
the end of the twentieth century, was called on to embrace them and
their ideals of equality and liberty. Another particularity of these memorials, perhaps more telling, is that, unlike all the other sites in the Panthéon, they contain no bones. Although it is assumed L'Ouverture was
buried near the Fort de Joux, his bones have not been recovered. (An urn
commemorating him in the Musée du Panthéon national in Haiti contains only dirt gathered from the area where it is believed his grave lies.)

FIGURE 23. Memorials in the Panthéon, Paris. L'Ouverture's and Delgrès's names are written upon the corridor walls. *Photograph by Gary Wilder*

And there has been no attempt to recover Delgrès's bones from Matouba. L'Ouverture and Delgrès have been powerfully acknowledged at the core site of France's official national memory in a way that spatially acknowledges them as precursors to the ultimate abolition of slavery in 1848. At the same time, their place in the Panthéon is no crypt and no grave but simply words in a hallway. They are present at the center, but in a way that emphasizes the complexities and contradictions of remembering the French Caribbean's Republican revolutions. For remembering these figures inevitably calls up not only the spirits of heroes who struggled for their rights but also the specter of a political order, driven by profit and sustained by lingering racism, that placed severe limits on these rights and ultimately ripped them away from those who had fought to gain them.[1]

The placement of an inscription for Delgrès in the Panthéon was part of a much larger endeavor organized to commemorate the 1848 abolition of slavery. The Guadeloupean writer Daniel Maximin coordinated this set of events from the Ministry of the *Départements d'outre-mer* in Paris. When the inscriptions went up, it was the culmination of a half-century of action on the part of Antilleans working on both sides of the Atlantic. In 1960, twelve years after the plaque to Delgrès was placed at Matouba, the Martinican poet and political leader Aimé Césaire published his "Memorial for Louis Delgrès," which invoked the Guadeloupean hero as a "fist" breaking the fog "that has haunted me forever." "Louis Delgrès, I say your name," Césaire wrote, "and lifting out of silence the pedestal of this name / I hit the precise thickness of night / With an ecstatic hive of fireflies." Césaire recounted the death of Del-

1. In 2003, L'Ouverture and Delgrès were joined by another man of African descent with roots in the Caribbean: the famous writer Alexandre Dumas, whose grandmother was a slave in Saint-Domingue and whose grandfather was her master. Dumas's father, also Alexandre, was an important general in France during the revolutionary period. Raised by his father in France, Dumas chose to take on his mother's last name, which was the one he passed on to his own son. When Alexandre Dumas's bones were transferred from his gravesite to the Panthéon, there was widespread and overdue acknowledgment of the African ancestry of one of France's most beloved writers. On Dumas's background, see H. Bernard Catus, "Thomas Alexandre Dumas, enfant de Saint-Domingue, général républicain, personnage littéraire et héros haïtien (mal connu)," in Michel Hector, ed., *La Révolution française et Haïti: Filiations, ruptures, nouvelles dimensions* (Port-au-Prince, Haiti, 1995), 360–383.

grès at the hands of "colonialistic bastards"—"everything blew up on the black Matouba"—when "history hoisted on its highest pyre / The drop of blood of which I speak." Ultimately, Césaire concluded, "today Delgrès / In the hollow of intersecting paths / Taking up this name outside the maremmas / I proclaim you and in any future wind / You the buccinator [trumpeter] of a distant vintage." Two years later, administrators in Guadeloupe ordered that Fort Richepance be given back its original name of Saint-Charles, presumably to end the provocative commemoration of a man who reenslaved much of the population of Guadeloupe. In 1989, a group of local administrators in Basse-Terre, including Daniel Maximin, decided to change the name of the fort once again, this time in memory of Louis Delgrès. As Maximin told me about his impulse to commemorate Delgrès by naming the fort after him: "It struck me that this was the only place I could think of where there were monuments to our oppressors. Are there statues of Hitler in France or of King George in the United States? Why should we honor a man who came to the island to reenslave us?" There are now new plaques inside the fort, one of which presents Delgrès's passionate 1802 plea for racial equality, a document that has also more recently been reproduced on posters in the main park of Basse-Terre.[2]

What does it mean to celebrate Delgrès in this way? What Maximin said of his novel *Lone Sun*—"The present always invents a past for itself out of its own desire"—could certainly be said of the commemoration. Delgrès can seem, as he did in 1998 in French official language, a symbol of heroism, idealism, and sacrifice for the Republic. To others, he stands for something quite different: the one moment when Guadeloupe could have become independent from France. Maximin's novel powerfully captures the complexity of remembering Delgrès, and the period out of which he emerged, in modern Guadeloupe. One character in the novel laments: "Do you realize that if the Soufrière had exploded on Basse-Terre in 1802, to the joyous applause of the insurgent population, we would have become free at the same time as Haiti?" Thinking of Del-

2. Aimé Césaire, "Memorial for Louis Delgrès," in Clayton Eshleman and Annette Smith, trans., *Aimé Césaire: The Collected Poetry* (Berkeley, Calif., 1983), 331–337. The poem was originally published in *Ferrements; poèmes* (Paris, 1960); the quotes from Daniel Maximin are from an interview I had with him in Basse-Terre, Apr. 23, 1996. In his 1986 book on Delgrès, Jacques Adélaïde-Mérlande had posed the question "Will the Fort St. Charles someday be called the Fort Delgrès?" in the caption to the cover of the work; see *Delgrès; ou, La Guadeloupe en 1802* (Paris, 1986).

grès's dramatic act at Matouba, the same character says: "Our rebels are in competition with the sun." But the main character, Marie-Gabriel, also wonders whether it is a mistake to celebrate Delgrès's grand, suicidal gesture rather than generations of women who struggled in other ways against reenslavement, notably by keeping the history of 1802 alive through the decades. Maximin's novel tells the story of Guadeloupe's revolutionary years, but it also shows how the myths of the past are reworked in modern culture. In present-day Guadeloupe, as his novel suggests, stories of the past are a way of grappling with an uncertain and ambiguous future as a department of France, politically integrated but excluded in various ways, and as a Caribbean island cut off politically and economically from the islands around it.[3]

Maximin's work in both Guadeloupe and the metropole represented well the tenor of Guadeloupe's local administration during the late 1980s. After 1981, President François Mitterand's encouragement of decentralization throughout France created a context in which certain projects initiated by pro-independence groups—the revitalization of Creole and *gwo-ka* music, for instance, as well as the recovery of histories of resistance—became part of official French policy. Whereas demands for political independence decreased, along with the bombings and strikes of earlier years, cultural nationalist claims became more and more accepted, legitimized and structured by local and government institutions. A crucial part of this has been the work of various groups to recover and revitalize Guadeloupeans' understanding of their island's past.

One group that exemplified the cultural politics of the island during this period is the *Mouvman Kiltirel Voukoum*, which became a major force in the public life of Guadeloupe. Presenting themselves as a cultural movement, Voukoum maintained a center in Basse-Terre and worked to bring back lost carnival traditions—notably the aspects of political satire that had dropped away in recent years. They developed a unique musical style by adapting the rhythms of traditional, African-based gwo-ka drumming (which is played sitting down) for marching and by using conch shells and a new style of incantatory, improvisational singing; they also spurned the official carnival routes in favor of long and unpredictable treks through marginal neighborhoods. As Voukoum marched through the streets, they were preceded by young men with long rope whips who cleared the crossroads with stinging, earsplitting blows to the pavement.

3. Daniel Maximin, *Lone Sun*, trans. Clarisse Zimra (Charlottesville, Va., 1989); see esp. Zimra, introduction, xxvii, 85.

FIGURE 24. Fort Delgrès. *Photograph by Laurent Dubois*

Voukoum took particular care, in both their lyrics and their public perfor-mances, to address the history of the island. In 1996, Voukoum, with the support of the local government, organized a procession in honor of Del-grès's last combat. The group marched from Fort Delgrès through the town of Basse-Terre and up the slopes of the Soufrière volcano toward Matouba. Along the way, they read poems and historical descriptions and accompanied the march with music.[4]

Voukoum's evocation of Delgrès sought to reverse the usual under-

4. I am drawing here on fieldwork in Guadeloupe during 1992 and 1996–1997. According to Voukoum's website, http://art.rue.free.fr/voukoum/index vouk.html: "Voukoum, as a Movement, means a disturbance of the cultural order established by the cultural, political, and administrative authorities" and is also a way to "valorize some popular aspects of GUADELOUPE'S CULTURAL HERI-TAGE." For a pan-Caribbean discussion of the politics of music and carnival, see Richard D. E. Burton, *Afro-Creole: Power, Opposition, and Play in the Caribbean* (Ithaca, N.Y., 1997).

standing of the course of emancipation in Guadeloupe. News of the 1848 abolition arrived in Guadeloupe in late May, during the same season that the 1802 reestablishment of slavery occurred. So, during the time set aside to celebrate the abolition decreed from France, Voukoum marched in memory of 1802 and its historical martyrs. Like the inscriptions in the Panthéon, then, Voukoum's work is an attempt to reorient the historical focus away from 1848 and from an emancipation traditionally represented, through the large-scale presence of monuments and streets dedicated to the memory of Victor Schoelcher, as a generous act on the part of the French metropole. They wish to place the focus, instead, upon the historical figures of the 1790s and the early 1800s. Edouard Glissant noted that the "noise of the explosion" at Matouba had long been absent from the consciousness of Martinicans and Guadeloupeans, in part silenced through official means. In 1848, for instance, the French government asserted to slaves in Martinique that the Guadeloupeans had themselves demanded the reimposition of slavery in 1802. It is up to writers, Glissant suggested, to confront such silences and bring to life those who had been forgotten. This is precisely what happened in 1998 — in part through the work of writers. Rather than focus on Schoelcher, Antilleans made clear their desire to focus on their own heroes and did so by insistently talking not of 1848 but of the earlier period of insurrection, revolution, and reenslavement. In addition to the plaques in the Panthéon, two statues erected in Pointe-à-Pitre were both figures from the revolutionary period—the mulâtresse Solitude and Delgrès's comrade Ignace. In Basse-Terre, an addition to a mural from the 1970s also recalls the revolutionary period. The original mural, painted on the outside wall of the town prison, tells the story of slavery and the slave trade, depicting a caravan of slaves and the famous French slave fortress of Gorée. In the 1990s, someone conspicuously painted the date "1794" on the wall next to the mural. As they struggle with the problems posed by their ambiguous place within the French nation and within the Caribbean, Guadeloupeans increasingly call upon dates such as 1794 and 1802 as a way of producing a history for the present.[5]

This book, researched and written in the midst of—and inspired by—these changes in the French Caribbean, has also focused attention on this earlier period in the history of the region, and particularly Guadeloupe. Like the Antilleans who have insisted on the importance of the 1790s, I

5. Edouard Glissant, *Caribbean Discourse: Selected Essays*, trans. J. Michael Dash (Charlottesville, Va., 1989), 62.

have shown the ways in which slaves, ex-slaves, and gens de couleur confronted, embraced, and transformed republicanism during this period. Rather than see their struggles as marginal to the course of the Age of Revolution in the Atlantic world, I have highlighted the ways in which the Caribbean was a crucial testing ground for emerging ideas and assertions of rights. I have emphasized the political culture of this period as being defined in multiple sites and by multiple actors. Though they rarely left written records of their political visions, slaves, ex-slaves, and gens de couleur participated in defining the Republic, rights, and citizenship. The history of rights and citizenship during this revolutionary era cannot be told without their story.

The emancipation of 1794, I explained in Part I, emerged from the actions of slave insurgents in the Caribbean, who gave new content to the idea of rights and made universal and immediate emancipation imaginable and necessary. In Part II, I described how, confronted with a kind of abolition not even abolitionists had argued for, French administrators such as Victor Hugues sought to maintain the plantation economy. Operating with almost no direction from the metropole, Hugues drew on the writings of gradual abolitionists as he constructed an order bent on sustaining the production of colonial commodities despite the end of slavery. In doing so, he justified new forms of exclusion that tied the ex-slaves to their plantations as the only way to save a threatened Republic. Yet, notwithstanding the limits placed on their freedom, through military service, new economic opportunities, and the new legal rights they gained, ex-slaves sought to shape freedom in their own ways. Finally, as I explored in Part III, the international situation and the ideologies of planters, who retooled old arguments about the morality and necessity of slavery in the tropics—as well as former gradual abolitionists dismayed by what they saw as the disastrous results of a sudden abolition—propelled a retreat from policies of emancipation. As they watched these alarming changes, the citizens of the Antilles struggled to sustain a Republican vision against a metropole that sought to dismantle what was in many ways the most radical experiment of the revolutionary era.

The fight over slavery and emancipation during the revolutionary period was a global affair. It involved political debates and alliances on both sides of the Atlantic, military conflicts not only in France and Britain but also in Spain and the United States. Its economic disruptions reshaped patterns of production in the Caribbean, opening the way for the dramatic expansion of Cuban sugar in the early nineteenth century as well as for the Louisiana Purchase. These broader developments were driven by the revolution within the societies of the French Caribbean, where slaves, gens de couleur, and some whites took to heart the possibilities embedded in republicanism and ultimately brought about the most radical social and political transformation of the Age of Revolution. To understand the larger history of democracy—of its contentious meanings, its unstoppable divagations—we must expand our historical vision and incorporate, as a central part of this history, the ideals and actions of those who produced emancipation from within slavery.

Slavery was an affront to the ideal that all people were born with certain natural rights, and the triumph of 1794 was in instituting a political order worthy of the claims of universalism despite its profound danger to the reigning order of the day. That slaves succeeded in their revolts was a remarkable enough achievement of the period; that their revolt ultimately was embraced by the French Republic and transformed into a new political order is just as notable. But this radical order fell prey to other visions. Productivity and profit were seen as dependent on racial hierarchy and slavery, and dreams of racial equality collapsed as racial solidarity became the basis for the defense of liberty. The struggle of slaves enabled political principle to overtake, but not defeat, the forces of inequality. The insurgents left a legacy of possibility that long remained— that still remains—unfulfilled.

I have insisted on the place of the history of slavery, and of slaves, in the history of the French Republic, presenting throughout these pages the argument summed up by the location of Delgrès and L'Ouverture on the way to Schoelcher in the French Panthéon. But perhaps the Panthéon, and the broader narrative of which it is a part, cannot—or should not be allowed to—contain the past I have returned to here. Certainly, some in 1998 critiqued the placement of L'Ouverture and Delgrès in the Panthéon as a dishonest gesture of co-optation by a republic that continues to practice racial exclusion on a variety of levels. Elsewhere in Paris that year and since, slave revolt and slave victory are also evoked, but in a very different way. In basement temples and around altars squeezed into small apartments, Haitians who practice Vodou, along with many Guadeloupeans and Martinicans, worship and speak to spirits who carry the wounds and the hopes of the past that emerged from slavery and emancipation. Although Haitians, many of whom are undocumented immigrants, face very different problems than individuals from the French overseas departments, members of both groups have found a vehicle for dialogue in this religion born out of a common past. As they practice this religion and form new communities in doing so, they draw on and reconfigure the past of the revolutionary period in the service of the present. The ancestors they commune with take on a form quite different from the still inscriptions in the stone Panthéon, for these are spirits who dance, speak, argue, and bring concrete advice to those who worship them.

Those who practice Vodou in Paris are led in this practice by a variety of oungans and manbos. One of these is Erol Josué, who combines his spiritual work with his career as a singer and dancer. It was with his story that I began this book. In 1997 and 1998, through his work in the sans-papiers movement, Josué expressed his own vision of the ways his culture and his history should be part of the Republic. At twenty-seven years of age, Josué was one of the younger oungan practicing in Paris at the time and took a leading public role in confronting the often-hostile reaction to Vodou on the part of mainstream French society. His goal was to make it easier for the *sévité* (worshippers) to serve the lwa openly. "We have to stop practicing Vodou in marronnage," he explained to me. "We have to work with people in this culture so that they will accept us and our religion. This is a democratic society, and people must accept us with our culture."[6]

In one of his songs, Josué describes his departure into exile: "I left Port-au-Prince, I arrived in Paris, with all my *divisions* supporting me." In bringing his "divisions," a military term referring to the lwa, with him, he imported the culture of Vodou into his new life in France. These divisions are, for Josué, particularly adapted to confronting the problems of "occidental society" and the "spiritual and moral crisis that it is going through." Vodou, he notes, was forged in a context of dehumanization and slavery, and worshipers had to live through the "hell of enslavement" so that they could refuse it at night and preserve their culture and themselves. The religion survived and grew stronger through the time of slavery, he argues, but was consolidated and reborn as a united religion through revolution. The Vodou ceremony that launched the 1791 insurrection in Saint-Domingue was therefore, as he sees it, a foundational moment both for the nation of Haiti and the practice of Vodou. "Haitian Vodou, and the solidarity of Haitians, was born in August 1791, at the Bois-Caïman ceremony," he says.

On that day, the slaves began to realize that they all were part of the same cause, that they had to fight together. It was both a religious and

6. The quotes in this paragraph, like those below, are drawn from a series of interviews conducted with Josué during 1997–1999.

a political economy. From there, a language was born, Creole, and a religion was born, Vodou, and, eventually, a nation was born, Haiti. All the slaves had come from different tribes, and these different tribes all had their different practices; but starting with the Bois-Caïman ceremony they mixed their cultures to create a force we call Haitian Vodou, the assembly of the lwa. The slaves merged together to create Haiti.

Josué associates the three elements of religion, language, and political unity to narrate Haiti's past in a way that provides a history for his own practice as an oungan. When I asked him about the argument, made famously by one scholar, that there is no historical evidence the Bois-Caïman ceremony ever occurred, and that it is in fact a "historical myth," Josué responded by calling on a different kind of historical evidence. "You can't do anything about it because it's not written," he told me. "If it's written it is they who write it down — the historians, always the historians."[7]

But the evidence is there because, in the songs of Vodou, in the history of Haiti, the evidence is there. The evidence is there, it is alive, and it is not we who have created all this. We inherited this power from the ancestors; there had to be a ceremony to bring together the slaves, to create a culture, a religion, to enable religious and political consolidation. Of course there was resistance before that; it prepared the ceremony, and afterward there were many other events . . . but I refer particularly to the Bois-Caïman ceremony because, as an oungan, it has a great deal of importance for me, because it is there that the religion I have inherited was born. But also because I am Haitian and I believe in the Bois-Caïman ceremony, and every day of my life I live the Bois-Caïman ceremony, and in every one of my ceremonies I live the Bois-Caïman ceremony.

7. See Léon-François Hoffman, "Un Mythe national: La Cérémonie du Bois-Caïman," in Gérard Barthélemy and Christian A. Girault, eds., *La République haïtienne: Etat des lieux et perspectives* (Paris, 1993), 434–448. Hoffman pointed out that the first written account of the ceremony appeared in a memoir of a Saint-Domingue planter who described it as the expression of an "absurd and bloody religion" and used it as part of his argument in favor of a French reconquest of Haiti (Antoine Dalmas, *Histoire de la révolution de Saint-Domingue . . . suivi d'un mémoire sur le rétablissement de cette colonie* [Paris, 1814], 117–118). Hoffman's dismissal of the ceremony as a "historical myth" earned him many vociferous attacks at the time.

For Josué, Bois-Caïman symbolizes the creation of Vodou—the act of diverse nations of slaves coming together in revolution. Each ceremony recalls and reenacts that convergence and therefore deepens the historical reality of the revolution. Ceremonies represent a dialogue with the history, and the symbols, of the nation of Haiti. The symbol of the lwa Aizan, for instance, is a palm tree. The palm tree is also found on the Haitian flag, and, as Josué told me, on the flag "there is a little bonnet on top of the palm, and we call this the bonnet of Aizan." "You see," he continued, "once again it's the history of Haiti that comes back. Aizan is a lwa of virtue but also of liberty, and when in a ceremony all the people tear the palms of Aizan and distribute them, they are sharing liberty, tearing liberty, and sharing, it giving liberty. . . . Every day you see the flag, every day you see Aizan, every day there is a *chiré Aizan* [the tearing of palm fronds for Aizan]—liberty is there." The red and blue of the flag's colors also evoke, according to Josué, the lwa Ogou and Erzulie.

"The lwa are the mirror of society," he says. "The history of Haiti resides in them." Vodou songs "tell the story of the lwa, and they tell the story of society at the same time." Songs sung to the lwa carry histories of slavery and of revolution, sometimes evoking the names of Boukman, who led the first revolts in 1791, or of L'Ouverture and Jean-Jacques Dessalines. The internal conflicts of the revolutionary period are remembered, for instance, in a song that describes how "Dessalines left the north, carrying an *ouanga nibo* [a kind of charm]" in order to kill an enemy. The lwa Ogou, in particular, embodies the complex ambivalence that military figures hold in Haiti, both as defenders and as enemies of the people, as ancestors of independence and contemporary destroyers of freedom.[8]

The lwa of Vodou are divided into nations, the most important of which are the Petwo and Rada. In the 1950s, the ethnographer Maya Deren argued that the lwa of the Petwo nation were born in the Americas out of enslavement and revolution. She noted the repetition of the chant "Vive la liberté!" in Petwo rituals, which she saw as a remembrance of

8. Joan Dayan, *Haiti, History, and the Gods* (Berkeley, Calif., 1995), 31; Karen McCarthy Brown, "Systematic Remembering, Systematic Forgetting: Ogou in Haiti," in Sandra T. Barnes, ed., *Africa's Ogoun: Old World and New* (Bloomington, Ind., 1989), 65–89; Sidney Mintz and Michel-Rolph Trouillot, "The Social History of Haitian Vodou," Donald J. Cosentino, "It's All for You, Sen Jak!" Patrick Polk, "Sacred Banners and the Divine Cavalry Charge," in Cosentino, ed., *The Sacred Arts of Haitian Vodou* (Los Angeles, Calif., 1995), 123–147, 243–264, 325–347.

"the raging revolt of the slaves against the Napoleonic forces" and a celebration of "the delirium of triumph." She was struck by the presence of the "slave-whip sounding constantly, a never-to-be-forgotten ghost." But if, for an observer like Deren (or myself), the shock of the whip hitting the dirt floor brings the violent past of slavery into the present, such a connection is not necessarily made by those who practice the religion. Josué told me that the whip may of course carry that connotation, but in his mind it is a part of the ritual, a means of opening the way for the lwa, of calling them to the ceremony. The whip is multivalent in its meanings, its resounding crack speaking both of oppression and resistance as it calls the spirits down. Born of Saint-Domingue's plantation society and the political revolution that emerged from it, Vodou provides a means of rereading this history; it does so not only through the memory carried in songs but also through the poetry of dance and the manipulation and placement of objects such as the Haitian flag, the palm, the machete, and the elements of altars.[9]

The memory present in Vodou is perhaps most powerfully evoked through possession by the lwa. The act of possession—by an Ogou imaged as Dessalines, by an ancestor spirit returning to the land—literalizes the invocation of history reappearing in the present, always reshaped. When the lwa possess a person, they come to dance, to chide, and to speak with the living. They may give advice, tell stories, criticize the ceremony, interrogate someone about his or her behavior. They may

9. Maya Deren, *Divine Horsemen: The Living Gods of Haiti* (New York, 1953), 62. See also Alfred Métraux, *Voodoo in Haiti* (New York, 1959), and Karen McCarthy Brown, *Mama Lola: A Vodou Priestess in Brooklyn* (Berkeley, Calif., 1991), 252–257. Modern work has linked Petwo to the Kongo; see Luc de Heusch, "Kongo in Haiti: A New Approach to Religious Syncretism," *Journal of the Royal Anthropological Institute*, XXIV (1989), 290–303. Paul Gilroy suggests that, in their "quest for citizenship," former slaves depended on the preserved memory of slavery, often maintained in religious practice; he notes W. E. B. Dubois's observation: "It was in religious practices that the buried social memory of the original terror had been preserved. It was frequently revisited by ritual means" (Gilroy, *The Black Atlantic: Modernity and Double Consciousness* [Cambridge, Mass., 1993], 122, 129). On the way rituals carry history, see also J. Lorand Matory, *Sex and the Empire That Is No More: Gender and the Politics of Metaphor in Oyo Yoruba Religion* (Minneapolis, Minn., 1994), chap. 1; Paul Stoller, *Embodying Colonial Memories: Spirit Possession, Power, and the Hauka in West Africa* (New York, 1995); Michael Taussig, *Shamanism, Colonialism, and the Wild Man: A Study in Terror and Healing* (Chicago, 1986); Barbara Browning, *Samba: Resistance in Motion* (Bloomington, Ind., 1995).

demand a spiritual marriage with one of those present or may simply bless them with a mist of rum. The major lwa can have many manifestations; Ogou can be dangerous, but he can also be a calming and positive presence as he touches chins with the base of his sword or delivers someone a military salute that is promptly returned. Erzulie, too, has many faces, as Erzulie Freda, a coquettish white figure who speaks French and demands perfume, or as the black Erzulie Dantor, who is voiceless but speaks through her dancing and demands that worshipers approach by holding a knife to her chest. The lwa carry the hidden and unfulfilled possibilities of a revolution that asserted the equality of blacks and whites as it brought together multiple nations of African gods, allowing for their difference and continued transformation yet uniting them in a struggle for liberty.[10]

When he brings down Ogou, Erzulie, and other lwa in the banlieue of Paris, Josué welcomes powerful divisions who embody many of the struggles of the women and men who formed the history of the Republic. According to Josué, the lessons they bring from the past have a great deal to contribute to the future. The growing number of initiates he greets—including, in addition to Haitians and French Antilleans, whites from France—seem to agree. He hopes that the ideals of openness and toleration that he sees as fundamental to Vodou can help "make people understand they are all united . . . that we may be of different colors but blood has only one color." For French Antilleans, Paris provides access to religious practices that are almost entirely absent in the islands of Guadeloupe and Martinique themselves. Although many in the French Caribbean perform traditional healing, which can include various forms of spirit possession, larger ceremonies involving sacrifice and possession are not part of this practice. It is in Paris that they can become part of a wider French community solidified by its ties to the lwa born of the history of slavery and struggle in the French Caribbean.

Vodou crosses boundaries, travels from the countryside of Haiti to the streets of Brooklyn and Paris, and carries with it the marks of the history it helped forge. It is a transnational and transcultural religion, one

10. "Gods were born in the memories of those who served," Dayan writes, and became "tough revenants carried in the memories of the descendants of slaves." She argues that the lwa are "deposits of history" and carry stories that are often silenced in the official histories of the revolution. See Dayan, "Erzulie: A Women's History of Haiti," *Research in African Literatures*, II, no. 25 (Summer 1994), 5–31; Dayan, *Haiti, History, and the Gods*, 29, 35–36; see also Brown, *Mama Lola*, 220–257.

that provides another image of the universalist Republic whose contradictions—at the end of the eighteenth century and at the beginning of the twenty-first—I have explored here. For in a sense Vodou is a republic, a religion created from enslavement and revolution against it, a religion that unites different nations of African and New World deities within shifting but solid *règlements* (laws). The distance between the secular republic worshiped in the Panthéon and the vision of responsibility enacted in the Vodou ceremonies of the Parisian banlieue may seem unbridgeable. Yet their history is inseparable, and so, inevitably, is their future.

CHRONOLOGY

1635	Guadeloupe and Martinique settled by French
1660s–1670s	Informal settlement of Hispaniola by French
1685	Code noir issued
1697	Spain officially cedes western half of Hispaniola to French in Treaty of Rhyswick
1734	Revolt in Danish colony of Saint John
1759–1763	British occupation of Guadeloupe
1788	Founding of the Société des amis des noirs in Paris
1789	Beginning of French Revolution
May	Meeting of Estates-General
June	Tennis Court Oath yields formation of National Assembly
July	Storming of the Bastille
August	Declaration of the Rights of Man adopted; slave insurrection in Martinique
1790	
8 March	Law on the colonies cedes power over "internal regime," including treatment of gens de couleur, to colonies
October	Revolt of Vincent Ogé in Saint-Domingue
1791	
15 May	Decree grants political rights to some gens de couleur
June	Flight and capture of Louis XVI
August	Slave insurrection in Saint-Domingue
1792	
28 March/4 April	Decree grants political rights to all gens de couleur
August	Royalists hold Guadeloupe
September	National Convention proclaims France a republic
October	Exiled Republicans from Guadeloupe hold election in Dominica
December	Royalist control of Guadeloupe broken
1793	
January	Execution of Louis XVI
April	Slave insurrection in Trois-Rivières, Guadeloupe

June	Liberty offered to "warriors" who will fight for the Republic in Saint-Domingue
August–September	
	Insurrection in Sainte-Anne, Guadeloupe; abolition of slavery in Saint-Domingue
December	British invasion of Saint-Domingue

1794

4 February	Abolition of slavery in French Empire
March–April	
	Occupation of Guadeloupe and Martinique by British
May	Toussaint L'Ouverture allies with the French in Saint-Domingue
June–August	
	Reconquest of Guadeloupe by Victor Hugues
July	Fall of Robespierre

1795

January–June	
	French attacks on Grenada and Saint Vincent; capture of Saint Lucia
August	New constitution for France makes colonies departments
October	Directory Regime begins
1796	British recapture Saint Lucia and defeat insurrection in Grenada
1797	British defeat insurrection in Saint Vincent

1798

January	Law on the colonies confirms them as departments of France
August	L'Ouverture negotiates final British withdrawal from Saint-Domingue
October	L'Ouverture expels General Hédouville from Saint-Domingue
November	Hugues removed from Guadeloupe

1799

June	War between André Rigaud and L'Ouverture begins in Saint-Domingue
November	Bonaparte's coup replaces Directory with Consulate
December	New constitution proclaims colonies will be governed by "particular laws"

1800
- May — Lacrosse arrives in Guadeloupe
- August — L'Ouverture triumphs over Rigaud

1801
- July — L'Ouverture declares constitution for Saint-Domingue
- October — France and Britain sign preliminaries of Treaty of Amiens; soldiers rise up against Lacrosse in Guadeloupe
- November — Leclerc mission leaves for Saint-Domingue

1802
- February — Leclerc expedition arrives in Saint-Domingue
- March — Treaty of Amiens ends war between France and Britain
- April — Richepance expedition leaves for Guadeloupe
- May — Richepance expedition arrives in Guadeloupe; Delgrès and partisans are defeated
- June — Deportation of L'Ouverture from Saint-Domingue
- July — Consulate decrees reestablishment of slavery in Guadeloupe, Guiana, and Saint-Domingue

1803
- May — Slavery officially reestablished in Guadeloupe
- November — French troops surrender in Saint-Domingue

1804
- January — Haitian independence declared

GLOSSARY OF FRENCH TERMS

africain/africaine: African

ancien libre: after general emancipation, an individual who was free before 1794

ancien régime: Old Regime; in France, the order that preceded the revolution of 1789; in the colonies, often used to refer to the regime of slavery

bourg: town

câpre/câpresse: generally used to describe a child of a *noir* and a *mulâtre*, i.e., a person of three-quarters African and one-quarter European descent

chouan: counterrevolutionary insurgent; originally coined for rebels of France's western provinces, particularly the Vendée, but also used in other contexts, notably the Caribbean

citoyen/citoyenne: citizen

Code noir: 1685 royal code setting out laws surrounding the treatment of slaves and the process of emancipation for the French colonies

conducteur: driver who oversaw plantation work, often himself a slave

cultivateur: after 1794, ex-slave plantation laborer

décadi: the tenth day of the ten-day week in the Republican calendar

de la Côte: "from the coast"; a designation sometimes used to refer to individuals who were African-born

divagation: rambling; term used by administrators to describe the departure of cultivateurs from plantations and their movement within the colony

engagé/engagée: indentured laborer

esclave: slave

état civil: register kept by priests and, during the revolutionary period, officials documenting births, marriages, and deaths

gens de couleur: free people of color; those of varying African descent freed by masters or born of two free parents

métis/métisse: generally, but not exclusively, used to describe a child of a *blanc* and a *mulâtre*, i.e., a person of three-quarters European and one-quarter African descent

mulâtre/mulâtresse: mulatto; generally, but not exclusively, used to describe a child of a *blanc* and a *noir*, i.e., a person of half European and half African ancestry

nègre: negro; generally more pejorative than *noir*

nègre libre: free black; a person of entirely African descent freed by a master or born of two free parents

noir: black person; generally less pejorative than *nègre*

nonédi: the ninth day of the ten-day week in the Republican calendar

nouveau citoyen/nouvelle citoyenne: new citizen; used to refer to gens de couleur after the granting of political rights in 1792 and to the formerly enslaved after 1794

quarteron/quarteronne: a child of a *métis* and a *blanc*, i.e., a person of one-eighth African ancestry

sang-mêlé: mixed-blood

sans-papiers: "without papers," i.e., undocumented immigrants; term used by social movement started in France in the 1990s that pushed for immigrants' rights

scélérat: villain

séquestres: state-appointed managers of confiscated property

INDEX

insurrection), 24, 126, 131–133, 135, 140, 151, 153–154, 357, 418–419